Essential Algorithms

Essential Algorithms

A Practical Approach to Computer Algorithms Using Python® and C#

Rod Stephens

WILEY

Essential Algorithms: A Practical Approach to Computer Algorithms Using Python® and C#

Published by
John Wiley & Sons, Inc.
10475 Crosspoint Boulevard
Indianapolis, IN 46256
www.wiley.com

Copyright © 2019 by John Wiley & Sons, Inc., Indianapolis, Indiana

Published simultaneously in Canada

ISBN: 978-1-119-57599-3
ISBN: 978-1-119-57596-2 (ebk)
ISBN: 978-1-119-57598-6 (ebk)

Manufactured in the United States of America

V10009977_050219

For general information on our other products and services please contact our Customer Care Department within the United States at (877) 762-2974, outside the United States at (317) 572-3993 or fax (317) 572-4002.

Wiley publishes in a variety of print and electronic formats and by print-on-demand. Some material included with standard print versions of this book may not be included in e-books or in print-on-demand. If this book refers to media such as a CD or DVD that is not included in the version you purchased, you may download this material at http://booksupport.wiley.com. For more information about Wiley products, visit www.wiley.com.

Library of Congress Control Number: 2019933736

For Maki

About the Author

Rod Stephens started out as a mathematician, but while studying at MIT, he discovered how much fun algorithms are. He took every algorithms course MIT offered, and he has been writing complex algorithms ever since.

During his career, Rod has worked on an eclectic assortment of applications in fields such as telephone switching, billing, repair dispatching, tax processing, wastewater treatment, concert ticket sales, cartography, and training for professional football players.

Rod was a Microsoft Visual Basic Most Valuable Professional (MVP) for 15 years and has taught introductory programming courses. He has written more than 30 books that have been translated into languages from all over the world. He has also written more than 250 magazine articles covering C#, Visual Basic, Visual Basic for Applications, Delphi, and Java.

Rod's popular C# Helper website (http://www.csharphelper.com) receives millions of hits per year and contains tips, tricks, and example programs for C# programmers. His VB Helper website (http://www.vb-helper.com) contains similar material for Visual Basic programmers.

You can contact Rod at: RodStephens@csharphelper.com.

About the Technical Editor

John Mueller is a freelance author and technical editor. He has writing in his blood, having produced 112 books and more than 600 articles to date. The topics range from networking to artificial intelligence and from database management to heads-down programming. Some of his current books include discussions of data science, machine learning, and algorithms. His technical editing skills have helped more than 70 authors refine the content of their manuscripts. John has provided technical editing services to numerous magazines, performed various types of consulting, and he writes certification exams as well.

Be sure to read John's blog at: `http://blog.johnmuellerbooks.com/`. You can reach John on the Internet at `John@JohnMuellerBooks.com`. John also has a website at `http://www.johnmuellerbooks.com/`. Be sure to follow John on Amazon at `https://www.amazon.com/John-Mueller/`.

Credits

Senior Acquisitions Editor
Kenyon Brown

Editorial Manager
Pete Gaughan

Associate Publisher
Jim Minatel

Production Manager
Kathleen Wisor

Project Editor
Gary Schwartz

Production Editor
Athiyappan Lalith Kumar

Technical Editor
John Muller

Copy Editor
Kim Wimpsett

Proofreader
Nancy Bell

Indexer
Potomac Indexing, LLC

Cover Designer
Wiley

Acknowledgments

Thanks to Ken Brown, Devon Lewis, Gary Schwartz, Pete Gaughan, Jim Minatel, Athiyappan Lalitkumar, and everyone else at Wiley that helped make this book possible.

Thanks to longtime friend John Mueller, who provided his technical expertise to help make the information in this book as accurate as possible. (Any remaining mistakes are mine, not his.)

Thanks also to Sunil Kumar for his generous feedback on the first edition.

Contents at a glance

Introduction		xxix
Chapter 1	Algorithm Basics	1
Chapter 2	Numerical Algorithms	23
Chapter 3	Linked Lists	71
Chapter 4	Arrays	103
Chapter 5	Stacks and Queues	135
Chapter 6	Sorting	167
Chapter 7	Searching	201
Chapter 8	Hash Tables	209
Chapter 9	Recursion	227
Chapter 10	Trees	285
Chapter 11	Balanced Trees	349
Chapter 12	Decision Trees	367
Chapter 13	Basic Network Algorithms	403
Chapter 14	More Network Algorithms	451
Chapter 15	String Algorithms	493
Chapter 16	Cryptography	519
Chapter 17	Complexity Theory	543

Chapter 18   Distributed Algorithms   561

Chapter 19   Interview Puzzles   595

Appendix A   Summary of Algorithmic Concepts   607

Appendix B   Solutions to Exercises   623

Glossary   711

Index   739

Contents

Introduction		**xxix**
Chapter 1	**Algorithm Basics**	**1**
	Approach	2
	Algorithms and Data Structures	2
	Pseudocode	3
	Algorithm Features	6
	Big O Notation	7
	Rule 1	8
	Rule 2	8
	Rule 3	9
	Rule 4	9
	Rule 5	10
	Common Run Time Functions	11
	1	11
	Log N	11
	Sqrt N	14
	N	14
	N log N	15
	N^2	15
	2^N	15
	N!	16
	Visualizing Functions	16
	Practical Considerations	18
	Summary	19
	Exercises	20

Chapter 2	**Numerical Algorithms**	**23**
	Randomizing Data	23
	Generating Random Values	23
	Generating Values	24
	Ensuring Fairness	26
	Getting Fairness from Biased Sources	28
	Randomizing Arrays	29
	Generating Nonuniform Distributions	30
	Making Random Walks	31
	Making Self-Avoiding Walks	33
	Making Complete Self-Avoiding Walks	34
	Finding Greatest Common Divisors	36
	Calculating Greatest Common Divisors	36
	Extending Greatest Common Divisors	38
	Performing Exponentiation	40
	Working with Prime Numbers	42
	Finding Prime Factors	42
	Finding Primes	44
	Testing for Primality	45
	Performing Numerical Integration	47
	The Rectangle Rule	48
	The Trapezoid Rule	49
	Adaptive Quadrature	50
	Monte Carlo Integration	54
	Finding Zeros	55
	Gaussian Elimination	57
	Forward Elimination	58
	Back Substitution	60
	The Algorithm	61
	Least Squares Fits	62
	Linear Least Squares	62
	Polynomial Least Squares	64
	Summary	67
	Exercises	68
Chapter 3	**Linked Lists**	**71**
	Basic Concepts	71
	Singly Linked Lists	72
	Iterating Over the List	73
	Finding Cells	73
	Using Sentinels	74
	Adding Cells at the Beginning	75
	Adding Cells at the End	76
	Inserting Cells After Other Cells	77
	Deleting Cells	78
	Doubly Linked Lists	79
	Sorted Linked Lists	81

Self-Organizing Linked Lists	82
Move To Front (MTF)	83
Swap	83
Count	84
Hybrid Methods	84
Pseudocode	85
Linked-List Algorithms	86
Copying Lists	86
Sorting with Insertionsort	87
Sorting with Selectionsort	88
Multithreaded Linked Lists	90
Linked Lists with Loops	91
Marking Cells	92
Using Hash Tables	93
List Retracing	94
List Reversal	95
Tortoise and Hare	98
Loops in Doubly Linked Lists	100
Summary	100
Exercises	101
Chapter 4 Arrays	**103**
Basic Concepts	103
One-Dimensional Arrays	106
Finding Items	106
Finding Minimum, Maximum, and Average	107
Finding Median	108
Finding Mode	109
Inserting Items	112
Removing Items	113
Nonzero Lower Bounds	114
Two Dimensions	114
Higher Dimensions	115
Triangular Arrays	118
Sparse Arrays	121
Find a Row or Column	123
Get a Value	124
Set a Value	125
Delete a Value	127
Matrices	129
Summary	131
Exercises	132
Chapter 5 Stacks and Queues	**135**
Stacks	135
Linked-List Stacks	136
Array Stacks	138
Double Stacks	139
Stack Algorithms	141

Reversing an Array	141
Train Sorting	142
Tower of Hanoi	143
Stack Insertionsort	145
Stack Selectionsort	146
Queues	147
Linked-List Queues	148
Array Queues	148
Specialized Queues	151
Priority Queues	151
Deques	152
Binomial Heaps	152
Binomial Trees	152
Binomial Heaps	154
Merging Trees	155
Merging Heaps	156
Merging Tree Lists	156
Merging Trees	158
Enqueue	161
Dequeue	162
Runtime	163
Summary	163
Exercises	164

Chapter 6	**Sorting**	**167**
	$O(N^2)$ Algorithms	168
	Insertionsort in Arrays	168
	Selectionsort in Arrays	170
	Bubblesort	171
	$O(N \log N)$ Algorithms	174
	Heapsort	175
	Storing Complete Binary Trees	175
	Defining Heaps	176
	Implementing Heapsort	180
	Quicksort	181
	Analyzing Quicksort's Run Time	182
	Picking a Dividing Item	184
	Implementing Quicksort with Stacks	185
	Implementing Quicksort in Place	185
	Using Quicksort	188
	Mergesort	189
	Sub $O(N \log N)$ Algorithms	192
	Countingsort	192
	Pigeonhole Sort	193
	Bucketsort	195
	Summary	197
	Exercises	198

Chapter 7	**Searching**	**201**
	Linear Search	202
	Binary Search	203
	Interpolation Search	204
	Majority Voting	205
	Summary	207
	Exercises	208
Chapter 8	**Hash Tables**	**209**
	Hash Table Fundamentals	210
	Chaining	211
	Open Addressing	213
	Removing Items	214
	Linear Probing	215
	Quadratic Probing	217
	Pseudorandom Probing	219
	Double Hashing	219
	Ordered Hashing	219
	Summary	222
	Exercises	222
Chapter 9	**Recursion**	**227**
	Basic Algorithms	228
	Factorial	228
	Fibonacci Numbers	230
	Rod-Cutting	232
	Brute Force	233
	Recursion	233
	Tower of Hanoi	235
	Graphical Algorithms	238
	Koch Curves	239
	Hilbert Curve	241
	Sierpiński Curve	243
	Gaskets	246
	The Skyline Problem	247
	Lists	248
	Divide and Conquer	249
	Backtracking Algorithms	252
	Eight Queens Problem	254
	Knight's Tour	257
	Selections and Permutations	260
	Selections with Loops	261
	Selections with Duplicates	262
	Selections Without Duplicates	264
	Permutations with Duplicates	265
	Permutations Without Duplicates	266
	Round-Robin Scheduling	267
	Odd Number of Teams	268

Even Number of Teams   270
Implementation   271
Recursion Removal   273
Tail Recursion Removal   274
Dynamic Programming   275
Bottom-Up Programming   277
General Recursion Removal   277
Summary   280
Exercises   281

Chapter 10   Trees   **285**
Tree Terminology   285
Binary Tree Properties   289
Tree Representations   292
Building Trees in General   292
Building Complete Trees   295
Tree Traversal   296
Preorder Traversal   297
Inorder Traversal   299
Postorder Traversal   300
Breadth-First Traversal   301
Traversal Uses   302
Traversal Run Times   303
Sorted Trees   303
Adding Nodes   303
Finding Nodes   306
Deleting Nodes   306
Lowest Common Ancestors   309
Sorted Trees   309
Parent Pointers   310
Parents and Depths   311
General Trees   312
Euler Tours   314
All Pairs   316
Threaded Trees   317
Building Threaded Trees   318
Using Threaded Trees   320
Specialized Tree Algorithms   322
The Animal Game   322
Expression Evaluation   324
Interval Trees   326
Building the Tree   328
Intersecting with Points   329
Intersecting with Intervals   330
Quadtrees   332
Adding Items   335
Finding Items   336

	Tries	337
	Adding Items	339
	Finding Items	341
	Summary	342
	Exercises	342
Chapter 11	**Balanced Trees**	**349**
	AVL Trees	350
	Adding Values	350
	Deleting Values	353
	2-3 Trees	354
	Adding Values	355
	Deleting Values	356
	B-Trees	359
	Adding Values	360
	Deleting Values	361
	Balanced Tree Variations	362
	Top-down B-trees	363
	B+trees	363
	Summary	365
	Exercises	365
Chapter 12	**Decision Trees**	**367**
	Searching Game Trees	368
	Minimax	369
	Initial Moves and Responses	373
	Game Tree Heuristics	374
	Searching General Decision Trees	375
	Optimization Problems	376
	Exhaustive Search	377
	Branch and Bound	379
	Decision Tree Heuristics	381
	Random Search	381
	Improving Paths	382
	Simulated Annealing	384
	Hill Climbing	385
	Sorted Hill Climbing	386
	Other Decision Tree Problems	387
	Generalized Partition Problem	387
	Subset Sum	388
	Bin Packing	388
	Cutting Stock	389
	Knapsack	390
	Traveling Salesman Problem	391
	Satisfiability	391
	Swarm Intelligence	392
	Ant Colony Optimization	393

General Optimization   393
Traveling Salesman   393
Bees Algorithm   394
Swarm Simulation   394
Boids   395
Pseudoclassical Mechanics   396
Goals and Obstacles   397
Summary   397
Exercises   398

Chapter 13   Basic Network Algorithms   403
Network Terminology   403
Network Representations   407
Traversals   409
Depth-First Traversal   410
Breadth-First Traversal   412
Connectivity Testing   413
Spanning Trees   416
Minimal Spanning Trees   417
Euclidean Minimum Spanning Trees   418
Building Mazes   419
Strongly Connected Components   420
Kosaraju's Algorithm   421
Algorithm Discussion   422
Finding Paths   425
Finding Any Path   425
Label-Setting Shortest Paths   426
Label-Correcting Shortest Paths   430
All-Pairs Shortest Paths   431
Transitivity   436
Transitive Closure   437
Transitive Reduction   438
Acyclic Networks   439
General Networks   440
Shortest Path Modifications   441
Shape Points   441
Early Stopping   442
Bidirectional Search   442
Best-First Search   442
Turn Penalties and Prohibitions   443
Geometric Calculations   443
Expanded Node Networks   444
Interchange Networks   445
Summary   447
Exercises   447

Chapter 14	**More Network Algorithms**	**451**
	Topological Sorting	451
	Cycle Detection	455
	Map Coloring	456
	Two-Coloring	456
	Three-Coloring	458
	Four-Coloring	459
	Five-Coloring	459
	Other Map-Coloring Algorithms	462
	Maximal Flow	464
	Work Assignment	467
	Minimal Flow Cut	468
	Network Cloning	470
	Dictionaries	471
	Clone References	472
	Cliques	473
	Brute Force	474
	Bron–Kerbosch	475
	Sets R, P, and X	475
	Recursive Calls	476
	Pseudocode	476
	Example	477
	Variations	480
	Finding Triangles	480
	Brute Force	481
	Checking Local Links	481
	Chiba and Nishizeki	482
	Community Detection	483
	Maximal Cliques	483
	Girvan–Newman	483
	Clique Percolation	485
	Eulerian Paths and Cycles	485
	Brute Force	486
	Fleury's Algorithm	486
	Hierholzer's Algorithm	487
	Summary	488
	Exercises	489
Chapter 15	**String Algorithms**	**493**
	Matching Parentheses	494
	Evaluating Arithmetic Expressions	495
	Building Parse Trees	496
	Pattern Matching	497
	DFAs	497
	Building DFAs for Regular Expressions	500
	NFAs	502

String Searching   504
Calculating Edit Distance   508
Phonetic Algorithms   511
   Soundex   511
   Metaphone   513
Summary   514
Exercises   515

Chapter 16 **Cryptography**   **519**
Terminology   520
Transposition Ciphers   521
   Row/Column Transposition   521
   Column Transposition   523
   Route Ciphers   525
Substitution Ciphers   526
   Caesar Substitution   526
   Vigenère Cipher   527
   Simple Substitution   529
   One-Time Pads   530
Block Ciphers   531
   Substitution-Permutation Networks   531
   Feistel Ciphers   533
Public-Key Encryption and RSA   534
   Euler's Totient Function   535
   Multiplicative Inverses   536
   An RSA Example   536
   Practical Considerations   537
Other Uses for Cryptography   538
Summary   539
Exercises   540

Chapter 17 **Complexity Theory**   **543**
Notation   544
Complexity Classes   545
Reductions   548
   3SAT   549
   Bipartite Matching   550
NP-Hardness   550
Detection, Reporting, and Optimization Problems   551
   Detection $\leq_p$ Reporting   552
   Reporting $\leq_p$ Optimization   552
   Reporting $\leq_p$ Detection   552
   Optimization $\leq_p$ Reporting   553
   Approximate Optimization   553
NP-Complete Problems   554
Summary   557
Exercises   558

Chapter 18	**Distributed Algorithms**	**561**
	Types of Parallelism	562
	Systolic Arrays	562
	Distributed Computing	565
	Multi-CPU Processing	567
	Race Conditions	567
	Deadlock	571
	Quantum Computing	572
	Distributed Algorithms	573
	Debugging Distributed Algorithms	573
	Embarrassingly Parallel Algorithms	574
	Mergesort	576
	Dining Philosophers	577
	Randomization	578
	Resource Hierarchy	578
	Waiter	579
	Chandy/Misra	579
	The Two Generals Problem	580
	Byzantine Generals	581
	Consensus	584
	Leader Election	587
	Snapshot	588
	Clock Synchronization	589
	Summary	591
	Exercises	591
Chapter 19	**Interview Puzzles**	**595**
	Asking Interview Puzzle Questions	597
	Answering Interview Puzzle Questions	598
	Summary	602
	Exercises	604
Appendix A	**Summary of Algorithmic Concepts**	**607**
	Chapter 1: Algorithm Basics	607
	Chapter 2: Numeric Algorithms	608
	Chapter 3: Linked Lists	609
	Chapter 4: Arrays	610
	Chapter 5: Stacks and Queues	610
	Chapter 6: Sorting	610
	Chapter 7: Searching	611
	Chapter 8: Hash Tables	612
	Chapter 9: Recursion	612
	Chapter 10: Trees	614
	Chapter 11: Balanced Trees	615
	Chapter 12: Decision Trees	615
	Chapter 13: Basic Network Algorithms	616
	Chapter 14: More Network Algorithms	617
	Chapter 15: String Algorithms	618

Chapter 16: Cryptography   618
Chapter 17: Complexity Theory   619
Chapter 18: Distributed Algorithms   620
Chapter 19: Interview Puzzles   621

Appendix B   Solutions to Exercises   623
Chapter 1: Algorithm Basics   623
Chapter 2: Numerical Algorithms   626
Chapter 3: Linked Lists   633
Chapter 4: Arrays   638
Chapter 5: Stacks and Queues   648
Chapter 6: Sorting   650
Chapter 7: Searching   653
Chapter 8: Hash Tables   655
Chapter 9: Recursion   658
Chapter 10: Trees   663
Chapter 11: Balanced Trees   670
Chapter 12: Decision Trees   675
Chapter 13: Basic Network Algorithms   678
Chapter 14: More Network Algorithms   681
Chapter 15: String Algorithms   686
Chapter 16: Encryption   689
Chapter 17: Complexity Theory   692
Chapter 18: Distributed Algorithms   697
Chapter 19: Interview Puzzles   701

Glossary   711
Index   739

Introduction

Algorithms are the recipes that make efficient programming possible. They explain how to sort records, search for items, calculate numeric values such as prime factors, find the shortest path between two points in a street network, and determine the maximum flow of information possible through a communications network. The difference between using a good algorithm and a bad one can mean the difference between solving a problem in seconds, hours, or never.

Studying algorithms lets you build a useful toolkit of methods for solving specific problems. It lets you understand which algorithms are most effective under different circumstances so that you can pick the one best suited for a particular program. An algorithm that provides excellent performance with one set of data may perform terribly with other data, so it is important that you know how to pick the algorithm that is the best match for your scenario.

Even more important, by studying algorithms, you can learn general problem-solving techniques that you can apply to other problems—even if none of the algorithms you already know is a perfect fit for your current situation. These techniques let you look at new problems in different ways so that you can create and analyze your own algorithms to solve your problems and meet unanticipated needs.

In addition to helping you solve problems while on the job, these techniques may even help you land the job where you can use them! Many large technology companies, such as Microsoft, Google, Yahoo!, IBM, and others, want their programmers to understand algorithms and the related problem-solving techniques. Some of these companies are notorious for making job applicants work through algorithmic programming and logic puzzles during interviews.

The better interviewers don't necessarily expect you to solve every puzzle. In fact, they will probably learn more about you when you don't solve a puzzle. Rather than wanting to know the answer, the best interviewers want to see how you approach an unfamiliar problem. They want to see whether you throw up your hands and say the problem is unreasonable in a job interview. Or perhaps you analyze the problem and come up with a promising line of reasoning for using algorithmic approaches to attack the problem. "Gosh, I don't know. Maybe I'd search the Internet," would be a bad answer. "It seems like a recursive divide-and-conquer approach might work" would be a much better answer.

This book is an easy-to-read introduction to computer algorithms. It describes a number of important classical algorithms and tells when each is appropriate. It explains how to analyze algorithms to understand their behavior. Most importantly, it teaches techniques that you can use to create new algorithms on your own.

Here are some of the useful algorithms that this book describes:

- Numerical algorithms, such as randomization, factoring, working with prime numbers, and numeric integration
- Methods for manipulating common data structures, such as arrays, linked lists, trees, and networks
- Using more-advanced data structures, such as heaps, trees, balanced trees, and B-trees
- Sorting and searching
- Network algorithms, such as shortest path, spanning tree, topological sorting, and flow calculations

Here are some of the general problem-solving techniques this book explains:

- Brute-force or exhaustive search
- Divide and conquer
- Backtracking
- Recursion
- Branch and bound
- Greedy algorithms and hill climbing
- Least-cost algorithms
- Constricting bounds
- Heuristics

To help you master the algorithms, this book provides exercises that you can use to explore ways that you can modify the algorithms to apply them to new situations. This also helps solidify the main techniques demonstrated by the algorithms.

Finally, this book includes some tips for approaching algorithmic questions that you might encounter in a job interview. Algorithmic techniques let you solve many interview puzzles. Even if you can't use algorithmic techniques to solve every puzzle, you will at least demonstrate that you are familiar with approaches that you can use to solve other problems.

Why You Should Study Algorithms

There are several reasons why you should study algorithms. First, they provide useful tools that you can use to solve particular problems such as sorting or finding shortest paths. Even if your programming language includes tools to perform tasks that are handled by an algorithm, it's useful to learn how those tools work. For example, understanding how array and list sorting algorithms work may help you decide which of those data structures would work best in your programs.

Algorithms also teach you methods that you may be able to apply to other problems that have a similar structure. They give you a collection of techniques that you can apply to other problems. Techniques such as recursion, divide and conquer, Monte Carlo simulation, linked data structures, network traversal, and others apply to a wide variety of problems.

Perhaps most importantly, algorithms are like a workout for your brain. Just as weight training can help a football or baseball player build muscle, studying algorithms can build your problem-solving abilities. A professional athlete probably won't need to bench press weights during a game. Similarly, you probably won't need to implement a simple sorting algorithm in your project. In both cases, however, practice can help improve your game, whether it's baseball or programming.

Finally, algorithms can be interesting, satisfying, and sometimes surprising. It never ceases to amaze me when I dump a pile of data into a program and a realistic three-dimensional rendering pops out. Even after decades of study, I still feel the thrill of victory when a particularly complicated algorithm produces the correct result. When all of the pieces fit together perfectly to solve an especially challenging problem, it feels like something at least is right in the world.

Algorithm Selection

Each of the algorithms in this book was included for one or more of the following reasons:

- The algorithm is useful, and a seasoned programmer should be expected to understand how it works and how to use it correctly in programs.

- The algorithm demonstrates important algorithmic programming techniques that you can apply to other problems.

- The algorithm is commonly studied by computer science students, so the algorithm or the techniques it uses could appear in a technical interview.

After reading this book and working through the exercises, you will have a good foundation in algorithms and techniques that you can use to solve your own programming problems.

Who This Book Is For

This book is intended primarily for three kinds of readers: professional programmers, programmers preparing for job interviews, and programming students.

Professional programmers will find the algorithms and techniques described in this book useful for solving problems they face on the job. Even when you encounter a problem that isn't directly addressed by an algorithm in this book, reading about these algorithms will give you new perspectives from which to view problems so that you can find new solutions.

Programmers preparing for job interviews can use this book to hone their algorithmic skills. Your interviews may not include any of the problems described in this book, but they may contain questions that are similar enough so that you can use the techniques you learned in this book to solve them. Even if you can't solve a problem, if you recognize a structure similar to those used in one of the algorithms, you can suggest similar strategies and perhaps get partial credit.

For all the reasons explained in the earlier section "Why You Should Study Algorithms," all programming students should study algorithms. Many of the approaches described in this book are simple, elegant, and powerful, but they're not all obvious, so you won't necessarily stumble across them on your own. Techniques such as recursion, divide and conquer, branch and bound, and using well-known data structures are essential to anyone who has an interest in programming.

NOTE   Personally, I think algorithms are just plain fun! They're my equivalent of crossword puzzles or Sudoku. I love the feeling of successfully assembling a complicated algorithm and watching it work.

They also make great conversation starters at parties. "What do you think about label setting versus label-correcting, shortest path algorithms?"

Getting the Most Out of This Book

You can learn some new algorithms and techniques just by reading this book, but to really master the methods demonstrated by the algorithms, you need to work with them. You need to implement them in some programming language. You also need to experiment, modify the algorithms, and try new variations on old problems. The book's exercises and interview questions can give you ideas for new ways to use the techniques demonstrated by the algorithms.

To get the greatest benefit from the book, I highly recommend that you implement as many of the algorithms as possible in your favorite programming language or even in more than one language to see how different languages affect implementation issues. You should study the exercises and at least write down outlines for solving them. Ideally, you should implement them, too. Often there's a reason why an exercise is included, and you may not discover it until you take a hard look at the problem. The exercises may lead you down paths that are very interesting but that are too long to squeeze into the book.

Finally, look over some of the other interview questions available on the Internet and figure out how you would approach them. In many interviews, you won't be required to implement a solution, but you should be able to sketch out solutions. And if you have time to implement solutions, you will learn even more.

Understanding algorithms is a hands-on activity. Don't be afraid to put down the book, break out a compiler, and write some actual code!

This Book's Websites

Actually, this book has two websites: Wiley's version and my version. Both sites contain the book's source code.

The Wiley web page for this book is `www.wiley.com/go/essentialalgorithms`. You also can go to `www.wiley.com` and search for the book by title or ISBN. Once you've found the book, click the Downloads tab to obtain all of the source code for the book. Once you download the code, just decompress it with your favorite compression tool.

NOTE At the Wiley website, you may find it easiest to search by ISBN. This book's ISBN is 978-1-119-57599-3.

The C# programs are named with a Pascal case naming convention. For example, the program that displays graphical solutions to the Tower of Hanoi puzzle for Exercise 4 in Chapter 9 is named `GraphicalTowerOfHanoi`. The corresponding Python programs are named with underscore casing as in `graphical_tower_of_hanoi.py`.

To find my web page for this book, go to `http://www.CSharpHelper.com/algorithms2e.html`.

How This Book Is Structured

This section describes the book's contents in detail.

Chapter 1, "Algorithm Basics," explains concepts you must understand to analyze algorithms. It discusses the difference between algorithms and data structures, introduces Big O notation, and describes times when practical considerations are more important than theoretical runtime calculations.

Chapter 2, "Numerical Algorithms," explains several algorithms that work with numbers. These algorithms randomize numbers and arrays, calculate greatest common divisors and least common multiples, perform fast exponentiation, and determine whether a number is prime. Some of the algorithms also introduce the important techniques of adaptive quadrature and Monte Carlo simulation.

Chapter 3, "Linked Lists," explains linked-list data structures. These flexible structures can be used to store lists that may grow, shrink, and change in structure over time. The basic concepts are also important for building other linked data structures, such as trees and networks.

Chapter 4, "Arrays," explains specialized array algorithms and data structures, such as triangular and sparse arrays, which can save a program time and memory.

Chapter 5, "Stacks and Queues," explains algorithms and data structures that let a program store and retrieve items in first-in, first-out (FIFO) or last-in, first-out (LIFO) order. These data structures are useful in other algorithms and can be used to model real-world scenarios such as checkout lines at a store.

Chapter 6, "Sorting," explains sorting algorithms that demonstrate a wide variety of useful algorithmic techniques. Different sorting algorithms work best for different kinds of data and have different theoretical run times, so it's good to understand an assortment of these algorithms. These are also some of the few algorithms for which exact theoretical performance bounds are known, so they are particularly interesting to study.

Chapter 7, "Searching," explains algorithms that a program can use to search sorted lists. These algorithms demonstrate important techniques such as binary subdivision and interpolation.

Chapter 8, "Hash Tables," explains hash tables—data structures that use extra memory to allow a program to locate specific items very quickly. They powerfully demonstrate the space-time trade-off that is so important in many programs.

Chapter 9, "Recursion," explains recursive algorithms—those that call themselves. Some problems are naturally recursive, so these techniques make solving them easier. Unfortunately, recursion can sometimes lead to problems, so this chapter also describes how to remove recursion from an algorithm when necessary.

Chapter 10, "Trees," explains highly recursive tree data structures, which are useful for storing, manipulating, and studying hierarchical data. Trees also have applications in unexpected places, such as evaluating arithmetic expressions.

Chapter 11, "Balanced Trees," explains trees that remain balanced as they grow over time. In general, tree structures can grow very tall and thin, and that can ruin the performance of tree algorithms. Balanced trees solve this problem by ensuring that a tree doesn't grow too tall and skinny.

Chapter 12, "Decision Trees," explains algorithms that attempt to solve problems that can be modeled as a series of decisions. These algorithms are often used on very hard problems, so they often find only approximate solutions rather than the best solution possible. However, they are very flexible and can be applied to a wide range of problems.

Chapter 13, "Basic Network Algorithms," explains fundamental network algorithms such as visiting all the nodes in a network, detecting cycles, creating spanning trees, and finding paths through a network.

Chapter 14, "More Network Algorithms," explains more network algorithms, such as topological sorting to arrange dependent tasks, graph coloring, network cloning, and assigning work to employees.

Chapter 15, "String Algorithms," explains algorithms that manipulate strings. Some of these algorithms, such as searching for substrings, are built into tools that most programming languages can use without customized programming. Others, such as parenthesis matching and finding string differences, require some extra work and demonstrate useful techniques.

Chapter 16, "Cryptography," explains how to encrypt and decrypt information. It covers the basics of encryption and describes several interesting encryption techniques, such as Vigenère ciphers, block ciphers, and public key encryption. This chapter does not go into all the details of modern encryption algorithms such as Data Encryption Standard (DES) and Advanced Encryption Standard (AES) because they are more appropriate for a book on encryption.

Chapter 17, "Complexity Theory," explains two of the most important classes of problems in computer science: P (problems that can be solved in deterministic polynomial time) and NP (problems that can be solved in nondeterministic polynomial time). This chapter describes these classes, ways to prove that a problem is in one or the other, and the most profound question in computer science: is P equal to NP?

Chapter 18, "Distributed Algorithms," explains algorithms that run on multiple processors. Almost all modern computers contain multiple processors, and computers in the future will contain even more, so these algorithms are essential for getting the most out of a computer's latent power.

Chapter 19, "Interview Puzzles," describes tips and techniques that you can use to attack puzzles and challenges that you may encounter during a programming interview. It also includes a list of some websites that contain large lists of puzzles that you can use for practice.

Appendix A, "Summary of Algorithmic Concepts," summarizes the ideas and strategies used by the algorithms described in this book. Using these, you can build solutions to other problems that are not specifically covered by the algorithms described here.

Appendix B, "Solutions to Exercises," contains the solutions to the exercises at the end of each chapter.

The **Glossary** defines important algorithmic terms that are used in this book. You may want to review the glossary before going on programming interviews so the terms are fresh in your mind.

What You Need to Use This Book

To read this book and understand the algorithms, you don't need any special equipment, except perhaps for reading glasses and a caffeinated beverage. If you really want to master the material, however, you should implement as many of the algorithms as possible in an actual programming language. It doesn't matter which language you use. Working through the implementation details in any language will help you better understand the algorithms and any special treatment required by the language.

Of course, if you plan to implement the algorithms in a programming language, you need a computer and whatever development environment is appropriate.

The book's websites contain sample implementations that you can download and examine written in C# with Visual Studio 2017 and Python 3.7. If you want to run those, you need to install either C# 2017 or Python 3.7 on a computer that can run them reasonably well.

Running any version of Visual Studio requires that you have a reasonably fast, modern computer with a large hard disk and lots of memory. For example, I'm fairly happy running my Intel Core 2 system at 1.83 GHz with 2 GB of memory and a spacious 500 GB hard drive. That's a lot more disk space than I need, but disk space is relatively cheap, so why not buy a lot?

You can run Visual Studio on much less powerful systems, but using an underpowered computer can be extremely slow and frustrating. Visual Studio has a big memory footprint, so if you're having performance problems, installing more memory may help.

The C# programs will load and execute with Visual Studio Community Edition, so there's no need to install a more expensive version of Visual Studio. You can get more information and download the Community Edition for free at `https://visualstudio.microsoft.com/downloads`.

You can download Python at `https://www.python.org/downloads/`. Python version 3.7 or later should be able to run this book's Python examples. Instead of downloading Python, you run it in the cloud without installing it on your local system. For example, Google Colaboratory (`https://colab.research.google.com`) is a free environment that lets you run Python programs on any Android device.

I built the book's examples in Windows 10, so there may be some differences if you are running Python on some other platform, such as Linux, OS X, or the cloud. Unfortunately, I can't help you much if you have problems in those environments.

Your performance will vary depending on the speed of the environment and device that you use to run the examples. If you're unsure of a program's performance, start small and then make the problem larger when you know how the program behaves. For example, try exhaustively solving a 10-item partition problem (which should run pretty quickly) before you try solving a 100-item problem (which probably won't finish before the sun burns out).

Conventions

To help you get the most from the text and keep track of what's happening, I've used several conventions throughout the book.

SPLENDID SIDEBARS

Sidebars such as this one contain additional information and side topics.

WARNING Warning boxes like this hold important, not-to-be forgotten information that is directly relevant to the surrounding text.

NOTE Boxes like this hold notes, tips, hints, tricks, and asides to the current discussion.

As for styles in the text:

- New terms and important words are *italicized* when they are introduced. You also can find many of them in the glossary.
- Keyboard strokes look like this: Ctrl+A. This one means to hold down the Ctrl key and then press the A key.
- URLs, code, and email addresses within the text are shown in monofont type, as in: `http://www.CSharpHelper.com`, `x = 10`, and `RodStephens@CSharpHelper.com`.

```
I use a monofont type with no highlighting for most code examples.
```

```
I use bold text to emphasize code that's particularly important
in the present context.
```

How to Contact the Author

If you have questions, comments, or suggestions, please feel free to email me at `RodStephens@CSharpHelper.com`. I can't promise to solve all of your algorithmic problems, but I do promise to try to point you in the right direction.

CHAPTER 1

Algorithm Basics

Before you jump into the study of algorithms, you need a little background. To begin with, you need to know that, simply stated, an *algorithm* is a recipe for getting something done. It defines the steps for performing a task in a certain way.

That definition seems simple enough, but no one writes algorithms for performing extremely simple tasks. No one writes instructions for how to access the fourth element in an array. It is just assumed that this is part of the definition of an array and that you know how to do it (if you know how to use the programming language in question).

Normally, people write algorithms only for difficult tasks. Algorithms explain how to find the solution to a complicated algebra problem, how to find the shortest path through a network containing thousands of streets, or how to find the best mix of hundreds of investments to optimize profits.

This chapter explains some of the basic algorithmic concepts you should understand if you want to get the most out of your study of algorithms.

It may be tempting to skip this chapter and jump to studying specific algorithms, but you should at least skim this material. Pay close attention to the section "Big O Notation," because a good understanding of run time performance can mean the difference between an algorithm performing its task in seconds, hours, or not at all.

Approach

To get the most out of an algorithm, you must be able to do more than simply follow its steps. You need to understand the following:

The algorithm's behavior   Does it find the best possible solution, or does it just find a good solution? Could there be multiple best solutions? Is there a reason to pick one "best" solution over the others?

The algorithm's speed   Is it fast? Slow? Is it usually fast but sometimes slow for certain inputs?

The algorithm's memory requirements   How much memory will the algorithm need? Is this a reasonable amount? Does the algorithm require billions of terabytes more memory than a computer could possibly have (at least today)?

The main techniques the algorithm uses   Can you reuse those techniques to solve similar problems?

This book covers all of these topics. It does not, however, attempt to cover every detail of every algorithm with mathematical precision. It uses an intuitive approach to explain algorithms and their performance, but it does not analyze performance in rigorous detail. Although that kind of proof can be interesting, it can also be confusing and take up a lot of space, providing a level of detail that is unnecessary for most programmers. This book, after all, is intended primarily for programmers who need to get a job done.

This book's chapters group algorithms that have related themes. Sometimes the theme is the task that they perform (sorting, searching, network algorithms), sometimes it's the data structures they use (linked lists, arrays, hash tables, trees), and sometimes it's the techniques they use (recursion, decision trees, distributed algorithms). At a high level, these groupings may seem arbitrary, but when you read about the algorithms, you'll see that they fit together.

In addition to those categories, many algorithms have underlying themes that cross chapter boundaries. For example, tree algorithms (Chapters 10, 11, and 12) tend to be highly recursive (Chapter 9). Linked lists (Chapter 3) can be used to build arrays (Chapter 4), hash tables (Chapter 8), stacks (Chapter 5), and queues (Chapter 5). The ideas of references and pointers are used to build linked lists (Chapter 3), trees (Chapters 10, 11, and 12), and networks (Chapters 13 and 14). As you read, watch for these common threads. Appendix A summarizes common strategies programs use to make these ideas easier to follow.

Algorithms and Data Structures

An *algorithm* is a recipe for performing a certain task. A *data structure* is a way of arranging data to make solving a particular problem easier. A data structure could be a way of arranging values in an *array*, a linked list that connects items in a certain pattern, a tree, a graph, a network, or something even more exotic.

Algorithms are often closely tied to data structures. For example, the edit distance algorithm described in Chapter 15, "String Algorithms," uses a network to determine how similar two strings are. The algorithm is tied closely to the network and won't work without it. Conversely, the algorithm builds and uses the network, so the network isn't useful (or really even built) without the algorithm.

Often an algorithm says, "Build a certain data structure and then use it in a certain way." The algorithm can't exist without the data structure, and there's no point in building the data structure if you don't plan to use it with the algorithm.

Pseudocode

To make the algorithms described in this book as useful as possible, they are first described in intuitive English terms. From this high-level explanation, you should be able to implement the algorithm in most programming languages.

Often, however, an algorithm's implementation contains petty details that can make implementation hard. To make handling those details easier, many algorithms are also described in pseudocode. *Pseudocode* is text that is a lot like a programming language but is not really a programming language. The idea is to give you the structure and details you would need to implement the algorithm in code without tying the algorithm to a particular programming language. Ideally, you can translate the pseudocode into actual code to run on your computer.

The following snippet shows an example of pseudocode for an algorithm that calculates the greatest common divisor (GCD) of two integers:

```
// Find the greatest common divisor of a and b.
// GCD(a, b) = GCD(b, a Mod b).
Integer: Gcd(Integer: a, Integer: b)
    While (b != 0)
        // Calculate the remainder.
        Integer: remainder = a Mod b

        // Calculate GCD(b, remainder).
        a = b
        b = remainder
    End While

    // GCD(a, 0) is a.
    Return a
End Gcd
```

THE MOD OPERATOR

The modulus operator, which is written as Mod in the pseudocode, means the remainder after division. For example, "13 Mod 4" is 1 because 13 divided by 4 is 3 with a remainder of 1.

The statement "13 Mod 4" is usually pronounced "13 mod 4" or "13 modulo 4."

The pseudocode starts with a comment. Comments begin with the characters // and extend to the end of the line.

The first actual line of code is the algorithm's declaration. This algorithm is called Gcd and returns an integer result. It takes two parameters named a and b, both of which are integers.

NOTE   Chunks of code that perform a task, optionally returning a result, are variously called *routines, subroutines, methods, procedures, subprocedures,* or *functions*.

The code after the declaration is indented to show that it is part of the method. The first line in the method's body begins a While loop. The code indented below the While statement is executed as long as the condition in the While statement remains true.

The While loop ends with an End While statement. This statement isn't strictly necessary, because the indentation shows where the loop ends, but it provides a reminder of what kind of block of statements is ending.

The method exits at the Return statement. This algorithm returns a value, so this Return statement indicates which value the algorithm should return. If the algorithm doesn't return any value, such as if its purpose is to arrange values or build a data structure, the Return statement isn't followed by a return value, or the method may have no Return statement.

The code in this example is fairly close to actual programming code. Other examples may contain instructions or values described in English. In those cases, the instructions are enclosed in angle brackets (<>) to indicate that you need to translate the English instructions into program code.

Normally, when a parameter or variable is declared (in the Gcd algorithm, this includes the parameters a and b and the variable remainder), its data type is given before it followed by a colon, as in Integer: remainder. The data type may be omitted for simple integer looping variables, as in For i = 1 To 10.

One other feature that is different from some programming languages is that a pseudocode For loop may include a Step statement indicating the value by which the looping variable is changed after each trip through the loop. A For loop ends with a Next i statement (where i is the looping variable) to remind you which loop is ending.

For example, consider the following pseudocode:

```
For i = 100 To 0 Step -5
    // Do something...
Next i
```

This code is equivalent to the following C# code:

```
for (int i = 100; i >= 0; i -= 5)
{
    // Do something...
}
```

Both of those are equivalent to the following Python code:

```
for i in range(100, -1, -5):
    # Do something...
```

The pseudocode used in this book uses If-Then-Else statements, Case statements, and other statements as needed. These should be familiar to you from your knowledge of real programming languages. Anything else that the code needs is spelled out in English.

Many algorithms in this book are written as methods or functions that return a result. The method's declaration begins with the result's data type. If a method performs some task and doesn't return a result, it has no data type.

The following pseudocode contains two methods:

```
// Return twice the input value.
Integer: DoubleIt(Integer: value)
    Return 2 * value
End DoubleIt

// The following method does something and doesn't return a value.
DoSomething(Integer: values[])
    // Some code here.
    ...
End DoSomething
```

The DoubleIt method takes an integer as a parameter and returns an integer. The code doubles the input value and returns the result.

The DoSomething method takes as a parameter an array of integers named values. It performs a task and doesn't return a result. For example, it might randomize or sort the items in the array. (Note that this book assumes that arrays start with the index 0. For example, an array containing three items has indices 0, 1, and 2.)

Pseudocode should be intuitive and easy to understand, but if you find something that doesn't make sense to you, feel free to post a question on the book's discussion forum at www.wiley.com/go/essentialalgorithms or e-mail me at RodStephens@CSharpHelper.com. I'll point you in the right direction.

One problem with pseudocode is that it has no compiler to detect errors. As a check of the basic algorithm and to give you some actual code to use for a reference, C# and Python implementations of many of the algorithms and exercises are available for download on the book's website.

Algorithm Features

A good algorithm must have three features: correctness, maintainability, and efficiency.

Obviously, if an algorithm doesn't solve the problem for which it was designed, it's not much use. If it doesn't produce correct answers, there's little point in using it.

NOTE   Interestingly, some algorithms produce correct answers only some of the time but are still useful. For example, an algorithm may be able to give you some information with a certain probability. In that case, you may be able to rerun the algorithm many times to increase your confidence that the answer is correct. Fermat's primality test, described in Chapter 2, "Numerical Algorithms," is this kind of algorithm.

If an algorithm isn't maintainable, it's dangerous to use in a program. If an algorithm is simple, intuitive, and elegant, you can be confident that it is producing correct results and you can fix it if it doesn't. If the algorithm is intricate, confusing, and convoluted, you may have a lot of trouble implementing it, and you will have even more trouble fixing it if a bug arises. If it's hard to understand, how can you know if it is producing correct results?

NOTE   This doesn't mean that it isn't worth studying confusing and difficult algorithms. Even if you have trouble implementing an algorithm, you may learn a lot in the attempt. Over time, your algorithmic intuition and skill will increase, so algorithms you once thought were confusing will seem easier to handle. You must always test all algorithms thoroughly, however, to make sure that they are producing correct results.

Most developers spend a lot of effort on efficiency, and efficiency is certainly important. If an algorithm produces a correct result and is simple to implement and debug, it's still not much use if it takes seven years to finish or if it requires more memory than a computer can possibly hold.

To study an algorithm's performance, computer scientists ask how its performance changes as the size of the problem changes. If you double the number of values the algorithm is processing, does the run time double? Does it increase by a factor of 4? Does it increase exponentially so that it suddenly takes years to finish?

You can ask the same questions about memory usage or any other resource that the algorithm requires. If you double the size of the problem, does the amount of memory required double?

You can also ask the same questions with respect to the algorithm's performance under different circumstances. What is the algorithm's worst-case performance? How likely is the worst case to occur? If you run the algorithm on a large set of random data, what is its average-case performance?

To get a feeling for how problem size relates to performance, computer scientists use Big O notation, which is described in the following section.

Big O Notation

Big O notation uses a function to describe how the algorithm's worst-case performance relates to the problem size as the size grows very large. (This is sometimes called the program's *asymptotic performance*.) The function is written within parentheses after a capital letter O.

For example, $O(N^2)$ means that an algorithm's run time (or memory usage or whatever you're measuring) increases as the square of the number of inputs N. If you double the number of inputs, the run time increases by roughly a factor of 4. Similarly, if you triple the number of inputs, the run time increases by a factor of 9.

NOTE   Often $O(N^2)$ is pronounced "order N squared." For example, you might say, "The quicksort algorithm described in Chapter 6, 'Sorting,' has a worst-case performance of order N squared."

There are five basic rules for calculating an algorithm's Big O notation.

1. If an algorithm performs a certain sequence of steps $f(N)$ times for a mathematical function f, then it takes $O(f(N))$ steps.

2. If an algorithm performs an operation that takes $O(f(N))$ steps and then performs a second operation that takes $O(g(N))$ steps for functions f and g, then the algorithm's total performance is $O(f(N) + g(N))$.

3. If an algorithm takes $O(f(N) + g(N))$ time and the function $f(N)$ is greater than $g(N)$ for large N, then the algorithm's performance can be simplified to $O(f(N))$.

4. If an algorithm performs an operation that takes $O(f(N))$ steps, and for every step in that operation it performs another $O(g(N))$ steps, then the algorithm's total performance is $O(f(N) \times g(N))$.

5. Ignore constant multiples. If C is a constant, $O(C \times f(N))$ is the same as $O(f(N))$, and $O(f(C \times N))$ is the same as $O(f(N))$.

These rules may seem a bit formal, with all that talk of f(N) and g(N), but they're fairly easy to apply. If they seem confusing, a few examples should make them easier to understand.

Rule 1

If an algorithm performs a certain sequence of steps f(N) times for a mathematical function f, *then* it takes O(f(N)) steps.

Consider the following algorithm, written in pseudocode, for finding the largest integer in an array:

```
Integer: FindLargest(Integer: array[])
    Integer: largest = array[0]
    For i = 1 To <largest index>
        If (array[i] > largest) Then largest = array[i]
    Next i
    Return largest
End FindLargest
```

The `FindLargest` algorithm takes as a parameter an array of integers and returns an integer result. It starts by setting the variable `largest` equal to the first value in the array.

It then loops through the remaining values in the array, comparing each to `largest`. If it finds a value that is larger than `largest`, the program sets `largest` equal to that value.

After it finishes the loop, the algorithm returns `largest`.

This algorithm examines each of the N items in the array once, so it has O(N) performance.

> **NOTE**   Often algorithms spend most of their time in loops. There's no way an algorithm can execute more than a few steps with a fixed number of code lines unless it contains some sort of loop.
>
> Study an algorithm's loops to figure out how much time it takes.

Rule 2

If an algorithm performs an operation that takes O(f(N)) steps and then performs a second operation that takes O(g(N)) steps for functions f and g, *then* the algorithm's total performance is O(f(N) + g(N)).

If you look again at the `FindLargest` algorithm shown in the preceding section, you'll see that a few steps are not actually inside the loop. The following pseudocode shows the same steps, with their run time order shown to the right in comments:

```
Integer: FindLargest(Integer: array[])
    Integer: largest = array[0]                          // O(1)
    For i = 1 To <largest index>                         // O(N)
        If (array[i] > largest) Then largest = array[i]
    Next i
    Return largest                                        // O(1)
End FindLargest
```

This algorithm performs one setup step before it enters its loop and then performs one more step after it finishes the loop. Both of those steps have performance O(1) (they're each just a single step), so the total run time for the algorithm is really O(1 + N + 1). You can use normal algebra to combine terms to rewrite this as O(2 + N).

Rule 3

If an algorithm takes O(f(N) + g(N)) time and the function f(N) is greater than g(N) for large N, *then* the algorithm's performance can be simplified to O(f(N)).

The preceding example showed that the FindLargest algorithm has run time O(2 + N). When N grows large, the function N is larger than the constant value 2, so O(2 + N) simplifies to O(N).

Ignoring the smaller function lets you focus on the algorithm's asymptotic behavior as the problem size becomes very large. It also lets you ignore relatively small setup and cleanup tasks. If an algorithm spends some time building simple data structures and otherwise getting ready to perform a big computation, you can ignore the setup time as long as it's small compared to the length of the main calculation.

Rule 4

If an algorithm performs an operation that takes O(f(N)) steps, and for every step in that operation it performs another O(g(N)) steps, *then* the algorithm's total performance is O(f(N) × g(N)).

Consider the following algorithm that determines whether an array contains any duplicate items. (Note that this isn't the most efficient way to detect duplicates.)

```
Boolean: ContainsDuplicates(Integer: array[])
    // Loop over all of the array's items.
    For i = 0 To <largest index>
        For j = 0 To <largest index>
            // See if these two items are duplicates.
            If (i != j) Then
                If (array[i] == array[j]) Then Return True
            End If
        Next j
    Next i
```

```
    // If we get to this point, there are no duplicates.
    Return False
End ContainsDuplicates
```

This algorithm contains two nested loops. The outer loop iterates over all the array's N items, so it takes O(N) steps.

For each trip through the outer loop, the inner loop also iterates over the N items in the array, so it also takes O(N) steps.

Because one loop is nested inside the other, the combined performance is $O(N \times N) = O(N^2)$.

Rule 5

Ignore constant multiples. If C is a constant, $O(C \times f(N))$ is the same as $O(f(N))$, and $O(f(C \times N))$ is the same as $O(f(N))$.

If you look again at the `ContainsDuplicates` algorithm shown in the preceding section, you'll see that the inner loop actually performs one or two steps. It performs an `If` test to see if the indices i and j are the same. If they are different, it compares `array[i]` and `array[j]`. It may also return the value `True`.

If you ignore the extra step for the `Return` statement (it happens at most only once) and you assume that the algorithm performs both of the `If` statements (as it does most of the time), then the inner loop takes $O(2 \times N)$ steps. Therefore, the algorithm's total performance is $O(N \times 2 \times N) = O(2 \times N^2)$.

Rule 5 lets you ignore the factor of 2, so the run time is $O(N^2)$.

This rule really goes back to the purpose of Big O notation. The idea is to get a feeling for the algorithm's behavior as N increases. In this case, suppose that you increase N by a factor of 2.

If you plug the value $2 \times N$ into the equation $2 \times N^2$, you get the following:

$$2 \times (2 \times N)^2 = 2 \times 4 \times N^2 = 8 \times N^2$$

This is four times the original value $2 \times N^2$, so the run time has increased by a factor of 4.

Now try the same thing with the run time simplified by rule 5 to $O(N^2)$. Plugging $2 \times N$ into this equation gives the following:

$$(2 \times N)^2 = 4 \times N^2$$

This is four times the original value N^2, so this also means that the run time has increased by a factor of 4.

Whether you use the formula $2 \times N^2$ or just N^2, the result is the same: increasing the size of the problem by a factor of 2 increases the run time by a factor of 4. The important thing here isn't the constant; it's the fact that the run time increases as the square of the number of inputs N.

> **NOTE** It's important to remember that Big O notation is just intended to give you an idea of an algorithm's theoretical behavior. Your results in practice may be different.

For example, suppose an algorithm's performance is O(N), but if you don't ignore the constants, the actual number of steps executed is something like 100,000,000 + N. Unless N is really big, you may not be able to safely ignore the constant.

Common Run Time Functions

When you study the run time of algorithms, some functions occur frequently. The following sections give some examples of a few of the most common functions. They also give you some perspective so that you'll know, for example, whether an algorithm with $O(N^3)$ performance is reasonable.

1

An algorithm with O(1) performance takes a constant amount of time no matter how big the problem is. These sorts of algorithms tend to perform relatively trivial tasks because they cannot even look at all of the inputs in O(1) time.

For example, at one point the `quicksort` algorithm needs to pick a number that is in an array of values. Ideally, that number should be somewhere in the middle of all of the values in the array, but there's no easy way to tell which number might fall nicely in the middle. (For example, if the numbers are evenly distributed between 1 and 100, 50 would make a good dividing number.) The following algorithm shows one common approach for solving this problem:

```
Integer: DividingPoint(Integer: array[])
    Integer: number1 = array[0]
    Integer: number2 = array[<last index of array>]
    Integer: number3 = array[<last index of array> / 2]

    If (<number1 is between number2 and number3>) Then Return number1
    If (<number2 is between number1 and number3>) Then Return number2
    Return number3
End MiddleValue
```

This algorithm picks the values at the beginning, end, and middle of the array; compares them; and returns whichever item lies between the other two. This may not be the best item to pick out of the whole array, but there's a decent chance that it's not too terrible a choice.

Because this algorithm performs only a few fixed steps, it has O(1) performance and its run time is independent of the number of inputs N. (Of course, this algorithm doesn't really stand alone. It's just a small part of a more complicated algorithm.)

Log N

An algorithm with O(log N) performance typically divides the number of items it must consider by a fixed fraction at every step.

For example, Figure 1.1 shows a sorted complete binary tree. It's a *binary tree* because every node has at most two branches. It's a *complete tree* because every level (except possibly the last) is completely full, and all the nodes in the last level are grouped on the left side. It's a *sorted tree* because every node's value is at least as large as its left child and no larger than its right child. (Chapter 10, "Trees," has a lot more to say about trees.)

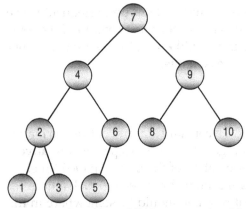

Figure 1.1: Searching a full binary tree takes O(log N) steps.

LOGARITHMS

The logarithm of a number in a certain log base is the power to which the base must be raised to get a certain result. For example, $\log_2(8)$ is 3 because $2^3 = 8$. Here, 2 is the log base.

Often in algorithms the base is 2 because the inputs are being divided into two groups repeatedly. As you'll see shortly, the log base isn't really important in Big O notation, so it is usually omitted.

The following pseudocode shows one way you might search the tree shown in Figure 1.1 to find a particular item:

```
Node: FindItem(Integer: target_value)
    Node: test_node = <root of tree>

    Do Forever
        // If we fell off the tree. The value isn't present.
        If (test_node == null) Then Return null

        If (target_value == test_node.Value) Then
            // test_node holds the target value.
            // This is the node we want.
            Return test_node
        Else If (target_value < test_node.Value) Then
            // Move to the left child.
```

```
            test_node = test_node.LeftChild
        Else
            // Move to the right child.
            test_node = test_node.RightChild
        End If
    End Do
End FindItem
```

Chapter 10, "Trees," covers tree algorithms in detail, but you should be able to get the gist of the algorithm from the following discussion.

The algorithm declares and initializes the variable `test_node` so that it points to the root at the top of the tree. (Traditionally, trees in computer programs are drawn with the root at the top, unlike real trees.) It then enters an infinite loop.

If `test_node` is `null`, then the target value isn't in the tree, so the algorithm returns `null`.

> **NOTE**   The value `null` is a special value that you can assign to a variable that should normally point to an object such as a node in a tree. The value `null` means "This variable doesn't point to anything."

If `test_node` holds the target value, then `test_node` is the node that you're seeking, so the algorithm returns it.

If `target_value` is less than the value in `test_node`, then the algorithm sets `test_node` equal to its left child. (If `test_node` is at the bottom of the tree, its `LeftChild` value is `null`, and the algorithm handles the situation the next time it goes through the loop.)

If `test_node`'s value does not equal `target_value` and is not less than `target_value`, then it must be greater than `target_value`. In that case, the algorithm sets `test_node` equal to its right child. (Again, if `test_node` is at the bottom of the tree, its `RightChild` is `null`, and the algorithm handles the situation the next time it goes through the loop.)

The variable `test_node` moves down through the tree and eventually either finds the target value or falls off the tree when `test_node` is `null`.

Understanding this algorithm's performance becomes a question of how far down the tree `test_node` must move before it either finds `target_value` or it falls off the tree.

Sometimes the algorithm gets lucky and finds the target value right away. If the target value is 7 in Figure 1.1, the algorithm finds it in one step and stops. Even if the target value isn't at the root node—for example, if it's 4—the program might have to check only a small piece of the tree before stopping.

In the worst case, however, the algorithm needs to search the tree from top to bottom.

In fact, roughly half the tree's nodes are the nodes at the bottom that have missing children. If the tree were a full complete tree, with every node having exactly zero or two children, then the bottom level would hold exactly half the tree's nodes. That means if you search for randomly chosen values in the tree, the algorithm will have to travel through most of the tree's height most of the time.

Now the question is, "How tall is the tree?" A full complete binary tree of height H has $2^{H+1} - 1$ nodes. To look at it from the other direction, a full complete binary tree that contains N nodes has height $\log_2(N + 1) - 1$. Because the algorithm searches the tree from top to bottom in the worst (and average) case and because the tree has a height of roughly $\log_2(N)$, the algorithm runs in $O(\log_2(N))$ time.

At this point, a curious feature of logarithms comes into play. You can convert a logarithm from base A to base B using this formula:

$$\log_B(x) = \log_A(x) / \log_A(B)$$

Setting $B = 2$, you can use this formula to convert the value $O(\log_2(N))$ into any other log base A:

$$O\big(\log_2(N)\big) = O\big(\log_A(N) / \log_A(2)\big)$$

The value $1 / \log_A(2)$ is a constant for any given A, and Big O notation ignores constant multiples, so that means $O(\log_2(N))$ is the same as $O(\log_A(N))$ for any log base A. For that reason, this run time is often written $O(\log N)$ with no indication of the base (and no parentheses to make it look less cluttered).

This algorithm is typical of many algorithms that have $O(\log N)$ performance. At each step, it divides the number of items that it must consider into two, roughly equal-sized groups.

Because the log base doesn't matter in Big O notation, it doesn't matter which fraction the algorithm uses to divide the items that it is considering. This example divides the number of items in half at each step, which is common for many logarithmic algorithms. But it would still have $O(\log N)$ performance if it divided the remaining items by a factor of 1/10th and made lots of progress at each step or if it divided the items by a factor of 9/10ths and made relatively little progress.

The logarithmic function $\log(N)$ grows relatively slowly as N increases, so algorithms with $O(\log N)$ performance generally are fast enough to be useful.

Sqrt N

Some algorithms have $O(\text{sqrt}(N))$ performance (where sqrt is the square root function), but they're not common, and they are not covered in this book. This function grows very slowly but a bit faster than $\log(N)$.

N

The `FindLargest` algorithm described in the earlier section "Rule 1" has $O(N)$ performance. See that section for an explanation of why it has $O(N)$ performance.

The function N grows more quickly than $\log(N)$ and $\text{sqrt}(N)$ but still not very quickly, so most algorithms that have $O(N)$ performance work quite well in practice.

N log N

Suppose an algorithm loops over all of the items in its problem set and then, for each loop, performs some sort of O(log N) calculation on that item. In that case, the algorithm has O(N × log N) or O(N log N) performance.

Alternatively, an algorithm might perform some sort of O(log N) operation and, for each step in it, do something to each of the items in the problem.

For example, suppose that you have built a sorted tree containing N items as described earlier. You also have an array of N values and you want to know which values in the array are also in the tree.

One approach would be to loop through the values in the array. For each value, you could use the method described earlier to search the tree for that value. The algorithm examines N items, and for each it performs log(N) steps so the total run time is O(N log N).

Many sorting algorithms that work by comparing items to each other have an O(N log N) run time. In fact, it can be proven that any algorithm that sorts by comparing items must use at least O(N log N) steps, so this is the best you can do, at least in Big O notation. Some of those algorithms are still faster than others because of the constants that Big O notation ignores. Some algorithms that don't use comparisons can sort even more quickly. Chapter 6 talks more about algorithms with various run times.

N^2

An algorithm that loops over all of its inputs and then for each input loops over the inputs again has O(N^2) performance. For example, the ContainsDuplicates algorithm described earlier in the section "Rule 4" runs in O(N^2) time. See that section for a description and analysis of the algorithm.

Other powers of N, such as O(N^3) and O(N^4), are possible and are obviously slower than O(N^2).

An algorithm is said to have *polynomial run time* if its run time involves any polynomial involving N. O(N), O(N^2), O(N^6), and even O(N^{4000}) are all polynomial run times.

Polynomial run times are important because in some sense these problems can still be solved. The exponential and factorial run times described next grow extremely quickly, so algorithms that have those run times are practical for only very small numbers of inputs.

2^N

Exponential functions such as 2^N grow extremely quickly, so they are practical for only small problems. Typically algorithms with these run times look for optimal selections of the inputs.

For example, in the *knapsack problem*, you are given a set of objects that each has a weight and a value. You also have a knapsack that can hold a certain amount of weight. You can put a few heavy items in the knapsack, or you can put lots of lighter items in it. The challenge is to select the items with the greatest total value that fit in the knapsack.

This may seem like an easy problem, but the only known algorithms for finding the best possible solution essentially require you to examine every possible combination of items.

To see how many combinations are possible, note that each item is either in the knapsack or out of it, so each item has two possibilities. If you multiply the number of possibilities for the items, you get $2 \times 2 \times \ldots \times 2 = 2^N$ total possible selections.

Sometimes, you don't have to try every possible combination. For example, if adding the first item fills the knapsack completely, you don't need to add any selections that include the first item plus another item. In general, however, you cannot exclude enough possibilities to narrow the search significantly.

For problems with exponential run times, you often need to use *heuristics*— algorithms that usually produce good results but that you cannot guarantee will produce the best possible results.

N!

The *factorial function*, written N! and pronounced "N factorial," is defined for integers greater than 0 by $N! = 1 \times 2 \times 3 \times \ldots \times N$. This function grows much more quickly than even the exponential function 2^N. Typically, algorithms with factorial run times look for an optimal arrangement of the inputs.

For example, in the *traveling salesman problem* (TSP), you are given a list of cities. The goal is to find a route that visits every city exactly once and returns to the starting point while minimizing the total distance traveled.

This isn't too hard with just a few cities, but with many cities the problem becomes challenging. The most obvious approach is to try every possible arrangement of cities. Following that algorithm, you can pick N possible cities for the first city. After making that selection, you have $N - 1$ possible cities to visit next. Then there are $N - 2$ possible third cities, and so forth, so the total number of arrangements is $N \times (N - 1) \times (N - 2) \times \ldots \times 1 = N!$.

Visualizing Functions

Table 1.1 shows a few values for the run time functions described in the preceding sections so that you can see how quickly these functions grow.

Figure 1.2 shows a graph of these functions. Some of the functions have been scaled so that they fit better on the graph, but you can easily see which grows fastest when x grows large. Even dividing by 100 doesn't keep the factorial function on the graph for very long.

Table 1.1: Function Values for Various Inputs

N	$\log_2(N)$	sqrt(N)	N	N^2	2^N	N!
1	0.00	1.00	1	1.00	2	1
5	2.32	2.23	5	25	32	625
10	3.32	3.16	10	100	1,024	1.0×10^9
15	3.90	3.87	15	225	3.3×10^4	2.9×10^{16}
20	4.32	4.47	20	400	1.0×10^6	5.24×10^{24}
50	5.64	7.07	50	2,500	1.1×10^{15}	1.8×10^{83}
100	6.64	10.00	100	1×10^4	1.3×10^{30}	1.0×10^{198}
1000	9.96	31.62	1,000	1×10^6	1.1×10^{301}	—
10000	13.28	100.00	1×10^4	1×10^8	—	—
100000	16.60	316.22	1×10^5	1×10^{10}	—	—

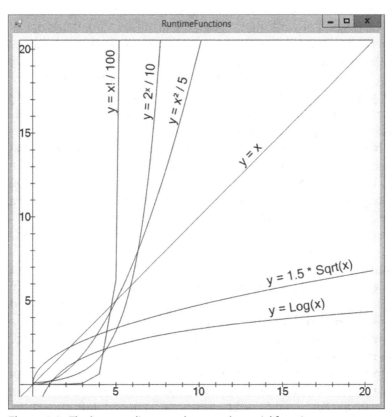

Figure 1.2: The log, sqrt, linear, and even polynomial functions grow at a reasonable pace, but exponential and factorial functions grow incredibly quickly.

Practical Considerations

Although theoretical behavior is important in understanding an algorithm's run time behavior, practical considerations also play an important role in real-world performance for several reasons.

The analysis of an algorithm typically considers all steps as taking the same amount of time even though that may not be the case. Creating and destroying new objects, for example, may take much longer than moving integer values from one part of an array to another. In that case, an algorithm that uses arrays may outperform one that uses lots of objects even though the second algorithm does better in Big O notation.

Many programming environments also provide access to operating system functions that are more efficient than basic algorithmic techniques. For example, part of the insertionsort algorithm requires you to move some of the items in an array down one position so that you can insert a new item before them. This is a fairly slow process and contributes greatly to the algorithm's $O(N^2)$ performance. However, many programs can use a function (such as RtlMoveMemory in .NET programs and MoveMemory in Windows C++ programs) that moves blocks of memory all at once. Instead of walking through the array, moving items one at a time, a program can call these functions to move the whole set of array values at once, making the program much faster.

Just because an algorithm has a certain theoretical asymptotic performance doesn't mean that you can't take advantage of whatever tools your programming environment offers to improve performance. Some programming environments also provide tools that can perform the same tasks as some of the algorithms described in this book. For example, many libraries include sorting routines that do a very good job of sorting arrays. Microsoft's .NET Framework, used by C# and Visual Basic, includes an Array.Sort method that uses an implementation that you are unlikely to beat using your own code—at least in general. Similarly, Python lists have a sort method that sorts the items in the list.

For specific problems, you can still sometimes beat built-in sorting methods if you have extra information about the data. (For example, read about countingsort in Chapter 6.)

Special-purpose libraries may also be available that can help you with certain tasks. For example, you may be able to use a network analysis library instead of writing your own network tools. Similarly, database tools may save you a lot of work building trees and sorting things. You may get better performance building your own balanced trees, but using a database is a lot less work.

If your programming tools include functions that perform the tasks of one of these algorithms, by all means use them. You may get better performance than you could achieve on your own, and you'll certainly have less debugging to do.

Finally, the best algorithm isn't always the one that is fastest for very large problems. If you're sorting a huge list of numbers, quicksort usually provides good performance. If you're sorting only three numbers, a simple series of If statements will probably give better performance and will be a lot simpler. Even if quicksort does give better performance, does it matter whether the program finishes sorting in 1 millisecond or 2? Unless you plan to perform the sort many times, you may be better off going with the simpler algorithm that's easier to debug and maintain rather than the complicated one to save 1 millisecond.

If you use libraries such as those described in the preceding paragraphs, you may not need to code all of these algorithms yourself, but it's still useful to understand how the algorithms work. If you understand the algorithms, you can take better advantage of the tools that implement them even if you don't write them. For example, if you know that relational databases typically use B-trees (and similar trees) to store their indices, you'll have a better understanding of how important pre-allocation and fill factors are. If you understand quicksort, you'll know why some people think the .NET Framework's Array .Sort method is not cryptographically secure. (This is discussed in the section "Using Quicksort" in Chapter 6.)

Understanding the algorithms also lets you apply them to other situations. You may not need to use mergesort, but you may be able to use its divide-and-conquer approach to solve some other problem on multiple processors.

Summary

To get the most out of an algorithm, you not only need to understand how it works, but you also need to understand its performance characteristics. This chapter explained Big O notation, which you can use to study an algorithm's performance. If you know an algorithm's Big O run time behavior, you can estimate how much the run time will change if you change the problem size.

This chapter also described some algorithmic situations that lead to common run time functions. Figure 1.2 showed graphs of these equations so that you can get a feel for just how quickly each grows as the problem size increases. As a rule of thumb, algorithms that run in polynomial time are often fast enough that you can run them for moderately large problems. Algorithms with exponential or factorial run times, however, grow extremely quickly as the problem size increases, so you can run them only with relatively small problem sizes.

Now that you have some understanding of how to analyze algorithm speeds, you're ready to study some specific algorithms. The next chapter discusses numerical algorithms. They tend not to require elaborate data structures, so they usually are quite fast.

Exercises

You can find the answers to these exercises in Appendix B. Asterisks indicate particularly difficult problems.

1. The section "Rule 4" described a ContainsDuplicates algorithm that has run time $O(N^2)$. Consider the following improved version of that algorithm:

```
Boolean: ContainsDuplicates(Integer: array[])
    // Loop over all of the array's items except the last one.
    For i = 0 To <largest index> - 1
        // Loop over the items after item i.
        For j = i + 1 To <largest index>
            // See if these two items are duplicates.
            If (array[i] == array[j]) Then Return True
        Next j
    Next i

    // If we get to this point, there are no duplicates.
    Return False
End ContainsDuplicates
```

What is the run time of this new version?

2. Table 1.1 showed the relationship between problem size N and various run time functions. Another way to study that relationship is to look at the largest problem size that a computer with a certain speed could execute within a given amount of time.

For example, suppose a computer can execute 1 million algorithm steps per second. Consider an algorithm that runs in $O(N^2)$ time. In one hour, the computer could solve a problem where $N = 60,000$ (because $60,000^2 = 3,600,000,000$, which is the number of steps the computer can execute in one hour).

Make a table showing the largest problem size N that this computer could execute for each of the functions listed in Table 1.1 in one second, minute, hour, day, week, and year.

3. Sometimes the constants that you ignore in Big O notation are important. For example, suppose that you have two algorithms that can do the same job. The first requires $1,500 \times N$ steps, and the other requires $30 \times N^2$ steps. For what values of N would you choose each algorithm?

4. *Suppose you have two algorithms—one that uses $N^3 / 75 - N^2 / 4 + N + 10$ steps, and one that uses $N / 2 + 8$ steps. For what values of N would you choose each algorithm?

5. Suppose a program takes as inputs N letters and generates all possible unordered pairs of the letters. For example, with inputs ABCD, the program generates the combinations AB, AC, AD, BC, BD, and CD. (Here unordered means that AB and BA count as the same pair.) What is the algorithm's run time?

6. Suppose an algorithm with N inputs generates values for each unit square on the surface of an $N \times N \times N$ cube. What is the algorithm's run time?

7. Suppose an algorithm with N inputs generates values for each unit cube on the edges of an $N \times N \times N$ cube, as shown in Figure 1.3. What is the algorithm's run time?

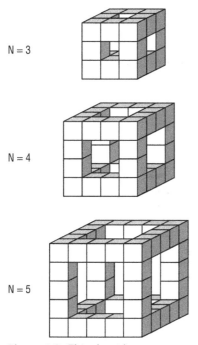

N = 3

N = 4

N = 5

Figure 1.3: This algorithm generates values for cubes on a cube's "skeleton."

8. *Suppose you have an algorithm that, for N inputs, generates a value for each small cube in the shapes shown in Figure 1.4. Assuming that the obvious hidden cubes are present so that the shapes in the figure are not hollow, what is the algorithm's run time?

9. Can you have an algorithm without a data structure? Can you have a data structure without an algorithm?

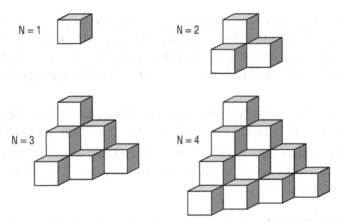

N = 1

N = 2

N = 3

N = 4

Figure 1.4: This algorithm adds one more level to the shape as N increases.

10. Consider the following two algorithms for painting a fence:

```
Algorithm1()
    For i = 0 To <number of boards in fence> - 1
        <paint board number i>
    Next i
End Algorithm1

Algorithm2(Integer: first_board, Integer: last_board)
    If (first_board == last_board) Then
        // There's only one board. Just paint it.
        <paint board number first_board>
    Else
        // There's more than one board. Divide the boards
        // into two groups and recursively paint them.
        Integer: middle_board = (first_board + last_board) / 2
        Algorithm2(first_board, middle_board)
        Algorithm2(middle_board + 1, last_board)
    End If
End Algorithm2
```

What are the run times for these two algorithms, where N is the number of boards in the fence? Which algorithm is better?

11. *You can define Fibonacci numbers recursively by the following rules:

```
Fibonacci(0) = 1
Fibonacci(1) = 1
Fibonacci(n) = Fibonacci(n - 1) + Fibonacci(n - 2)
```

The Fibonacci sequence starts with the values 1, 1, 2, 3, 5, 8, 13, 21, 34, 55, 89. How does the Fibonacci function compare to the run time functions shown in Figure 1.2?

Numerical Algorithms

Numerical algorithms calculate numbers. They perform such tasks as randomizing values, breaking numbers into their prime factors, finding greatest common divisors, and computing geometric areas.

All of these algorithms are useful occasionally, but they also demonstrate useful algorithmic techniques such as adaptive algorithms, Monte Carlo simulation, and using tables to store intermediate results.

Randomizing Data

Randomization plays an important role in many applications. It lets a program simulate random processes, test algorithms to see how they behave with random inputs, and search for solutions to difficult problems. Monte Carlo integration, which is described in the later section "Performing Numerical Integration," uses randomly selected points to estimate the size of a complex geometric area.

The first step in any randomized algorithm is generating random numbers.

Generating Random Values

Even though many programmers talk about "random" number generators, any algorithm used by a computer to produce numbers is not truly random. If you knew the details of the algorithm and its internal state, you could correctly predict the "random" numbers it generates.

To get truly unpredictable randomness, you need to use a source other than a computer program. For example, you could use a radiation detector that measures particles coming out of a radioactive sample to generate random numbers. Because no one can predict exactly when the particles will emerge, this is truly random.

Other possible sources of true randomness include rolling dice, analyzing static in radio waves, and studying Brownian motion. Random.org measures atmospheric noise to generate random numbers. (You can go to `https://www.random.org` to get true random numbers.) You may also be able to use a *hardware random number generator* (HRNG). Search the Internet or look at `https://en.wikipedia.org/wiki/Hardware_random_number_generator` for more information on those.

Unfortunately, because these sorts of *true random-number generators* (TRNGs) are relatively complicated and slow, most applications use a faster *pseudorandom number generator* (PRNG) instead. For many applications, if the numbers are in some sense "random enough," a program can still make use of them and get good results.

Generating Values

One simple and common method of creating pseudorandom numbers is a *linear congruential generator*, which uses the following relationship to generate numbers:

$$X_{n+1} = (A \times X + B) \, \text{Mod} \, M$$

Here A, B, and M are constants.

The value X_0 initializes the generator so that different values for X_0 produce different sequences of numbers. A value that is used to initialize the pseudorandom number generator, such as X_0 in this case, is called the *seed*.

Because all the values in the number sequence are taken modulo M, after at most M numbers, the generator produces a number it produced before, and the sequence of numbers repeats from that point.

As a small example, suppose $A = 7$, $B = 5$, and $M = 11$. If you start with $X_0 = 0$, the previous equation gives you the following sequence of numbers:

$$X_0 = 0$$
$$X_1 = (7 \times 0 + 5) \, \text{Mod} \, 11 = 5$$
$$X_2 = (7 \times 5 + 5) \, \text{Mod} \, 11 = 40 \, \text{Mod} 11 = 7$$
$$X_3 = (7 \times 7 + 5) \, \text{Mod} \, 11 = 54 \, \text{Mod} 11 = 10$$
$$X_4 = (7 \times 10 + 5) \, \text{Mod} \, 11 = 75 \, \text{Mod} 11 = 9$$
$$X_5 = (7 \times 9 + 5) \, \text{Mod} \, 11 = 68 \, \text{Mod} 11 = 2$$
$$X_6 = (7 \times 2 + 5) \, \text{Mod} \, 11 = 19 \, \text{Mod} 11 = 8$$
$$X_7 = (7 \times 8 + 5) \, \text{Mod} \, 11 = 61 \, \text{Mod} 11 = 6$$
$$X_8 = (7 \times 6 + 5) \, \text{Mod} \, 11 = 47 \, \text{Mod} 11 = 3$$
$$X_9 = (7 \times 3 + 5) \, \text{Mod} \, 11 = 26 \, \text{Mod} 11 = 4$$
$$X_{10} = (7 \times 4 + 5) \, \text{Mod} \, 11 = 33 \, \text{Mod} 11 = 0$$

Because $X_{10} = X_0 = 0$, the sequence repeats.

The values 0, 5, 7, 10, 9, 2, 8, 6, 3, 4 appear to be fairly random. But now that you know the method that the program uses to generate the numbers, if someone tells you the method's current number, you can correctly predict those that follow.

Some PRNG algorithms use multiple linear congruential generators with different constants and then select from among the values generated at each step to make the numbers seem more random and to increase the sequence's repeat period. That can make programs produce more random-seeming results, but those methods are still not truly random.

> **NOTE**   Most programming languages have built-in PRNG methods that you can use instead of writing your own. Those methods generally are reasonably fast and produce very long sequences of numbers before they repeat, so for most programs you can simply use them instead of writing your own.

One feature of PRNGs that is sometimes an advantage is that you can use a particular seed value to generate the same sequence of "random" values repeatedly. That may seem like a disadvantage because it means that the numbers are more predictable, but being able to use the same numbers repeatedly can make some programs much easier to debug.

Being able to repeat sequences of numbers also lets some applications store complex data in a very compact form. For example, suppose a program needs to make an object perform a long and complicated pseudorandom walk on a map. The program could generate the walk and save all of its coordinates so that it can redraw the route later. Alternatively, it could just save a seed value. Then, whenever it needs to draw the route, it can use the seed to reinitialize a PRNG so that it produces the same walk each time.

The `RandomTrees` and `random_trees` programs, shown in Figure 2.1, use seed values to represent random trees. Enter a seed and click Go to generate a random tree. If two seed values differ by even 1, they produce very different results.

Figure 2.1: Even slightly different seeds lead to very different random trees.

These programs use the seed value you enter to generate drawing parameters such as the number of branches the tree creates at each step, the angle at which the branches bend from their parent branch, and how much shorter each branch is than its parent. You can download the programs from the book's website to see the details.

If you enter the same seed number twice, you produce the same tree both times.

CRYPTOGRAPHICALLY SECURE PRNGs

Any linear congruential generator has a period over which it repeats, and that makes it unusable for cryptographic purposes.

For example, suppose you encrypt a message by using a PRNG to generate a value for each letter in the message and then add that value to the letter. For example, the letter A plus 3 would be D, because D is three letters after A in the alphabet. If you get to Z, you wrap around to A. So, for example, Y + 3 = B.

This technique works quite well as long as the sequence of numbers is random, but a linear congruential generator has a limited number of seed values. All you need to do to crack the code is to try to decrypt the message with every possible seed value. For each possible decryption, the program can look at the distribution of letters to see whether the result looks like real text. If you picked the wrong seed, every letter should appear with roughly equal frequency. If you guessed the right seed, some letters, such as E and T, will appear much more often than other letters, such as J and X. If the letters are very unevenly distributed, you have probably guessed the seed.

This may seem like a lot of work, but on a modern computer it's not very hard. If the seed value is a 32-bit integer, only about 4 billion seed values are possible. A modern computer can check every possible seed in just a few seconds or, at most, minutes.

A *cryptographically secure pseudorandom number generator* (CSPRNG) uses more complicated algorithms to generate numbers that are harder to predict and to produce much longer sequences without entering a loop. They typically have much larger seed values. A simple PRNG might use a 32-bit seed. A CSPRNG might use keys that are 3,072 bits long to initialize its algorithm.

CSPRNGs are interesting and very "random," but they have a couple of disadvantages. They are complicated, so they're slower than simpler algorithms. They also may not allow you to do all of the initialization manually, so you may be unable to generate a repeatable sequence easily. If you want to use the same sequence more than once, you should use a simpler PRNG. Fortunately, most algorithms don't need a CSPRNG, so you can use a simpler algorithm.

Ensuring Fairness

Usually programs need to use a fair PRNG. A *fair PRNG* is one that produces all of its possible outputs with the same probability. A PRNG that is unfair is called a *biased PRNG*. For example, a coin that comes up heads two-thirds of the time is biased.

Many programming languages have methods that produce random numbers within any desired range. But if you need to write the code to transform the PRNG's values into a specific range, you need to be careful to do so in a fair way.

A linear congruential generator produces a number between 0 (inclusive) and M (exclusive), where M is the modulus used in the generator's equation:

$$X_{n+1} = (A \times X_n + B) \operatorname{Mod} M$$

Usually, a program needs a random number within a range other than 0 to M. An obvious but bad way to map a number produced by the generator into a range Min to Max is to use the following equation:

$$result = Min + number \operatorname{Mod} (Max - Min + 1)$$

For example, to get a value between 1 and 100, you would calculate the following:

$$result = 1 + number \operatorname{Mod} (100 - 1 + 1)$$

The problem with this is that it may make some results more likely than others.

To see why, consider a small example where $M = 3$, $Min = 0$, and $Max = 1$. If the generator does a reasonable job, it produces the values 0, 1, and 2 with roughly equal probability. If you plug these three values into the preceding equation, you get the values shown in Table 2.1.

Table 2.1: PRNG Values and Results Mapped with a Modulus

GENERATOR VALUE	RESULT
0	0
1	1
2	0

The result 0 occurs twice as often as the result 1 in Table 2.1, so the final result is biased.

In a real PRNG where the modulus M is very large, the problem is smaller, but it's still present.

A better approach is to convert the value produced by the PRNG into a fraction between 0 and 1 and then multiply that by the desired range, as in the following formula:

$$result = Min + (number \div M) \times (Max - Min)$$

Another method of converting a pseudorandom value from one range to another is simply to ignore any results that fall outside the desired range. In the previous example, you would use the limited PRNG to generate a value between 0 and 2. If you get a 2, which is outside the desired range, you ignore it and get another number.

For a slightly more realistic example, suppose that you want to give a cookie to one of four friends, and you have a six-sided die. In that case, you could simply roll the die repeatedly until you get a value between 1 and 4.

Getting Fairness from Biased Sources

Even if a PRNG is unfair, there may be a way to generate fair numbers. For example, suppose that you think a coin is unfair. You don't know the probabilities of getting heads or tails, but you suspect the probabilities are not 0.5. In that case, the following algorithm produces a fair coin flip:

```
Flip the biased coin twice.
    If the result is {Heads, Tails}, return Heads.
    If the result is {Tails, Heads}, return Tails.
    If the result is something else, start over.
```

To see why this works, suppose the probability of the biased coin coming up heads is P, and the probability of its coming up tails is $1 - P$. Then the probability of getting heads followed by tails is $P \times (1 - P)$. The probability of getting tails followed by heads is $(1 - P) \times P$. The two probabilities are the same, so the probability of the algorithm returning heads or tails is the same, and the result is fair.

If the biased coin gives you heads followed by heads or tails followed by tails, you need to repeat the algorithm. If you are unlucky or the coin is very biased, you may need to repeat the algorithm many times before you get a fair result. For example, if $P = 0.9$, 81% of the time the coin will give you heads followed by heads, and 1% of the time it will give you tails followed by tails. That means that you would fail to generate a fair flip and need to repeat the algorithm roughly 82% of the time.

> ■ **WARNING**   Using a biased coin to produce fair coin flips is unlikely to be useful in a real program. But it's a good use of probabilities and would make an interesting interview question, so it's worth understanding.

You can use a similar technique to expand the range of a PRNG. For example, suppose you want to give one of your five friends a cookie and your only source of randomness is a fair coin. In that case, you can flip the coin three times and treat the results as a binary number with heads representing 1 and tails representing 0. For example, {heads, tails, heads} corresponds to the value 101 in binary, which is 5 in decimal. If you get a result that is outside the desired range (in this example, {heads, heads, heads} gives the result 111 binary or 7 decimal, which is greater than the number of friends present), you discard the result and try again.

In conclusion, the PRNG tools that come with your programming language are probably good enough for most programs. If you need better randomness, you may need to look at CSPRNGs. Using a fair coin to pick a random number between 1 and 100 or using a biased source of information to generate fair numbers are situations that are more useful under weird circumstances or as interview questions than they are in real life.

Randomizing Arrays

Randomizing the items in an array is a fairly common task in programs. In fact, it's so common that Python's random module includes a shuffle method that does exactly that.

For example, suppose a scheduling program needs to assign employees to work shifts. If the program assigns the employees alphabetically, in the order in which they appear in the database or in some other static order, the employee who always gets assigned to the late-night shift will complain.

Some algorithms can also use randomness to prevent a worst-case situation. For example, the standard quicksort algorithm usually performs well, but if the values it must sort are initially already sorted, the algorithm performs terribly. One way to avoid that situation would be to randomize the values before sorting them.

The following algorithm shows one way to randomize an array:

```
RandomizeArray(String: array[])
    Integer: max_i = <Upper bound of array>
    For i = 0 To max_i - 1
        // Pick the item for position i in the array.
        Integer: j = <random number between i and max_i>
        <Swap array[i] and array[j]>
    Next i
End RandomizeArray
```

This algorithm visits every position in the array once, so it has a run time of $O(N)$, which should be fast enough for most applications.

Note that repeating this algorithm does not make the array "more random." When you shuffle a deck of cards, items that start near each other tend to remain near each other (although possibly less near each other), so you need to shuffle several times to get a reasonably random result. This algorithm completely randomizes the array in a single pass, so running it again just wastes time.

A task similar to randomizing an array is picking a certain number of random items from an array without duplication.

A FAIRLY RANDOM ARRAY

One other important consideration of this algorithm is whether it produces a fair arrangement. In other words, is the probability that an item ends up in any given position the same for all positions? For example, it would be bad if the item that started in the first position finished in the first position half of the time.

I said in the introduction that this book doesn't include long mathematical proofs, so if you want you can skip the following discussion and take my word for it that the randomness algorithm is fair. If you know some probability, however, you may find the discussion interesting.

For a particular item in the array, consider the probability of its being placed in position k. To be placed in position k, it must not have been placed in positions $1, 2, 3, \ldots, k-1$ and then placed in position k.

Define P_{-i} to be the probability of the item's *not* being placed in position i given that it was not previously placed in positions $1, 2, \ldots, i-1$. Also, define P_k to be the probability of the item's being placed in position k given that it was not placed in positions $1, 2, \ldots, k-1$. Then the total probability that the item is placed in position k is $P_{-1} \times P_{-2} \times P_{-3} \times \ldots \times P_{-(k-1)} \times P_k$.

P_1 is $1/N$, so P_{-1} is $1 - P_1 = 1 - 1/N = (N-1)/N$.

After the first item is assigned, $N-1$ items could be assigned to position 2, so P_2 is $1/(N-1)$, and P_{-2} is $1 - P_2 = 1 - 1/(N-1) = (N-2)/(N-1)$.

More generally, $P_i = 1/(N-(i-1))$ and

$P_{-i} = 1 - P_i = 1 - 1/(N-(i-1)) = (N-(i-1)-1)/(N-(i-1)) = (N-i)/(N-i+1)$.

If you multiply the probabilities together, $P_{-1} \times P_{-2} \times P_{-3} \times \ldots \times P_{-(k-1)} \times P_k$ gives the following equation:

$$\frac{N-1}{N} \times \frac{N-2}{N-1} \times \frac{N-3}{N-2} \times \ldots \frac{N-(k-1)}{N-(k-1)+1} \times \frac{1}{(N-(k-1))}$$

If you look at the equation, you'll see that the numerator of each term cancels out with the denominator of the following term. When you make all the cancelations, the equation simplifies to $1/N$.

This means that the probability of the item being placed in position k is $1/N$ no matter what k is, so the arrangement is fair.

For example, suppose you're holding a drawing to give away five copies of your book (something I do occasionally), and you get 100 entries. One way to pick five names is to put the 100 names in an array, randomize it, and then give the books to the first five names in the randomized list. The probability that any particular name is in any of the five winning positions is the same, so the drawing is fair.

Generating Nonuniform Distributions

Some programs need to generate pseudorandom numbers that are not uniformly distributed. Often these programs simulate some other form of random-number generation. For example, a program might want to generate numbers between 2 and 12 to simulate the roll of two six-sided dice.

You can't simply pick pseudorandom numbers between 2 and 12, because you won't have the same probability of getting each number that you would get by rolling two dice.

The solution is actually to simulate the dice rolls by generating two numbers between 1 and 6 and adding them together.

Occasionally, you might want to select random items with specific probabilities. For example, you might like to pick one of the three colors. You want to pick red with probability 0.25 (25%), green with probability 0.30 (30%), and blue with probability 0.45 (45%).

One way to do that is to pick a random value between 0 and 1. Then loop through the probabilities subtracting each from the random value. When the result drops to zero or lower, you select the corresponding color. The following pseudocode shows this algorithm:

```
// Pick an item from a array with given probabilities.
Item: PickItemWithProbabilities(Item: items[],
        Float: probabilities[])
    Float: value = <PRNG value where 0 <= value < 1>
    For i = 0 To items.Length - 1
        value = value - probabilities[i]
        If (value <= 0) Then Return items[i]
    Next i
End PickItemWithProbabilities
```

For this method to work, the `items` and `probabilities` arrays must have the same lengths. The values in the `probabilities` arrays must also add up to 1.

Making Random Walks

As you can probably guess from the name, a *random walk* is a path generated at random. Usually the path consists of steps with a fixed length that move the path along some sort of lattice, such as a rectangular or hexagonal grid. The following pseudocode shows a method that generates points in a random walk on a rectangular grid:

```
Point[]: MakeWalk(Integer: num_points)
    Integer: x = <X coordinate of starting point>
    Integer: y = <Y coordinate of starting point>

    List Of Point: points
    points.Add(x, y)

    For i = 1 To num_points - 1
        direction = random(0, 3)
        If (direction == 0) Then          // Up
            y -= step_size
        Else If (direction == 1) Then    // Right
            x += step_size
```

```
        Else If (direction == 2) Then    // Down
            y += step_size
        Else                             // Left
            x -= step_size
        End If

        points.Add(x, y)
    Next i

    Return points
End MakeWalk
```

This method sets variables x and y to the coordinates of the starting point, possibly in the center of the drawing area. It then enters a loop where it picks a random integer between 0 and 3 and uses that value to move the point (x, y) up, down, left, or right. After the loop ends, the method returns the walk's points.

Figure 2.2 shows the RandomWalk example program using this algorithm to create a random walk.

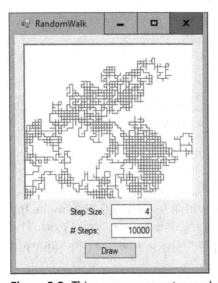

Figure 2.2: This program generates random walks on a square grid.

You can make similar random walks on other grids. For example, you can make a walk on a triangular lattice by picking random directions, as shown in Figure 2.3.

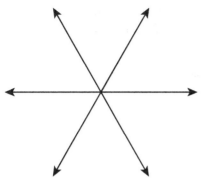

Figure 2.3: These random directions produce a walk on a triangular lattice.

Making Self-Avoiding Walks

A *random self-avoiding walk,* which is also called a *non-self-intersecting walk,* is a random walk that is not allowed to intersect itself. Usually, the walk continues on a finite lattice until no more moves are possible.

Figure 2.4 shows the SelfAvoidingWalk example program displaying a random self-avoiding walk on a 6×6 grid. The walk started at the circled node and continued until it got stuck at a point where it had no unvisited neighboring nodes.

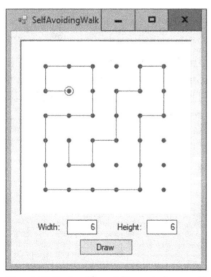

Figure 2.4: A self-avoiding random walk moves randomly but does not visit any node twice.

The algorithm is similar to the one used to build a random walk, except it only allows the walk to move to unvisited lattice points. The following pseudocode code shows the new algorithm:

```
Point[]: SelfAvoidingWalk(Integer: num_points)
    Integer: x = <X coordinate of starting point>
    Integer: y = <Y coordinate of starting point>

    List Of Point: points
    Points.Add(x, y)

    For i = 1 To num_points - 1
        List Of Point: neighbors = <unvisited neighbors of (x, y)>
        If (neighbors Is Empty) Then Return points
        <Move to a random unvisited neighboring point>
    Next i

    Return points
End SelfAvoidingWalk
```

At each step, the new algorithm makes a list of the points that are neighbors to the walk's most recent point. If the neighbor list is empty, then the walk cannot continue, so the method returns the walk so far. If the neighbor list is not empty, the algorithm moves to a random neighbor and continues.

Making Complete Self-Avoiding Walks

The self-avoiding random walk shown in Figure 2.4 eventually got stuck, so it did not visit every node in the lattice. A *complete random self-avoiding walk* is a walk that visits every node in a finite lattice. The CompleteSelfAvoidingWalk example program shown in Figure 2.5 draws complete self-avoiding walks.

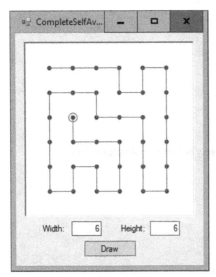

Figure 2.5: A complete self-avoiding random walk visits every node in the lattice.

> **NOTE** Depending on the size of the lattice and the starting point, it may be impossible to find a complete self-avoiding walk. For example, try building a walk on a lattice with two rows and three columns and starting from a point in the middle column.

Building a complete walk is a bit trickier than building any old random walk because many paths lead to dead ends where the walk cannot be extended. For example, the walk shown in Figure 2.4 starts at the circled node and then wanders around randomly until it reaches a point where it has no unvisited neighbors.

To avoid getting stuck in a dead end, the algorithm must be able to unwind bad decisions. It needs to be able to undo previous moves so that it can return to a state where a complete walk is possible. That strategy of unwinding bad decisions in a program is called *backtracking*.

The following pseudocode shows one possible backtracking approach to building complete walks:

```
Point[]: CompleteSelfAvoidingWalk(Integer: num_points)
    Integer: x = <X coordinate of starting point>
    Integer: y = <Y coordinate of starting point>

    List Of Point: points
    Points.Add(x, y)

    ExtendWalk(points, num_points)

    Return points
End CompleteSelfAvoidingWalk

// Extend a walk that we have built so far.
// Return True if we find a complete walk.
Boolean: ExtendWalk(Point[] walk, Integer: num_points)
    If (points.Length == num_points) Then Return True

    List Of Point: neighbors = <unvisited neighbors of (x, y)>
    If (neighbors Is Empty) Then Return False
    <Randomize neighbors>

    For Each neighbor In neighbors
        <Add neighbor to points>
        If (ExtendWalk(points, num_points) Then Return True
        <Remove neighbor from points>
    Next i

    Return False
End ExtendWalk
```

This `CompleteSelfAvoidingWalk` method creates a list of points and adds the starting point to it. It then calls the `ExtendWalk` method to try to extend the walk that it has created so far to a complete walk.

The `ExtendWalk` method first checks the length of the current walk. If the walk contains `num_points` steps, then it is a complete walk, so the method returns `True` to indicate that it found a complete walk.

If the walk is not complete, the method builds a list of points that neighbor the walk's current last point (x, y) and that have not been visited yet. If that list is empty, then the current walk cannot be extended, so the method returns `False` to indicate that no complete walk is possible starting from that initial walk.

If the neighbor list is not empty, the method randomizes the list and loops through them. It tries adding each neighbor to the walk and calls `ExtendWalk` to see whether the new partial walk can be extended to a complete walk. If any of the calls to `ExtendWalk` returns `True`, then it has found a solution, so the current call to `ExtendWalk` also returns `True`.

If a particular neighbor cannot lead to a complete walk, the method removes that point from the walk and tries again with the next neighbor.

If none of the neighbors leads to a complete walk, then no complete walk is possible from the starting walk, so the method returns `False`.

Finding Greatest Common Divisors

The *greatest common divisor* (GCD) of two integers is the largest integer that evenly divides both of the numbers. For example, GCD(60, 24) is 12 because 12 is the largest integer that evenly divides both 60 and 24. (The GCD may seem like an esoteric function, but it is actually quite useful in cryptographic routines that are widely used in business to keep such things as financial communications secure.)

NOTE   If GCD$(A, B) = 1$, A and B are said to be *relatively prime* or *coprime.*

The following section explains an algorithm for finding greatest common divisors. The section after that describes an extension that lets you find an equation related to greatest common divisors.

Calculating Greatest Common Divisors

One way to find the GCD is to factor the two numbers and see which factors they have in common. However, the Greek mathematician Euclid recorded a faster method in his treatise, *Elements,* circa 300 BC.

The following pseudocode shows the modern version of the algorithm. Because it is based on Euclid's work, this algorithm is called the *Euclidian algorithm* or *Euclid's algorithm.*

```
Integer: GCD(Integer: A, Integer: B)
    While (B != 0)
```

```
            Integer: remainder = A Mod B
            // GCD(A, B) = GCD(B, remainder)
            A = B
            B = remainder
        End While
        Return A
    End GCD
```

For example, consider GCD(4851, 3003). Table 2.2 shows the values for A, B, and A Mod B at each step.

Table 2.2: Values Used to Calculate GCD(4851, 3003)

A	B	A MOD B
4,851	3,003	1,848
3,003	1,848	1,155
1,848	1,155	693
1,155	693	462
693	462	231
462	231	0
231	0	

When B becomes 0, the variable A holds the GCD—in this example, 231. To verify the result, note that $4,851 = 231 \times 21$ and $1,848 = 231 \times 8$, so 231 divides both numbers. The values 21 and 8 have no common factors (they are relatively prime), so 231 is the largest integer that divides 4,851 and 1,848.

GREAT GCDs

This is another mathematical explanation that you can skip if you really want.

The key to Euclid's algorithm is the fact that GCD(A, B) = GCD(B, A Mod B).

To understand why this is true, consider the definition of the modulus operator. If the remainder R = A Mod B, then $A = m \times B + R$ for some integer m. If g is the GCD of A and B, then g divides B evenly, so it must also divide $m \times B$ evenly. Because g divides A evenly and $A = m \times B + R$, g must also divide $m \times B + R$ evenly. Because g divides $m \times B$ evenly, it must also divide R evenly.

This proves that g divides both B and R. To say $g = GCD(B, R)$ you still need to know that g is the *largest* integer that divides B and R evenly.

Suppose G is an integer larger than g, and G divides both B and R. Then G also divides $m \times B + R$. But $A = m \times B + R$, so G divides A as well. This means that g is not $GCD(A, B)$. This contradicts the assumption that $g = GCD(A, B)$. Because the assumption that $G > g$ leads to a contradiction, there must be no such G, and g is $GCD(A, B)$.

This algorithm is quite fast because the value B decreases by at least a factor of $1/2$ for every two trips through the `While` loop. Because the size of B decreases by a factor of at least $1/2$ for every two iterations, the algorithm runs in time at most $O(\log B)$.

THE NEED FOR SPEED

The value B in Euclid's algorithm decreases by at least a factor of $1/2$ for every two trips through the `While` loop. To see why, let A_k, B_k, and R_k be the A, B, and R values for the kth iteration, and consider $A_1 = m_1 \times B_1 + R_1$ for some integer m_1. In the second iteration, $A_2 = B_1$ and $B_2 = R_1$.

If $R_1 \le B_1/2$, then $B_2 \le B_1/2$, and B has been cut in half as desired.

Suppose $R_1 > B_1/2$. In the third iteration, $A_3 = B_2 = R_1$, and $B_3 = R_2$. By definition, $R_2 = A_2 \bmod B_2$, which is the same as $B_1 \bmod R_1$. We're assuming that $R_1 > B_1/2$, so R_1 divides into B_1 exactly once with a remainder of $B_1 - R_1$. Because we're assuming that $R_1 > B_1/2$, we know that $B_1 - R_1 \le B_1/2$. Working back through the equations:

$$B_1 - R_1 = B_1 \ \textbf{Mod} \ R_1 = A_2 \ \textbf{Mod} \ B_2 = R_2 = B_3$$

Therefore, $B_3 \le B_1/2$ and B has again been cut in half as desired.

Extending Greatest Common Divisors

In addition to being the largest integer that divides evenly into two values A and B, the GCD also plays a role in an interesting theorem called *Bézout's identity*. That theorem states that, for any integers A and B, there are other integers X and Y such that $A \times X + B \times Y = GCD(A, B)$.

For example, $GCD(210, 154) = 14$. You can set $X = 3$ and $Y = -4$ in Bézout's identity to get the equation $210 \times 3 + 154 \times -4 = 14$.

NOTE   Note: Bézout's identity is named after French mathematician Étienne Bézout (1730–1783), who proved the identity for polynomials. The identity was previously discussed for integers by the earlier French mathematician Claude Gaspard Bachet de Méziriac (1581–1638), but Bézout gets all the publicity. (Perhaps he had a better public relations firm.)

You can use an extended version of Euclid's GCD algorithm to find the integers X and Y that satisfy Bézout's identity. The extended algorithm defines four values at each step of the calculation.

The values Q and R are the quotient and remainder that you get after dividing one number by the other. The remainder plays the role of A and B in Euclid's algorithm.

You calculate the values X and Y by adding combinations of previous values multiplied by the current value of Q.

The following equations show how you initialize the first values for R, X, and Y:

$$R_0 = A$$
$$R_1 = B$$
$$X_0 = 1$$
$$X_1 = 0$$
$$Y_0 = 0$$
$$Y_1 = 1$$

The following equations show how you calculate Q, R, X, and Y for the algorithm's subsequent rounds:

$$R_i = R_{i-2} \% R_{i-1}$$
$$Q_i = R_{i-2} / R_{i-1}$$
$$X_i = X_{i-2} - Q_{i\times} X_{i-1}$$
$$Y_i = Y_{i-2} - Q_{i\times} Y_{i-1}$$

Here, / represents integer division, and the algorithm discards any remainder. The % symbol represents the modulus operator.

When R_i equals 0, the algorithm stops and the current values of X and Y, which are X_{i-1} and Y_{i-1}, are the values that satisfy Bézout's identity. The value R_{i-1} holds the GCD.

For an example, let's work through the algorithm's calculations where A = 210 and B = 154. The following table shows the values of Q, R, X, and Y for the algorithm's rounds:

ROUND	Q	R	X	Y
0		210	1	0
1		154	0	1
2	$210/154=1$	$210\%154=56$	$1-1\times0=1$	$0-1\times1=-1$
3	$154/56=2$	$154\%56=42$	$0-2\times1=-2$	$1-2\times-1=3$
4	$56/42=1$	$56\%42=\mathbf{14}$	$1-1\times-2=\mathbf{3}$	$-1-1\times3=-\mathbf{4}$
5	$42/14=3$	$42\%14=0$		

At this point, R_5 equals 0, so the algorithm stops. The bold value R_4 is 14, which is GCD(210, 154). The bold values X_4 and Y_4 are 3 and –4. The following equation shows those values plugged into Bézout's identity:

$$210*3+154*-4=14$$

The extended GCD algorithm's pseudocode simply implements the algorithm described in the preceding paragraphs, so I won't show it here.

Performing Exponentiation

Sometimes a program needs to calculate a number raised to an integer power. That's not hard if the power is small. For example, 7^3 is easy to evaluate by multiplying $7 \times 7 \times 7 = 343$.

For larger powers such as $7^{102,187,291}$, however, this would be fairly slow.

> **NOTE**   Calculating large powers such as $7^{102,187,291}$ might be slow, but people probably wouldn't care very much if it weren't for the fact that this kind of large exponentiation is used in some important kinds of cryptography.

Fortunately, there's a faster way to perform this kind of operation. This method is based on the fact that you can quickly calculate powers of a number that are themselves powers of 2. For example, consider the value A^1, which is simply A. From that, you can calculate A^2 because $A^2 = A^1 \times A^1$. Similarly, you can calculate A^4 because $A^4 = A^2 \times A^2$. You can then calculate A^8 because $A^8 = A^4 \times A^4$, and so on.

Now that you know how to calculate some large powers of A quickly, you need to figure out how to assemble them to produce any large power. To do that, consider the binary representation of the exponent. Each of the digits in that representation correspond to the powers of $A: A^0, A^1, A^2, A^4$, and so on.

For example, suppose you want to calculate A^{18}. The binary representation of 18 is 10010. Reading the binary digits from right to left, the digits correspond to the values A^0, A^1, A^2, A^4, and A^8. You can use those special powers of A to calculate A^{18}. In this case, $A^{18} = 0 \times A^0 + 1 \times A^1 + 0 \times A^2 + 0 \times A^4 + 1 \times A^8$.

That's the basis for the fast exponentiation algorithm. You build bigger and bigger powers of A and use the binary digits of the exponent to decide which of those should be multiplied into the final result. The following pseudocode shows the algorithm:

```
// Perform the exponentiation.
Integer: Exponentiate(Integer: value, Integer: exponent)
    Integer: result = 1
    Integer: factor = value
    While (exponent != 0)
        If (exponent Mod 2 == 1) Then result *= factor
        factor *= factor
        exponent /= 2
    End While

    Return result
End Exponentiate
```

The algorithm sets `result` to 1. Initially, this holds `value` to the 0th power, which is 1 for any value.

The algorithm also sets `factor` equal to `value`. This will represent the powers of `value`. Initially, it holds `value` to the first power.

The code then enters a loop that executes as long as the exponent is not zero. Inside the loop, the algorithm uses the modulus operator to see whether the exponent is odd. If it is odd, then its binary representation ends with a 1. In that case, the algorithm multiplies `result` by the current value of `factor` to include that power of `value` in the result.

The algorithm then multiplies `factor` by itself so that it represents `value` raised to the next power of 2. It also divides the exponent by 2 to remove its least significant binary digits.

When the exponent reaches zero, the algorithm returns the result.

The algorithm's loop executes once for each binary digit in the exponent. If the exponent is P, then it has $\log_2(P)$ binary digits, so the algorithm runs in $O(\log P)$ time. That's fast enough to calculate some pretty large values. For example, if P is 1 million, $\log(P)$ is about 20, so this algorithm uses about 20 steps.

One limitation of this algorithm is that values raised to large powers grow extremely large. Even a "small" value such as 7^{300} has 254 decimal digits. This means that multiplying the huge numbers needed to calculate large powers is slow and takes up quite a bit of space.

NOTE   C# has a `BigInteger` data type that you can use to calculate extremely large integer values. To use `BigInteger`, give the program a reference to the `System.Numerics` namespace. You may also want to include a `using System .Numerics` directive in the code to make using the `BigInteger` type easier.

Fortunately, the most common applications for these kinds of huge powers are cryptographic algorithms that perform all of their operations in a modulus. The modulus is large, but it still limits the numbers' size. For example, if the modulus has 100 digits, the product of two 100-digit numbers can have no more than 200 digits. You then reduce the result with the modulus to again get a number with no more than 100 digits. Reducing each number with the modulus makes each step slightly slower, but it means you can calculate values of practically unlimited size.

NOTE   In C#, the `BigInteger` data type has a `ModPow` method that performs this kind of exponentiation for you.

In Python, the built-in `pow` function allows you to include a third parameter that indicates the modulus for this kind of exponentiation.

Working with Prime Numbers

As you probably know, a *prime number* (or simply *prime*) is a counting number (an integer greater than 0) greater than 1 whose only factors are 1 and itself. A *composite number* is a counting number greater than 1 that is not prime.

Prime numbers play important roles in some applications where their special properties make certain operations easier or more difficult. For example, some kinds of cryptography use the product of two large primes to provide security. The fact that it is hard to factor a number that is the product of two large primes is what makes the algorithm secure.

The following sections discuss common algorithms that deal with prime numbers.

Finding Prime Factors

The most obvious way to find a number's prime factors is to try dividing the number by all of the numbers between 2 and 1 less than the number. When a possible factor divides the number evenly, save the factor, divide the number by it, and continue trying more possible factors. Note that you need to try the same factor again before moving on in case the number contains more than one copy of the factor.

For example, to find the prime factors of 127, you would try to divide 127 by 2, 3, 4, 5, and so on, until you reach 126.

The following pseudocode shows this algorithm:

```
List Of Integer: FindFactors(Integer: number)
    List Of Integer: factors
    Integer: i = 2
    While (i < number)
        // Pull out factors of i.
        While (number Mod i == 0)
            // i is a factor. Add it to the list.
            factors.Add(i)

            // Divide the number by i.
            number = number / i
        End While

        // Check the next possible factor.
        i = i + 1
    End While

    // If there's anything left of the number, it is a factor, too.
    If (number > 1) Then factors.Add(number)

    Return factors
End FindFactors
```

If the number is N, this algorithm has run time $O(N)$.

You can improve this method considerably with these three key observations:

- You don't need to test whether the number is divisible by any even number other than 2 because, if it is divisible by any even number, it is also divisible by 2. This means you only need to check divisibility by 2 and then by odd numbers instead of by all possible factors. Doing so cuts the run time roughly in half.

- You only need to check for factors up to the square root of the number. If $n = p \times q$, then either p or q must be less than or equal to $sqrt(n)$. (If both are greater than $sqrt(n)$, then their product is greater than n.) If you check possible factors up to $sqrt(n)$, you will find the smaller factor, and when you divide n by that factor, you will find the other one. This reduces the run time to $O(sqrt(n))$.

- Every time you divide the number by a factor, you can update the upper bound on the possible factors that you need to check.

These observations lead to the following improved algorithm:

```
List Of Integer: FindFactors(Integer: number)
    List Of Integer: factors

    // Pull out factors of 2.
    While (number Mod 2 == 0)
        factors.Add(2)
        number = number / 2
    End While

    // Look for odd factors.
    Integer: i = 3
    Integer: max_factor = Sqrt(number)
    While (i <= max_factor)
        // Pull out factors of i.
        While (number Mod i == 0)
            // i is a factor. Add it to the list.
            factors.Add(i)

            // Divide the number by i.
            number = number / i

            // Set a new upper bound.
            max_factor = Sqrt(number)
        End While

        // Check the next possible odd factor.
        i = i + 2
    End While
```

```
      // If there's anything left of the number, it is a factor, too.
      If (number > 1) Then factors.Add(number)

      Return factors
  End FindFactors
```

NOTE   This prime factoring algorithm has run time $O\left(sqrt(N)\right)$, where N is the number it is factoring, so it is reasonably fast for relatively small numbers. If N gets really large, even $O\left(sqrt(N)\right)$ isn't fast enough. For example, if N is 100 digits long, $sqrt(N)$ has 50 digits. If N happens to be prime, even a fast computer won't be able to try all of the possible factors in a reasonable amount of time. This is what makes some cryptographic algorithms secure.

The method of trying all the possible factors smaller than a number is called *trial division*. There are other factoring methods, such as *wheel factorization* and various field sieves. For information on those, search the Internet or look at such pages as the following: https://en.wikipedia.org/wiki/Integer_factorization and http://mathforum.org/library/drmath/view/65801.html. All of these methods depend on the size of the number and its factors, so a number's size gives you an idea of how hard a number might be to factor.

Finding Primes

Suppose that your program needs to pick a large prime number (yet another task required by some cryptographic algorithms). One way to find prime numbers is to use the algorithm described in the preceding section to test a bunch of numbers to see whether they are prime. For reasonably small numbers, that works, but for large numbers, it can be prohibitively slow.

The *sieve of Eratosthenes* is a simple method you can use to find all of the primes up to a given limit. This method works well for reasonably small numbers, but it requires a table with entries for every number that is considered. Therefore, it uses an unreasonable amount of memory if the numbers are too large.

The basic idea is to make a table with one entry for each of the numbers between 2 and the upper limit. Cross out all of the multiples of 2 (not counting 2 itself). Then, starting at 2, look through the table to find the next number that is not crossed out (3 in this case). Cross out all multiples of that value (not counting the value itself). Note that some of the values may already be crossed out because they were also a multiple of 2. Repeat this step, finding the next value that is not crossed out and crossing out its multiples until you reach the square root of the upper limit. At that point, any numbers that are not crossed out are prime.

The following pseudocode shows the basic algorithm:

```
// Find the primes between 2 and max_number (inclusive).
List Of Integer: FindPrimes(long max_number)
```

```
    // Allocate an array for the numbers.
    Boolean: is_composite = New Boolean[max_number + 1]

    // "Cross out" multiples of 2.
    For i = 4 to max_number Step 2
        is_composite[i] = true
    Next i

    // "Cross out" multiples of primes found so far.
    Integer: next_prime = 3
    Integer: stop_at = Sqrt(max_number)
    While (next_prime <= stop_at)
        // "Cross out" multiples of this prime.
        For i = next_prime * 2 To max_number Step next_prime Then
            is_composite[i] = true
        Next i

        // Move to the next prime, skipping the even numbers.
        next_prime = next_prime + 2
        While (next_prime <= max_number) And (is_composite[next_prime])
            next_prime = next_prime + 2
        End While
    End While

    // Copy the primes into a list.
    List Of Integer: primes
    For i = 2 to max_number
        If (Not is_composite[i]) Then primes.Add(i)
    Next i

    // Return the primes.
    Return primes
End FindPrimes
```

It can be shown that this algorithm has run time $O(N \times \log(\log N))$, but that is beyond the scope of this book.

Testing for Primality

The algorithm described in the earlier section "Finding Prime Factors" factors numbers. One way to determine whether a number is prime is to use that algorithm to try to factor it. If the algorithm doesn't find any factors, then the number is prime.

As that section mentioned, the algorithm works well for relatively small numbers. However, if the number has 100 digits, the number of steps the program must execute is a 50-digit number. Not even the fastest computers can perform that many operations in a reasonable amount of time. (A computer executing 1 trillion steps per second would need more than 3×10^{30} years.)

Some cryptographic algorithms need to use large prime numbers, so this method of testing whether a number is prime won't work. Fortunately, there are other methods. The *Fermat primality test* is one of the simpler.

Fermat's "little theorem" states that if p is prime and $1 \le n < p$, then n^{p-1} Mod $p = 1$ In other words, if you raise n to the $p - 1$ power and then take the result modulo p, the result is 1.

For example, suppose $p = 11$ and $n = 2$. Then n^{p-1} Mod $p = 2^{10}$ Mod 11=1,024 Mod 11. The value $1,024 = 11 \times 93 + 1$, so $1,024$ Mod $11 = 1$. as desired.

Note that it is possible for n^{p-1} Mod $p = 1$, even if p is not prime. In that case, the value n is called a *Fermat liar* because it incorrectly implies that p is prime.

If n^{p-1} Mod $p \ne 1$, then n is called a *Fermat witness* because it proves that p is not prime.

It can be shown that, for a natural number p, at least half of the numbers n between 1 and p are Fermat witnesses. In other words, if p is not prime and you pick a random number n between 1 and p, there is a 0.5 probability that n is a Fermat witness, so n^{p-1} Mod $p \ne 1$.

Of course, there is also a chance you'll get unlucky and randomly pick a Fermat liar for n. If you repeat the test many times, you can increase the chances that you'll pick a witness if one exists.

It can be shown that at each test, there is a 50% chance that you'll pick a Fermat witness. So, if p passes k tests, there is a $1/2^k$ chance that you got unlucky and picked Fermat liars every time. In other words, there is a $1/2^k$ chance that p is actually a composite number pretending to be prime.

For example, if p passes the test 10 times, there is a $1/2^{10} \approx 0.00098$ probability that p is not prime. If you want to be even more certain, repeat the test 100 times. If p passes all 100 tests, there is only a $1/2^{100} \approx 7.8 \times 10^{-31}$ probability that p is not prime.

The following pseudocode shows an algorithm that uses this method to decide whether a number is probably prime:

```
// Return true if the number p is (probably) prime.
Boolean: IsPrime(Integer: p, Integer: max_tests)
    // Perform the test up to max_tests times.
    For test = 1 To max_tests
        <Pick a pseudorandom number n between 1 and p (exclusive)>
        If (n^(p-1) Mod p != 1) Then Return false
    Next test

    // The number is probably prime.
    // (There is a 1/2^max_tests chance that it is not prime.)
    Return true
End IsPrime
```

NOTE This is an example of a *probabilistic algorithm*—one that produces a correct result with a certain probability. There's still a slim chance that the algorithm is wrong, but you can repeat the tests until you reach whatever level of certainty you want.

If the number p is very large—which is the only time when this whole issue is interesting—calculating n^{p-1} by using multiplication could take quite a while. Fortunately, you know how to do this quickly by using the fast exponentiation algorithm described in the earlier section, "Performing Exponentiation."

Once you know how to determine whether a number is (probably) prime, you can write an algorithm to pick prime numbers.

```
// Return a (probable) prime with max_digits digits.
Integer: FindPrime(Integer: num_digits, Integer: max_tests)
    Repeat
        <Pick a pseudorandom number p with num_digits digits>
        If (IsPrime(p, max_tests)) Then Return p
End FindPrime
```

Performing Numerical Integration

Numerical integration, which is also sometimes called *quadrature* or *numeric quadrature*, is the process of using numerical techniques to approximate the area under a curve defined by a function. Often, the function has one variable so it looks like $y = F(x)$ and the result is a two-dimensional area, but some applications might need to calculate the three-dimensional volume under a surface defined by a function $z = F(x, y)$. You could even calculate areas defined by higher-dimensional functions.

If the function is easy to understand, you may be able to use calculus to find the exact area. Unfortunately, you may not always be able to calculate the function's antiderivative. For example, the function's equation might be very complicated, or you might have data generated by some physical process, so you don't know the function's equation. In that case, you can't use calculus, but you *can* use numerical integration.

There are several ways to perform numerical integration. The most straightforward involve Newton-Cotes formulas, which use a series of polynomials to approximate the function. The two most basic kinds of Newton-Cotes formulas are the rectangle rule and the trapezoid rule.

The Rectangle Rule

The *rectangle rule* uses a series of rectangles of uniform width to approximate the area under a curve. Figure 2.6 shows the RectangleRule sample program (which is available for download on the book's website) using the rectangle rule. The program also uses calculus to find the exact area under the curve so that you can see how far the rectangle rule is from the correct result.

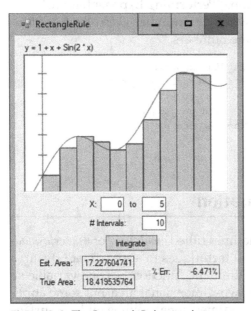

Figure 2.6: The RectangleRule sample program uses the rectangle rule to approximate the area under the curve $y = 1 + x + Sin(2x)$.

The following pseudocode shows an algorithm for applying the rectangle rule:

```
Float: UseRectangleRule(Float: function(), Float: xmin, Float: xmax,
    Integer: num_intervals)
    // Calculate the width of a rectangle.
    Float: dx = (xmax - xmin) / num_intervals

    // Add up the rectangles' areas.
    Float: total_area = 0
    Float: x = xmin
    For i = 1 To num_intervals
        total_area = total_area + dx * function(x)
        x = x + dx
    Next i

    Return total_area
End UseRectangleRule
```

The algorithm simply divides the area into rectangles of constant width and with height equal to the value of the function at the rectangle's left edge. It then loops over the rectangles and adds their areas.

The Trapezoid Rule

You can see in Figure 2.6 where the rectangles don't fit the curve exactly, producing an error in the total calculated area. You can reduce the error by using more, skinnier rectangles. In this example, increasing the number of rectangles from 10 to 20 reduces the error from roughly –6.5% to –3.1%.

An alternative strategy is to use trapezoids to approximate the curve instead of using rectangles. Figure 2.7 shows the TrapezoidRule sample program (which is available for download on the book's website) using the *trapezoid rule*.

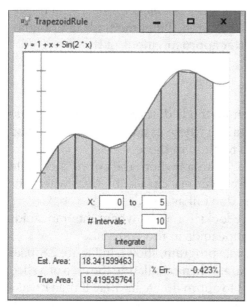

Figure 2.7: The TrapezoidRule sample program uses the trapezoid rule to make a better approximation than the RectangleRule program does.

The following pseudocode shows an algorithm for applying the trapezoid rule:

```
Float: UseTrapezoidRule(Float: function(), Float: xmin, Float: xmax,
    Integer: num_intervals)
    // Calculate the width of a trapezoid.
    Float: dx = (xmax - xmin) / num_intervals

    // Add up the trapezoids' areas.
    Float: total_area = 0
    Float: x = xmin
```

```
    For i = 1 To num_intervals
     total_area = total_area + dx * (function(x) + function(x + dx)) / 2
     x = x + dx
    Next i

    Return total_area
End UseTrapezoidRule
```

The only difference between this algorithm and the rectangle rule algorithm is in the statement that adds the area of each slice. This algorithm uses the formula for the area of a trapezoid: area = width × average of the lengths of the parallel sides.

You can think of the rectangle rule as approximating the curve with a step function that jumps from one value to another at each rectangle's edge. The trapezoid rule approximates the curve with line segments.

Another example of a Newton-Cotes formula is *Simpson's rule*, which uses polynomials of degree 2 to approximate the curve. Other methods use polynomials of even higher degree to make better approximations of the curve.

Adaptive Quadrature

A variation on the numerical integration methods described so far is *adaptive quadrature*, in which the program detects areas where its approximation method may produce large errors and refines its method in those areas.

For example, look again at Figure 2.7. In areas where the curve is close to straight, the trapezoids approximate the curve very closely. In areas where the curve is bending sharply, the trapezoids don't fit as well.

A program using adaptive quadrature looks for areas where the trapezoids don't fit the curve well and uses more trapezoids in those areas.

The AdaptiveMidpointIntegration sample program, shown in Figure 2.8, uses the trapezoid rule with adaptive quadrature. When calculating the area of a slice, this program first uses a single trapezoid to approximate its area. It then breaks the slice into two pieces and uses two smaller trapezoids to calculate their areas. If the difference between the larger trapezoid's area and the sum of the areas of the smaller trapezoids is more than a certain percentage, the program divides the slice into two pieces and calculates the areas of the pieces in the same way.

The following pseudocode shows this algorithm:

```
// Integrate by using an adaptive midpoint trapezoid rule.
Float: IntegrateAdaptiveMidpoint(Float: function(),
   Float: xmin, Float: xmax, Integer: num_intervals,
 Float: max_slice_error)
     // Calculate the width of the initial trapezoids.
     Float: dx = (xmax - xmin) / num_intervals
     double total = 0
```

```
    // Add up the trapezoids' areas.
    Float: total_area = 0
    Float: x = xmin
    For i = 1 To num_intervals
        // Add this slice's area.
        total_area = total_area +
            SliceArea(function, x, x + dx, max_slice_error)
        x = x + dx
    Next i

    Return total_area
End IntegrateAdaptiveMidpoint


// Return the area for this slice.
Float: SliceArea(Float: function(),Float: x1, Float: x2,
  Float: max_slice_error)
    // Calculate the function at the endpoints and the midpoint.
    Float: y1 = function(x1)
    Float: y2 = function(x2)
    Float: xm = (x1 + x2) / 2
    Float: ym = function(xm)

    // Calculate the area for the large slice and two subslices.
    Float: area12 = (x2 - x1) * (y1 + y2) / 2.0
    Float: area1m = (xm - x1) * (y1 + ym) / 2.0
    Float: aream2 = (x2 - xm) * (ym + y2) / 2.0
    Float: area1m2 = area1m + aream2

    // See how close we are.
    Float: error = (area1m2 - area12) / area12

    // See if this is small enough.
    If (Abs(error) < max_slice_error) Then Return area1m2

    // The error is too big. Divide the slice and try again.
    Return
        SliceArea(function, x1, xm, max_slice_error) +
        SliceArea(function, xm, x2, max_slice_error)
End SliceArea
```

If you run the AdaptiveMidpointIntegration program and start with only two initial slices, the program divides them into the 24 slices shown in Figure 2.8 and estimates the area under the curve with –0.035% error. If you use the TrapezoidRule program with 24 slices of uniform width, the program has an error of –0.072%, roughly twice as much as that produced by the adaptive program. The two programs use the same number of slices, but the adaptive program positions them more effectively.

The AdaptiveTrapezoidIntegration sample program uses a different method to decide when to break a slice into subslices. It calculates the second derivative

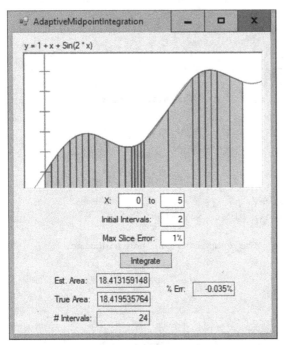

Figure 2.8: The AdaptiveMidpointIntegration program uses an adaptive trapezoid rule to make a better approximation than the TrapezoidRule program.

of the function at the slice's starting x value and divides the interval into one slice plus 1 per second derivative value. For example, if the second derivative is 2, the program divides the slice into three pieces. (The formula for the number of slices was chosen somewhat arbitrarily. You might get better results with a different formula.)

> **NOTE**   In case your calculus is a bit rusty, a function's derivative tells you its slope at any given point. Its second derivative tells you the slope's rate of change, or how fast the curve is bending. A higher second derivative means that the curve is bending relatively tightly, so the AdaptiveTrapezoidIntegration program uses more slices.

Of course, this technique won't work if you can't calculate the curve's second derivative. The technique used by the AdaptiveMidpointIntegration program seems to work fairly well in any case, so you can fall back on that technique.

Adaptive techniques are useful in many algorithms because they can produce better results without wasting effort in areas where it isn't needed. The AdaptiveGridIntegration program shown in Figure 2.9 uses adaptive techniques to estimate the area in the shaded region. This region includes the union of vertical and horizontal ellipses, minus the areas covered by the three circles inside the ellipses.

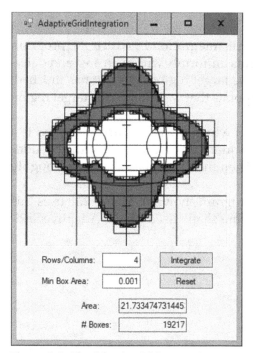

Figure 2.9: The AdaptiveGridIntegration program uses adaptive integration to estimate the area in the shaded region.

This program divides the whole image into a single box and defines a grid of points inside the box. In Figure 2.9, the program uses a grid with four rows and columns of points. For each point in the grid, the program determines whether the point lies inside or outside the shaded region.

If none of the points in the box lies within the shaded region, the program assumes that the box is not inside the region and ignores it.

If every point in the box lies inside the shaded region, the program considers the box to lie completely within the region and adds the box's area to the region's estimated area.

If some of the points in the box lie inside the shaded region and some lie outside the region, the program subdivides the box into smaller boxes and uses the same technique to calculate the smaller boxes' areas.

In Figure 2.9, the AdaptiveGridIntegration program has drawn the boxes it considered so that you can see them. You can see that the program considered many more boxes near the edges of the shaded region than far inside or outside the region. In total, this example considered 19,217 boxes, mostly focused on the edges of the area it was integrating.

Monte Carlo Integration

Monte Carlo integration is form of numeric integration in which the program generates a series of pseudorandom points uniformly within an area and determines whether each point lies within the target region. When it has finished, the program uses the percentage of the points that were inside the target region to estimate the region's total area.

For example, suppose the area within which the points are generated is a 20×20 square, so it has an area of 400 square units, and 37% of the pseudorandom points are within the region. Then the region has an area of roughly $0.37 \times 400 = 148$ square units.

The MonteCarloIntegration sample program shown in Figure 2.10 uses this technique to estimate the area of the same shape used by the AdaptiveGridIntegration program.

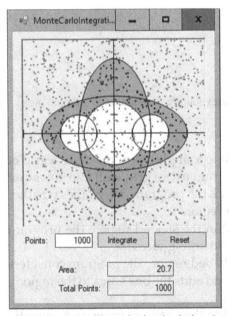

Figure 2.10: Points inside the shaded region are black, and points outside the region are gray.

Monte Carlo integration generally is more prone to error than more methodical approaches such as trapezoid integration and adaptive integration. However, it is sometimes easier to implement because it doesn't require you to know much about the nature of the shape you're measuring. You simply throw points at the shape and see how many hit it.

Finding Zeros

Sometimes a program needs to figure out where an equation crosses the x-axis. In other words, given an equation $y = f(x)$, you may want to find x where $f(x) = 0$. Values such as this are called the equation's *roots*.

Newton's method, which is sometimes called the *Newton-Raphson method*, is a way to approximate an equation's roots successively.

The method starts with an initial guess X_0 for the root. If $f(X_0)$ is not close enough to 0, the algorithm follows a line that is tangent to the function at the point X_0 until the line hits the x-axis. It uses the x-coordinate at the intersection as a new guess X_1 for the root.

The algorithm then repeats the process starting from the new guess X_1. The algorithm continues the process of following tangents to the function to find new guesses until it finds a value X_k where $f(X_k)$ is sufficiently close to 0.

The only tricky part is figuring out how to follow tangent lines. If you use a little calculus to find the derivative of the function $f(x)$, which is also written $df/dx(x)$, then the following equation shows how the algorithm can update its guess by following a tangent line:

$$X_{i+1} = X_i = -\frac{f(X_i)}{f'(X_i)}$$

Figure 2.11 shows the process graphically. The point corresponding to the initial guess is labeled 1. That point's y value is far from 0, so the algorithm follows the tangent line until it hits the x-axis. It then calculates the function at the new guess to get the point labeled 2 in Figure 2.11. This point's y-coordinate is also far from 0, so the algorithm repeats the process to find the next guess, labeled 3. The algorithm repeats the process one more time to find the point labeled 4. Point 4's y-coordinate is close enough to 0, so the algorithm stops.

The following pseudocode shows the algorithm:

```
// Use Newton's method to find a root of the function f(x).
Float: NewtonsMethod(Float: f(), Float: dfdx(), Float: initial_guess,
    Float: maxError)

    float x = initial_guess
    For i = 1 To 100  // Stop at 100 in case something goes wrong.
        // Calculate this point.
        float y = f(x)

        // If we have a small enough error, stop.
        if (Math.Abs(y) < maxError) break

        // Update x.
        x = x - y / dfdx(x)
    Next i

    Return x
End NewtonsMethod
```

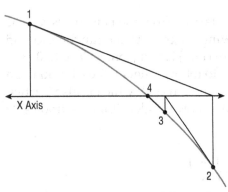

Figure 2.11: Newton's method follows a function's tangent lines to zero in on the function's roots.

The algorithm takes as parameters a function y = f(x), the function's derivative dfdx, an initial guess for the root's value, and a maximum acceptable error.

The code sets the variable x equal to the initial guess and then enters a For loop that repeats, at most, 100 times. Normally, the algorithm quickly finds a solution. But sometimes, if the function has the right curvature, the algorithm can diverge and not zero in on a solution. Or it can get stuck jumping back and forth between two different guesses. The maximum of 100 iterations means the program cannot get stuck forever.

Within the For loop, the algorithm calculates f(x). If the result isn't close enough to 0, the algorithm updates x and tries again.

Note that some functions have more than one root. In that case, you need to use the FindZero algorithm repeatedly with different initial guesses to find each root.

Figure 2.12 shows the NewtonsMethod sample program, which is available for download on this book's website. This program uses Newton's method three times to find the three roots of the function $y = x^3 / 5 - x^2 + x$. Circles show the program's guesses as it searches for each root.

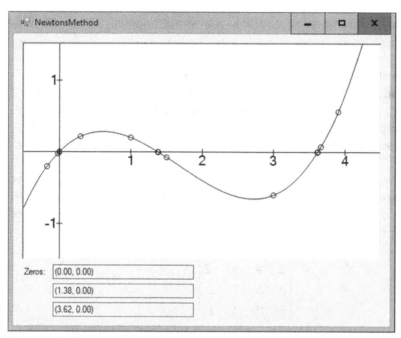

Figure 2.12: The NewtonsMethod sample program demonstrates Newton's method to find the three roots of the function $y = x^3 / 5 - x^2 + x$.

Gaussian Elimination

Root finding algorithms let you find values for X that make the equation $y = f(x)$ equal to zero. *Gaussian elimination* is a technique that does something similar for a system of linear equations. It attempts to find values for the x's in the following equations to make all of the equations true simultaneously:

$$A_{11} \cdot x_1 + A_{12} \cdot x_2 + \ldots + A_{1n} \cdot x_n = C_1$$

$$A_{21} \cdot x_1 + A_{22} \cdot x_2 + \ldots + A_{2n} \cdot x_n = C_2$$

$$\ldots$$

$$A_{n1} \cdot x_1 + A_{n2} \cdot x_2 + \ldots + A_{nn} \cdot x_n = C_n$$

Here all of the A and C values are numbers given by the problem. For a concrete example, consider the following system of equations:

$$2x_1 + 4x_2 + 6x_3 = -2$$

$$3x_1 + 6x_2 + 7x_3 = 2$$

$$6x_1 + 10x_2 + 4x_3 = 1$$

The goal is to find numbers x_1, x_2, and x_3 that simultaneously satisfy all three equations.

> **NOTE**   Gaussian elimination was named after German mathematician and phys-
> icist Johann Carl Friedrich Gauss. The technique has a long history dating back to as
> early as 179 CE when it was included in a Chinese mathematical text. It was described
> and elaborated upon many times, including by Gauss in 1810. It wasn't until the 1950s
> that it took Gauss's name because of confusion about the method's history.

It's easier to work with the equations if you represent them as an augmented matrix. The first entries in each row hold the equations' coefficients (the A values). An extra final column holds the C values. The following shows the augmented matrix for the preceding equations:

$$\begin{vmatrix} 2 & 4 & 6 & -2 \\ 3 & 6 & 7 & 2 \\ 6 & 10 & 4 & 1 \end{vmatrix}$$

> **NOTE**   Often, people draw a vertical line separating the final column containing
> the C values from the other columns that hold the A values.

Gaussian elimination works in two stages that are sometimes called *forward elimination* and *back substitution*.

Forward Elimination

During *forward elimination*, you use two operations to rearrange the matrix until it has the following upper-triangular form:

$$\begin{vmatrix} * & * & * & \cdots & * \\ 0 & * & * & \cdots & * \\ 0 & 0 & * & \cdots & * \\ & & \ddots & \cdots & * \\ 0 & 0 & 0 & \cdots & * \end{vmatrix}$$

The entries on the matrix's lower left are all zeros. The other entries are any numbers and may or may not be zero. (That's what the asterisks mean.)

You can use the following two row operations to manipulate the matrix during forward elimination:

1. Swap the positions of two rows.

2. Add a nonzero multiple of one row to another row.

Each of these operations preserves the truth of the equations. If the x values satisfy the original equations, then they also satisfy the matrix's modified equations.

For an example, consider the following augmented matrix, which was shown earlier:

$$\begin{vmatrix} 2 & 4 & 6 & -2 \\ 3 & 6 & 7 & 2 \\ 6 & 10 & 4 & 1 \end{vmatrix}$$

We start by using the first entry in the first row (highlighted in bold) to zero out the entries in that column in lower rows. The first entry in the first row is 2, and the first entry in the second row is 3. We can zero out the 3 by multiplying the first row by $-3/2 = -1.5$ and then adding it to the second row. The following matrix shows the calculation:

$$\begin{vmatrix} 2 & 4 & 6 & -2 \\ 3-1.5*2 & 6-1.5*4 & 7-1.5*6 & 2-1.5*(-2) \\ 6 & 10 & 4 & 1 \end{vmatrix} = \begin{vmatrix} 2 & 4 & 6 & -2 \\ 0 & 0 & -2 & 5 \\ 6 & 10 & 4 & 1 \end{vmatrix}$$

Next, we perform a similar operation to zero out the first entry in the last row. This time, we multiply the first row by $-6/2 = -3$ and add it to the final row as shown here:

$$\begin{vmatrix} 2 & 4 & 6 & -2 \\ 0 & 0 & -2 & 5 \\ 6-3*2 & 10-3*4 & 4-3*6 & 1-3*(-2) \end{vmatrix} = \begin{vmatrix} 2 & 4 & 6 & -2 \\ 0 & 0 & -2 & 5 \\ 0 & -2 & -14 & 7 \end{vmatrix}$$

Now that we've zeroed out the entries in the first column after the first row, we turn to the second column. We want to zero out the entries in the second column below the second row.

Unfortunately, to do that we would need to multiply the second row by 2/0. That's a problem because we cannot divide by zero.

NOTE   In practice, an entry doesn't need to be exactly zero to cause problems. If the value is close enough to zero, dividing by it might cause an arithmetic overflow error. To prevent that, swap rows if the value is close to zero.

In cases like this one, where the next entry that we want to use to zero out a column is already 0, we swap that row with one of the later rows that does not have a zero in that column. In this example, the third row has –2 in its second column, so we swap the second and third rows to get the following:

$$\begin{vmatrix} 2 & 4 & 6 & -2 \\ 0 & -2 & -14 & 7 \\ 0 & 0 & -2 & 5 \end{vmatrix}$$

NOTE Sometimes you may find that no later row has a nonzero entry in the column that you're trying to zero out. In that case, the system of equations has no unique solution.

Now that you have a nonzero entry in the column, you can use it to continue forward elimination. In this example, the final row already has a zero in its second column, so the matrix is in upper triangular form, and we can move on to back substitution.

Back Substitution

During *back substitution*, you work through the matrix from the bottom up to find the values for the x's that satisfy the equations. Each time you examine a row, you learn one more x value. You can then plug in the x values that you know to find the next value in the row above.

For a concrete example, consider the previous augmented matrix in upper-triangular form:

$$\begin{vmatrix} 2 & 4 & 6 & -2 \\ 0 & -2 & -14 & 7 \\ 0 & 0 & -2 & 5 \end{vmatrix}$$

The last row in the matrix represents the following equation:

$$0x_1 + 0x_2 - 2x_3 = 5$$

Because the first two coefficients are zero, their x terms drop out leaving $-2x_3 = 5$. You can easily solve this by dividing both sides of the equation by –2 to get $x_3 = -2.5$. You have your first x value!

Now you move up a row. The matrix's second row represents the following equation:

$$0x_1 - 2x_2 - 14x_3 = 7$$

But you now know that $x_3 = -2.5$. Plugging that value into the equation gives the following:

$$0\,x_1 - 2\,x_2 - 14 \cdot \left(-2.5\right) = 7$$

This simplifies to the following equation:

$$-2\,x_2 = 7 - 35 = -28$$

Now you can divide both sides of the equation by –2 to get $x_2 = 14$.

You move up a row again to the top row, which corresponds to the following equation:

$$2\,x_1 + 4\,x_2 + 6\,x_3 = -2$$

Plugging in the values that you now have for x_3 and x_2 gives the following:

$$2\,x_1 + 4 \cdot 14 + 6 \cdot \left(-2.5\right) = -2$$

Rearranging this gives the following:

$$2\,x_1 = -2 - 4 \cdot 14 - 6 \cdot \left(-2.5\right) = -2 - 56 + 15 = -43$$

Now you can divide both sides of the equation by 2 to learn $x_1 = -21.5$.

The complete solution to the original system of equations is $x_1 = -21.5$, $x_2 = 14$, $x_3 = -2.5$. If you plug those values into the original equations, you'll see that they are correct.

The Algorithm

Gaussian elimination is a nice, straightforward, methodical way to solve a system of linear equations. Unfortunately, it requires you to perform a long sequence of relatively simple steps, so you have many chances to make small arithmetic errors. This is exactly the kind of situation that a computer handles well because it can quickly perform any number of simple arithmetic calculations without making mistakes.

The following pseudocode shows the Gaussian elimination algorithm at a high level:

```
// Solve a linear system of equations.
Item: GaussianEliminate(Float: As[,], Float: Cs[])
    <Use the As and Cs to build the augmented matrix.>
    <Use row operations to put the matrix in upper triangular form.>
    <Perform back substitution to find the Xs.>
End GaussianEliminate
```

The details involve some long but relatively straightforward sequences of loops to perform the calculations.

Least Squares Fits

A *least squares fit* attempts to find a function $y = f(x)$ to fit a collection of data values. The result is called a least squares fit because it finds the least possible sum of the squares of the distances between the data points and the corresponding points on the function.

Figure 2.13 shows a function approximating a set of data values. The vertical lines show the distances between the data points and the corresponding points on the function. A least squares fit considers variations of the function and finds the one that minimizes the sum of the squares of those vertical distances.

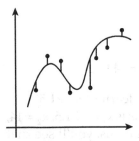

Figure 2.13: A least squares fit minimizes the sum of the squares of the distances between the data points and the function.

Calculating a least squares fit can be intimidating, mostly because it can involve a lot of terms. Fortunately, those terms are often relatively simple. They can look scary when they're all arranged in one grand equation, but individually the terms are easy to manage. I admit that you need to use a little calculus to find a least squares fit. Fortunately, it's pretty easy calculus, so you should be able to understand the following discussion even if you haven't taken a derivative in a while.

The following sections describe two kinds of least squares fits. In the first, the function that approximates the data is a line. In the second, the function is a polynomial of any degree.

Linear Least Squares

In a *linear least squares fit*, the goal is to find a line that minimizes the sum of the squares of the vertical distances between the data points and the line. It's the same situation shown in Figure 2.13, except the curve is a line.

You can represent a line with the equation $y = mx + b$ where m is the line's slope and b is its Y-intercept. (The point where the line crosses the y-axis.)

Suppose that you have a set of n data points $(x_0, y_0), (x_1, y_1), \ldots, (x_n, y_n)$ Then the vertical distance between one of the points (x_i, y_i) and the line is simply $y_i - (mx_i + b)$. The square of that distance is $(y_i - (mx_i + b))^2$. If you add up all of the squared terms for all of the points, you get the following equation:

$$E = (y_0 - (mx_0 + b))^2 + (y_1 - (mx_1 + b))^2 + \ldots + (y_n - (mx_n + b))^2$$

You can write this more concisely by using the mathematical summation symbol Σ:

$$E = \Sigma(y_i - (mx_i + b))^2$$

Here the symbol Σ simply means that you should add up all of the values for $i = 0, 1, 2, \ldots, n$.

This equation looks pretty intimidating in both forms. After all, they include two variables, m and b, plus a bunch of x_i and y_i values. Things are simpler if you remember that the x_i and y_i values are part of the data—they're just numbers like 6 and –13.

Now it's time for the calculus. To find the minimum value for this equation, you take its partial derivatives with respect to the variables m and b, set the derivatives equal to zero, and solve for m and b.

The following equation shows the error equation's derivative with respect to m:

$$\frac{\partial E}{\partial m} = \Sigma 2 \cdot (y_i - (m \cdot x_i + b)) \cdot (-x_i)$$

Multiplying this out and rearranging a bit gives the following:

$$\frac{\partial E}{\partial m} = \Sigma 2 \cdot (-y_i \cdot x_i + m \cdot x_i^2 + b \cdot x_i)$$
$$= 2(m\Sigma x_i^2 + b\Sigma x_i - \Sigma(y_i - x_i))$$

The following equation shows the error equation's derivative with respect to b:

$$\frac{\partial E}{\partial b} = \Sigma 2 \cdot (y_i - (m \cdot x_i + b)) \cdot (-1)$$

Multiplying this out and rearranging a bit gives the following:

$$\frac{\partial E}{\partial b} = \Sigma 2 \cdot (-y_i + m \cdot x_i + b)$$
$$= 2(m\Sigma x_i + b\Sigma 1 - \Sigma y_i)$$

These new equations don't look any simpler until you remember that only the m and b terms are variables. All of the x_i and y_i values are numbers that you're given by the data. To make it easier to work with the equations, let's make the following substitutions:

$$S_x = \Sigma x_i$$
$$S_{xx} = \Sigma x_i^2$$
$$S_{xy} = \Sigma x_i \cdot y_i$$
$$S_y = \Sigma y_i$$
$$S_1 = \Sigma 1$$

If we plug those values into the partial derivatives and set them equal to zero, we get the following:

$$2\left(m \cdot S_{xx} + b \cdot S_x - S_{xy}\right) = 0$$
$$2\left(m \cdot S_x + b \cdot S_1 - S_x\right) = 0$$

Now you can solve these two equations for m and b to get the following:

$$m = \frac{\left(S_{xy} \cdot S_1 - S_x \cdot S_y\right)}{\left(S_{xx} \cdot S_1 - S_x \cdot S_x\right)}$$
$$b = \frac{\left(S_{xy} \cdot S_x - S_y \cdot S_{xx}\right)}{\left(S_x \cdot S_x - S_1 \cdot S_{xx}\right)}$$

All of the S terms are easy to calculate from the data values, so now you can find m and b to minimize the error squared.

The follow pseudocode shows the algorithm for finding a linear least squares fit at a high level:

```
Float[]: FindLinearLeastSquaresFit(Point[]: points)
    <Calculate the sums Sx, Sxx, Sxy, Sy, and S1.>
    <Use the S values to callculate m and b.>
End FindLinearLeastSquaresFit
```

This code simply performs the calculations described in the preceding paragraphs.

Polynomial Least Squares

A linear least squares fit uses a line to fit a set of data points. A *polynomial least squares fit* uses a polynomial of the form $A_0 \cdot x^0 + A_1 \cdot x^1 + A_2 \cdot x^2 + \ldots + A_d \cdot x^d$ to fit the data points.

The *degree* of the polynomial is the largest power of x used by the equation. The preceding equation has degree d. You can pick the degree to fit the data. In general, higher degrees will fit the data points more closely, although they may imply an artificially-high accuracy.

For example, a degree d – 1 polynomial can fit d data points exactly, but it may need to wiggle all over the place to do so. Figure 2.14 shows a degree 5 polynomial that exactly fits six data points.

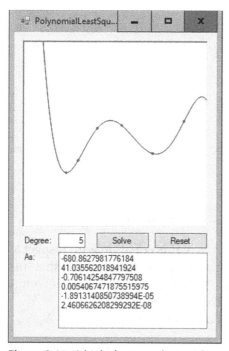

Figure 2.14: A high-degree polynomial may match a set of data values very closely but misleadingly.

It's usually better to pick the smallest degree that fits the data reasonably well. Figure 2.15 shows the same data points as shown in Figure 2.14, but this time fit by a degree 3 polynomial that probably does a better job of representing the data.

You find a polynomial fit in the same way that you find a linear fit: you take the partial derivatives of the error function with respect to the A values, set the derivatives equal to zero, and solve for the A values.

The following equation shows the error function:

$$E = \sum \left(y_i - \left(A_0 * x_i^0 + A_1 * x_i^1 + A_2 * x_i^2 + \ldots + A_n * x_i^d \right) \right)^2$$

$$= \sum \left(y_i - A_0 * x_i^0 - A_1 * x_i^1 - A_2 * x_i^2 - \ldots - A_d * x_i^d \right)^2$$

Here the sum is taken over all of the data points (x_i, y_i).

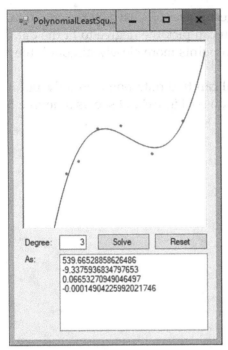

Figure 2.15: You should use lowest-degree polynomial that fits the data reasonably well.

The next step is to take the partial derivatives of this equation with respect to the A values. This is a pretty complicated equation, so you might think that this will be hard. Fortunately, only a few terms in the equation involve any given A value, so most of the terms become zero in the partial derivatives.

The following equation shows the partial derivative with respect to A_k:

$$\frac{\partial E}{\partial A_k} = \sum 2\left(y_i - A_0 * x_i^0 - A_1 * x_i^1 - A_2 * x_i^2 - \ldots - A_n * x_i^d\right)\left(-x_i^k\right)$$

If you multiply the $-x_i^k$ term through and add up the A_i terms separately, you get the following:

$$\frac{\partial E}{\partial A_k} = 2 * \left(\sum y_i * x_i^k - A_0 \sum x_i^k - A_1 \sum x_i^{k+1} - A_2 \sum x_i^{k+2} - \ldots - A_d \sum x_i^{k+d}\right)$$

This equation also looks intimidating, but if you look closely, you'll see that most of the terms are sums that you can calculate by using the data points (x_i, y_i). For example, in the partial derivative with respect to A_k, the A_2 term is the sum of the x_i values raised to the $k + 2$ power.

If you replace the sums with the values $S, S_0, S_1, \ldots, S_d$, then the equation simplifies to the following:

$$\frac{\partial E}{\partial A_k} = 2 * \left(S - A_0 * S_0 - A_1 * S_1 - \ldots - A_d * S_d\right)$$

Now you have n + 1 linear equations with n + 1 unknowns A_0 through A_d. To finish solving the problem, you set the equations equal to zero and then use Gaussian elimination to solve them for the A_i values.

When you set a partial derivative equal to zero, you can divide both sides of the equation by 2 and then move the A terms to the other side of the equals sign to get the following equation:

$$A_0 * S_0 + A_1 * S_1 + \ldots + A_d * S_d = S$$

This has the format used in the earlier section on Gaussian elimination.

All of this leads to the following high-level algorithm for finding a polynomial least squares fit to a set of data points:

```
// Find a polynomial least squares fit to a set of data points.
Float[]: FindPolynomialLeastSquaresFit(Point[]: points)
    <Calculate the sums S, S0, S1, ..., Sn.>
    <Use the S values to build coefficients for
    a system of linear equations.>
    <Use Gaussian elimination to solve the system
    of equations and find the A values.>
End FindPolynomialLeastSquaresFit
```

This code simply performs the calculations described in the preceding text.

Summary

Some numerical algorithms, such as randomization, are useful in a wide variety of applications. Other algorithms, such as prime factoring and finding the greatest common divisor, have more limited use. If your program doesn't need to find greatest common divisors, the GCD algorithm won't be much help.

However, the techniques and concepts demonstrated by these algorithms can be useful in many other situations. For example, the idea that an algorithm can be probabilistic is very important in many applications. That idea can help you devise other algorithms that don't work with perfect certainty (and that could easily be the subject of an interview question).

This chapter explained the ideas of fairness and bias, two important concepts for any sort of randomized algorithm, such as the Monte Carlo integration algorithm, which also was described in this chapter.

This chapter also explained adaptive quadrature, a technique that lets a program focus most of its work on areas that are the most relevant and pay less attention to areas that are easy to manage. This idea of making a program adapt to spend the most time on the most important parts of the problem is applicable to many algorithms.

Many numerical algorithms, such as GCD, Fermat's primality test, the rectangle and trapezoid rules, and Monte Carlo integration, don't need complex data structures. In contrast, most of the other algorithms described in this book do require specialized data structures to produce their results.

The next chapter explains one kind of data structure: linked lists. These are not the most complicated data structures you'll find in this book, but they are useful for many other algorithms. Also, the concept of linking data is useful in other data structures, such as trees and networks.

Exercises

You can find the answers to these exercises in Appendix B. Asterisks indicate particularly difficult problems.

1. Write an algorithm to use a fair six-sided die to generate coin flips.

2. The section "Getting Fairness from Biased Sources" explains how you can use a biased coin to get fair coin flips by flipping the coin twice. However, sometimes doing two flips produces no result, so you need to repeat the process. Suppose that the coin produces heads three-fourths of the time and tails one-fourth of the time. In that case, what is the probability that you'll get no result after two flips and have to try again?

3. Again, consider the coin described in Exercise 2. This time, suppose you were wrong and the coin is actually fair but you're still using the algorithm to get fair flips from a biased coin. In that case, what is the probability that you'll get no result after two flips and have to try again?

4. Write an algorithm to use a biased six-sided die to generate fair values between 1 and 6. How efficient is this algorithm?

5. Write an algorithm to pick M random values from an array containing N items (where $M \leq N$). What is its run time? How does this apply to the example described in the text where you want to give books to five people selected from 100 entries? What if you got 10,000 entries?

6. Write an algorithm to deal five cards to players for a poker program. Does it matter whether you deal one card to each player in turn until every player has five cards or whether you deal five cards all at once to each player in turn?

7. Write a program that simulates rolling two six-sided dice and draws a bar chart or graph showing the number of times each roll occurs. Compare the number of times each value occurs with the number you would expect for two fair dice in that many trials. How many trials do you need to perform before the results fit the expected distribution well?

8. In the complete self-avoiding random walk algorithm, what is the key backtracking step? In other words, exactly where does the backtracking occur?

9. When building a complete self-avoiding random walk, what happens if the algorithm does not randomize the neighbor list? Would that change the algorithm's performance?

10. What happens to Euclid's algorithm if A < B initially?

11. The *least common multiple (LCM)* of integers A and B is the smallest integer that A and B both divide into evenly. How can you use the GCD to calculate the LCM?

12. How would you need to change the fast exponentiation algorithm to implement *modular* fast exponentiation?

13. *Write a program that calculates the GCD for a series of pairs of pseudorandom numbers and graphs the number of steps required by the GCD algorithm versus the average of the two numbers. Does the result look logarithmic?

14. The following pseudocode shows how the sieve of Eratosthenes crosses out multiples of the prime next_prime:

```
// "Cross out" multiples of this prime.
For i = next_prime * 2 To max_number Step next_prime Then
    is_composite[i] = true
Next i
```

The first value crossed out is next_prime * 2. But you know that this value was already crossed out because it is a multiple of 2; the first thing the algorithm did was cross out multiples of 2. How can you modify this loop to avoid revisiting that value and many others that you have already crossed out?

15. *In an infinite set of odd composite numbers, called *Carmichael numbers*, every relatively prime smaller number is a Fermat liar. In other words, p is a Carmichael number if p is odd and every n where $1 < n < p$ and $GCD(p, n) = 1$ is a Fermat liar. Write an algorithm to list the Carmichael numbers between 1 and 10,000 and their prime factors.

16. When you use the rectangle rule, parts of some rectangles fall above the curve, increasing the estimated area, and parts of some rectangles fall below the curve, reducing the estimated area. What do you think would happen if you used the function's value at the midpoint of the rectangle for the rectangle's height instead of the function's value at the rectangle's left edge? Write a program to check your hypothesis.

17. Could you make a program that uses adaptive Monte Carlo integration? Would it be effective?

18. Write a high-level algorithm for performing Monte Carlo integration to find the volume of a three-dimensional shape.

19. How could you use Newton's method to find the points where two functions intersect?

20. Could you use least squares with functions other than lines and polynomials?

21. What happens to the linear least squares calculation if you have only two data points and they have the same x-coordinate? What causes that behavior?

22. What line best fits two data points that have the same x-coordinate? How does that line relate to your answer to Exercise 21?

Linked Lists

Linked lists are probably the simplest data structures you'll build. However, some of the concepts you use to build them are also used to build the most sophisticated data structures described in this book. To use a linked list, you need to understand cells and links in addition to methods of finding, inserting, and deleting cells. You use those same concepts to build complicated networks, trees, and balanced trees, which can be extremely confusing.

This chapter explains the ideas you need to master to use linked lists. Later chapters (in particular, Chapters 4, 5, 8, and 10 through 14) revisit these ideas.

Basic Concepts

A *linked list* is built of objects that are often called *cells*. The cell's class contains whatever data the list must store plus a *link* to another cell. The link is simply a reference or pointer to another object of a cell's class. Often, the pointer field in the cell class is called Next.

For example, the following code shows the definition of an IntegerCell class in C#. The cell holds an integer value and a pointer to the next IntegerCell object in the linked list.

```
class IntegerCell
{
    public int Value;
    public IntegerCell Next;
}
```

Linked lists are often represented graphically, with boxes representing cells and arrows representing links.

To indicate a link that doesn't point to anything, I use a small box with an X in it. (In a programming language, the value of the pointer corresponding to the link would be nothing, null, none, or some other language-specific value indicating that the pointer doesn't point to anything.)

In addition to the list itself, a program needs a variable that points to the list so that the code can find it. Often, this variable is named `top` to indicate that it represents the top of the list. The `top` variable could be a variable of the cell's class, or it might be a pointer to the first cell in the list.

Figure 3.1 shows two linked lists holding the numbers 31, 72, 47, and 9. In the list on the top, the program has a variable named `top` that is a pointer to the list's first cell. In the list on the bottom, the program's `top` variable is the first cell in the list. Both lists end with a box containing an X to represent a null pointer.

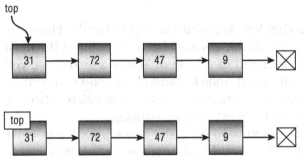

Figure 3.1: These linked lists hold the numbers 31, 72, 47, and 9.

Linked lists are a good way to store a list of items that can grow or shrink over time. To add a new cell, you just add it at the beginning or end of the linked list. In contrast, an array has a fixed size, so it may be hard to enlarge if you need to add more items.

The following sections explain some of the algorithms that you can use to manipulate linked lists. Many of them are most easily described with figures that show the list before and after an operation has been performed.

Singly Linked Lists

In a *singly linked list*, each cell is connected to the following cell by a single link. The lists shown in Figure 3.1 are singly linked lists.

To use a linked list, you need a set of algorithms for iterating over a list, adding items to the list, finding items in the list, and removing items from the list. The following sections describe some of the algorithms that you might want to use.

Iterating Over the List

Assuming that a program has built a linked list, iterating over its cells is relatively easy. The following algorithm shows how you can iterate over the cells in a list and use some sort of method to do something with the values in the cells. This example uses a `Print` method to display the cells' values, but you could replace `Print` with any method that does something with the cells.

```
Iterate(Cell: top)
    While (top != null)
        Print(top.Value)
        top = top.Next
    End While
End Iterate
```

> **NOTE** These algorithms assume that the parameter `top` is passed by value, so the code can modify it without changing the value of `top` in the calling code.

This algorithm starts with a `While` loop that executes as long as the `top` cell pointer is not `null`. Inside the loop, the algorithm calls the `Print` method to display the `top` cell's value. It then sets `top` to point to the next cell in the linked list.

This process continues until `top` is set to the `null` pointer at the end of the list and the `While` loop stops.

This algorithm examines every cell in the linked list, so if the list contains N cells, it has run time O(N).

Finding Cells

Finding a cell in a linked list is simply a matter of iterating over the list and stopping when you find the cell you want. The following algorithm looks through a list and returns the cell that contains a target value:

```
Cell: FindCell(Cell: top, Value: target)
    While (top != null)
        If (top.Value == target) Then Return top
        top = top.Next
    End While

    // If we get this far, the target is not in the list.
    Return null
End FindCell
```

The algorithm enters a While loop that executes as long as top is not null. Inside the loop, the algorithm compares the top cell's value to the target value. If the values match, the algorithm returns top. If the values do not match, the algorithm moves top to point to the next cell in the list.

If top runs all the way through the list and becomes null, then the target value is not in the list, so the algorithm returns null. (Alternatively, the algorithm could throw an exception or raise some kind of error, depending on your programming language.)

As you'll see in some of the following sections, it's often easiest to work with a cell in a linked list if you have a pointer to the cell *before* that cell. The following algorithm finds the cell before the cell that contains a target cell:

```
Cell: FindCellBefore(Cell: top, Value: target)
    // If the list is empty, the target value isn't present.
    If (top == null) Return null

    // Search for the target value.
    While (top.Next != null)
        If (top.Next.Value == target) Then Return top
        top = top.Next
    End While

    // If we get this far, the target is not in the list.
    Return null
End FindCellBefore
```

This code is similar to the previous version—with two exceptions. First it must check that top is not null before it starts so that it knows it can look at top.Next safely. If top is null, then top.Next is undefined, and a program that implemented the algorithm would fail and probably crash.

If top is not null, the algorithm enters a While loop as before, but this time it looks at top.Next.Value instead of top.Value. When it finds the value, top points to the cell before the one that holds the target value, and the algorithm returns top.

Using Sentinels

If you study the preceding algorithm closely, you'll find one situation where it fails. If the first cell in the linked list contains the target value, then there is no cell before that one, so the algorithm cannot return it. The first value that the algorithm examines is in the list's second cell, and the algorithm never looks back.

One way to handle this situation is to add special-purpose code that explicitly looks for the target value in the first cell and then handles that case separately. The program would probably need to handle this situation as a special case, and it could get messy.

Another approach is to create a sentinel at the beginning of the list. A *sentinel* is a cell that is part of the linked list but that doesn't contain any meaningful data. It is used only as a placeholder so that algorithms can refer to a cell that comes before the first cell.

The following pseudocode shows the previous `FindCellBefore` algorithm modified to use a sentinel:

```
Cell: FindCellBefore(Cell: top, Value: target)
    // Search for the target value.
    While (top.Next != null)
        If (top.Next.Value == target) Then Return top
        top = top.Next
    End While

    // If we get this far, the target is not in the list.
    Return null
End FindCellBefore
```

This version doesn't need to check whether `top` is `null`. Because the linked list always has at least a sentinel, `top` cannot be `null`. This means that the `While` loop can begin right away.

This version also starts by checking the value in the first cell in the list, not the second, so it can detect the case where the first cell contains the target value.

This version of the algorithm can return the sentinel cell before the first real cell if appropriate. Therefore, the program using the algorithm doesn't need customized code to handle the special case in which the target value is at the beginning of the list.

When searching for a target value, the algorithm might get lucky and find it right away. But in the worst case it may have to search most of the linked list before it finds the target value. If the target value isn't in the list, the algorithm needs to search every cell in the list. If the list contains N cells, that means this algorithm has run time O(N).

A sentinel may seem like a waste of space, but it removes the need for special-purpose code and makes the algorithm simpler and more elegant.

The following sections assume that linked lists have sentinels.

Adding Cells at the Beginning

One use for linked lists is to provide a data structure where you can store items. This is sort of like an array that you can expand whenever you need more space.

The easiest way to add an item to a linked list is to place a new cell at the beginning, right after the sentinel. The following algorithm adds a new item at the beginning of a linked list:

```
AddAtBeginning(Cell: sentinel, Cell: new_cell)
    new_cell.Next = sentinel.Next
sentinel.Next = new_cell
End AddAtBeginning
```

This algorithm sets the new cell's Next pointer so that it points to the first cell in the list after the sentinel. It then sets the sentinel's Next pointer to point to the new cell. That places the new cell after the sentinel so that it becomes the new first cell in the linked list.

Figure 3.2 shows a linked list before and after a new cell is added at the top of the list.

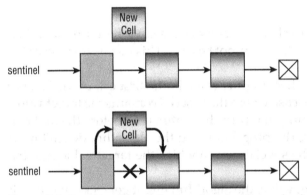

Figure 3.2: To add an item at the top of a linked list, make the new cell's Next link point to the old top of the list and then make the sentinel's Next link point to the new cell.

This algorithm performs only two steps, so its run time is O(1) no matter how many cells the list contains.

Adding Cells at the End

Adding a cell at the end of the list is a bit more difficult than adding it at the beginning because the algorithm must first traverse the list to find the last cell.

The following pseudocode shows an algorithm for adding a new cell at the end of a list:

```
AddAtEnd(Cell: sentinel, Cell: new_cell)
    // Find the last cell.
    While (sentinel.Next != null)
sentinel = sentinel.Next
    End While
```

```
        // Add the new cell at the end.
    sentinel.Next = new_cell
        new_cell.Next = null
    End AddAtEnd
```

The code iterates through the linked list until it finds the last cell. It makes the last cell's Next link point to the new cell and then sets the new cell's Next link to point to null.

This code would be messier if the list didn't have a sentinel. In that case, you would have to use special code to handle the case when the list is empty so sentinal points to null.

Figure 3.3 shows the process graphically.

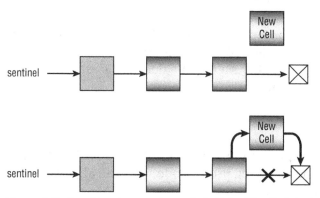

Figure 3.3: To add an item at the end of a linked list, find the last cell and make its Next link point to the new cell. Then make the new cell's Next link point to null.

This algorithm must traverse the entire list, so if the list contains N cells, it has run time O(N).

Inserting Cells After Other Cells

The preceding sections explained how you can add cells at the beginning or end of a linked list, but sometimes you may want to insert an item in the middle of the list. Assuming you have a variable named after_me that points to the cell after which you want to insert the item, the following pseudocode shows an algorithm for inserting a cell after after_me:

```
    InsertCell(Cell: after_me, Cell: new_cell)
        new_cell.Next = after_me.Next
        after_me.Next = new_cell
    End InsertCell
```

This algorithm makes the new cell's Next link point to the cell that follows after_me and then makes after_me's Next link point to the new cell. Figure 3.4 shows the process graphically.

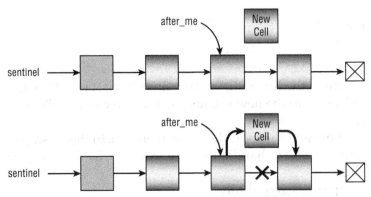

Figure 3.4: Inserting a cell after a given cell takes $O(1)$ time.

This algorithm takes only two steps, so it runs in $O(1)$ time, although you may need to use $O(N)$ time to find the cell `after_me`. For example, if you want to insert a cell after the cell that contains a target value, first you need to find the cell that contains the target value.

Deleting Cells

To delete a target cell, you simply set the previous cell's `Next` link to the cell that follows the target cell. The following pseudocode shows an algorithm that deletes the cell after the cell `after_me`:

```
DeleteAfter(Cell: after_me)
    Cell: target = after_me.Next
    after_me.Next = target.Next
End DeleteAfter
```

Figure 3.5 shows this algorithm graphically.

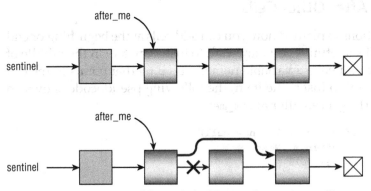

Figure 3.5: To remove a cell from a linked list, set the previous cell's `Next` link to point to the cell after the target cell.

Programming languages such as Python, C#, and Visual Basic use automatic memory management, so the deleted cell is eventually recycled automatically. In some other programming languages, such as C and C++, you may need to perform extra work to free the deleted cell properly. For example, in C++ you would need to free the target cell, as in the following version of the algorithm:

```
DeleteAfter(Cell: after_me)
    Cell: target_cell = after_me.Next
    after_me.Next = after_me.Next.Next
    free(target_cell)
End DeleteAfter
```

How you destroy a linked list also depends on your language. In Python, C#, and Visual Basic, you can simply set all of the program's references to the list to null, and the garbage collector eventually reclaims the list. In a language such as C++, where you need to free each cell explicitly, you need to walk through the list, freeing each cell, as shown in the following pseudocode:

```
DestroyList(Cell: sentinel)
    While (sentinel != null)
        // Save a pointer to the next cell.
        Cell: next_cell = sentinel.Next

        // Free sentinel.
        free(sentinel)

        // Move to the next cell.
        sentinel = next_cell
    End While
End DestroyList
```

How you free resources is language-dependent, so this book doesn't say anything more about it here or in later chapters. Just be aware that you may need to do some extra work whenever you remove a cell or other object from a data structure.

Doubly Linked Lists

In a *doubly linked list*, the cells have links that point to both the next and previous cells in the list. The link to the previous cell is often called Prev or Previous.

Often, it is convenient to have both top and bottom sentinels for doubly linked lists so that the program can easily manipulate the list from either end. For example, this lets you add items to and remove items from either end in O(1) time.

Figure 3.6 shows a doubly linked list with top and bottom sentinels.

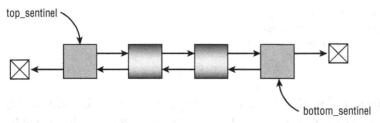

Figure 3.6: Doubly linked lists often have top and bottom sentinels.

Algorithms for manipulating doubly linked lists are similar to those that work with singly linked lists, except that they must do some extra work to manage the second set of links. For example, the following pseudocode shows an algorithm for inserting a cell after a given cell:

```
InsertCell(Cell: after_me, Cell: new_cell)
    // Update Next links.
    new_cell.Next = after_me.Next
    after_me.Next = new_cell

    // Update Prev links.
    new_cell.Next.Prev = new_cell
    new_cell.Prev = after_me
End InsertCell
```

The only really tricky part of these algorithms is keeping track of which links have been updated at any point in time. For example, in the preceding algorithm, the second-to-last statement sets the Prev link that should point to the new cell. You might be tempted to do this by using the following statement:

```
after_me.Next.Prev = new_cell
```

However, when this statement executes, after_me.Next has already been updated to point to the new cell, so this won't work. The algorithm needs to use new_cell.Next instead.

Figure 3.7 shows the algorithm graphically.

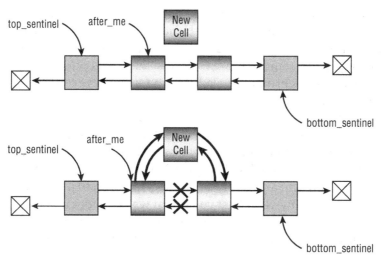

Figure 3.7: When updating a doubly linked list, a program must update both the `Next` and `Prev` links.

Sorted Linked Lists

Sometimes, it's convenient to keep the items in a linked list in sorted order. When you add a new item to the list, you need to search through the list to find the position where the item belongs and update the appropriate links to insert it there.

The following pseudocode shows an algorithm for inserting an item into a sorted singly linked list:

```
// Insert a cell into a sorted singly linked list.
InsertCell(Cell: sentinel, Cell: new_cell)
    // Find the cell before where the new cell belongs.
    While (sentinel.Next != null) And
          (sentinel.Next.Value < new_cell.Value)
sentinel = sentinel.Next
    End While

    // Insert the new cell after sentinel.
    new_cell.Next = sentinel.Next
    sentinel.Next = new_cell
End InsertCell
```

In the worst case, this algorithm might need to cross the whole list before finding the correct location for the new item. Therefore, if the list holds N cells, its run time is $O(N)$.

Although you cannot improve the theoretical run time, you can make the algorithm simpler and slightly faster in practice by adding a bottom sentinel. If you set the bottom sentinel's `Value` to a value larger than any `Value` that could be stored in a cell, then you can remove the `sentinel.Next != null` test because you know that the code will eventually find a location for the new cell, even if it's right before the bottom sentinel.

For example, if the cells hold names that use ASCII characters, you can set the bottom sentinel's `Value` to ~ because the ~ character comes alphabetically after any valid name. If the cells hold integers, you can set the bottom sentinel's `Value` to the largest possible integer value. (On most 32-bit systems, that value is 2,147,483,647. Python can represent arbitrarily large integers, so you'll just have to pick a value that is larger than any value that you might want to store in the list.)

The following pseudocode shows the revised algorithm, assuming that the list has a bottom sentinel holding a value larger than any value that could be held in the cells:

```
// Insert a cell into a sorted singly linked list.
InsertCell(Cell: sentinel, Cell: new_cell)
    // Find the cell before where the new cell belongs.
    While (sentinel.Next.Value < new_cell.Value)
        sentinel = sentinel.Next
    End While

    // Insert the new cell after sentinel.
    new_cell.Next = sentinel.Next
    sentinel.Next = new_cell
End InsertCell
```

Self-Organizing Linked Lists

A *self-organizing linked list* is a list that uses some sort of heuristic to rearrange its items to improve expected access times. For example, if the program searches the list for a specific item a large number of times, it would make sense to move that item to the beginning of the list so that it is easier to find.

> **NOTE** A *heuristic* is an algorithm that is likely but not guaranteed to produce a good result. For example, a heuristic for not getting speeding tickets is to drive no more than 5 miles per hour over the speed limit. You still *might* get a ticket, but you probably won't. (But don't take my word as legal advice! Don't blame me if you get a ticket.) You'll learn a lot more about heuristic algorithms later in this book.

If you number the items in the list 1, 2, ..., N, and the probability that you need to find item i is P_i, then the expected number of steps that you need to move down the list to find an item is given by the following formula:

$$Expected\,Search\,Length =$$
$$1 \cdot P_1 + 2 \cdot P_2 + 3 \cdot P_3 + \cdots + N \cdot P_N$$

If it is equally likely that you'll want to find any given item, then all of the probabilities P_i have the same value $1 / N$ and the expected search length is the following:

$$Expected\,Search\,Length = \frac{1}{N} + \frac{2}{N} + \frac{3}{N} + \cdots + \frac{N}{N} =$$
$$\frac{1}{N} \sum i = \frac{N(N+1)}{2N} = \frac{N+1}{2}$$

This value depends only on the length of the list, so it doesn't matter how the items are arranged. Because the P_i values are all the same, you will need to search roughly halfway through the list on average to find any given item.

In contrast, if the P_i values are different, then it makes sense to move the more popular items to the front of the list. If you knew the P_i values ahead of time, then you could arrange the list optimally. Unfortunately, you usually won't know the actual probabilities until after you perform some searches.

A self-organizing list rearranges its items as it goes along to try to improve the order of its items. The following sections describe several ways that a self-organizing list can rearrange its items to improve search times.

Move To Front (MTF)

In the *move to front method*, the list moves the most recently accessed item to the front of the list. Moving an item to the front of a link list only takes a few steps, so this is relatively fast and easy. Frequently accessed items will tend to remain near the top of the list while those that are accessed less often will usually be near the bottom of the list.

One drawback to this method is that an infrequently accessed item will occasionally jump to the front of the list and slow down subsequent searches until it is pushed back down the list. Still, this kind of list gives a significant improvement for little extra work.

Swap

The *swap method* or *transpose method* swaps the most recently accessed item with the item before it so that frequently accessed items gradually move toward the front of the list. It takes only a few steps to swap two items in a linked list, so this method is fast and easy. It also prevents an infrequently accessed item from jumping to the front of the list and slowing down later searches.

One drawback to this method is that items move slowly. That means frequently accessed items can take a long time to move to the front of the list, so it can take a while before the items reach an effective arrangement. In turn, that means the MTF method may give better results if you are only going to perform a smaller number of searches.

Count

In the *count method*, you keep track of the number of times each item is accessed. When you search for an item, you increment its count and then move it up in the list until it lies before any items that have smaller counts. Over time, the items move close to their optimal arrangement where they are sorted by their probabilities.

One drawback to this method is that it requires extra storage to hold the item counts. It also takes more work to move an item several positions through the list than it does simply to move it to the front of the list or to swap it with one neighboring item.

Despite the fact that it may take a relatively large amount of work to rearrange the list, the items move into near-optimal positions fairly quickly, and after that, the items should require little rearrangement.

Hybrid Methods

The MTF, swap, and count methods have different behaviors during different parts of the list's lifetime. For example, the MTF method makes large adjustments to the items' order relatively quickly, but later searches for less commonly accessed items can mess up the arrangement. Swapping produces a better arrangement but is slower. Counting produces a very good arrangement but requires extra storage.

You may be able to use a combination of techniques to produce a better overall result. For example, you might use an MTF strategy to move the most commonly accessed items quickly to the front part of the list. Then you could switch to a swapping strategy to adjust the list more slowly.

Another approach might initially use MTF while updating item counts. After performing enough searches to get useful statistics, you could sort the items by their counts and then switch to a counting strategy.

Figure 3.8 shows the SelfOrganizingLists example program after it has searched a list of 100 values 1 million times. You can see that the MTF list was much faster than the nonarranging list, the swapping list was even faster, and the counting list was the fastest of all.

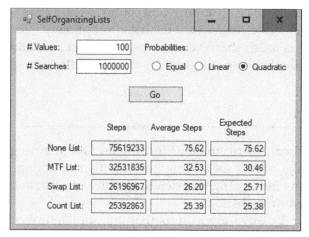

Figure 3.8: Self-arranging lists are much faster than fixed lists.

The program's radio buttons determine how the items' probabilities are distributed. If you check the Equal button, all of the items are selected with equal probability.

If you check the Linear button, then an item's probability is proportional to its value. For example, the value 10 is selected 10 times as often as the value 1.

If you check the Quadratic button, an item is selected with probability equal to its square divided by the total of all of the numbers squared. For example, the value 17 is selected with probability 17×17 / total.

Pseudocode

You can use the following high-level pseudocode for any self-organizing list:

```
// Find an item and rearrange the linked list.
Item: FindItem(Value: value)
    <Find the item.>
    <Rearrange the list for the desired self-organizing strategy.>
    <Return the item.>
End FindItem
```

You can use the techniques described earlier in this chapter to find the item.

For an MTF or swapping list, you can find the linked-list cell before the target item so that you can move or swap the item more easily.

For a counting list, you can use a doubly linked list so that you can easily swap the found item toward the front of the list as far as necessary.

To implement the algorithm in C#, Python, or another object-oriented language, you can make a self-organizing list parent class that provides basic list methods to add and remove items. Its `Find` method can call a `Rearrange` method that does nothing in the parent class. Then the MTF, swapping, and counting child classes can override the `Rearrange` method to restructure the list appropriately. That allows the parent class to hold as much shared code as possible, and the child classes only need to contain code that is specific to their arranging strategies.

Linked-List Algorithms

So far, this chapter has described algorithms for building and maintaining linked lists. It has described algorithms for adding items at the top, bottom, and interior of a list; algorithms for finding and deleting items in a list; and algorithms for making self-organizing lists.

The following sections describe other algorithms that manipulate linked lists in other ways.

Copying Lists

Some algorithms rearrange a list. For example, the next two sections describe algorithms that sort the items in a list. If you want to keep the original list intact, you must make a copy of the list before you sort it.

The following pseudocode shows how you can copy a singly linked list:

```
// Copy a list.
Cell: CopyList(Cell: old_sentinel)
    // Make the new list's sentinel.
    Cell: new_sentinel = New Cell()

    // Keep track of the last item we've added so far.
    Cell: last_added = new_sentinel

    // Skip the sentinel.
    Cell: old_cell = old_sentinel.Next

    // Copy items.
    While (old_cell != null)
        // Make a new item.
        last_added.Next = New Cell

        // Move to the new item.
        last_added = last_added.Next

        // Set the new item's value.
        last_added.Value = old_cell.Value

        // Get ready to copy the next cell.
        old_cell = old_cell.Next
    End While
```

```
        // End with null.
        last_added.Next = null

        // Return the new list's sentinel.
        Return new_sentinel
}
```

This algorithm is reasonably straightforward, but it contains one feature worth mentioning. The algorithm uses the variable `last_added` to keep track of the cell that was most recently added to the new copy of the list. To copy a new item to the list, the algorithm sets `last_added.Next` equal to a new cell object. That puts the new object at the end of the list. The algorithm then updates `last_added` to point to the new item and copies the original cell's value into it.

This lets the list grow at the bottom instead of at the top. This is similar to how you can easily add items to the end of a list if you keep track of the last item in the list, as described in Exercise 1.

Sorting with Insertionsort

Chapter 6, "Sorting," says a lot about sorting algorithms, but two are worth discussing here: `insertionsort` and `selectionsort`.

The basic idea behind `insertionsort` is to take an item from the input list and insert it into the proper position in a sorted output list (which initially starts empty).

The following pseudocode shows the `insertionsort` algorithm, where the items to sort are stored in a singly linked list that has a top sentinel:

```
// Use insertionsort to sort the list.
Cell: Insertionsort(Cell: old_sentinel)
    // Make a sentinel for the sorted list.
    Cell new_sentinel = New Cell()
    new_sentinel.Next = null

    // Skip the input list's sentinel.
    old_sentinel = old_sentinel.Next

    // Repeat until we have inserted all of the items in the new list.
    While (old_sentinel != null)
        // Get the next cell to add to the list.
        Cell: next_cell = old_sentinel

        // Advance old_sentinel for the next trip through the loop.
        old_sentinel = old_sentinel.Next

        // See where to add the next item in the sorted list.
        Cell: after_me = new_sentinel
        While (after_me.Next != null) And
```

```
            (after_me.Next.Value < next_cell.Value)
            after_me = after_me.Next
        End While

        // Insert the item in the sorted list.
        next_cell.Next = after_me.Next
        after_me.Next = next_cell
    End While

    // Return the sorted list.
    return new_sentinel
End Insertionsort
```

This algorithm starts by building an empty list to hold the sorted output. It then loops through the unsorted list of input cells. For each input cell, it looks through the growing sorted list and finds the cell after which the new value belongs. It then inserts the cell there.

You can simplify the code if you call the InsertCell algorithm described in the earlier section "Inserting Cells After Other Cells."

The algorithm's best case occurs if the items in the input list are initially sorted in largest-to-smallest order. In that case, each time the algorithm considers a new item, it is smaller than all of the items that have already been added to the sorted list. That means the new item belongs at the top of the sorted list, so you can insert it in O(1) time. That in turn means you can "sort" the already-sorted items in a total of O(N) time.

The algorithm's worst case occurs when the items are initially sorted in smallest-to-largest order. In that case, when the algorithm considers an item, it is larger than all the items that have already been moved to the new list, and you need to insert it at the end of the list. That means inserting all of the items takes $1 + 2 + 3 + \ldots + N = N \times (N - 1) / 2 = O(N^2)$ steps.

In the average case, with the items initially randomly arranged, the algorithm can insert some items quickly, but others take longer. The result is that the algorithm's run time is still $O(N^2)$, although in practice it won't take as long as the worst case.

Many other sorting algorithms take only O(N log N) time, so this algorithm's $O(N^2)$ performance is relatively slow. That makes this algorithm ineffective for large lists. However, it runs reasonably quickly for small lists, and it works for linked lists, which many of the other algorithms don't.

Sorting with Selectionsort

The basic idea behind the selectionsort algorithm is to search the input list for the largest item it contains and then add it to the front of a growing sorted list.

The following pseudocode shows the selectionsort algorithm for a singly linked list holding integers:

```
// Use selectionsort to sort the list.
Cell: Selectionsort(Cell: old_sentinel)
    // Make a new_sentinel for the sorted list.
    Cell: new_sentinel = New Cell
    new_sentinel.Next = null

    // Repeat until the old list is empty.
    While (old_sentinel.Next != null)
        // Find the largest item in the old list.
        // The cell best_after_me will be the cell before
        // the one with the largest value.
        Cell: best_after_me = old_sentinel
        Integer: best_value = best_after_me.Next.Value

        // Start looking with the next item.
        Cell: after_me = old_sentinel.Next
        While (after_me.Next != null)
            If (after_me.Next.Value > best_value) Then
                best_after_me = after_me
                best_value = after_me.Next.Value
            End If
            after_me = after_me.Next
        End While

        // Remove the best cell from the unsorted list.
        Cell: best_cell = best_after_me.Next
        best_after_me.Next = best_cell.Next

        // Add the best cell at the beginning of the sorted list.
        best_cell.Next = new_sentinel.Next
        new_sentinel.Next = best_cell
    End While

    // Return the sorted list.
    Return new_sentinel
End Selectionsort
```

You can simplify this algorithm somewhat if you extract the code that finds the largest cell in the input list, place that code in a new algorithm, and then invoke the new algorithm from this one.

When the input list contains K items, finding the largest item in the list takes K steps. Adding the largest item to the sorted list takes only a few steps. As the algorithm progresses, the input list shrinks. Therefore, if it originally holds N items, the total number of steps is $N + (N-1) + (N-2) + \ldots + 2 + 1 = N \times (N-1) / 2 = O(N^2)$, the same run time given by the insertionsort algorithm.

Multithreaded Linked Lists

In a singly linked list, a cell has a link to the next cell in the list. In a doubly linked list, each cell has links to the cell before and after it in the list. The doubly linked list uses two links to provide two different ways to move through the cells it contains: forward or backward.

There's no reason why you can't add other links to a list's cells to provide other ways to move through the cells. For example, suppose you build a Planet class to hold information about the solar system's planets. You can give the Planet class a field named NextDistance that is a link to the Planet that is the next nearest to the sun. Following the NextDistance links would list the planets in the order Mercury, Venus, Earth, Mars, Jupiter, Saturn, Uranus, and Neptune (and optionally Pluto, if you're a Pluto fan).

Similarly, you could add other fields to list the planets ordered by mass, diameter, and other characteristics. Each path through the cells defined by a set of links is called a *thread*.

It's easy enough to work with a single thread, thinking of it as a simple linked list, although visualizing all of the threads at the same time can be messy. For example, Figure 3.9 shows a linked list of planets with three threads. The thin links visit the planets ordered by distance to the sun, the dashed links visit the planets ordered by mass, and the thick links visit the planets ordered by diameter.

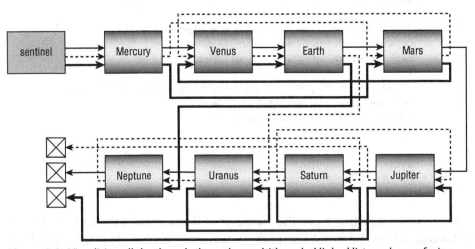

Figure 3.9: Visualizing all the threads through a multithreaded linked list can be confusing.

NOTE   Other data structures can also have threads. For example, a tree might provide threads to let a program visit its nodes in orders that are not typical for a tree.

Linked Lists with Loops

A *circular linked list* is a linked list in which the last link points back to the first item in the list. Figure 3.10 shows a circular linked list.

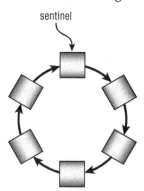

Figure 3.10: Circular linked lists let a program easily loop through a sequence of objects indefinitely.

Circular linked lists can be useful when you need to loop through a sequence of items indefinitely. For example, an operating system might repeatedly loop through a list of processes to give each a chance to execute. If a new process started, it could be added anywhere in the list, perhaps right after the sentinel so that it would have a chance to execute right away.

As another example, a game might loop indefinitely through a list of objects, allowing each to move on the screen. Again, new objects could be added anywhere to the list.

Figure 3.11 shows a linked list that contains a loop, but the loop doesn't include all of the list's cells.

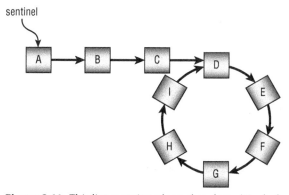

Figure 3.11: This list contains a loop that doesn't include all of the list's cells.

The kind of linked list shown in Figure 3.10 is interesting, mostly because it presents you with two thought-provoking problems. First, how can you tell whether a linked list contains such a loop? Second, if a linked list contains such a loop, how can you find where the loop starts and break it there to "fix" the list? This is roughly the same question as asking where the "bottom" of the list is. In Figure 3.11, you might define the bottom of the list to be cell I because it is the last cell you visit while traversing the list before cells start repeating.

The following sections describe some of the most interesting algorithms that answer these questions.

Marking Cells

Probably the easiest way to tell whether a linked list has a loop is to traverse its cells, marking each as you visit it. If you come to a cell that is already marked, you know that the list has a loop and that it starts at that point.

The following pseudocode shows this algorithm:

```
// Return true if the list has a loop.
// If the list has a loop, break it.
Boolean: HasLoopMarking(Cell: sentinel)
    // Assume there is no loop.
    Boolean: has_loop = false

    // Loop through the list.
    Cell: cell = sentinel
    While (cell.Next != null)
        // See if we already visited the next cell.
        If (cell.Next.Visited)
            // This is the start of a loop.
            // Break the loop.
            cell.Next = null
            has_loop = true
            <Break out of the While loop>
        End If

        // Move to the next cell.
        cell = cell.Next

        // Mark the cell as visited.
        cell.Visited = true
    End While

    // Traverse the list again to clear the Visited flags.
    cell = sentinel
    While (cell.Next != null)
        cell.Visited = false
        cell = cell.Next
    End While
```

```
    // Return the result.
    Return has_loop
End HasLoopMarking
```

The BreakLoopMarking sample program, which is available for download on the book's website, demonstrates this algorithm.

This algorithm must traverse the loop twice—once to set the cells' `Visited` flags to `true` and again to reset them to `false`. So, if the list contains N cells, this algorithm takes $2 \times N$ steps and runs in O(N) time.

This algorithm also requires that each cell have an added `Visited` field, so it requires O(N) space. The list already takes up O(N) space to hold the cells and their links, so this shouldn't be a problem, but it's worth acknowledging that the algorithm has some memory requirements.

> **NOTE**   Marking cells is a simple technique that is also useful for other data structures, particularly networks. Some of the algorithms described in Chapters 13 and 14 use marking techniques.

Often, a problem such as this one has the additional requirement that you are not allowed to change the definition of the cell class. In this case, that means you aren't allowed to add a `Visited` field. The following algorithms satisfy that additional restriction.

Using Hash Tables

Hash tables are described in detail in Chapter 8. For now, all you need to know is that a hash table can quickly store items, retrieve items, and tell you whether an item is present in the hash table.

This algorithm moves through the list, adding each cell to a hash table. When it visits a cell, it checks the hash table to see whether the cell is already in the table. If it comes to a cell that is already in the hash table, the list contains a loop that starts at that cell.

The following pseudocode shows this algorithm:

```
// Return true if the list has a loop.
// If the list has a loop, break it.
Boolean: HasLoopHashTable(Cell: sentinel)
    // Make a hash table.
    Hashtable: visited

    // Loop through the list.
    Cell: cell = sentinel
    While (cell.Next != null)
        // See if we already visited the next cell.
        If (visited.Contains(cell.Next))
            // This is the start of a loop.
            // Break the loop and return true.
```

```
            cell.Next = null
            Return true
        End If


        // Add the cell to the hash table.
        visited.Add(cell)

        // Move to the next cell.
        cell = cell.Next
    End While

    // If we get this far, there is no loop.
    Return false
End HasLoopHashTable
```

The BreakLoopHashtable sample program, which is available for download on the book's website, demonstrates this algorithm.

This algorithm traverses the list's cells once, so if the list contains N cells, this algorithm takes N steps and runs in O(N) time.

This algorithm also requires a hash table. For the best performance, a hash table must have extra space beyond what it needs to store the values. If the list contains N items, the hash table must have room for more than N entries. A hash table with room for 1.5 × N entries will give good performance and still use O(N) space.

This algorithm obeys the restriction that it isn't allowed to modify the cell class, but it uses extra storage. The following sections describe some algorithms that detect loops without using extra storage.

List Retracing

The *list retracing algorithm* uses two objects that traverse the list. It starts the first object (call it leader) on a normal traversal. Each time that object visits a new cell, the algorithm starts a second object (call it tracer) on a traversal. If tracer ever reaches the cell leader.Next before it comes to the cell leader, then the list contains a loop.

For example, look again at the list shown in Figure 3.11, and suppose leader is pointing to cell I. Then tracer will reach leader.Next, which is cell D, before it reaches cell I. That shows there is a loop starting at node D and ending at node I.

The following code shows the algorithm in pseudocode:

```
// Return true if the list has a loop.
// If the list has a loop, break it.
Boolean: HasLoopRetracing(Cell: sentinel)
    // Loop through the list.
    Cell: cell = sentinel
    While (cell.Next != null)
        // See if we already visited the next cell.
        Cell: tracer = sentinel
        While (tracer != cell)
            If (tracer.Next == cell.Next)
```

```
            // This is the start of a loop.
            // Break the loop and return true.
            cell.Next = null
            Return true
        End If
        tracer = tracer.Next
    End While

    // Move to the next cell.
    cell = cell.Next
End While

// If we get here, the list has no loop.
Return false
End HasLoopRetracing
```

The BreakLoopHashtable sample program, which is available for download on the book's website, demonstrates this algorithm.

Assume that the list contains N cells. When the algorithm's cell object examines the Kth cell in the list, the tracer object must traverse the list up to that point, so it must perform K steps. That means the algorithm's total run time is $1 + 2 + 3 + \ldots + N = N \times (N - 1) / 2 = O(N^2)$.

This is slower than the previous algorithms, but, unlike those algorithms, the only additional space it requires is for the two cell pointers that traverse the list.

List Reversal

Like the preceding list retracing algorithm, the *list reversal algorithm* uses only a small amount of extra space to hold some pointers. This algorithm, however, works in O(N) time.

This algorithm traverses the list, reversing each cell's Next link so that it points to the cell before it in the list instead of the one after it. If the algorithm ever reaches the list's sentinel, then the list contains a loop. If the algorithm reaches a null link without reaching the sentinel, then the list doesn't contain a loop.

Of course, moving through the list reversing links messes up the links. To restore them, the algorithm then moves back through the list a second time, reversing the links again so that they point back to where they did originally.

To see how this works, look at the list shown in Figure 3.12.

The top image in Figure 3.12 shows the original list. The algorithm starts at cell A and moves through the list, reversing the links.

The middle image in Figure 3.12 shows the algorithm when it has reached cell I. The links that have been reversed are shown in bold. Next, the algorithm follows the link out of cell I to cell D. It then follows the reversed links from cell D to cells C, B, and A. As it follows those links, the algorithm reverses them again to give the image shown at the bottom of Figure 3.12. Here the links that have been reversed twice are shown with dotted arrows.

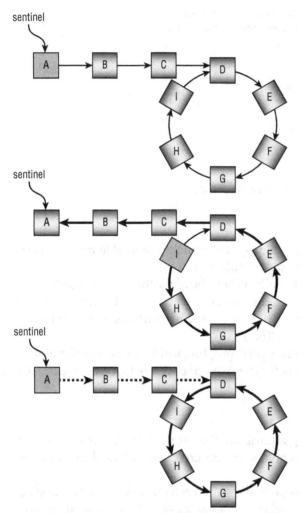

Figure 3.12: An algorithm can detect a loop by reversing the links in a linked list.

At this point, the algorithm returns to the first cell in the list so that it knows the list contains a loop. Notice that the new list is the same as the old one, except that the links in the loop are reversed.

The algorithm finishes by reversing the links again to restore their original links.

Because this algorithm must reverse the list twice, it makes sense to move that operation into a separate method that you can call twice. The following pseudocode shows how the algorithm reverses the list's links:

```
// Reverse the loop once and return the new top of the list.
Cell: ReverseList(Cell: sentinel)
    Cell: prev_cell = null
    Cell: curr_cell = sentinel
```

```
    While (curr_cell != null)
        // Reverse the link out of this cell.
        Cell: next_cell = curr_cell.Next
        curr_cell.Next = prev_cell

        // Move to the next cell.
        prev_cell = curr_cell
        curr_cell = next_cell
    End While

    // Return the last cell we visited.
    Return prev_cell
End ReverseList
```

This pseudocode moves through the list, reversing the links, and returns the last node visited, which is the first node in the reversed list.

The following algorithm uses the previous pseudocode to determine whether the list contains a loop:

```
// Return true if the list has a loop.
Boolean: HasLoopReversing(Cell: sentinel)
{
    // If the list is empty, it has no loops.
    If (sentinel.Next == null) Then Return false

    // Loop through the list, reversing links.
    Cell: new_sentinel = ReverseList(sentinel)

    // Loop through the list again to restore the links.
    ReverseList(new_sentinel)

    // If the reversed list starts with the same cell
    // as the original list, there is a loop.
    If (new_sentinel == sentinel) Then Return true
    Return false
End HasLoopReversing
```

This algorithm calls the ReverseList method to reverse the list and get the reversed list's first cell. It then calls ReverseList again to re-reverse the list and restore the links to their original values.

If the sentinel is the same as the first cell in the reversed list, the algorithm returns true. If the sentinel is different from the first cell in the reversed list, the algorithm returns false.

This algorithm traverses the list twice—once to reverse links and once to restore them—so it performs $2 \times N = O(N)$ steps.

This algorithm runs in $O(N)$ time without requiring additional space. Unfortunately, it only detects loops; it doesn't provide a way to break them. The next algorithm solves that problem, although it is the most confusing of the algorithms described here.

Tortoise and Hare

This algorithm is called the *tortoise-and-hare algorithm* or *Floyd's cycle-finding algorithm* after Robert Floyd, who invented it in the 1960s. The algorithm itself isn't too complicated, but its explanation is pretty confusing, so if you don't want to see the math, skip to the following pseudocode.

The algorithm starts two objects called `tortoise` and `hare` moving through the list at different speeds starting at the beginning of the list. The tortoise moves one cell per step. The hare moves two cells per step.

If the hare reaches a link that is `null`, then the list has an end, so there is no loop.

If the list does contain a loop, the hare eventually enters the loop and starts running laps around it.

Meanwhile, the tortoise plods along until it eventually reaches the loop, too. At that point, both the tortoise and hare are inside the loop.

Let T be the number of steps that pass before the tortoise enters the loop, and let H be the distance from the beginning of the loop to the hare's location after T steps, as shown in Figure 3.13. Let L be the number of cells inside the loop.

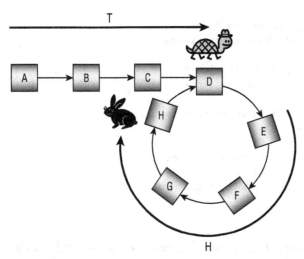

Figure 3.13: T is the distance the tortoise travels to get to the loop, and H is the distance from the start of the loop to the hare at that time.

In Figure 3.13, T = 4, H = 4, and L = 5.

Because the hare moves twice as fast as the tortoise, it reaches the loop after moving T cells. It then crosses T more cells inside the loop to reach the position shown in Figure 3.13. This leads to the following Important Fact #1.

IMPORTANT FACT #1

If you move across T cells within the loop, you end up H cells away from where you started.

Note that the hare may have run several laps around the loop if L is much smaller than T. For example, if T is 102 and L is 5, the tortoise reaches the loop after 102 steps. The hare reaches the loop after 51 steps, spends the next 50 steps (100 cells) running 20 laps around the loop, and then moves one more step (two cells) inside the loop. In this case, H = 2.

The next question is, "When will the hare catch the tortoise?" When the tortoise enters the loop, the hare is H cells ahead, as shown in Figure 3.13. Because the tortoise and hare are in a loop, you can also think of the hare as L – H cells behind the tortoise. Because the hare moves two cells for every one that the tortoise moves, it gains one cell per step. That means the hare will catch the tortoise in L – H more steps.

In Figure 3.13, H = 4 and L = 5, so the hare will catch the tortoise in 5 – 4 = 1 more step when both animals meet at cell E.

This means that, at the point of collision, the tortoise will have moved L – H cells into the loop. When the two animals meet, they are L – (L – H) = H cells short of the beginning of the loop. This is Important Fact #2.

IMPORTANT FACT #2

When the hare catches the tortoise, the two animals are H cells short of the beginning of the loop.

Now, if you could move the tortoise H cells from the point of collision, the tortoise would be at the beginning of the loop, and you would know where the loop starts. Unfortunately, you don't know the value of H, so you can't simply move the tortoise that far.

However, you do know from Important Fact #1 that if the tortoise moves T cells around the loop, it will end up H cells ahead of where it started. In this case, it will end up at the start of the loop!

Unfortunately, you also don't know the value of T, so you can't simply move the tortoise that far either. However, if you start the hare at the beginning of the linked list and make it move only one cell at a time instead of two (it's probably tired after running around in the loop for so long), it will also reach the start of the loop after it crosses T cells. That means the two will meet again after crossing T cells, when they will be at the start of the loop.

The following pseudocode shows the algorithm at a high level:

1. Start the tortoise moving through the list at one cell per step. Start the hare moving through the list at two cells per step.

2. If the hare finds a `null` link, then the list has no loop, so stop.

3. Otherwise, when the hare catches the tortoise, restart the hare at the beginning of the list, moving one cell per step this time. Continue moving the tortoise at one cell per step.

4. When the tortoise and hare meet again, they are at the start of the loop. Leave the hare at the loop's starting point to take a well-deserved rest while the tortoise takes one more lap around the loop. When the tortoise's `Next` pointer gives the cell where the hare is waiting, the tortoise is at the end of the loop.

5. To break the loop, set the tortoise's cell's `Next` pointer to `null`.

> **WARNING**   I've never met a program that really needed to use the tortoise-and-hare algorithm. If you're careful, there's no excuse for letting a linked list become corrupted by an accidental loop. However, detecting loops seems to be a popular interview question and brainteaser, so it's good to know about this solution.

Loops in Doubly Linked Lists

Detecting loops in a doubly linked list is easy. If there is a loop, somewhere a `Next` pointer jumps back to an earlier part of the list. The `Prev` pointer in that cell points to an earlier cell, not the one that created the loop.

So, to detect a loop, simply traverse the list, and for each cell, verify that `cell.Next.Prev == cell`.

This all assumes that the cells form a normal doubly linked list and that a loop, if it exists, is a simple loop. If the `Next` and `Prev` lists are completely out of sync, this method detects the mess but doesn't help you fix it. This is more of a case of two threads through the same cells than a doubly linked list with a loop.

Summary

This chapter explained linked lists and some of the things that you can do with them. It explained singly and doubly linked lists and threaded lists. It also explained basic list-manipulation algorithms such as adding, finding, and deleting items. Finally, it described some more advanced algorithms to manage self-organizing lists and to detect and remove loops.

All of this work with pointers is a kind of preview for later chapters that deal with trees, balanced trees, networks, and other linked data structures. In fact, the next chapter uses linked data structures to implement sparse arrays.

Exercises

You can find the answers to these exercises in Appendix B. Asterisks indicate particularly difficult problems.

1. The section "Adding Cells at the End" gives an O(N) algorithm for adding an item at the end of a singly linked list. If you keep another variable, bottom, that points to the last cell in the list, then you can add items to the end of the list in O(1) time. Write such an algorithm. How does this complicate other algorithms that add an item at the beginning or end of the list, find an item, and remove an item? Write an algorithm for removing an item from this kind of list.

2. Write an algorithm to find the largest item in an unsorted singly linked list with cells containing integers.

3. Write an algorithm to add an item at the top of a doubly linked list.

4. Write an algorithm to add an item at the bottom of a doubly linked list.

5. If you compare the algorithms you wrote for Exercises 3 and 4 to the InsertCell algorithm shown in the section "Doubly Linked Lists," you should notice that they look very similar. Rewrite the algorithms you wrote for Exercises 3 and 4 so that they call the InsertCell algorithm instead of updating the list's links directly.

6. Write an algorithm that deletes a specified cell from a doubly linked list. Draw a picture that shows the process graphically.

7. Suppose you have a sorted doubly linked list holding names. Can you think of a way to improve search performance by starting the search from the bottom sentinel instead of the top sentinel? Does that change the Big O run time?

8. Write an algorithm for inserting an item in a sorted doubly linked list where the top and bottom sentinels hold the minimum and maximum possible values.

9. Write an algorithm that determines whether a linked list is sorted.

10. Write a program similar to the one shown in Figure 3.14 that compares the times needed by selectionsort and insertionsort to sort a list of items. Which is faster?

Figure 3.14: This program compares the performance of insertionsort and selectionsort.

11. Insertionsort and selectionsort both have a run time of $O(N^2)$. Explain why selectionsort takes longer in practice.

12. In what state is the input list after executing the insertionsort and selectionsort algorithms? Can you think of a way to make them both leave the input list unchanged?

13. Write a program that builds a multithreaded linked list of the planets, as described in the section "Multithreaded Linked Lists." Let the user click a radio button or select from a combo box to display the planets ordered by the different threads. (*Hint*: Make a `Planet` class with fields `Name`, `DistanceToSun`, `Mass`, `Diameter`, `NextDistance`, `NextMass`, and `NextDiameter`. Then make an `AddPlanetToList` method that adds a planet to the threads in sorted order.)

14. *Write a program similar to the SelfOrganizingLists program shown in Figure 3.8. For bonus points, you might try making a program that graphs the average expected steps as the number of searches grows for the various list types and probability distributions.

15. The swapping self-organizing list moves items slowly, so it is less effective than the MTF list until the items move into good positions. Use the program that you wrote for Exercise 14 to determine the number of searches required with a 100-item list before the swapping list starts to outperform the MTF list.

16. *Write a program that implements the tortoise-and-hare algorithm.

Arrays

Arrays are extremely common data structures. They are intuitive, easy to use, and supported well by most programming languages. In fact, arrays are so common and well understood that you may wonder whether there's much to say about them in an algorithms book. Most applications use arrays in a relatively straightforward manner, but special-purpose arrays can be useful in certain cases, so they deserve some attention here.

This chapter explains algorithmic techniques that you can use to make arrays with nonzero lower bounds, save memory, and manipulate arrays more quickly than you can normally.

NOTE Python does not have arrays, but lists can do the same things in most cases. Python also does not have multidimensional lists, but you can use a list of lists instead. For example, instead of an array with an entry at position [i, j], you can use a list of lists with an entry at position [i][j].

Basic Concepts

An *array* is a chunk of contiguous memory that a program can access by using indices—one index per dimension in the array. You can think of an array as an arrangement of boxes where a program can store values.

Figure 4.1 illustrates one-, two-, and three-dimensional arrays. A program can define higher-dimensional arrays, but trying to represent them graphically is hard.

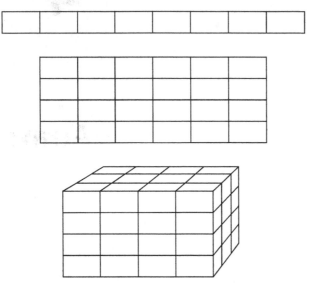

Figure 4.1: You can think of one-, two-, and three-dimensional arrays as arrangements of boxes where a program can store values.

Typically, a program declares a variable to be an array with a certain number of dimensions and certain bounds for each dimension. For example, the following code shows how a C# program might declare and allocate an array named `numbers` that has 10 rows and 20 columns:

```
int[,] numbers = new int[10, 20];
```

In C#, array bounds are zero-based, so this array's row indices range from 0 to 9, and its column indices range from 0 to 19.

NOTE   The following Python code allocates a list of lists that you can use much as you can use a C# array:

```
numbers = [[0 for c in range(num_columns)] for r in range(num_rows)]
```

This isn't quite the same as the preceding C# array, but you can use similar indices to get and set its elements.

Behind the scenes, the program allocates enough contiguous memory to hold the array's data. Logically, the memory looks like a long series of bytes, and the program maps the array's indices to positions in this series of bytes, as explained in the following list:

- For one-dimensional arrays, the mapping from array indices to memory entries is simple: index i maps to entry i.

- For two-dimensional arrays, the program can map the array entries in one of two ways: row-major order or column-major order.

  - In *row-major order*, the program maps the first row of array entries to the first set of memory locations. It then maps the second row to the set of memory locations after the first. It continues mapping one row at a time until all of the entries are mapped.

  - In *column-major order*, the program maps the first column of array entries to the first set of memory locations. It then maps the second column to the second set of memory locations, and so forth.

Figure 4.2 shows row-major and column-major mappings.

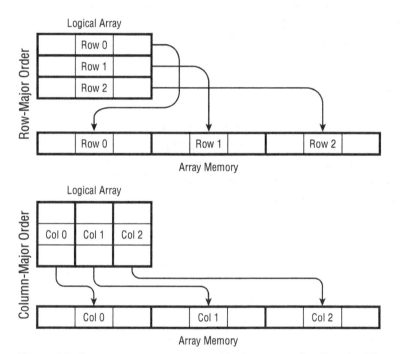

Figure 4.2: A program can map array entries to memory locations in either row-major or column-major order.

You can extend the ideas of row-major and column-major ordering for higher-dimensional arrays. For example, to store a three-dimensional array in row-major order, the program would map the first two-dimensional "slice" of the array where the third dimension's index is 0. It would map that slice in row-major order as usual. It would then similarly map the second slice where the third index is 1, and so on, for the remaining slices.

Another way to think of this is as an algorithm for mapping a three-dimensional array. Suppose you have defined a Map2DArray method that maps a two-dimensional array. The following algorithm uses Map2DArray to map a three-dimensional array:

```
For i = 0 To <upper bound of array's third coordinate>
    Map2DArray(<array with the third coordinate set to i>)
Next i
```

Similarly, you could use this algorithm to define algorithms for mapping arrays with even more dimensions.

Normally, how a program maps array entries to memory locations is irrelevant to how a program works, and there's no reason why you should care. Your code manipulates the array entries, and you don't need to know how they are stored. However, understanding how the row-major and column-major orders work is useful when you try to create your own array-mapping data structures to implement triangular arrays. (Triangular arrays are discussed later in this chapter in the section "Triangular Arrays.")

One-Dimensional Arrays

Algorithms that involve one-dimensional or *linear* arrays tend to be so straightforward that they're almost trivial. They often come up in programming interviews, however, so they're worth a brief discussion here. Linear array operations also provide a preview of operations used by more interesting data structures such as stacks and queues, so it's worth covering these operations now for completeness.

Finding Items

Chapter 7, "Searching," covers some interesting algorithms for finding a target item in a sorted array. If the items in the array are not sorted, however, finding an item is a matter of performing a *linear search* or *exhaustive search*. You look at every element in the array until you find the target item, or you conclude that the item is not in the array. The following algorithm finds a target item:

```
Integer: IndexOf(Integer: array[], Integer: target)
    For i = 0 to array.Length - 1
        If (array[i] == target) Return i
    Next i

    // The target isn't in the array.
    Return -1
End IndexOf
```

In the worst case, the target item may be the very last item in the array. If the array has N items, the algorithm ends up examining all of them. That makes the algorithm's run time O(N).

The worst case also occurs if the target item is not in the array. In that case, the algorithm must examine all N items to conclude that the item is not present.

If you were to search for every item in the array, you would find some items near the beginning of the array and some near the end. It would take one step to find the first item, two steps to find the second item, and so forth. Finding every item would take a total of $1 + 2 + 3 + \ldots + N = N(N + 1) / 2$ steps. If you divide that by the number of searches, N, you get the average number of steps to find an item in the array: $(N + 1) / 2$. This means that the average run time for finding an item in the array is O(N).

Finding Minimum, Maximum, and Average

If the array contains numbers, you might want to find the minimum, maximum, and average values in the array. As is the case for finding an item, you cannot avoid looking at every item in the array when you want to find those values.

The following algorithms find the minimum, maximum, and average values for a one-dimensional array of integers:

```
Integer: FindMinimum(Integer: array[])
    Integer: minimum = array[0]
    For i = 1 To array.Length - 1
        If (array[i] < minimum) Then minimum = array[i]
    Next i
    Return minimum
End FindMinimum

Integer: FindMaximum(Integer: array[])
    Integer: maximum = array[0]
    For i = 1 To array.Length - 1
        If (array[i] > maximum) Then maximum = array[i]
    Next i
    Return maximum
End FindMaximum

Float: FindAverage(Integer: array[])
    Integer: total = 0
    For i = 0 To array.Length - 1
        total = total + array[i]
    Next i
    Return total / array.Length
End FindMaximum
```

As is the case for the algorithm that finds a specific item, these algorithms must visit every item in the array, so they have run time O(N).

Finding Median

You can use code similar to the preceding algorithms to calculate other statistical values such as the standard deviation and variance if you need them. One value that isn't as easy to calculate is the median, the value that lies in the middle of the values when they are sorted. For example, the median of the values $\{3, 1, 7, 8, 4, 8, 9\}$ is 7, because there are three smaller values $(1, 3, 4)$ and three larger values $(8, 8, 9)$.

A single pass through the array won't give you all of the information you need to calculate the median because in some sense you need more global information about the values to find the median. You can't simply adjust a "running" median by looking at values one at a time.

One approach might be to think about each value in the list. For each test value, reconsider all of the values and keep track of those that are larger and smaller than the test value. If you find a test value where the number of smaller and larger entries is equal, then the test value is the median.

The following pseudocode shows the basic algorithm:

```
Integer: FindMedian(Integer: array[])
    For i = 0 To array.Length - 1
        // Find the number of values greater than and
        // less than array[i].
        Integer: num_larger = 0
        Integer: num_smaller = 0
        For j = 0 To array.Length - 1
            If (array[j] < array[i]) Then num_smaller++
            If (array[j] > array[i]) Then num_larger++
        Next j

        If (num_smaller = num_larger) Then
            Return array[i]
        End If
    Next i
End FindMedian
```

This algorithm has a few flaws. For example, it doesn't handle the case in which multiple items have the same value, as in $\{1, 2, 3, 3, 4\}$. It also doesn't handle arrays with an even number of items, which have no item in the middle. If an array has an even number of items, its median is defined as the average of the two middlemost items. For example, the median of $\{1, 4, 6, 9\}$ is $(4 + 6) / 2 = 5$.

This algorithm isn't efficient enough to be worth fixing, but its run time is worth analyzing.

If the array contains N values, the outer `For i` loop executes N times. For every one of those iterations, the inner `For j` loop executes N times. That means the steps inside the inner loop execute $N \times N = N^2$ times, giving the algorithm a run time of $O(N^2)$.

A much faster algorithm is first to sort the array and then to find the median directly by looking at the values in the middle of the sorted array. Chapter 6, "Sorting," describes several algorithms for sorting an array containing N items in $O(N \log N)$ time. That's a lot faster than $O(N^2)$.

Finding Mode

Another value that's hard to calculate with a single pass through the array is the mode. The *mode* is the value that occurs most often. For example, if the array contains the values $\{A, C, A, B, E, B, C, F, B, G\}$, then the mode is B because that value occurs more times than the other values.

There are several approaches that you can take to find the mode. For example, you could loop through the items. For each item, you could loop through the items again and count the number of times that particular item appears. You would then keep track of the item that appeared most often. Because that method uses two nested loops that each cover N items, this method has run time $O(N^2)$.

A second approach would be to use one of the algorithms described in Chapter 6 to sort the items in $O(N \log N)$ time. Then you can perform a pass through the array, keeping track of the longest run of adjacent matching items. The following pseudocode uses this approach:

```
Integer: FindModeSort(Data: array[])
    <Sort the array>

    // Keep track of the best run.
    Integer: best_run_start = -1
    Integer: best_run_length = 0

    Integer: run_start = 0
    Data: current_value = array[0]
    For i = 1 To array.Length - 1
        If (array[i] != current_value) Then
            // We've found a new value.
            Integer: run_length = i - run_start
            If (run_length > best_run_length) Then
                best_run_start = run_start
                best_run_length = run_length
            End If

            // Save the new item.
            current_value = array[i]
        End If
```

```
    Next i

    // Check the last run.
    Integer: run_length = array.Length - run_start
    If (run_length > best_run_length) Then
        best_run_start = run_start
        best_run_length = run_length
    End If

    // Return the item at the best start position.
    Return array[best_run_start]
End FindModeSort
```

This algorithm uses variable `run_start` to keep track of the index where the current run started. It uses variable `current_value` to keep track of the current run's value. Note that the values may not be numbers. Quantities such as the average or median are defined only for numbers, but the mode is defined for strings or any other kind of data.

After initializing `run_start` and `current_value`, the algorithm loops through the array. Each time it encounters a new value, it calculates the length of the current run and updates the `best_run_start` and `best_run_length` values if this run is a new best.

After it finishes its loop, the algorithm considers the array's final run (in case the mode is at the end of the array). It finishes by returning the value at the start of the longest run.

This algorithm sorts the array's values in O(N log N) time. It then loops through the array in O(N) time, so its total run time is O(N + N log N) = O(N log N).

Unfortunately, this algorithm works only if you can sort the items in the array. If the items are unsortable, for example if they are `Customer` objects, then you need to use a different approach.

A third method for finding the mode works only if the values in the array span a relatively small range of integer values. For example, you might have 10,000 items that lie between 0 and 100.

This algorithm uses a technique similar to the one used by the countingsort algorithm described in Chapter 6. It allocates a new array to hold the number of times each item occurs in the array. The following pseudocode shows the algorithm:

```
Integer: FindModeCounts(Data: array[])
    // Make an array to hold item counts.
    Integer: counts[] = New Integer[<maximum value> + 1]

    // Keep track of the largest count.
    Integer: best_value = -1
    Integer: best_count = 0
```

```
    // Count the items.
    For Each value In array
        // Increment this value's count.
        counts[value]++

        // See if it's the biggest.
        If (counts[value] > best_count) Then
            best_value = value
            best_count = counts[value]
        End If
    Next value

    Return best_value
End FindModeCounts
```

This algorithm creates a `counts` array that is big enough to hold the range of the values in the array. It then loops through the array and updates each value's count. If a count is greater than the values stored in the `best_count` variable, the code updates `best_count`. After it finishes counting the values, the code returns the best value that it found.

This algorithm loops through the values in the array once, so it has O(N) run time. It is faster than the previous methods, but it requires extra memory to build the `counts` array. This is an example of the kind of space/time trade-off that is common in algorithms. The algorithm is faster than the previous ones, but it uses more memory.

A fourth method for finding the mode, and the last one described here, uses a hash table similar to the ones described in Chapter 8, "Hash Tables." A hash table lets you quickly associate a value with a key. Later, you can look up a key's associated value much like you can look up a word's definition in a dictionary.

NOTE   In C# and Python, a dictionary is a type of hash table.

The advantage to a hash table is that it can use just about anything as a key. The preceding algorithm worked only if the values in the array were integers that spanned a fairly limited range. The new algorithm will work even if the items span a large range, aren't integers, or aren't sortable.

The following pseudocode shows how this algorithm works:

```
Integer: FindMode(Data: array[])
    // Make a hash table to hold item counts.
    HashTable<Data>: counts[] = New HashTable<Data>

    // Keep track of the largest count.
    Integer: best_value = -1
    Integer: best_count = 0
```

```
    // Count the items.
    For Each value In array
        // Increment this value's count.
        counts[value]++

        // See if it's the biggest.
        If (counts[value] > best_count) Then
            best_value = value
            best_count = counts[value]
        End If
    Next value

    Return best_value
End FindMode
```

This algorithm is almost the same as the FindModeCounts algorithm, except that it stores the item counts in a hash table instead of an array. Like the earlier algorithm, it loops through the array once.

During each trip through the main loop, it uses the hash table. If the hash table is properly designed, it should have a lookup time of O(1), so the algorithm will have a total run time of O(N).

The hash table does take up extra space, however. If an array contains M different values, then the hash table needs O(M) extra memory to hold the values. This is another example of the space/time trade-off demonstrated by the previous algorithm.

Inserting Items

Inserting an item at the end of a linear array is easy, assuming that the underlying programming language can extend the array by one item. Simply extend the array and insert the new item at the end.

Inserting an item anywhere else in the array is more difficult. The following algorithm inserts a new item at location position in a linear array:

```
InsertItem(Integer: array[], Integer: value, Integer: position)
    <Resize the array to add 1 item at the end>

    // Move down the items after the target position
    // to make room for the new item.
    For i = array.Length - 1 To position + 1 Step -1
        array[i] = array[i - 1]
    Next i

    // Insert the new item.
    array[position] = value
End InsertItem
```

Notice that this algorithm's For loop starts at the end of the array and moves toward the beginning. That lets it fill in the new location at the end of the array first and then fill each preceding spot right after its value has been copied to its new location.

NOTE These operations are trivial in Python. You simply use a list's `append` method to add a new item at the end or its `insert` method to add an item in the middle of the list.

If the array initially holds N items, this algorithm's For loop executes N − position times. In the worst case, when you're adding an item at the beginning of the array, position $= 0$ and the loop executes N times, so the algorithm's run time is O(N).

NOTE Many programming languages have methods for moving blocks of memory that would make moving the items down one position much faster.

In practice, inserting items in a linear array isn't all that common, but the technique of moving over items in an array to make room for a new one is useful in other algorithms.

Removing Items

Removing the item with index k from an array is about as hard as adding an item. The code first moves the items that come after position k one position closer to the beginning of the array. The code then resizes the array to remove the final unused entry.

In the worst case, when you're removing the first item from the array, the algorithm may need to move all the items in the array. That means it has a run time of O(N).

NOTE In some cases, it may be possible to flag an entry as unused instead of actually removing it. For example, if the values in the array are references or pointers to objects, you may be able to set the removed entry to `null`. That technique can be particularly useful in hash tables, where resizing the array and rebuilding the hash table would be time-consuming.

If you flag many entries as unused, however, the array could eventually fill up with unused entries. Then, to find an item, you would need to examine a lot of empty positions. At some point, you may want to compress the array to remove the empty entries.

Nonzero Lower Bounds

Many programming languages require that all arrays use 0 for a lower bound in every dimension. For example, a linear array can have indices ranging from 0 to 9, but it cannot have indices ranging from 1 to 10 or 101 to 200.

Sometimes it's convenient to treat an array's dimension as if it had nonzero lower bounds. For example, suppose you're writing a sales program that needs to record sales figures for 10 employees with IDs between 1 and 10 for the years 2000 through 2010. In that case, it might be nice to declare the array like this:

```
Double: sales[1 to 10, 2000 to 2010]
```

You can't do that in languages such as C# and Python, which require 0 lower bounds, but you can translate the more convenient bounds into bounds that start with 0 fairly easily. The following two sections explain how to use nonzero lower bounds for arrays with two or more dimensions.

NOTE   Many languages have features that let you create arrays with nonzero lower bounds. For example, Python's NumPy library can create multidimensional array objects, and C#'s `Array` class can build arrays with nonzero lower bounds.

Two Dimensions

Managing arrays with nonzero lower bounds isn't too hard for any given number of dimensions.

Consider again the example where you want an array indexed by employee ID and year, where the employee ID ranges from 1 to 10 and the year ranges from 2000 to 2010. These ranges include 10 employee ID values and 11 years, so the program would allocate an array with 10 rows and 11 columns, as shown in the following pseudocode:

```
Double: sales[10, 11]
```

To access an entry for employee e in year y, you calculate the row and column in the actual array as follows:

```
row = e - 1
column = y - 2000
```

Now the program simply works with the entry array[row, column] (or array[row][column] in Python).

This is easy enough, but you can make it even easier by wrapping the array in a class. You can make a constructor to give the object the bounds for its dimensions. It can then store the lower bounds so that it can later calculate the corresponding rows and columns in the storage array.

In some programming languages, you can even make `get` and `set` methods (`__getitem__` and `__setitem__` in Python) to be the class's indexers, so you can treat objects almost as if they were arrays. For example, in C# you could use the following code to set and get values in an array:

```
array[6, 2005] = 74816
MessageBox.Show("In 2005 employee 6 had " +
    array[6, 2005].ToString() + " in sales."
```

The details of a particular programming language are specific to that language, so they aren't shown here. You can download the TwoDArray and two_d_array sample programs from the book's website to see the details in C# and Python.

Higher Dimensions

The method described in the preceding section works well if you know the number of dimensions the array should have. Unfortunately, generalizing this technique for any number of dimensions is difficult because, for N dimensions, you need to allocate an N-dimensional array to hold the data. You could make separate classes to handle two, three, four, and more dimensions, but it would be better to find a more generalizable approach.

Instead of storing the values in a two-dimensional array, you could pack them into a one-dimensional array in row-major order. (See? I told you it would be good to know how row-major order worked.) You would start by allocating an array big enough to hold all of the items. If there are N rows and M columns, you would allocate an array with $N \times M$ entries.

```
Double: values[N * M]
```

To find an item's position in this array, first you calculate the row and column as before. If an item corresponds to employee ID `e` and year `y`, the row and column are given by the following:

```
row = e - <employee ID lower bound>
column = y - <year lower bound>
```

Now that you know the item's row and column, you need to find its index in the `values` array. To find that index, you first need to know how many complete rows fit into the array before this item. If the item's row number is r, then there are r complete rows before this item, and they are numbered $0, 1, ..., r - 1$. Because there are `<row size>` items in each row, that means those rows account for $r \times$ `<row size>` items before this one.

After you know the number of entries before this item that are due to complete rows, you need to know how many items come before this one in this item's row. If this item's column number is c, then there are c items before this item in its row numbered $0, 1, ..., c - 1$. Those items take up c positions in the values array.

The total number of items that come before this one in the values array is given by this:

```
index = row × <row size> + column
```

Now you can find this item at location `values[index]`.

This technique is a bit more complicated than the technique described in the preceding section, but it is easier to generalize for any number of dimensions.

Suppose you want to create an array with N dimensions, with lower bounds stored in the `lower_bounds` array and with upper bounds stored in the `upper_bounds` array.

The first step is to allocate a one-dimensional array with enough space to store all the values. Simply subtract each lower bound from each upper bound to see how "wide" the array must be in that dimension and then multiply the resulting "widths" together:

```
Integer: ArraySize(Integer: lower_bounds[], Integer: upper_bounds[])
    Integer: total_size = 0
    For i = 0 To lower_bounds.Length - 1
        total_size = total_size * (upper_bounds[i] - lower_bounds[i])
    Next i
    Return total_size
End ArraySize
```

The next step, mapping a row and column to a position in the one-dimensional array, is a bit more confusing. Recall how the preceding example mapped row and column to an index in the `values` array. First the code determined how many complete rows should come before the item in question and multiplied that number by the number of items in a row. The code then added 1 for each position in the item's row that was before the item.

Moving to three dimensions isn't much harder. Figure 4.3 shows a $4 \times 4 \times 3$ three-dimensional array with dimensions labeled height, row, and column. The entry with coordinates $(1, 1, 3)$ is highlighted in gray.

To map the item's coordinates $(1, 1, 3)$ to an index in the `values` array, first determine how many complete "slices" come before the item. Because the item's height coordinate is 1, there is one complete slice before the item in the array. The size of a slice is `<row size> × <column size>`. If the item has coordinates (h, r, c), then the number of items that come before this one due to slices is given by the following:

```
index = h × <row size> × <column size>
```

Next you need to determine how many items come before this one due to complete rows. In this example, the item's row is 1, so one row comes before the item in the `values` array. If the item has row r, you need to add r times the size of a row to the index.

```
index = index + r × <row size>
```

Finally, you need to add 1 for each item that comes before this one in its column. If the item has column c, this is simply c.

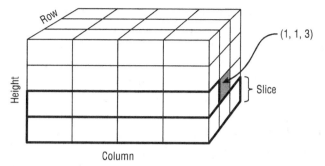

Figure 4.3: The first step in mapping an item to the `values` array is determining how many complete "slices" come before it.

```
index = index + c
```

You can extend this technique to work in even higher dimensions. To make calculating indices in the `values` array easier, you can make a `slice_sizes` array that holds the size of the "slice" at each of the dimensions. In the three-dimensional case, these values are `<row size> × <column size>`, `<column size>`, and 1.

To move to higher dimensions, you can find a slice size by multiplying the next slice size by the size of the current dimension. For example, for a four-dimensional array, the next slice size would be `<height size> × <row size> × <column size>`.

With all of this background, you're ready to see the complete algorithm. Suppose the `bounds` array holds alternating lower and upper bounds for the desired N-dimensional array. Then the following pseudocode initializes the array:

```
InitializeArray(Integer: bounds[])
    // Get the bounds.
    Integer: NumDimensions = bounds.Length / 2
    Integer: LowerBound[NumDimensions]
    Integer: SliceSize[NumDimensions]

    // Initialize LowerBound and SliceSize.
    Integer: slice_size = 1
    For i = NumDimensions - 1 To 0 Step -1
        SliceSize[i] = slice_size

        LowerBound[i] = bounds[2 * i]
        Integer: upper_bound = bounds[2 * i + 1]
        Integer: bound_size = upper_bound - LowerBound[i] + 1
        slice_size *= bound_size
    Next i

    // Allocate room for all of the items.
    Double: Values[slice_size]
End InitializeArray
```

This code calculates the number of dimensions by dividing the number of values in the `bounds` array by 2. It creates a `LowerBound` array to hold the lower bounds and a `SliceSize` array to hold the sizes of slices at different dimensions.

Next the code sets `slice_size` to 1. This is the size of the slice at the highest dimension, which is a column in the preceding example.

The code then loops through the dimensions, starting at the highest and looping toward dimension 0. (This corresponds to looping from column to row to height in the preceding example.) It sets the current slice size to `slice_size` and saves the dimension's lower bound. It then multiplies `slice_size` by the size of the current dimension to get the slice size for the next-smaller dimension.

After it finishes looping over all of the dimensions, `slice_size` holds the sizes of all of the array's dimensions multiplied together. That is the total number of items in the array, so the code uses it to allocate the `Values` array, where it will store the array's values.

The following deceptively simple pseudocode uses the `LowerBound` and `SliceSize` arrays to map the indices in the `indices` array to an index in the `Values` array:

```
Integer: MapIndicesToIndex(Integer: indices[])
    Integer: index = 0
    For i = 0 to indices.Length - 1
        index = index +
            (indices[i] - LowerBound[i]) * SliceSize[i]
    Next i
    Return index
End MapIndicesToIndex
```

The code initializes `index` to 0. It then loops over the array's dimensions. For each dimension, it multiplies the number of slices at that dimension by the size of a slice at that dimension and adds the result to `index`.

After it has looped over all of the dimensions, `index` holds the item's index in the `Values` array.

You can make using the algorithm easier by encapsulating it in a class. The constructor can tell the object what dimensions to use. Depending on your programming language, you may be able to make `get` and `set` methods that are used as accessors so that a program can treat an object as if it actually were an array.

Download the NDArray and n_d_array sample programs from the book's website to see a C# and Python implementations of this algorithm.

Triangular Arrays

Some applications can save space by using triangular arrays instead of normal rectangular arrays. In a *triangular array,* the values on one side of the diagonal have some default value, such as 0, null, or blank. In an *upper-triangular array,* the real values lie on or above the diagonal. In a *lower-triangular array,* the non-default values lie on or below the diagonal. For example, Figure 4.4 shows a lower-triangular array.

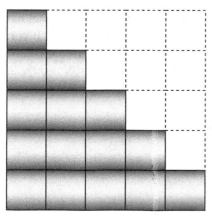

Figure 4.4: In a lower-triangular array, values above the diagonal have a default value.

For example, a *connectivity matrix* represents the connections between points in some sort of network. The network might be an airline's flight network that indicates which airports are connected to other airports. The array's entry connected[i, j] is set to true if there is a flight from airport i to airport j. If you assume that there is a flight from airport j to airport i whenever there is a flight from airport i to airport j, then connected [i, j] = connected[j, i]. In that case, there's no need to store both connected[i, j] and connected[j, i] because they are the same.

In cases such as this, the program can save space by storing the connectivity matrix in a triangular array.

NOTE   It's probably not worth going to the trouble of making a 3×3 triangular array because you would save only three entries. In fact, it's probably not worth making a 100×100 triangular array because you would save only 4,960 entries, which still isn't all that much memory, and working with the array would be harder than using a normal array. However, a 10,000×10,000 triangular array would save about 50 million entries, which begins to add up to real memory savings, so it may be worth making it into a triangular array.

Building a triangular array isn't too hard. Simply pack the array's values into a one-dimensional array, skipping the entries that should not be included. The challenges are to figure out how big the one-dimensional array must be and to figure out how to map rows and columns to indices in the one-dimensional array.

Table 4.1 shows the number of entries needed for triangular arrays of different sizes.

If you study Table 4.1 for a while, you'll see a pattern. The number of cells needed for N rows equals the number needed for N − 1 rows plus N.

If you think about triangular arrays for a while, you'll realize that they contain roughly half the number of the entries in a square array with the same number of rows. A square array containing N rows holds N^2 entries, so it seems likely that the number of entries in the corresponding triangular array would involve N^2. If you start with a general quadratic equation $A \times N^2 + B \times N + C$ and plug in the values from Table 4.1, you can solve for A, B, and C to find that the equation is $(N^2 + N) / 2$.

Table 4.1: Entries in Triangular Arrays

NUMBER OF ROWS	NUMBER OF ENTRIES
1	1
2	3
3	6
4	10
5	15
6	21
7	28

That solves the first challenge. To build a triangular array with N rows, allocate a one-dimensional array containing $(N^2 + N) / 2$ items.

The second challenge is to figure out how to map rows and columns to indices in the one-dimensional array. To find the index for an entry with row r and column c, you need to figure out how many entries come before that one in the one-dimensional array.

To answer that question, look at the array shown in Figure 4.5 and consider the number of entries that come before entry (3, 2).

The entries due to complete rows are highlighted with a thick border in Figure 4.5. The number of those entries is the same as the number of all entries in a triangular array with three rows, and you already know how to calculate that number.

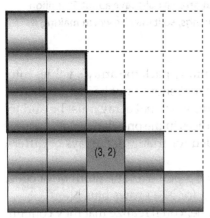

Figure 4.5: To find the index of an entry, you must figure out how many entries come before it in the one-dimensional array.

The entries that come before the target entry (3, 2) that are not due to complete rows are those to the left of the entry in its row. In this example, the target entry is in column 2, so there are two entries to its left in its row.

In general, the formula for the index of the entry with row r and column c is $\left((r-1)^2 + (r-1)\right)/2 + c$.

With these two formulas, working with triangular arrays is easy. Use the first formula, $(N^2 + N)/2$, to figure out how many items to allocate for an array with N rows. Use the second formula, $\left((r-1)^2 + (r-1)\right)/2 + c$, to map rows and columns to indices in the one-dimensional array.

You can make this easier by wrapping the triangular array in a class. If you can make get and set indexers for the class, a program can treat a triangular array object as if it were a normal array.

One last detail is how the triangular array class should handle requests for entries that do not exist in the array. For example, what should the class do if the program tries to access entry (1, 4), which lies in the missing upper half of the array? Depending on the application, you might want to return a default value, switch the row and column and return that value, or throw an exception.

Sparse Arrays

Triangular arrays let a program save memory if you know that the array will not need to hold values above its diagonal. If you know that an array will hold very few entries, you may be able to save even more memory.

For example, consider again an airline connectivity matrix that holds the value true in the [i, j] entry to indicate that there is a flight between city i and city j. The airline might have only 600 flights connecting 200 cities. In that case, there would be only 600 nonzero values in an array of 40,000 entries. Even if the flights are symmetrical (for every i–j flight there is a j–i flight) and you store the connections in a triangular array, the array would hold only 300 nonzero entries out of a total of 20,100 entries. The array would be almost 99 percent unused.

A *sparse array* lets you save even more space than a triangular array by not representing the missing entries. To get an item's value, the program searches for the item in the array. If the item is present, the program returns its value. If the item is missing, the program returns a default value for the array. For the connectivity matrix example, the default value would be false.

One way to implement a sparse array is to make a linked list of linked lists. The first list holds information about rows. Each item in that list points to another linked list holding information about the array's columns for that row.

You can build a sparse array with two cell classes—an ArrayRow class to represent a row and an ArrayEntry class to represent a value in a row.

The ArrayRow class stores a row number, a reference or pointer to the next ArrayRow object, and a reference to the first ArrayEntry in that row. The following pseudocode shows the ArrayRow class's layout:

```
ArrayRow:
    Integer: RowNumber
    ArrayRow: NextRow
    ArrayEntry: RowSentinel
```

The `ArrayEntry` class stores the entry's column number, whatever value the entry should hold for the array, and a reference to the next `ArrayEntry` object in this row. The following shows the `ArrayEntry` class's layout, where `T` is whatever type of data the array must hold:

```
ArrayEntry:
    Integer: ColumnNumber
    T: Value
    ArrayEntry: NextEntry
```

To make adding and removing rows easier, the list of rows can start with a sentinel, and each list of values in a row can start with a sentinel. Figure 4.6 shows a sparse array with the sentinels outlined in bold.

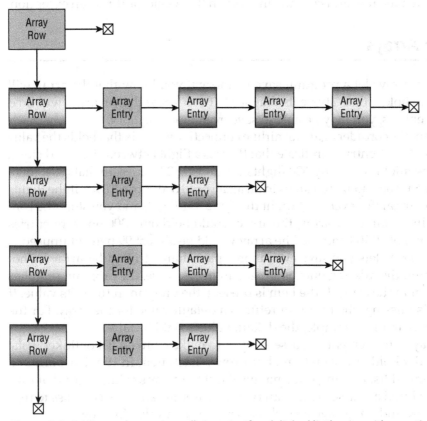

Figure 4.6: Adding and removing cells is easier if each linked list begins with a sentinel.

To make it easier to determine when a value is missing from the array, the Array-Row objects are stored in increasing order of RowNumber. If you're searching the list for a particular row number and you come to an ArrayRow object that has a greater RowNumber, you know that the row number you're looking for isn't in the array.

Similarly, the ArrayEntry objects are stored in increasing order of ColumnNumber.

Note that the RowEntry objects that seem to be aligned vertically in Figure 4.6 do not necessarily represent the same columns. The first RowEntry object in the first row might represent column 100, and the first RowEntry object in the second row might represent column –50.

The arrangement shown in Figure 4.6 looks complicated, but it's not too hard to use. To find a particular value, look down the row list until you find the right row. Then look across that row's value list until you find the column you want. If you fail to find the row or column, then the value isn't in the array.

This arrangement requires some ArrayRow objects and sentinels that don't hold values, but it's still more efficient than a triangular array if the array really is sparse. For example, in the worst case, a sparse array would contain one value in each row. In that case, an $N \times N$ array would use $N + 1$ ArrayRow objects and $2 \times N$ ArrayEntry objects. Of those objects, only N would contain actual values and the rest would be sentinels or used to navigate through the array. The fraction of objects containing array values is $N / (N + 1 + 2 * N) = N / (3 * N + 1)$, or approximately $1 / 3$. Compare that to the triangular array described previously, which was almost 99 percent empty.

With the data structure shown in Figure 4.6, you still need to write algorithms to perform three array operations.

1. Get the value at a given row and column or return a default value if the value isn't present.

2. Set a value at a given row and column.

3. Delete the value at a given row and column.

These algorithms are a bit easier to define if you first define methods for finding a particular row and column.

Find a Row or Column

To make finding values easier, you can define the following FindRowBefore method. This method finds the ArrayRow object *before* the spot where a target row should be. If the target row is not in the array, this method returns the ArrayRow before where the target row would be if it were present.

```
ArrayRow: FindRowBefore(Integer: row, ArrayRow: array_row_sentinel)
    ArrayRow: array_row = array_row_sentinel
    While (array_row.NextRow != null) And
        (array_row.NextRow.RowNumber < row))
```

```
        array_row = arrayRow.NextRow
    End While

    Return array_row
End FindRowBefore
```

This algorithm sets variable `array_row` equal to the array's row sentinel. The algorithm then repeatedly advances `array_row` to the next `ArrayRow` object in the list until either the next object is `null` or the next object's `RowNumber` is at least as large as the target row number.

If the next object is `null`, the program has reached the end of the row list without finding the desired row. If the row were present, it would belong after the current `array_row` object.

If the next object's `RowNumber` value equals the target row, then the algorithm has found the target row.

If the next object's `RowNumber` value is greater than the target row, the target row is not present in the array. If the row were present, it would belong after the current `array_row` object.

Similarly, you can define a `FindColumnBefore` method to find the `ArrayEntry` object before the spot where a target column should be in a row.

```
FindColumnBefore(Integer: column, ArrayEntry: row_sentinel)
    ArrayEntry: array_entry = row_sentinel
    While (array_entry.NextEntry != null) And
            (array_entry.NextEntry.ColumnNumber < column))
        array_entry = array_entry.NextEntry
    Return array_entry
End FindColumnBefore
```

If the array holds N `ArrayRow` objects, the `FindRowBefore` method takes O(N) time. If the row holding the most nondefault items contains M of those items, then the `FindColumnBefore` method runs in O(M) time. The exact run time for these methods depends on the number and distribution of nondefault values in the array.

Get a Value

Getting a value from the array is relatively easy once you have the `FindRowBefore` and `FindColumnBefore` methods.

```
GetValue(Integer: row, Integer: column)
    // Find the row.
    ArrayRow: array_row = FindRowBefore(row)
    array_row = array_row.NextRow
    If (array_row == null) Return default
    If (array_row.RowNumber > row) Return default
```

```
    // Find the column in the target row.
    ArrayEntry: array_entry =
        FindColumnBefore(column, array_row.RowSentinel)
    array_entry = array_entry.NextEntry
    If (array_entry == null) Return default
    If (array_entry.ColumnNumber > column) Return default
    Return array_entry.Value
End GetValue
```

This algorithm uses `FindRowBefore` to set `array_row` to the row before the target row. It then advances `array_row` to the next row, which is ideally the target row. If `array_row` is `null` or refers to the wrong row, the `GetValue` method returns the array's default value.

If the algorithm finds the correct row, it uses `FindColumnBefore` to set `array_entry` to the column before the target column. It then advances `array_entry` to the next column, which is ideally the target column. If `array_entry` is `null` or refers to the wrong column, the `GetValue` method again returns the array's default value.

If the algorithm gets this far, it has found the correct `ArrayEntry` object, so it returns that object's value.

This algorithm calls the `FindRowBefore` and `FindColumnBefore` methods. If the array has N rows that contain nondefault values, and the row with the most nondefault values contains M of those values, then the total run time for the `GetValue` method is $O(N + M)$. This is much longer than the $O(1)$ time needed to get a value from a normal or triangular array, but the sparse array uses much less space.

This is the reverse of the space/time trade-off demonstrated by some of the mode-finding algorithms described earlier in this chapter. This time, the algorithm reduces speed to save space.

Set a Value

Setting a value is similar to finding a value, except that the algorithm must be able to insert a new row or column into the array if necessary.

```
SetValue(Integer: row, Integer: column, T: value)
    // If the value we're setting is the default,
    // delete the entry instead of setting it.
    If (value == default)
        DeleteEntry(row, column)
        Return
    End If

    // Find the row before the target row.
    ArrayRow: array_row = FindRowBefore(row)

    // If the target row is missing, add it.
    If (array_row.NextRow == null) Or
        (array_row.NextRow.RowNumber > row)
```

```
Then
    ArrayRow: new_row
    new_row.NextRow = array_row.NextRow
    array_row.NextRow = new_row

    ArrayEntry: sentinel_entry
    new_row.RowSentinel = sentinel_entry
    sentinel_entry.NextEntry = null
End If

// Move to the target row.
array_row = array_row.NextRow

// Find the column before the target column.
ArrayEntry: array_entry =
    FindColumnBefore(column, array_row.RowSentinel)

// If the target column is missing, add it.
If (array_entry.NextEntry == null) Or
   (array_entry.NextEntry.ColumnNumber > column)
Then
    ArrayEntry: new_entry
    new_entry.NextEntry = array_entry.NextEntry
    array_entry.NextEntry = new_entry
End If

// Move to the target entry.
array_entry = array_entry.NextEntry

// Set the value.
array_entry.Value = value
End SetValue
```

The algorithm starts by checking the value it is setting in the array. If the value is the default value, the program should delete it from the array to minimize the array's size. To do that, it calls the DeleteEntry method, which is described in the next section, and returns.

If the new value isn't the default value, the algorithm calls the FindRowBefore method to find the row before the target row. If the row after the one returned by FindRowBefore isn't the target row, then either the algorithm reached the end of the row list or the next row comes after the target row. In either case, the algorithm inserts a new ArrayRow object between the row before and the row that follows it.

Figure 4.7 shows this process. In the list on the left, the target row is missing, but it should go where the dashed ellipse is shown.

To insert the new ArrayRow object, the algorithm creates the new object, sets its NextRow reference to array_row.NextRow, and sets array_row.NextRow to the new object. It then gives the new object a new row sentinel.

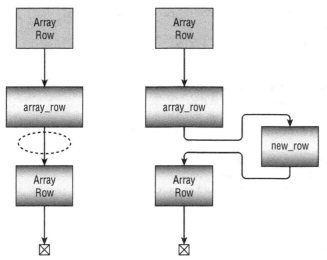

Figure 4.7: If the target row is missing, the `SetValue` method inserts a new `ArrayRow`.

When it has finished, the list looks like the right side of Figure 4.7, with `array_row`'s `NextRow` reference pointing to the new object.

Having found the target row, creating it if necessary, the algorithm calls the `FindColumnBefore` method to find the `ArrayEntry` object that represents the target column. If that object doesn't exist, the algorithm creates it and inserts it into the linked list of the `ArrayEntry` object, much as it inserted the `ArrayRow` if necessary.

Finally, the algorithm moves the variable `array_entry` to the `ArrayEntry` corresponding to the column and sets its value.

The `SetValue` algorithm may call the `DeleteEntry` algorithm, described in the following section. That algorithm calls the `FindRowBefore` and `FindColumnBefore` methods. If the `SetValue` algorithm does not call `DeleteEntry`, it calls `FindRowBefore` and `FindColumnBefore`. In either case, the method calls `FindRowBefore` and `FindColumnBefore` either directly or indirectly.

Suppose the array has N rows that contain nondefault values and the row with the most nondefault values contains M of those values. In that case, those `FindRowBefore` and `FindColumnBefore` methods give the `SetValue` algorithm a total run time of O(N + M).

Delete a Value

The algorithm to delete a value follows the same general approach used to get or set a value.

```
DeleteEntry(Integer: row, Integer column)
    // Find the row before the target row.
    ArrayRow: array_row = FindRowBefore(row)
```

```
    // If the target row is missing, we don't need to delete it.
    If (array_row.NextRow == null) Or
            (array_row.NextRow.RowNumber > row)
                Return

    // Find the entry before the target column in the next row.
    ArrayRow: target_row = array_row.NextRow
    ArrayEntry: array_entry =
        FindColumnBefore(column, target_row.RowSentinel)

    // If the target entry is missing, we don't need to delete it.
    If (array_entry.NextRow == null) Or
            (array_entry.NextRow.ColumnNumber > column)
                Return

    // Delete the target column.
    array_entry.NextColumn = array_entry.NextColumn.NextColumn

    // If the target row has any columns left, we're done.
    If (target_row.RowSentinel.NextColumn != null) Return

    // Delete the empty target row.
    array_row.NextRow = array_row.NextRow.NextRow
End DeleteEntry
```

This algorithm calls `FindRowBefore` to find the row before the target row. If the target row doesn't exist, the algorithm doesn't need to delete anything, so it returns.

Next, the algorithm calls `FindColumnBefore` to find the column before the target column in the target row. If the target column doesn't exist, again the algorithm doesn't need to delete anything, so it returns.

At this point, the algorithm has found the `ArrayEntry` object before the target entry in the row's linked list of entries. It removes the target entry from the list by setting the `NextColumn` reference of the previous entry to refer to the object after the target entry.

Figure 4.8 shows this operation. The list at the top is the original list. The variable `array_entry` refers to the entry before the target entry. To remove the target entry, the algorithm makes that entry's `NextColumn` reference point to the following entry.

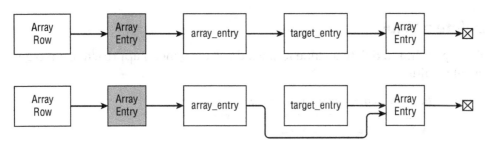

Figure 4.8: To remove a target entry, the algorithm sets the preceding entry's `NextColumn` reference to the entry after the target entry.

The algorithm does not change the target entry's NextColumn reference. That reference still refers to the following entry, but the algorithm no longer has a reference that can refer to the target entry, so it is essentially lost to the program.

> **NOTE** When this algorithm deletes a row or column object, that object's memory must be freed. Depending on the programming language, that may require more action. For example, a C++ program must explicitly call the free function for the removed object to make that memory available for reuse.
>
> Other languages take other approaches. For example, C#, Visual Basic, and Python use garbage collection, so the next time the garbage collector runs, it automatically frees any objects that the program can no longer access.

After it has removed the target entry from the row's linked list, the program examines the row's ArrayRow sentinel. If that object's NextColumn reference is not null, then the row still holds other column entries, so the algorithm is finished, and it returns.

If the target row no longer contains any entries, then the algorithm removes it from the linked list of ArrayRow objects, much as it removed the target column entry.

The DeleteEntry algorithm calls FindRowBefore and FindColumnBefore. If the array has N rows that contain nondefault values and the row with the most nondefault values contains M of those values, the total run time for the Delete-Entry method is O(N + M).

Matrices

One application of arrays is to represent matrices. If you use normal arrays, it's fairly easy to perform operations on matrices. For example, to add two 3×3 matrices, you simply add the corresponding entries.

> **NOTE** If you're unfamiliar with matrices and matrix operations, you may want to review the article on the Math Is Fun website (https://www.mathsisfun .com/algebra/matrix-introduction.html). For a more in-depth discussion, see the Wikipedia article "Matrix" at https://en.wikipedia.org/wiki/ Matrix(mathematics).

The following pseudocode shows how you can add two normal matrices that are stored in two-dimensional arrays:

```
AddArrays(Integer: array1[], Integer: array2[], Integer: result[])
    For i = 0 To <maximum bound for dimension 1>
        For j = 0 To <maximum bound for dimension 2>
```

```
            result[i, j] = array1[i, j] + array2[i, j]
        Next i
    Next i
End AddArrays
```

The following algorithm shows how you can multiply two normal two-dimensional matrices:

```
MultiplyArrays(Integer: array1[], Integer: array2[], Integer: result[])
    For i = 0 To <maximum bound for dimension 1>
        For j = 0 To <maximum bound for dimension 2>
            // Calculate the [i, j] result.
            result[i, j] = 0
            For k = 0 To <maximum bound for dimension 2>
                result[i, j] = result[i, j] +
                    array1[i, k] * array2[k, j]
            Next k
        Next j
    Next i
End MultiplyArrays
```

These algorithms work with triangular or sparse arrays, but they are inefficient because they examine every item in both input arrays—even if those entries aren't present.

For example, a triangular array is missing all values [i, j] where j > i, so adding or multiplying those entries takes on special meaning. If the missing entries are assumed to be 0, then adding or multiplying them doesn't contribute to the result. (If those entries are assumed to have some other default value, then adding or multiplying the arrays will result in a nontriangular array, so you may need to add or multiply the arrays completely.)

Instead of considering every entry, the algorithms should consider only the entries that are actually present. For triangular arrays, this isn't too confusing. I'll let you write addition and multiplication algorithms for triangular arrays as exercises.

The situation is a bit more confusing for sparse arrays, but the potential time savings is even greater. For example, when you add two sparse matrices, there's no need to iterate over rows and columns that are not present in either of the input arrays.

The following high-level algorithm adds two sparse matrices:

```
AddArrays(SparseArray: array1[], SparseArray: array2[],
        SparseArray: result[])
    // Get pointers into the the matrices' row lists.
    ArrayRow: array1_row = array1.Sentinel.NextRow
    ArrayRow: array2_row = array2.Sentinel.NextRow
    ArrayRow: result_row = result.Sentinel

    // Repeat while both input rows have items left.
    While (array1_row != null) And (array2_row != null)
        If (array1_row.RowNumber < array2_row.RowNumber) Then
```

```
            // array1_row's RowNumber is smaller. Copy it.
            <copy array1_row's row to the result>
            array1_row = array1_row.NextRow
        Else If (array2_row.RowNumber < array1_row.RowNumber) Then
            // array2_row's RowNumber is smaller. Copy it.
            <copy array2_row's row to the result>
            array2_row = array2_row.NextRow
        Else
            // The input rows have the same RowNumber.
            // Add the values in both rows to the result.
            <add the values in both array1_row and array2_row to the
             result>
            array1_row = array1_row.NextRow
            array2_row = array2_row.NextRow
        End If
    End While

    // Copy any remaining items from either input matrix.
    If (array1_row != null) Then
        <copy array1_row's remaining rows to the result>
    End If
    If (array2_row != null) Then
        <copy array2_row's remaining rows to the result>
    End If
End AddArrays
```

Similarly, you can write an algorithm to multiply two sparse matrices without examining all the missing rows and columns. I'll save that for an exercise, too.

COLUMN-ORDERED SPARSE MATRICES

In some algorithms, it may be more convenient to access the entries in a sparse matrix by columns instead of by rows. For example, when you're multiplying two 2D matrices, you multiply the entries in the rows of the first matrix by the entries in the columns of the second matrix.

To make that easier, you can use a similar technique where you use linked lists to represent columns instead of rows. If you need to access a sparse matrix in both row and column order, you can use both representations. The result is similar to a threaded linked list.

Summary

Normal arrays are simple, intuitive, and easy to use, but for some applications they can be awkward. In some applications, it may be more natural to work with an array that has nonzero lower bounds. By using the techniques described in the section "Nonzero Lower Bounds," you can effectively do just that.

Normal arrays are also inefficient for some applications. If an array holds entries in only its lower-left half, you can use a triangular array to save roughly half of the array's memory. If an array contains even fewer entries, you may be able to save even more space by using a sparse array.

Arrays with nonzero lower bounds, triangular arrays, and sparse arrays are more complicated than the normal arrays provided by most programming languages, but in some cases, they offer greater convenience and large memory savings.

An array provides random access to the elements that it contains. It lets you get or set any item if you know its indices in the array.

The next chapter explains two different kinds of containers: stacks and queues. Like arrays, these data structures hold collections of items. Unlike arrays, with their random access behavior, they have very constrained methods for inserting and removing items.

Exercises

You can find the answers to these exercises in Appendix B. Asterisks indicate particularly difficult problems.

1. Write an algorithm to calculate the sample variance of a one-dimensional array of numbers where the sample variance for an array containing N items is defined by this equation:

$$S = \frac{1}{N} \sum_{i=0}^{N-1} (x_i - \bar{x})^2$$

   Here $\bar{x}$ is the mean (average) of the values in the array, and the summation symbol Σ means to add up all of the x_i values as i varies from 0 to $N - 1$.

2. Write an algorithm to calculate the sample standard deviation of a one-dimensional array of numbers where the sample standard deviation is defined to be the square root of the sample variance.

3. Write an algorithm to find the median of a sorted one-dimensional array. (Be sure to handle arrays holding an even or odd number of items.)

4. If more than one value occurs the most in a one-dimensional array, then all such items are modes. For example, in the values $\{A, B, A, C, A, B, B\}$, both A and B occur three times, so they are both modes. How do the mode-finding algorithms described in this chapter handle that issue? How could you modify them to return all of the modes?

5. The FindModeCounts algorithm checks to see whether a count is the new largest count every time it increases a count. Would it be better to save those comparisons for the end after all of the counts are complete?

6. The FindModeCounts algorithm uses a counts array to find an array's mode in O(N) time. How would that compare to the FindModeSort algorithm if that algorithm used a sorting method, such as countingsort, which can sort in O(N) time?

7. The FindModeCounts algorithm works only if the range of values is relatively limited and starts at 0. How would you modify it if the range did not start at 0? For example, what if the values ranged from 1,000 to 2,000?

8. The section "Removing Items" explained how to remove an item from a linear array. Write the algorithm in pseudocode.

9. The triangular arrays discussed in this chapter are sometimes called *lower-triangular arrays* because the values are stored in the lower-left half of the array. How would you modify that kind of array to produce an upper-triangular array with the values stored in the upper-right corner?

10. How would you modify the lower-triangular arrays described in this chapter to make an "upper-left" array where the entries are stored in the upper-left half of the array? What is the relationship between row and column for the entries in the array?

11. Suppose you define the main diagonal of a rectangular (and nonsquare) array to start in the upper-left corner and extend down and to the right until it reaches the bottom or right edge of the array. Write an algorithm that fills entries on or below the main diagonal with 1s and entries above the main diagonal with 0s.

12. Consider the diagonal of a rectangular array that starts in the last column of the first row and extends left and down until it reaches the bottom or left edge of the array. Write an algorithm that fills the entries on or above the diagonal with 1s and entries below the diagonal with 0s.

13. Write an algorithm that fills each item in a rectangular array with the distance from that entry to the nearest edge (left, right, top, or bottom) of the array.

14. *Generalize the method for building triangular arrays to build three-dimensional tetrahedral arrays that contain entries value[i, j, k] where j ≤ i and k ≤ j. How would you continue to extend this method for even higher dimensions?

15. How could you make a sparse triangular array?

16. Write an algorithm that adds two triangular arrays.

17. Write an algorithm that multiplies two triangular arrays.

18. The algorithm described for adding two sparse matrices is fairly high level. Expand the algorithm to provide details in place of the instructions inside the angle brackets (<>). (*Hint*: You may want to make a separate CopyEntries method to copy entries from one list to another and a separate AddEntries method to combine the entries in two rows that have the same row number.)

19. Write a high-level algorithm that efficiently multiplies two sparse matrices that have default value 0.

Stacks and Queues

Stacks and queues are relatively simple data structures that store objects in either first-in-first-out order or last-in-first-out order. They expand as needed to hold additional items, much like linked lists can, as described in Chapter 3, "Linked Lists." In fact, you can use linked lists to implement stacks and queues.

You can also use stacks and queues to model analogous real-world scenarios, such as service lines at a bank or supermarket. Usually, however, they are used to store objects for later processing by other algorithms, such as shortest-path algorithms.

This chapter describes stacks and queues. It explains what they are, explains stack and queue terminology, and describes the methods that you can use to implement them.

Stacks

A *stack* is a data structure where items are added and removed in last-in-first-out order. Because of this last-in-first-out (LIFO, usually pronounced "life-oh") behavior, stacks are sometimes called *LIFO lists* or *LIFOs*.

A stack is similar to a pile of books on a desk. You can add a book to the top of the pile or remove the top book from the pile, but you can't pull a book out of the middle or bottom of the pile without making the whole thing topple over.

A stack is also similar to a spring-loaded stack of plates at a cafeteria. If you add plates to the stack, the spring compresses so that the top plate is even with the countertop. If you remove a plate, the spring expands so that the plate that is now on top is still even with the countertop. Figure 5.1 shows this kind of stack.

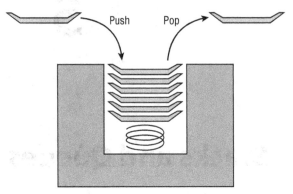

Figure 5.1: A stack is similar to a stack of plates at a cafeteria.

Because this kind of stack pushes plates down into the counter, this data structure is also sometimes called a *pushdown stack*. Adding an object to a stack is called *pushing* the object onto the stack, and removing an object from the stack is called *popping* the object off of the stack. A stack class typically provides Push and Pop methods to add items to and remove items from the stack.

> **NOTE** Python lists even provide a pop method. It can take the index of the item that you want to remove from the list as a parameter. If you omit the index, then the method removes and returns the last item in the list, just like a stack should.
>
> Python lists don't provide a push method, but the append method does what push would do.
>
> One important difference between the C# Stack class and a Python list is the position where they add and remove items. The C# Stack class's Push and Pop methods add and remove items at the beginning of its list. In contrast, a Python list's append and pop methods add and remove items from the end of the list.
>
> This doesn't matter if you only access the stacks' items via the push and pop methods, but it makes a difference if you examine the items inside the stacks. The two kinds of stacks store their items in opposite orders. For example, if you use the algorithms described later in this chapter to sort items in increasing order, the items will actually appear in decreasing order in a Python list.

The following sections describe a few of the more common methods for implementing a stack.

Linked-List Stacks

Implementing a stack is easy using a linked list. The Push method simply adds a new cell to the top of the list, and the Pop method removes the top cell from the list.

The following pseudocode shows the algorithm for pushing an item onto a linked-list stack:

```
Push(Cell: sentinel, Data: new_value)
    // Make a cell to hold the new value.
    Cell: new_cell = New Cell
    new_cell.Value = new_value

    // Add the new cell to the linked list.
    new_cell.Next = sentinel.Next
    sentinel.Next = new_cell
End Push
```

The following pseudocode shows the algorithm for popping an item off of a linked-list stack:

```
Data: Pop(Cell: sentinel)
    // Make sure there is an item to pop.
    If (sentinel.Next == null) Then <throw an exception>

    // Get the top cell's value.
    Data: result = sentinel.Next.Value

    // Remove the top cell from the linked list.
    sentinel.Next = sentinel.Next.Next

    // Return the result.
    Return result
End Pop
```

Figure 5.2 shows the process. The top image shows the stack after the program has pushed the letters *A, P, P, L,* and *E* onto it. The middle image shows the stack

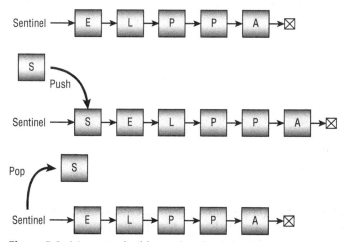

Figure 5.2: It's easy to build a stack with a linked list.

after the new letter *S* has been pushed onto the stack. The bottom image shows the stack after the *S* has been popped off of the stack.

NOTE   See Chapter 3 for more details about using linked lists.

With a linked list, pushing and popping items both have O(1) run times, so both operations are quite fast. The list requires no extra storage aside from the links between cells, so linked lists are also space-efficient.

Array Stacks

Implementing a stack in an array is almost as easy as implementing one with a linked list. Allocate space for an array that is large enough to hold the number of items that you expect to put in the stack. Then use a variable to keep track of the next empty position in the stack.

The following pseudocode shows the algorithm for pushing an item onto an array-based stack:

```
Push(Data: stack_values [], Integer: next_index, Data: new_value)
    // Make sure there's room to add an item.
    If (next_index == <length of stack_values>) Then
        <throw an exception>

    // Add the new item.
    stack_values[next_index] = new_value

    // Increment next_index.
    next_index = next_index + 1
End Push
```

The following pseudocode shows the algorithm for popping an item off of an array-based stack:

```
Data: Pop(Data: stack_values[], Integer: next_index)
    // Make sure there is an item to pop.
    If (next_index == 0) Then <throw an exception>

    // Decrement next_index.
    next_index = next_index - 1

    // Return the top value.
    Return stack_values[next_index]
End Pop
```

Figure 5.3 shows the process graphically. The top image shows the stack after the program has pushed the letters *A, P, P, L,* and *E* onto it. The middle image shows the stack after the new letter *S* has been pushed onto the stack. The bottom image shows the stack after the *S* has been popped off of the stack.

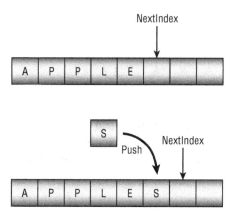

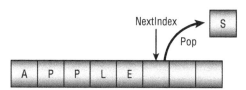

Figure 5.3: It's easy to build a stack with an array.

With an array-based stack, adding and removing an item both have O(1) run times, so both operations are quite fast. Setting and getting a value from an array generally is faster than creating a new cell in a linked list, so this method may be slightly faster than using a linked list. The array-based stack also doesn't need extra memory to store links between cells.

Unlike a linked-list stack, however, an array-based stack requires extra space to hold new items. How much extra space depends on your application and whether you know in advance how many items might need to fit in the stack. If you don't know how many items you might need to store in the array, you can resize the array if needed, although that will take extra time. If the array holds N items when you need to resize it, it will take O(N) steps to copy those items into the newly resized array.

Depending on how the stack is used, allowing room for extra items may be very inefficient. For example, suppose an algorithm occasionally needs to store 1,000 items in a stack, but most of the time it stores only a few. In that case, most of the time the array will take up much more space than necessary. If you know the stack will never need to hold more than a few items, however, an array-based stack can be fairly efficient.

Double Stacks

Suppose an algorithm needs to use two stacks whose combined size is bounded by some amount. In that case, you can store both stacks in a single array, with one at each end and both growing toward the middle, as shown in Figure 5.4.

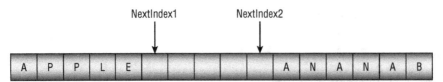

Figure 5.4: Two stacks can share an array if their combined size is limited.

The following pseudocode shows the algorithms for pushing and popping items with two stacks contained in a single array. To make the algorithm simpler, the Values array and the NextIndex1 and NextIndex2 variables are stored outside of the Push methods.

```
Data: StackValues [<max items>]
Integer: NextIndex1, NextIndex2

// Initialize the array.
Initialize()
    NextIndex1 = 0
    NextIndex2 = <length of StackValues> - 1
End Initialize

// Add an item to the top stack.
Push1(Data: new_value)
    // Make sure there's room to add an item.
    If (NextIndex1 > NextIndex2) Then <throw an exception>

    // Add the new item.
    StackValues[NextIndex1] = new_value

    // Increment NextIndex1.
    NextIndex1 = NextIndex1 + 1
End Push1

// Add an item to the bottom stack.
Push2(Data: new_value)
    // Make sure there's room to add an item.
    If (NextIndex1 > NextIndex2) Then <throw an exception>

    // Add the new item.
    StackValues[NextIndex2] = new_value

    // Decrement NextIndex2.
    NextIndex2 = NextIndex2 - 1
End Push2

// Remove an item from the top stack.
Data: Pop1()
    // Make sure there is an item to pop.
    If (NextIndex1 == 0) Then <throw an exception>
```

```
    // Decrement NextIndex1.
    NextIndex1 = NextIndex1 - 1

    // Return the top value.
    Return StackValues[NextIndex1]
End Pop1

// Remove an item from the bottom stack.
Data: Pop2()
    // Make sure there is an item to pop.
    If (NextIndex2 == <length of StackValues> - 1)
    Then <throw an exception>

    // Increment NextIndex2.
    NextIndex2 = NextIndex2 + 1

    // Return the top value.
    Return StackValues[NextIndex2]
End Pop2
```

Stack Algorithms

Many algorithms use stacks. For example, some of the shortest path algorithms described in Chapter 13, "Basic Network Algorithms," can use stacks. The following sections describe a few other algorithms that you can implement by using stacks.

Reversing an Array

Reversing an array is simple with a stack. Just push each item onto the stack and then pop it back off. Because of the stack's LIFO nature, the items come back out in reverse order.

The following pseudocode shows this algorithm:

```
ReverseArray(Data: values[])
    // Push the values from the array onto the stack.
    Stack: stack = New Stack
    For i = 0 To <length of values> - 1
        stack.Push(values[i])
    Next i

    // Pop the items off the stack into the array.
    For i = 0 To <length of values> - 1
        values[i] = stack.Pop()
    Next i
End ReverseArray
```

If the array contains N items, this algorithm takes $2 \times N$ steps, so it has run time O(N).

Train Sorting

Suppose a train contains cars bound for several different destinations, and it enters a train yard. Before the train leaves the yard, you need to use holding tracks to sort the cars so that the cars going to the same destination are grouped together.

Figure 5.5 shows a train with cars bound for cities 3, 2, 1, 3, and 2 entering from the left on the input track. The train can move onto a holding track and move its rightmost car onto the left end of any cars on that holding track. Later, the train can go back to the holding track and move a car from the holding track's left end back onto the train's right end. The goal is to sort the cars.

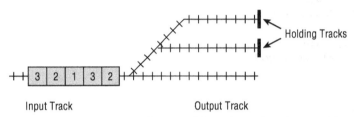

Figure 5.5: You can use stacks to model a train yard sorting a train's cars.

You can directly model this situation by using stacks. One stack represents the incoming train. Its Pop method removes a car from the right of the train, and its Push method moves a car back onto the right end of the train.

Other stacks represent the holding tracks and the output track. Their Push methods represent moving a car onto the left end of the track, and the Pop method represents moving a car off of the left end of the track.

The following pseudocode shows how a program could use stacks to model sorting the train shown in Figure 5.5. Here train is the train on the input track, track1 and track2 are the two holding tracks, and output is the output track on the right.

```
holding1.Push(train.Pop())    // Step 1: Car 2 to holding 1.
holding2.Push(train.Pop())    // Step 2: Car 3 to holding 2.
output.Push(train.Pop())      // Step 3: Car 1 to output.
holding1.Push(train.Pop())    // Step 4: Car 2 to holding 1.
train.Push(holding2.Pop())    // Step 5: Car 3 to train.
train.Push(holding1.Pop())    // Step 6: Car 2 to train.
train.Push(holding1.Pop())    // Step 7: Car 2 to train.
train.Push(output.Pop())      // Step 8: Car 1 to train.
```

Figure 5.6 shows this process. The car being moved in each step has a bold outline. An arrow shows where each car moves.

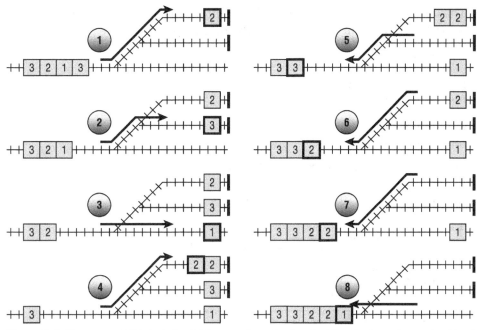

Figure 5.6: You can sort this train in eight moves by using two holding tracks and an output track.

NOTE A real train yard might need to sort several trains containing many more cars all at once using many more holding tracks that may connect in unique configurations. All of these considerations make the problem much harder than this simple example.

Of course, in a real train yard, each move requires shuffling train cars, and that can take several minutes. Therefore, finding a solution with the fewest possible moves is very important.

Tower of Hanoi

The Tower of Hanoi puzzle (also called the Tower of Brahma or Lucas' Tower), shown in Figure 5.7, has three pegs. One peg holds a stack of disks of different sizes, ordered from smallest to largest. The goal is to move all the disks from one peg to another. You must move disks one at a time, and you cannot place a disk on top of another disk that has a smaller radius.

You can model this puzzle using three stacks in a fairly obvious way. Each stack represents a peg. You can use numbers giving the disks' radii for objects in the stacks.

Figure 5.7: The goal in the Tower of Hanoi puzzle is to restack disks from one peg to another without placing a disk on top of a smaller disk.

The following pseudocode shows how a program could use stacks to model moving the disks from the left peg to the middle peg in Figure 5.7:

```
peg2.Push(peg1.Pop())
peg3.Push(peg1.Pop())
peg3.Push(peg2.Pop())
peg2.Push(peg1.Pop())
peg1.Push(peg3.Pop())
peg2.Push(peg3.Pop())
peg2.Push(peg1.Pop())
```

Figure 5.8 shows the process graphically.

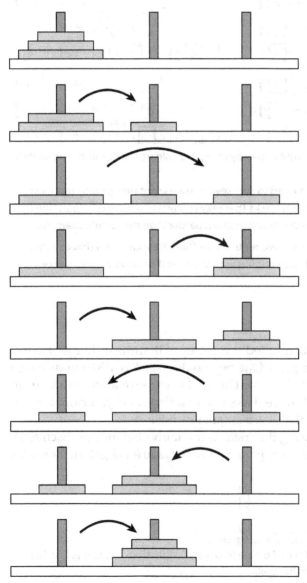

Figure 5.8: You can model the Tower of Hanoi puzzle with three stacks.

NOTE The example shown in Figure 5.8 uses only three disks so that the solution can fit easily into a figure. In general, the number of steps required to move N disks is $2^N - 1$, so the number of steps grows very quickly as N increases.

The puzzle was invented by French mathematician Edouard Lucas (1842–1891). The legend (which may have been invented by Lucas) says that there is an Indian temple containing three large posts and 64 golden disks. The temple's priests follow the bigger-disks-on-the-bottom rule to move the whole stack.

The bad news is that, when the priests finish, the world will end. The good news is that $2^{64} - 1$ is more than 1.8×10^{19}, so this will take a while. If the priests can move one disk per second, then this will take nearly 585 billion years.

One solution to the Tower of Hanoi puzzle is a nice example of recursion, so it is discussed in greater detail in Chapter 9, "Recursion."

Stack Insertionsort

Chapter 6, "Sorting," focuses on sorting algorithms, but Chapter 3 briefly explained how to implement insertionsort with linked lists. The basic idea behind insertionsort is to take an item from the input list and insert it into the proper position in a sorted output list (which initially starts empty). Chapter 3 explained how to implement insertionsort with linked lists, but you also can implement it with stacks.

The original stack holds items in two sections. The items farthest down in the stack are sorted, and those near the top of the stack are not. Initially, no items are sorted, and all of the items are in the "not sorted" section of the stack.

The algorithm uses a second, temporary stack. For each item in the original stack, the algorithm pops the top item off of the stack and stores it in a variable. It then moves all of the other unsorted items onto the temporary stack. By "moves," I mean the algorithm pops a value from one stack and pushes it onto another stack.

Next the algorithm starts moving sorted items onto the temporary stack until it finds the position where the new item belongs within the sorted items. At that point, the algorithm inserts the new item onto the original stack and then moves all of the items from the temporary stack back onto the original stack. The algorithm repeats this process until all of the items have been added to the sorted section of the stack.

The following pseudocode shows the insertionsort algorithm at a fairly high level:

```
// Sort the items in the stack.
StackInsertionsort(Stack: items)
    // Make a temporary stack.
    Stack: temp_stack = New Stack
```

```
Integer: num_items = <number of items>
For i = 0 To num_items - 1
    // Position the next item.
    // Pull off the first item.
    Data: next_item = items.Pop()

    <Move the items that have not yet been sorted to temp_stack.
     At this point there are (num_items - i - 1) unsorted items.>

    <Move sorted items to the second stack until
     you find out where next_item belongs.>

    <Add next_item at this position.>

    <Move the items back from temp_stack to the original stack.>
Next i
End StackInsertionsort
```

For each item, this algorithm moves the unsorted items to the temporary stack. Next it moves some of the sorted items to the temporary stack, and then it moves all of the items back to the original stack. At different steps, the number of unsorted items that must be moved is $N, N - 1, N - 2, \ldots, 2, 1$ so the total number of items moved is $N + (N - 1) + (N - 2) + \ldots + 2 + 1 = N \times (N + 1) / 2 = O(N^2)$. This means that the algorithm has a run time of $O(N^2)$.

Stack Selectionsort

In addition to describing a linked-list insertionsort, Chapter 3 explained how to implement selectionsort with linked lists. The basic idea behind selectionsort is to search through the unsorted items to find the largest item and then move it to the front end of the sorted output list. Chapter 3 explained how to implement selectionsort with linked lists, but you can also implement it with stacks.

As in the insertionsort algorithm, the original stack holds items in two sections. The items farthest down in the stack are sorted, and those near the top of the stack are not. Initially, no items are sorted, and all of the items are in the "not sorted" section of the stack.

The algorithm uses a second temporary stack. For each position in the original stack, the algorithm moves all of the still unsorted items to the temporary stack, keeping track of the largest item.

After it has moved all of the unsorted items to the temporary stack, the program pushes the largest item it found onto the original stack in its correct position. It then moves all of the unsorted items from the temporary stack back to the original stack.

The algorithm repeats this process until all of the items have been added to the sorted section of the stack.

The following pseudocode shows the selectionsort algorithm at a fairly high level:

```
// Sort the items in the stack.
StackSelectionsort(Stack: items)
    // Make the temporary stack.
    Stack: temp_stack = New Stack

    Integer: num_items = <number of items>
    For i = 0 To num_items - 1
        // Position the next item.
        // Find the item that belongs in sorted position i.

        <Move the items that have not yet been sorted onto the
         temp_stack, keeping track of the largest. Store the
         largest item in variable largest_item.
         At this point there are (num_items - i - 1) unsorted items.>

        <Add largest_item to the original stack
         at the end of the previously sorted items.>

        <Move the unsorted items back from temp_stack to the
         original stack, skipping largest_item when you find it>
    Next i
End StackSelectionsort
```

For each item, this algorithm moves the unsorted items to the temporary stack, adds the largest item to the sorted section of the original stack, and then moves the remaining unsorted items back from the temporary stack to the original stack. For each position in the array, it must move the unsorted items twice. At different steps, there are $N, N-1, N-2, \ldots, 1$ unsorted items to move, so the total number of items moved is $N + (N-1) + (N-2) + \ldots + 1 = N \times (N+1) / 2 = O(N^2)$, and the algorithm has run time $O(N^2)$.

Queues

A *queue* is a data structure where items are added and removed in first-in-first-out order. Because of this first-in-first-out (FIFO, usually pronounced "fife-oh") behavior, stacks are sometimes called *FIFO lists* or *FIFOs*.

A queue is similar to a store's checkout queue. You join the end of the queue and wait your turn. When you get to the front of the queue, the cashier takes your money and gives you a receipt.

Usually, the method that adds an item to a queue is called `Enqueue`, and the item that removes an item from a queue is called `Dequeue`.

The following sections describe a few of the more common methods for implementing a queue.

Linked-List Queues

Implementing a queue is easy using a linked list. To make removing the last item from the queue easy, the queue should use a doubly linked list.

The `Enqueue` method simply adds a new cell to the top of the list, and the `Dequeue` method removes the bottom cell from the list.

The following pseudocode shows the algorithm for enqueueing an item in a linked-list stack:

```
Enqueue(Cell: top_sentinel, Data: new_value)
    // Make a cell to hold the new value.
    Cell: new_cell = New Cell
    new_cell.Value = new_value

    // Add the new cell to the linked list.
    new_cell.Next = top_sentinel.Next
    top_sentinel.Next = new_cell
    new_cell.Prev = top_sentinel
End Enqueue
```

The following pseudocode shows the algorithm for dequeueing an item from a linked-list stack:

```
Data: Dequeue(Cell: bottom_sentinel)
    // Make sure there is an item to dequeue.
    If (bottom_sentinel.Prev == top_sentinel) Then <throw an exception>

    // Get the bottom cell's value.
    Data: result = bottom_sentinel.Prev.Value

    // Remove the bottom cell from the linked list.
    bottom_sentinel.Prev = bottom_sentinel.Prev.Prev
    bottom_sentinel.Prev.Next = bottom_sentinel

    // Return the result.
    Return result
End Dequeue
```

NOTE See Chapter 3 for more details about using linked lists.

With a doubly linked list, enqueueing and dequeueing items have O(1) run times, so both operations are quite fast. The list requires no extra storage aside from the links between cells, so linked lists are also space-efficient.

Array Queues

Implementing a queue in an array is a bit trickier than implementing one with a linked list. To keep track of the array positions that are in use, you can use two variables: `Next`, to mark the next open position, and `Last`, to mark the position that has been in use the longest. If you simply store items at one end of an array and remove them from the other, however, the occupied spaces move down through the array.

For example, suppose that a queue is implemented in an array with eight entries. Consider the following series of enqueue and dequeue operations:

```
Enqueue (M)
Enqueue (O)
Enqueue (V)
Dequeue ()        // Remove M.
Dequeue ()        // Remove O.
Enqueue (I)
Enqueue (N)
Enqueue (G)
Dequeue ()        // Remove V.
Dequeue ()        // Remove I.
```

Figure 5.9 shows this sequence of operations. Initially, Next and Last refer to the same entry. This indicates that the queue is empty. After the series of Enqueue and Dequeue operations, only two empty spaces are available for adding new items. After that, it will be impossible to add new items to the queue.

One approach to solving this problem is to enlarge the array when Next falls off the end of the array. Unfortunately, that would make the array grow bigger over time, and all the space before the Last entry would be unused.

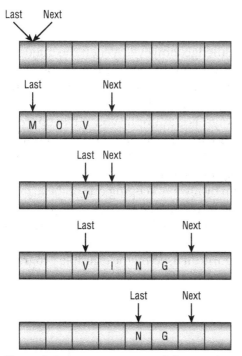

Figure 5.9: As you enqueue and dequeue items in an array-based queue, the occupied spaces move down through the array.

Another approach would be to move all of the array's entries back to the beginning of the array whenever Last falls off the array. That would work, but it would be relatively slow.

A more effective approach is to build a *circular array*, in which you treat the last item as if it were immediately before the first item. Now when Next falls off the end of the array, it wraps around to the first position, and the program can store new items there.

Figure 5.10 shows a circular queue holding the values M, O, V, I, N, and G.

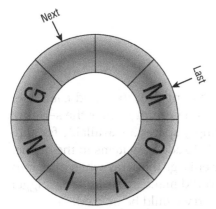

Figure 5.10: In a circular queue, you treat the array's last item as if it comes right before the first item.

A circular array does present a new challenge, however. When the queue is empty, Next is the same as Last. If you add enough items to the queue, Next goes all the way around the array and catches up to Last again, so there's no obvious way to tell whether the queue is empty or full.

You can handle this problem in a few ways. For example, you can keep track of the number of items in the queue, keep track of the number of unused spaces in the queue, or keep track of the number of items added to and removed from the queue. The CircularQueue sample program, which is available for download on the book's website, handles this problem by always keeping one of the array's spaces empty. If you added another value to the queue shown in Figure 5.10, the queue would be considered full when Next is just before Last, even though there was one empty array entry.

The following pseudocode shows the algorithm used by the example program for enqueueing an item:

```
// Variables to manage the queue.
Data: Queue[<queue size>]
Integer: Next = 0
Integer: Last = 0
```

```
// Enqueue an item.
Enqueue(Data: value)
    // Make sure there's room to add an item.
    If ((Next + 1) Mod <queue size> == Last) Then <throw an exception>

    Queue[Next] = value
    Next = (Next + 1) Mod <queue size>
End Enqueue
```

The following pseudocode shows the algorithm for dequeueing an item:

```
// Dequeue an item.
Data: Dequeue()
    // Make sure there's an item to remove.
    if (Next == Last) Then <throw an exception>

    Data: value = Queue[Last]
    Last = (Last + 1) Mod <queue size>

    Return value
End Dequeue
```

A circular queue still has a problem if it becomes completely full. If the queue is full and you need to add more items, then you need to allocate a larger storage array, copy the data into the new array, and then use the new array instead of the old one. This can take some time, so you should try to make the array big enough in the first place.

Specialized Queues

Queues are fairly specialized, but some applications use even more specialized queues. Two of these kinds of queues are priority queues and deques.

Priority Queues

In a priority queue, each item has a priority, and the dequeue method removes the item that has the highest priority. Basically, high-priority items are handled first.

One way to implement a priority queue is to keep the items in the queue sorted by priority. For example, you can use the main concept behind insertionsort to keep the items sorted. When you add a new item to the queue, you search through the queue until you find the position where it belongs and you place it there. To dequeue an item, you simply remove the top item from the queue. With this approach, enqueueing an item takes O(N) time, and dequeueing an item takes O(1) time.

Another approach is to store the items in whatever order they are added to the queue and then have the dequeue method search for the highest-priority item. With this approach, enqueueing an item takes O(1) time, and dequeueing an item takes O(N) time.

Both of these approaches are reasonably straightforward if you use linked lists.

The heap data structure described in the "Heapsort" section of Chapter 6 provides a more efficient way of implementing a priority queue. A heap-based priority queue can enqueue and dequeue items in $O(\log N)$ time.

Deques

Deque, which is usually pronounced "deck," stands for double-ended queue. A *deque* is a queue that allows you to add items to and remove items from either end of the queue.

Deques are useful in algorithms where you have partial information about the priority of items. For example, you might know that some items are high priority and others are low priority, but you might not necessarily know the exact relative priorities of every item. In that case, you can add high-priority items to one end of the deque and low-priority items to the other end of the deque.

Deques are easy to build with doubly linked lists.

Binomial Heaps

You can use a linked list to make a simple priority queue, but then you need either to keep the list sorted (which is slow) or to dig through the list to find the highest-priority item when needed (which is also slow). A *binomial heap* lets you insert new items and remove the highest priority item relatively quickly.

A binomial heap contains a collection of *binomial trees* that contain the heap's values. To make rearranging the trees easier, the heap normally stores the tree roots in a linked list. You may want to use a list sentinel to make it easier to manage the list.

> **NOTE** A disjoint union of trees, such as the ones used by a binomial heap, is sometimes called a *forest*.

Chapters 10 and 11 have a lot more to say about trees, but I wanted to describe binomial heaps here near the discussion of priority queues.

Binomial Trees

You can define a binomial tree recursively by using the following rules:

1. A binomial tree with order 0 is a single node.
2. A binomial tree with order k has child nodes that are roots of subtrees that have orders $k - 1, k - 2, ..., 1, 0$ in that order from left to right.

Figure 5.11 shows binomial trees with orders between 0 and 3. Dashed lines show how the order 3 contains trees of order 2, 1, and 0.

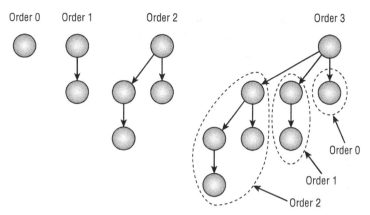

Figure 5.11: A binomial tree of order k contains binomial subtrees of order $k-1, k-2, \ldots, 0$.

> **NOTE** These trees are called binomial trees because the number of nodes at a certain level in a tree is given by the binomial formula. If a tree has order n, then it has $\binom{n}{d}$ nodes at depth d. The value $\binom{n}{d}$, which is pronounced "n choose d," is given by the following formula:

$$\binom{n}{d} = \frac{n!}{d!(n-d)!}$$

For example, consider the order 3 tree shown in Figure 5.11. The following equations calculate the number of nodes that this tree should have on each of its four levels (numbered 0 through 3).

$$\binom{3}{0} = \frac{3!}{0!(3-0)!} = \frac{6}{1(3)!} = \frac{6}{6} = 1$$

$$\binom{3}{1} = \frac{3!}{1!(3-1)!} = \frac{6}{1(2)!} = \frac{6}{2} = 3$$

$$\binom{3}{2} = \frac{3!}{2!(3-2)!} = \frac{6}{2(1)!} = \frac{6}{2} = 3$$

$$\binom{3}{3} = \frac{3!}{3!(3-3)!} = \frac{6}{6(0)!} = 1$$

If you look again at Figure 5.11, you'll see that the order 3 tree has 1, 3, 3, and 1 node on its four levels.

Binomial trees have a couple of interesting properties. A tree of order k contains 2^k nodes and has a height of k. (A tree's *height* is the number of links between the root node and the tree's deepest leaf node.)

A feature of binomial trees that is particularly important for building a binomial heap is that you can combine two trees of order k by making one of the roots be a child of the other in order to produce a new tree of order k + 1. Figure 5.12 shows how you can turn two order 2 trees into an order 3 tree.

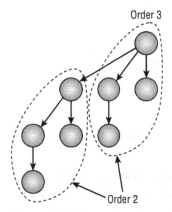

Figure 5.12: If you make the root of an order 2 tree (in the left dashed circle) into a child of the root of another order 2 tree (in the right dashed circle), you get an order 3 tree.

Binomial Heaps

A binomial heap contains a forest of binomial trees that follows these three additional rules:

1. Each binomial tree obeys the *minimum heap property*. That means every node's value is less than or equal to the values of its children. In particular, this means that the tree's root holds the smallest value in the tree.

2. The forest contains at most one binomial tree of any given order. For example, the forest might contain trees of order 0, 3, and 7, but it cannot contain a second tree with order 3.

3. The forest's trees are sorted by their orders, so those with the smallest orders come first.

The first rule makes it easy to find the node with the smallest value in the forest—simply loop through the trees and pick the smallest root value.

> **NOTE**   This discussion assumes that items with higher priorities have smaller values, so, for example, the value 1 might mean top priority and the value 2 might mean second priority. If you regard larger numbers as having higher priority, simply reverse the discussion.

The second property ensures that the heap cannot grow too wide and force you to examine a lot of trees when you need to find the smallest element.

In fact, the number of values in the heap uniquely determines the number of trees and their orders! Because a binomial tree of order k contains 2^k nodes, you can use the binary representation of the number of values to determine which trees it must contain.

For example, suppose a heap contains 13 nodes. The binary representation of 13 is 1101, so the heap must contain a tree of order 3 (containing eight nodes), a tree of order 2 (containing four nodes), and a tree of order 0 (containing one node).

All of this means that a binomial heap containing N nodes can hold at most $1 + \log_2(N)$ trees, so it cannot be too wide.

That's enough background about binomial trees and heaps. The following sections explain how you perform the key operations necessary to make a binomial heap work as a priority queue.

Merging Trees

As I mentioned earlier, you can merge two trees with the same order by making one tree's root a child of the other tree's root. The only trick here is that you need to maintain the minimum heap property. To do that, simply use the root node that has the smaller value as the parent so that it becomes the root of the new tree.

The following pseudocode shows the basic idea. Here I assume that the nodes in the trees are contained in BinomialNode objects. Each BinomialNode object has a NextSibling field that points to the node's sibling and a FirstChild field that points to the node's first child.

```
// Merge two trees that have the same order.
BinomialNode: MergeTrees(BinomialNode: root1, BinomialNode: root2)
    If (root1.Value < root2.Value) Then
        // Make root1 the parent.
        root2.NextSibling = root1.FirstChild
        root1.FirstChild = root2
        Return root1
    Else
        // Make root1 the parent.
        root1.NextSibling = root2.FirstChild
        root2.FirstChild = root1
        Return root2
    End If
End MergeTrees
```

The algorithm compares the values of the trees' root nodes. If the value of root1 is smaller, the algorithm makes root2 a child of root1. To do that, it first sets the next sibling of root2 equal to the current first child of root1. It then sets the first child of root1 equal to root2, so root2 is the first child of root1 and its NextSibling pointer leads to the other children of root1. The algorithm then returns the new tree's root.

If the value of `root2` is smaller than the value of `root1`, the algorithm performs the same steps with the roles of the two roots reversed.

Figure 5.13 shows this operation. The root nodes in the two trees on the left have values 24 and 16. Because 16 is smaller, that node becomes the root of the new tree and the node with value 24 becomes that node's child.

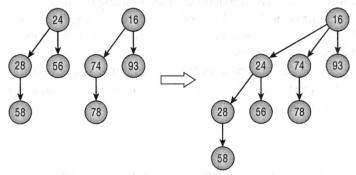

Figure 5.13: Merge two trees with the same order by making one tree's root become a child of the other tree's root.

Notice that the new tree satisfies the minimum heap property.

Merging Heaps

Merging two binomial heaps is the most important, interesting, and confusing operation required to maintain a binomial heap. The process works in two phases. First, you merge the tree lists. Then, you merge trees that have the same order.

Merging Tree Lists

In the first phase of merging two heaps, you merge the trees in each of the heaps into a single list where the trees are sorted in increasing order. Because each heap stores its trees in sorted order, you can loop through the two tree lists simultaneously and move the trees into the merged list in order.

The following pseudocode shows the basic idea. Here I assume that heaps are represented by `BinomialHeap` objects that have a `RootSentinel` property that points to the first tree in the heap's forest.

```
// Merge two heaps' tree lists.
List Of BinomialTree: MergeHeapLists(BinomialHeap: heap1,
    BinomialHeap: heap2)
    // Make a list to hold the merged roots.
    BinomialNode: mergedListSentinel = New BinomialNode(int.MinValue)
    BinomialNode: mergedListBottom = mergedListSentinel
```

```
        // Remove the heaps' root list sentinels.
        heap1.RootSentinel = heap1.RootSentinel.NextSibling
        heap2.RootSentinel = heap2.RootSentinel.NextSibling

        // Merge the two heaps' roots into one list in ascending order.
        While ((heap1.RootSentinel != null) And
               (heap2.RootSentinel != null))
            // See which root has the smaller order.
            BinomialHeap moveHeap = null
            If (heap1.RootSentinel.Order <= heap2.RootSentinel.Order) Then
                moveHeap = heap1
            Else
                moveHeap = heap2
            End If

            // Move the selected root.
            BinomialNode: moveRoot = moveHeap.RootSentinel
            moveHeap.RootSentinel = moveRoot.NextSibling
            mergedListBottom.NextSibling = moveRoot
            mergedListBottom = moveRoot
            mergedListBottom.NextSibling = null
        End While

        // Add any remaining roots.
        If (heap1.RootSentinel != null) Then
            mergedListBottom.NextSibling = heap1.RootSentinel
            heap1.RootSentinel = null
        Else If (heap2.RootSentinel != null) Then
            mergedListBottom.NextSibling = heap2.RootSentinel
            heap2.RootSentinel = null
        End If

        // Return the merged list sentinel.
        Return mergedListSentinel
    End MergeHeapLists
```

This algorithm starts by setting each heap's `RootSentinel` value to the first actual tree in the heap. As long as both heaps contain trees, the code compares the first trees in the heaps (which will have the smallest orders in their respective heaps) and moves the one with the smaller order into the merged list.

After one of the heaps has run out of trees, the algorithm adds the other heap's remaining trees to the end of the merged list.

Figure 5.14 shows two heaps that should be merged.

Figure 5.15 shows the merged tree list.

If you look at the merged tree list in Figure 5.15, you'll see that it violates second heap rule, which requires that a heap cannot contain more than one tree with the same order. This list contains two trees of order 1 and two trees of order 2. That brings us to the second phase of the merge process, merging trees that have the same order.

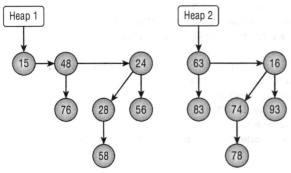

Figure 5.14: The goal is to merge these two heaps.

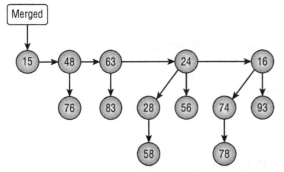

Figure 5.15: This list contains the heaps' merged tree lists.

Merging Trees

In the second phase of merging two heaps, you merge any trees that have the same order. The trees in the merged list shown in Figure 5.15 are sorted by their orders. This means that if there are any trees with the same degree, then they are adjacent to each other in the list.

To merge the trees, you scan through the list looking for adjacent trees that have the same order. When you find a matching pair, you simply make one tree's root the child of the other tree's root as described earlier.

Unfortunately, there is a catch. When you merge two trees of order k, you create a new tree of order k + 1. If the list happens to include two other trees of order k + 1, then you now have three trees with the same order in a row. In that case, simply leave the first (new) tree alone and merge the following two trees into a new tree of degree k + 2.

The following pseudocode shows how to merge adjacent trees with the same order:

```
// Sift through the list and merge roots with the same order.
MergeRootsWithSameOrder(BinomialNode: listSentinel)
    BinomialNode: prev = listSentinel
    BinomialNode: node = prev.NextSibling
```

```
BinomialNode: next = null
If (node != null) Then next = node.NextSibling

While (next != null)
    // See if we need to merge node and next.
    If (node.Order != next.Order) Then
        // Move to consider the next pair.
        prev = node
        node = next
        next = next.NextSibling
    Else
        // Remove them from the list.
        prev.NextSibling = next.NextSibling

        // Merge node and next.
        node = MergeTrees(node, next)

        // Insert the new root where the old ones were.
        next = prev.NextSibling
        node.NextSibling = next
        prev.NextSibling = node

        // If we have three matches in a row,
        // skip the first one so we can merge
        // the other two in the next round.
        // Otherwise consider node and next
        // again in the next round.
        If ((next != null) And
            (node.Order == next.Order) And
            (next.NextSibling != null) And
            (node.Order == next.NextSibling.Order))
        Then
            prev = node
            node = next
            next = next.NextSibling
        End If
    End If
End While
End MergeRootsWithSameOrder
```

The algorithm uses three variables to keep track of its position in the merged tree list. The variable `node` points to the tree that the algorithm is considering. Variables `prev` and `next` point to the trees before and after `node` in the linked list.

The algorithm then enters a loop that executes as long as `next` is not `null`. If the `node` and `next` trees have different orders, the algorithm simply advances `prev`, `node`, and `next` to examine the next pair of trees.

If the `node` and `next` trees have the same order, then the algorithm calls the `MergeTrees` method described earlier to merge them. That may create a new tree with the same order as the next two trees. If that is the case, the algorithm advances prev, node, and next to move past the new tree so that it can merge the other two during the next pass through the While loop.

If the merge did not create three trees in a row with the same order, the algorithm leaves prev, node, and next so that node is pointing to the new tree. During the next trip through the loop, the algorithm will compare the new tree to the next one and merge them if they have the same order.

The next few figures show how the MergeRootsWithSameOrder algorithm works. Figure 5.16 shows the previous merged tree list, which contains some trees that have the same order.

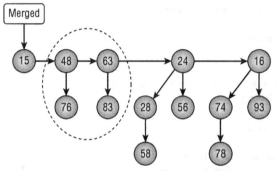

Figure 5.16: Some of these trees have the same order, so they must be merged.

When the algorithm loops through the list, it finds that the trees inside the dashed ellipse shown in Figure 5.16 both have order 1, so it merges them into a tree with order 2. Figure 5.17 shows the new list.

When it merges the two trees with order 1, the algorithm notices that the list now contains three trees with order 2. It skips the first one and merges the second and third, which are surrounded by dashed lines in Figure 5.17.

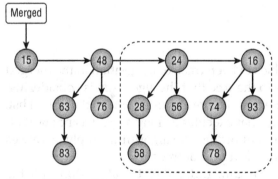

Figure 5.17: The list now contains three trees in a row that have order 2.

Figure 5.18 shows the list after the latest merge.

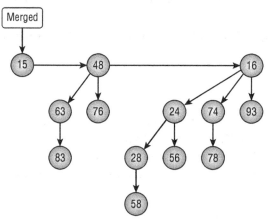

Figure 5.18: At this point, the list ready to be used by a binomial heap.

Recall that the point of this exercise was to merge two binomial heaps. The MergeHeapLists algorithm merged their tree lists. Then the MergeRoots-WithSameOrder algorithm merged any trees in the list that had the same order. At this point, the tree list satisfies the binomial heap properties, so you can use it to build the new merged heap. You'll see in the following sections how you can use this process to implement the final heap features: adding an item to the heap and removing the item with the smallest value from the heap.

Enqueue

After you know how to merge heaps, adding an item to a heap is relatively easy. Simply create a new heap that contains the new item and then merge the new heap with the existing one. The following pseudocode shows how to perform this operation:

```
Enqueue(Integer: value)
    // If this heap is empty, just add the value.
    If (RootSentinel.NextSibling == null) Then
        RootSentinel.NextSibling = New BinomialNode(value)
    Else
        // Make a new heap containing the new value.
        BinomialHeap newHeap = New BinomialHeap()
        newHeap.Enqueue(value)

        // Merge with the new heap.
        MergeWithHeap(newHeap)
    End If
End Enqueue
```

This algorithm checks the heap's tree list to see whether it is empty. If the list is empty, it creates a new single-node (order 0) tree containing the new value and adds it to the top of the list.

If the tree list isn't empty, the algorithm makes a new single-item heap and then merges it with the existing heap.

Dequeue

After you know how to merge tree lists, removing the item with the smallest value is also easy. First, find the item with the smallest value and remove that item's tree from the tree list. Next, add the removed tree's child subtrees to a new heap and merge the new heap with the original one. The following pseudocode shows the steps in more detail:

```
// Remove the smallest value from the heap.
Integer: Dequeue()
    // Find the root with the smallest value.
    BinomialNode: prev = FindRootBeforeSmallestValue()

    // Remove the tree containing the value from our list.
    BinomialNode: root = prev.NextSibling
    prev.NextSibling = root.NextSibling

    // Make a new heap containing the
    // removed tree's subtrees.
    BinomialHeap: newHeap = New BinomialHeap()
    BinomialNode: subtree = root.FirstChild
    While (subtree != null)
        // Add this subtree to the top of the new heap's root list.
        BinomialNode: next = subtree.NextSibling
        subtree.NextSibling = newHeap.RootSentinel.NextSibling
        newHeap.RootSentinel.NextSibling = subtree
        subtree = next
    End While

    // Merge with the new heap.
    MergeWithHeap(newHeap)

    // Return the removed root's value.
    Return root.Value
End Dequeue
```

This algorithm finds the tree root that has the smallest value. Because each of the trees satisfies the minimum heap property, that is the item with the smallest value in the entire heap.

Next, the algorithm removes that tree from the tree list. It then creates a new heap and loops through the removed tree's subtrees adding them to the new heap. The subtrees of a binomial tree are stored sorted by increasing tree order, so it's easy to add them to the new heap in increasing order by simply adding them to the top of the new heap's tree list.

After it finishes adding the subtrees to the new heap, the algorithm calls the `MergeWithHeap` method to merge the new heap with the original one. The code finishes by returning the smallest item that it found.

Runtime

The longest operations on a binomial heap loop through the heap's tree list, so their runtimes depend on the length of that list. I mentioned earlier that the tree list can hold at most $1 + \log_2(N)$ trees if the heap contains N items, so the time needed to loop through the list can take at most O(log N) time.

More precisely, to enqueue an item, you create a new heap containing the item and then merge the new heap with the existing one. To merge the heaps, you combine their tree lists in O(log N) time. You then loop through the merged tree list to combine any trees that have the same order, again taking O(log N) time. That makes the total time to insert an item O(log N) + O(log N) = O(log N).

To dequeue an item, you first spend O(log N) time looping through the heap's tree list to find the root with the smallest value. You then remove that tree and add its subtrees to a new heap. The removed tree can have at most O(log N) subtrees, so that takes at most O(log N) time. Finally, you spend O(log N) time merging the two heaps, so the total run time is O(log N) + O(log N) + O(log N) = O(log N).

The worst case time for inserting an item is O(log n), but in the long run the average time is smaller because a long operation tends to reduce the time needed for later operations.

For example, suppose a heap contains 15 items. Remember that the number of items uniquely determines the number and orders of the trees in the heap. If the heap contains 15 items, then it contains four trees with orders 0, 1, 2, and 3.

When you add another item, the new item will force all of those trees to merge together into a single tree of order 4 containing all 16 items. That operation will take the full O(log N) steps because the heap initially contained O(log N) trees. However, after that, the heap contains only one tree, so future insertions will be much quicker.

This kind of study of performance over a long sequence of operations is called *amortized analysis*. It turns out that the amortized runtime for inserting items in a binomial heap is O(1).

Summary

This chapter explained stacks and queues, two data structures that are often used by other algorithms to store items. In a stack, items are added to and then removed from the same "end" of the data structure in last-in-first-out order.

In a queue, items are added at one end and removed from the other in first-in-first-out order.

You can use an array to build a stack fairly easily, as long as it doesn't run out of space. If you build a stack with a linked list, you don't need to worry about running out of space.

You can also use an array to build a queue, although in that approach the items move through the array until they reach the end and you need to resize the array. You can solve that problem by using a circular array. You can also avoid the whole issue by using a doubly linked list to build a queue.

You can use stacks and queues to sort items in $O(N^2)$ time, although those algorithms are more exercises in using stacks and queues than in efficient sorting. The next chapter describes several sorting algorithms that give much better performance, with some running in $O(N \log N)$ time and others even running in $O(N)$ time.

This chapter also explained binomial heaps, which are the most complicated data structures described by this book so far. They let you add and remove items from a heap in $O(\log N)$ time. That makes them a useful method for building a priority queue.

Exercises

You can find the answers to these exercises in Appendix B. Asterisks indicate particularly difficult problems.

1. When you use a double stack, what is the relationship between the variables NextIndex1 and NextIndex2 when one of the stacks is full?

2. Write an algorithm that takes as input a stack and returns a new stack containing the same items but in reverse order.

3. Write a program that implements insertionsort with stacks.

4. For each item, the stack insertionsort algorithm moves the unsorted items to the temporary stack. Next, it moves some of the sorted items to the temporary stack, and then it moves all of the items back to the original stack. Does it really need to move all of the items back to the original stack? Can you improve the algorithm's performance by modifying that step? What does that do to the algorithm's Big O run time?

5. What does the stack insertionsort algorithm mean in terms of train sorting?

6. Write a program that implements selectionsort with stacks.

7. What does the stack selectionsort algorithm mean in terms of train sorting?

8. Write a program that implements a priority queue.

9. Write a program that implements a deque.

10. *Consider a bank where customers enter a single line that is served by several tellers. You enter the line at the end, and when you get to the front of the line, you are served by the next available teller. You can model this "multiheaded queue" with a normal queue that serves multiple tellers.

    Make a program similar to the one shown in Figure 5.19 to simulate a multiheaded queue in a bank. Give the user controls to adjust the number of tellers, the amount of time between customer arrivals, the amount of time each customer stays, and the speed of the simulation. After the user specifies the parameters, run a simulation to see how the queue behaves. How does the number of tellers affect the average wait time?

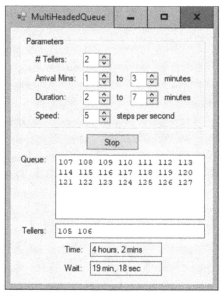

Figure 5.19: In a bank queue, customers stand in a single line and then are helped by the next available teller.

11. Write a program that implements insertionsort with queues.

12. Write a program that implements selectionsort with queues.

13. *Write a program that implements a binomial heap.

Sorting

Sorting algorithms are usually covered in great detail in algorithms books for several reasons.

- They are interesting and demonstrate several useful techniques, such as recursion, divide and conquer, heaps, and trees.

- Sorting algorithms are well-studied and are some of the few algorithms for which exact run times are known. It can be shown that the fastest possible algorithm that uses comparisons to sort N items must use O(N log N) time. Several sorting algorithms actually achieve that performance, so in some sense they are optimal.

- Sorting algorithms are useful. Almost any data is more useful when it is sorted in various ways, so sorting algorithms play an important role in many applications.

This chapter describes several different sorting algorithms. Some, such as insertionsort, selectionsort, and bubblesort, are relatively simple but slow. Others, such as heapsort, quicksort, and mergesort, are more complicated but much faster. Still others, such as countingsort and pigeonhole sort, don't use comparisons to sort items, so they can break the O(N log N) barrier and perform amazingly fast under the right circumstances.

The following sections categorize the algorithms by their run-time performance.

> **NOTE**   Many programming libraries, such as C# and Python, include sorting tools, and they usually are quite fast. In practice, you may want to use those tools to save time writing and debugging the sorting code. It's still important to understand how sorting algorithms work, however, because sometimes you can do even better than the built-in tools. For example, a simple bubblesort algorithm may beat a more complicated library routine for very small lists, and countingsort often beats the tools if the data being sorted has the right characteristics.

O(N²) Algorithms

O(N^2) algorithms are relatively slow but fairly simple. In fact, their simplicity sometimes lets them outperform faster but more complicated algorithms for very small arrays.

Insertionsort in Arrays

Chapter 3 described an insertionsort algorithm that sorts items in linked lists. Chapter 5 described insertionsort algorithms that use stacks and queues. The basic idea is to take an item from the input list and insert it into the proper position in a sorted output list (which initially starts empty).

Chapter 3 explained how to do this in linked lists, but you can use the same steps to sort an array. The following pseudocode shows the algorithm for use with arrays:

```
Insertionsort(Data: values[])
    For i = 0 To <length of values> - 1
        // Move item i into position in the sorted part of the array.
        < Find  the first index j where
          j < i and values[j] > values[i].>
        <Move the item into position j.>
    Next i
End Insertionsort
```

As the code loops through the items in the array, the index i separates the items that have been sorted from those that have not. The items with an index less than i have already been sorted, and those with an index greater than or equal to i have not yet been sorted.

As i goes from 0 to the last index in the array, the code moves the item at index i into the proper position in the sorted part of the array.

To find the item's position, the code looks through the already sorted items and finds the first item that is greater than the new value values[i].

The code then moves values[i] into its new position. Unfortunately, this can be a time-consuming step. Suppose that the item's new index should be j. In that case, the code must move the items between indices j and i, one position to the right to make room for the item at position j.

Figure 6.1 shows the algorithm's key steps. The image at the top shows the original unsorted array. In the middle image, the first four items (outlined in bold) have been sorted, and the algorithm is preparing to insert the next item (which has value 3) into the sorted part of the array. The algorithm searches through the sorted items until it determines that the value 3 should be inserted before the value 5. At the bottom of the figure, the algorithm has moved the values 5, 6, and 7 to the right to make room for value 3. The algorithm inserts value 3 and continues the For loop to insert the next item (which has value 2) into its correct position.

This algorithm sorts the items in the original array, so it doesn't need any additional storage (aside from a few variables to control loops and move items).

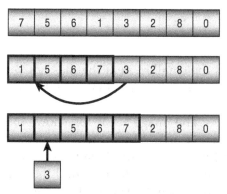

Figure 6.1: Insertionsort inserts items into the sorted part of the array.

If the array contains N items, the algorithm considers each of the N positions in the array. For each position i, it must search the previously sorted items in the array to find the ith item's new position. It must then move the items between that location and index i one position to the right. If the item i should be moved to position j, it takes j steps to find the new location j and then i − j more steps to move items over, resulting in a total of i steps. That means in total it takes i steps to move item i into its new position.

Adding up all the steps required to position the items, the total run time is as follows:

$$1 + 2 + 3 + \ldots + N = (N^2 + N) / 2$$

This means that the algorithm has run time $O(N^2)$. This isn't a very fast run time, but it's fast enough for reasonably small arrays (fewer than 10,000 or so items). It's also a relatively simple algorithm, so it may sometimes be faster than more complicated algorithms for very small arrays. How small an array must be for this algorithm to outperform more complicated algorithms depends on your system. Typically, this algorithm is only faster for arrays holding fewer than 5 or 10 items.

Selectionsort in Arrays

In addition to describing insertionsort for linked lists, Chapter 3 also described selectionsort for linked lists. Similarly, Chapter 5 described selectionsort algorithms that use stacks and queues.

The basic idea is to search the input list for the largest item it contains and then add it to the end of a growing sorted list. The following pseudocode shows the algorithm for use with arrays:

```
Selectionsort(Data: values[])
    For i = 0 To <length of values> - 1
        // Find the item that belongs in position i.
        <Find the smallest item with index j >= i.>
        <Swap values[i] and values[j].>
    Next i
End Selectionsort
```

The code loops through the array to find the smallest item that has not yet been added to the sorted part of the array. It then swaps that smallest item with the item in position i.

Figure 6.2 shows the algorithm's key steps. The image at the top shows the original unsorted array. In the middle image, the first three items (outlined in bold) have been sorted, and the algorithm is preparing to swap the next item into position. The algorithm searches the unsorted items to find the one with the smallest value (3 in this case). The algorithm then swaps the item that has the smallest value into the next unsorted position. The image at the bottom of the figure shows the array after the new item has been moved to the sorted part of the array. The algorithm now continues the For loop to add the next item (which has value 5) to the growing sorted portion of the array.

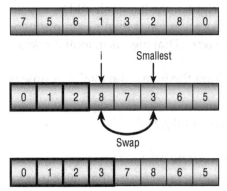

Figure 6.2: Selectionsort moves the smallest unsorted item to the end of the sorted part of the array.

Like insertionsort, this algorithm sorts the items in the original array, so it doesn't need any additional storage (aside from a few variables to control loops and move items).

If the array contains N items, the algorithm considers each of the N positions in the array. For each position i, it must search the N − i items that have not yet been sorted to find the item that belongs in position i. It then swaps the item into its final position in a small constant number of steps. Adding up the steps to move all of the items gives the following run time:

$$(N-1)+(N-2)+\ldots+2+1=(N^2+N)/2$$

This means that the algorithm has run time $O(N^2)$—the same run time as insertionsort.

Like insertionsort, selectionsort is fast enough for reasonably small arrays (fewer than 10,000 or so items). It's also a fairly simple algorithm, so it may sometimes be faster than more complicated algorithms for very small arrays (typically 5 to 10 items).

Bubblesort

Bubblesort uses the fairly obvious fact that if an array is not sorted, then it must contain two adjacent elements that are out of order. The algorithm repeatedly passes through the array, swapping items that are out of order, until it can't find any more swaps.

The following pseudocode shows the bubblesort algorithm:

```
Bubblesort(Data: values[])
    // Repeat until the array is sorted.
    Boolean: not_sorted = True
    While (not_sorted)
        // Assume we won't find a pair to swap.
        not_sorted = False

        // Search the array for adjacent items that are out of order.
        For i = 0 To <length of values> - 1
            // See if items i and i - 1 are out of order.
            If (values[i] < values[i - 1]) Then
                // Swap them.
                Data: temp = values[i]
                values[i] = values[i - 1]
                values[i - 1] = temp

                // The array isn't sorted after all.
                not_sorted = True
            End If
        Next i
    End While
End Bubblesort
```

The code uses a Boolean variable named `not_sorted` to keep track of whether it has found a swap in its most recent pass through the array. As long as `not_sorted` is true, the algorithm loops through the array, looking for adjacent pairs of items that are out of order and swaps them.

Figure 6.3 shows an example. The array on the far left is mostly sorted. During the first pass through the array, the algorithm finds that the 6/3 pair is out of order (6 should come after 3), so it swaps 6 and 3 to get the second arrangement of values. During the second pass through the array, the algorithm finds that the 5/3 pair is out of order, so it swaps 5 and 3 to get the third arrangement of values. During the third pass through the array, the algorithm finds that the 4/3 pair is out of order, so it swaps 4 and 3, giving the arrangement on the far right in the figure. The algorithm performs one final pass, finds no pairs that are out of order, and ends.

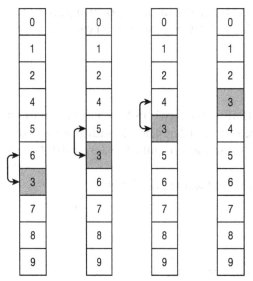

Figure 6.3: In bubblesort, items that are farther down than they should be slowly "bubble up" to their correct positions.

The fact that item 3 seems to bubble up slowly to its correct position gives the bubblesort algorithm its name.

During each pass through the array, at least one item reaches its final position. In Figure 6.3, item 6 reaches its final destination during the first pass, item 5 reaches its final destination during the second pass, and items 3 and 4 reach their final destinations during the third pass.

If the array holds N items and at least one item reaches its final position during each pass through the array, then the algorithm can perform, at most, N passes. (If the array is initially sorted in reverse order, the algorithm needs all N passes.) Each pass takes N steps, so the total run time is $O(N^2)$.

Like insertionsort and selectionsort, bubblesort is fairly slow but may provide acceptable performance for small lists (fewer than 1,000 or so items). It is also sometimes faster than more complicated algorithms for very small lists (five or so items).

You can make several improvements to bubblesort. First, in Figure 6.3, the item with value 3 started out below its final correct position. However, consider what happens if an item starts above its final position. In that case, the algorithm finds that the item is out of position and swaps it with the following item. It then considers the next position in the array and considers the item again. If the item is still out of position, the algorithm swaps it again. The algorithm continues swapping that item down through the list until it reaches its final position in a single pass through the array. You can use this fact to speed up the algorithm by alternating downward and upward passes through the array. Downward passes quickly move items that are too high in the array, and upward passes quickly move items that are too low in the array.

This upward and downward version of bubblesort is sometimes called *cocktail shaker sort*.

To make a second improvement, notice that some items may move through several swaps at once. For example, during a downward pass, a large item (call it K) may be swapped several times before it reaches a larger item, and it stops for that pass. You can save a little time if you don't put item K back in the array for every swap. Instead, you can store K in a temporary variable and move other items up in the array until you find the spot where K stops. You then put K in that position and continue the pass through the array.

To make a final improvement, consider the largest item (call it L) that is not in its final position. During a downward pass, the algorithm reaches that item (possibly making other swaps beforehand) and swaps it down through the list until it reaches its final position. During the next pass through the array, no item can swap past L because L is in its final position. That means the algorithm can end its pass through the array when it reaches item L.

More generally, the algorithm can end its pass through the array when it reaches the position of the last swap that it made during the previous pass. If you keep track of the last swaps made during downward and upward passes through the array, you can shorten each pass.

Figure 6.4 shows these three improvements. During the first pass down through the array, the algorithm swaps item 7 with items 4, 5, 6, and 3. It holds the value 7 in a temporary variable, so it doesn't need to save it back into the array until it reaches its final position.

After placing 7 after 3, the algorithm continues moving through the array and doesn't find any other items to swap, so it knows that item 7 and those that follow are in their final positions and don't need to be examined again. If some item nearer to the top of the array were larger than 7, the first pass

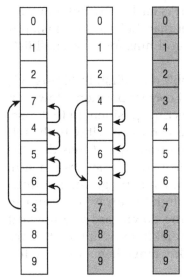

Figure 6.4: Improvements make bubblesort faster, but it still has $O(N^2)$ performance.

would have swapped it down past 7. In the middle image shown in Figure 6.4, the final items are shaded to indicate that they don't need to be checked during later passes.

The algorithm knows that item 7 and the items after it are in their final positions, so it starts its second pass, moving upward through the array at the first item before item 7, which is item 3. It swaps that item with items 6, 5, and 4, this time holding item 3 in a temporary variable until it reaches its final position.

Now item 3 and those that come before it in the array are in their final positions, so they are shaded in the last image in Figure 6.4.

The algorithm makes one final downward pass through the array, starting the pass at value 4 and ending at value 6. No swaps occur during this pass, so the algorithm ends.

These improvements make bubblesort faster in practice. (In one test sorting 10,000 items, bubblesort took 2.50 seconds without improvements and 0.69 seconds with improvements.) But it still has $O(N^2)$ performance, so there's a limit to the size of the list you can sort with bubblesort.

O(N log N) Algorithms

$O(N \log N)$ algorithms are much faster than $O(N^2)$ algorithms, at least for larger arrays. For example, if N is 1,000, N log N is less than 1×10^4, but N^2 is roughly 100 times as big at 1×10^6. That difference in speed makes $O(N \log N)$ algorithms more useful in everyday programming, at least for large arrays.

Heapsort

Heapsort uses a data structure called a *heap*, which also demonstrates a useful technique for storing a complete binary tree in an array.

Storing Complete Binary Trees

A *binary tree* is a tree where every node is connected to, at most, two children. In a *complete tree* (binary or otherwise), all of the tree's levels are completely filled, except possibly the last level, where all of the nodes are pushed to the left.

Figure 6.5 shows a complete binary tree holding 12 nodes. The tree's first three levels are full. The fourth level contains five nodes pushed to the left side of the tree.

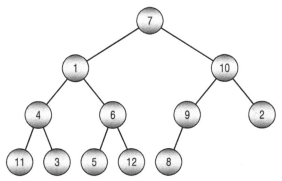

Figure 6.5: In a complete binary tree, every level is full, except possibly the last.

One useful feature of complete binary trees is that you can easily store them in an array using a simple formula. Start by placing the root node at index 0. Then, for any node with index i, place its children at indices $2 \times i + 1$ and $2 \times i + 2$.

If a node has index j, then its parent has index $\lfloor (j - 1) / 2 \rfloor$, where $\lfloor \ \rfloor$ means to truncate the result to the next-smallest integer. In other words, round down. For example, $\lfloor 2.9 \rfloor$ is 2, and $\lfloor 2 \rfloor$ is also 2.

Figure 6.6 shows the tree shown in Figure 6.5 stored in an array, with the entries' indices shown on top.

0	1	2	3	4	5	6	7	8	9	10	11
7	1	10	4	6	9	2	11	3	5	12	8

Figure 6.6: You can easily store a complete binary tree in an array.

For example, the value 6 is at index 4, so its children should be at indices $4 \times 2 + 1 = 9$ and $4 \times 2 + 2 = 10$. Those items have values 5 and 12. If you look at the tree shown in Figure 6.5, you'll see that those are the correct children.

If the index of either child is greater than the largest index in the array, then the node doesn't have that child in the tree. For example, the value 9 has index 5. Its right child has index $2 \times 5 + 2 = 12$, which is beyond the end of the array. If you look at Figure 6.5, you'll see that the item with value 9 has no right child.

For an example of calculating a node's parent, consider the item with value 12 stored at index 10. The index of the parent is $\lfloor (10 - 1)/2 \rfloor = \lfloor 4.5 \rfloor = 4$. The value at index 4 is 6. If you look at the tree shown in Figure 6.5, you'll see that the node with value 12 does have as its parent the node with value 6.

Defining Heaps

A *heap,* shown in Figure 6.7, is a complete binary tree where every node holds a value that is at least as large as the values in all of its children. Figure 6.5 is not a heap, however, because the root node has a value of 7 and its right child has a value of 10, which is greater.

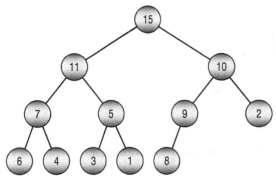

Figure 6.7: In a heap, the value of every node is at least as large as the values of its children.

You can build a heap one node at a time. Start with a tree consisting of a single node. Because the single node has no children, it satisfies the heap property.

Now suppose you have built a heap, and you want to add a new node to it. Add the new node at the end of the tree. There is only one place where you can add this node to keep the tree a complete binary tree—to the right of the nodes already in the bottom level of the tree.

Now compare the new value to the value of its parent. If the new value is larger than the parent's, swap them. Because the tree was previously a heap, you know that the parent's value was already larger than its other child (if it has one). By swapping it with an even larger value, you know that the heap property is preserved at this point.

However, you have changed the value of the parent node, so that might break the heap property farther up in the tree. Move up the tree to the parent node and compare its value to the value of its parent, swapping their values if necessary.

Continue up the tree, swapping values if necessary, until you reach a node where the heap property is satisfied. At that point, the tree is again a heap.

Figure 6.8 shows this process when you add the value 12 to the tree shown in Figure 6.7. Figure 6.9 shows the new heap.

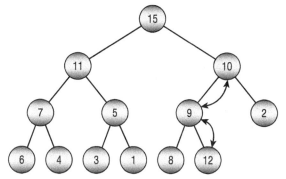

Figure 6.8: To add a new value to a heap, place the value at the end of the tree and move it up as needed to restore the heap property.

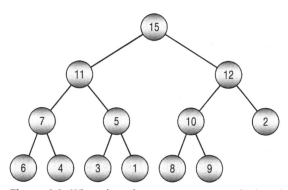

Figure 6.9: When the value moves up to a node that already satisfies the heap property, the tree is once again a heap.

Storing the heap in an array makes this process particularly easy because when you need to add a new item to the end of the tree, it's already in the proper position in the array. When you store a complete binary tree in an array, the next item belongs on the right, on the tree's bottom level. In the array, that's the position that comes after the last entry that is already in the tree. This means you don't need to do anything to place the next item in the tree. All you need to do is to swap it up through the tree to restore the heap property.

The following pseudocode shows the algorithm to turn an array into a heap:

```
MakeHeap(Data: values[])
    // Add each item to the heap one at a time.
    For i = 0 To <length of values> - 1
        // Start at the new item, and work up to the root.
        Integer: index = i
        While (index != 0)
            // Find the parent's index.
            Integer: parent = (index - 1) / 2

            // If child <= parent, we're done, so
            // break out of the While loop.
            If (values[index] <= values[parent]) Then Break

            // Swap the parent and child.
            Data: temp = values[index]
            values[index] = values[parent]
            values[parent] = temp

            // Move to the parent.
            index = parent
        End While
    Next i
End MakeHeap
```

You may recall from Chapter 5, "Stacks and Queues," that a *priority queue* is a queue that returns objects in the order of their priorities. Heaps are useful for creating priority queues because the largest item in the tree is always at the root node. If you use the items' priorities to build the heap, then the item with the highest priority is at the top. To remove an item from the priority queue, you simply use the item at the root.

Unfortunately, that breaks the heap, so it has no root and is therefore no longer a tree. Fortunately, there's an easy way to fix it: move the last item in the tree to the root.

Doing that breaks the tree's heap property, but you can fix that by using a method similar to the one you used to build the heap. If the new root value is smaller than one of its child values, swap it with the larger child. That fixes the heap property at this node, but it may have broken it at the child's level, so move down to that node and repeat the process. Continue swapping the node down into the tree until you find a spot where the heap property is already satisfied or you reach the bottom of the tree.

The following pseudocode shows the algorithm to remove an item from the heap and restore the heap property:

```
Data: RemoveTopItem(Data: values[], Integer: count)
    // Save the top item to return later.
    Data: result = values[0]
```

```
    // Move the last item to the root.
    values[0] = values[count - 1]

    // Restore the heap property.
    Integer: index = 0
    While (True)
        // Find the child indices.
        Integer: child1 = 2 * index + 1
        Integer: child2 = 2 * index + 2

        // If a child index is off the end of the tree,
        // use the parent's index.
        If (child1 >= count) Then child1 = index
        If (child2 >= count) Then child2 = index

        // If the heap property is satisfied,
        // we're done, so break out of the While loop.
        If ((values[index] >= values[child1]) And
            (values[index] >= values[child2])) Then Break

        // Get the index of the child with the larger value.
        Integer: swap_child
        If (values[child1] > values[child2]) Then
            swap_child = child1
        Else
            swap_child = child2

        // Swap with the larger child.
        Data: temp = values[index]
        values[index] = values[swap_child]
        values[swap_child] = temp

        // Move to the child node.
        index = swap_child
    End While

    // Return the value we removed from the root.
    return result
End RemoveTopItem
```

This algorithm takes as a parameter the size of the tree, so it can find the location where the heap ends within the array.

The algorithm starts by saving the value at the root node so that it later can return the highest-priority value. It then moves the last item in the tree to the root node.

The algorithm sets the variable `index` to the index of the root node and then enters an infinite `While` loop.

Inside the loop, the algorithm calculates the indices of the children of the current node. If either of those indices is off the end of the tree, then it is set to the current node's index. In that case, when the node's values are compared later, the current node's value is compared to itself. Because any value is greater than or equal to itself, that comparison satisfies the heap property, so the missing node does not make the algorithm swap values.

After the algorithm calculates the child indices, it checks whether the heap property is satisfied at this point. If it is, then the algorithm breaks out of the While loop. (If both child nodes are missing or if one is missing and the other satisfies the heap property, then the While loop also ends.)

If the heap property is not satisfied, the algorithm sets swap_child to the index of the child that holds the larger value and swaps the parent node's value with that child node's value. It then updates the index variable to move down to the swapped child node and continues down the tree.

Implementing Heapsort

Now that you know how to build and maintain a heap, implementing the heap-sort algorithm is easy. The algorithm builds a heap. It then repeatedly swaps the first and last items in the heap and rebuilds the heap excluding the last item. During each pass, one item is removed from the heap and added to the end of the array where the items are placed in sorted order.

The following pseudocode shows how the algorithm works:

```
Heapsort(Data: values)
    <Turn the array into a heap.>

    For i = <length of values> - 1 To 0 Step -1
        // Swap the root item and the last item.
        Data: temp = values[0]
        values[0] = values[i]
        values[i] = temp

        <Consider the item in position i to be removed from the heap,
         so the heap now holds i - 1 items. Push the new root value
         down into the heap to restore the heap property.>
    Next i
End Heapsort
```

This algorithm starts by turning the array of values into a heap. It then repeatedly removes the top item, which is the largest, and moves it to the end of the heap. It reduces the number of items in the heap by one and restores the heap property, leaving the newly positioned item beyond the end of the heap in its proper sorted order.

When it is finished, the algorithm has removed the items from the heap in largest-to-smallest order and placed them at the end of the ever-shrinking heap. That leaves the array holding the values in smallest-to-largest order.

The space required by heapsort is easy to calculate. The algorithm stores all the data inside the original array and uses only a fixed number of extra variables for counting and swapping values. If the array holds N values, the algorithm uses O(N) space.

The run time required by the algorithm is slightly harder to calculate. To build the initial heap, the algorithm adds each item to a growing heap. Each time it adds an item, it places the item at the end of the tree and swaps the item upward until the tree is again a heap. Because the tree is a complete binary tree, it is up to O(log N) levels tall, so pushing the item up through the tree can take, at most, O(log N) steps. The algorithm performs this step of adding an item and restoring the heap property N times, so the total time to build the initial heap is O(N log N).

To finish sorting, the algorithm removes each item from the heap and then restores the heap property. It does that by swapping the last item in the heap with the root node and then swapping the new root down through the tree until the heap property is restored. The tree is up to O(log N) levels tall, so this can take up to O(log N) time. The algorithm repeats this step N times, so the total number of steps required is O(N log N).

Adding the time needed to build the initial heap and the time to finish sorting gives a total time of O(N log N) + O(N log N) = O(N log N).

Heapsort is an elegant "sort-in-place" algorithm that takes no extra storage. It also demonstrates some useful techniques such as heaps and storing a complete binary tree in an array.

Even though heapsort's O(N log N) run time is asymptotically the fastest possible for an algorithm that sorts by using comparisons, the quicksort algorithm described in the next section usually runs slightly faster.

Quicksort

The *quicksort algorithm* uses a divide-and-conquer strategy. It subdivides an array into two pieces and then calls itself recursively to sort the pieces. The following pseudocode shows the algorithm at a high level:

```
Quicksort(Data: values[], Integer: start, Integer: end)
    <Pick a dividing item from the array. Call it divider.>

    <Move items < divider to the front of the array.
     Move items >= divider to the end of the array.
     Let middle be the index between the pieces where divider is put.>

    // Recursively sort the two halves of the array.
    Quicksort(values, start, middle - 1)
    Quicksort(values, middle + 1, end)
End Quicksort
```

For example, the top of Figure 6.10 shows an array of values to sort. In this case, I picked the first value, 6, for divider.

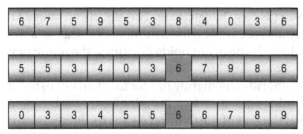

Figure 6.10: When the value moves up to a node that already satisfies the heap property, the tree is once again a heap.

In the middle image, values less than `divider` have been moved to the beginning of the array, and values greater than or equal to `divider` have been moved to the end of the array. The divider item is shaded at index 6. Notice that one other item has value 6, and it comes after the `divider` in the array.

The algorithm then calls itself recursively to sort the two pieces of the array before and after the `divider` item. The result is shown at the bottom of Figure 6.10.

Before moving into the implementation details, let's study the algorithm's run-time behavior.

Analyzing Quicksort's Run Time

First, consider the special case in which the dividing item divides the part of the array that is of interest into two exactly equal halves at every step. Figure 6.11 shows the situation.

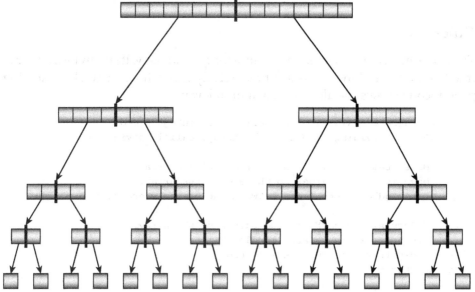

Figure 6.11: If the divider item divides the array into equal halves, the algorithm progresses quickly.

Each of the "nodes" in the tree shown in Figure 6.11 represents a call to the quicksort algorithm. The thick line in the middle of the node shows how the array was divided into two equal halves. The two arrows out of the node represent the quicksort algorithm calling itself twice to process the two halves.

The nodes at the bottom of the tree represent calls to sort a single item. Because a list holding a single item is already sorted, those calls simply return without doing anything.

After the calls work their way to the bottom of the tree, they begin returning to the methods that called them, so control moves back up the tree.

If the array originally holds N items and the items divide exactly evenly, as shown in Figure 6.11, then the tree of quicksort calls is log N levels tall.

Each call to quicksort must examine all the items in the piece of the array it is sorting. For example, a call to quicksort represented by a group of four boxes in Figure 6.11 would need to examine those four boxes to divide its values further.

All of the items in the original array are present at each level of the tree, so each level of the tree contains N items. If you add up the items that each call to quicksort must examine at any level of the tree, you get N items. That means the calls to quicksort on any level require N steps.

The tree is log N levels tall, and each level requires N steps, so the algorithm's total run time is O(N log N).

All of this analysis assumes that the quicksort algorithm divides its part of the array into two equal-sized pieces at every step. In practice, that would be extremely unlikely.

Most of the time, however, the dividing item will belong somewhere more or less in the middle of the items that it is dividing. It won't be in the exact middle, but it won't be near the edges either. For example, in Figure 6.10, the dividing item 6 ended up close to but not exactly in the middle in the second image. If the dividing item is usually somewhere near the middle of the values that it is dividing, then in the expected case, the quicksort algorithm still has O(N log N) performance.

In the worst case, suppose the dividing item is less than any of the other items in the part of the array that it is dividing. That happens if the items are already sorted when the algorithm begins. (The worst case also occurs if all of the items in the array have the same value.) In that case, none of the items goes into the left piece of the array, and all of the other items (except the dividing item) go into the right piece of the array. The first recursive call returns immediately because it doesn't need to sort any items, but the second call must process almost all the items. If the first call to quicksort had to sort N items, this recursive call must sort N − 1 items.

If the dividing item is always less than the other items in the part of the array being sorted, then the algorithm is called to sort N items, then N − 1 items, then N − 2 items, and so on. In that case, the call tree shown in Figure 6.11 is extremely tall and thin, with a height of N.

The calls to quicksort at level i in the tree must examine N − i items. Adding up the items that all of the calls must examine gives $N + (N-1) + (N-2) + \ldots + 1 = N \times (N+1) / 2$, which is $O(N^2)$, so the algorithm's worst-case behavior is $O(N^2)$.

In addition to examining the algorithm's run-time performance, you should consider the space it needs. This depends partly on the method you use to divide parts of the array into halves, but it also depends on the algorithm's depth of recursion. If the sequence of recursive calls is too deep, the program will exhaust its stack space and crash.

For the tree shown in Figure 6.11, the quicksort algorithm calls itself recursively to a depth of log N calls. In the expected case, that means the program's call stack will be O(log N) levels deep. That shouldn't be a problem for most computers. Even if the array holds 1 billion items, log N is only about 30, and the call stack should be able to handle 30 recursive method calls.

For the tall thin tree created in the worst case, however, the depth of recursion is N. Few programs will be able to build a call stack safely with 1 billion recursive calls.

You can help avoid the worst-case scenario to make the algorithm run in a reasonable amount of time and with a reasonable depth of recursion by picking the dividing item carefully. The following section describes some strategies for doing that. The sections after that one describe two methods for dividing a section of an array into two halves. The final quicksort section summarizes issues with using quicksort in practice.

Picking a Dividing Item

One method of picking the dividing item is simply to use the first item in the part of the array being sorted. This is quick, simple, and usually effective. Unfortunately, if the array happens to be initially sorted or sorted in reverse, the result is the worst case. If the items are randomly arranged, this worst-case behavior is extremely unlikely, but it seems reasonable that the array of items might be initially sorted or mostly sorted for some applications.

One solution is to randomize the array before calling quicksort. If the items are randomly arranged, it is extremely unlikely that this method will pick a bad dividing item every time and result in worst-case behavior. Chapter 2, "Numerical Algorithms," explains how to randomize an array in O(N) time so that this won't add to quicksort's expected O(N log N) run time, at least in Big O notation. In practice, however, it could still take a fair amount of time to randomize a large array, so most programmers don't use this approach.

Another approach is to examine the first, last, and middle items in the part of the array being sorted and use the value that is between the other two for the dividing item. This doesn't guarantee that the dividing item isn't close to the largest or smallest in this part of the array, but it does make it less likely.

A final approach is to pick a random index from the part of the array being sorted and then use the value at that index as the dividing item. It would be extremely unlikely that every such random selection would produce a bad dividing value and result in worst-case behavior.

Implementing Quicksort with Stacks

After you have picked a dividing item, you must divide the items into two sections to be placed at the front and back of the array. One easy way to do this is to move items into one of two stacks, depending on whether the item you are considering is greater than or less than the dividing item. The following pseudocode shows the algorithm for this step:

```
Stack of Data: before = New Stack of Data
Stack of Data: after = New Stack of Data

// Gather the items before and after the dividing item.
// This assumes the dividing item has been moved to values[start].
For i = start + 1 To end
    If (values[i] < divider) Then before.Push(values[i])
    Else after.Push(values[i])
Next i

<Move items in the "before" stack back into the array.>
<Add the dividing item to the array.>
<Move items in the "after" stack back into the array.>
```

At this point, the algorithm is ready to recursively call itself to sort the two pieces of the array on either side of the dividing item.

Implementing Quicksort in Place

Using stacks to split the items in the array into two groups as described in the preceding section is easy, but it requires you to allocate extra space for the stacks. You can save some time if you allocate the stacks at the beginning of the algorithm and then let every call to the algorithm share the same stacks instead of creating their own, but this still requires the stacks to hold O(N) memory.

With a little more work, you can split the items into two groups without using any extra storage. The following high-level pseudocode shows the basic approach:

```
<Swap the dividing item to the beginning of the array.>
<Remove the dividing item from the array.
 This leaves a hole at the beginning where you can place another item.>

Repeat:
    <Search the array from back to front to find
     the last item in the array less than "divider.">
    <Move that item into the hole. The hole is now where that item was.>
```

```
<Search the array from front to back to find
    the first item in the array greater than or equal to "divider.">
<Move that item into the hole. The hole is now where that item was.>
```

This code uses the first item as the dividing item. It places that item in a temporary variable and removes it from the array, leaving a hole.

The algorithm then searches the array from the back to the front until it finds a value that is less than the dividing item. It removes that value from its current location and moves it into the hole. Removing the item from its original location creates a new hole.

Next, the algorithm searches from the point of the old hole (now filled with the newly moved item) toward the back of the array until it finds an item that is greater than the dividing item. It moves that item to the current hole, creating a new hole where the item was originally.

The code continues searching back and forth through this section of the array, moving items into the holes left by previously moved items, until the two regions that it is searching meet somewhere in the middle. The algorithm deposits the dividing item in the hole, which is now between the two pieces, and recursively calls itself to sort the two pieces.

This is a fairly confusing step, but the actual code isn't all that long. If you study it closely, you should be able to figure out how it works.

```
<Search the array from back to front to find
    the last item in the array less than "divider.">
<Move that item into the hole. The hole is now where that item was.>

    <Search the array from front to back to find
    the first item in the array greater than or equal to "divider.">
<Move that item into the hole. The hole is now where that item was.>
```

The following pseudocode shows the entire quicksort algorithm at a low level:

```
// Sort the indicated part of the array.
Quicksort(Data: values[], Integer: start, Integer: end)
    // If the list has no more than one element, it's sorted.
    If (start >= end) Then Return

    // Use the first item as the dividing item.
    Integer: divider = values[start]

    // Move items < divider to the front of the array and
    // items >= divider to the end of the array.
    Integer: lo = start
    Integer: hi = end
    While (True)
        // Search the array from back to front starting at "hi"
        // to find the last item where value < "divider."
        // Move that item into the hole. The hole is now where
```

```
            // that item was.
            While (values[hi] >= divider)
                hi = hi - 1
                If (hi <= lo) Then <Break out of the inner While loop.>
            End While
            If (hi <= lo) Then
                // The left and right pieces have met in the middle
                // so we're done. Put the divider here, and
                // break out of the outer While loop.
                values[lo] = divider
                <Break out of the outer While loop.>
            End If

            // Move the value we found to the lower half.
            values[lo] = values[hi]

            // Search the array from front to back starting at "lo"
            // to find the first item where value >= "divider."
            // Move that item into the hole. The hole is now where
            // that item was.
            lo = lo + 1
            While (values[lo] < divider)
                lo = lo + 1
                If (lo >= hi) Then <Break out of the inner While loop.>
            End While
            If (lo >= hi) Then
                // The left and right pieces have met in the middle
                // so we're done. Put the divider here, and
                // break out of the outer While loop.
                lo = hi
                values[hi] = divider
                <Break out of the outer While loop.>
            End If

            // Move the value we found to the upper half.
            values[hi] = values[lo]
        End While

    // Recursively sort the two halves.
    Quicksort(values, start, lo - 1)
    Quicksort(values, lo + 1, end)
End Quicksort
```

This algorithm starts by checking whether the section of the array contains one or fewer items. If it does, then it is sorted, so the algorithm simply returns.

If the section of the array contains at least two items, the algorithm saves the first item as the dividing item. You can use some other dividing item selection method if you like. Just swap the dividing item you pick to the beginning of the section so that the algorithm can find it in the following steps.

Next the algorithm uses variables `lo` and `hi` to hold the highest index in the lower part of the array and the lowest index in the upper part of the array. It uses those variables to keep track of which items it has placed in the two halves. Those variables also alternately track where the hole is left after each step.

The algorithm then enters an infinite `While` loop that continues until the lower and upper pieces of the array grow to meet each other.

Inside the outer `While` loop, the algorithm starts at index `hi` and searches the array backward until it finds an item that should be in the lower piece of the array. It moves that item into the hole left behind by the dividing item.

Next the algorithm starts at index `lo` and searches the array forward until it finds an item that should be in the upper piece of the array. It moves that item into the hole left behind by the previously moved item.

The algorithm continues searching backward and then forward through the array until the two pieces meet. At that point, it puts the dividing item between the two pieces and recursively calls itself to sort the pieces.

Using Quicksort

If you divide the items in place instead of by using stacks or queues, quicksort doesn't use any extra storage (beyond a few variables).

Like heapsort, quicksort has O(N log N) expected performance, although quicksort can have $O(N^2)$ performance in the worst case. Heapsort has O(N log N) performance in all cases, so it is in some sense safer and more elegant. However, in practice, quicksort is usually faster than heapsort, so it is the algorithm of choice for many programmers.

In addition to greater speed, quicksort has another advantage over heapsort: it is parallelizable. Suppose a computer has more than one processor, which is increasingly the case these days. Each time the algorithm splits a section of the array into two pieces, it can use different processors to sort the two pieces. Theoretically, a highly parallel computer could use O(N) processors to sort the list in O(log N) time. In practice, most computers have a fairly limited number of processors (for example, two or four), so the run time would be divided by the number of processors plus some additional overhead to manage the different threads of execution. That won't change the Big O run time, but it should improve performance in practice.

Because it has $O(N^2)$ performance in the worst case, the implementation of quicksort provided by a library may be cryptographically insecure. If the algorithm uses a simple dividing item selection strategy, such as picking the first item, an attacker might be able to create an array holding items in an order that gives worst-case performance. The attacker might be able to launch a denial-of-service (DOS) attack by passing your program that array and ruining your performance. Most programmers don't worry about this possibility, but if this is a concern, you can use a randomized dividing item selection strategy.

Mergesort

Like quicksort, *mergesort* uses a divide-and-conquer strategy. Instead of picking a dividing item and splitting the items into two groups holding items that are larger and smaller than the dividing item, mergesort splits the items into two halves holding an equal number of items. It then recursively calls itself to sort the two halves. When the recursive calls to mergesort return, the algorithm merges the two sorted halves into a combined sorted list.

The following pseudocode shows the algorithm:

```
Mergesort(Data: values[], Data: scratch[], Integer: start, Integer: end)
    // If the array contains only one item, it is already sorted.
    If (start == end) Then Return

    // Break the array into left and right halves.
    Integer: midpoint = (start + end) / 2

    // Call Mergesort to sort the two halves.
    Mergesort(values, scratch, start, midpoint)
    Mergesort(values, scratch, midpoint + 1, end)

    // Merge the two sorted halves.
    Integer: left_index = start
    Integer: right_index = midpoint + 1
    Integer: scratch_index = left_index
    While ((left_index <= midpoint) And (right_index <= end))
        If (values[left_index] <= values[right_index]) Then
            scratch[scratch_index] = values[left_index]
            left_index = left_index + 1
        Else
            scratch[scratch_index] = values[right_index]
            right_index = right_index + 1
        End If
        scratch_index = scratch_index + 1     End While

    // Finish copying whichever half is not empty.
    For i = left_index To midpoint
        scratch[scratch_index] = values[i]
        scratch_index = scratch_index + 1
    Next i
    For i = right_index To end
        scratch[scratch_index] = values[i]
        scratch_index = scratch_index + 1
    Next i

    // Copy the values back into the original values array.
    For i = start To end
        values[i] = scratch[i]
    Next i
End Mergesort
```

In addition to the array and the start and end indices to sort, the algorithm also takes as a parameter a scratch array that it uses to merge the sorted halves.

This algorithm starts by checking whether the section of the array contains one or fewer items. If it does, then it is trivially sorted, so the algorithm returns.

If the section of the array contains at least two items, the algorithm calculates the index of the item in the middle of the section of the array and recursively calls itself to sort the two halves.

After the recursive calls return, the algorithm merges the two sorted halves. It loops through the halves, copying the smaller item from whichever half holds it into the scratch array. When one-half is empty, the algorithm copies the remaining items from the other half.

Finally, the algorithm copies the merged items from the scratch array back into the original `values` array.

> **NOTE**   It is possible to merge the sorted halves without using a scratch array, but it's more complicated and slower, so most programmers use a scratch array.

The "call tree," shown in Figure 6.11, shows calls to quicksort when the values in the array are perfectly balanced, so the algorithm divides the items into equal halves at every step. The mergesort algorithm *does* divide the items into exactly equal halves at every step, so Figure 6.11 applies even more to mergesort than it does to quicksort.

The same run-time analysis shown earlier for quicksort also works for mergesort, so this algorithm also has O(N log N) run time. Like heapsort, mergesort's run time does not depend on the initial arrangement of the items, so it always has O(N log N) run time and doesn't have a disastrous worst case like quicksort does.

Like quicksort, mergesort is parallelizable. When a call to mergesort calls itself recursively, it can make those calls on different processors. This requires some coordination, however, because the original call must wait until both recursive calls finish before it can merge their results. In contrast, quicksort can simply tell its recursive calls to sort a particular part of the array, and it doesn't need to wait until those calls return.

Mergesort is particularly useful when all the data to be sorted won't fit in memory at once. For example, suppose a program needs to sort 1 million customer records, each of which occupies 1 MB. Loading all that data into memory at once would require 10^{18} bytes of memory, or 1,000 TB, which is much more than most computers have.

Fortunately, the mergesort algorithm doesn't need to load that much memory all at once. The algorithm doesn't even need to look at any of the items in the array until after its recursive calls to itself have returned.

At that point, the algorithm walks through the two sorted halves in a linear fashion and merges them. Moving through the items linearly reduces the computer's need to page memory to and from disk. When quicksort moves items into the two halves of a section of an array, it jumps from one location in the array to another, increasing paging and greatly slowing down the algorithm.

Mergesort was even more useful in the days when large data sets were stored on tape drives, which work most efficiently if they keep moving forward with few rewinds. (Sorting data that cannot fit in memory is called *external sorting*.) Specialized versions of mergesort were even more efficient for tape drives. They're interesting but not commonly used anymore, so they aren't described here.

NOTE For some interesting background on external sorting on tape drives, see `https://en.wikipedia.org/wiki/Merge_sort#Use_with_tape_drives`. **For more general information on tape drives, see** `https://en.wikipedia.org/wiki/Tape_drive`.

A more common approach to sorting enormous data sets is to sort only the items' keys. For example, a customer record might occupy 1 MB, but the customer's name might occupy only 100 bytes. A program can make a separate index that matches names to record numbers and then sort only the names. Then, even if you have 1 million customers, sorting their names requires only about 100 MB of memory, an amount that a computer could reasonably hold. (Chapter 11, "Balanced Trees," describes B-trees and B+ trees, which are often used by database systems to store and sort record keys in this manner.)

STABLE SORTING

A *stable sorting algorithm* is one that maintains the original relative positioning of equivalent values. For example, suppose that a program is sorting `Car` objects by their `Cost` properties and that `Car` objects A and B have the same `Cost` values. If object A initially comes before object B in the array, then in a stable sorting algorithm, object A still comes before object B in the sorted array.

If the items you are sorting are value types such as integers, dates, or strings, then two entries with the same values are equivalent, so it doesn't matter if the sort is stable. For example, if the array contains two entries that have value 47, it doesn't matter which 47 comes first in the sorted array.

In contrast, you might care if `Car` objects are rearranged unnecessarily. For example, a stable sort lets you arrange the array multiple times to get a result that is sorted on multiple keys (such as `Maker` and `Cost` for the `Car` example).

Mergesort is easy to implement as a stable sort (the algorithm described earlier is stable). It is also easy to parallelize, so it may be useful on computers that have more than one CPU. See Chapter 18, "Distributed Algorithms," for information on implementing mergesort on multiple CPUs.

Quicksort may often be faster, but mergesort still has some advantages.

Sub O(N log N) Algorithms

Earlier in this chapter, I said that the fastest possible algorithm that uses comparisons to sort N items must use at least O(N log N) time. Heapsort and mergesort achieve that bound, and so does quicksort in the expected case, so you might think that's the end of the sorting story. The loophole is in the phrase "that uses comparisons." If you use a technique other than comparisons to sort, you can beat the O(N log N) bound.

The following sections describe some algorithms that sort in less than O(N log N) time.

Countingsort

Countingsort is a specialized algorithm that works well if the values you are sorting are integers that lie in a relatively small range. For example, if you need to sort 1 million integers with values between 0 and 1,000, countingsort can provide amazingly fast performance.

The basic idea behind countingsort is to count the number of items in the array that have each value. Then it is relatively easy to copy each value, in order, the required number of times back into the array.

The following pseudocode shows the countingsort algorithm:

```
Countingsort(Integer: values[], Integer: max_value)
    // Make an array to hold the counts.
    Integer: counts[0 To max_value]

    // Initialize the array to hold the counts.
    // (This is not necessary in all programming languages.)
    For i = 0 To max_value
        counts[i] = 0
    Next i

    // Count the items with each value.
    For i = 0 To <length of values> - 1
        // Add 1 to the count for this value.
        counts[values[i]] = counts[values[i]] + 1
    Next i

    // Copy the values back into the array.
    Integer: index = 0
    For i = 0 To max_value
        // Copy the value i into the array counts[i] times.
        For j = 1 To counts[i]
            values[index] = i
            index = index + 1
        Next j
    Next i
End Countingsort
```

The `max_value` parameter gives the largest value in the array. (If you don't pass it in as a parameter, you can modify the algorithm to figure it out by looking through the array.)

Let M be the number of items in the counts array (so M = `max_value` + 1) and let N be the number of items in the `values` array. If your programming language doesn't automatically initialize the `counts` array so that it contains 0s, the algorithm spends M steps initializing the array. It then takes N steps to count the values in the `values` array.

The algorithm finishes by copying the values back into the original array. Each value is copied once, so that part takes N steps. If any of the entries in the `counts` array is still 0, the program also spends some time skipping over that entry. In the worst case, if all of the values are the same so that the `counts` array contains mostly 0s, it takes M steps to skip over the 0 entries.

That makes the total run time $O(2 \times N + M) = O(N + M)$. If M is relatively small compared to N, this is much smaller than the $O(N \log N)$ performance given by heapsort and the other algorithms described previously.

In one test, quicksort took 4.29 seconds to sort 1 million items with values between 0 and 1,000, but it took countingsort only 0.03 seconds. Note that this is a bad case for quicksort because the values include many duplicates. With 1 million values between 0 and 1,000, roughly 1,000 items have each value, and quicksort doesn't handle lots of duplication well.

With similar values, heapsort took roughly 1.02 seconds. This is a big improvement on quicksort, but it is still much slower than countingsort.

Pigeonhole Sort

Like countingsort, *pigeonhole sort* works well when the range of possible values is limited. Countingsort counts the number of items with each given value. To do that, it uses the values as indices into the `counts` array. Unfortunately, that won't work if the items that you are sorting are not integers, so you can't use them as indices.

Pigeonhole sort works by placing the items in pigeonholes corresponding to their key values. The pigeonhole approach makes it easier to sort more complicated items than simple numeric values. For example, suppose that you want to sort a set of words by their lengths. Countingsort would give you an array holding the number of words with each length, but it's not immediately obvious how you would convert that into the ordered list of words.

In contrast, pigeonhole sort groups words with the same length in the same pigeonhole, so it is easier to put them in order.

The following pseudocode shows how pigeonhole sort works. The algorithm assumes that you have defined a `Cell` class with `Value` and `Next` properties that you can use to build a linked list of values in each pigeonhole.

```
PigeonholeSort(Integer: values[], Integer: max)
    // Make the pigeonholes.
    Cell: pigeonholes[] = new Cell[max + 1]

    // Initialize the linked lists.
    For i = 0 To max
        pigeonholes[i] = null
    Next i

    // Move items into the pigeonholes.
    For Each value in values
        // Add this item to its pigeonhole.
        Cell: cell = new Cell(value)
        cell.Next = pigeonholes[value]
        pigeonholes[value] = cell
    Next value

    // Copy the items back into the values array.
    Integer: index = 0
    For i = 0 To max
        // Copy the items in pigeonhole i into the values array.
        Cell: cell = pigeonholes[i]
        While (cell != null)
            values[index] = cell.Value
            index++
            cell = cell.Next
        End While
    Next i
End PigeonholeSort
```

The `values` parameter gives the values to sort. The `max` parameter gives the maximum value that the `values` array could hold. Here I'm assuming the values are integers starting at zero. If they include values between lower and upper bounds, you'll have to adjust the code accordingly. If the values are non-numeric, for example if they are strings, then you'll need to use some sort of algorithm to map each value to its pigeonhole.

The algorithm first creates a pigeonhole array of pointers to `Cell` objects and initializes them to `null`. It then loops through the items and adds each to the top of its pigeonhole's linked list. The code then loops through the pigeonholes and copies the items in each linked list back into the `values` array.

To analyze the algorithm's run time, suppose that the `values` array contains N items that span a range of M possible values. The algorithm uses O(M) steps to initialize its pigeonhole linked lists. It then loops through the values and adds them to their pigeonholes in O(N) steps.

The algorithm finishes by looping through the pigeonholes again, this time moving the items back into the values array. It must spend O(M) steps examining each linked list whether or not that list is empty. During this stage, it also must move every item back into the `values` array, and that takes O(N) steps, so the total steps to perform this final stage is O(M + N).

That means the total run time for the algorithm is O(M) + O(N) + O(M + N) = O(M + N).

If the number of values N is roughly the same as the size of the range of values M, then this becomes O(N), and that is much faster than O(N log N).

Bucketsort

The countingsort and pigeonhole sort algorithms work well if the values include only a relatively small range. Bucketsort works even if the values span a large range.

The *bucketsort algorithm*, which is also called *binsort*, works by dividing items into buckets. It sorts the buckets either by recursively calling bucketsort or by using some other algorithm. It then concatenates the buckets' contents back into the original array in sorted order. The following pseudocode shows the algorithm at a high level:

```
Bucketsort(Data: values[])
    <Make buckets.>
    <Distribute the items into the buckets.>
    <Sort the buckets.>
    <Gather the bucket values back into the original array.>
End Bucketsort
```

If the values in an array holding N items are reasonably uniformly distributed, if you use M buckets, and if the buckets divide the range of values evenly, then you should expect roughly N / M items per bucket.

For example, consider the array shown at the top of Figure 6.12, which contains 10 items with values between 0 and 99. In the distribution step, the algorithm moves the items into the buckets. In this example, each bucket represents 20 values: 0 to 19, 20 to 39, and so on. In the sorting step, the algorithm sorts each bucket. The gathering step concatenates the values in the buckets to build the sorted result.

The buckets can be stacks, linked lists, queues, arrays, or any other data structure that you find convenient.

If the original array contains N fairly evenly distributed items, then distributing them into the buckets requires N steps times whatever time it takes to place an item in a bucket. Normally this mapping can be done in constant time. For example, suppose the items are integers between 0 and 99, as in the example shown in Figure 6.12. You would place an item with value v in bucket number $\lfloor v / 20 \rfloor$. You can calculate this number in constant time, so distributing the items takes O(N) steps.

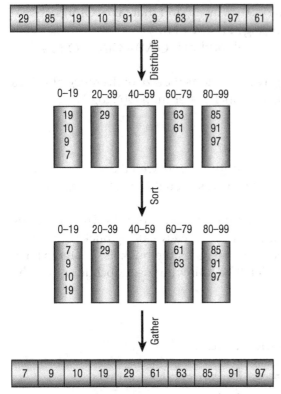

Figure 6.12: Bucketsort moves items into buckets, sorts the buckets, and then concatenates the buckets to get the sorted result.

If you use M buckets, sorting each bucket requires an expected F(N/M) steps, where F is the run-time function of the sorting algorithm that you use to sort the buckets. Multiplying this by the number of buckets M, the total time to sort all the buckets is $O(M \times F(N/M))$.

After you have sorted the buckets, gathering their values back into the array requires N steps to move all of the values. It could require an additional O(M) steps to skip empty buckets if many of the buckets are empty, but if M < N, the whole operation requires O(N) steps.

Adding the times needed for the three stages gives a total run time of $O(N) + O(M \times F(N/M)) + O(N) = O(N + M \times F(N/M))$.

If M is a fixed fraction of N, then N / M is a constant, so F(N / M) is also a constant, and this simplifies to O(N + M).

In practice, M must be a relatively large fraction of N for the algorithm to perform well. If you are sorting 10 million records and you use only 10 buckets, then you need to sort buckets containing an average of 1 million items each.

In contrast, if M equals N, then each bucket should hold only a few items and sorting them should take a small constant amount of time. In that case, the algorithm's O(N + M) run time simplifies to O(N), and the algorithm runs very quickly.

Unlike countingsort and pigeonhole sort, bucketsort's performance does not depend on the range of the values. Instead, it depends on the number of buckets that you use.

Summary

The sorting algorithms described in this chapter demonstrate different techniques and have different characteristics. Table 6.1 summarizes the algorithms.

Table 6.1: Algorithm Characteristics

ALGORITHM	RUN TIME	TECHNIQUES	USEFUL FOR
Insertionsort	$O(N^2)$	Insertion	Very small arrays
Selectionsort	$O(N^2)$	Selection	Very small arrays
Bubblesort/ Cocktail Shaker Sort	$O(N^2)$	Two-way passes, restricting bounds of interest	Very small arrays, mostly sorted arrays
Heapsort	O(NlogN)	Heaps, storing complete trees in an array	Large arrays with unknown distribution
Quicksort	O(NlogN) expected, $O(N^2)$ worst case	Divide-and-conquer, swapping items into position, randomization to avoid worst-case behavior	Large arrays without too many duplicates, parallel sorting
Mergesort	O(NlogN)	Divide-and-conquer, merging, external sorting	Large arrays with unknown distribution, huge amounts of data, parallel sorting
Countingsort	O(N+M)	Counting	Large arrays of integers with a limited range of values
Pigeonhole sort	O(N+M)	Pigeonholes	Large arrays of possibly noninteger values within a limited range
Bucketsort	O(N+M)	Buckets	Large arrays with reasonably uniform value distribution

These algorithms demonstrate an assortment of useful techniques and provide good performance for a wide variety of problems, but they're far from the end of the story. There are dozens of other sorting algorithms. Some are minor modifications of these algorithms, and others use radically different approaches. Chapter 10 discusses trees, which are also extremely useful for sorting data. Search the Internet for other algorithms.

This chapter explained several ways to sort data, but it didn't explain why you should want to do that. Simply having data sorted often makes it more useful to a user. For example, viewing customer accounts sorted by balance makes it much easier to determine which accounts need special attention.

Another good reason to sort data is so that you can later find specific items within it. For example, if you sort customers by their names, it's easier to locate a specific customer. The next chapter explains methods that you can use to search a sorted set of data to find a specific value.

Exercises

You can find the answers to these exercises in Appendix B. Asterisks indicate particularly difficult problems.

1. Write a program that implements insertionsort.

2. The For i loop used by the insertionsort algorithm runs from 0 to the array's last index. What happens if it starts at 1 instead of 0? Does that change the algorithm's run time?

3. Write a program that implements selectionsort.

4. What change to selectionsort could you make that corresponds to the change described in Exercise 2? Would it change the algorithm's run time?

5. Write a program that implements bubblesort.

6. Add the first and third bubblesort improvements described in the section "Bubblesort" (downward and upward passes and keeping track of the last swap) to the program you built for Exercise 5.

7. Write a program that uses an array-based heap to build a priority queue. So that you don't need to resize the array, allocate it at some fixed size, perhaps 100 items, and then keep track of the number of items that are used by the heap. (To make the queue useful, you can't just store priorities. Use two arrays—one to store string values and another to store the corresponding priorities. Order the items by their priorities.) (For more practice, use a class to store items with their priorities and wrap the priority queue in a second class.)

8. What is the run time for adding items to and removing items from a heap-based priority queue?

9. Write a program that implements heapsort.

10. Can you generalize the technique used by heapsort for holding a complete binary tree so that you can store a complete tree of degree d? Given a node's index p, what are its children's indices? What is its parent's index?

11. Write a program that implements quicksort with stacks. (You can use the stacks provided by your programming environment or build your own.)

12. Write a program that implements quicksort with queues instead of stacks. (You can use the queues provided by your programming environment or build your own.) Is there any advantage or disadvantage to using queues instead of stacks?

13. Write a program that implements quicksort with in-place partitioning. Why is this version faster than the version that uses stacks or queues?

14. Quicksort can display worst-case behavior if the items are initially sorted, if the items are initially sorted in reverse order, or if the items contain many duplicates. You can avoid the first two problems if you choose random dividing items. How can you avoid the third problem?

15. Write a program that implements countingsort.

16. If an array's values range from 100,000 to 110,000, allocating a counts array with 110,001 entries with indices 0 through 110,000 would slow down countingsort considerably, particularly if the array holds a relatively small number of items. How could you modify countingsort to give good performance in this situation?

17. Write a program that implements pigeonhole sort.

18. If an array holds N items that span the range 0 to M − 1, what happens to bucketsort if you use M buckets?

19. Write a program that implements bucketsort. Allow the user to specify the number of items, the maximum item value, and the number of buckets.

20. Explain the space/time trade-off that you should consider when picking the number of buckets used by bucketsort.

21. For the following data sets, which sorting algorithms would work well, and which would not?
    a. 10 floating-point values
    b. 1,000 integers
    c. 1,000 names
    d. 100,000 integers with values between 0 and 1,000
    e. 100,000 integers with values between 0 and 1 billion

     f. 100,000 names

     g. 1 million floating-point values

     h. 1 million names

     i. 1 million integers with uniform distribution

     j. 1 million integers with nonuniform distribution

Searching

The preceding chapter explained how you can sort data. Algorithms such as quicksort and heapsort let you sort large amounts of data quickly. Algorithms such as countingsort and bucketsort let you sort data almost as quickly as a program can examine it, but only under certain special circumstances.

One of the advantages of sorted data is that it lets you find specific items relatively quickly. For example, you can locate a particular word in a dictionary containing tens of thousands of words in just a minute or two because all the words are arranged in sorted order. (Imagine trying to find a word if the dictionary wasn't sorted!)

This chapter explains algorithms that you can use to find a particular piece of data in a sorted array.

> **NOTE** The algorithms described in this chapter work with simple arrays, not more specialized data structures. Specialized data structures such as trees also let you quickly find an item with a specific value. Chapter 10, "Trees," discusses algorithms for working with trees.

Some programming libraries include searching tools that locate items in a sorted array. For example, the .NET Framework's `Array` class provides a `Binary-Search` method. These methods generally are fast, so in practice you may want to use those tools to save time writing and debugging the searching code.

It's still important to understand how searching algorithms work, however, because sometimes you can do even better than the tools. For example, interpolation search is much faster than binary search when it is applicable.

Linear Search

As you may be able to guess from its name, a *linear search* or *exhaustive search* simply loops through the items in the array, looking for the target item. Figure 7.1 shows a linear search for the value 77.

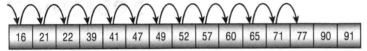

| 16 | 21 | 22 | 39 | 41 | 47 | 49 | 52 | 57 | 60 | 65 | 71 | 77 | 90 | 91 |

Figure 7.1: A linear search examines every item in the array until it finds the target item.

Unlike binary search and interpolation search, linear search works on linked lists, where you cannot easily jump from one part of the list to another, as you can in an array.

Linear search also works on unsorted lists. If the items are sorted, however, the algorithm can stop if it ever comes to an item with a value greater than the target value. That lets the algorithm stop early and save a little time if the target value isn't in the list.

The following pseudocode shows the linear search algorithm for an array:

```
// Find the target item's index in the sorted array.
// If the item isn't in the array, return -1.
Integer: LinearSearch(Data values[], Data target)
    For i = 0 To <length of values> - 1
        // See if this is the target.
        If (values[i] == target) Then Return i

        // See if we have passed where the target would be.
        If (values[i] > target) Then Return -1
    Next i

    // If we get here, the target is not in the array.
    Return -1
End LinearSearch
```

This algorithm may need to loop through the entire array to conclude that an item isn't there, so its worst-case behavior is O(N).

Even in the average case, the algorithm's run time is O(N). If you add up the number of steps required to search for every item in the array, you get

$1 + 2 + 3 + \ldots + N = N \times (N + 1) / 2$. If you divide that total by N to get the average search time for all the N items, you get $(N + 1) / 2$, which is still O(N).

This algorithm is much slower than binary search or interpolation search, but it has the advantage that it works on linked lists and unsorted lists.

Binary Search

A *binary search algorithm* uses a divide-and-conquer strategy to narrow down quickly the part of the array that might contain the target value. The algorithm keeps track of the largest and smallest indices that the target item might have in the array. Initially, those bounds (call them `min` and `max`) are set to 0 and the largest index in the array.

The algorithm then calculates the index halfway between `min` and `max` (call it `mid`). If the target is less than the array's value at `mid`, the algorithm resets `max` to search the left half of the array and starts over. If the target is greater than the array's value at `mid`, the algorithm resets `min` to search the right half of the array and starts over. If the target equals the array's value at `mid`, the algorithm returns the index `mid`.

Figure 7.2 shows a binary search for the value 77.

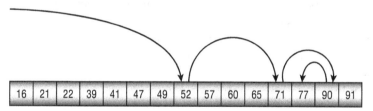

Figure 7.2: A binary search repeatedly divides the part of the array that might contain the target item into two halves and then searches the appropriate half.

The following pseudocode shows the algorithm:

```
// Find the target item's index in the sorted array.
// If the item isn't in the array, return -1.
Integer: BinarySearch(Data values[], Data target)
    Integer: min = 0
    Integer: max = <length of values> - 1
    While (min <= max)
        // Find the dividing item.
        Integer: mid = (min + max) / 2

        // See if we need to search the left or right half.
        If (target < values[mid]) Then max = mid - 1
```

```
            Else If (target > values[mid]) Then min = mid + 1
            Else Return mid
        End While

        // If we get here, the target is not in the array.
        Return -1
    End BinarySearch
```

At each step, this algorithm halves the number of items that might contain the target. If the array contains N items, then after O(log N) steps, the section of the array that might hold the target contains only one item, so the algorithm either finds the item or concludes that it isn't in the array. This means that the algorithm has O(log N) run time.

Interpolation Search

At every step, binary search examines the item in the middle of the section of the array that it is considering. In contrast, *interpolation search* uses the value of the target item to guess where in the array it might lie and achieve much faster search times.

For example, suppose that the array contains 1,000 items with values between 1 and 100. If the target value is 30, then it should lie about 30 percent of the way from the smallest to the largest value, so you can guess that the item may be somewhere near index 300. Depending on the distribution of the numbers in the array, this may not be exactly correct, but it should get you fairly close to the target item's position.

Figure 7.3 shows an interpolation search for the value 77.

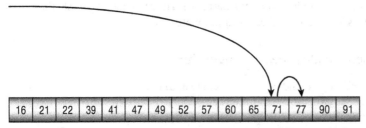

Figure 7.3: Interpolation search uses the target item's value to calculate where it should be in the remaining part of the array.

The following pseudocode shows the algorithm at a high level:

```
Integer: InterpolationSearch(Data values[], Data target)
    Integer: min = 0
    Integer: max = values.Length - 1
    While (min <= max)
```

```
        // Find the dividing item.
        Integer: mid = min + (max - min) *
            (target - values[min]) / (values[max] - values[min])

        If (values[mid] == target) Then Return mid

        <Set min or max to search the left or right half.>
    End While

    Return -1
End InterpolationSearch
```

This high-level description leaves a couple of problems unsolved. The `mid` calculation can result in an overflow or a value of `mid` that is not between `min` and `max`. Solving those problems is left as part of Exercise 6 in this chapter.

The trickiest part of this algorithm is the statement that calculates `mid`. The value is set to the current value of `min` plus the distance between `min` and `max` when scaled by the expected fraction of the distance between `values[min]` and `values[max]` where `target` should lie.

For example, if `values[min]` is 100, `values[max]` is 200, and `target` is 125, then you would use the following calculation to decide where to look for the target value:

```
(target - values[min]) / (values[max] - values[min]) =
(125 - 100) / (200 - 100) =
25 / 100 =
0.25
```

That puts the new value for `mid` one-quarter of the way from `min` to `max`.

In the worst case, if the data is extremely unevenly distributed and you're looking for the worst possible target value, this algorithm has O(N) performance. If the distribution is reasonably uniform, the expected performance is O(log(log N)). (Proving that, however, is outside the scope of this book.)

Majority Voting

Voting is basically a specialized kind of searching. The goal in the *majority voting problem* is to determine a sequence's majority item—the item that appears more than half of the time. For example, suppose you poll 30 students and ask them whether they prefer chocolate, strawberry, or vanilla ice cream. The majority voting problem asks you to determine the majority opinion.

Note that there may not be a majority item. For example, suppose 14 students pick chocolate, 6 pick strawberry, and 10 pick vanilla. In that case, none of the choices receives more than half of the votes, so there is no majority.

One obvious majority voting algorithm is to loop through the list of items and keep a counter indicating the number of times each was chosen. If there are M possible values (chocolate, strawberry, and vanilla) and the list contains N items (30 students give 30 results in this example), then this algorithm takes O(N) time to scan the results and O(M) space to hold the counters.

Each of the O(N) steps will also require some time to find the appropriate counter. For example, if you use a hash table to store the counters, then finding them will be relatively quick. If you store the counters in an array or linked list, then finding the appropriate counter to increment will be slower.

This algorithm has the advantage of being very simple and intuitive. It can also find the mode of the votes, in case no item occurs more than half of the time. (The *mode* is the outcome that occurred most often.) For example, if 14 students pick chocolate, 6 pick strawberry, and 10 pick vanilla, then this algorithm can fairly easily determine that chocolate was the mode even though it didn't receive a majority of the votes.

The Boyer-Moore majority vote algorithm is an interesting algorithm that can find the majority item in O(N) time using only O(1) space. To find the majority, the algorithm uses two variables: Majority to hold an outcome and Count to hold a counter. The following pseudocode shows how the algorithm works:

```
Outcome: BoyerMooreVote(List<Outcome> outcomes)
    Outcome: majority = ""
    Integer: counter = 0
    For Each outcome In outcomes
        If (counter == 0) Then
            majority = outcome
            counter = 1
        Else If (outcome == majority) Then
            counter++
        Else
            counter--
        End If
    Next outcome

    Return majority
End BoyerMooreVote
```

The algorithm initializes variable counter to 0 and then loops through the list of items. When it examines an item, if counter is currently 0, then the algorithm saves the current item in variable majority and sets counter to 1.

If counter is not 0 when it examines an item, the algorithm compares the new item to the one stored in majority. If the new item matches majority, then the algorithm increments counter, essentially casting another vote for this item.

If counter is not 0 and the new item is different from majority, then the algorithm decrements count, essentially removing a vote for majority.

After the algorithm finishes, the variable `majority` holds the result. If there is a majority item, then the result is correct. If there is no majority item, then the algorithm returns something, but the result is not guaranteed to be the mode.

To understand why the algorithm works, suppose that the majority item is m. During any step of the algorithm, define the value C to be the value in `counter` if `majority` currently holds m, and let C be the negative of the value in `counter` otherwise. Whenever the algorithm sees m, it increases C. When the algorithm sees some other item, it either increases or decreases C, depending on whether the new outcome matches the value currently stored in `majority`.

Because m is the majority item, the algorithm must increase C more than it decreases C, so when the algorithm finishes, C will be positive. That happens only when `majority` holds m, so m must hold that value when the algorithm finishes.

Summary

Table 7.1 shows the values of N, log N, and log(log N) for different values of N so that you can compare the speeds of linear search, binary search, and interpolation search.

Table 7.1: Algorithm Characteristics

N	$\log_2 N$	$\log_2(\log_2 N)$
1,000	10.0	3.3
1,000,000	19.9	4.3
1,000,000,000	29.9	4.9
1,000,000,000,000	39.9	5.3

Linear search is useful only for relatively small arrays. Table 7.1 shows that binary search works well even for very large arrays. It can search an array containing 1 trillion items in only about 40 steps.

Interpolation search works well for arrays of any size that you can reasonably fit on a computer. It can search an array containing 1 trillion items in only about five steps. In fact, an array would need to hold more than 1×10^{154} items before interpolation search would require an expected number of steps greater than nine.

However, the exact number of steps for interpolation search depends on the distribution of the values. Sometimes the algorithm gets lucky and finds the target in one or two steps. At other times, it might need four or five steps. On average, however, it is extremely fast.

The Boyer-Moore majority voting algorithm is a particularly odd algorithm because it produces the correct result only sometimes, and it doesn't tell you whether the result is correct.

Exercises

You can find the answers to these exercises in Appendix B. Asterisks indicate particularly difficult problems.

If you're not familiar with recursion, skip Exercises 2, 5, and 7 and come back to them after you read Chapter 9.

1. Write a program that implements linear search.

2. Write a program that implements linear search recursively. Does this version have any advantages or disadvantages compared to the nonrecursive version?

3. Write a program that implements linear search with sorted linked lists.

4. Write a program that implements binary search.

5. Write a program that implements binary search recursively. Does this version have any advantages or disadvantages compared to the nonrecursive version?

6. Write a program that implements interpolation search.

7. Write a program that implements interpolation search recursively. Does this version have any advantages or disadvantages compared to the nonrecursive version?

8. Which sorting algorithm described in Chapter 6, "Sorting," uses a technique reminiscent of the technique used by interpolation search?

9. If an array contains duplicates, the binary search and interpolation search algorithms described in this chapter don't guarantee that they return the first instance of the target item. How could you modify them to return the first occurrence of the target item? What is the run time for the modified version?

10. In the Boyer-Moore majority voting algorithm, what happens if outcome M occurs exactly half of the time in the list of outcomes? Can you make two example lists, one that causes the algorithm to return M and one that returns some other value?

11. The Boyer-Moore majority voting algorithm always returns an outcome, but if there is no majority, the result is not guaranteed to be the most common outcome in the list. How could you modify that algorithm to indicate whether the result is really a majority without changing the O(N) run time and O(1) memory characteristics?

Hash Tables

The preceding chapter explained binary search, an O(log N) algorithm for locating an item in a sorted list. The algorithm repeatedly examines a test item in the middle of the part of the list where the target item must be. It compares the test item to the target item and then recursively examines the left or right half of the region, depending on whether the test item is greater than or less than the target item.

Chapter 7 also explained interpolation search, which uses a mathematical calculation to predict where the target item will be. That algorithm has O(log (log N)) time and is so much faster than binary search that it almost seems like magic.

The reason why interpolation search is so much faster than binary search is that it uses the data's special structure to find values by calculation instead of by making comparisons. The countingsort, pigeonhole sort, and bucketsort algorithms described in Chapter 6 do that too.

Hash tables also use the data's structure to locate values quickly. Instead of storing items in a sorted list, a hash table stores them in a way that lets you calculate an item's location in the table directly.

NOTE Python's version of a hash table is a dictionary.

In C#, you can use the `HashTable` class to store weakly typed objects with keys.

The `Dictionary` class is a strongly typed hash table where the data types of the items and keys are defined. Because the objects in a Dictionary have a known data type, a Dictionary gives faster performance than a nonspecific HashTable.

Dictionaries in both C# and Python allow you to look up items by using a key. The prebuilt dictionary classes work well, so feel free to use them in your programs. This chapter explains some of the methods that those classes use and how you can implement hash tables in your code.

For a simple example of a hash table, suppose that you have a small company with 20 employees, and you want to be able to look up an employee's information by searching for that person's employee ID. One way you could store the information is to allocate an array of 100 items and then store an employee with employee ID N in position N mod 100 in the array. For example, an employee with ID 2190 would go in position 90, an employee with ID 2817 would go in position 17, and an employee with ID 3078 would go in position 78.

To find a particular employee, you would simply calculate the ID mod 100 and look at the corresponding array entry. This is an O(1) operation that's even faster than interpolation search.

In a real program, things aren't quite so simple. If you have enough employees, you will eventually get two with IDs that map to the same value. For example, if two employees have IDs 2817 and 1317, they both map to position 17 in the table.

Still, this idea of mapping values into a table is a pretty good start, and it is the basic concept behind hash tables. The rest of this chapter describes hash tables more precisely and explains ways that you can implement hash tables in a program.

Hash Table Fundamentals

A *hash table* maps data to locations in a data structure. Often it associates a key value such as an ID or name to a larger record such as an employee or customer record. Because hash tables associate a key to a value, they are sometimes called *associative arrays* or, less formally, *dictionaries*.

The process of mapping a key value for use by the hash table is called *hashing*. Good hashing functions spread out key values so that they don't all go to the same position in the table. In particular, key values are often similar, so a good hashing function maps similar key values to dissimilar locations in the table.

For example, suppose that you want to store customer records in a hash table and look them up by name. If two customers have the last names Richards and Richardson, ideally the hashing function should map them to two different locations.

To achieve this, hashing functions often generate a value that looks something like gibberish, as if the key value had been chopped into hash.

If you put enough values in a hash table, eventually you'll find two keys that hash to the same value. That's called a *collision*. When that occurs, you need a *collision-resolution policy* that determines what to do. Often the collision resolution policy maps the key to a series of new positions in the table until it finds an empty position.

A hash table's *fill percentage*, the percentage of the table that contains entries, influences the chance of collisions occurring. Adding a new key to a hash table is more likely to cause a collision if the table's data structure is 95 percent full than if it's only 10 percent full.

To summarize, a hash table needs the following:

- A data structure to hold the data
- A hashing function to map keys to locations in the data structure
- A collision-resolution policy that specifies what to do when keys collide

To be useful, a hash table must be able to at least add new items and locate items that were previously stored. Another feature that is useful but not provided by some hash tables is the ability to remove a hashed key.

RESIZING HASH TABLES

Eventually a hash table may become completely full, or at least so full that collisions are likely and performance suffers. In that case, you need a resize algorithm to determine when and how the hash table is resized to make it larger.

You can also have an algorithm for determining when and how to make the hash table smaller. For example, if a hash table can hold 1 million entries but currently holds only 10 entries, you might want to make it smaller to reclaim unused space.

One simple method of resizing a hash table is to create a new hash table of the desired size and then rehash all the items in the original data structure into the new table. Some types of hash tables, such as hash tables with chaining, offer other methods, but this one should work for almost any hash table.

Different kinds of hash tables use different methods to provide these features. The following sections describe some common methods of building hash tables.

Chaining

A hash table with chaining uses a collection of entries called *buckets* to hold key values. Each bucket is the top of a linked list holding the items that map to that bucket.

Typically the buckets are arranged in an array, so you can use a simple hashing function to determine a key's bucket. For example, if you have N buckets and the keys are numeric, you could map the key K to bucket number K mod N.

Figure 8.1 shows a hash table with chaining.

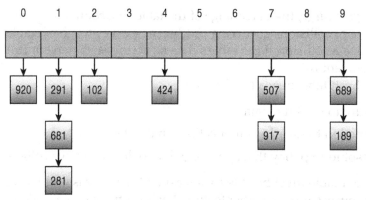

Figure 8.1: In a hash table with chaining, each bucket is the top of a linked list.

To add a key to the hash table, you map the key to a bucket using the hash function and then add a new cell to the bucket's linked list. Hashing the key to find its bucket takes O(1) steps. Adding the value to the top of the linked list takes O(1) steps, so this operation is very fast.

However, to be useful, a hash table cannot hold duplicate values. This means that before you can add a new item to a bucket, you should verify that it is not already present. If the hash table uses B buckets and holds a total of N items and the items are reasonably evenly distributed, each bucket's linked list holds roughly N/B items. If you need to verify that a key is not in the hash table, you need to examine the roughly N/B items in that key's bucket. All of this means that adding an item to the hash table takes a total of O(1) + O(N/B) = O(N/B) steps.

> **NOTE** You can make searching for items in the hash table a little faster if the linked lists hold keys in sorted order. Then, if a key isn't present, you only need to search until you find a value greater than the target key instead of searching all the way to the end of the list. The run time is still O(N/B), but in practice it will be a bit faster.

To find an item, you hash its key to see which bucket should hold it and then traverse that bucket's linked list until you find the item or come to the end of the list. If you get to the end of the list, you can conclude that the item isn't in the hash table. As is the case when adding an item to the hash table, this takes O(N/B) steps.

A hash table with chaining supports item removal quite well. To remove an item, hash its key as usual to find its bucket. Then remove the item from the bucket's linked list. Hashing the item takes O(1) steps and removing it takes O(N/B) steps, so the total time is O(N/B).

A hash table with chaining can expand and shrink as needed, so you don't need to resize it if you don't want to. If the linked lists become too long, however, finding and removing items will take a long time. In that case, you may want to enlarge the table to make more buckets. When you rehash the table, you know that you will not be adding any duplicate items, so you don't need to search to the end of each bucket's linked list to look for duplicates. That allows you to rehash all of the items in O(N) time.

Open Addressing

Chaining has some nice advantages, such as the fact that it can hold any number of values without changing the number of buckets, but it has some disadvantages as well. For example, if you put too many items in the buckets, then searching through the buckets can take a fair amount of time. You can reduce the search time by adding more buckets, but then you might have lots of empty buckets taking up space, and there's no way for the hash table to use those empty buckets.

Another strategy for building hash tables is called open addressing. In *open addressing*, the values are stored in an array, and some sort of calculation serves as the hashing function, mapping values into positions in the array. For example, if a hash table uses an array with M entries, a simple hashing function might map the key value K into array position K mod M.

Different variations of open addressing use different hashing functions and collision-resolution policies. In all cases, however, the collision-resolution policy produces a sequence of locations in the array for a value. If a value maps to a location that is already in use, the algorithm tries another location. If that location is also in use, the algorithm tries again. The algorithm continues trying new locations until it either finds an empty location or concludes that it cannot find one.

The sequence of locations that the algorithm tries for a value is called the value's *probe sequence*. The average length of probe sequences for values that may or may not be in the hash table gives a good estimate of the efficiency of the hash table. Ideally, the average probe sequence length should be only 1 or 2. If the table becomes too full, the average probe sequence may become very long.

Depending on the collision-resolution policy, a probe sequence might be unable to find an empty location for an item even if there are empty items in the hash table's array. If the probe sequence repeats itself before visiting every entry, some entries may remain unused.

To locate an item in the hash table, the algorithm follows the value's probe sequence until one of three things happens. First, if the probe sequence finds the item, the job is done. Second, if the probe sequence finds an empty entry in the array, the item is not present. (Otherwise, it would have been placed in the empty position.)

The third possibility is that the probe sequence could visit M entries, where M is the size of the array. In that case, the algorithm can conclude that the value is not present. The probe sequence might not visit every entry in the array, but after visiting M entries, you know that it has either visited every entry or that it is unlikely to find the target value. The probe sequence may even be following a loop, visiting the same positions repeatedly. In any case, the value must not be present because, if it were, it would have been added to the array using the same probe sequence.

At a reasonable fill percentage, open addressing is extremely fast. If the average probe sequence length is only 1 or 2, then adding and locating items has run time O(1).

Open addressing is fast, but it does have some disadvantages. The most obvious problem is that the hash table's performance degrades if its array becomes too full. In the worst case, if the array contains N items and is completely full, it takes O(N) time to conclude that an item is not present in the array. Even finding items that are present can be very slow.

If the array becomes too full, you can resize it to make it bigger and give the hash table a smaller fill percentage. To do that, create a new array and rehash the items into it. If the new array is reasonably large, it should take O(1) time to rehash each item, for a total run time of O(N).

The following section discusses another important problem with open addressing: removing items.

Removing Items

Although open addressing lets you add and find items reasonably quickly, at least if the array isn't too full, it doesn't allow you to remove items the way chaining does. An item in the array might be part of another item's probe sequence. If you remove that item, then you will break the other item's probe sequence so you can no longer find the second value.

For example, suppose items A and B both map to the same index I_A in the array. Item A is added first at index I_A, so when you try to add item B, it goes to the second position in its probe sequence, I_B.

Now suppose you remove item A. If you then try to find item B, you initially look at index I_A. Because that entry is now empty, you incorrectly conclude that item B isn't present.

One solution to this problem is to mark the item as deleted instead of resetting the array's entry to the empty value. For example, if the array holds 32-bit integers, you might use the value −2,147,483,648 to mean that an entry has no value and −2,147,483,647 to mean that the value has been deleted.

When you search for a value, you continue searching if you find the deleted value. When you insert a new value into the hash table, you can place it in a previously deleted entry if you find one in the probe sequence.

One drawback of this approach is that if you add and then remove many items, the table may become full of deleted entries. That will make searching for items slower. In the worst case, if the array is completely full of current and deleted items, you might have to search the entire array to find an item or to conclude that it isn't present.

If you delete many items, you can rehash the current values and reset the deleted array locations so that they hold the special empty value. If the array contains N items and has a reasonable fill percentage, this should take O(N) time.

Linear Probing

In *linear probing*, the collision-resolution policy adds a constant number, called the *stride* and usually set to 1, to each location to generate a probe sequence. Each time the algorithm adds 1, it takes the result modulus the size of the array, so the sequence wraps around to the beginning of the array if necessary.

For example, suppose the hash table's array contains 100 items and the hashing rule is as follows: N maps to location N mod 100. Then the probe sequence for the value 2,197 would visit locations 97, 98, 99, 0, 1, 2, and so forth.

Figure 8.2 shows a linear probe sequence for inserting the value 71.

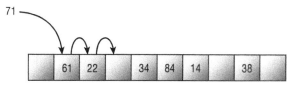

Figure 8.2: In linear probing, the algorithm adds a constant amount to locations to produce a probe sequence.

Here the table already contains several values when you want to add item 71. This table's array has 10 entries, so 71 maps to location 71 mod 10 = 1. That location already contains the value 61, so the algorithm moves to the next location in the value's probe sequence: location 2. That location is also occupied, so the algorithm moves to the next location in the probe sequence: location 3. That location is empty, so the algorithm places 71 there.

This method has the advantages that it is very simple and that a probe sequence will eventually visit every location in the array. Therefore, the algorithm can insert an item if any space is left in the array.

However, it has a disadvantage called *primary clustering,* an effect in which items added to the table tend to cluster to form large blocks of contiguous array entries that are all full. This is a problem because it leads to long probe sequences. If you try to add a new item that hashes to any of the entries in a cluster, the item's probe sequence will not find an empty location for the item until it crosses the whole cluster.

The LinearProbing example program shown in Figure 8.3 demonstrates primary clustering. This hash table's array has 101 entries and currently holds 50 values. If the items were evenly distributed within the array, the probe sequence for every item that is in the table would have a length of 1. The probe sequences for items that are not in the table would have lengths of 1 or 2, depending on whether the initial hashing mapped an item to an occupied location.

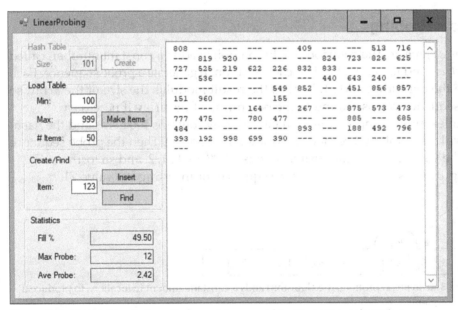

Figure 8.3: Hash tables that use linear probing are subject to primary clustering.

However, in Figure 8.3 the program shows that the hash table's average probe sequence length is 2.42, which is a bit above what you would get with an even distribution. The situation is worse with higher load factors.

NOTE   The program shown in Figure 8.3 is a solution to Exercise 8.3. See Appendix B for more information.

To understand how clusters form, consider an empty hash table with N entries. If you add a random number to the table, there's a $1/N$ chance that it will end up in any given position. Suppose it ends up in position K.

Now suppose that you add another random number to the table. There's a $1/N$ chance that this item will also map to position K, and in that case, linear probing will put the item in position $K + 1$. There's also a $1/N$ chance that the item will map directly to position $K + 1$. Between the two possibilities, there's a $2/N$ chance that the item will end up in position $K + 1$ and a small cluster will form.

Over time, more clusters will form. The larger a cluster is, the greater the probability that a new item will add to the end of the cluster. Eventually, clusters will expand until they merge and form bigger clusters. Soon the array is full of clusters and long probe sequences.

The following two sections describe ways you can reduce the primary clustering effect.

Quadratic Probing

The reason linear probing produces clusters is that items that map to any location within a cluster end up at the end of the cluster, making it larger. One way to prevent that is *quadratic probing*. Instead of adding a constant stride to locations to create a probe sequence, the algorithm adds the square of the number of locations it has tried to create the probe sequence.

In other words, if $K, K + 1, K + 2, K + 3, \ldots$ is the probe sequence created by linear probing, the sequence created by quadratic probing is $K, K + 1^2, K + 2^2, K + 3^2, \ldots$.

Now, if two items map to different positions in the same cluster, they don't follow the same probe sequences, so they don't necessarily end up adding to the cluster.

Figure 8.4 shows an example. Initially, the table has a cluster containing five items. The value 71 has the probe sequence $1, 1 + 1^2 = 2, 1 + 2^2 = 5, 1 + 3^2 = 10$, so it doesn't add to the cluster. The value 93 initially maps to the same cluster but has the probe sequence $3, 3 + 1^2 = 4, 3 + 2^2 = 7$, so it doesn't add to the cluster, either.

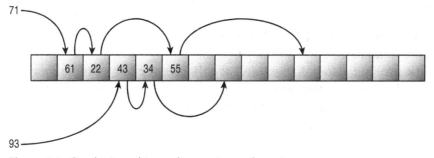

Figure 8.4: Quadratic probing reduces primary clustering.

The QuadraticProbing example program, shown in Figure 8.5, uses quadratic probing to store random values in a hash table. If you compare this figure to Figure 8.3, you'll see that quadratic probing gives a shorter average probe sequence length than linear probing. In this example, linear probing gave an average probe sequence length of 2.42 but quadratic probing gave an average probe sequence length of only 1.92.

NOTE   The program shown in Figure 8.5 is part of the solution to Exercise 8.4. See Appendix B for more information.

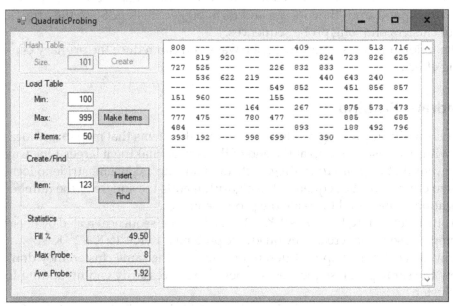

Figure 8.5: The average probe sequence length is shorter with quadratic probing than it is with linear probing.

Quadratic probing reduces primary clustering, but it can suffer from secondary clustering. In *secondary clustering*, values that map to the same initial position in the array follow the same probe sequence, so they create a cluster. This cluster is spread out through the array, but it still results in longer probe sequences for the items that map to the same initial position.

Quadratic probing also has the drawback that it may fail to find an empty entry for a value even if a few empty positions are left in the table. Because of how a quadratic probe sequence jumps farther and farther through the array, it may jump over an empty position and not find it.

Pseudorandom Probing

Pseudorandom probing is similar to linear probing, except that the stride is given by a pseudorandom function of the initially mapped location. In other words, if a value initially maps to position K, its probe sequence is $K, K + p, K + 2 \times p, \ldots$, where p is determined by a pseudorandom function of K.

Like quadratic probing, pseudorandom probing prevents primary clustering. Also like quadratic probing, pseudorandom probing is subject to secondary clustering, because values that map to the same initial position follow the same probe sequences.

Pseudorandom probing may also skip over some unused entries and fail to insert an item even though the table isn't completely full.

The result is similar to that of quadratic probing; you're just using a different method for building the probe sequence.

Double Hashing

The reason quadratic probing and pseudorandom probing suffer from secondary clustering is that values that map to the same initial location then follow the same probe sequence. You can reduce that effect if you make values that map to the same location follow different probe sequences.

Double hashing is similar to pseudorandom probing. However, instead of using a pseudorandom function of the initial location to create a stride value, it uses a second hashing function to map the original value to a stride.

For example, suppose the values A and B both initially map to position K. In pseudorandom probing, a pseudo-random function F_1 generates a stride $p = F_1(K)$. Then both values use the probe sequence $K, K + p, K + 2 \times p, K + 3 \times p, \ldots$.

In contrast, double hashing uses a pseudorandom hash function F_2 to map the original values A and B to two different stride values $p_A = F_2(A)$ and $p_B = F_2(B)$. The two probe sequences start at the same value K, but after that they are different.

Double hashing eliminates primary and secondary clustering. However, like pseudorandom probing, double hashing may skip some unused entries and fail to insert an item even though the table isn't completely full.

Ordered Hashing

In some applications, values are hashed once and then looked up many times. For example, a program that uses a dictionary, address book, or product lookup table might follow this approach. In that case, it is more important that the program be able to find values quickly than to insert them quickly.

A hash table with chaining can find items more quickly if its linked lists are sorted. When searching for an item, the algorithm can stop if it ever finds an item that is larger than the target item.

Similarly, you can arrange a hash table in an ordered manner. Suppose the probe sequence for value K visits array locations with values V_1, V_2, and so forth, where all of the V_i are less than K. In other words, all of the values along K's probe sequence are less than K.

Note that the values need not be in a strictly increasing order. For example, the probe sequence for the value 71 might encounter the values 61, 32, and then 71. That's okay as long as the probe sequence for 32 doesn't follow the same path so that it visits 61 before 32.

If you can arrange the array in this way, you can make searching for an item faster by stopping if you ever find a value greater than the target value.

The following pseudocode shows at a high level how you can find an item in an ordered hash table:

```
// Return the location of the key in the array or -1 if it is
// not present.
Integer: FindValue(Integer: array[], Integer: key)
    Integer: probe = <Initial location in key's probe sequence.>

    // Repeat forever.
    While true
        // See if we found the item.
        If (array[probe] == key) Then Return probe

        // See if we found an empty spot.
        If (array[probe] == EMPTY) Then Return -1

        // See if we passed where the item should be.
        If (array[probe] > key) Then Return -1

        // Try the next location in the probe sequence.
        probe = <Next location in key's probe sequence.>
    End While
End FindValue
```

The exact arrangements of the hash tables described so far depend on the order in which items are added to the table. For example, suppose a hash table's array has 10 entries and the hashing function maps the value K to K mod 10. If you add the values 11, 21, 31, 41 to the hash table, they are stored in that order in positions 1 through 4. However, if you add the same items in the order 41, 31, 21, 11, they are stored in the same positions, but in reverse order.

Suppose that you can add the values to the hash table in sorted order, smallest to largest. Then, when you add a value, if the table already holds any values in the new value's probe sequence, they must be smaller than the new value, because you're adding the values in sorted order. That means each probe sequence must be properly ordered so that you can search the table quickly.

Unfortunately, you often cannot add the items to a hash table in sorted order because you don't know that order when you start. For example, you may only add a few items at a time to the table over a long period. Fortunately, there is a way to create an ordered hash table no matter how you add the items.

To add an item, follow its probe sequence as usual. If you find an empty spot, insert the item and you're done. If you find a spot containing a value that is larger than the new value, replace it with the new value and then rehash the larger value.

As you rehash the larger value, you may encounter another, even larger value. If that happens, drop the item you're hashing in the new position and rehash the larger value. Continue the process until you find an empty spot for whatever item you're currently hashing.

The following pseudocode shows the process at a high level:

```
AddItem(Integer: array[], Integer: key)
    Integer: probe = <Initial location in key's probe sequence.>

    // Repeat forever.
    While true
        // See if we found an empty spot.
        If (array[probe] == EMPTY) Then
            array[probe] = key
            Return
        End If

        // See if we found a value greater than "key."
        If (array[probe] > key) Then
            // Place the key here and rehash the other item.
            Integer: temp = array[probe]
            array[probe] = key
            key = temp
        End If

        // Try the next location in the probe sequence.
        probe = <Next location in key's probe sequence.>
    End While
End AddItem
```

The final step inside the `While` loop sets `probe` equal to the next location in the current key's probe sequence. For linear probing, pseudorandom probing, and double hashing, you can figure out the next item in the probe sequence even if you switched the `key` value you're hashing for a larger value. For example, with double hashing, you can apply the second hashing function to the new `key` value to find the new probe sequence's stride. You can then use the new stride to follow the new item's probe sequence from that point.

That doesn't work for quadratic probing, because you would need to know how far the algorithm had searched the new key's probe sequence to get to that point.

The reason this method works is that you only replace values with smaller values. If you replace a value in an ordered probe sequence with a smaller value, the probe sequence is still ordered.

The only value that might still be in question is the new larger value you're rehashing. When you rehash that value, it ends up in a position that makes its probe sequence ordered.

Summary

Hash tables allow you to store and locate values very quickly. If a hash table has a reasonably low fill percentage, finding an item may require only a couple calculations.

It is important to maintain a reasonable fill percentage, however, because if a hash table becomes too full, its performance suffers. A lower fill percentage gives better performance but requires extra space that isn't used to hold data, so in some sense it is wasted. Too high a fill percentage can slow performance and increases the risk that the hash table will become full. This requires you to resize the hash table, which can take a considerable amount of time and memory.

This is a good example of a space/time trade-off that is common in algorithms. By using extra space, you can improve an algorithm's performance.

Ordered hashing provides another kind of trade-off. If you spend extra time up front building a hash table, later searching is much faster. When inserting a value, the program may find a value that is larger than the one it is inserting. In that case, it switches values and continues to rehash the larger one. One way to do that is recursion: making the insertion algorithm call itself. The next chapter discusses recursion in detail. It covers good and bad uses of recursion and explains how you can remove recursion from a program if deep call stacks or frequent recalculation of values cause problems.

Exercises

You can find the answers to these exercises in Appendix B. Asterisks indicate particularly difficult problems.

For the exercises that ask you to build a hash table, create an interface similar to Figure 8.6. The example shown in the figure sets each item's value to its key value with a v added in front so that you can tell it's a string. It displays an entry's value in the format [key:value].

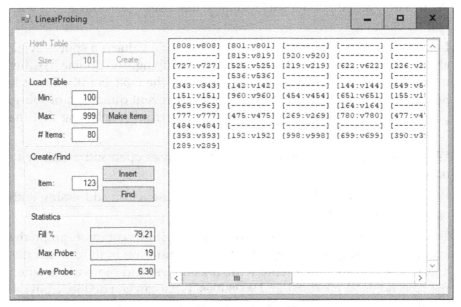

Figure 8.6: This interface lets you build and test hash tables.

The Create button creates a new hash table. The Make Items button lets you add many random items to the hash table all at once. The Insert and Find buttons add or find a single item. After each change to the table or its data, display the number of keys per bucket for chaining algorithms or the fill percentage for open addressing algorithms. Also display the maximum and average probe length when you try to find all of the values between the minimum and maximum values used to fill the table.

1. Write a program that implements a hash table with chaining.

2. Modify the program you wrote for Exercise 1 to use sorted chains. Compare the average probe lengths of the two programs when the hash tables use 10 buckets and hold 100 items.

3. Graph the average probe sequence length for the programs you built for Exercises 1 and 2 when the hash tables use 10 buckets and hold 50, 100, 150, 200, and 250 items. What can you deduce from the graph?

4. Write a program that builds a hash table that uses open addressing with linear probing.

5. Write a program that builds a hash table that uses open addressing with quadratic probing.

6. Write a program that builds a hash table that uses open addressing with pseudorandom probing.

7. Write a program that builds a hash table that uses open addressing with double hashing.

8. Linear probing always finds an empty spot for a value if a spot is available, but quadratic probing, pseudorandom probing, and double hashing may all skip empty entries and conclude that the table is full when it is not. How can you pick the table size N to prevent quadratic probing, pseudorandom probing, and double hashing from concluding that the hash table is full even if it is not?

9. Write a program that builds a hash table that uses open addressing with ordered quadratic hashing.

10. Write a program that builds a hash table that uses open addressing with ordered double hashing.

11. To see how the different open addressing algorithms compare, graph the average probe sequence length for the programs you built for Exercises 4, 5, 6, 7, 9, and 10. Use a table with 101 entries, and plot values when the table holds 50, 60, 70, 80, and 90 values. What can you deduce from the graph?

12. Suppose a hash table uses buckets with sorted chaining. To insert a key, you need to search its bucket to verify that it is not present. If the table uses B buckets and contains N items, that takes roughly $O(N/B/2)$ steps on average. After you verify that the key is not present, you need to insert it in the correct position in its chain, which takes another $O(N/B/2)$ steps. Why is this faster than the $O(N/B)$ steps needed to insert an item if the chains are not sorted?

13. Suppose you want to double the number of buckets used by a hash table that uses buckets with chaining. How would you split a bucket in two? What if the chains are sorted?

14. Suppose that you're using a hash table with open addressing and you mark removed entries with a special value such as –2,147,483,647. When you insert a new item, you can place it in a spot that has been marked as deleted if you find such a spot. Now suppose you add and remove many items so that the table is full of marked entries. Why does that slow down inserting new items?

15. In open addressing with linear probing, what is the probability that two random values will land adjacent to each other and start a small cluster if the table is initially empty?

16. When you insert an item in an ordered hash table that uses open address-ing, you sometimes find a larger value along an item's probe sequence. In that case, you deposit the new item and rehash the larger value. How do you know that this process will eventually stop? What is the largest number of items that you might move during this process?

17. In ordered hashing, what happens if the algorithm is unable to find an empty position to add a new item even if the table isn't full?

Recursion

Recursion occurs when a method calls itself. The recursion can be direct (when the method calls itself) or indirect (when the method calls some other method that then calls the first method).

Recursion can also be single (when the method calls itself once) or multiple (when the method calls itself multiple times).

Recursive algorithms can be confusing because people don't naturally think recursively. For example, to paint a fence, you probably would start at one end and start painting until you reach the other end. It is less intuitive to think about breaking the fence into left and right halves and then solving the problem by recursively painting each half.

However, some problems are naturally recursive. They have a structure that allows a recursive algorithm to easily keep track of its progress and find a solution. For example, trees are naturally recursive because branches divide into smaller branches that divide into still smaller branches and so on. For that reason, algorithms that build, draw, and search trees are often recursive.

This chapter explains some useful algorithms that are naturally recursive. Some of these algorithms are useful by themselves, but learning how to use recursion in general is far more important than learning how to solve a single problem. Once you understand recursion, you can find it in many programming situations.

Recursion is not always the best solution, however, so this chapter also explains how you can remove recursion from a program when recursion might cause poor performance.

Basic Algorithms

Some problems have naturally recursive solutions. The following sections describe several naturally recursive algorithms for calculating factorials, finding Fibonacci numbers, solving the rod-cutting problem, and moving disks in the Tower of Hanoi puzzle.

These relatively straightforward algorithms demonstrate important concepts used by recursive algorithms. Once you understand them, you'll be ready to move on to the more complicated algorithms described in the rest of this chapter.

Factorial

The factorial of a number N is written N! and pronounced "N factorial." You can define the `factorial` function recursively as follows:

$$0! = 1$$
$$N! = N \times (N-1)!$$

For example, the following equations show how you can use this definition to calculate 3!:

$$3! = 3 \times 2! = 3 \times 2 \times 1! = 3 \times 2 \times 1 \times 0! = 3 \times 2 \times 1 \times 1$$

This definition leads to the following simple recursive algorithm:

```
Integer: Factorial(Integer: n)
    If (n == 0) Then Return 1
    Return n * Factorial(n - 1)
End Factorial
```

First, if the input value n equals 0, the algorithm returns 1. This corresponds to the first equation that defines the `factorial` function. That equation is called the *base case*. It represents the situation where the algorithm does not call itself recursively.

NOTE   It is important that any recursive algorithm have a base case to prevent it from recursively calling itself forever.

Otherwise, if the input is not 0, the algorithm returns the number n times the factorial of n - 1. This step corresponds to the second equation that defines the `factorial` function.

This is a simple algorithm, but it demonstrates two important features that all recursive algorithms must have.

- Each time the method executes, it reduces the current problem to a smaller instance of the same problem and then calls itself to solve the smaller problem. In this example, the method reduces the problem of computing n! to the problem of computing (n - 1)! and then multiplying by n.

- The recursion must eventually stop. In this example, the input parameter n decreases with each recursive call until it equals 0. At that point, the algorithm reaches its base case, returns 1, and does not call itself recursively, so the process stops.

Note that even this simple algorithm can create problems. If a program calls the `Factorial` method, passing it the parameter –1, the recursion never ends. Instead, the algorithm begins the following series of calculations:

$$-1! =$$
$$-1 \times -2! =$$
$$-1 \times -2 \times -3! =$$
$$-1 \times -2 \times -3 \times -4! = \ldots$$

One method that some programmers use to prevent this is to change the first statement in the algorithm to `If (n <= 0) Then Return 1`. Now if the algorithm is called with a negative parameter, it simply returns 1.

> **NOTE** From a software engineering point of view, this may not be the best solution because it hides a problem in the program that called the algorithm. It also returns the misleading value 1 when the true factorial of a negative number is undefined.
>
> To detect problems in the calling code quickly, it may be better to check the value explicitly to make sure that it is at least 0 and raise an error or throw an exception if it is not.

Analyzing the run-time performance of recursive algorithms is sometimes tricky, but it is easy for this particular algorithm. On input N, the Factorial algorithm calls itself $N + 1$ times to evaluate $N!, (N - 1)!, (N - 2)!, \ldots, 0!$. Each call to the algorithm does a small constant amount of work, so the total run time is $O(N)$.

Because the algorithm calls itself N + 1 times, the maximum depth of recursion is also O(N). In some programming environments, the maximum possible depth of recursion may be limited, so this might cause a problem.

SERIOUS STACK SPACE

Normally, a computer allocates two areas of memory for a program: the stack and the heap.

The stack is used to store information about method calls. When a piece of code calls a method, information about the call is placed on the stack. When the method returns, that information is popped off the stack, so the program can resume execution just after the point where it called the method. (The stack is the same kind of stack described in Chapter 5.) The list of methods that were called to get to a particular point of execution is called the *call stack*.

The heap is another piece of memory that the program can use to create variables and perform calculations.

Typically, the stack is much smaller than the heap. The stack usually is large enough for normal programs because your code typically doesn't include methods calling other methods to a very great depth. However, recursive algorithms can sometimes create extremely deep call stacks and exhaust the stack space, causing the program to crash.

For this reason, it's important to evaluate the maximum depth of recursion that a recursive algorithm requires in addition to studying its run time and memory requirements.

The `factorial` function grows very quickly, so there's a practical limit to how big N can be in a normal program. For example, $20! \approx 2.4 \times 10^{18}$, and 21! is too big to fit in a 64-bit long integer. If a program never calculates values larger than 20!, the depth of recursion can be only 20 and there should be no problem with stack space.

If you really need to calculate larger factorials, you can use other data types that can hold even larger values. For example, a 64-bit double-precision floating-point number can hold $170! \approx 7.3 \times 10^{306}$. Some data types, such as the .NET `BigInteger` type and Python's integer types, can hold arbitrarily large numbers. In those cases, the maximum depth of recursion could be a problem. The section "Tail Recursion Removal" later in this chapter explains how you can prevent this kind of deep recursion from exhausting the stack space and crashing the program.

Fibonacci Numbers

The Fibonacci numbers (named after the Italian mathematician Leonardo of Pisa, c. 1170–c. 1250, who was later known as Fibonacci) are defined by these equations:

Fibonacci(0) = 0

Fibonacci(1) = 1

Fibonacci(n) = Fibonacci(n − 1) + Fibonacci(n − 2) for n > 1

To calculate a new Fibonacci number, you add the two preceding values. For example, the first 12 Fibonacci numbers are 0, 1, 1, 2, 3, 5, 8, 13, 21, 34, 55, 89.

NOTE   Some people define Fibonacci(0) = 1 and Fibonacci(1) = 1. This gives the same values as the definition shown here, just skipping the value 0.

The recursive definition leads to the following recursive algorithm:

```
Integer: Fibonacci(Integer: n)
    If (n <= 1) Then Return n
    Return Fibonacci(n - 1) + Fibonacci(n - 2);
End Fibonacci
```

If the input n is 0 or 1, the algorithm returns 0 or 1. (If the input is 1 or less, the algorithm just returns the input.)

Otherwise, if the input is greater than 1, the algorithm calls itself for inputs n - 1 and n - 2, adds them together, and returns the result.

This recursive algorithm is reasonably easy to understand but is very slow. For example, to calculate Fibonacci(6) the program must calculate Fibonacci(5) and Fibonacci(4). But before it can calculate Fibonacci(5), the program must calculate Fibonacci(4) and Fibonacci(3). Here Fibonacci(4) is being calculated twice. As the recursion continues, the same values must be calculated many times. For large values of N, Fibonacci(N) calculates the same values an enormous number of times, making the program take a very long time.

Figure 9.1 shows the Fibonacci algorithm's call tree when it evaluates Fibonacci(6). Each node in the tree represents a call to the algorithm with the indicated number as a parameter. The figure shows, for example, that the call to Fibonacci(6) in the top node calls Fibonacci(5) and Fibonacci(4). If you look at the figure, you can see that the tree is filled with duplicated calls. For example, Fibonacci(0) is calculated five times, and Fibonacci(1) is calculated eight times.

This algorithm's run time is more complicated than that of the Factorial algorithm because this algorithm is multiply-recursive. To understand the run time, suppose T(N) is the run time for the algorithm on input N. If N > 1, the algorithm calculates Fibonacci(N − 1) and Fibonacci(N − 2), performs an extra step to add those values, and returns the result. That means T(N) = T(N − 1) + T(N − 2) + 1.

This is slightly greater than T(N − 1) + T(N − 2). If you ignore the extra constant 1 at the end, this is the same as the definition of the Fibonacci function, so the algorithm has a run time at least as large as the function itself.

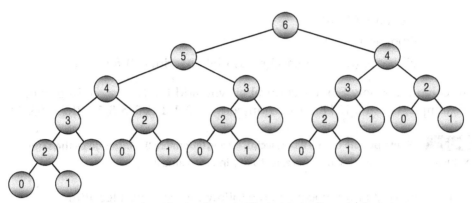

Figure 9.1: The Fibonacci algorithm's call tree is filled with duplicated calculations.

The Fibonacci function doesn't grow as quickly as the Factorial function, but it still grows very quickly. For example, Fibonacci(92) $\approx 7.5 \times 10^{18}$ and Fibonacci(93) doesn't fit in a long integer. That means you can calculate up to Fibonacci(92) with a maximum depth of recursion of 92, which shouldn't be a problem for most programming environments.

However, the run time of the Fibonacci algorithm grows quickly. On my computer, calculating Fibonacci(44) takes more than a minute, so calculating much larger values of the function is impractical anyway. (Don't worry. All is not lost. Techniques later in this chapter explain how you can calculate much larger Fibonacci numbers.)

Rod-Cutting

In the *rod-cutting problem*, the goal is to cut a wooden or metal rod into pieces. Pieces of different lengths have different values, so you must decide the best way to cut the rod to maximize the total value.

> **NOTE**   The rod-cutting problem assumes that the rod and pieces all have integer lengths. I'll also assume that the piece values are integers, although you could use floating-point values without changing the solution.

For example, suppose the following table shows the values of pieces with different lengths:

Length:	1	2	3	4	5	6	7	8
Value:	1	5	8	9	10	17	17	20

Now suppose that the original rod is 10 inches long. You could cut it into ten 1-inch pieces. Each 1-inch piece has a value of 1, so the divided rod would have a total value of $10 \times 1 = 10$.

Another solution would be to divide the rod into two 5-inch pieces. Each of those would have a value of 10, so the divided rod would have a total value of $2 \times 10 = 20$.

There are many other ways that you could divide the rod. You could divide the rod into pieces with lengths $1 + 2 + 7, 3 + 3 + 4, 4 + 6$, or any other combination of lengths that add up to 10.

The following sections describe three approaches that you can take to find the best combination of cuts to maximize the total value.

Brute Force

In the *brute-force* approach, you simply examine every possible combination of cuts, evaluate their values, and pick the one that gives the best result. If the rod initially has length N, then there are $N - 1$ places where you could make cuts. At each of those places, you either make a cut or not, so there are 2^{N-1} possible combinations of cuts.

In the brute-force solution, you examine all 2^{N-1} possible cuts, evaluate their total values, and pick the best one. Because this requires you to examine 2^{N-1} possible solutions, it has a run time of $O(2^N)$.

This approach includes some duplication. For example, the cuts $1 + 1 + 8, 1 + 8 + 1$, and $8 + 1 + 1$ all produce pieces with the same lengths. Even if you eliminate duplicates, however, the number of possible cuts is still exponential, so this is a relatively slow approach.

Recursion

There are many ways that you could enumerate all of the possible cuts to use in the brute-force approach. One method is to use recursion. Instead of trying to enumerate all possible cuts for a rod of a given length, you examine each possible single cut and then recursively find the optimal cuts for the two pieces on either side of that cut.

For example, suppose that the initial rod has length 10. You would consider the cuts $0 + 10, 1 + 9, 2 + 8, 3 + 7, 4 + 6$, and $5 + 5$. You don't need to consider making any other single because they give you the same results as their reverses. For example, you don't need to consider $7 + 3$, because it gives you the same result as $3 + 7$.

For each off those single cuts, you recursively consider the best way to divide the two pieces. For example, when you examine the $4 + 6$ cut, you recursively ask the method to find the optimal cuts for rods of lengths 4 and 6.

At this point, you can write an algorithm that uses recursion to find optimal cuts. Suppose `values` is an array giving the values of pieces of different lengths.

For example, `values[2]` is the value of a piece with length 2. The following pseudocode shows a recursive method for finding optimal cuts:

```
FindOptimalCuts(Integer: length, List Of Integer: values,
    Output Integer: bestValue, Output List Of Integer: bestCuts)

    // Assume we make no cuts.
    bestValue = values[length]
    bestCuts = New List Of Integer()
    bestCuts.Add(length)

    // Try possible single cuts.
    For i = 1 to length / 2
        // Try pieces with lengths i and length - i.
        Integer: value1, value2
        List Of Integer: cuts1, cuts2
        FindOptimalCuts(i, values, Output value1, Output cuts1)
        FindOptimalCuts(length - i, values,
            Output value2, Output cuts2)

        // See if this is an improvement.
        If (value1 + value2 > bestValue) Then
            bestValue = value1 + value2
            bestCuts = cuts1
            cuts1.AddRange(cuts2)
        End If
    Next i
End FindOptimalCuts
```

The algorithm first considers the case where the rod is not cut, in which case the full rod is worth `values[length]`.

Next, the algorithm loops through possible lengths for the first piece of a single cut. As I mentioned in the preceding section, the code only needs to check cuts where the first piece has length between 1 and `length / 2` because other cuts are reversed versions of those.

Each time through the loop, the algorithm recursively calls itself to find optimal cuts for the two pieces. If the sum of the two piece values is greater than the current best value, the algorithm saves the new value.

After it has examined all of the possible single cuts, the algorithm returns the greatest value that it found.

Figure 9.2 shows the algorithm's call tree when the initial rod has length 5. Notice that the calls come in pairs that evaluate the two pieces that form a single cut.

If you study the tree shown in Figure 9.2, you'll see that it contains a lot of duplication. For example, the algorithm is called twice for pieces of length 3, five times for pieces of length 2, and a whopping 14 times for pieces of length 1.

This is the same problem that spoiled the performance of the recursive Fibonacci number calculation. In fact, if you compare this tree to the branch of the tree in Figure 9.1 that calculates Fibonacci(5), you'll see that the problem is even larger here. My computer takes around 15 seconds to solve the problem for a rod of length 30, so this algorithm is too slow to calculate values for much longer rods.

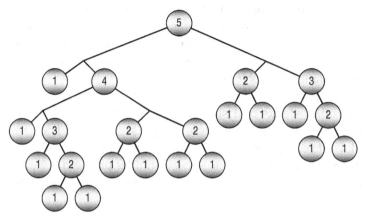

Figure 9.2: Calls to the `RecursiveFindOptimalCuts` algorithm come in pairs.

Tower of Hanoi

Chapter 5 introduced the Tower of Hanoi puzzle, in which a stack of disks sits on one of three pegs. The goal is to transfer the disks from their starting peg to another peg by moving them one at a time and never placing a disk on top of a smaller disk. Figure 9.3 shows the puzzle from the side.

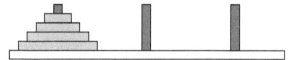

Figure 9.3: In the Tower of Hanoi puzzle, the goal is to move disks from one peg to another without placing a disk on top of a smaller disk.

Trying to solve the puzzle with a grand plan can be confusing, but there is a simple recursive solution. Instead of trying to think of solving the problem as a whole, you can reduce the problem size and then recursively solve the rest of the problem. The following pseudocode uses this approach to provide a simple recursive solution:

```
// Move the top n disks from peg from_peg to peg to_peg
// using other_peg to hold disks temporarily as needed.
TowerOfHanoi(Peg: from_peg, Peg: to_peg, Peg: other_peg, Integer: n)
    // Recursively move the top n - 1 disks from from_peg to other_peg.
    If (n > 1) Then TowerOfHanoi(from_peg, other_peg, to_peg, n - 1)

    // Move the last disk from from_peg to to_peg.
    <Move the top disk from from_peg to to_peg.>

    // Recursively move the top n - 1 disks back
    // from other_peg to to_peg.
```

```
        If (n > 1) Then TowerOfHanoi(other_peg, to_peg, from_peg, n - 1)
End TowerOfHanoi
```

The first step requires faith in the algorithm that seems to beg the question of how the algorithm works. That step moves the top n – 1 disks from the original peg to the peg that isn't the destination peg. It does this by recursively calling the TowerOfHanoi algorithm. At this point, how can you know that the algorithm works and can handle the smaller problem?

The answer is that the method recursively calls itself repeatedly if needed to move smaller and smaller stacks of disks. At some point in the sequence of recursive calls, the algorithm is called to move only a single disk. Then the algorithm doesn't call itself recursively. It simply moves the disk and returns.

The key is that each recursive call is used to solve a smaller problem. Eventually, the problem size is so small that the algorithm can solve it without calling itself recursively.

As each recursive call returns, the algorithm's calling instance moves a single disk and then calls itself recursively again to move the smaller stack of disks to its final destination peg.

Figure 9.4 shows the series of high-level steps needed to move the stack from the first peg to the second. The first step recursively moves all but the bottom disk from the first peg to the third. The second step moves the bottom disk from the first peg to the second. The final step recursively moves the disks from the third peg to the second.

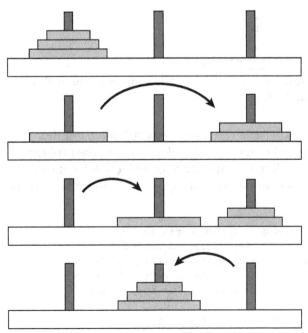

Figure 9.4: To move n disks, recursively move the upper n – 1 disks to the temporary peg. Then move the remaining disk to the destination peg. Finally, move the n – 1 upper disks from the temporary peg to the destination peg.

Figure 9.5 shows the entire sequence of moves needed to transfer a stack of three disks from the first peg to the second.

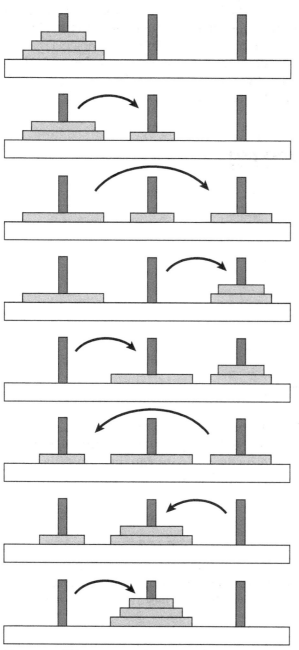

Figure 9.5: This sequence of steps transfers three disks from the first peg to the second.

To analyze the algorithm's run time, let T(N) be the number of steps required to move N disks from one peg to another. Clearly $T(1) = 1$, because it takes one step to move a single disk from one peg to another.

For $N > 0$, $T(n) = T(N-1) + 1 + T(N-1) = 2 \times T(N-1) + 1$. If you ignore the extra constant 1, $T(N) = 2 \times T(N-1)$, so the function has exponential run time $O(2^N)$.

To see this in another way, you can make a table similar to Table 9.1, giving the number of steps for various values of N. In the table, each value with $N > 1$ is calculated from the previous value by using the formula $T(N) = 2 \times T(N-1) + 1$. If you study the values, you'll see that $T(N) = 2^N - 1$.

Table 9.1: Run Times for the Tower of Hanoi Puzzle

N	T(N)
1	1
2	3
3	7
4	15
5	31
6	63
7	127
8	255
9	511
10	1023

Like the Fibonacci algorithm, the maximum depth of recursion for this algorithm on input N is N. Also like the Fibonacci algorithm, this algorithm's run time increases very quickly as N increases, so the run time limits the effective problem size long before the maximum depth of recursion does.

Graphical Algorithms

Several interesting graphical algorithms take advantage of recursion to produce intricate pictures with surprisingly little code. Although these algorithms are short, generally they are more confusing than the basic algorithms described in the previous sections.

Koch Curves

The Koch curve (named after Swedish mathematician Helge von Koch, 1870–1924) is good example of a particular kind of *self-similar fractal*, a curve in which pieces of the curve resemble the curve as a whole. These fractals start with an *initiator*, a curve that determines the fractal's basic shape. At each level of recursion, some or all of the initiator is replaced by a suitably scaled, rotated, and translated version of a curve called the *generator*. At the next level of recursion, pieces of the generator are then similarly replaced by new versions of the generator.

The simplest Koch curve uses a line segment as an initiator. Then, at each level of recursion, the segment is replaced with four segments that are one-third of the original segment's length. The first segment is in the direction of the original segment, the next is rotated −60 degrees, the third is rotated 120 degrees, and the final segment is in the original direction. Figure 9.6 shows this curve's initiator (top) and generator (bottom).

Figure 9.6: This initiator (top) and generator (bottom) create the Koch curve.

At the next level of recursion, the program takes each of the segments in the generator and replaces them with a new copy of the generator. Figure 9.7 shows the curve with levels of recursion 0 through 5.

Looking at Figure 9.7, you can see why the curve is called self-similar. Parts of the curve look like smaller versions of the whole curve.

Let pt1, pt2, pt3, pt4, and pt5 be the points connected by the segments in the generator on the bottom in Figure 9.6. The following pseudocode shows how you might draw Koch curves:

```
// Draw a Koch curve with the given depth starting at point p1
// and going the distance "length" in the direction "angle."
DrawKoch(Integer: depth, Point: pt1, Float: angle, Float: length)
    If (depth == 0) Then
        <Draw the line segment>
    Else
        <Find the points pt2, pt3, and pt4.>
```

```
            // Recursively draw the pieces of the curve.
            DrawKoch(depth - 1, pt1, angle, length / 3);
            DrawKoch(depth - 1, pt2, angle - 60, length / 3);
            DrawKoch(depth - 1, pt3, angle + 60, length / 3);
            DrawKoch(depth - 1, pt4, angle, length / 3);
        End If
    End DrawKoch
```

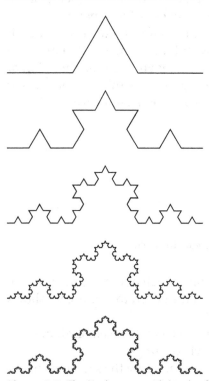

Figure 9.7: The Koch curve with levels of recursion 0 through 5 produces these shapes.

If depth is 0, the algorithm simply draws a line segment starting at point p1 going in direction angle for the distance length. (Exactly how you draw the segment depends on your programming environment.)

If depth is greater than 0, the algorithm finds the points pt2, pt3, and pt4. It then draws a line segment starting at point pt1 going in direction angle for one-third of the original distance. From the new end point at pt2, it turns 60 degrees left and draws another segment one-third of the original distance. From the new end point at pt3, it turns 120 degrees right (to an angle 60 degrees greater than the original angle) and draws another segment one-third of the original distance. Finally, from the last end point, pt4, the algorithm draws a segment at the original angle for one-third of the original distance.

If the depth is greater than 0, the algorithm calls itself recursively four times. If $T(N)$ is the number of steps the algorithm uses for depth N, $T(N) = 4 \times T(N - 1) + C$ for some constant C. If you ignore the constant, $T(N) = 4 \times T(N - 1)$, so the algorithm has run time $O(4^N)$.

The maximum depth of recursion required to draw a depth N Koch curve is only N. Like the Fibonacci and Tower of Hanoi algorithms, this algorithm's run time grows so quickly that the maximum depth of recursion should never be a problem.

If you connect the edges of three Koch curves so that their initiators form a triangle, the result is called a *Koch snowflake*. Figure 9.8 shows a level 3 Koch snowflake.

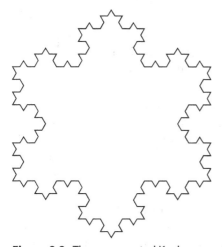

Figure 9.8: Three connected Koch curves form a Koch snowflake.

Hilbert Curve

Like the Koch curve, the Hilbert curve starts with a simple initiator curve. To move to a deeper level of recursion, the algorithm breaks the initiator into pieces and uses an appropriately rotated smaller version of the Hilbert curve to draw the pieces. (The curve was named after German mathematician David Hilbert, 1862–1943.)

Figure 9.9 shows level 0, 1, and 2 Hilbert curves. In the level 1 and 2 curves, the lines connecting the lower-level curves are gray so that you can see how the pieces are connected to build the higher-level curves.

The following pseudocode shows the remarkably simple Hilbert curve algorithm:

```
// Draw the Hilbert initially moving in the direction <dx, dy>.
Hilbert(Integer: depth, Float: dx, Float: dy)
    If (depth > 0) Then Hilbert(depth - 1, dy, dx)
```

```
    DrawRelative(dx, dy)
    If (depth > 0) Then Hilbert(depth - 1, dx, dy)
    DrawRelative(dy, dx)
    If (depth > 0) Then Hilbert(depth - 1, dx, dy)
    DrawRelative(-dx, -dy)
    If (depth > 0) Then Hilbert(depth - 1, -dy, -dx)
End Hilbert
```

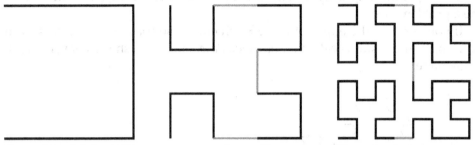

Figure 9.9: High-level Hilbert curves are made up of four connected lower-level curves.

The algorithm assumes that the program has defined a current drawing location. The DrawRelative method draws from that current position to a new point relative to that position and updates the current position. For example, if the current position is (10, 20), the statement DrawRelative(0, 10) would draw a line segment between (10, 20) and (10, 30) and leave the new current position at (10, 30).

If the depth of recursion is greater than 0, the algorithm calls itself recursively to draw a version of the curve with one lower level of recursion and with the dx and dy parameters switched so that the smaller curve is rotated 90 degrees. If you compare the level 0 and level 1 curves shown in Figure 9.9, you can see that the level 0 curve drawn at the beginning of the level 1 curve is rotated.

Next the program draws a line segment to connect the first lower-level curve to the next one.

The algorithm then calls itself again to draw the next subcurve. This time it keeps dx and dy in their original positions so that the second subcurve is not rotated.

The algorithm draws another connecting line segment and then calls itself, again keeping dx and dy in their original positions so that the third subcurve is not rotated.

The algorithm draws another connecting line segment and then calls itself a final time. This time it replaces dx with -dy and dy with -dx so that the smaller curve is rotated –90 degrees.

Sierpiński Curve

Like the Koch and Hilbert curves, the Sierpiński curve (named after Polish mathematician Wacław Sierpiński, 1882–1969) draws a higher-level curve by using lower-level copies of itself. Unlike the other curves, however, the simplest method of drawing a Sierpiński curve uses four indirectly recursive routines that call each other rather than a single routine.

Figure 9.10 shows level 0, 1, 2, and 3 Sierpiński curves. In the level 1, 2, and 3 curves, the lines connecting the lower-level curves are gray so that you can see how the pieces are connected to build the higher-level curves.

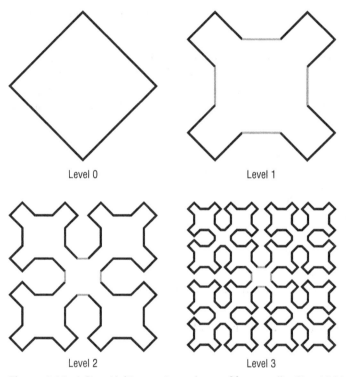

Figure 9.10: A Sierpiński curve is made up of four smaller Sierpiński curves.

Figure 9.11 shows the pieces of the level 1 Sierpiński curve. The curve consists of four sides that are drawn by four different routines and connected by line segments. The four routines draw curves that move the current drawing position in the right, down, left, and up directions. For example, the Right routine draws a series of segments that leaves the drawing position moved to the right. In Figure 9.11, the connecting line segments are drawn in gray.

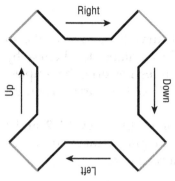

Figure 9.11: The level 1 Sierpiński curve is made up of pieces that go right, down, left, and up.

To draw a higher-level version of one of the pieces of the curve, the algorithm breaks that piece into smaller pieces that have a lower level. For example, Figure 9.12 shows how you can make a depth 2 Right piece out of four depth 1 pieces. If you study Figure 9.10, you can figure out how to make the other pieces.

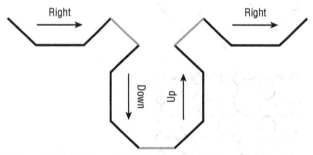

Figure 9.12: The level 2 Right piece is made up of pieces that go right, down, up, and right.

The following pseudocode shows the main algorithm:

```
// Draw a Sierpiński curve.
Sierpinski(Integer: depth, Float: dx, Float: dy)
    SierpRight(depth, dx, dy)
    DrawRelative(dx, dy)
    SierpDown(depth, dx, dy)
    DrawRelative(-dx, dy)
    SierpLeft(depth, dx, dy)
    DrawRelative(-dx, -dy)
    SierpUp(depth, dx, dy)
    DrawRelative(dx, -dy)
End Sierpiński
```

The algorithm calls the methods `SierpRight`, `SierpDown`, `SierpLeft`, and `SierpUp` to draw the pieces of the curve. Between those calls, the algorithm calls

DrawRelative to draw the line segments connecting the pieces of the curve. As was the case with the Hilbert curve, the DrawRelative method draws from that current position to a new point relative to that position and updates the current position. These calls to DrawRelative are the only places where the algorithm actually does any drawing.

The following pseudocode shows the SierpRight algorithm:

```
// Draw right across the top.
SierpRight(Integer: depth, Float: dx, Float: dy)
    If (depth > 0) Then
        depth = depth - 1

        SierpRight(depth, dx, dy)
        DrawRelative(dx, dy)
        SierpDown(depth, dx, dy)
        DrawRelative(2 * dx, 0)
        SierpUp(depth, dx, dy)
        DrawRelative(dx, -dy)
        SierpRight(depth, dx, dy)
    End If
End SierpRight
```

You can follow this method's progress in Figure 9.12. First this method calls SierpRight to draw a piece of the curve moving to the right at a smaller depth of recursion. It then draws a segment down and to the right to connect to the next piece of the curve.

Next the method calls SierpDown to draw a piece of the curve moving downward at a smaller depth of recursion. It draws a segment to the right to connect to the next piece of the curve.

The method then calls SierpUp to draw a piece of the curve moving upward at a smaller depth of recursion. It draws a segment up and to the right to connect to the next piece of the curve.

The method finishes by calling SierpRight to draw the final piece of the curve moving to the right at a smaller depth of recursion.

Figuring out the other methods that draw pieces of the Sierpiński curve is left as an exercise for you.

Because the Sierpiński methods call each other multiple times, they are multiply and indirectly recursive. Coming up with a nonrecursive solution from scratch would be difficult.

APPROXIMATE ROUTING

The Hilbert and Siepiński curves are two examples of *space-filling curves*. Intuitively, a space-filling curve is one that, in the limit, approaches arbitrarily closely to every point in the area that it covers. For example, suppose that you draw a Hilbert curve in the square $-1 \le x, y \le 1$. If you pick any point in that rectangle, then for a sufficiently high level of recursion, the Hilbert curve passes within any desired distance of that point. (One of my old math professors used to say, "Pick *any* distance. Could be one over infinity billion! The curve will pass that close to the point.)

Space-filling curves such as these provide a simple method of approximate routing. Suppose that you need to visit a group of stops in a city. If you draw a Hilbert or Sierpiński curve over the map of the city, then you can visit the stops in the order in which they are visited by the curve. (You don't need to drive along the curve. You just use it to generate the ordering.)

The result probably won't be optimal, but it probably will be reasonably good. You can use it as a starting point for the traveling salesperson problem (TSP) described in Chapter 17, "Complexity Theory."

Gaskets

A *gasket* is another type of self-similar fractal. To draw a gasket, you start with a geometric shape such as a triangle or square. If the desired depth of recursion is 0, the method simply fills the shape. If the desired depth is greater than 0, the method subdivides the shape into smaller, similar shapes and then calls itself recursively to draw some but not all of them.

For example, Figure 9.13 shows depth 0 through 3 triangular gaskets that are often called Sierpiński gaskets (or Sierpiński sieves or Sierpiński triangles).

Figure 9.13: To create a Sierpiński gasket, divide a triangle into four pieces and recursively color the three at the triangle's corners.

Figure 9.14 shows a square gasket that is often called the Sierpiński carpet. (Yes, named after the same Sierpiński whose name is attached to the Sierpiński curve. He studied many of these sorts of shapes, so his name is attached to several of them.)

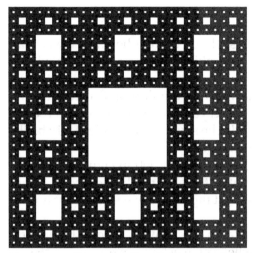

Figure 9.14: To create a Sierpiński carpet, divide a square into nine pieces, remove the center one, and recursively color the rest.

Writing low-level pseudocode to draw the Sierpiński gasket and carpet are left as Exercises 10 and 11 at the end of this chapter.

The Skyline Problem

In the *skyline problem*, you are given a collection of rectangles that have a common baseline, and you need to find an outline for them. Figure 9.15 shows a collection of rectangles on the left and their skyline on the right. The small circles show places where the skyline moves to a new height.

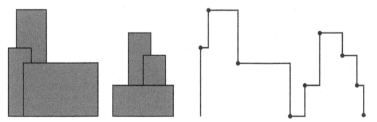

Figure 9.15: The skyline problem produces an outline similar to the outline of skyscrapers in a city.

The following two sections describe different approaches to the skyline problem.

Lists

One relatively straightforward approach to solving this problem is to create a `HeightChange` object to represent places where a rectangle begins or ends. You can then sort those objects by their X coordinates and loop through them in order from left to right.

Each time you reach a `HeightChange` object, you update the skyline's current height appropriately. For example, if the skyline's current height is lower than the height given by the new `HeightChange` object, you increase the skyline's current height.

Unfortunately, if the new height is lower than the skyline's current height, you have some extra work to do. In that case, you need to know which rectangles have been started but not yet finished. The skyline's new height will be the largest height of any of those "active" rectangles.

For example, consider the group of rectangles on the left in Figure 9.15. When the tallest rectangle ends, the new height of the skyline should be the height of the short, wide rectangle because that rectangle has been started but not yet finished.

You can keep track of the active rectangles in several ways. One of the simplest is to add each rectangle to an active list when you reach its starting `HeightChange` object. When you need to find the tallest active rectangle, you simply loop through the list. Later, when you reach an active rectangle's ending `HeightChange` object, you remove it from the list.

If there are N rectangles, then the algorithm needs O(N) `HeightChange` objects to represent the places where the rectangles start and stop. Sorting those objects takes O(N log N) steps.

The algorithm then processes the O(N) sorted objects. Each time an object's height is smaller than the skyline's current height, you need to search through the list of active objects. That list could hold up to O(N) objects at a time, so that step might take up to O(N) steps. Because the algorithm performs that O(N) search for O(N) objects, the total time for the processing step is $O(N^2)$.

That makes the total time to build the skyline $O(N) + O(\log N) + O(N^2) = O(N^2)$.

The following pseudocode shows the algorithm at a high level:

```
List<Point>: MakeSkyline(List<Rectangle>: rectangles)
    <Make HeightChange objects to represent each rectangle's
     start and stop.>
    <Place the HeightChange objects in a list named changes.>
    <Sort the changes list.>

    <Make an empty list activeTops to hold active rectangles.>
    Integer: currentY = <ground height>
    For Each change In changes
        // See if we are starting or stopping a building.
        If (change.Starting) Then
```

```
        // Starting a building.
        <Add new points to increase the skyline's height.>
    Else
        // Ending a building.
        <Remove this rectangle from the active list.>
        <Find the tallest active rectangle.>
        <Add new points to the skyline to move to that
         building's height.>
    End If
Next change

Return <The skyline points>
End MakeSkyline
```

NOTE   This algorithm talks about height as you would normally think of it in Figure 9.15. In most programming languages, however, Y coordinates usually increase downward. That means when the algorithm says, "Find the tallest active rectangle," you actually need to look for the rectangle with an upper edge having the smallest Y coordinate.

In practice, this algorithm is relatively simple and fast, but it still has $O(N^2)$ performance.

One of the most potentially time-consuming operations performed by the algorithm is finding the tallest currently active rectangle. Because the rectangles are stored in a simple list, that task takes $O(N)$ steps. If you store the active rectangles in a priority queue instead of a list, then you can find the tallest item in a single step, plus $O(\log N)$ steps to rearrange the queue. With that change, the algorithm's run time becomes $O(N) + O(\log N) + O(N \log N) = O(N \log N)$.

Divide and Conquer

The algorithm described in the preceding section processes HeightChange objects in order from left to right. It's reasonably straightforward, but it requires the algorithm to examine the rectangles that are active at any given step. Because there could be many active rectangles, that process can take a long time.

Another strategy is to use a divide-and-conquer approach, similar to the one used by mergesort. Instead of considering the rectangles' edges in sorted order, you divide the rectangles into two groups, recursively create skylines for the two groups, and then merge those two skylines.

The hardest part of this approach is merging two skylines. For example, suppose you are working on the rectangles shown on the left in Figure 9.16. Also suppose that the algorithm has created the two skylines on the right, one for the lighter set of rectangles and one for the darker set of rectangles.

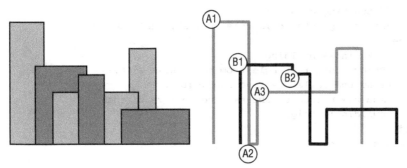

Figure 9.16: The light and dark skylines on the right correspond to the light and dark rectangles on the left.

To merge the two skylines, make three variables: one to keep track of the new merged skyline's height and two to keep track of the smaller skylines' left edges. Initially, the left edge variables indicate the leftmost points on the skylines, which are labeled A1 and B1 in the figure. (The labels in the figure show places where the skylines' heights change.)

The algorithm compares the X coordinates of the left edge variables and finds that point A1 has a smaller X coordinate. The result skyline currently has height 0, so the algorithm updates it to the height of point A1. It also moves the left edge variable for the lighter skyline to the next point on that skyline, which is point A2.

The algorithm again compares the left edge variables, which now refer to points A2 and B1. Point B1 has the smaller X coordinate, so the algorithm uses that one next. The height at point B1 is less than the height of the other skyline, so the algorithm does not change the result skyline's height.

This is one place where this algorithm has an advantage over the previous one. At the corresponding point in the previous algorithm, the program needed to search a list of active rectangles to see which one is currently highest. The new algorithm needs to consider only two partial skylines at a time.

After considering point B1, the algorithm moves the darker skyline's left edge variable to point B2. It then considers points A2 and B2. Point A2 comes first. That point's height is less than the height of the dark skyline, so the algorithm moves the result skyline's height to the height of the dark skyline.

The algorithm continues tracing its way through the two partial skylines until it has processed them both.

The following pseudocode shows the main MakeSkyline method, which implements the algorithm except for the merge step:

```
// Make the skyline points.
List<Point>: MakeSkyline(List<Rectangle>: rectangles,
    Integer: mini, Integer: maxi)
    // See if we need to process a single rectangle.
    If (mini == maxi) Then
        <Make and return a skyline representing the single rectangle.>
    End If
```

```
        // Process the two halves.
        Integer: midi = (mini + maxi) / 2
        List<Point>: skyline1 = MakeSkyline(rectangles, mini, midi)
        List<Point>: skyline2 = MakeSkyline(rectangles, midi + 1, maxi)

        // Merge and return the result.
        Return MergeSkylines(skyline1, skyline2)
    End MakeSkyline
```

This method's `rectangles` parameter holds the rectangles that define the skyline. The `mini` and `maxi` parameters give the minimum and maximum indices of the rectangles that this call to `MakeSkyline` should consider.

If `mini` equals `maxi`, then the method is building a skyline for a single rectangle. In that case, it simply builds the one-rectangle skyline and returns it.

If `mini` does not equal `maxi`, then the method sets variable `midi` to the average of `mini` and `maxi`. It then divides the rectangles into two groups and recursively calls itself to make skylines for the two groups. When the recursive calls return, the method calls the `MergeSkylines` method to merge the two skylines and then returns the combined result.

The following pseudocode shows the `MergeSkylines` method:

```
// Merge two skylines.
List<Point>: MergeSkylines(List<Point>: skyline1,
    List<Point>: skyline2)
        List<Point>: results = new List<Point>()

        <Set index1 and index2 to the indices of the leftmost
         skyline points.>
        <Set y1 and y2 equal to the ground's Y coordinate.>
        <Set currentY equal to the ground's Y coordinate.>
        While (index1 < skyline1.Length) Or (index2 < skyline2.Length)
            <Compare the next point in each skyline.>
            <Add the appropriate point to resuls.>
            <Update currentY, index1, and index2.>
        End While

        // Add any remaining points.
        For i = index1 To skyline1.Length - 1
            <Add skyline1[index1] to results.>
            index1++
        Next i
        For i = index2 To skyline2.Length - 1
            <Add skyline2[index2] to results.>
            index2++
        Next i

        Return results
    End MergeSkylines
```

This method performs some initialization and then enters a loop that executes as long as there are unmerged points in both of the input skylines. Inside the loop, it compares the two skylines' left edge points and the `currentY` value to determine the result skyline's correct height. It then updates `index1`, `index2`, and `currentY` appropriately.

After the method finishes processing one of the input skylines, it adds the other skyline's remaining points to the result skyline. It then returns the result.

This algorithm's structure is similar to that of the mergesort algorithm, so it has a similar run time of O(N log N). In practice, both this algorithm and the previous one are quite fast, so the difference isn't obvious until you use a large number of rectangles. In one set of tests, both algorithms were able to build a skyline from 100,000 rectangles in less than one second.

With 500,000 rectangles, the difference was obvious. With that many rectangles, the divide and conquer algorithm took around 0.57 seconds while the active list algorithm took roughly 16.79 seconds.

Backtracking Algorithms

Backtracking algorithms use recursion to search for the best solution to complicated problems. These algorithms recursively build partial test solutions to solve the problem. When they find that a test solution cannot lead to a usable final solution, they backtrack, discarding that test solution and continuing the search from an earlier test solution.

Backtracking is useful when you can incrementally build partial solutions, and you can sometimes quickly determine that a partial solution cannot lead to a complete solution. In that case, you can stop improving that partial solution, backtrack to the previous partial solution, and continue the search from there.

The following pseudocode shows the general backtracking approach at a high level:

```
// Explore this test solution.
// Return false if it cannot be extended to a full solution.
// Return true if a recursive call to LeadsToSolution finds
// a full solution.
Boolean: LeadsToSolution(Solution: test_solution)
    // If we can already tell that this partial solution cannot
    // lead to a full solution, return false.
    If <test_solution cannot solve the problem> Then Return false

    // If this is a full solution, return true.
    If <test_solution is a full solution> Then Return true
```

```
      // Extend the partial solution.
      Loop <over all possible extensions to test_solution>
          <Extend test_solution>

          // Recursively see if this leads to a solution.
          If (LeadsToSolution(test_solution)) Then Return true

          // This extension did not lead to a solution. Undo the change.
          <Undo the extension>
      End Loop

      // If we get here, this partial solution cannot
      // lead to a full solution.
      Return false
  End LeadsToSolution
```

The LeadsToSolution algorithm takes as a parameter whatever data it needs to keep track of a partial solution. It returns `true` if that partial solution leads to a full solution.

The algorithm begins by testing the partial solution to see if it is illegal. If the test solution so far cannot lead to a feasible solution, the algorithm returns `false`. The calling instance of LeadsToSolution abandons this test solution and works on others.

If the test solution looks valid so far, the algorithm loops over all the possible ways that it can extend the solution toward a full solution. For each extension, the algorithm calls itself recursively to see whether the extended solution will work. If the recursive call returns `false`, that extension doesn't work, so the algorithm undoes the extension and tries again with a new extension.

If the algorithm tries all possible extensions to the test solution and cannot find a feasible solution, it returns `false` so that the calling instance of Leads-ToSolution can abandon this test solution.

You can think of the quest for a solution as a search through a hypothetical decision tree. Each branch in the tree corresponds to a particular decision attempting to solve the problem. For example, an optimal chess game tree would contain branches for every possible move at a given point in the game. If you can use a relatively quick test to realize that a partial solution cannot produce a full solution, then you can trim the corresponding branch off of the tree without searching it exhaustively. That can remove huge chunks from the tree and save a lot of time. (The idea of decision trees is described further in Chapter 12.)

The following sections describe two problems that have natural backtracking algorithms: the eight queens problem and the knight's tour problem. When you study the algorithms for those problems, the more general backtracking approach described here should be easier to understand.

Eight Queens Problem

In the eight queens problem, the goal is to position eight queens on a chessboard so that none of them can attack any of the other queens. In other words, no two queens can be in the same row, column, or diagonal. Figure 9.14 shows one solution to the eight queens problem.

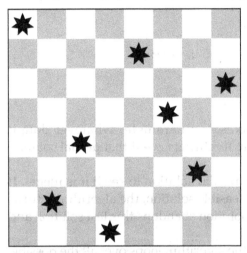

Figure 9.17: In the eight queens problem, you must position eight queens on a chessboard so that none can attack any of the others.

One way to solve this problem would be to try every possible arrangement of eight queens on a chessboard. Unfortunately, $\binom{64}{8} = 4,426,165,368$ arrangements are possible. You could enumerate all of them, but doing so would be time-consuming.

COUNTING COMBINATIONS

The reason why there are so many possible arrangements of queens is that you can position 8 queens in any of 64 squares. The queens are identical, so it doesn't matter which queen you use in a given location. That means the number of possible arrangements is the same as the number of ways that you can pick 8 squares out of the possible 64.

The number of selections of k items from a set of n without duplicates is given by the binomial coefficient. That value is written $\binom{n}{k}$ and is pronounced "n choose k." You can calculate the value with this formula:

$$\binom{n}{k} = \frac{n!}{k!(n-k)!}$$

For example, this equation gives the number of different selections of three items from a set of five without duplicates:

$$\binom{5}{3} = \frac{5!}{3!(5-3)!} = \frac{5!}{3!2!} = \frac{120}{6 \times 2} = 10$$

The number of selections of k items from a set of n allowing duplicates (if you are allowed to pick the same item more than once in a selection) is given by this formula:

$$\binom{n+k-1}{k}$$

For example, this equation gives the number of different selections of three items from a set of five allowing duplicates:

$$\binom{5+3-1}{3} = \binom{7}{3} = \frac{7!}{3!(7-3)!} = \frac{7!}{3!4!} = \frac{5040}{6 \times 24} = 35$$

In the eight queens problem, you need to find the number of ways to pick 8 of the squares without duplicates (you can't put more than one queen on the same square). That means the number of possible selections is as follows:

$$\binom{64}{8} = \frac{64!}{8!(64-8)!} = \frac{64!}{8!56!} = 4,426,165,368$$

Backtracking works well for this problem because it allows you to eliminate certain possibilities from consideration. For example, you could start with a partial solution that places a queen on the board's upper-left corner. You might try adding another queen just to the right of the first queen, but you know that placing two queens on the same row isn't allowed. This means you can eliminate every possible solution that has the first two queens next to each other in the upper-left corner. The program can backtrack to the point before it added the second queen and search for more promising solutions.

This may seem like a trivial benefit. After all, you know a solution cannot have two queens side by side in the upper-left corner. However, $\binom{62}{6} = 61,474,519$ possible arrangements of eight queens on a chessboard have queens in those positions, so one backtracking step saves you the effort of examining more than 61 million possibilities.

In fact, if the first queen is placed in the upper-left corner, then no other queen can be placed in the same row, column, or diagonal. This means that there are a total of 21 places where the second queen cannot be placed. Eliminating all of those partial solutions removes almost 1.3 billion possible arrangements from consideration.

Later tests remove other partial solutions from consideration. For example, after you place the second queen somewhere legal, it further restricts where the third queen can be placed.

The following pseudocode shows how you can use backtracking to solve the eight queens problem:

```
Boolean: EightQueens(Boolean: spot_taken[,],
    Integer: num_queens_positioned)
        // See If the test solution is already illegal.
        If (Not IsLegal(spot_taken)) Then Return false

        // See if we have positioned all of the queens.
        If (num_queens_positioned == 8) Then Return true

        // Extend the partial solution.
        // Try all positions for the next queen.
        For row = 0 to 7
            For col = 0 to 7
                // See if this spot is already taken.
                If (Not spot_taken[row, col]) Then
                    // Put a queen here.
                    spot_taken[row, col] = true

                    // Recursively see if this leads to a solution.
                    If (EightQueens(spot_taken, num_queens_positioned + 1))
                        Then Return true

                    // The extension did not lead to a solution.
                    // Undo the change.
                    spot_taken[row, col] = false
                End If
            Next col
        Next row

        // If we get here, we could not find a valid solution.
        Return false
End EightQueens
```

The algorithm takes as a parameter a two-dimensional array of Booleans named spot_taken. The entry spot_taken[row, col] is true if there is a queen in row row and column col.

The algorithm's second parameter, num_queens_positioned, specifies how many queens have been placed in the test solution.

The algorithm starts by calling IsLegal to see if the test solution so far is legal. The IsLegal method, which isn't shown here, simply loops through the spot_taken array to see if there are two queens in the same row, column, or diagonal.

Next the algorithm compares num_queens_positioned with the total number of queens, 8. If all of the queens have been positioned, then this test solution is a full solution, so the algorithm returns true. (The spot_taken array is not modified after that point, so when the first call to EightQueens returns, the array holds the solution.)

If this is not a full solution, the algorithm loops over all of the rows and columns. For each row/column pair, it checks spot_taken to see if that spot already contains a queen. If the spot doesn't hold a queen, the algorithm puts the next queen there and calls itself recursively to see if the extended solution leads to a full solution.

If the recursive call returns true, then it found a full solution, so this call also returns true.

If the recursive call returns false, the extended solution does not lead to a full solution, so the algorithm removes the queen from its new position and tries the next possible position.

If the algorithm tries all possible locations for the next queen and none of them work, this test solution (before the new queen is added) cannot lead to a full solution, so the algorithm returns false.

You can improve this algorithm's performance in a couple of interesting ways. See Exercises 13 and 14 at the end of this chapter for details.

Knight's Tour

In the *knight's tour problem*, the goal is to make a knight visit every position on a chessboard without visiting any square twice. A tour is considered *closed* if the final position is one move away from the starting position, and the knight could immediately start the tour again. A tour that is not closed is considered open.

NOTE   In case you don't remember, a knight moves two squares horizontally or vertically and then one square perpendicularly from its current position, as shown in Figure 9.18.

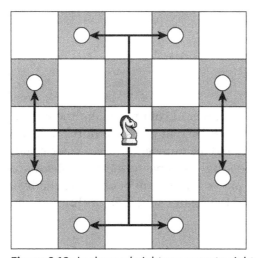

Figure 9.18: In chess, a knight can move to eight places if none of them lies off the board.

The following pseudocode shows a backtracking solution to the knight's tour problem:

```
// Move the knight to position [row, col]. Then recursively try
// to make other moves. Return true if we find a valid solution.
Boolean: KnightsTour(Integer: row, Integer: col,
  Integer: move_number[,], Integer: num_moves_taken)
    // Move the knight to this position.
    num_moves_taken = num_moves_taken + 1
    move_number[row, col] = num_moves_taken

    // See if we have made all the required moves.
    If (num_moves_taken == 64) Then Return true

    // Build arrays to determine where legal moves are
    // with respect to this position.
    Integer: dRows[] = { -2, -2, -1, 1, 2, 2, 1, -1 }
    Integer: dCols[] = { -1, 1, 2, 2, 1, -1, -2, -2 }

    // Try all legal positions for the next move.
    For i = 0 To 7
        Integer: r = row + d_rows[i]
        Integer: c = col + d_cols[i]
        If ((r >= 0) And (r < NumRows) And
            (c >= 0) And (c < NumCols) And
            (move_number[r, c] == 0))
        Then
            // This move is legal and available. Make this move
            // and then recursively try other assignments.
            If (KnightsTour(r, c, move_number, num_moves_taken))
                Then Return true
        End If
    Next i

    // This move didn't work out. Undo it.
    move_number[row, col] = 0

    // If we get here, we did not find a valid solution.
    return false
End KnightsTour
```

This algorithm takes as parameters the row and column where the knight should move next, an array named move_number that gives the number of the move when the knight visited each square, and the number of moves made so far.

The algorithm starts by recording the knight's move to the current square and incrementing the number of moves made. If the number of moves made is 64, then the knight has finished a tour of the board, so the algorithm returns true to indicate success.

If the tour is not finished, the algorithm initializes two arrays to represent the moves that are possible from the current square. For example, the first entries in the arrays are –2 and –1, indicating that the knight can move from square (row, col) to (row - 2, col - 1) if that square is on the board.

Next the algorithm loops through all of the possible moves from the position (row, col). If a move is on the board and has not already been visited in the test tour, the algorithm recursively calls itself to see if that move leads to a full solution.

If none of the possible moves from the current position leads to a solution, the algorithm sets move_number[row, col] = 0 to undo the current move and returns false to indicate that moving the knight to square (row, col) does not lead to a solution.

Unfortunately, the knight's tour problem isn't as easy to constrain as the eight queens problem. With the eight queens problem, it's fairly easy to tell whether a new position is under attack by another queen and therefore unavailable for a new queen. In that case, you can eliminate that position from consideration. A queen also attacks many squares, so it restricts later queens significantly.

In the knight's tour, any position the knight can reach that has not yet been visited gives a new test solution. There may be some cases where you can easily conclude that a test solution won't work, such as if the board has an unvisited square that is more than one move away from any other unvisited square but recognizing that situation is difficult.

The fact that it's hard to eliminate test solutions early on means that the algorithm often follows a test solution for a long while before discovering that the solution is infeasible. A knight can have up to eight legal moves, so an upper bound on the number of potential tours is 8^{64}, or roughly 6.3×10^{57}. You can study the positions on the board to get a better estimate of the potential number of tours (for example, a knight in a corner has only two possible moves), but the total number of potential tours is an enormous number in any case.

All this means is that it's difficult to solve the knight's tour problem for a normal 8×8 chessboard. In one set of tests, a program solved the problem on a 6×6 board almost instantly and on a 7×6 board in about 2 seconds. It still hadn't found a solution on a 7×7 board after an hour.

Although solving the knight's tour using only backtracking is difficult, a particular heuristic solves the problem extremely well. A *heuristic* is an algorithm that often produces a good result but that is not guaranteed to produce the best possible result. For example, a driving heuristic might be to add 10 percent to expected travel time to allow for traffic delays. Doing so doesn't guarantee that you'll always be on time, but it increases the chances.

Way back in 1823, H. C. von Warnsdorff suggested an amazingly effective knight's tour heuristic. At each step, the algorithm should select the next possible move that has the lowest number of possible moves leading out of it.

For example, suppose that the knight is in a position where it has only two possible moves. If the knight makes the first move, then it will have five possible locations for its next move. If the knight makes the second move, then it will have only one possible move for its next move. In that case, the heuristic says the algorithm should try the second move first.

This heuristic is so good that it finds a complete tour with no backtracking for boards of size up to 75×75. (In my tests, the program found a solution on a 57×57 board almost instantly and then crashed with a stack overflow on a 58×58 board.)

Selections and Permutations

A *selection* or *combination* is a subset of a set of objects. For example, in the set {A, B, C}, the subset {A,B} is a selection. All the two-item selections for the set {A, B, C} are {A,B}, {A,C}, and {B,C}.

In a selection, the ordering of the items doesn't matter, so {A, B} is considered the same as {B, A}. You can think of this as being similar to a menu selection at a restaurant. Selecting a cheese sandwich and milk is the same as selecting milk and a cheese sandwich.

In contrast, a *permutation* is an ordered arrangement of a subset of items taken from a set. This is similar to a selection, except that the ordering matters. For example, (A, B) and (B, A) are two permutations of two items taken from the set {A, B, C}. All of the permutations of two items taken from the set {A, B, C} are (A, B), (A, C), (B, A), (B, C), (C, A), and (C, B). (Notice the notation uses brackets { } for unordered selections and parentheses ( ) for ordered permutations.)

One other factor determines which groups of items are included in a particular kind of selection or permutation, that is, whether duplicates are allowed or not. For example, the two-item selections for the set {A, B, C} allowing duplicates include {A, A}, {B, B}, and {C, C} in addition to the other selections listed earlier.

The special case of a permutation that takes all of the items in the set and doesn't allow duplicates gives all of the possible arrangements of the items. For the set {A, B, C}, all the arrangements are (A, B, C), (A, C, B), (B, A, C), (B, C, A), (C, A, B), and (C, B, A). Many people think of the permutations of a set to be this collection of arrangements, rather than the more general case in which you may not be taking all of the items from the set and you may allow duplicates.

The following sections describe algorithms that you can use to generate selections and permutations with and without duplicates.

Selections with Loops

If you know how many items you want to select from a set when you are writing a program, you can use a series of `For` loops to generate combinations easily. For example, the following pseudocode generates all of the selections of three items taken from a set of five items allowing duplicates:

```
// Generate selections of 3 items allowing duplicates.
List<string>: Select3WithDuplicates(List<string> items)
    List<string>: results = New List<string>
    For i = 0 To <Maximum index in items>
        For j = i To <Maximum index in items>
            For k = j To <Maximum index in items>
                results.Add(items[i] + items[j] + items[k])
            Next k
        Next j
    Next i
    Return results
End Select3WithDuplicates
```

This algorithm takes as a parameter a list of `strings`. It then uses three `For` loops to select the three choices that make up each selection.

Each loop starts with the current value of the previous loop's counter. For example, the second loop starts with `j` equal to `i`. That means the second letter chosen for the selection will not be a letter that comes before the first letter in the items. For example, if the items include the letters *A*, *B*, *C*, *D*, and *E*, and the first letter in the selection is *C*, then the second letter won't be A or B. That keeps the letters in the selection in alphabetical order and prevents the algorithm from selecting both {A, B, C} and {A, C, B}, which are the same set.

Within the innermost loop, the algorithm combines the items selected by each loop variable to produce an output that includes all three selections.

Modifying this algorithm to prevent duplicates is simple. Just start each loop at the value 1 greater than the current value in the next outer loop. The following pseudocode shows the algorithm with this modification highlighted:

```
// Generate selections of 3 items without allowing duplicates.
List<string>: Select3WithoutDuplicates(List<string> items)
    List<string>: results = new List<string>()
    For i = 0 To <Maximum index in items>
        For j = i + 1 To <Maximum index in items>
            For k = j + 1 To <Maximum index in items>
                results.Add(items[i] + items[j] + items[k])
            Next k
```

```
            Next j
        Next i
        Return results
    End Select3WithoutDuplicates
```

This time, each loop starts at 1 greater than the previous loop's current value, so a loop cannot select the same item as a previous loop and that prevents duplicates.

Selections with Duplicates

The problem with the algorithms described in the preceding section is that they require you to know how many items you will select when you write the code, and sometimes that may not be the case. If you don't know how many items are in the original set of items, the program can figure that out. However, if you don't know how many items to select, you can't program the right number of For loops.

You can solve this problem recursively. Each call to the algorithm is responsible for adding a single selection to the result. Then, if the result doesn't include enough selections, the algorithm calls itself recursively to make more. When the selection is complete, the algorithm does something with it, such as printing the list of items selected.

The following pseudocode shows a recursive algorithm that generates selections allowing duplicates:

```
// Generate combinations allowing duplicates.
SelectKofNwithDuplicates(Integer: index, Integer: selections[],
    Data: items[], List<List<Data>> results)
    // See if we have made the last assignment.
    If (index == <Length of selections>) Then
        // Add the result to the result list.
        List<Data> result = New List<Data>()
        For i = 0 To <Largest index in selections>
            result.Add(items[selections[i]])
        Next i
        results.Add(result)
    Else
        // Get the smallest value we can use for the next selection.
        Integer: start = 0    // Use this value the first time through.
        If (index > 0) Then start = selections[index - 1]

        // Make the next assignment.
        For i = start To <Largest index in items>
            // Add item i to the selection.
            selections[index] = i
```

```
        // Recursively make the other selections.
        SelectKofNwithDuplicates(index + 1, selections,
            items, results)
    Next i
  End If
End SelectKofNwithDuplicates
```

This algorithm takes the following parameters:

- `index` gives the index of the item in the selection that this recursive call should set. If `index` is 2, then this call to the algorithm fills in `selections [2]`.

- `selections` is an array to hold the indices of the selected items. For example, if `selections` holds two entries with values 2 and 3, then the selection includes the items with indices 2 and 3.

- `items` is an array of the items from which selections should be made.

- `results` is a list of lists of items representing the complete selections. For example, if a selection is $\{A, B, D\}$, then `results` holds a list including the indices of A, B, and D.

When the algorithm starts, it checks the index of the item in the selection that it should make. If this value is greater than the length of the `selections` array, the selection is complete, so the algorithm adds it to the `results` list.

If the selection is incomplete, the algorithm determines the smallest index in the `items` array that it could use for the next choice in the selection. If this call to the algorithm is filling in the first position in the `selections` array, it could use any value in the `items` array, so `start` is set to 0. If this call does not set the first item in the selection, the algorithm sets `start` to the index of the last value chosen.

For example, suppose the items are $\{A, B, C, D, E\}$ and the algorithm has been called to fill in the third choice. Suppose also that the first two selected items were those with indices 0 and 2, so the current selection is $\{A, C\}$. In that case, the algorithm sets `start` to 3, so the items it considers for the next position have indices of 3 or greater. That makes it pick between D and E for this selection.

Setting `start` in this way keeps the items in the selection in order. In this example, that means the letters in the selection are always in alphabetical order. That prevents the algorithm from picking two selections such as $\{A, C, D\}$ and $\{A, D, C\}$, which are the same items in different orders.

Having set `start`, the algorithm loops from `start` to the last index in the `items` array. For each of those values, the algorithm places the value in the `selections` array to add the corresponding item to the selection and then calls itself recursively to assign values to the other entries in the `selections` array.

Selections Without Duplicates

To produce selections without duplicates, you need to make only one minor change to the previous algorithm. Instead of setting the start variable equal to the index that was last added to the selections array, you set it to 1 greater than that index. That prevents the algorithm from selecting the same value again.

The following pseudocode shows the new algorithm with the modified line highlighted:

```
// Generate combinations allowing duplicates.
SelectKofNwithoutDuplicates(Integer: index, Integer: selections[],
  Data: items[], List<List<Data>> results)
    // See if we have made the last assignment.
    If (index == <Length of selections>) Then
        // Add the result to the result list.
        List<Data> result = New List<Data>()
        For i = 0 To <Largest index in selections>
            Result.Add(items[selections[i]])
        Next i
        results.Add(result)
    Else
        // Get the smallest value we can use for the next selection.
        Integer: start = 0 // Use this value the first time through.
        If (index > 0) Then start = selections[index - 1] + 1

        // Make the next assignment.
        For i = start To <Largest index in items>
            // Add item i to the selection.
            selections[index] = i

            // Recursively make the other selections.
            SelectKofNwithoutDuplicates(
                index + 1, selections, items, results)
        Next i
    End If
End SelectKofNwithoutDuplicates
```

The algorithm works the same way as before, but this time each choice for an item in the selection must come after the one before it in the items list. For example, suppose the items are {A, B, C, D}, the algorithm has already chosen {A, B} for the partial selection, and now the algorithm has been called to make the third selection. In that case, the algorithm considers only the items that come after B, which are C and D.

Permutations with Duplicates

The algorithm for generating permutations is similar to the previous ones for generating selections. The following pseudocode shows the algorithm for generating permutations allowing duplicates:

```
// Generate permutations allowing duplicates.
PermuteKofNwithDuplicates(Integer: index, Integer: selections[],
  Data: items[], List<List<Data>> results)
    // See if we have made the last assignment.
    If (index == <Length of selections>) Then
        // Add the result to the result list.
        List<Data> result = New List<Data>()
        For i = 0 To <Largest index in selections>
            Result.Add(items[selections[i]])
        Next i
        results.Add(result)
    Else
        // Make the next assignment.
        For i = 0 To <Largest index in items>
            // Add item i to the selection.
            selections[index] = i

            // Recursively make the other assignments.
            PermuteKofNwithDuplicates(index + 1, selections, items, results)
        Next i
    End If
End PermuteKofNwithDuplicates
```

The main difference between this algorithm and the earlier one for generating selections with duplicates is that this algorithm loops through all of the items when it makes its assignment instead of starting the loop at a start value. This allows the algorithm to pick items in any order, so it generates all of the permutations.

COUNTING PERMUTATIONS WITH DUPLICATES

Suppose you're making permutations of k out of n items allowing duplicates. For each item in a permutation, the algorithm could pick any of the n choices. It makes k independent choices (in other words, one choice does not depend on the previous choices), so there are $n * n * \ldots * n = n^k$ possible permutations.

In the special case where you want to generate permutations that select all n of the n items, n^n results are possible.

Just as you can define selections without duplicates, you can define permutations without duplicates.

Permutations Without Duplicates

To produce permutations without duplicates, you need to make only one minor change to the preceding algorithm. Instead of allowing all of the items to be selected for each assignment, the algorithm excludes any items that have already been used.

The following pseudocode shows the new algorithm with the modified lines highlighted:

```
// Generate permutations not allowing duplicates.
PermuteKofNwithoutDuplicates(Integer: index, Integer: selections[],
  Data: items[], List<List<Data>> results)
    // See if we have made the last assignment.
    If (index == <Length of selections>) Then
        // Add the result to the result list.
        List<Data> result = New List<Data>()
        For i = 0 To <Largest index in selections>
            Result.Add(items[selections[i]])
        Next i
        results.Add(result)
    Else
        // Make the next assignment.
        For i = 0 To <Largest index in items>
            // Make sure item i hasn't been used yet.
            Boolean: used = false
            For j = 0 To index - 1
                If (selections[j] == i) Then used = true
            Next j

            If (Not used) Then
                // Add item i to the selection.
                selections[index] = i

                // Recursively make the other assignments.
                PermuteKofNwithoutDuplicates(
                    index + 1, selections, items, results)
            End If
        Next i
    End If
End PermuteKofNwithoutDuplicates
```

The only change is that this version of the algorithm checks that an item has not already been used in the permutation before adding it.

> **COUNTING PERMUTATIONS WITHOUT DUPLICATES**
>
> Suppose that you're making permutations of k out of n items without duplicates. For the first item in a permutation, the algorithm could pick any of the n choices. For the second item, it could pick any of the remaining n − 1 items. Multiplying the number of choices at each step gives the total number of possible permutations:
> $n \times (n - 1) \times (n - 2) \times ... \times (n - k + 1)$.

> In the special case where k = n, so that you are generating permutations that select all n of the items without duplicates, this formula becomes n × (n − 1) × (n − 2) ×...1 = n!. This is the number most people think of as the number of permutations of a set.

Round-Robin Scheduling

Round-robin scheduling is a special kind of permutation. For a two-team (or two-player) sport, a *round-robin tournament* is a tournament where every team plays every other team once. A *round-robin schedule* consists of a collection of rounds during which every team plays another team. If the number of teams is odd, then one team in each round receives a *bye* when they don't play.

The result is a set of very specific permutations of the teams. To make the schedule as short as possible, no two teams should play against each other twice, and no team should have more than one bye. Each team either plays a new team or has a bye in each round. If the number of teams N is even, then there are no byes, so it takes N − 1 rounds for every team to play each of the other N − 1 teams. If N is odd, then it takes N rounds for every team to play each of the other N − 1 teams and have a bye.

For example, the following list shows a schedule for five teams:

Round 1

- Team 1 versus Team 4
- Team 2 versus Team 3
- Team 5 has a bye

Round 2

- Team 5 versus Team 3
- Team 1 versus Team 2
- Team 4 has a bye

Round 3

- Team 4 versus Team 2
- Team 5 versus Team 1
- Team 3 has a bye

Round 4

- Team 3 versus Team 1
- Team 4 versus Team 5
- Team 2 has a bye

Round 5

- Team 2 versus Team 5
- Team 3 versus Team 4
- Team 1 has a bye

One way that you could schedule a round robin tournament would be to try all possible random assignments until you find one that works. As you can probably imagine, that would be slow.

The following sections describe a better approach called the *polygon method*. The method works differently depending on whether you're scheduling an odd or even number of teams, so those cases are described separately.

Odd Number of Teams

To use the polygon method with an odd number of teams, draw a regular polygon with one vertex for each team and place the teams on the vertices. Then draw horizontal lines connecting teams that have the same Y coordinate. For example, Figure 9.19 shows the polygon for five teams labeled A, B, C, D, and E.

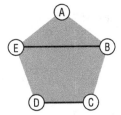

Figure 9.19: In the polygon method, horizontal lines represent matches in a tournament round.

The horizontal lines define the matches for the tournament's first round. In Figure 9.19, the lines indicate that team E plays team B, team D plays team C, and team A at the top of the polygon gets a bye in the round.

Now rotate the lines one position around the polygon's center. The lines now show the matches for round 2. Continue rotating the lines until they have defined all the tournament's matches.

More precisely, if there are N teams, then the polygon has N sides, the schedule includes N rounds, you rotate the lines $N-1$ times, and you rotate the lines by $360 / N$ degrees between rounds.

Figure 9.20 shows the rotations for five teams. The lines are rotated $5-1=4$ times by $360 / 5 = 72°$ each time.

The rotations shown in Figure 9.20 produce the following tournament schedule:

Round 1

- B versus E
- C versus D
- A has a bye

Round 2

- A versus C
- D versus E
- B has a bye

Round 3

- A versus E
- B versus D
- C has a bye

Round 4

- A versus B
- C versus E
- D has a bye

Round 5

- A versus D
- B versus C
- E has a bye

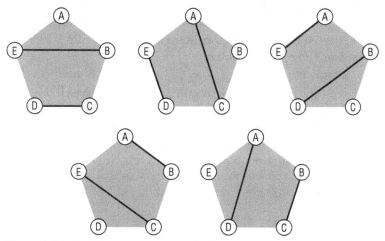

Figure 9.20: For N teams, you rotate the lines 360 / N degrees between rounds.

This technique clearly produces some sort of schedule. Now you need to ask, "Is this schedule valid and optimal?" To be valid and optimal, the schedule needs to satisfy the following requirements:

- In each round, each team plays exactly one other team or has a bye.
- Every team has exactly one bye.
- No team plays the same opponent twice.

The way the lines are constructed guarantees that the first requirement is satisfied. The number of teams is odd, so there is always one team that is not connected to a line, and that team gets the bye. Every other team is connected to exactly one line, so it plays exactly one opponent.

The second requirement is satisfied because, each time you rotate the lines, a different team is *not* connected to a line and therefore gets a bye. Because there are N arrangements, each team gets a turn being the one that gets the bye.

Another way to think of this is to leave the lines stationary and rotate the teams instead. (Whether you rotate the vertices or lines is just a matter of perspective. The resulting matchups are the same.) In that case, each team sits at the top of the polygon during one round, and that's when it gets its bye. Either way you think about it, this shows that every team gets exactly one bye, so the second requirement is satisfied.

The third requirement is a bit trickier. It is satisfied because each of the rotations produces different lines with no repetitions or reflections. For example, the first pentagon shown in Figure 9.20 includes a line between teams B and E, and no later rotation includes a line between those teams.

We know that there are no repeated lines because the lines are rotated by different angles after each round. After K rounds, the lines are rotated by $360 \times K / N$ degrees. Here $K < N$, so this angle is always less than $360°$, and we know that the lines have not rotated all the way around to their original angles.

There's one other case to consider: the rotation angle might be $180°$. In that case, the lines would be mirror images of their original positions. For example, the first pentagon in Figure 9.20 includes a line from team E to team B. If we rotate the lines by $180°$, then the result would contain a line from team B to team E and that would represent a repeated match.

Fortunately, that cannot happen because N is odd. After K rounds, the lines are rotated by the angle $360 \times K / N$ degrees. If that angle is $180°$, then $360 \times K / N = 180$. Solving this equation for N gives $N = 2K$. Because K is an integer, that means N is even, which contradicts our assumption that N is odd. That means there is no value for K that will rotate the lines by $180°$, at least as long as N is odd. The following section explains how to schedule a tournament when N is even.

Even Number of Teams

Scheduling a tournament for an even number of teams is easy if you know how to handle an odd number of teams. Simply remove one of the teams and schedule the remaining teams as described in the preceding section. Then replace the byes with the team you removed.

For example, suppose you want to schedule a tournament for six teams labeled A through F. First build a schedule for the five teams A through E. Then replace the byes with matches against team F.

Implementation

The previous sections show that the polygon method works. Fortunately, you don't actually need to draw a bunch of polygons to implement the method. Instead, think of the teams as sitting in an array that wraps around halfway through, as shown in Figure 9.21.

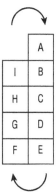

Figure 9.21: You can use a wrapped array to model the polygon method.

You can see how the elements in the array map to the polygon's vertices. The rows in Figure 9.21 correspond to the horizontal rows of vertices in Figure 9.20, so they give you the team matchups. For example, the first row in Figure 9.21 (not counting the odd team A at the top, which gets the bye) tells you that team I plays team B.

When you're ready for the next round, rotate the teams in the array, wrapping the last team back into the first position. Figure 9.22 shows the array during the second round.

Figure 9.22: After each round, move the teams down one position in the array, wrapping the last team around to the beginning.

Understanding the polygon method takes some work, but the algorithm is surprisingly short. The following pseudocode shows the algorithm that schedules an odd number of teams. The `MatchUp` class simply holds two teams that should play each other. (In C# Python you could use a tuple instead of a class.)

```
// Find a round robin schedule for the teams.
List Of List Of MatchUp: ScheduleRoundRobinOdd(
  List Of String: teams, String: bye_team)
    Integer: num_teams = <length of teams>
    Integer: mid = num_teams / 2

    // Loop.
    List Of List Of MatchUp: schedule = New List Of List Of MatchUp()
    For i = 0 to num_teams -1
        // Save this arrangement.
        List Of MatchUp: round = New List Of MatchUp()
        For j = 1 to mid
            round.Add(New MatchUp(teams[j], teams[num_teams - j]))
        Next j
        round.Add(New MatchUp(teams[0], bye_team))
        schedule.Add(round)

        // Rotate.
        teams.Insert(0, teams[num_teams - 1])
        teams.RemoveAt(num_teams)
    Next i

    return schedule
End ScheduleRoundRobinOdd
```

The algorithm calculates the number of teams and the index of the array's halfway point. The code assumes that integer division rounds down, so the midpoint index `mid` is the position of the last team in the first column of the wrapped array. For example, in Figure 9.21, `mid` is that index of team E.

The algorithm then creates a list to hold the tournament's rounds and enters a loop to generate the rounds.

Inside the loop, the algorithm creates a list to hold the matches for the current round. It then loops through the rows in the array, as shown in Figure 9.21, and saves the pairs of teams in the `round` list. This is the trickiest part of the algorithm and is basically bookkeeping.

After it finishes processing the round's matchups, the algorithm adds another matchup for the odd team (team A in Figure 9.21). It matches that team with the team in the `bye_team` parameter. That value should be either a team or a special value (such as `null`, `None`, or the string BYE) representing a bye. (You'll see how that works shortly.)

After it has built the round, the algorithm adds it to the `schedule` list.

Next, the algorithm rotates the array. To do that, it adds a copy of the last team to the beginning of the `teams` list and then removes the last team from the list. This operation is easy if the teams are stored in a queue. Then you can simply dequeue the first item and enqueue it at the end of the queue.

If the teams are stored in an array, then you'll need to move each of the teams into its new position.

The following pseudocode shows how you can use the `ScheduleRoundRobinOdd` method to build a schedule for any number of teams:

```
// Find a round robin schedule for the teams.
List Of List Of MatchUp: ScheduleRoundRobin(List Of String: teamList)
    // Copy the team list.
    List Of String: teams = <copy of teamList>

    // See if the number of teams is odd or even.
    String: byeTeam = "BYE"
    If (teams.Count % 2 == 0) Then
        // Even. Use the first item as the bye team.
        byeTeam = teams[0]
        teams.RemoveAt(0)
    End If

    // Make the schedule.
    return ScheduleRoundRobinOdd(teams, byeTeam)
End ScheduleRoundRobin
```

This algorithm makes a copy of the team list and works on the copy. It then determines whether the list contains an even or odd number of teams. If the number of teams is odd, it sets the variable bye_team to the string BYE. If the number of teams is even, it sets the variable bye_team to the first team and removes that team from the list.

The algorithm then calls `ScheduleRoundRobinOdd` to build a schedule for the team list. It passes that algorithm the bye_team variable so that it can pair unmatched teams with either the original first team or the special team named BYE.

The `ScheduleRoundRobin` algorithm then simply returns the schedule returned by `ScheduleRoundRobinOdd`.

Recursion Removal

Recursion makes some problems easier to understand. For example, the recursive solution to the Tower of Hanoi problem is simple and elegant.

Unfortunately, recursion has some drawbacks. Sometimes it leads to solutions that are natural but inefficient. For example, the recursive algorithm for generating Fibonacci numbers requires that the program calculate the same values many times. This slows it down so much that calculating more than the 50th or so value is impractical.

Other recursive algorithms cause a deep series of method calls, which can exhaust the call stack. The knight's tour with Warnsdorff's heuristic demonstrates that problem. The heuristic can solve the knight's tour problem for boards up to 57×57 on my computer, but beyond that it exhausts the call stack, at least in C#.

Fortunately, you can do a few things to address these problems. The following sections describe some approaches that you can take to restructure or remove recursion to improve performance.

Tail Recursion Removal

Tail recursion occurs when the last thing a singly recursive algorithm does before returning is call itself. For example, consider the following implementation of the Factorial algorithm:

```
Integer: Factorial(Integer: n)
    If (n == 0) Then Return 1

    Integer: result = n * Factorial(n - 1)
    Return result
End Factorial
```

The algorithm starts by checking to see whether it needs to call itself recursively or whether it can simply return the value 1. If the algorithm must call itself, it does so, multiplies the returned result by n, and returns the result.

You can convert this recursive version of the algorithm into a nonrecursive version by using a loop. Within the loop, the algorithm performs whatever tasks the original algorithm did.

Before the end of the loop, the algorithm should set its parameters to the values they had during the recursive call. If the algorithm returns a value, as the Factorial algorithm does, you need to create a variable to keep track of the return value.

When the loop repeats, the parameters are set for the recursive call, so the algorithm does whatever the recursive call did.

The loop should end when the condition occurs that originally ended the recursion.

For the Factorial algorithm, the stopping condition is n == 0 so that condition controls the loop.

When the algorithm calls itself recursively, it decreases its parameter n by 1, so the non-recursive version should also decrease n by 1 before the end of the loop.

The following pseudocode shows the new nonrecursive version of the Factorial algorithm:

```
Integer: Factorial(Integer: n)
    // Make a variable to keep track of the returned value.
    // Initialize it to 1 so we can multiply it by returned results.
    // (The result is 1 if we do not enter the loop at all.)
    Integer: result = 1

    // Start a loop controlled by the recursion stopping condition.
    While (n != 0)
        // Save the result from this "recursive" call.
        result = result * n

        // Prepare for "recursion."
        n = n - 1
    Loop

    // Return the accumulated result.
    Return result
End Factorial
```

This algorithm looks a lot longer than it really is because of all the comments.

Removing tail recursion is straightforward enough that some compilers can do it automatically to reduce stack space requirements.

Of course, the problem with the Factorial algorithm isn't the depth of recursion, it's the fact that the results become too big to store in data types of fixed size. Tail recursion is still useful for other algorithms and usually improves performance, because checking a `While` loop's exit condition is faster than performing a recursive method call.

Dynamic Programming

Unfortunately, tail recursion won't help the Fibonacci algorithm for two reasons. First, it is multiply recursive, so tail recursion doesn't really apply. Perhaps, more importantly, its problem isn't great depth of recursion. Its problem is that it calculates too many intermediate results repeatedly, so it takes a long time to calculate results.

One solution to this problem is to record values as they are calculated so that the algorithm doesn't need to calculate them again later. The following pseudocode shows one way to do that:

```
// Calculated values.
Integer: FibonacciValues[100]

// The maximum value calculatued so far.
Integer: MaxN
```

```
// Set Fibonacci[0] and Fibonacci[1].
InitializeFibonacci()
    FibonacciValues[0] = 0
    FibonacciValues[1] = 1
    MaxN = 1
End InitializeFibonacci


// Return the nth Fibonacci number.
Integer: Fibonacci(Integer: n)
    // If we have not yet calculated this value, calculate it.
    If (MaxN < n) Then
        FibonacciValues[n] = Fibonacci(n - 1) + Fibonacci(n - 2)
        MaxN = n
    End If

    // Return the calculated value.
    Return FibonacciValues[n]
End Fibonacci
```

This algorithm starts by declaring a globally visible FibonacciValues array to hold calculated values. The variable MaxN keeps track of the largest value N for which Fibonacci(N) has been stored in the array.

Next, the algorithm defines an initialization method called InitializeFibonacci. The program must call this method to set the first two Fibonacci values before it calls the Fibonacci function.

The Fibonacci function compares MaxN to its input parameter n. If the program has not yet calculated the nth Fibonacci number, it recursively calls itself to calculate that value, stores it in the FibonacciValues array, and updates MaxN.

Next the algorithm simply returns the value stored in the FibonacciValues array. At this point, the algorithm knows the value is in the array either because it was before or because the previous lines of code put it there.

In this program, each Fibonacci number is calculated only once. After that, the algorithm simply looks it up in the array instead of recursively calculating it.

NOTE   This approach is called *dynamic programming*. The technique probably seemed dynamic when it was invented in the 1950s, but it seems downright static compared to modern techniques such as neural networks, genetic programming, and other machine learning techniques that basically reprogram themselves on the fly.

This approach solves the original Fibonacci algorithm's problem by letting it avoid calculating intermediate values a huge number of times. The original algorithm can calculate Fibonacci(44) in about a minute on my computer and cannot reasonably calculate values that are much larger. The new algorithm can calculate Fibonacci(92) almost instantly. It cannot calculate Fibonacci(93) in C# because the result doesn't fit in a 64-bit-long integer. If you use the BigInteger data type or integers in Python, the algorithm can easily calculate Fibonacci(100) or more.

Bottom-Up Programming

Dynamic programming makes the Fibonacci algorithm much faster, but it doesn't remove the recursion. It allows the program to calculate much larger values, but that also means it can enter deeper levels of recursion and exhaust the stack space.

To solve that problem, you need to remove the recursion. You can do that by thinking about how this particular program works.

To calculate a particular value Fibonacci(n), the program first recursively calculates Fibonacci(n – 1), Fibonacci(n – 2),..., Fibonacci(2). It then looks up Fibonacci(1) and Fibonacci(0) in the `FibonacciValues` array.

As each recursive call finishes, it saves its value in the `FibonacciValues` array so that it can be used by calls to the algorithm higher up the call stack. To make this work, the algorithm saves new values into the array in increasing order. As the recursive calls finish, they save Fibonacci(2), Fibonacci(3), . . ., Fibonacci(n) in the array.

Knowing this, you can remove the recursion by making the algorithm follow similar steps to create the Fibonacci values in increasing order. Instead of starting with the highest-level call to calculate Fibonacci(n), you use a bottom-up approach. You start by calculating the smallest value Fibonacci(2) and work your way up.

The following pseudocode shows this approach:

```
// Return the nth Fibonacci number.
Integer: Fibonacci(Integer: n)
    If (n > MaxN) Then
        // Calculate values between Fibonacci(MaxN) and Fibonacci(n).
        For i = MaxN + 1 To n
            FibonacciValues[i] = Fibonacci(i - 1) + Fibonacci(i - 2)
        Next i

        // Update MaxN.
        MaxN = n
    End If

    // Return the calculated value.
    Return FibonacciValues[n]
End Fibonacci
```

This version of the algorithm starts by precalculating all the Fibonacci values up to the one it needs. It then returns that value.

General Recursion Removal

The previous sections explained how you can remove tail recursion, how dynamic programming lets you save previously calculated values, and how you can remove recursion from the Fibonacci algorithm, but they didn't give a general algorithm for removing recursion in other situations. For example, the Hilbert curve algorithm is multiply recursive, so you can't use tail recursion removal on it. You might be able to work on it long enough to come up with a nonrecursive version, but that would be hard.

A more general way to remove recursion is to mimic what the program does when it performs recursion. Before making a recursive call, the program stores information about its current state on the stack. Then, when the recursive call returns, the program pops the saved information off of the stack so that it can resume execution where it left off.

To mimic this behavior, divide the algorithm into sections that come before each recursive call, and name them 1, 2, 3, and so forth.

Next, create a variable named section that indicates which section the algorithm should execute next. Set this variable to 1 initially so that the algorithm starts with the first section of code.

Create a While loop that executes as long as section is greater than 0.

Now move all the algorithm's code inside the While loop and place it inside a series of If-Else statements. Make each If statement compare the variable section to a section number and execute the corresponding code if they match. (You can use a Switch or Select Case statement instead of a series of If-Else statements if that makes sense for your programming language.)

When the algorithm enters a section of code, increment the variable section so that the algorithm knows which section to execute the next time it passes through the loop.

When the algorithm would normally call itself recursively, push all of the parameters' current values onto stacks. Also, push section onto a stack so that the algorithm will know which section to execute when it returns from the simulated recursion. Update any parameters that should be used by the simulated recursion. Finally, set section = 1 to begin the simulated recursive call at the first section of code.

The following pseudocode shows the original Hilbert curve algorithm presented earlier in this chapter broken into sections after each recursion:

```
Hilbert(Integer: depth, Float: dx, Float: dy)
    // Section 1.
    If (depth > 0) Then Hilbert(depth - 1, dy, dx)

    // Section 2.
    DrawRelative(dx, dy)
    If (depth > 0) Then Hilbert(depth - 1, dx, dy)

    // Section 3.
    DrawRelative(dy, dx)
    If (depth > 0) Then Hilbert(depth - 1, dx, dy)
```

```
    // Section 4.
    DrawRelative(-dx, -dy)
    If (depth > 0) Then Hilbert(depth - 1, -dy, -dx)

    // Section 5.
End Hilbert
```

The following pseudocode shows this code translated into a nonrecursive version:

```
// Draw the Hilbert curve.
Hilbert(Integer: depth, Float: dx, Float: dy)
    // Make stacks to store information before recursion.
    Stack<Integer> sections = new Stack<int>();
    Stack<Integer> depths = new Stack<int>();
    Stack<Float> dxs = new Stack<float>();
    Stack<Float> dys = new Stack<float>();

    // Determine which section of code to execute next.
    Integer: section = 1

    While (section > 0)
        If (section == 1) Then
            section = section + 1
            If (depth > 0) Then
                sections.Push(section)
                depths.Push(depth)
                dxs.Push(dx)
                dys.Push(dy)
                // Hilbert(depth - 1, gr, dy, dx)
                depth = depth - 1
                float temp = dx
                dx = dy
                dy = temp
                section = 1
            End If
        Else If (section == 2) Then
            DrawRelative(gr, dx, dy)
            section = section + 1
            If (depth > 0) Then
                sections.Push(section)
                depths.Push(depth)
                dxs.Push(dx)
                dys.Push(dy)
                // Hilbert(depth - 1, gr, dx, dy)
                depth = depth - 1
                section = 1
            End If
        Else If (section == 3) Then
            DrawRelative(gr, dy, dx)
            section = section + 1
```

```
            If (depth > 0) Then
                sections.Push(section)
                depths.Push(depth)
                dxs.Push(dx)
                dys.Push(dy)
                // Hilbert(depth - 1, gr, dx, dy)
                depth = depth - 1
                section = 1
            End If
        Else If (section == 4) Then
            DrawRelative(gr, -dx, -dy)
            section = section + 1
            If (depth > 0) Then
                sections.Push(section)
                depths.Push(depth)
                dxs.Push(dx)
                dys.Push(dy)
                // Hilbert(depth - 1, gr, -dy, -dx)
                depth = depth - 1
                float temp = dx
                dx = -dy
                dy = -temp
                section = 1
            End If
        Else If (section == 5) Then
            // Return from a recursion.
            // If there's nothing to pop, we're at the top.
            If (sections.Count == 0) Then section = -1
            Else
                // Pop the previous parameters.
                section = sections.Pop()
                depth = depths.Pop()
                dx = dxs.Pop()
                dy = dys.Pop()
            End If
    End While
End Hilbert
```

This version is quite a bit longer, because it contains several copies of code to push values onto stacks, update parameters, and pop values back off stacks.

The technique doesn't really help much for the Hilbert curve because a level 8 or 9 curve will fill every pixel on your computer's screen, so there's no reason to go to any greater depth of recursion. It's still a useful technique to know when you want to remove deep levels of recursion.

Summary

Recursion is a powerful technique. Some problems are naturally recursive, and when they are, a recursive algorithm is often much easier to design than a nonrecursive version. For example, recursion makes the Tower of Hanoi puzzle relatively easy to solve. Recursion also lets you create interesting pictures such as self-similar curves and gaskets with little code.

Recursion lets you implement backtracking algorithms and solve problems in which you need to repeat certain steps an unknown number of times. For example, generating selections or permutations is easy if you know how many items you will need to pick when you write the code. If you don't know beforehand how many items to pick, generating solutions is easier with recursion.

Despite its usefulness, recursion can sometimes cause problems. Using recursion indiscriminately can make a program repeat the same calculation many times, as does the most obvious implementation of the Fibonacci algorithm. Deep levels of recursion can also exhaust the stack space and make a program crash. In cases such as these, you can remove recursion from a program to improve performance.

Aside from these few instances, recursion is an extremely powerful and useful technique. It's particularly useful when you're working with naturally recursive data structures, such as the trees described in the next three chapters.

Exercises

You can find the answers to these exercises in Appendix B. Asterisks indicate particularly difficult problems.

Some of the following exercises require graphic programming. Exactly how you build them depends on your programming environment. They also require graphic programming experience, so they are marked with asterisks to indicate that they are harder than the other problems.

Other programs, such as the eight queens problem and the knight's tour, can be implemented graphically or just with textual output. Start with text output and then implement the programs graphically if you want an extra challenge.

1. Write a program that implements the original recursive Factorial algorithm. Experiment with it to see how large a factorial you can reasonably calculate on your computer.

2. Write a program that implements the original recursive Fibonacci algorithm. Experiment with it to see how large a value you can calculate on your computer in around 10 seconds.

3. Write a program that implements the Tower of Hanoi algorithm. The result should be text that shows the series of moves in the form A-->B where this represents moving the top disk from peg A to peg B. For example, here is the result for moving three disks:

```
A-->B A-->C B-->C A-->B C-->A C-->B A-->B
```

4. *Write a program that solves the Tower of Hanoi puzzle and then displays the moves by graphically drawing disks moving between the pegs. (For hints, see Appendix B.)

5. *Write a program that draws Koch snowflakes. What is the maximum depth beyond which you can't really see any difference in the curve?

6. *In the standard Koch snowflake, the generator's corners are 60-degree angles, but you can use other angles to produce interesting results. Write a program that lets the user specify the angle as a parameter and that produces a result similar to the one shown in Figure 9.23 for 80-degree angles.

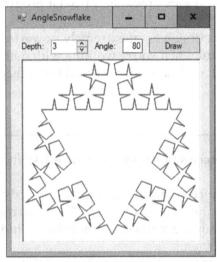

Figure 9.23: Giving the Koch snowflake's generator 80-degree turns creates a spiky result.

7. *Write a program that draws Hilbert curves. (For a hint about how to set `dx`, see Appendix B.)

8. Write pseudocode for the algorithms that draw the Sierpiński curve pieces down, left, and up.

9. *Write a program that draws Sierpiński curves. (For a hint about how to set `dx`, see Appendix B.)

10. Write low-level pseudocode to draw the Sierpiński gasket.

11. Write low-level pseudocode to draw the Sierpiński carpet.

12. *Write a program that solves the eight queens problem. In addition to the solution, display the number of queen positions examined and the time the program takes to solve the problem.

13. *One improvement that you can make to the eight queens problem is to keep track of how many queens can attack a particular position on the board. Then, when you are considering adding a queen to the board, you can ignore any positions where this value isn't 0. Modify the program you wrote for Exercise 12 to use this improvement.

14. *To make another improvement to the eight queens problem, notice that every row on the chessboard must hold a single queen. Modify the program you wrote for Exercise 13 so that each call to the EightQueens method searches only the next row for the new queen's position.

15. Compare the number of queen positions examined and the elapsed time for the programs that you wrote for Exercises 12, 13, and 14, respectively.

16. *Write a program that uses backtracking (but not Warnsdorff's heuristic) to solve the knight's tour problem. Let the user specify the board's width and height. What is the size of the smallest square board larger than 1×1 for which a knight's tour is possible? What is the size of the largest board for which the program can find a solution in under 10 seconds?

17. Write a program that solves the knight's tour problem by using Warnsdorff's heuristic. How large a board can the program handle?

18. How are a selection without duplicates and a permutation without duplicates related?

19. Write a program that implements the SelectKofNwithDuplicates and SelectKofNwithoutDuplicates algorithms.

20. Write a program that implements the PermuteKofNwithDuplicates and PermuteKofNwithoutDuplicates algorithms.

21. Write a program that implements the nonrecursive Factorial algorithm. What is the largest factorial that you can calculate with your program?

22. Write a program that uses dynamic programming to calculate Fibonacci numbers. What is the largest value that you can calculate with an initially empty table of values?

23. Write a program that implements the nonrecursive, bottom-up Fibonacci algorithm. What is the largest value that you can calculate with this program?

24. The nonrecursive Fibonacci algorithm calculates Fibonacci numbers up to the one it needs and then looks up the value in its array. In fact, the algorithm doesn't really need the array. Instead, it can calculate the smaller Fibonacci values whenever they are needed. This takes a little longer but

avoids the need for a globally available array. Write a program that implements a nonrecursive Fibonacci algorithm that uses this approach. Does this change the values that you can calculate?

25. *Write a program that implements the nonrecursive Hilbert curve algorithm.

This chapter explains trees, which are highly recursive data structures that you can use to store hierarchical data and model decision processes. For example, a tree can store a company organizational chart or the parts that make up a complex machine such as a car.

This chapter explains how to build relatively simple trees and provides the background that you need to understand the more complicated trees described in Chapter 11 and Chapter 12.

Tree Terminology

Tree terminology includes a hodgepodge of terms taken from genealogy, horticulture, and computer science. Trees use a lot of terms, but many of them are intuitive because you probably already understand what they mean in another context.

A tree consists of *nodes* connected by *branches*. Usually, the nodes contain some sort of data, and the branches do not.

NOTE Trees are a special type of network or graph, so sometimes network and graph terms leak into discussions of trees. For example, branches are sometimes called *links* or *edges*, although those terms are more appropriate for networks and graphs. Chapter 13 and Chapter 14 have more to say about networks.

The branches in a tree are usually *directed* so that they define a parent-child relationship between the nodes that they connect. Normally, branches are drawn as arrows pointing from the *parent node* to the *child node*. Two nodes that have the same parent are sometimes called *siblings*.

Each node in the tree has exactly one parent node, except for a single, unique *root node*, which has no parent.

The children, the children's children, and so on, for a node are that node's *descendants*. A node's parent, its parent's parent, and so on, up to the root are that node's *ancestors*.

All of these relationship-oriented terms make sense if you think of the tree as a family tree. You can even define terms such as cousin, nephew, and grandparent without confusing anyone, although those terms are uncommon.

Depending on the type of tree, nodes may have any number of children. The number of children a node has is the node's *degree*. A tree's degree is the maximum degree of its nodes. For example, in a degree 2 tree, which is usually called a *binary tree*, each node can have at most two children.

A node with no children is called a *leaf node* or an *external node*. A node that has at least one child is called an *internal node*.

Unlike real trees, tree data structures usually are drawn with the root at the top and the branches growing downward, as shown in Figure 10.1.

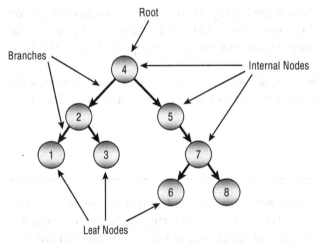

Figure 10.1: Tree data structures usually are drawn with the root at the top.

All of these definitions explain what a tree is intuitively. You can also recursively define a tree to be either

- A single root node
- A root node connected by branches to one or more smaller trees

A node's *level* or *depth* in the tree is the distance from the node to the root. To think of this in another way, a node's depth is the number of links between it and the root node. In particular, the root's level is 0.

A node's *height* is the length of the longest path from the node downward through the tree to a leaf node. In other words, it's the distance from the node to the bottom of the tree.

A tree's *height* is the same as the height of the root node.

A *subtree* of a tree T rooted at the node R is the node R and all of its descendants. For example, in Figure 10.1, the subtree rooted at node 5 is the tree containing the nodes 5, 7, 6, and 8.

An *ordered tree* is one in which the order of the children is important in some way. For example, many algorithms treat the left and right children in a binary tree differently. An *unordered tree* is one in which the order of the children doesn't matter. (Usually, a tree has an ordering, even if it's not particularly important to the algorithm. This is true simply because the children or branches are stored in a list, array, or some other collection that imposes an ordering on them.)

For any two nodes, the *lowest common ancestor* (or *first common ancestor*) is the node that is the ancestor of both nodes that is closest to those nodes. Another way to think about this is to start at one node and move up toward the root until you reach the first node that is an ancestor of the other node. For example, in Figure 10.1, the lowest common ancestor of nodes 3 and 5 is the root 4.

Note that the lowest common ancestor of two nodes might be one of those two nodes. For example, in Figure 10.1, the lowest common ancestor of nodes 5 and 6 is node 5.

Note also that there is a unique path between any two nodes in a tree that doesn't cross any branch more than once. The path starts at the first node, moves up the tree to the nodes' lowest common ancestor, and then moves down the tree to the second node.

A *full tree* is one in which every node has either zero children or as many children as the tree's degree. For example, in a full binary, every node has either zero or two children. The tree shown in Figure 10.1 is not full because node 5 has only one child.

A *complete tree* is one in which every level is completely full, except possibly the bottom level where all the nodes are pushed as far to the left as possible. Figure 10.2 shows a complete binary tree. Notice that this tree is not full because node I has only one child.

A *perfect tree* is full, and all the leaves are at the same level. In other words, the tree holds every possible node for a tree of its height.

Figure 10.3 shows examples of full, complete, and perfect binary trees.

That's a lot of terminology all at once, so Table 10.1 summarizes these tree terms to make remembering them a bit easier.

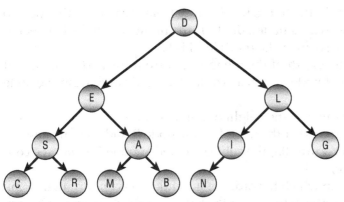

Figure 10.2: In a complete binary tree, every level is completely full, except possibly the bottom level, where the nodes are pushed as far to the left as possible.

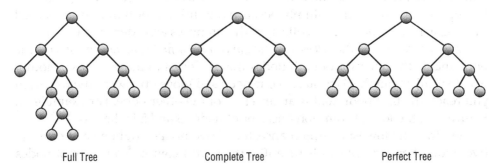

Full Tree   Complete Tree   Perfect Tree

Figure 10.3: Full, complete, and perfect binary trees contain an increasing number of nodes for a given height.

Table 10.1: Summary of Tree Terminology

TERM	MEANING
Ancestor	A node's parent, grandparent, great grandparent, and so on, up to the root are the node's ancestors.
Binary tree	A tree with degree 2.
Branch	Connects nodes in a tree.
Child	A child node is connected to its parent in the tree. Normally, a child is drawn below its parent.
Complete tree	A tree in which every level is completely full, except possibly the bottom level, where all the nodes are pushed as far to the left as possible.
Degree	For a node, the number of children the node has. For a tree, the maximum degree of any of its nodes.
Depth	Level.

TERM	MEANING
Descendant	A node's children, grandchildren, great grandchildren, and so on, are the node's descendants.
External node	A leaf node.
Lowest (or first) common ancestor	For any two nodes, the node that is the ancestor of both nodes that is closest to those nodes.
Full tree	A tree in which every node has either zero children or as many children as the tree's degree.
Height	For a node, the length of the longest path from the node downward through the tree to a leaf node. For a tree, this is the same as the root's height.
Internal node	A tree node that has at least one child.
Leaf node	A tree node with no children.
Level	A tree node's level is the distance (in links) between it and the root node.
Node	An object that holds data in a tree. Connected to other nodes by branches.
Ordered tree	A tree in which the ordering of each node's children matters.
Parent	A parent node is connected to its child nodes by branches. Every node has exactly one parent, except the root node, which has no parent. Normally, the parent is drawn above its children.
Perfect tree	A full tree where all of the leaves are at the same level.
Root	The unique node at the top of the tree that has no parent.
Sibling	Two nodes in a tree that have the same parent are siblings.
Subtree	A node and all of its descendants in a tree.

Having learned all of these terms, you're ready to start learning some of the properties and uses of trees.

Binary Tree Properties

Binary trees are useful in many algorithms, partly because lots of problems can be modeled using binary choices and partly because binary trees are relatively easy to understand. The following are some useful facts about binary trees:

■ The number of branches B in a binary tree containing N nodes is $B = N - 1$.

■ The number of nodes N in a perfect binary tree of height H is $N = 2^{H+1} - 1$.

- Conversely, if a perfect binary tree contains N nodes, it has a height of $\log_2(N+1)-1$.

- The number of leaf nodes L in a perfect binary tree of height H is $L = 2^H$. Because the total number of nodes in a perfect binary tree of height H is $2^{H+1}-1$, the number of internal nodes I is $I = N - L = (2^{H+1}-1) - 2^H = (2^{H+1}-2^H) - 1 = 2^H \times (2-1) - 1 = 2^H - 1$.

- This means that in a perfect binary tree, almost exactly half of the nodes are leaves, and almost exactly half are internal nodes. More precisely, $I = L - 1$.

- The number of missing branches (places where a child could be added) M in a binary tree that contains N nodes is $M = N + 1$.

- If a binary tree has N_0 leaf nodes and N_2 nodes with degree 2, then $N_0 = N_2 + 1$. In other words, there is one more leaf node than nodes with degree 2.

LEAF AND FULL NODES

The last fact is not very intuitive, so here's a proof:

1. Let N be the total number of nodes; B the total number of branches; and N0, N1, and N2 the number of nodes of degree 0, 1, and 2, respectively.

2. Consider the branches leading into nodes. Every node except the root has a single branch leading into it from its parent, so B = N − 1.

3. Next consider the branches leading out of nodes. The N0 nodes have no branches leading out of them, the N1 nodes have one branch leading out of them, and the N2 nodes have two branches leading out of them. This means that the total number of branches B = N1 + 2 × N2.

4. Setting these two equations for B equal to each other gives N − 1 = N1 + 2 × N2. Adding 1 to both sides of the equation changes this to N = N1 + 2 × N2 + 1.

5. Adding up the three kinds of nodes, you know that N = N0 + N1 + N2.

6. Setting these two equations for N equal to each other gives N1 + 2 × N2 + 1 = N0 + N1 + N2. Then subtracting N1 + N2 from both sides makes this N2 + 1 = N0.

These facts often make it easier to calculate the run time for algorithms that work with trees. For example, if an algorithm must search a perfect binary tree containing N nodes from the root to a leaf node, then you know that the algorithm needs only $O(\log N)$ steps.

INDUCTIVE REASONING

You can prove many of these properties of binary trees inductively. In an inductive proof, you first establish a base case for a small problem. Then you make an inductive step in which you prove that the property being true for some value K means that it must also be true for the value K + 1. Those two steps show that the property holds for all values K.

For example, consider the first property described a moment ago: The number of nodes N in a perfect binary tree of height H is $N = 2^{H+1} - 1$. The following shows an inductive proof. (Here H plays the role of K in the general description of an inductive proof.)

Base Case

Consider a perfect tree of height H = 0. This tree has a single root node and no branches. In that case, the number of nodes N is 1. Note that $2^{H+1} - 1 = 2^{0+1} - 1 = 2^1 - 1 = 2 - 1 = 1$, so $N = 2^{H+1} - 1$ as desired.

Inductive Step

Suppose that the property holds true for perfect binary trees of height H. A perfect binary tree of height H + 1 consists of a root node connected to two perfect binary subtrees of height H. Because we assume that the property is true for trees of height H, the total number of nodes in each subtree is $2^{H+1} - 1$. Adding the root node means the total number of nodes in the tree of height H + 1 is $2 \times (2^{H+1} - 1) + 1$. Rearranging this a bit gives $(2^{(H+1)} + 1 - 2) + 1 = 2^{(H+1)} + 1 - 1$. This is the formula for the number of nodes for a perfect binary tree of height H + 1 (just plug H + 1 into the formula), so the property is true for a tree of height H + 1.

This proves that the number of nodes in a perfect binary tree of height H is $2^{H+1} - 1$ for all H.

If a binary tree containing N nodes is fat (isn't too tall and skinny), such as if it's a complete tree, its statistics are similar to those of a perfect binary tree in terms of Big O notation. For example, if a fat binary tree contains N nodes, it has $O(\log N)$ height, $O(N \div 2) = O(N)$ leaves, $O(N \div 2) = O(N)$ internal nodes, and $O(N)$ missing branches.

These properties are also true for fat trees of higher degrees but with different log bases. For example, a fat degree 10 tree containing N nodes has height $O(\log_{10} N)$. Because all log bases are the same in Big O notation, this is the same as $O(\log N)$, although in practice the constants ignored by Big O notation may make a big difference.

Chapter 11 describes balanced trees that do not to grow too tall and thin in order to guarantee that these properties are true.

Tree Representations

You can use a class to represent a tree's nodes. For complete trees, you can also store the tree in an array. The following two sections describe these approaches.

Building Trees in General

You can use a class to represent a tree's nodes much as you can use them to make the cells in a linked list. Give the class whatever properties it needs to hold data. Also give it object references to represent the branches to the node's children.

In a binary tree, you can use separate properties named `LeftChild` and `RightChild` for the branches.

The following pseudocode shows how you might create a binary node class. The details will differ depending on your programming language.

```
Class BinaryNode
    String: Name
    BinaryNode: LeftChild
    BinaryNode: RightChild

    Constructor(String: name)
        Name = name
    End Constructor
End Class
```

The class begins by declaring a public property called `Name` to hold the node's name. It then defines two properties named `LeftChild` and `RightChild` to hold references to the node's children.

The class's constructor takes a string as a parameter and saves it in the node's `Name` property.

The following pseudocode shows how you could use this class to build the tree shown in Figure 10.1:

```
BinaryNode: root = New BinaryNode("4")
BinaryNode: node1 = New BinaryNode("1")
BinaryNode: node2 = New BinaryNode("2")
BinaryNode: node3 = New BinaryNode("3")
BinaryNode: node5 = New BinaryNode("5")
BinaryNode: node6 = New BinaryNode("6")
BinaryNode: node7 = New BinaryNode("7")
BinaryNode: node8 = New BinaryNode("8")
root.LeftChild = node2
root.RightChild = node5
node2.LeftChild = node1
node2.RightChild = node3
node5.RightChild = node7
```

```
node7.LeftChild = node6
node7.RightChild = node8
```

This code first creates a `BinaryNode` object to represent the root. It then creates other `BinaryNode` objects to represent the tree's other nodes. After it has created all the nodes, the code sets the nodes' left and right child references.

Sometimes, it may be useful to make the constructor take as parameters references to the node's children. If one of those values should be undefined, you can pass the value `null`, `None`, or your programming language's equivalent into the constructor. The following pseudocode shows how you might build the same tree if the constructor takes a node's children as parameters:

```
BinaryNode: node1 = New BinaryNode("1", null, null)
BinaryNode: node3 = New BinaryNode("3", null, null)
BinaryNode: node1 = New BinaryNode("6", null, null)
BinaryNode: node3 = New BinaryNode("8", null, null)
BinaryNode: node2 = New BinaryNode("2", node1, node3)
BinaryNode: node7 = New BinaryNode("7", node6, node8)
BinaryNode: node5 = New BinaryNode("5", null, node7)
BinaryNode: root = New BinaryNode("4", node2, node5)
```

If the tree's degree is greater than 2 or if it is unordered (so that the order of a node's children is unimportant), it is usually more convenient to put the child references in an array, list, or some other collection. That lets the program loop through the children, doing something to each, instead of requiring you to write a separate line of code for each child.

The following pseudocode shows how you could create a `TreeNode` class that allows each node to have any number of children:

```
Class TreeNode
    String: Name
    List Of TreeNode: Children

    Constructor(String: name)
        Name = name
    End Constructor
End Class
```

This class is similar to the preceding one, except that it stores its children in a `List` of references to `TreeNode` objects instead of in separate properties.

The following pseudocode shows another approach for creating a `TreeNode` class that allows nodes to have any number of children:

```
Class TreeNode
    String: Name
    TreeNode: FirstChild, NextSibling
    Constructor(String: name)
```

```
            Name = name
        End Constructor
    End Class
```

In this version, the `FirstChild` field provides a link to the first of the node's children. The `NextSibling` field is a link to the next sibling in the child nodes of this node's parent. Basically, this treats a node's child list as a linked list of nodes.

Figure 10.4 shows these two representations of trees where nodes can have any number of children. The version on the left is often easier to understand. However, the version on the right lets you treat child nodes as linked lists, so it may make rearranging children easier.

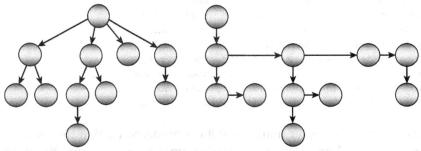

Figure 10.4: These are two representations of the same tree.

Occasionally, it may be useful to make a node class's constructor take a parameter giving the node's parent. It can then add the child to the parent's `Children` list.

Notice that these representations only have links from a node to its child nodes. They don't include a link from a node up to its parent. Most tree algorithms work in a top-down manner, so they move from parent to child down into the tree. If you really need to be able to find a node's parent, however, you can add a `Parent` property to the node class.

Most tree algorithms store data in each node, but a few store information in the branches. If you need to store information in the branches, you can add the information to the child nodes. The following pseudocode demonstrates this approach:

```
Class TreeNode
    String: Name
    List Of TreeNode: Children
    List Of Data: BranchData

    Constructor(String: name)
        Name = name
    End Constructor
End Class
```

Now when you add a node to the tree, you also need to add data for the branch that leads to that child.

Often, an algorithm will need to use the branch data to decide which path to take down through the tree. In that case, it can loop through a node's children and examine their branch data to pick the appropriate path.

XML AND TREES

Extensible Markup Language (*XML*) is a markup language for representing data. XML documents are hierarchical. You define tokens nested within other tokens.

XML's hierarchical structure makes it a natural choice for storing trees persistently and for transmitting trees from one program or computer to another. For example, you could build a large tree representing your company's organizational chart, save it in an XML file, and then share that file with other programs throughout your company.

For more information on XML, see http://en.wikipedia.org/wiki/XML or http://www.w3schools.com/xml/xml:whatis.asp, or get a book about XML such as *Beginning XML*, 5th edition, by Joe Fawcett, *et al.* (Wrox, 2012).

Building Complete Trees

The heapsort algorithm described in Chapter 6 uses a complete binary tree stored in an array to represent a heap, a binary tree in which every node holds a value that is at least as large as the values in all of its children. Figure 10.5 shows a heap represented as a tree and stored in an array.

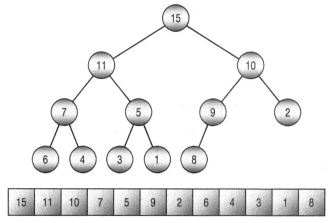

Figure 10.5: You can store a heap, or any complete binary tree, conveniently in an array.

If a node is stored at index i in the array, the indices of its children are $2 \times i + 1$ and $2 \times i + 2$.

Conversely, if a node has index j, its parent has index $\lfloor (j - 1) \div 2 \rfloor$ where $\lfloor \ \rfloor$ means to truncate the result to the next-smaller integer. For example, $\lfloor 2.9 \rfloor$ is 2 and $\lfloor 2 \rfloor$ is also 2.

This provides a concise format for storing any complete binary tree in an array. Working with this kind of tree can be a bit awkward and confusing, however, particularly if you need to resize the array frequently. For those reasons, you may want to stick to using classes to build trees.

> **NOTE** Now that you know more about trees, you may want to reread the section "Heapsort" in Chapter 6 to see how you can use classes instead of an array to build a heap.

Tree Traversal

One of the most basic and important tree operations is traversal. In a *traversal*, the goal is for the algorithm to visit all the nodes in the tree in some order and perform an operation on them. The most basic traversal simply enumerates the nodes so that you can see their ordering in the traversal.

> **TRAVERSAL AND SEARCHING**
>
> Many algorithms search a tree for a particular node. In general, these searches are traversals, and you can use any traversal as the basis for a search.
>
> Chapter 11 describes some special cases in which you can use the structure of the data in a tree to search it efficiently.

Binary trees have four kinds of traversals.

Preorder: This traversal visits a node before visiting its children.

Inorder: This traversal visits a node's left child, then the node, then its right child.

Postorder: This traversal visits a node's children before visiting the node.

Breadth-first: This traversal visits all the nodes at a given level in the tree before visiting any nodes at lower levels.

Preorder, postorder, and breadth-first traversals make sense for any kind of tree. Inorder traversals are usually only defined for binary trees.

Because the preorder, inorder, and postorder traversals all dive deeply into the tree before backtracking up to visit other parts of the tree, they are sometimes called *depth-first traversals*.

The following sections describe the four kinds of traversals in greater detail.

Preorder Traversal

In a *preorder traversal*, the algorithm processes a node followed by its left child and then its right child. For example, consider the tree shown in Figure 10.6 and suppose that you're writing an algorithm simply to display the tree's nodes in a preorder traversal.

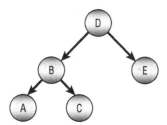

Figure 10.6: Traversals process a tree's nodes in different orders.

To produce the tree's preorder traversal, the algorithm first visits the root node, so it immediately outputs the value D. The algorithm then moves to the root node's left child.

It visits that node, so it outputs B and then moves to that node's left child.

There the algorithm outputs A. That node has no children, so the algorithm returns to the previous node, B, and visits that node's right child.

There the algorithm outputs C. That node also has no children, so the algorithm returns to the previous node, B. It has finished visiting that node's children, so the algorithm moves up the tree again to node D and visits that node's right child.

The algorithm outputs the next node, E. That node also has no children, so the algorithm returns to the previous node, which is the root node. It has finished visiting the root's children, so the algorithm is done producing the traversal.

The full traversal order is D, B, A, C, E.

Notice that the algorithm examines or visits the nodes in one order but processes the nodes to produce an output in a different order. The following list shows the series of steps the algorithm follows while producing the preorder traversal for the tree shown in Figure 10.6:

1. Visit D

2. Output D

3. Visit B

4. Output B

5. Visit A

6. Output A

7. Visit B

8. Visit C

9. Output C

10. Visit B

11. Visit D

12. Visit E

13. Output E

14. Visit D

The following pseudocode shows a natural recursive implementation of this algorithm:

```
TraversePreorder(BinaryNode: node)
    <Process node>
    If (node.LeftChild != null) Then TraversePreorder(node.LeftChild)
    If (node.RightChild != null) Then TraversePreorder(node.RightChild)
End TraversePreorder
```

This algorithm simply follows the definition of a preorder traversal. It starts by processing the current node. In a real program, you would insert whatever code you needed to execute for each node here. For example, you might use code that adds the current node's label to an output string, you might examine the node to see whether you had found a particular target item, or you might add the node itself to an output list.

Next the algorithm determines whether the node has a left child. If it does, the algorithm calls itself recursively to traverse the left child's subtree. The algorithm then repeats that step for the right child and is done.

The algorithm is extremely short and simple.

To traverse the entire tree, a program would simply call TraversePreorder, passing it the root node as a parameter.

This algorithm works quite well, but its code must be placed somewhere in the program—perhaps in the main program, in a code module, or in a helper class. Usually, it is more convenient to place code that manipulates a tree inside its node class. The following pseudocode shows the same algorithm implemented inside the BinaryNode class:

```
Class BinaryNode
    ...
    TraversePreorder()
```

```
        <Process this node>
        If (LeftChild != null) Then TraversePreorder(LeftChild)
        If (RightChild != null) Then TraversePreorder(RightChild)
    End TraversePreorder
End Class
```

This is almost the same as the previous version, except that the code is running within a `BinaryNode` object, so it has direct access to that object's `LeftChild` and `RightChild` properties. This makes the code slightly simpler and keeps it nicely encapsulated within the `BinaryNode` class (thus making it more object-oriented'ish).

Now, to traverse the entire tree, you simply invoke the root node's `Traverse-Preorder` method.

PASSING METHODS

In most programming languages, you can pass a reference to a method as a parameter to a method. In this example, this means that you could pass a method to use on a node into the `TraversePreorder` method. When `TraversePreorder` reaches the step `<Process this node>`, it would call the method that was passed into it as a parameter.

This lets you use a single `TraversePreorder` method to do pretty much anything you want to the tree by passing it an appropriate node processing method.

You can use a similar technique to make other traversal algorithms perform arbitrary actions on a tree's nodes.

Although this discussion is about binary trees, you can also define a preorder traversal for trees of higher degrees. The only rule is that you visit the node first and then visit its children.

Inorder Traversal

In an *inorder traversal* or *symmetric traversal*, the algorithm processes a node's left child, the node, and then the node's right child. For the tree shown in Figure 10.6, the algorithm starts at the root node and moves to its left child B. To process node B, the algorithm first moves to that node's left child A.

Node A has no left child, so the algorithm visits the node and outputs A. Node A also has no right child, so the algorithm returns to the parent node B.

Having finished with node B's left child, the algorithm processes node B and outputs B. It then moves to that node's right child C.

Node C has no left child, so the algorithm visits the node and outputs C. The node also has no right child, so the algorithm returns to the parent node B.

The algorithm has finished with node B's right child, so it returns to the root node D. The algorithm has finished with D's left child, so it outputs D and then moves to its right child E.

Node E has no left child, so the algorithm visits the node and outputs E. The node also has no right child, so the algorithm returns to the parent node D.

The full traversal order is A, B, C, D, E. Notice that this outputs the tree's nodes in sorted order. Normally the term *sorted tree* means that the tree's nodes are arranged so that an inorder traversal processes them in sorted order like this.

The following pseudocode shows a recursive implementation of this algorithm inside the `BinaryNode` class:

```
Class BinaryNode
    . . .
    TraverseInorder()
        If (LeftChild != null) Then TraverseInorder(LeftChild)
        <Process this node>
        If (RightChild != null) Then TraverseInorder(RightChild)
    End TraverseInorder
End Class
```

This algorithm simply follows the definition of an inorder traversal. It recursively processes the node's left child if it exists, processes the node itself, and then recursively processes the node's right child if it exists.

To traverse the entire tree, a program would simply call the root node's `TraverseInorder` method.

Unlike the preorder traversal, it's unclear how you would define an inorder traversal for a tree with a degree greater than 2. You could define it to mean that the algorithm processes the first half of a node's children, then the node, and then the remaining children. That's an unusual traversal, however.

Postorder Traversal

In a *postorder traversal*, the algorithm processes a node's left child, then its right child, and then the node. By now you should be getting the hang of traversals, so you should be able to verify that the postorder traversal for the tree shown in Figure 10.6 is A, C, B, E, D.

The following pseudocode shows a recursive implementation of this algorithm inside the `BinaryNode` class:

```
Class BinaryNode
    . . .
    TraverseInorder()
        If (LeftChild != null) Then TraversePostorder(LeftChild)
        If (RightChild != null) Then TraversePostorder(RightChild)
        <Process this node>
    End TraversePostorder
End Class
```

This algorithm recursively processes the node's children if they exist and then processes the node. To traverse the entire tree, a program would simply call the root node's `TraversePostorder` method.

Like the preorder traversal, you can define a postorder traversal for trees with a degree greater than 2. The algorithm simply visits all of a node's children before visiting the node itself.

Breadth-First Traversal

In a *breadth-first traversal* or *level-order traversal*, the algorithm processes all the nodes at a given level of the tree in left-to-right order before processing the nodes at the next level. For the tree shown in Figure 10.6, the algorithm starts at the root node's level and outputs D.

The algorithm then moves to the next level and outputs B and E.

The algorithm finishes at the bottom level by outputting the nodes A and C. The full traversal is D, B, E, A, C.

This algorithm does not naturally follow the structure of the tree as the previous traversal algorithms do. The tree shown in Figure 10.6 has no child link from node E to node A, so it's not obvious how the algorithm moves from node E to node A.

One solution is to add a node's children to a queue and then process the queue later, after you've finished processing the parents' level. The following pseudocode uses this approach:

```
TraverseDepthFirst(BinaryNode: root)
    // Create a queue to hold children for later processing.
    Queue<BinaryNode>: children = New Queue<BinaryNode>()

    // Place the root node on the queue.
    children.Enqueue(root)

    // Process the queue until it is empty.
    While (children Is Not Empty)
        // Get the next node in the queue.
        BinaryNode: node = children.Dequeue()

        // Process the node.
        <Process node>

        // Add the node's children to the queue.
        If (node.LeftChild != null) children.Enqueue(node.LeftChild)
        If (node.RightChild != null) children.Enqueue(node.RightChild)
    End While
End TraverseDepthFirst
```

This algorithm starts by making a queue and placing the root node in it. It then enters a loop that continues until the queue is empty.

Inside the loop, the algorithm removes the first node from the queue, processes it, and adds the node's children to the queue.

Because a queue processes items in first-in, first-out order, all of the nodes at a particular level in the tree are processed before any of their child nodes are processed. Because the algorithm adds each node's left child to the queue before it adds the right node to the queue, the nodes on a particular level are processed in left-to-right order. (If you want to be more precise, you can prove these facts by induction.)

Traversal Uses

Tree traversals are often used by other algorithms to visit the tree's nodes in various orders. The following list describes a few situations when a particular traversal might be handy:

- If you want to copy a tree, then you need to create each node before you can create that node's children. In that case, a preorder traversal is helpful because it visits the original tree's nodes before visiting their children.

- Preorder traversals are also useful for evaluating mathematical equations written in *Polish notation*. (See https://en.wikipedia.org/wiki/ Polish_notation.)

- If the tree is sorted, then an inorder traversal *flattens* the tree and visits its nodes in their sorted order.

- Inorder traversals are also useful for evaluating normal mathematical expressions. The section "Expression Evaluation," later in this chapter, explains that technique.

- A breadth-first traversal lets you find a node that is as close to the root as possible. For example, if you want to find a particular value in the tree and that value may occur more than once, then a breadth-first traversal will let you find the value that is closest to the root. (This same approach is even more useful in some network algorithms, such as certain shortest path algorithms.)

- Postorder traversals are useful for evaluating mathematical equations written in *reverse Polish notation*. (See https://en.wikipedia.org/wiki/ Reverse_Polish_notation.)

- Postorder traversals are also useful for destroying trees in languages, such as C and C++, which do not have garbage collection. In those languages, you must free a node's memory *before* you free any objects that might be pointing to it. In a tree, a parent node holds references to its children, so you must free the children first. A postorder traversal lets you visit the nodes in the correct order.

Traversal Run Times

The three recursive algorithms for preorder, inorder, and postorder traversal all travel down the tree to the leaf nodes. Then, as the recursive calls unwind, they travel back up to the root. After an algorithm visits a node and then returns to the node's parent, the algorithm doesn't visit that node again. That means the algorithms visit each node once. So, if a tree contains N nodes, they all have O(N) run time.

Another way to see this is to realize that the algorithms cross each link once. A tree with N nodes has N − 1 links, so the algorithms cross O(N) links and therefore have O(N) run time.

Those three algorithms don't need any extra storage space, because they use the tree's structure to keep track of where they are in the traversal. They do, however, have depths of recursion equal to the tree's height. If the tree is very tall, that could cause a stack overflow.

The breadth-first traversal algorithm processes nodes as they move through a queue. Each node enters and leaves the queue once, so if the tree has N nodes, the algorithm takes O(N) time.

This algorithm isn't recursive, so it doesn't have problems with large depths of recursion. Instead, it needs extra space to build its queue. In the worst case, if the tree is a perfect binary tree, its bottom level holds roughly half the total number of nodes (see the earlier section "Facts About Binary Trees"), so if the tree holds N nodes, the queue holds up to O(N ÷ 2) = O(N) nodes at one time.

More generally, a tree of arbitrary degree might consist of a root node that has every other node as a child. In that case, the queue might need to hold N − 1 nodes, so the space requirement is still O(N).

Sorted Trees

As mentioned earlier, a sorted tree's nodes are arranged so that an inorder traversal processes them in sorted order. Another way to think of this is that each node's value is larger than the value of its left child and less than (or equal to) the value of its right child. Figure 10.7 shows a sorted tree.

To use a sorted tree, you need three algorithms to add, delete, and find nodes.

Adding Nodes

Building a sorted tree is fairly easy. To add a value to a node's subtree, compare the new value to the node's value and recursively move down the left or right branch as appropriate. When you try to move down a missing branch, add the new value there.

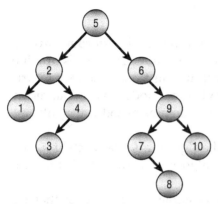

Figure 10.7: In a sorted tree, a node's value lies between the values of its left child and its right child.

The following pseudocode shows the algorithm for a `BinaryNode` class. The code assumes that the class has a `Value` property to hold the node's data.

```
// Add a node to this node's sorted subtree.
AddNode(Data: new_value)
    // See if this value is smaller than ours.
    If (new_value < Value) Then
        // The new value is smaller. Add it to the left subtree.
        If (LeftChild == null) LeftChild = New BinaryNode(new_value)
        Else LeftChild.AddNode(new_value)
    Else
        // The new value is not smaller. Add it to the right subtree.
        If (RightChild == null) RightChild = New BinaryNode(new_value)
        Else RightChild.AddNode(new_value)
    End If
End AddNode
```

The algorithm compares the new value to the current node's value. If the new value is smaller than the node's value, the algorithm should place the new value in the left subtree. If the left child reference is `null`, the algorithm gives the current node a new left child node and places the new value there. If the left child is not `null`, the algorithm calls the child node's `AddNode` method recursively to place the new value in the left subtree.

If the new value is not smaller than the node's value, the algorithm should place the new value in the right subtree. If the right child reference is `null`, the algorithm gives the current node a new right child node and places the new value there. If the right child is not `null`, the algorithm calls the child node's `AddNode` method recursively to place the new value in the right subtree.

> **NOTE**   As was the case for the linked lists described in Chapter 3, it is sometimes helpful to use a sentinel at the top of a tree. For a sorted tree, if you set the root node's value to something smaller than any possible value the tree might need to contain, you can simply add nodes to the tree without worrying about whether it is empty. All of the nodes that you add end up in the right subtree below the root.

The run time for this algorithm depends on the order in which you add the items to the tree. If the items are initially ordered in a reasonably random way, the tree grows relatively short and wide. In that case, if you add N nodes to the tree, it has height $O(\log N)$. When you add an item to the tree, you must search to the bottom of the tree, and that takes $O(\log N)$ steps. Adding N nodes at $O(\log N)$ steps each makes the total time to build the tree $O(N \log N)$.

RANDOM TREE HEIGHT

When you build a nice, wide sorted tree, it may not be obvious that you're adding $O(N)$ nodes at a height of $O(\log N)$. After all, what if most of the nodes fit near the top of the tree so that the tree is short while you're adding most of the nodes?

Recall from the earlier section "Facts About Binary Trees" that roughly half of the nodes in a perfect binary tree are at the bottom of the tree. This means that after you have added half of the nodes to the tree, you have built all but the last level of the tree, so it already has height $\log(N)-1$. Now you need to add the remaining half of the nodes at a depth of $\log(N)-1$. The total number of steps for that part of the algorithm is $N/2 \times \log(N)-1$, which is still $O(N \log N)$.

If the values in the tree are initially randomly ordered, you get a reasonably wide tree. However, if you add the values in certain orders, you get a tall, thin tree. In the worst case, if you add the values in sorted or reverse sorted order, every node has a single child, and you get a tree containing N nodes that has height N.

In that case, adding the nodes takes $1 + 2 + 3 + \ldots + N = N(N+1)/2$ steps, so the algorithm runs in $O(N^2)$ time.

You can use the `AddNode` algorithm to build a sorting algorithm called treesort. In the *treesort algorithm*, you use the previous `AddNode` algorithm to add values to a sorted tree. You then use an inorder traversal to output the items in sorted order. If the items are initially arranged randomly, then using the `AddNode` algorithm to build the tree takes expected time $O(N \log N)$, and the inorder traversal takes $O(N)$ time, so the total run time is $O(N \log N + N) = O(N \log N)$.

In the worst case, building the sorted tree takes $O(N^2)$ time. Adding the $O(N)$ time for the inorder traversal gives a total run time of $O(N^2 + N) = O(N^2)$.

Finding Nodes

After you build a sorted tree, you can search for specific items in it. For example, nodes might represent employee records, and the values used to order the tree might be a record's employee ID. The following pseudocode shows a method provided by the `BinaryNode` class that searches a node's subtree for a target value:

```
// Find a node with a given target value.
BinaryNode: FindNode(Key: target)
    // If we've found the target value, return this node.
    If (target == Value) Then Return <this node>

    // See if the desired value is in the left or right subtree.
    If (target < Value) Then
        // Search the left subtree.
        If (LeftChild == null) Then Return null
        Return LeftChild.FindNode(target)
    Else
        // Search the right subtree.
        If (RightChild == null) Then Return null
        Return RightChild.FindNode(target)
    End If
End FindNode
```

First the algorithm checks the current node's value. If that value equals the target value, the algorithm returns the current node.

Next, if the target value is less than the current node's value, the desired node lies in this node's left subtree. If the left child branch is `null`, the algorithm returns `null` to indicate that the target item isn't in the tree. If the left child isn't `null`, the algorithm recursively calls the left child's `FindNode` method to search that subtree.

If the target value is greater than the current node's value, the algorithm performs similar steps to search the right subtree.

If the tree contains N nodes and is reasonably balanced so that it isn't tall and thin, it has height O(log N), so this search takes O(log N) steps.

Deleting Nodes

Deleting a node from a sorted tree is a bit more complicated than adding one.

The first step is finding the node to delete. The preceding section explained how to do that.

The next step depends on the position of the target node in the tree. To understand the different situations, consider the tree shown in Figure 10.8.

If the target node is a leaf node, you can simply delete it, and the tree is still sorted. For example, if you remove node 89 from the tree shown in Figure 10.8, you get the tree shown in Figure 10.9.

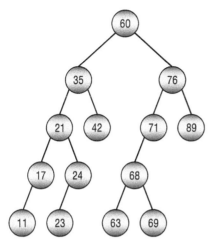

Figure 10.8: How you delete a node from a sorted binary tree depends on the node's position in the tree.

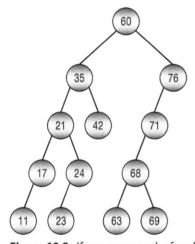

Figure 10.9: If you remove a leaf node from a sorted binary tree, it remains a sorted binary tree.

If the target node is not a leaf and it has only one child, you can replace the node with its child. For example, if you remove node 71 from the tree shown in Figure 10.9, you get the tree shown in Figure 10.10.

The trickiest case occurs when the target node has two children. In that case, the general strategy is to replace the node with its left child, but that leads to two subcases.

First, if the target node's left child has no right child, you can simply replace the target node with its left child. For example, if you remove node 21 from the tree shown in Figure 10.10, you get the tree shown in Figure 10.11.

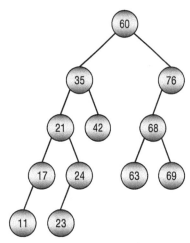

Figure 10.10: To remove an internal node that has one child, replace it with its child.

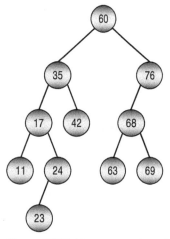

Figure 10.11: To remove a target node with two children and whose left child has no right child, replace the target node with its left child.

The final case occurs when the target node has two children and its left child has a right child. In that case, search down the tree to find the rightmost node below the target node's left child. If that node has no children, simply replace the target node with it. If that node has a left child, replace it with its left child and then replace the target node with the rightmost node.

Figure 10.12 shows this case where you want to remove node 35. Now 35 has two children, and its left child (17) has a right child (24). The algorithm moves down from the left child (17) as far as possible by following right child links. In this example, that leads to node 24, but in general that rightmost child could be farther down the tree.

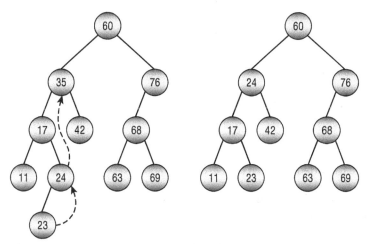

Figure 10.12: Removing a target node with two children whose left child has a right child is the most complicated operation for a sorted binary tree.

To delete the target node, the algorithm replaces the rightmost node with its child (if it has one) and then replaces the target node with the rightmost node. In this example, the program replaces node 24 with node 23 and then replaces node 35 with node 24, resulting in the tree on the right in Figure 10.12.

Lowest Common Ancestors

There are several ways that you can find the *lowest common ancestor* (LCA) of two nodes. Different LCA algorithms work with different kinds of trees and produce different desired behaviors. For example, some algorithms work on sorted trees, others work when child nodes have links to their parents, and some preprocess the tree to provide faster lookup of lowest common ancestors later.

The following sections describe several lowest common ancestor algorithms that work under different circumstances.

Sorted Trees

In a sorted tree, you can use a relatively simple top-down algorithm to find the lowest common ancestor of two nodes. Start at the tree's root and recursively move down through the tree. At each node, determine the child branch down which the two nodes lie. If they lie down the same branch, recursively follow it. If they lie down different child branches, then the current node is the lowest common ancestor.

For example, suppose that you want to find the lowest common ancestor of the nodes 3 and 7 in the sorted binary tree shown in Figure 10.13.

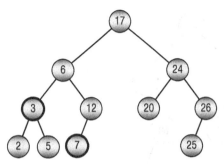

Figure 10.13: You can search a sorted tree from the top down to find lowest common ancestors.

You start at the root, which has value 17. That value is greater than both 3 and 7. Both of those values lie down the left child branch, so that's the branch you follow.

Now you compare the node's value, 6, to 3 and 17. The value 6 is greater than 3 and less than 7, so this is the lowest common ancestor.

The following pseudocode shows this algorithm:

```
// Find the LCA for the two nodes.
TreeNode: FindLcaSortedTree(Integer: value1, Integer: value2)
    // See if both nodes belong down the same child branch.
    If ((value1 < Value) && (value2 < Value)) Then
        Return LeftChild.FindLca(value1, value2)
    End If
    If ((value1 > Value) && (value2 > Value)) Then
        Return RightChild.FindLca(value1, value2)
    End If

    // This is the LCA.
    Return <this node>
End FindLcaSortedTree
```

This algorithm is implemented as a method in the `TreeNode` class. It compares the current node's value to the two descendant node values. If both of the target values are less than the node's value, then they both lie down the node's left child subtree, so the algorithm recursively calls itself on the left child. Similarly, if both values are greater than the node's value, then they both lie down the node's right child subtree, so the algorithm recursively calls itself on the right child.

If the target values do not both lie down the same child subtree, then either they are in different child subtrees or the current node holds one of the values. In either of those cases, the current node is the lowest common ancestor, so the algorithm returns the current node.

Parent Pointers

Suppose the tree's nodes include references to their parent nodes. In that case, you can use a simple marking strategy to find the lowest common ancestor of two nodes. Follow the parent pointers from the first node to the root marking each node as visited. Then follow parent pointers from the second node to the root until you reach a marked node. The first marked node that you reach is the LCA. Finish by following the parent pointers above the first node again to reset their marked flags so the tree will be ready for future operations.

The following pseudocode shows this algorithm:

```
TreeNode: FindLcaParentPointers(TreeNode: node1, TreeNode: node2)
    # Mark nodes above node1.
    TreeNode: node = node1
    While (node != null)
        node.Marked = True
        node = node.Parent
    End While

    # Search nodes above node2 until we find a marked node.
    TreeNode: lca = null
    node = node2
    While (node != null)
        If (node.Marked) Then
            lca = node
            Break
        End If
        node = node.Parent

    # Unmark nodes above node1.
    node = node1
    While (node != null)
        node.Marked = False
        node = node.Parent
    End While

    # Return the LCA.
    Return lca
End FindLcaParentPointers
```

This code simply follows the algorithm described earlier.

This algorithm has the drawback that it requires extra storage for the `Marked` field in the `TreeNode` class.

Parents and Depths

If the `TreeNode` class contains a `Depth` field that indicates the node's depth in the tree in addition to a parent reference, then you can you can use that field to implement another method for finding the LCA without using marking. Starting at the node with the greater depth, follow parent nodes up the tree until you reach the other node's depth. Then move up both nodes' parent chains until the two paths meet at the same node. The following pseudocode shows this algorithm:

```
TreeNode: FindLcaParentsAndDepths(TreeNode: node1, TreeNode: node2)
    // Climb up until the nodes have the same depth.
    While (node1.Depth > node2.Depth) node1 = node1.Parent
    While (node2.Depth > node1.Depth) node2 = node2.Parent

    // Climb up until the nodes match.
    While (node1 != node2)
        node1 = node1.Paren
        node2 = node2.Parent
    End While

    Return node1
FindLcaParentsAndDepths
```

This algorithm has a couple of advantages over the preceding approach. In this algorithm, the Depth field basically replaces the Marked field, so it doesn't use any extra space. It is slightly faster because it doesn't need to retrace the first node's path to the root to unmark previously marked nodes. It also only traces the paths until they meet, so it doesn't need to go all the way to the root.

The preceding version may still be useful, however, if you want the TreeNode class to have a Marked field for use by some other algorithm.

General Trees

The first LCA algorithm described in this chapter used a top-down search through a sorted binary tree to find the LCA of two nodes. You can also use a top-down approach to find the LCA for two values in an unsorted tree.

The previous algorithm compared the target values at each node to the node's value to see which branch it should move down in its search. Because the tree in the new scenario is unsorted, comparing values won't tell you which branch to move down. Instead, you basically need to perform a search of the complete tree to find the nodes containing the target values. That idea leads to the following straightforward algorithm:

```
TreeNode: FindLcaExhaustively(Integer: value1, Integer: value2)
    <Traverse the tree to find the path from the root to value1.>
    <Traverse the tree to find the path from the root to value2.>
    <Follow the two paths until they diverge.>
    <Return the last node that is on both paths.>
FindLcaExhaustively
```

In some sense, this algorithm is optimal. You don't know where the values might be in the tree, so in the worst case you might need to search the entire

tree before you find them. If the tree contains N nodes, then this is an O(N) algorithm.

Although you can't change that algorithm's big O run time, you can improve the real-world performance slightly by searching for both values at the same time and stopping when you find the LCA.

The basic idea is similar to the one used by the algorithm for the sorted tree. At each node, you determine down which child branch the two values lie. The LCA is the first node where the values lie down different child branches.

However, because this tree isn't sorted, you can't use the nodes' values to determine which child subtrees contain them. Instead, you need to perform a traversal of the subtrees, but you need to be careful. If you simply traverse the subtrees at every step, then you will end up traversing the same parts of the tree many times.

For example, suppose that the target values are near the rightmost edge of the tree. At the root node, you would traverse most of the tree before learning that you need to move down to the rightmost child. Then at the root's right child node, you would traverse most of its subtree to learn that you need to move down to its rightmost child. You would repeatedly traverse smaller and smaller pieces of the right part of the tree until you finally reached the LCA.

You can avoid those repeated traversals if you keep track of both values as you traverse the tree only once. The following pseudocode demonstrates that approach:

```
TreeNode: FindLca(Integer: value1, Integer: value2)
    Boolean: contains1, contains2
    Return ContainsNodes(value1, value2,
        Output contains1, Output contains2)
End FindLca
```

This algorithm simply calls the root node's ContainsNodes algorithm, shown in the following pseudocode, to do all of the actual work:

```
// Find the LCA for the two nodes.
TreeNode: ContainsNodes(Integer: value1, Integer: value2,
    Output Boolean: contains1, Output Boolean: contains2)

    // Assume we won't find the target values.
    contains1 = (Value == value1)
    contains2 = (Value == value2)
    If (contains1 && contains2) Then Return <this node>

    // See which children contain the values.
    For Each child In Children
        // Check this child.
        Boolean: has1, has2
```

```
        TreeNode: lca = child.ContainsNodes(value1, value2,
            Output has1, Output has2)

        // If we have found the LCA, return it.
        If (lca != null) Then Return lca

        // Update contains1 and contains2.
        If (has1) Then contains1 = True
        If (has2) Then contains2 = True

        // If we found both values in different
        // children, then this is the LCA.
        If (contains1 && contains2) Then Return <this node>
    Next child
    Return null
End ContainsNodes
```

This algorithm takes two output parameters that it uses to keep track of whether a particular node's subtree contains the target values. Alternatively, you could make the method return a tuple containing the LCA and those two values instead of using output parameters.

The code first sets the Boolean variables contains1 and contains2 to true if the current node equals either of the target values. If both of those values are true, then the two values are the same and they equal the node's value, so the code returns the node as the LCA.

Next, the code loops through the node's children. It recursively calls the ContainsNodes algorithm to look for the LCA in that child's subtree. The recursive call sets the has1 and has2 variables to indicate whether the subtree contains the target values.

If the recursive call returns an LCA, then the current instance of the algorithm returns it.

Otherwise, if the recursive call returns null, the current instance of the algorithm uses has1 and has2 to update contains1 and contains2. If contains1 and contains2 are now both true, the algorithm returns the current node as the LCA.

If the algorithm finishes examining all of the current node's children without finding the LCA, then the algorithm returns null.

Euler Tours

The previous LCA algorithms use the tree's structure to find the LCA. Other algorithms preprocess the tree to make it easier to find LCAs later. One approach that makes it at least conceptually easier to find LCAs is to look at the tree's Euler tour.

An *Euler tour* or *Eulerian path* is a path through a network that crosses every edge once. (Euler is pronounced "oiler.") To make an Euler tour in a tree, you double each branch so that there is an upward and downward branch. You then traverse the tree as shown in Figure 10.14.

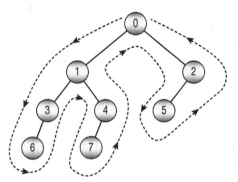

Figure 10.14: This tree's Euler tour visits the nodes in the order 0, 1, 3, 6, 3, 1, 4, 7, 4, 1, 0, 2, 5, 2, 0.

The dashed path in Figure 10.14 shows the Euler tour. Notice that nonleaf nodes are visited multiple times as the path moves up and down the tree. For example, the tour visits node 1 three times: on the way down to node 3, on the way back up from node 3 and down to node 4, and on the way back up from node 4. The complete tour visits the tree's nodes in the order 0, 1, 3, 6, 3, 1, 4, 7, 4, 1, 0, 2, 5, 2, 0.

A useful feature of the Euler tour is that the LCA of two nodes lies between their entries in the tour. For example, consider nodes 3 and 7 in Figure 10.14, and look at their positions in the Euler tour. First, notice that all of node 3s entries in the tour (it appears twice) come before all of node 7s entries in the tour (it appears only once). If you look at the interval between any of node 3s entries and any of node 7s entries, then that interval contains the LCA of nodes 3 and 7. For example, the longest such interval visits the nodes 3, 6, 3, 1, 4, 7 and node 1 is the LCA.

These observations lead to the following high-level steps for finding LCAs.

1. Preprocessing:
    a. Add two new fields to the node class.
        i. Depth is the node's depth in the tree.
        ii. TourLocation is the index of the node's first position in the Euler tour.
    b. Perform a traversal of the tree to assign each node's Depth.
    c. Build the Euler tour and save it as a list containing the nodes in the order in which they are visited. Set each node's TourLocation value to the index of the node's first occurrence in the tour.

2. To find the LCA, loop between the two nodes' `TourLocation` values to examine the nodes that appear between them in the tour. The node with the smallest `Depth` is the LCA.

This algorithm requires some preprocessing, but scanning the tour is much easier to understand than the recursive ContainsNode algorithm described in the preceding section. One drawback to this approach is that you need to update the tour information if you modify the tree.

Chapter 14, "More Network Algorithms," explains how you can find Eulerian paths through a network.

All Pairs

The fastest and easiest possible way to find LCAs would be simply to look up the LCA in an array. For example, the value `LCA[i, j]` would return the LCA of nodes i and j.

The following pseudocode snippet shows how you might build that array:

```
// Allocate the array.
Lcas = new TreeNode[numNodes, numNodes]

// Fill in the array values.
For i = 0 to <number of nodes - 1>
    For j = i to <number of nodes - 1>
        Lcas[i, j] = FindLca(i, j)
        Lcas[j, i] = Lcas[i, j]
    Next j
Next i
```

This code allocates the array and then loops through all of the pairs of node values. For each pair, it uses some other method such as the Euler tour to find the LCA and saves the result in the array.

Building the array requires you to examine $O(N^2)$ pairs of nodes, so it is relatively slow. The array also uses $O(N^2)$ memory, so it takes up a lot of space. You will also need to restructure or rebuild the array if you modify the tree. All of those factors make this method impractical for large trees.

The key to the Euler Tour approach is finding the minimum depth of the nodes within a range of values given by part of the Euler tour. The general problem of finding the minimum value in a range of values such as this is called the *range minimum query problem*. Other versions of this algorithm use special techniques to solve the range minimum query problem quickly. They allow the algorithm to find LCAs in constant time with only $O(N)$ amount of extra storage. Unfortunately, those algorithms are too complicated to include here.

Threaded Trees

A *thread* is a sequence of links that allows you to move through the nodes in a tree or network in a way other than by following normal branches or links. A *threaded tree* is a tree that contains one or more threads.

For example, Figure 10.15 shows a tree with threads represented by dashed arrows.

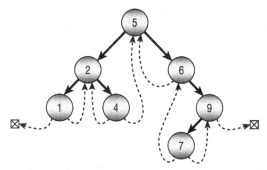

Figure 10.15: A threaded tree contains references that let you move through the tree without following its normal branches.

The threads shown in Figure 10.15 point from a node to the nodes that come before and after it in an inorder traversal. The first and last threads shown in Figure 10.15 don't have nodes to point to, so they are set to null. The threads allow an algorithm to perform an inorder traversal or reverse traversal more quickly than is possible by using the branches alone.

> **NOTE** You can define other threads in a tree, but this type is the most common. Because it includes threads forward and backward through the tree's inorder traversal, this kind of tree is sometimes called a *symmetrically threaded tree*.

> **NOTE** Notice that all of the nodes shown in Figure 10.15 have either a left branch or a left thread and a right branch or a right thread. You can use the same references for both branches and threads if you can somehow distinguish between them. For example, if you give the node class two Boolean variables, `HasLeftBranch` and `HasRightBranch`, you can store threads in the child links if you set those variables to `True`.
>
> You can even pack the two Boolean values into a byte and use byte operations to see if they are set.
>
> In practice, the savings in memory may not be worth the extra complexity and potential confusion unless you're working with an extremely large tree.

To use this kind of threaded tree, you need to know two things: how to build the tree and how to traverse it.

Building Threaded Trees

A threaded tree starts with a single node that has no branches and with threads set to `null`. Creating that node is simple.

The trick is adding new nodes to the tree. There are two cases, depending on whether you add a new node as the left or right child of its parent.

First, suppose that you're adding the new node as a left child. Suppose that you're adding the node 3 as the left child of node 4 in the tree shown in Figure 10.15.

Because of where the new node is placed, its value is the next smaller value compared to its parent's value. (In this example, 3 is the next smaller value before 4.) That means the node before the new one in the traversal is the node that was formerly the node before the parent. In this example, the node before 3 is the node that was before 4—in this case, 2. When creating the new node, set the new node's left thread equal to the value of the parent's left thread.

The parent's predecessor in the traversal is now the new node. The parent's left branch points to the new node, so the parent no longer needs its left thread and you should set it equal to `null`.

The new node's right thread should point to the next node in the tree's traversal. Because of where the new node is placed, that is the parent node, so you should set the new node's right thread to its parent. In this example, node 3's right thread should point to node 4. The parent's right child link or right thread is still correct, so you don't change it.

Figure 10.16 shows the updated tree with node 3 added.

When you add a node as the right child of an existing node, the steps are similar, with the roles of the left and right branches and threads reversed. The new node's right thread takes the value that the parent's right thread had, and the parent's right thread is set to `null`. The new node's left thread points to the parent node.

Figure 10.17 shows the tree in Figure 10.16 with the new node 8 inserted.

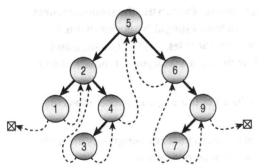

Figure 10.16: When you insert a node as a left child, its left thread points where the parent's left thread used to point.

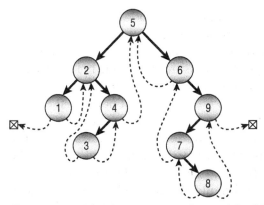

Figure 10.17: When you insert a node as a right child, its right thread points where the parent's right thread used to point.

The following pseudocode shows an algorithm for inserting a node into a threaded sorted tree:

```
// Add a node to this node's sorted subtree.
AddNode(Data: new_value)
    // See if the new value is smaller than ours.
    If (new_value < this.Value)
        // The new value is smaller. Add it to the left subtree.
        If (this.LeftChild != null)
        Then this.LeftChild.AddNode(new_value)
        Else
            // Add the new child here.
            ThreadedNode child = new ThreadedNode(new_value)
            child.LeftThread = this.LeftThread
            child.RightThread = this
            this.LeftChild = child
            this.LeftThread = null
        End If
    Else
        // The new value is not smaller. Add it to the right subtree.
        If (this.RightChild != null)
        Then this.RightChild.AddNode(new_value)
        Else
            // Add the new child here.
            ThreadedNode child = new ThreadedNode(new_value)
            child.LeftThread = this
            child.RightThread = this.RightThread
            this.RightChild = child
            this.RightThread = null
        End If
    End If
End AddNode
```

The algorithm first compares the new value to the node's value. If the new value is smaller, the algorithm adds it to the left subtree.

If the node has a left child, the algorithm recursively calls its AddNode method.

If the node has no left child, the algorithm adds the new node here. It creates the new node, sets its left thread equal to the current node's left thread, and sets its right thread equal to the current node. It sets the current node's left branch to point to the new node and sets the current node's left thread to null.

If the new value is greater than or equal to the current node's value, the algorithm performs similar steps to place the new value in the right subtree. The steps are the same as the case when the new value is smaller than the current node's value, with the roles of the left and right branches and threads reversed.

This algorithm is similar to the previous algorithm for adding a node to a sorted tree. Both versions recursively search down through the tree to find the new node's location. The only difference is that this version takes extra action to sort out threads when it finally creates the new node.

As with the previous version, if you use this method to build a threaded sorted tree containing N nodes, this algorithm takes O(N log N) time if the values are initially arranged randomly. The algorithm takes $O(N^2)$ time in the worst case when the values are initially sorted or sorted in reverse order.

Using Threaded Trees

The following pseudocode uses threads to perform an inorder traversal:

```
InorderWithThreads(BinaryNode: root)
    // Start at the root.
    BinaryNode: node = root

    // Remember whether we got to a node via a branch or thread.
    // Pretend we go to the root via a branch so we go left next.
    Boolean: via_branch = True

    // Repeat until the traversal is done.
    While (node != null)
        // If we got here via a branch, go
        // down and to the left as far as possible.
        If (via_branch) Then
            While (node.LeftChild != null)
                node = node.LeftChild
            End While
        End If

        // Process this node.
        <Process node>
```

```
        // Find the next node to process.
        If (node.RightChild == null) Then
            // Use the thread.
            node = node.RightThread
            via_branch = False
        Else
            // Use the right branch.
            node = node.RightChild
            via_branch = True
        End If
    End While
End InorderWithThreads
```

The algorithm starts by initializing the variable node to the root node. It also initializes the variable via_branch to True to indicate that the algorithm got to the current node via a branch. Treating the root node in this way makes the algorithm move to the leftmost node in the tree in the next step.

The algorithm then enters a loop that continues until the variable node drops off the tree at the end of the traversal.

If the algorithm got to the current node via a branch, it should not necessarily process that node just yet. If that node has a left branch, the nodes down that subtree have values smaller than the current node, so the algorithm must visit them first. To do that, the algorithm moves as far down the left branches as possible. For example, in Figure 10.15 this occurs when the algorithm moves from node 6 to node 9. The algorithm must first move down to node 7 before it processes node 9.

The algorithm then processes the current node.

Next, if the node's right branch is null, the algorithm follows the node's right thread. If the right thread is also null, the algorithm sets node to null and the While loop ends.

If the node does have a right thread, the algorithm sets via_branch to False to indicate that it got to the new node via a thread, not a branch. In Figure 10.15, this happens several times, such as when the algorithm moves from node 4 to node 5. Because via_branch is False, the algorithm will process node 5 next.

If the current node's right branch is not null, the algorithm follows it and sets via_branch to True so that it moves down that node's left subtree during the next trip through the While loop.

The following list describes the steps taken by this algorithm to traverse the tree shown in Figure 10.15:

1. Start at the root, and set via_branch to True.

2. Variable via_branch is True, so follow the left branches to 2 and then 1. Process node 1.

3. Follow the right thread to 2, and set via_branch to False.

4. Variable via_branch is False, so process node 2.

5. Follow the right branch to 4, and set `via_branch` to `True`.

6. Variable `via_branch` is `True`, so try to move down the left branches. There is no left branch here, so stay at node 4 and process node 4.

7. Follow the right thread to 5 and set `via_branch` to `False`.

8. Variable `via_branch` is `False`, so process node 5.

9. Follow the right branch to 6, and set `via_branch` to `True`.

10. Variable `via_branch` is `True`, so try to move down the left branches. There is no left branch here, so stay at node 6 and process node 6.

11. Follow the right branch to 9, and set `via_branch` to `True`.

12. Variable `via_branch` is `True`, so follow the left branch to 7 and process node 7.

13. Follow the right thread to 9, and set `via_branch` to `False`.

14. Variable `via_branch` is `False`, so process node 9.

15. Follow the right thread to `null`, and set `via_branch` to `False`.

16. Variable `node` is now `null`, so the `While` loop ends.

This algorithm still follows all of the nodes' branches, and it visits every node, so it has run time O(N). However, it doesn't need to let recursive calls unwind back up the child branches, so it saves a bit of time over a normal traversal. It also doesn't use recursion, so it doesn't have problems with deep levels of recursion. It also doesn't need any extra storage space, unlike a breadth-first traversal.

Specialized Tree Algorithms

Over the years, programmers have developed many specialized tree algorithms to solve specific problems. This chapter can't possibly describe every algorithm, but the following sections describe four algorithms that are particularly interesting. They demonstrate the useful techniques of updating a tree to include new data, evaluating recursive expressions, and subdividing geometric areas. The final section explains tries, which are well-known in algorithmic studies.

The Animal Game

In the animal game, the user thinks of an animal. The program's simple artificial intelligence tries to guess what it is. The program is a learning system, so over time it gets better at guessing the user's animal.

The program stores information about animals in a binary tree. Each internal node holds a yes-or-no question that guides the program down the left or right branch. Leaf nodes represent specific animals.

The program asks the questions at each of the nodes that it visits and follows the appropriate branch until it reaches a leaf node where it guesses that node's animal.

If the program is wrong, it asks the user to type a question that it can ask to differentiate between the animal it guessed and the correct answer. It adds a new internal node containing the question and gives that node leaves holding the correct and incorrect animals.

Figure 10.18 shows a small knowledge tree for the game.

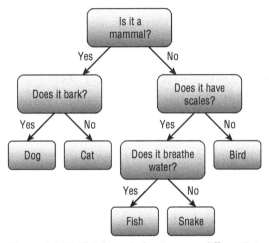

Figure 10.18: This knowledge tree can differentiate among dog, cat, fish, snake, and bird.

For example, suppose that the user is thinking about a snake. Table 10.2 shows the questions that the program asks and the answers the user gives.

Table 10.2: The Animal Game Trying to Guess Snake

THE PROGRAM ASKS:	THE USER ANSWERS:
Is it a mammal?	No
Does it have scales?	Yes
Does it breathe water?	No
Is it a snake?	Yes

For another example, suppose that the user is thinking about a giraffe. Table 10.3 shows the questions the program asks and the answers the user gives in this example.

Table 10.3: The Animal Game Trying to Guess Giraffe

THE PROGRAM ASKS:	THE USER ANSWERS:
Is it a mammal?	Yes
Does it bark?	No
Is it a cat?	No
What is your animal?	Giraffe
What question could I ask to differentiate between a cat and a giraffe?	Does it have a long neck?
Is the answer to this question true for a giraffe?	Yes

The program then updates its knowledge tree to hold the new question and animal. The new tree is shown in Figure 10.19.

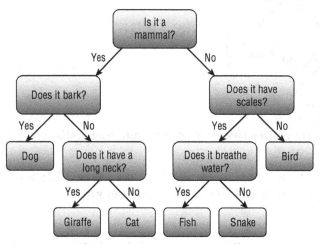

Figure 10.19: This knowledge tree can now differentiate between cat and giraffe.

Expression Evaluation

You can model many situations with trees. You can model mathematical expressions by creating an internal node for each operator and a leaf node for each numeric value.

Mathematical expressions naturally break into subexpressions that you must evaluate before you can evaluate the expression as a whole. For example, consider the expression $(6 \times 14) \div (9 + 12)$. To evaluate this expression, you must first evaluate 6×14 and $9 + 12$. You can then divide the results of those calculations to get the final result.

To model this expression as a tree, you build subtrees to represent the sub-expressions. You then join the subtrees with a parent node that represents the operation that combines the subexpressions—in this case, division.

Figure 10.20 shows the tree representing the expression $(6 \times 14) \div (9 + 12)$.

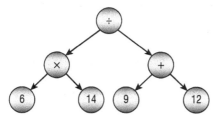

Figure 10.20: You can use trees to evaluate mathematical expressions.

Each internal node has children representing its operands. For example, binary operators such as + and / have left and right children, and the operator must combine the children's values.

You can think of the leaf nodes as special operators that convert a text value into a numeric one. In that case, the leaf nodes must hold their text.

The only thing missing from the arithmetic node class is a method to evaluate the node. That method should examine the type of node and then return an appropriate result. For example, if the operator is +, the method should recursively make its operands evaluate their subexpressions, and then it can add the results.

The following pseudocode creates an enumeration that defines values that indicate a node's operator type:

```
Enumeration Operators
    Literal
    Plus
    Minus
    Times
    Divide
    Negate
End Enumeration
```

This enumeration defines operator types for literal values such as 8, addition, subtraction, multiplication, division, and unary negation (as in –5). You can add other operators such as square root, exponentiation, sine, cosine, and others.

The following pseudocode shows an ExpressionNode class that represents a node in a mathematical expression tree:

```
Class ExpressionNode
    Operators: Operator
    ExpressionNode: LeftOperand, RightOperand
    String: LiteralText
```

```
        // Evaluate the expression.
    Float: Evaluate()
        Case Operator
            Literal:
                Return Float.Parse(LiteralText)
            Plus:
                Return LeftOperand.Evaluate() + RightOperand.Evaluate()
            Minus:
                Return LeftOperand.Evaluate() - RightOperand.Evaluate()
            Times:
                Return LeftOperand.Evaluate() * RightOperand.Evaluate()
            Divide:
                Return LeftOperand.Evaluate() / RightOperand.Evaluate()
            Negate:
                Return -LeftOperand.Evaluate()
        End Case
    End Evaluate
End ExpressionNode
```

The class begins by declaring its properties. The `Operator` property is a value from the `Operators` enumerated type.

The `LeftOperand` and `RightOperand` properties hold links to the node's left and right children. If the node represents a unary operator such as negation, only the left child is used. If the node represents a literal value, neither child is used.

The `LiteralText` property is used only by literal nodes. For a literal node, it contains the node's textual value, such as 12.

The `Evaluate` method examines the node's `Operator` property and takes appropriate action. For example, if `Operator` is `Plus`, the method calls the `Evaluate` method for its left and right children, adds their results, and returns the sum.

After you build an expression tree, evaluating it is easy. You simply call the root node's `Evaluate` method.

The hardest part of evaluating mathematical expressions is building the expression tree from a string such as $(6 \times 14) / (9 + 12)$. That is a string operation, not a tree operation, so this topic is deferred until Chapter 15, which covers strings in depth.

Interval Trees

Suppose that you have a collection of intervals with start and end points in a one-dimensional coordinate system. For example, if the intervals represent time spans, then their end points would be start and stop times. An appointment calendar application might need to search a collection of intervals to see whether a new appointment overlaps any existing appointment.

You can think of each interval as representing a range of values $[x1, x2]$ on the x-axis. After you have the intervals, you might want to find those that include a specific x-coordinate.

One approach to this problem would be simply to loop through the intervals and find those that include the target value. If there are N intervals, then that would take O(N) steps.

An *interval tree* is a data structure that makes this kind of lookup faster. Each node in an interval tree represents a single midpoint coordinate. The node holds two child pointers, one leading to intervals that lie entirely to the left of the midpoint and one leading to intervals that lie entirely to the right of the midpoint. The node also includes two lists of the intervals that surround the midpoint. One of those lists is sorted by their left end coordinates, and the other is sorted by their right end coordinates.

For example, consider the segments shown in Figure 10.21. The dark horizontal lines represent the intervals. (Ignore their y-coordinates.) The gray dots represent nodes in the interval tree. The vertical gray lines show which intervals surround the centers of the nodes.

Figure 10.22 shows a representation of this tree's root node.

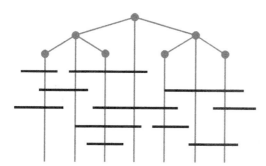

Figure 10.21: Horizontal lines represent intervals. Vertical lines show which intervals surround the tree nodes.

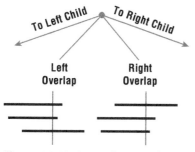

Figure 10.22: Interval tree nodes contain lists of overlapping intervals sorted by their left and right edges.

The node includes links to child nodes, plus two lists holding nodes that overlap with the node's midpoint. The left overlap list holds the intervals sorted by their left end points. The right overlap list holds the intervals sorted by their right end points. For example, the first interval in the right overlap list has a larger right coordinate than the other two intervals in that list.

The following sections explain how to build and use an interval tree.

Building the Tree

The following code snippet shows how you could define an `Interval` class to represent an interval:

```
Class Interval
    Integer: LeftCoordinate, RightCoordinate

    Constructor(Integer: coordinate1, Integer: coordinate2)
        // Save the points in order.
        If (coordinate1.X < coordinate2.X) Then
            LeftCoordinate = coordinate1
            RightCoordinate = coordinate2
        Else
            LeftCoordinate = coordinate2
            RightCoordinate = coordinate1
        End If
    End Constructor
End Class
```

The `Interval` class simply stores the interval's coordinates. Its constructor saves the new interval's coordinates where `LeftCoordinate` is smaller than `RightCoordinate`.

The following code snippet shows how you could define the `IntervalNode` class's fields:

```
Class IntervalNode
    Float: Min, Mid, Max
    List<Interval>: LeftOverlap = New List<Interval>
    List<Interval>: RightOverlap = New List<Interval>
    IntervalNode: LeftChild = null
    IntervalNode: RightChild = null

    Constructor(Float: xmin, Float: xmax)
        Xmin = xmin
        Xmax = xmax
        Xmid = (xmin + xmax) / 2
    End Constructor
    ...
End Class
```

For convenience, the node stores the minimum, maximum, and middle coordinates of the area that it represents. The constructor stores the minimum and maximum values and calculates the middle value.

To build an interval tree, start with a root node and then add the intervals to it. The following pseudocode shows the IntervalNode class's AddInterval method, which adds a new interval to the node:

```
// Add an interval to the node.
AddInterval(Interval: interval)
    If <interval lies to the left of Mid>
        If LeftChild == null Then <Create LeftChild>
        LeftChild.AddInterval(interval)
    Else If <interval lies to the right of Mid>
        If RightChild == null Then <Create RightChild>
        RightChild.AddInterval(interval)
    Else
        <Add interval to left overlap list>
        <Add interval to right overlap list>
    End If
End AddInterval
```

This method compares the new interval's coordinates to the node's Mid value. If the interval lies completely to the left of the node's Mid value, then the method adds the interval to the left child node. If the interval lies to the right of the node's Mid value, then the method adds the interval to the right child node.

If the interval spans the Mid value, then the method adds it to the node's left and right overlap lists. You can either add the interval to the lists in sorted order now or wait until the tree is finished and then sort the lists in O(K log K) time, where K is the number of items in the lists.

Intersecting with Points

The following pseudocode shows how an interval tree can search for intervals that contain a target coordinate value:

```
FindOverlappingIntervals(List<Interval>: results,
    Integer: target)
    // Check our overlap intervals.
    If (target <= Mid) Then
        <Search the left overlap list>
    Else
        <Search the right overlap list>
    End If

    // Check the children.
    If ((target < Mid) And (LeftChild != null)) Then
        LeftChild.FindOverlappingIntervals(results, target)
```

```
    Else If ((target > Mid) And (RightChild != null)) Then
        RightChild.FindOverlappingIntervals(results, target)
    End If
End FindOverlappingIntervals
```

This method takes as inputs a result list that will hold any intervals that intersect with the target coordinate and the target coordinate. It first checks the node's overlap lists to see whether any of the intervals in the lists contain the target value. The fact that the overlap lists are sorted makes searching them a bit easier.

For example, if `target` < `Mid`, then the method searches its left overlap list. The intervals in that list have `RightCoordinate` >= `Mid`, so an interval contains the target value if `LeftCoordinate` <= `target`. Because the intervals are sorted by increasing `LeftCoordinate` value, you only need to search the list until you find an interval with `LeftCoordinate` > `target`. Then you know that the later intervals also have `LeftCoordinate` > `target`, so they cannot contain the target value.

The same logic applies in reverse for the right overlap list.

After the method has searched the overlap lists for the target value, it recursively calls itself for the left or right child node as appropriate.

Intersecting with Intervals

The preceding section explained how you can search an interval tree to find intervals that overlap a target point. You can also use a recursive search to find intervals that overlap a target interval. Simply traverse the tree as before, this time examining any node that *might* overlap the target interval. The following pseudocode shows this technique:

```
FindOverlappingIntervals(List<Interval>: results,
    Integer: xmin, Integer: xmax)
    // Check our overlap intervals.
    If (xmax <= Mid) Then
        <Search the left overlap list>
    Else if (xmin >= Mid) Then
        <Search the right overlap list>
    Else
        <Add all node intervals to the results>
    End If

    // Check the children.
    If ((xmin < Mid) && (LeftChild != null)) Then
        LeftChild.FindOverlappingIntervals(results, xmin, xmax);
    End If
    If ((xmax > Mid) && (RightChild != null)) Then
        RightChild.FindOverlappingIntervals(results, xmin, xmax);
    End If
End FindOverlappingIntervals
```

The xmin and xmax parameters give the target interval's minimum and maximum coordinates. The algorithm first uses those values to decide whether its intervals might intersect the target interval.

If xmax <= Mid, then the target interval lies to the left of the node's midpoint. In that case, the method searches the node's left overlap list. If any of those intervals has left coordinate larger than the target interval's maximum coordinate, then that interval and those that come after it in the list are completely to the right of the target interval, so they do not overlap with it. That means the algorithm can break out of its loop and stop searching the left overlap list.

Figure 10.23 shows a left overlap list. The dark horizontal lines represent intervals in the tree. Recall that they are arranged in order of increasing left coordinate. The gray line in the upper left is the target interval. The dashed lines show the edges of that interval. The algorithm only needs to search through the list's intervals until it reaches one with left coordinate greater than the target interval's right coordinate. In Figure 10.23, the list's second-to-last interval lies to the right of the target interval, so the algorithm doesn't need to check the list further.

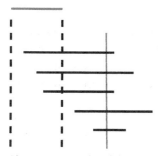

Figure 10.23: The algorithm only needs to check the left overlap list until it finds an interval with left coordinate greater than the target interval's right coordinate.

The same steps apply in reverse to the node's right intervals. If xmin >= Mid, then the target interval lies to the right of the node's midpoint. In that case, the method searches the node's right overlap list.

If neither of the previous two conditions is true, then the target interval spans the node's midpoint, so the algorithm adds all of its intervals to the results list.

After searching the node's overlap list, the algorithm considers its child subtrees. If the target interval's left coordinate is less than the node's midpoint, then it is possible that the left subtree might contain intervals that overlap with the target. In that case, the algorithm calls itself recursively to examine the left subtree.

Similarly, if the target interval's right coordinate is greater than the node's midpoint, then the algorithm recursively examines the node's right subtree.

One of the larger differences between this algorithm and the previous one that searched for intervals that overlap a point is in these recursive calls. Because the target point could not lie both to the left and the right of a node's mid-point, the previous algorithm needed to search only one of the node's subtrees. In contrast, a target interval can be both to the left and the right of the midpoint, so the new algorithm might search both child subtrees.

Quadtrees

Quadtrees are tree data structures that help locate objects in two-dimensional space. For example, suppose you have an application that displays several thousand delivery locations. If the user clicks the map, the program needs to search through all of the locations to find the one closest to where the user clicked. If the locations are stored in a simple list, the program must perform a sequential search to find the closest point. A quadtree can make the search much faster.

In a quadtree, a node represents a rectangle in two-dimensional space. The node contains a list of items that are contained within its rectangle.

If a quadtree node contains more than a predetermined number of items, it is split into four child nodes representing the parent node's northwest, northeast, southeast, and southwest quadrants. The items are then moved into the appropriate child nodes.

To use a quadtree to find an item with given x- and y-coordinates, you start at the root node. If the quadtree node has children, you use the item's coordinates to determine which child contains the item. You then recursively search that child for the item. If you reach a node that doesn't have children, you search the items it contains for an item at the target location.

To see why this makes the search faster, suppose that the mapping application described a moment ago contains a list of 1,500 locations. Searching that list linearly will require on average roughly 750 comparisons.

In contrast, suppose that you store the items in a quadtree where each node can hold at most 100 items. If the nodes are reasonably evenly distributed around the map, the quadtree would logically look like the one shown in Figure 10.24.

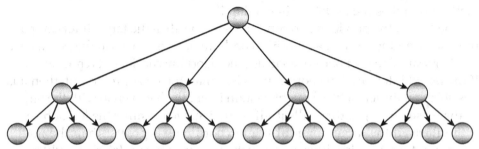

Figure 10.24: If each leaf node can hold 100 items and the items are evenly distributed, this quadtree can hold roughly 1,600 items.

The root node's area is divided into four quadrants, each of which is divided into four smaller quadrants. Each leaf node representing a smaller quadrant can hold up to 100 items. Its parent node holds four leaf nodes, so it contains up to 400 items. The root node holds four of those nodes, so the whole tree can contain up to 1,600 items.

To find the item that the user clicked in this quadtree, you need to determine which larger quadrant contains the item and then which smaller quadrant within the larger quadrant contains the item. Then you need to search up to 100 items in the leaf node. The result is an average of two quadrant tests plus roughly 50 item tests. The relative speed of the quadrant tests and item tests may vary depending on your implementation, but the speed is generally much faster than the 750 item tests required by a simple list.

If a quadtree contains N nodes, each of which can hold up to K items, and the items are distributed reasonably evenly in the map area, the tree has a height of roughly $\log_4 (N / K)$. In the previous example, $N = 1,500$ and $K = 100$, so the height should be roughly $\log_4 (1,500 / 100) = \log_4 (15) \approx 1.95$, which is close to the height of 2 for the tree shown in Figure 10.24.

Figure 10.25 shows another way to visualize a quadtree. In this figure, the quadtree contains 200 items, and each quadtree node can hold at most 10 items. (In a real program, you would probably want to let each node hold more items so that they don't split as often.) The program draws a box around each quadtree node so that you can see how the area is divided.

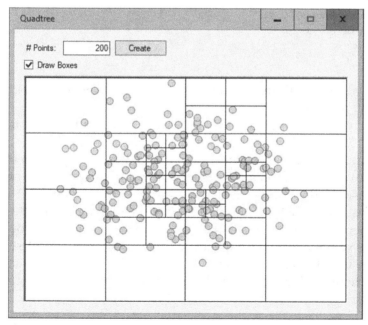

Figure 10.25: Each box shows a quadtree node's area.

In the tree shown in Figure 10.25, the full map area is divided into four quadrants, and each of these is divided into smaller quadrants. Some of the smaller quadrants are divided again, and some of those areas are divided one last time.

To manage a quadtree, you need algorithms to add a new item to a subtree and to find an item in a subtree. You may also want an algorithm to draw the items, as shown in Figure 10.25.

The following pseudocode shows the basic class definition for a quadtree node:

```
Class QuadtreeNode
    // The maximum number of points allowed in a quadtree node.
    Integer: MaxItems = 10

    // The items in this quadtree node.
    List Of Data: Items

    // The area's bounds and middle X and Y values.
    Float: Xmin, Ymin, Xmid, Ymid, Xmax, Ymax

    // The child quadtree nodes in order NW, NE, SW, SE.
    QuadtreeNode: Children[]

    // Initializing constructor.
    Constructor(Float: xmin, Float: ymin, Float: xmax, Float: ymax)
        Xmin = xmin
        Ymin = ymin
        Xmax = xmax
        Ymax = ymax
        Xmid = (xmin + xmax) / 2
        Ymid = (ymin + ymax) / 2
    End Constructor
End QuadtreeNode
```

The value MaxItems indicates the maximum number of items a node can hold before it must be split into quadrants.

The Items property contains the items that the node holds. If the node is internal, Items is null, and the items are stored in the node's child subtrees.

The Xmin, Ymin, Xmax, and Ymax values store the bounds of the area represented by the node. The Xmid and Ymid values give the middle X and Y coordinates of the area. These are used to determine which quadrant contains an item.

This class provides a constructor that initializes the node's bounds and the Xmid and Ymid properties. You could calculate Xmid and Ymid whenever you need them, but those values are used frequently (at least for nonleaf nodes), so you can save time by initializing them now.

The following sections explain how to add items to a quadtree and how to find items in a quadtree.

Adding Items

The following pseudocode shows how a `QuadtreeNode` can add a new item to its subtree:

```
// Add an item to this node.
AddItem(Item: new_item)
    // See if this quadtree node is full.
    If ((Items != null) And (Items.Count >= MaxItems)) Then
        // Divide this quadtree node.
        Children.Add(new QuadtreeNode(Xmin, Ymin, Xmid, Ymid)) // NW
        Children.Add(new QuadtreeNode(Xmid, Ymin, Xmax, Ymid)) // NE
        Children.Add(new QuadtreeNode(Xmin, Ymid, Xmid, Ymax)) // SW
        Children.Add(new QuadtreeNode(Xmid, Ymid, Xmax, Ymax)) // SE

        // Move the points into the appropriate subtrees.
        For Each item in Items
            AddItemToChild(point)
        Next item

        // Remove this node's points list.
        Points = null
    End If

    // Add the new item here or in the appropriate subtree.
    If (Items != null)
        Items.Add(new_item)
    Else
        AddItemToChild(new_item)
    End If
End AddItem
```

If the current node is a leaf node and adding one more item would give it too many items, the algorithm splits the node by creating four child nodes. It then loops through the items and calls the `AddItemToChild` method described shortly to move each item into the appropriate child subtree. It then sets the `Items` list to `null` to indicate that this is an internal node.

After splitting the node if necessary, the algorithm adds the new item. If the `Items` property is not `null`, then this is a leaf node, so the algorithm adds the new item to the `Items` list.

If the `Items` property is `null`, then this is an internal node. In that case, the algorithm calls the `AddItemToChild` method described next to move each item into the appropriate child subtree.

The following pseudocode shows the `AddItemToChild` method:

```
// Add an item to the appropriate child subtree.
AddItemToChild(Item: new_item)
    For Each child in Children
```

```
        If ((new_item.X >= child.Xmin) And
            (new_item.X <= child.Xmax) And
            (new_item.Y >= child.Ymin) And
            (new_item.Y <= child.Ymax))
        Then
            child.AddItem(new_item)
            Break
        End If
    Next child
End AddItemToChild
```

This algorithm loops through the node's children. When it finds the child with bounds that include the new item's location, it calls the child's `AddItem` method described earlier to add the new item to that child.

Finding Items

You can probably imagine how to use quadtree to find the item at a specific point. Starting at the root node, you determine which child node contains the target point. You then recursively search that child for the item.

That almost works, but there's a catch. Suppose that you want to find the item closest to a target point, but that point lies close to the edge between two quadtree nodes. In that case, the closest item might lie in the quadtree node that does not contain the target point.

Furthermore, the objects stored in the quadtree might not be simple points. They may be bigger objects such as circles, line segments, and polygons. In that case, where should you store an item that straddles the edges between two or more quadtree nodes?

One approach is to store the item in every quadtree node that overlaps the object so that the algorithm can find it no matter which area the user clicks. If you use this approach, you need to change the algorithms to work with two-dimensional items. For example, the search algorithm cannot simply compare the target point to the item's location. Instead, it must use some method to see whether the target point lies within the item.

One problem with this approach is that it requires duplicate items representing the same object in different quadtree nodes. That wastes space and fills quadtree nodes sooner than they would be filled otherwise, so they must split more often and that makes the tree deeper.

Another approach is to represent each item with a specific point, perhaps in its center or upper-left corner. Then, when you need to find an item, you search quadtree nodes with areas that overlap an area around the target point that is big enough to include the largest possible item.

For example, the program shown in Figure 10.25 stores circles with radius 5 that are represented by their center points. When searching for an item at location (A, B), the program examines any quadtree node with an area that intersects the rectangle $A - 5 \leq X \leq A + 5$ and $B - 5 \leq Y \leq B + 5$.

The changes to the algorithms aren't too complicated, but they make the code quite a bit longer.

OCTTREES

An *octtree* is similar to a quadtree, except that it stores objects in three dimensions instead of two. An octtree node represents a three-dimensional volume. When an octtree node contains too many items, its volume is divided into eight octants that are represented by eight child nodes, and the items are distributed among the child subtrees.

Tries

A *trie* (the word comes from "retrieval" but is usually pronounced "try") is a tree that holds strings. Each internal node represents a single letter. Leaf nodes may represent more than one letter. A path from the root to a leaf node corresponds to a string.

A partial path from the root to an internal node forms a prefix for longer paths, so tries are sometimes called *prefix trees*.

A path that represents a key string, whether it ends at an internal node or at a leaf node, has an associated value.

Figure 10.26 shows a trie that holds the keys and values shown in Table 10.4.

For example, consider the path from the root to the node E. The nodes visited correspond to the letters W, A, N, and E, so that node represents the key WANE. That key's value is 29.

Table 10.4: Keys and Values for the Example Trie

KEY	VALUE
WANE	29
WISP	72
WANT	36

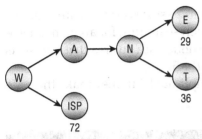

Figure 10.26: A path through a trie defines a string.

For another example, consider the path to the node T. The nodes visited correspond to the letters W, A, N, and T, so the node represents the key WANT. That key's value is 36.

Notice that the path to the node N forms the string WAN, which is a prefix of both WANE and WANT.

Notice also that a leaf node may represent more than one letter. In this example, the node ISP represents three letters. The path from the root to that node represents the key WISP and has value 72.

To add a new key to the trie, you use the key's letters to follow the appropriate path through the trie. If you reach a leaf node and the key has still more letters that are not represented by the current path, you add a new child node to represent the rest of the key.

For example, suppose that you want to add the key WANTED to the trie. You follow the path through the nodes W, A, N, and T. The key still has the letters ED, so you add a new node to hold them. Figure 10.27 shows the new trie.

Sometimes, when you add a new key to the trie, you find it early. For example, the trie shown in Figure 10.27 already has the nodes needed to represent the key WAN. In that case, all that you need to do is to add a value to the appropriate node, as shown in Figure 10.28.

Instead of storing a letter in each internal node, you can figure out the node's letter by keeping track of the path you took from the root to get there. For example, you could store a node's children in an array where `Children[0]` is the branch for the letter A, `Children[1]` is the branch for the letter B, and so forth.

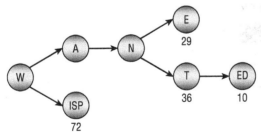

Figure 10.27: To add a key that is longer than the corresponding path through the tree, add a new leaf node.

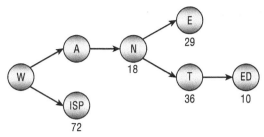

Figure 10.28: If a trie already contains nodes to represent a key, simply add a value to the key's final node.

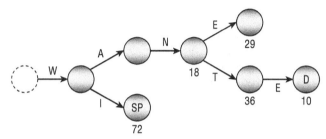

Figure 10.29: Instead of storing an internal node's letter in the node, you can figure out the node from the path to the node.

Figure 10.29 shows the trie from Figure 10.28 with internal node letters moved to the branches. Notice that the node with value 29 doesn't need any extra information because the key it represents is fully specified by the path to the node. In contrast, the path to the node with value 10 specifies only the letters *W, A, N, T,* and *E,* so the node needs to store the final *D.*

The following two sections explain how you can add items to a trie and find items in a trie.

Adding Items

The following pseudocode shows how you can add an item to a trie. In this code, the phrase *remaining node key* means part of a key stored in a leaf node, such as D and SP in Figure 10.29.

```
AddValue(string new_key, string new_value)
    <If new_key is not blank and matches the remaining node key,
     place the value in this node and return.>

    <If new_key is blank and the remaining node key is too,
     place the value here and return.>

    <If new_key is blank but the node's remaining key isn't blank,
     move the node's remaining key (minus the first letter) into
     a child, place the value here, and return.>
```

```
    // If we get to this point, we need a child node.
    If <The Children array is null> Then
        // Make the Children array.
        Children = New TrieNode[26]

        <If the node's remaining key is not blank,
         move it into the appropriate child.>
    End If

    // Convert the letter into an integer by "subtracting" A.
    Integer: index = new_key[0] - 'A'

    // Search the appropriate subtrie.
    If (Children[index] == null)
        // This child doesn't exist. Make it and
        // let it represent the rest of the new key.
        Children[index] = New TrieNode()
        Children[index].RemainingKey = new_key.Substring(1)
        Children[index].Value = new_value
        Return
    End If

    // Search the appropriate subtrie.
    Children[index].AddValue(new_key.Substring(1), new_value)
End AddValue
```

This is a fairly confusing algorithm. It may be easier to understand if you draw a tree and then walk through the algorithm, updating it in various ways.

As the algorithm moves through the trie, it removes the letters from the new key corresponding to the branches it crosses. The body of the algorithm then considers the current value of the new key.

First, if the new key is not blank and it matches the remaining node key, the algorithm places the new value in the current node. This would happen in Figure 10.29 if you were setting the value for WANTED. When the algorithm reached the node labeled D, the new key value will be D, and the node's remaining key is D.

Next, if the new key is blank and the node's remaining key is too, the algorithm places the value in this node. This occurs if you set the value of WAN in Figure 10.29. When the algorithm crosses the N branch, the new key is reduced to an empty string. The node at the end of that branch doesn't have any remaining key (only leaf nodes can have remaining key values), so this is where the value for WAN belongs.

Next, if the new key is blank but the node's remaining key isn't, the algorithm moves the node's remaining key into a child. This would happen if the trie contains WANE and WANTED but not WANT. In that case, the path for WANTED will be W, A, N, T, ED. When you add WANT and cross the T branch, the new key value is blank because the path represents the entire new key WANT. But that node has value ED. The algorithm moves the ED down to a child, creating a new E branch and a new node with D as its remaining key.

If the algorithm gets past all of the previous steps, the algorithm must move into a child node's subtrie. Before it tries to do that, it determines whether the node's `Children` array has been initialized. If it has not, the algorithm creates the array. If the node's remaining key is not blank, the algorithm also moves the remaining key (minus its first letter) into the appropriate child.

The algorithm then examines the child that should contain the new key. If that child doesn't exist, the algorithm creates it and stores the rest of the new key and the new value in it.

If that child does exist, the algorithm recursively calls itself to add the new key (minus its first letter) to that child's subtrie.

Finding Items

A search for a value in a trie follows the same path through the trie but uses a much simpler algorithm because there are fewer special cases to consider. The following pseudocode shows how a search algorithm might work in a trie:

```
// Find a value in this node's subtrie.
Data: FindValue(String: target_key)
    // If the remaining key matches the
    // remaining node key, return this node's value.
    If (target_key == RemainingKey) Then Return Value

    // Search the appropriate child.
    If (Children == null) Then Return null

    Integer: index = target_key[0] - 'A'
    If (Children[index] == null) Then Return null
    Return Children[index].FindValue(target_key.Substring(1))
End FindValue
```

The algorithm first compares the target key to the node's remaining key value. If these are the same, two things may have happened. First, the algorithm may have used up the target key and reached a node that doesn't have a remaining value. (This happens if you search for WAN in Figure 10.28.) Second, the algorithm may have reached a node where the remaining target key matches the node's remaining key. (This happens if you search for WANTED in Figure 10.28.) In either case, this code matches the target key, so the algorithm returns its value.

If the remaining target key doesn't match the node's remaining key, the algorithm must search a child node. If the current node has no children, then the target key isn't in the trie, so the algorithm returns `null`.

If the node has children, the algorithm calculates the index of the target key's child. If that child doesn't exist, the target key isn't in the trie, so the algorithm again returns `null`.

Finally, if the target key's child exists, the algorithm calls itself recursively for that child to find the target key (minus its first letter).

Summary

Trees can be useful for storing and manipulating hierarchical data. After you build a tree, you can enumerate its values in different orders and search for values within the tree.

The performance of many tree algorithms is related to the tree's height. If a tree holding N nodes is relatively short and wide, its height is O(log N), and those algorithms are fairly quick. If the tree is tall and thin, it could have height O(N), and some of those algorithms perform badly. For example, building a sorted binary tree takes O(N log N) time in the best case and O(N^2) time in the worst case.

Because a tree's height is important to these algorithms, special trees have been devised that rebalance themselves so that they cannot grow too tall and thin. The next chapter describes several kinds of balanced trees, including the B-trees and B+trees used by many database systems to store and search indices efficiently.

Exercises

You can find the answers to these exercises in Appendix B. Asterisks indicate particularly difficult problems. Two asterisks indicate extremely difficult or time-consuming problems.

1. Can a perfect binary tree hold an even number of nodes?

2. A perfect tree is full and complete, although not all full and complete trees are perfect. Draw a tree that is full and complete but not perfect.

3. Use induction to prove that the number of branches B in a binary tree containing N nodes is B = N – 1.

4. Prove that the number of branches B in a binary tree containing N nodes is B = N – 1 without using induction.

5. *Use induction to prove that the number of leaf nodes L in a perfect binary tree of height H is L = 2^H.

6. **Use induction to prove that the number of missing branches (places where a child could be added) M in a binary tree that contains N nodes is $M = N + 1$.

7. What is the preorder traversal for the tree shown in Figure 10.30?

8. What is the inorder traversal for the tree shown in Figure 10.30?

9. What is the postorder traversal for the tree shown in Figure 10.30?

10. What is the breadth-first traversal for the tree shown in Figure 10.30?

11. Write a program that finds the preorder, inorder, postorder, and breadth-first traversals for the tree shown in Figure 10.30.

12. What happens if you use a queue instead of a stack in the breadth-first traversal algorithm described in the "Breadth-First Traversal" section? How could you generate the same traversal recursively?

13. Write a program similar to the one shown in Figure 10.31 that uses a pre-order traversal to display a textual representation of the tree shown in Figure 10.30.

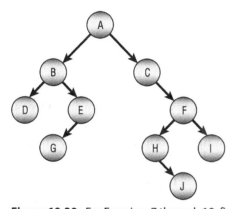

Figure 10.30: For Exercises 7 through 10, find this tree's traversals.

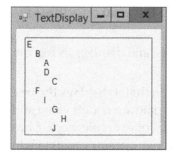

Figure 10.31: A preorder traversal can generate a textual display of a tree similar to the one used by Windows File Explorer to display a directory hierarchy.

14. **Write a program similar to the one shown in Figure 10.32 to display a more intuitive picture of a tree. (*Hints*: Give the node class a `PositionSubtree` method that positions the node's subtree. It should take as parameters the minimum x- and y-coordinates that the node's subtree can occupy, and it should calculate the rectangle that the subtree will cover. It will need to call the `PositionSubtree` method of its left and right child subtrees recursively and use the subtrees' sizes to see how big to make the original subtree. Also give the node class methods to draw the tree's links and nodes recursively.)

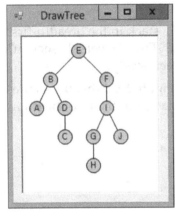

Figure 10.32: To draw a tree, a program must first position it.

15. *The tree shown in Figure 10.32 is particularly useful for unordered trees, but for ordered binary trees it can be hard to tell whether a node is the left or right child of its parent. For example, in Figure 10.32, it's unclear whether node C is the left or right child of node D.

    Modify the program you wrote for Exercise 14 to produce a display similar to the one shown in Figure 10.33. Here, if a node has only one child, the program allows some space for the missing child, so you can tell whether the other child is a left or right child.

16. Write pseudocode to perform a reverse inorder traversal on a threaded sorted tree.

17. *Write a program that builds a threaded sorted tree and displays its inorder and reverse inorder traversals.

18. **Expand the program you built for Exercise 17 so that it displays the tree shown in Figure 10.34. The circles in the drawing show a node's value and the values of the nodes to which its threads lead. For example, node 4 has its left thread set to `null` (displayed as -- in the program) and its right thread pointing to node 5.

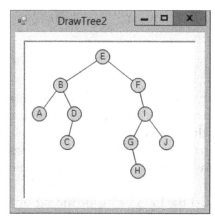

Figure 10.33: In an ordered binary tree, you can leave space to indicate missing children.

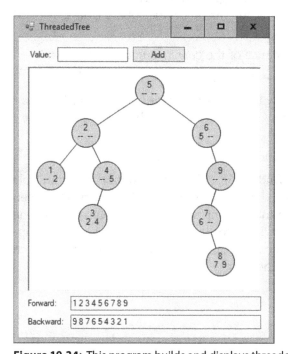

Figure 10.34: This program builds and displays threaded sorted trees.

19. What is the run time performance of the `FindLcaSortedTree` algorithm?

20. *Write a program that implements the `FindLcaSortedTree` algorithm.

21. What is the run time performance of the `FindLcaParentPointers` algorithm?

22. *Write a program that implements the `FindLcaParentPointers` algorithm.

23. What is the run time performance of the `FindLcaParentsAndDepths` algorithm?

24. *Write a program that implements the `FindLcaParentsAndDepths` algorithm.

25. In the `ContainsNodes` algorithm, the recursive call to the algorithm sets the values `has1` and `has2` to indicate whether a particular subtree contains either of the target values. The code uses those values to update `contains1` and `contains2`, and then it returns the current node if both of those values are true. In that case, how do we know that the current node is the LCA and not some other node deeper in the subtree? In other words, if `has1` and `has2` are both true, then shouldn't the LCA be inside the subtree and not at the current node?

26. If an instance of the `ContainsNodes` algorithm returns `null`, what can you tell about the location of the LCA for various values of the `contains1` and `contains2` variables?

27. What is the run time performance of the `ContainsNodes` algorithm?

28. *Write a program that implements the `ContainsNodes` algorithm.

29. If a tree contains N nodes, how long is its Euler tour? How does the Euler Tour method for finding LCAs compare to the `ContainsNodes` algorithm?

30. *Write a program that uses Euler tours to find LCAs.

31. When using an Euler tour to find LCAs, either node might appear multiple times in the tour. You can find the LCA by searching the interval between any of the two nodes' appearances in the tour. For example, consider the tour 0, 1, 3, 6, 3, 1, 4, 7, 4, 1, 0, 2, 5, 2, 0 for the tree in Figure 10.14, and suppose that you want to find the LCA of nodes 1 and 2. You could search any of the following parts of the tour.

    1, 3, 6, 3, 1, 4, 7, 4, 1, 0, 2, 5, 2
    1, 3, 6, 3, 1, 4, 7, 4, 1, 0, 2
    3, 6, 3, 1, 4, 7, 4, 1, 0, 2, 5, 2
    3, 6, 3, 1, 4, 7, 4, 1, 0, 2
    3, 1, 4, 7, 4, 1, 0, 2, 5, 2
    3, 1, 4, 7, 4, 1, 0, 2

    Each of those intervals begins with 3 and ends with 2, but some intervals are longer than others. How can you quickly determine which locations to use for each of the two nodes so that you search the shortest possible interval?

32. *Implement your solution to the previous exercise.

33. In general, is the knowledge tree used by the animal game full, complete, perfect, none of those, or a combination of those?

34. The animal game can use the following node class to store information:

```
Class AnimalNode
    String: Question
    AnimalNode: YesChild, NoChild
End Class
```

If you use this class, how can you tell whether a node represents a question or an animal?

35. Write a program that implements the animal game.

36. Draw expression trees for the following expressions:

$(15 \div 3) + (24 \div 6)$

$8 \times 12 - 14 \times 32$

$1 \div 2 + 1 \div 4 + 1 \div 20$

37. Write a program that evaluates mathematical expressions. Because parsing expressions to build mathematical expression trees is deferred until Chapter 15, this program doesn't need to do that. Instead, make the program use code to build and evaluate the expressions in Exercise 36.

38. Draw expression trees for the following expressions:

$\sqrt{(36 \times 2) \div (9 \times 32)}$

$5! \div ((5 - 3)! \times 3!)$

$\text{Sine}(45°)2$

39. *Extend the program you wrote for Exercise 37 above to evaluate the expressions in Exercise 38.

40. *Write a program that lets the user left click and drag to define horizontal intervals. When the user clicks a button, build an interval tree for the intervals. If the user right-clicks and the interval tree has been created, draw a vertical line through the point clicked and change the colors of the intervals that contain the point's x-coordinate.

41. *Copy the program you wrote for the preceding exercise and modify it so that it searches for intervals that overlap with a target interval that spans 25 pixels to either side of the target x-coordinate picked by the user.

42. **Write a program similar to the one shown in Figure 10.25. Let the user click to select a circle. If the user clicks outside all of the circles, select no circle. When you draw the map, draw the selected circle (if there is one) in a different color.

43. Draw a trie to represent the following keys and values:

KEY	VALUE
APPLE	10
APP	20
BEAR	30
ANT	40
BAT	50
APE	60

44. **Write a program that lets you add and find items in a trie.

CHAPTER 11

Balanced Trees

The previous chapter explained trees in general and some of the algorithms that use trees. Some algorithms, such as tree traversals, have run times that depend on the tree's total size. Other algorithms, such as one for inserting a node in a sorted tree, have run times that depend on the tree's height. If a sorted tree containing N nodes is relatively short and wide, inserting a new node takes O(log N) steps. However, if the nodes are added to the tree in sorted order, the tree grows tall and thin, so adding a new node takes O(N) time, which is much longer.

This chapter describes balanced trees. A *balanced tree* is one that rearranges its nodes as necessary to guarantee that it doesn't become too tall and thin. These trees may not be perfectly balanced or have the minimum height possible for a given number of nodes, but they are balanced enough that algorithms that travel through them from top to bottom run in O(log N) time.

> **NOTE** This chapter doesn't use the pseudocode that's included in much of the rest of the book. Balanced tree algorithms are much easier to explain and understand if you use pictures instead of code.

The following sections describe three kinds of balanced trees: AVL trees, 2-3 trees, and B-trees.

AVL Trees

An *AVL tree* is a sorted binary tree in which the heights of two subtrees at any given node differ by at most 1. For example, if a node's left subtree has height 10, then its right subtree must have height 9, 10, or 11. When a node is added or removed, the tree is rebalanced if necessary to ensure that the subtrees again have heights differing by at most 1.

> **NOTE**   AVL trees are named after their inventors, G. M. Adelson-Velskii and E. M. Landis. They were described in a 1962 paper and are the oldest type of balanced tree.

Because an AVL tree is a sorted binary tree, searching one is fairly easy. The previous chapter explained how to do that.

Adding values to and deleting values from an AVL tree is a bit more complicated. The following sections describe these two operations.

Adding Values

Usually, the implementation of the AVL tree node includes a balance factor that indicates whether the node's subtrees are left-heavy, balanced, or right-heavy. You can define the balance factor as `<height of left subtree>` − `<height of right subtree>`. This means that a balance factor of −1 indicates that the node is right-heavy, a balance factor of 0 means that the two subtrees have the same height, and a balance factor of +1 means that the node is left-heavy.

The basic strategy for adding a new node to an AVL tree is to climb down recursively into the tree until you find the location where the new node belongs. As the recursion unwinds and moves back up the nodes to the root, the program updates the balance factors at each node. If the program finds a node with a balance factor of less than −1 or greater than +1, it uses one or more "rotations" to rebalance the subtrees at that node.

Which rotations the algorithm uses depends on which grandchild subtree contains the new node. There are four cases, depending on whether the new node is in the left child's left subtree, the left child's right subtree, the right child's left subtree, or the right child's right subtree.

The tree shown in Figure 11.1 illustrates the situation in which the new node is in the left child's left subtree A1. This is called a *left-left case*.

The triangles in Figure 11.1 represent balanced AVL subtrees that could contain many nodes. In this example, the new node is in subtree A1. The tree is unbalanced at node B because the subtree rooted at node A, which includes subtree A1, is two levels taller than node B's other subtree, B2.

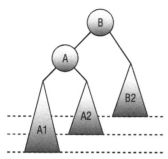

Figure 11.1: In the left-left case, the left child's left subtree contains the new node.

You can rebalance the tree by rotating it to the right, replacing node B with node A, and moving subtree A2 so that it becomes the new left subtree for node B. Figure 11.2 shows the result. This rebalancing is called a *right rotation*.

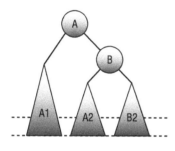

Figure 11.2: A right rotation rebalances the tree shown in Figure 11.1.

The right-right case is similar. You can rebalance the tree in that case with a left rotation, as shown in Figure 11.3.

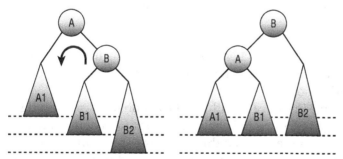

Figure 11.3: A left rotation rebalances the tree if the new node is in the right child's right subtree.

The top image in Figure 11.4 shows the left-right case in which the new node is in the left child's right subtree. That subtree includes node A and its two subtrees. It doesn't matter whether the new node is in subtree A1 or A2. In either

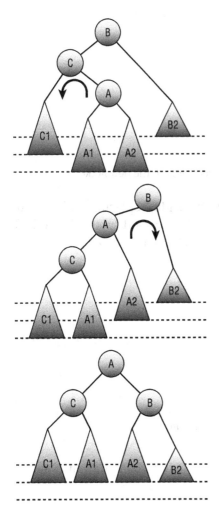

Figure 11.4: A left rotation followed by a right rotation rebalances the tree if the new node is in the left child's right subtree.

case, the subtree rooted at node A reaches two levels deeper than subtree B2. That means the subtree rooted at node C has depth 2 greater than subtree B2, so the tree is unbalanced at node B.

You can rebalance the tree in this case with a left rotation followed by a right rotation. The second image in Figure 11.4 shows the tree after a left rotation to change the positions of nodes A and C. At this point, the tree is in the left-left case, like the one shown in Figure 11.1. The left child's subtree is two levels deeper than node B's right subtree. Now you can rebalance the tree the same way you do in the left-left case by using a right rotation. The bottom image in Figure 11.4 shows the resulting balanced tree.

Similar techniques let you rebalance the tree in the right-left case. Use a right rotation to put the tree in the right-right case and then use a left rotation to rebalance the tree.

Deleting Values

You can use the same rotations to rebalance the tree whether you're adding new nodes or removing existing nodes. For example, Figure 11.5 shows the process of removing a node from an AVL tree. The top image shows the original tree. After node 1 is removed, the tree in the middle of the figure is unbalanced at node 3, because that node's left subtree has height 1 and its right subtree has height 3. A left rotation gives the rebalanced tree shown on the bottom.

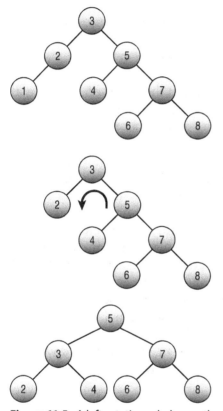

Figure 11.5: A left rotation rebalances the tree after node 1 is removed.

At all times, an AVL tree containing N nodes has height at most O(log N), so it is reasonably short and wide. This means that operations that climb the tree, such as searching for a value, take O(log N) time.

Rebalancing the tree also takes at most O(log N) time, so adding or removing a value takes O(log N) time.

2-3 Trees

To keep an AVL tree balanced, you consider the tree's structure at a relatively large scale. The subtrees at any node differ in height by at most 1. If you needed to examine the subtrees to determine their heights, you would need to search the subtrees to their leaf nodes.

To keep a 2-3 tree balanced, you consider its nodes at a smaller scale. Instead of considering entire subtrees at any given node, you consider the number of children each node has.

In a *2-3 tree*, every internal node has either two or three children. A node that has two children is called a *2-node*, and a node that has three children is called a *3-node*. Because every internal node has at least two children, a tree containing N nodes can have a height of at most $\log_2 (N)$.

Nodes with two children work the same way that the nodes do in a normal binary tree. Such a node holds a value. When you're searching the tree, you look down the node's left or right branch, depending on whether the target value is less than or greater than the node's value.

Nodes with three children hold two values. When you're searching the tree, you look down this node's left, middle, or right branch, depending on whether the target value is less than the node's first value, between its first and second values, or greater than its second value.

In practice, you can use the same class or structure to represent both kinds of nodes. Just create a node that can hold up to two values and three children. Then add a property that tells how many values are in use. (Note that a leaf node might hold one or two values but has no children.)

Figure 11.6 shows a 2-3 tree. To find the value 76, you would compare 76 to the root node's value 42. The target value 76 is greater than 42, so you move down the branch to the right of the value 42. At the next node, you compare 76 to 69 and 81. The target value 76 is between 69 and 81, so you move down the middle branch. You then find the value 76 in the leaf node.

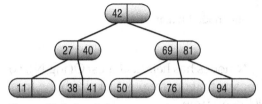

Figure 11.6: In a 2-3 tree, every internal node has either two or three children.

Searching a 2-3 tree is reasonably simple, but adding and deleting values is a bit harder than it is for a normal binary tree.

Adding Values

To add a new value to the tree, search the tree much as you would search any sorted tree to find the leaf node where the new value belongs. There are two cases, depending on whether the leaf node is full.

First, if the leaf node holds fewer than two values, simply add the new value to the node, keeping it in sorted order with the node's existing value and you're done.

Second, suppose that the leaf node that should hold the new value already holds two values, so it is full. In that case, you split the node into two new nodes, put the smallest value in the left node, put the largest value in the right node, and move the middle value up to the parent node. This is called a *node split*.

Figure 11.7 shows the process of adding the value 42 to the tree on the left. The value 42 is greater than the value 27 in the root node, so the new value should be placed down the root node's right branch. The node down that branch is a leaf node, so that is where the new value ideally belongs. That node is full, however, so adding the new value would give it three values: 32, 42, and 57. To make room, you split the leaf node into two new nodes holding the smaller and larger values 32 and 57, and you move the middle value up to the parent node. The resulting tree is shown on the right.

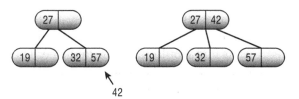

Figure 11.7: Adding a new value to a full leaf node forces a node split.

When a node splits, you need to move a value up to its parent node. That may cause the parent node to hold too many values, so it also splits. In the worst case, the series of splits cascades all the way up the tree to the root node, causing a *root split*. When a root split occurs, the tree grows taller. This is the only way a 2-3 tree grows taller.

In a sorted binary tree, adding values in sorted order is the worst-case scenario and results in a tall, thin tree. If you add N nodes to the tree, the tree has height N.

Figure 11.8 shows a 2-3 tree with the values 1 through 7 added in numeric order. The tree can hold the values 1 and 2 in the root node, so the first image shows the tree already containing those values. Each image shows the next value to be added and the location where it belongs in the tree. If you step through the stages, you'll see that adding the value 4 causes a node split and adding the value 7 causes a root split.

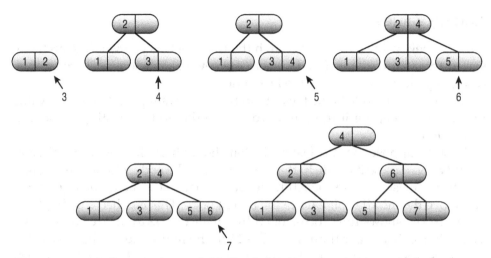

Figure 11.8: Adding a new value to a full leaf node forces a node split

Deleting Values

In theory, deleting a value from a 2-3 tree is about the same as adding one in reverse. Instead of node splits, you may have node merges. In practice, however, the details are fairly complicated.

You can simplify the problem if you can treat all deletions as if they are from a leaf node. If the target value is not in a leaf node, replace it with the right-most value to the left of it in the tree, just as you would in any sorted tree. The replacement node will be in a leaf node, so now you can treat the situation as if you had removed the rightmost value from that leaf node.

After you remove a value from a node, that node contains either zero values or one value. If it contains one value, you're done.

If the node now contains zero values, you may be able to borrow a value from its sibling node. If the node's sibling has two values, move one into the empty node, and again you're done.

For example, consider the tree shown at the top of Figure 11.9. Suppose you want to remove the value 4 from the root. Start by moving the value 3 into the deleted position to get the tree shown second in the picture.

This tree is no longer a 2-3 tree because the internal node A has only one child. In this example, node A's sibling node B has three children, so node A can take one. Move the node containing the value 5 so that it is a child of node A. When you remove that node, you must also remove the value 6 that was used to decide when to move left from node B to the node containing 5. The third tree in Figure 11.9 shows the new situation.

At this point, the value 6 doesn't have a node, and the values in the tree are no longer in sorted order because the value 5 is to the left of value 3. The value 6 is greater than any value in A's subtree, so move it to A's parent.

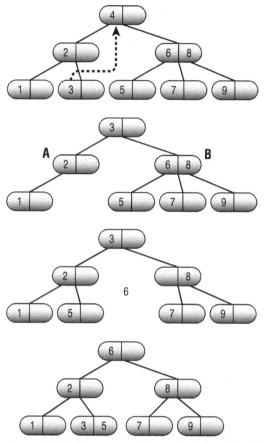

Figure 11.9: When you delete a value from a node in a 2-3 tree, sometimes a node that is too empty can borrow values from its sibling.

The value that was in that position (3 in this example) is greater than the values in A's original subtree and less than the value borrowed from its sibling (5), so put 3 to the left of the borrowed value.

The bottom tree in Figure 11.9 shows the final result.

One more situation may occur when you delete a value. Suppose that you remove a value from a node. If the node then has only one child and the node's sibling contains only one value, then you can't borrow a node from the sibling. In that case, you can merge the node and its sibling. Not surprisingly, this is called a *node merge*.

When you merge two nodes, their parent loses a child. If the parent had only two children, it now violates the condition that every internal node in a 2-3 tree must have either two or three children. In that case, you move up the tree and rebalance at that node's parent, either redistributing nodes or merging the parent with its sibling.

For example, consider the tree shown at the top of Figure 11.10 and suppose that you want to delete the value 3. Doing so results in the second tree shown in the figure. This tree is no longer a 2-3 tree because internal node A has only one child.

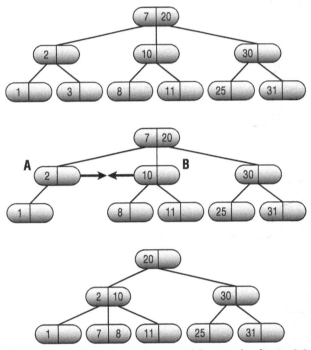

Figure 11.10: Sometimes when you delete a value from a 2-3 tree, you need to merge two nodes.

Node B also has only two children, so node A cannot borrow a child from it. Instead, you need to merge nodes A and B. Between them, nodes A and B contain two values and have three children, so that works from a space point of view.

When you merge the two nodes, their parent node loses a child, so it must also lose a value. You can move that value into the merged node's subtree.

After you make those rearrangements, the values are no longer in sorted order, so you need to rearrange them a bit. The bottom of Figure 11.10 shows the resulting tree.

In this example, the top node (which ends up holding the value 20) has two children. If it did not, you would have to rebalance the tree at that node's level, either borrowing a child or merging with that node's sibling.

In the worst case, a series of merges can cascade all the way to the tree's root, causing a root merge. This is the only way a 2-3 tree grows shorter.

B-Trees

B-trees (pronounced "bee trees") are an extension of 2-3 trees. (Or, if you prefer, 2-3 trees are a special case of B-trees.) In a 2-3 tree, every internal node holds one or two values and has two or three branches. In a B-tree of order K, every internal node (except possibly the root) holds between K and $2 \times K$ values and has between $K + 1$ and $2 \times K + 1$ branches.

Because they can hold many values, the internal nodes in a B-tree are often called *buckets*.

The number of values that a B-tree node can hold is determined by the tree's *order*. A B-tree of order K has these properties:

- Each node holds at most $2 \times K$ values.

- Each node, except possibly the root node, holds at least K values.

- An internal node holding M values has $M + 1$ branches leading to $M + 1$ children.

- All leaves are at the same level in the tree.

Because each internal node has at least $M + 1$ branches, the B-tree cannot grow too tall and thin. For example, every internal node in a B-tree of order 9 has at least 10 branches, so a tree holding 1 million values would need to be about $\log_{10} (1 \text{ million}) = 6$ levels tall. (A complete binary tree would need to be 20 levels tall to hold the same values.)

> **NOTE**   Recall that a tree's degree is the maximum number of branches that any of its nodes can have. That means a B-tree of order K has degree $2 \times K + 1$.

You search a B-tree much as you search a 2-3 tree. At each node, you find the values between which the target value lies and then move down the corresponding branch.

Figure 11.11 shows a B-tree node of order 2. If you were searching the tree for the value 35, you would move down branch B, because 35 is between the node's values 27 and 36, and branch B is between those values. If you wanted to find the value 50, you would move down branch D, because that is the node's last branch, and the value 50 is greater than all of the node's values.

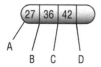

Figure 11.11: In a B-tree, internal nodes hold several values with branches between them.

Just as searching in a B-tree is similar to searching in a 2-3 tree, adding and removing values in a B-tree is similar to adding and removing values in a 2-3 tree.

Adding Values

To insert a value in a B-tree, locate the leaf node that should contain it. If that node contains fewer than $2 \times K$ values, simply add the new value.

If the node contains $2 \times K$ values, there's no room for a new value. If any one of the node's siblings contains fewer than $2 \times K$ values, you can rearrange the values in the siblings so that the new value will fit.

For example, consider the tree shown at the top of Figure 11.12 and suppose that you want to add the value 17. The leaf that should hold the new value is full. In the tree at the bottom of the figure, the values in the node and its right sibling have been rearranged to make room for the new value. Notice that the dividing value has been changed in the parent node.

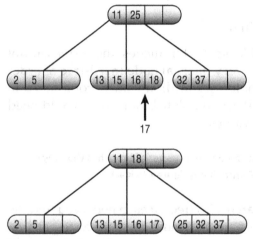

Figure 11.12: Sometimes when you add a value to a full B-tree node, you can redistribute values among the node's siblings to make room.

If all of the sibling nodes are full (or if you don't want to rearrange values among siblings, a potentially difficult task), you can split the node into two nodes that each contain $2 \times K$ values. Add the new value to the node's existing values, move the middle value up to be the dividing value in the parent node, and put the remaining values in the two new nodes.

For example, consider the tree shown at the top of Figure 11.13 and suppose that you want to add the value 34. The leaf node and its siblings are all full, so you cannot redistribute values to make room. Instead, you can split the node, as shown at the bottom of the figure.

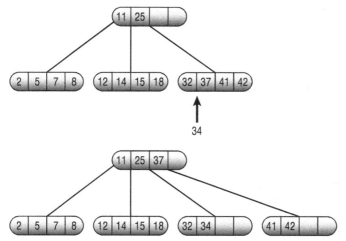

Figure 11.13: Sometimes when you add a value to a full B-tree node, you must split the node.

When you move a new value up to the parent node, that node may become too full. In that case, you must repeat the process with the parent node, either rearranging values among that node's siblings or splitting that node and moving a value up to its parent.

In the worst case, the split travels all of the way up the tree to the root, where it causes a root split. This is the only way a B-tree grows taller.

Deleting Values

To remove a value from an internal node, swap it with the rightmost value to the left in the tree, as you normally do for sorted trees. Then treat the case as if you were removing the value from a leaf node.

After you remove the value, if the leaf node contains at least K values, you're done. If the leaf node contains fewer than K values, you must rebalance the tree.

If any one of the node's siblings holds more than K values, you can redistribute the values to give the target node K values.

For example, consider the tree shown at the top of Figure 11.14 and suppose that you want to remove the value 32. That would leave its leaf node holding only one value, which is not allowed for a B-tree of degree 2. In the tree at the bottom of the figure, the values in the node and its siblings have been rearranged so that each holds two values.

If none of the node's siblings holds more than K values, you can merge the node with one of its siblings to make a node that holds 2×K values.

For example, consider the tree shown at the top of Figure 11.15 and suppose that you want to delete the value 12. Its leaf node and all of its siblings all hold K values, so you cannot redistribute values. Instead, you can merge the leaf with one of its siblings, as shown at the bottom of the figure.

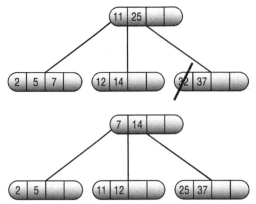

Figure 11.14: Sometimes when you delete a value from a B-tree node, you can redistribute values among the node's siblings to rebalance the tree.

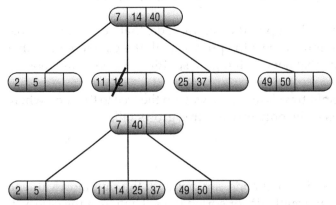

Figure 11.15: Sometimes when you delete a value from a B-tree node, you must merge the node with a sibling.

When you merge two nodes, the parent node may not hold K values. In that case, you must repeat the process with the parent node, either rearranging values among that node's siblings or merging that node with one of its siblings.

In the worst case, the merge travels all of the way up the tree to the root, where it causes a root merge. This is the only way a B-tree grows shorter.

Balanced Tree Variations

There are many other kinds of balanced tree structures and several variations on the ones that have already been described. The following sections cover two useful modifications that you can make to B-trees. These modifications are described for B-trees, but they also apply to some of the other kinds of balanced trees. In particular, because a 2-3 tree is really just a B-tree of order 1, these techniques apply directly to 2-3 trees.

Top-down B-trees

When you add an item to a B-tree, you first recursively move down into the tree to find the leaf node that should hold it. If that bucket is full, you may need to split it and move an item up to the parent node. As the recursive calls return, they can add a value that has been moved up to the current node and, if that node splits, move another value up the tree. Because these bucket splits occur as the recursive calls return up the tree, this data structure is sometimes called a *bottom-up B-tree*.

An alternative strategy is to make the algorithm split any full nodes on the way down into the tree. This creates room in the parent node if the algorithm must move a value up the tree. For example, if the leaf node that should hold the new value is full, the algorithm knows that the leaf's parent has room, because if it didn't, it would have been split already. Because these bucket splits occur as the recursion moves down into the tree, this variation is sometimes called a *top-down B-tree*.

In a top-down B-tree, bucket splits occur sooner than they might otherwise. The top-down algorithm splits a full node even if its children contain lots of unused entries. This means that the tree holds more unused entries than necessary, so it is taller than a bottom-up B-tree would be. However, all that empty space also reduces the chances that adding a new value will cause a long series of bucket splits.

Unfortunately, there is no top-down algorithm for bucket merging. As it moves down into the tree, the algorithm cannot tell if a node will lose a child, so it can't know if it should merge that node with a sibling.

B+trees

B-trees are often used to store large records. For example, a B-tree might hold employee records, each occupying several kilobytes of space. If the records include photographs of the employees, each might hold a few megabytes. The B-tree would organize its data by using some sort of key value, such as employee ID.

In that case, rearranging the items in a bucket would be fairly slow, because the program might need to shuffle many megabytes of data among several nodes. A cascading bucket split could make the algorithm move a huge amount of data.

One way to avoid moving large amounts of data is to place only the key values in the B-tree's internal nodes and then make each node also store a pointer to the rest of the record's data. Now when the algorithm needs to rearrange buckets, it moves only the keys and the record pointers instead of the whole record. This type of tree is called a *B+tree* (pronounced "bee plus tree").

Figure 11.16 shows the idea behind B+trees. Here dashed lines indicate links (pointers) from a key to the corresponding data, shown in a box.

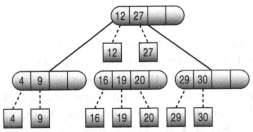

Figure 11.16: In a B+tree, values are linked to the corresponding data, shown here in boxes.

B+trees have a couple of advantages in addition to making it faster to rearrange values. First, they let a program easily use multiple trees to manage different keys for the same data. For example, a program might use one B+tree to arrange employee records by employee ID and another B+tree to arrange the same records by Social Security number. Each tree would use the same pointers to refer to the employee records. To find an employee by ID or Social Security number, you would search the appropriate tree and then follow the correct pointer to the actual data.

A second benefit of B+trees is that the nodes could hold more values in the same space. This means that you can increase the tree's degree and make the tree shorter.

For example, suppose that you build an order 2 B-tree so that each node has between three and five children. To hold 1 million records, this tree would need a height between $\log_5 (1,000,000) \approx 9$ and $\log_3 (1,000,000) \approx 13$. To find an item in this tree, the program might need to search as many as 13 nodes. It is unlikely that all of the tree's records would fit into memory all at once, so this might require 13 disk accesses, which would be relatively slow.

Now suppose that you store the same 1 million records in a B+tree using nodes that use the same number of kilobytes as the original nodes. Because the B+tree stores only key values in the nodes, its nodes may be able to hold far more keys.

Suppose the new B+tree can store up to 20 employee IDs in the same node space. (The actual value may be much larger, depending on the size of the employee records.) In that case, each node in the tree would have between 11 and 21 children, so the tree could store the same 1 million values with a height between $\log_{21} (1,000,000) \approx 5$ and $\log_{11} (1,000,000) \approx 6$. To find an item, the program would need to search only six nodes at most and perform six disk accesses at most, cutting the search time roughly in half.

> **NOTE**   Because B+trees provide fast search times with relatively few disk accesses, relational databases often use them to implement indices.

Summary

Like other sorted trees, balanced trees let a program store and find values quickly. By keeping themselves balanced, trees such as AVL trees, 2-3 trees, B-trees, and B+trees ensure that they don't grow too tall and thin, which would ruin their performance.

Adding and removing values in a balanced tree takes longer than it does in an ordinary (nonbalanced) sorted tree. Those operations still take only O(log N) time, however, so the theoretical run time is the same even if the actual time is slightly longer. Spending that extra time lets the algorithm guarantee that those operations don't grow to linear time.

Chapter 8 described hash tables, which store and retrieve values even more quickly than balanced trees do. However, hash tables don't allow some of the same features, such as quickly displaying all of the values in the data structure in sorted order.

This chapter and the preceding one describe generic tree algorithms that let you build and traverse trees and balanced trees. The next chapter describes decision trees, which you can use to model and solve a wide variety of problems.

Exercises

You can find the answers to these exercises in Appendix B. Asterisks indicate particularly difficult problems.

1. Draw a picture similar to Figure 11.4 showing how to rebalance an AVL tree in the right-left case.

2. Draw a series of pictures showing an AVL tree as you add the values 1 through 8 to it in numeric order.

3. Rebalance the AVL tree shown in Figure 11.17 after removing node 33.

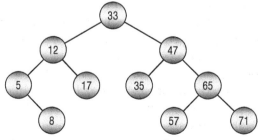

Figure 11.17: Remove value 33 from this AVL tree and rebalance it.

4. Draw a series of pictures similar to Figure 11.7 showing how to rebalance the 2-3 tree shown in Figure 11.18 after you add the value 24 to it.

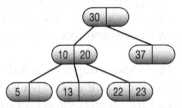

Figure 11.18: Add value 24 to this 2-3 tree and rebalance it.

5. Draw a series of pictures similar to Figure 11.9 showing how to remove the value 20 from the 2-3 tree shown in Figure 11.18.

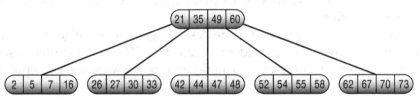

Figure 11.19: Add value 56 to this B-tree and rebalance it.

6. Draw a series of pictures similar to Figure 11.13 showing how to add the value 56 to the B-tree shown in Figure 11.19.

7. Draw a series of pictures similar to the one shown in Figure 11.14 illustrating how to delete the value 49 from the B-tree you got as the final solution in Exercise 6 above.

8. Draw a series of pictures that shows a B-tree of order 2 as you add consecutive numbers 1, 2, 3, and so forth until the root node has four children. How many values does the tree hold at that point?

9. Computers usually read data from a hard disk in blocks. Suppose that a computer has a 2 KB block size, and you want to build a B-tree or a B+tree that stores customer records using four blocks per bucket. Assume that each record occupies 1 KB, and you want the key value stored by the tree to be the customer's name, which occupies up to 100 bytes. Also assume that pointers between nodes (or to data in a B+tree) take 8 bytes each. What is the largest order you could use for a B-tree or a B+tree while using four-block buckets? What would be the maximum height of the B-tree and B+tree if they hold 10,000 records?

Decision Trees

Chapter 10 and Chapter 11 described tree algorithms in general and balanced trees in particular. They explained algorithms that you can use to build and maintain trees, but they didn't describe any algorithms that use trees to solve a particular problem.

This chapter describes *decision trees*, which you can use to model situations where you can solve a problem by making a series of decisions. Each branch in the tree represents a single choice. A leaf node represents a complete set of decisions that produces a final solution. The goal is to find the best possible set of choices or the best leaf node in the tree.

For example, in the *partition problem*, you want to divide a set of objects of various weights into two groups that have the same total weight. You could model this problem with a binary tree, where the left branch at level K of the tree corresponds to including the Kth object in the first pile and the right branch corresponds to including the Kth object in the second pile. A complete path through the tree corresponds to a complete assignment of objects to the two piles. The goal is to find a path that gives the most even distribution of weight.

Decision trees are extremely useful and can model all sorts of situations where you can use a series of steps to produce a solution. Unfortunately, decision trees are often truly enormous. For example, the binary tree described in the preceding paragraph representing the division of N objects into two piles has 2^N leaf nodes, so searching the entire tree may be impossible. For example, a tree representing the division of 50 objects has approximately 1.13×10^{15} leaf nodes.

Even if you could examine 1 million of those nodes per second, it would take more than 2,100 years to examine every node.

This chapter describes some different kinds of decision trees. It explains techniques that you can use to search these trees efficiently so that you can find solutions to larger problems than you could find by using a brute-force approach. It also explains heuristic methods that you can use to find approximate solutions to some problems when searching a tree completely isn't feasible.

The following section starts the discussion of decision tree search algorithms by covering a very specific kind of search: game tree searches.

Searching Game Trees

You can model games such as chess, checkers, Go, and tic-tac-toe (naughts and crosses) with a game tree where each branch represents a move by one of the players. If at some point in the game a player has 10 possible moves, then the tree at that point has 10 possible branches. A complete path through the tree corresponds to a complete game.

Like all decision trees, game trees grow extremely quickly. For example, suppose that a chess game lasts 40 moves (each player moves 20 times) and has an average of about 30 possible moves per turn. In that case, the total number of paths through the game tree is roughly $30^{40} \approx 1.2 \times 10^{59}$. Exhaustively searching such a tree with a computer that could examine 1 billion possible paths per second would take roughly 2.3×10^{44} years. (See https://en.wikipedia.org /wiki/Shannon_number for a discussion of the Shannon number, an estimate of the complexity of chess.)

Tic-tac-toe is a more tractable problem, although the game tree is still huge. In the first move, the X player initially has nine choices. In the second move, player O has eight choices because one square is already taken by X. At each move, the current player has one fewer choice than the other player had in the previous move, so a total of $9 \times 8 \times 7 \times \ldots \times 1 = 9! = 362,880$ paths are possible through the game tree.

Some of those paths are illegal. For example, if X takes the top three squares in the first moves, the game is over, so any paths through the tree that begin with X taking those squares don't go all the way to the ninth level of the tree.

If you remove all of the paths that end early, the game tree still contains roughly a quarter-million leaf nodes, so the tree is still fairly large.

The following sections describe algorithmic techniques that you can use to search a tic-tac-toe game tree. The discussion uses tic-tac-toe because that problem is reasonably small, but the same techniques apply to any similar game, such as chess, checkers, or Go.

Minimax

To decide whether one move is preferable to another during a game, you need to decide what value the different board positions have. For example, if you can place an X in a particular square in a tic-tac-toe game and doing so lets you win, then that board position has a high value. Conversely, if placing an X in a different position will allow O to win later, then that board position has a low value.

Other games such as chess use different board position values that can depend on many factors, such as whether you win, whether your opponent wins, whether your pieces occupy certain parts of the board, and whether your pieces can threaten certain positions. In tic-tac-toe, you can define four board values.

4: The board position will end in a win for this player.

3: It's unclear whether the current board position will result in a win, loss, or draw.

2: The board position will end in a draw.

1: The board position will end in a loss for this player.

Figure 12.1 shows board positions demonstrating each of these values. In the upper-left board position, X will win in the next move. The board position in the upper right gives a loss to X, because O will win no matter where X goes in the next turn. The lower-left board position is uncertain, assuming that you can search only a few levels into the game tree. Finally, the board position in the lower right will end in a draw no matter where X and O move on their final moves.

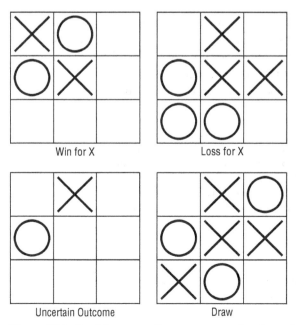

Figure 12.1: To pick a move, the program must assign values to board positions.

There's an obvious relationship among these values. If player 1 wins, then player 2 loses. If a game ends in a draw for player 1, it also ends in a draw for player 2. If the board value is unknown for player 1, then it's also unclear for player 2.

For complicated games, the outcome of a particular board position is often uncertain because the program cannot search the game tree thoroughly enough to examine all of the possible outcomes. In cases such as those, the program must assign approximate values to different positions so that the program can pick the best one.

On a reasonably fast computer, a tic-tac-toe program can search the entire game tree, so the value 3 isn't really necessary. It is included here so that you can see how to handle more complicated games. (You can get the same effect in a tic-tac-toe program by not allowing the program to search more than a few levels through the game tree.)

> **NOTE**   Because you can search the entire tic-tac-toe game tree, it's fairly obvious that, starting from the first move, X can force a win, O can force a win, or one of the players can force a draw. If both players understand the game tree completely, there's really no game. The only way there could be any doubt about the outcome is if one of the players makes a mistake.
>
> It's much less obvious that the same is true for more complicated games such as chess. If the players had perfect knowledge of the game tree, one or the other could force a win or draw with no doubt about the outcome. It's the fact that the game tree is too big to understand completely that makes the game interesting.

Minimax is a game tree search strategy in which, at each move, you try to minimize the maximum value your opponent can achieve. For example, if you can make two moves, the first giving your opponent a win and the second giving your opponent a loss, you should take the second move.

The following pseudocode shows the minimax algorithm at a high level:

```
// Find the best move for player1.
Minimax(Board: board_position, Move: best_move, Value: best_value,
    Player: player1, Player: player2, Integer: depth, Integer: max_depth)
    // See if we have exceeded our allowed depth of recursion.
    If (depth > max_depth) Then
        // We have exceeded the maximum allowed depth of recursion.
        // The outcome for this board position is unknown.
        best_value = Unknown
        Return
    End If

    // Find the move that gives player2 the lowest value.
    Value: lowest_value = Infinity
```

```
Move: lowest_move

For Each <possible test move>
    <Update board_position to make the test move>

    // Evaluate this board position.
    If <this is a win, loss, or draw> Then
        <Set lowest_value and lowest_move appropriately>
    Else
        // Recursively try other future moves.
        Value: test_value
        Move: test_move
        Minimax(board_position, test_move, test_value,
            player2, player1, depth, max_depth)

        // See if we found a worse move for player2.
        If (test_value < lowest_value) Then
            // This is an improvement. Save it.
            lowest_value = test_value
            lowest_move = test_move
        End If
    End If

    <Restore board_position to unmake the test move>
Next <possible test move>

// Save the best move.
best_move = lowest_move

// Convert board values for player2 into values for player 1.
If (lowest_value == Win)
    best_value = Loss
Else If (lowest_value == Loss)
    best_value = Win
Else
    ...
End If
End Minimax
```

The algorithm starts by checking its depth of recursion. If it has exceeded its maximum allowed depth of recursion, the algorithm cannot determine the game's eventual outcome from this board position, so it sets best_value to Unknown and returns.

To find the best move for player1, the algorithm must find the move that gives player2 the worst board value. The algorithm creates variables to keep track of the lowest board value found so far for player2. It sets lowest_value equal to Infinity so that any board value it finds replaces that initial value.

Next the algorithm loops through all the moves that player1 could make. The Minimax algorithm makes a move and then recursively calls itself to find the best move player2 could make after player1 makes that test move.

After the recursive call returns, the algorithm compares the best result player2 could obtain with the value saved in lowest_value. If the test value is lower, the algorithm updates lowest_value and lowest_move, so it knows that this move is preferable (to player1).

After it finishes examining all the possible test moves, the algorithm knows which move player1 should make to give player2 the worst possible board position. It saves that move and then converts the value of the board for player2 into the value for player1. For example, if the best board position makes player2 lose, then it makes player1 win and vice versa.

In cases where player2 doesn't win or lose, it's a little less clear how to convert from a player2 value to a player1 value. For tic-tac-toe, the Unknown and Draw values are the same for both players. For example, if a board position gives player2 a draw, it gives player1 a draw as well.

For a more complicated game such as chess, a board position's value might be a number between –100 and +100, where +100 represents a win and –100 represents a loss. In that case, player2's value for a board position might simply be the negative of player1's value for the same board position.

One side effect of a simple minimax strategy that can sometimes be a problem is that the program considers all solutions that have the same board value equally desirable. To see why that can be a problem, suppose that a game is close enough to the end for the program to realize that it will lose no matter what it does. In that case, it selects the first move it considers while searching the game tree, because all moves give the same result. The result may seem random or even foolish. For example, the program might pick a move that gives its opponent a win in the next move when a different move might have delayed the inevitable for two or three more moves. In contrast, a human would probably pick a move that made the game last longer, hoping the opponent will make a mistake or won't realize that the game is as good as over. Alternatively, a human might concede instead of delaying the inevitable or making seemingly-random moves.

Conversely, the program might find a way to win in six moves and pick that over another strategy that would win in only two moves. If the computer finds the six-move win first, it won't switch later to the two-move win because that doesn't improve the outcome.

You can address these problems by favoring longer sequences of moves that lead to losses or ties and shorter sequences of moves that lead to wins.

A simple minimax strategy is enough for a winning tic-tac-toe game, but for more complicated games, a program cannot search the entire game tree. The following sections describe some strategies that you can use to search larger game trees.

Initial Moves and Responses

One way to reduce the size of the game tree is to store precomputed initial moves and responses. If you search the game tree ahead of time to find the best possible initial move, then you can simply have the program make that move if it has the first turn. Instead of spending a noticeable amount of time searching for a first move, the program can move instantly.

The user moves next, so the computer doesn't need to move again until two moves have been made. The size of the game tree at that point depends on the particular moves made, but the tree will be much smaller than the original game tree. For example, the entire tic-tac-toe game tree contains 255,168 possible games. If X picks the upper-left square and O picks the upper-middle square, the remaining game tree contains only 3,668 possible games. That may still be too many to enumerate by hand, but it's small enough for a computer to search.

If the user moves first, the game tree also shrinks dramatically. If the user picks the upper-left square for the first move, the remaining game tree contains only 27,732 possible games. This is a lot more than the number of games after the second move, but it's still a lot smaller than the entire game tree. With one additional change, you can make that number even smaller.

X has only nine choices for a first move. If you precalculate all of the best responses to those first moves, you can make the program simply look up the appropriate response. Instead of searching a game tree containing 27,732 possible games, the program only needs to look up one of nine possible responses.

The user then moves again, so the program doesn't need to search the game tree until three moves have been made—one by the user, one a precalculated response, and another by the user. At that point, the game tree is much smaller. For example, if X takes the upper-left square, O takes the upper-middle square, and X takes the upper-right square, the remaining game tree contains only 592 possible games. That's actually small enough that you could search the tree by hand if you wanted.

In a more complicated game like chess, the game tree is infinitely large for practical purposes, so trimming the top few levels of the tree won't help as much. Skipping three moves might let you reduce the number of possible games from around 1.2×10^{59} to roughly 4.5×10^{54}, but that's still much too big to search completely.

Using precalculated moves and responses does let a chess program make its first few moves quickly, however. It lets you spend lots of time studying game openings so that you can invest extra time in planning those moves. It also lets the program avoid openings that would give it a big initial disadvantage.

Game Tree Heuristics

The game trees for all but the simplest games are much too big to search completely, so in general there's no way to know whether a particular move will lead to a better solution than another. Although you can't always know for certain that a particular move will be beneficial, sometimes you can use a heuristic to indicate a move's value.

A *heuristic* (pronounced "hyoo-riss-tik") is an algorithm that is likely to produce a good result but that is not guaranteed to do so. Heuristics can't help you search the entire game tree, but they can give you rules for deciding which parts of the tree to avoid and which parts deserve special attention.

One type of game heuristic is to look for patterns in the board position. For example, one heuristic that some chess players use is "When ahead, trade mercilessly." This means if you have the advantage and you can trade one of your pieces for a piece of equal value, you should do so. That can make your relative advantage greater and makes the game tree smaller so that it's easier to search in the future.

Other patterns that a chess program may seek out include long sequences of trades, castling moves, moves that threaten multiple pieces, discovered check, moves that threaten the king or queen, promotion, en passant, and so forth.

When a program recognizes one of these patterns, it can alter the strategy it uses to search the game tree. For example, if the program sees a long series of exchanges, it might exceed its normal maximum depth of recursion to follow the exchange to its end to see if it will come out ahead.

Another kind of heuristic assigns numeric values to locations on the board and then modifies a board's total value based on the values of the locations occupied or threatened by a player's pieces. For example, in tic-tac-toe you might assign each square a number indicating the number of wins that include it. The upper-left corner would have the value 3, because there are three ways to win by using that square. Figure 12.2 shows the square values for this heuristic.

In chess, the center four squares occupy a critical location, so you might give those squares more value. You also might want to assign different values for squares occupied by a piece and squares threatened by a piece.

3	2	3
2	4	2
3	2	3

Figure 12.2: The value of a tic-tac-toe square is the number of ways you can use that square to win.

In most games, the values of the board locations will change over time. For example, in the early stages of a chess game, the central four squares are important. At the very end of the game, however, it is whether a player can achieve a checkmate that is important, not whether the player controls those squares.

NOTE   Writing a Reversi game is an interesting exercise in game programming. The rules are much simpler than those for chess, but the game tree is much larger than the tree for tic-tac-toe, so you can't search it completely. The way pieces move is much simpler than chess, so some patterns at least are easier to recognize. By using board location values alone and some tree searching, you can build a reasonably strong Reversi program. For more information on Reversi, including the rules and some notes about strategy, see https://en.wikipedia.org/wiki/Reversi.

The later section "Decision Tree Heuristics" has more to say about heuristics.

Searching General Decision Trees

By modeling a game's moves as a tree, you convert the problem of picking a good move into a search for the best path through the tree. Similarly, you can model many other decision processes with a tree.

For example, consider the partition problem that I described at the beginning of this chapter. You have a collection of objects of a given weight (or cost or value or some other measure), and you need to divide them into two groups that have the same total weight. In some cases, this is easy. If you have four objects with weights 2, 4, 1, and 1, it's obvious that you can put the large object in the first group and the other objects in the second group. Similarly, if you have an even number of objects that all have the same weight, you can simply place half in one group and half in the other group.

The problem is much harder if you have a large number of objects with varying weights. In that case, you can model the process of deciding which objects go in which group with a binary decision tree. Here the Kth level of the tree represents a decision about the Kth object. A left branch represents putting the object in the first group, and a right branch represents putting the object in the second group.

Figure 12.3 shows a complete decision tree for a partition problem with four objects having weights 2, 4, 1, and 1. A path through the tree represents a complete assignment of objects to the two groups. For example, the path that follows the root's left branch and then the next three right branches puts the first object (weight 2) in the first group and the other objects (weights 4, 1, and 1) in the second group. The numbers below the tree show the total weights of the two groups—in this case, 2 and 6.

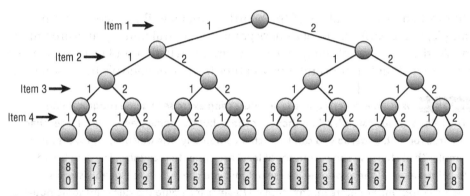

Figure 12.3: You use a decision tree to model the partition problem.

Notice that only two leaf nodes in Figure 12.3 correspond to dividing the objects' weights equally so that both groups have a total weight of 4. The two solutions are basically the same solution with the objects in the two groups switched.

> **NOTE**   In fact, any solution you find will have a complementary solution with the two groups switched. If you arbitrarily pick an item and place it in the first group before starting the search, you can shorten the tree by one level. This eliminates solutions that have the chosen item in the second group, but the tree will still contain solutions if there are any.

The decision tree shown in Figure 12.3 is fairly large even though it represents a problem with only four objects. For larger problems, the decision tree is enormous. For example, if you need to divide 50 objects into two groups, the tree holds 2^{50} leaf nodes, representing roughly 1.13×10^{15} possible solutions. If only a few of the arrangements produce an even division of weight, it could be very difficult to find a good solution.

The following section explains the difference between two versions of problems such as the partition problem—one that is hard to solve and one that is extremely hard to solve. The sections after that explain general methods that you can use to search decision trees efficiently.

Optimization Problems

Problems such as the partition problem often come in two closely related forms. The first form asks if a particular solution is possible. The second form asks you to find the best solution possible.

For the partition problem, the first question asks whether you can divide the objects into two groups with equal total weights. The second question asks you to divide the objects into two groups with total weights as close to equal as possible. The second question is called an *optimization problem* because you can divide the objects in many ways, and you must find the optimum division.

The optimization version of the problem is in some ways easier because it allows approximate solutions. The other version of the problem requires a strictly yes or no answer.

For example, suppose you need to divide into two groups—100 items with a total combined weight of 400. If you search the decision tree and find an exactly equal division, you know that the answer to the first question is yes. However, you might search the tree for hours or even days and never find a division that is exactly equal. In that case, you cannot conclude that no such division exists, only that you haven't found one.

In contrast, you can easily find solutions to the optimization version of the problem. Those solutions may not be very good, but at least you can find an answer that approximates the best possible solution. If you search the decision tree long enough, usually you can find a solution that is reasonably good, even if it isn't perfect. Of course, you might get lucky and find a solution that divides the objects exactly evenly. If you don't find such a solution, you cannot conclude that no such solution exists, but at least you've found an approximate solution.

The following sections discuss methods that you can use to search decision trees. The first two methods you can use to solve either the optimization or nonoptimization version of a problem. The final section, on decision tree heuristics, works only on the optimization version of a problem.

Exhaustive Search

The simplest way to search a decision tree is to visit all of its nodes, looking for the best solution. Note that you don't actually need to build a decision tree to search it. You just need a way to keep track of where you are in the tree. Many algorithms use recursion to pick branches at different levels of the tree, and those recursive calls can keep track of their positions in the tree.

For example, the following pseudocode shows a basic high-level algorithm that exhaustively searches for a solution to the optimization version of the partition problem:

```
StartExhaustiveSearch()
    <Initialize best solution so it is replaced by the first
    test solution>
    ExhaustiveSearch(0)
End StartExhaustiveSearch

ExhaustiveSearch(Integer: next_index)
    // See if we are done.
    If <next_index > max_index>
        // We have assigned all items, so we are at a leaf node.
```

```
            <If the test solution is better than the
             best solution found so far, save it>
        Else
            // We have not assigned all items,
            // so we are not at a leaf node.
            <Assign item next_index to group 0>
            ExhaustiveSearch(next_index + 1)
            <Unassign item next_index to group 0>

            <Assign item at next_index to group 1>
            ExhaustiveSearch(next_index + 1)
            <Unassign item next_index to group 1>
        End If
End ExhaustiveSearch
```

The StartExhaustiveSearch method initializes the best solution found so far. Normally, it simply sets the value of that solution (which, in the case of the partition problem, is the difference between the weights of the two groups) to a large number, so the first valid test solution will be an improvement.

The StartExhaustiveSearch method then calls ExhaustiveSearch to do all of the real work.

The ExhaustiveSearch method takes as a parameter the index of the item that it should assign to a group. This is the same as the depth of recursion and the level in the decision tree.

If ExhaustiveSearch has assigned all of the items to one group or another, it compares the test solution to see whether it is better than the best solution found so far. If the test solution is an improvement, the method saves it as the new best solution.

If ExhaustiveSearch has not yet assigned every item to a group, it tries assigning item number next_index to group 0 and then calls itself recursively to assign the remaining items. After the recursive call returns, the method tries assigning item number next_index to group 1 and again calls itself recursively to assign the remaining items.

Eventually, the recursive calls work their way down the tree until they reach leaf nodes and update the best solution if appropriate.

This basic algorithm is fairly flexible, and it can be adapted for many different problems.

For the partition problem, you can use an array to store the test solution and the best solution found so far. The Kth entry in the array should be a 0 or 1 to indicate whether the Kth item is assigned to group 0 or group 1. When the algorithm reaches a leaf node, it should add up the weights of the items in each group and compare the difference to the best difference found so far.

This algorithm is reasonably straightforward and works, but the fact that it searches the entire decision tree makes it relatively slow. This method will never be fast, but you can make one improvement that sometimes shortens the search considerably.

If the algorithm ever reaches a leaf node where the test assignment makes two groups with exactly equal total weights, the algorithm can stop without searching the rest of the decision tree. If the tree contains many optimal solutions, "short circuiting" a search in this way may let the algorithm find a solution relatively quickly and skip searching much of the tree.

For example, in one test, while trying to divide 20 items into two groups of equal weight, a full exhaustive search visited 2,097,150 nodes. When allowed to stop the search after finding an optimal solution, the algorithm visited only 4,098 nodes. The results vary greatly depending on the items' specific weights.

Branch and Bound

Branch and bound is a technique for searching trees more effectively than by an exhaustive search. After it moves down a branch in the tree, the algorithm calculates the best possible outcome that it could possibly achieve down that branch. If the best possible outcome won't be an improvement over the best solution that has already been found, the algorithm abandons that branch and doesn't continue down its subtree. Depending on the specific data values, this can save a huge amount of time.

For example, suppose that a partition problem algorithm keeps track of the current total weight in each of the two groups it is building and the total weight of the items that have not yet been assigned to a group. Now suppose that the algorithm has reached a point where group 0 has a total weight of 100, group 1 has a total weight of 50, and the unassigned items have a total weight of 20. Suppose also that the algorithm has already found a solution in which the two groups have weights that differ by 20.

If the algorithm were to assign all of the remaining items to group 1, then group 0 would have a total weight of 100 and group 1 would have a total weight of 70, a difference of 30. However, the algorithm has already found a solution in which the difference is only 20. The current test solution cannot be improved enough to make it better than the current best solution. In that case, the algorithm can stop working on its current solution without assigning the rest of the items.

The following pseudocode shows a high-level branch and bound algorithm for the optimization version of the partition problem:

```
StartBranchAndBound()
    <Initialize best solution so it is replaced by the first
    test solution>
    BranchAndBound(0)
End StartBranchAndBound

BranchAndBound(Integer: next_index)
    // See if we are done.
    If <next_index > max_index>
```

```
            // We have assigned all items, so we are at a leaf node.
            <If the test solution is an improvement, save it>
        Else
            // We have not assigned all items,
            // so we are not at a leaf node.

            If <the test solution cannot be improved enough
                to beat the current best solution>
                    Then Return

            <Assign item next_index to group 0>
            BranchAndBound(next_index + 1)
            <Unassign item next_index to group 0>

            <Assign item next_index to group 1>
            BranchAndBound(next_index + 1)
            <Unassign item next_index to group 1>
        End If
    End BranchAndBound
```

This algorithm is similar to the exhaustive search algorithm, except that it returns without recursion if the current test solution cannot be improved enough to beat the current best solution.

Branch and bound often trims many branches and their subtrees from the decision tree, so it can be much faster than an exhaustive search.

For example, in one test, while trying to divide 20 items into two groups of equal weight, a full exhaustive search visited 2,097,150 nodes, but a branch and bound search visited only 774,650 nodes. When both algorithms were allowed to use the "short circuit" described in the preceding section to stop early, the exhaustive search visited 4,082 nodes, but the branch and bound search visited only 298 nodes.

Branch and bound is a useful technique, but I want to mention two important facts before moving on to decision tree heuristics. First, branch and bound searches every path through the tree that might lead to a solution better than the best solution found so far. That means, like exhaustive search, it always finds the optimal solution.

The second important fact is that although branch and bound often avoids searching large parts of the decision tree, decision trees can be enormous, so branch and bound can still be fairly slow.

In one test, exhaustive search could search a decision tree for a 25-item partition problem in roughly 6.6 seconds. Branch and bound could search the same tree in roughly 2 seconds. That's a big improvement but adding a new item to the problem roughly doubles the tree's size. Adding one more item made branch and bound take about 4 seconds and adding a second item made it take 7.9 seconds.

Branch and bound is much faster than exhaustive search, but it still isn't fast enough to search a really big decision tree such as the 2.2 trillion node tree representing the partition problem with 40 items.

Decision Tree Heuristics

Exhaustive search and branch and bound find the best possible solution. Unfortunately, decision trees are so large that those algorithms work only for relatively small problems.

To search larger trees, you need to use heuristics. A heuristic won't necessarily find the best possible solution, but it may find a fairly good solution—at least for the optimization version of a problem where approximate solutions make sense.

The following sections describe four heuristics for use with the partition problem.

Random Search

One of the simplest heuristics for searching a decision tree is to follow random paths through it. At each node, simply pick a branch to follow randomly. If you try enough random paths, you may stumble across a reasonably good solution.

The following pseudocode shows how you might search a decision tree randomly:

```
RandomSearch()
    <Initialize best solution so it is replaced by the first
    test solution>
    For i = 1 To num_trials
        For index = 0 To max_index
            <Randomly assign item number index to group 0 or 1>
        Next index

        // See if this solution is an improvement.
        <If the test solution is an improvement, save it>
    Next i
End RandomSearch
```

The algorithm starts by initializing the best solution as usual. It then enters a loop that it executes for some number of trials.

For each trial, the algorithm loops over the indices of the items to be partitioned and randomly assigns each item to either group 0 or group 1.

After it has randomly assigned every item to a group, the algorithm checks the solution to see whether it is better than the best solution found so far and, if it is, saves the new solution.

If you are trying to partition N weights, each trial takes only N steps, so this heuristic is extremely fast. That's good, because in a large decision tree, the odds of your finding a good solution may be small, so you need to run a lot of trials.

There are several ways that you could pick the number of trials to run. You could just run a fixed number of trials—say, 1,000. That will work for small decision trees, but it might be better to pick a number that depends on the tree's size.

Another strategy is to make the number of trials a polynomial function of the number of weights being partitioned. For example, if you are partitioning N weights, you could use `num_trials` $= 3 \times N^3$. The function $3 \times N^3$ grows quickly as N increases but not nearly as quickly as 2^N, so this still searches only a tiny fraction of the decision tree.

Another approach is to continue trying random paths until a certain number of random paths in a row fail to find an improvement. With that approach, the algorithm won't stop as long as it's fairly easy to find improvements.

Perhaps the ideal approach is to let the algorithm run continuously, updating its best solution when it finds improvements, until you stop it. That way, if you don't need a solution in a hurry, you can let the algorithm run for hours or possibly even days.

Improving Paths

You can make random path selection more effective if you pick a random path and then try to improve it. Start with a random path. Then randomly pick an item, and switch it from the group it is in to the other group. If that improves the partitioning, keep that change. If that change doesn't help, undo it and try again. Repeat this process many times until you can't improve the path any more.

This technique has many variations. For example, instead of swapping random items, you could try swapping each item one at a time. You might want to repeat that process several times, because swapping one item may change the weights of the two groups so that it is now possible to swap some other item that you could not swap before.

The following pseudocode shows this algorithm:

```
MakeImprovements()
    <Initialize best solution so it is replaced by the first
    test solution>
    For i = 1 To num_trials
        // Make a random initial solution.
        For index = 0 To max_index
            <Randomly assign item number index to group 0 or 1>
        Next index

        // Try to improve the solution.
        Boolean: had_improvement = True
        While (had_improvement)
```

```
        // Assume this time we won't  have any improvement.
        had_improvement = False

        // Try swapping items.
        For index = 0 To max_index
            <Swap item number index into the other group>

            // See if this improves the test solution.
            If <this swap improves the test solution> Then
                had_improvement = True
            Else
                <Swap the item back>
            End If
        Next index
    Loop

    // See if this solution is an improvement.
    <If the test solution is an improvement, save it>
    Next i
End MakeImprovements
```

The algorithm enters a loop to perform a certain number of trials. For each trial, it picks a random test solution.

It then enters a loop that executes as long as the algorithm finds an improvement for the random test solution. Each time through this improvement loop, the algorithm tries swapping each item into the group to which it isn't currently assigned. If that swap improves the test solution, the algorithm keeps it. If that swap does not improve the test solution, the algorithm undoes it.

After it can find no more improvements, the algorithm compares the test solution to the best solution found so far and keeps it if it is better.

You can pick the number of trials to run in the same ways that you can for the random heuristic described in the previous section. You can let the algorithm run a fixed number of trials, a number of trials that depends on the number of weights being partitioned, until it finds no improved best solution, or until you stop it.

Sometimes, it is not possible to improve a path by making a single swap. For example, suppose you are partitioning the weights 6, 5, 5, 5, 3, and 3. Suppose also that you pick a random path that makes the two groups {6, 3, 3} and {5, 5, 5} so that the groups have total weights of 12 and 15. Therefore, their total weights differ by 3.

Moving an item from the first group to the second only makes the difference greater, so that won't improve the solution.

If you moved an item with weight 5 from the second group to the first, the groups would be {6, 5, 3, 3} and {5, 5}, so their total weights would be 17 and 10—also not an improvement.

No single swap can improve this solution. But if you move an item with weight 3 from the first group to the second and you also move an item with weight 5 from the second group to the first, you get the groups {6, 5, 3} and {5, 5, 3}. The groups would then have weights 14 and 13, an improvement over the original solution.

The single swap strategy described in this section won't find this improvement, because it requires you to make two swaps at the same time. Other improvement strategies try swapping two items at the same time. Of course, there are also improvements that you cannot make by swapping two items, which you can make by swapping three items, so that strategy doesn't always work either. Still, swapping two items at a time isn't too difficult and may result in some improvements, so it is worth implementing.

Simulated Annealing

Simulated annealing is an improved version of the simple improvement heuristic described in the preceding section. Simulated annealing initially makes large changes to a solution and then, over time, makes smaller and smaller changes to try to improve the solution.

As mentioned in the preceding section, one problem with the original improvement heuristic is that sometimes moving a single item from one group to the other won't let you improve the solution, but moving two items at the same time might. Even that method has limits. There may be cases where moving two items at the same time won't get you an improvement, but moving three will.

Simulated annealing addresses this issue by allowing the algorithm to make large changes to the initial solution. Over time, the size of the allowed changes is reduced. The algorithm tries smaller and smaller changes until finally it reaches a test solution that it compares to the best solution found so far.

> **NOTE** Simulated annealing is modeled on the way crystals grow in a cooling metal or mineral. When the material is very hot, the molecules move quickly, so their arrangement changes a lot. As the material cools, the molecular motion decreases and structures form, but there's still enough energy to allow some structures to merge with others if that forms a more stable arrangement. Eventually, the material cools enough so that there is insufficient energy to disrupt the molecular structure. If the cooling happened slowly enough, the material should contain only a few very large crystals representing a very stable arrangement of molecules.

Another way to implement simulated annealing is to consider random changes of any complexity. If a change results in an improvement, the algorithm accepts it and continues. If a change doesn't result in an improvement, the algorithm accepts it anyway with a certain probability. Over time that probability decreases, so initially the algorithm may make the solution worse so that it can later get to a better end result. Eventually, the probability of accepting a nonimproving change decreases until the algorithm accepts only changes that improve the solution.

Hill Climbing

Imagine that you're a lost hiker. It's nighttime, so you can't see very far, and you need to find the top of the mountain. One strategy that you could use would be always to move up the steepest slope. If the mountain has a reasonably smooth shape with no small peaks or hills on its side, you'll eventually reach the top. If there is a smaller hill on the side of the mountain, however, you may become stuck there and not know which way to go until morning.

This method is called a *hill-climbing heuristic*. It may also be called the *method of gradient ascent* or, if the goal is to minimize a value instead of maximizing one, *method of gradient descent*.

In a hill-climbing heuristic, the algorithm always makes a choice that moves it closer to a better solution. For the partitioning problem, that means placing the next item in the group that minimizes the difference in the groups' weights. That's equivalent to adding the item to the group that has the smaller total weight.

For example, suppose that the items have weights 3, 4, 1, 5, and 6. The first item can go in either group, so suppose that it's placed in the first group.

Now the algorithm considers the second item, with weight 4. If the algorithm places the second item in the first group, the groups are {3, 4} and {}, so the difference between their total weights is 7. If the algorithm places the second item in the second group, the groups are {3} and {4}, so the difference between their total weights is 1. To make the best choice at this time, the algorithm places the item in the second group.

Next the algorithm considers the third item with weight 1. If the algorithm places this item in the first group, the groups are {3, 1} and {4}, so the difference between their total weights is 0. If the algorithm places the item in the second group, the groups are {3} and {4, 1}, so the difference between their total weights is 2. To make the best choice at this time, the algorithm places the item in the first group.

The algorithm continues in this manner until it has placed all of the items in a group.

The following pseudocode shows the hill-climbing algorithm:

```
HillClimbing()
    For index = 0 To max_index
        Integer: difference_0 =
            <difference in group weights if item number index is in
            group 0>
        Integer: difference_1 =
            <difference in group weights if item number index is in
            group 1>
```

```
        If (difference_0 < difference_1)
            <Place item number index in group 0>
        Else
            <Place item number index in group 1>
        End If
    Next index
End HillClimbing
```

If you are partitioning N weights, this algorithm performs only N steps, so it is extremely fast. In a large decision tree, it is unlikely to find the best possible solution, but sometimes it finds a reasonable solution.

Hill climbing is so fast that you could spend some extra time improving its solution. For example, you could try using the techniques described in the preceding section to improve the initial solution.

Sorted Hill Climbing

One easy way to improve the hill-climbing algorithm is to sort the weights and then consider them in order of decreasing size. The idea is that the early stages of the algorithm place the heavier objects in groups and then the later stages use the smaller items to try to balance the groups.

The following pseudocode shows this algorithm:

```
SortedHillClimbing()
    <Sort the items in order of decreasing weight>

    For index = 0 To max_index
        Integer: difference_0 =
            <difference in group weights if item number index is in
            group 0>
        Integer: difference_1 =
            <difference in group weights if item number index is in
            group 1>

        If (difference_0 < difference_1)
            <Place item number index in group 0>
        Else
            <Place item number index in group 1>
        End If
    Next index
End SortedHillClimbing
```

This is the same as the hill-climbing algorithm described in the preceding section, with the addition of the sorting step.

This may seem like a small modification, but sorted hill climbing often finds a better solution than hill climbing.

If you are partitioning N weights, the sorted hill-climbing algorithm takes O(N log N) steps to sort the weights and then N steps to generate its solution. The sorting step makes it slower than the normal hill-climbing algorithm, but it's still extremely fast.

In fact, sorted hill climbing is so fast that you could spend some extra time improving its solution, just as you can improve the normal hill-climbing algorithm's solution.

Other Decision Tree Problems

The previous sections focused on the partition problem, but you can use decision trees to model many other difficult problems. The following sections describe some algorithmic problems that you can study with decision trees.

Many of the problems come in pairs—one problem that asks whether something is possible and an optimization version that asks for an optimal solution.

Generalized Partition Problem

In the partition problem, the goal is to divide a set of objects into two groups with equal weight. In the *generalized partition problem*, the goal is to divide a set of objects into K groups with equal weights.

The decision tree for this problem has K branches at each node corresponding to putting the item at that level of the tree into one of the K different partitions. If you have N items, then the tree is N levels tall, so it contains K^N leaf nodes.

The same heuristics that work for the partition problem also work for the generalized partition problem, although they are more complicated. For example, a random improvement for the partition problem might try moving an object from one group to the other. In the generalized partition problem, it would need to consider moving the object from one group into any of the other $K - 1$ groups.

The optimization version of the generalized partition problem asks you to find a way to divide the items into K groups, but you need to decide how to judge the best solution. For example, you might try to minimize the sum of the absolute values of the differences between the groups' weights and the average group weight. For example, suppose that you have four groups with total weights 15, 18, 22, and 25. The average of those weights is 20, so the absolute values of the differences between the group weights and the average are 5, 2, 2, and 5, making the sum of those differences 14. This measurement might allow some groups to have weights that are fairly far from the average if that allows other groups to have weights closer to the average.

Alternatively, you might want to minimize the sum of the squares of the differences between the group's weights and the average. For the preceding example, the squared differences would be 25, 4, 4, and 25, so the sum would be 58. This measurement would favor solutions where all of the group weights are close to the average.

Subset Sum

In the *subset sum problem*, you have a set of numbers, and you want to determine whether there is a subset whose sum is 0. For example, consider the set {–11, –7, –5, –3, 4, 6, 9, 12, 14}. This set has the zero-sum subset {–7, –5, –3, 6, 9}. A related optimization version of the problem would ask you to find a subset with a sum close to 0.

You can model this problem with a decision tree similar to the one you use for the partition problem. Essentially, you need to divide the items into two groups—one that holds objects to go into the zero-sum set and one that holds objects that will be discarded.

Like the decision tree for the partition problem, if you are working with N items, this tree has N levels and each node has two branches—one corresponding to adding an item to the zero-sum set and one corresponding to discarding the item, so the tree has 2^N leaf nodes.

You can use branch and bound and heuristics on the optimization version of this problem but not on the nonoptimization version.

Bin Packing

In the *bin-packing problem*, you have a set of items of different weights and a series of bins that have the same capacity. (In a generalized version, the bins could have different capacities.) The goal is to pack the items into the bins so that you use as few bins as possible.

You could model this as a decision tree in which each branch corresponds to putting an item in a particular bin. If you have N items and K bins, the tree would have N levels with K branches at each node, so the tree would have K^N leaf nodes.

This is an optimization problem. You can use branch and bound and heuristics to try to find good solutions.

A related problem is to find a way to pack the items into bins so that you use only ⌈`<total weight of all items>` ÷ `<bin capacity>`⌉ where ⌈ ⌉ means to round up. For example, if the total weight of the items is 115 and the bins have a capacity of 20, can you find a way to pack the items into only six bins? You can use heuristics to try to find a good solution, but if you don't find a solution, that doesn't mean one doesn't exist.

Cutting Stock

The *cutting stock problem* is basically a two-dimensional version of the bin-packing problem. In this problem, you need to cut out a collection of shapes (usually rectangles) from a set of boards, pieces of cloth, or other stock. The goal is to use as few pieces of stock as possible.

Modeling this problem as a decision tree is much harder than it is for the bin-packing problem, because how you position shapes on a piece of stock changes the number of pieces that you can fit on that piece. That means that assigning a shape to a piece of stock isn't enough. You must also assign a position to the shape within the stock.

If you make some simplifying assumptions, you can still use a decision tree for this problem. For example, if the pieces of stock are 36 inches by 72 inches and you allow a shape to be positioned at only an (X, Y) position where X and Y are integer numbers of inches, then there are $36 \times 72 = 2,592$ positions where you can place a shape on a particular piece of stock. This means that each node in the tree would have $K \times 2,592$ branches.

Fortunately, many of those branches are easy to trim from the tree. For example, some branches place a shape so close to an edge of the stock that it won't fit. Other branches make a shape overlap with another shape. If you avoid following those kinds of branches, you can search the tree to find at least some solution.

The tree will still be extremely large, however, so you'll need to use heuristics to find reasonable solutions.

Also note that the simplifying assumptions may exclude some solutions. For example, suppose that you want to fit five 7-inch-by-7-inch squares on 20-inch-by-20-inch sheets of stock. If you place the squares so that their edges are parallel to the sides of the stock, you can fit only two squares vertically and horizontally on each piece of stock, as shown on the left in Figure 12.4. If you rotate one of the squares, however, you can fit all five squares on a single piece of stock, as shown on the right.

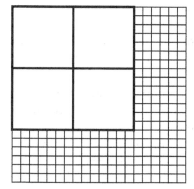 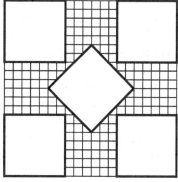

Figure 12.4: If you don't allow rotation, some solutions are impossible.

A common variation of the cutting stock problem involves a single very long piece of stock, such as a roll of paper. The goal is to minimize the number of linear inches of stock used.

Knapsack

In the *knapsack problem*, you are given a set of objects that have weights and values and a knapsack that holds a certain amount of weight. Your goal is to find the items with the maximum value that will fit in the knapsack. For example, you might fill the knapsack with a few heavy items that have high values, or you may be better off filling it with lots of lighter items that have lower values.

The knapsack problem is similar to the partition problem, in which you try to divide the items into two groups—one with items to go into the knapsack and one with items to remain outside. In the knapsack problem, the goal is to make the first group as valuable as possible and also to ensure that the first group fits inside the knapsack.

Because the knapsack's basic structure is similar to that of the partition problem, you can use a similar decision tree. The main differences are that not all assignments are legal due to the weight constraint, and the goal is different.

The same techniques that work well with the partition problem also work with the knapsack problem. Random solutions, improved solutions, and simulated annealing work in much the same way as they do for the partition problem.

Branch and bound could stop examining a partial solution if its total weight already exceeded the knapsack's capacity.

Branch and bound could also stop if the total value of the unconsidered items was insufficient to raise the current solution's value enough to beat the best solution found so far. For example, suppose that you've found a solution worth $100 and you're examining a partial solution that has a value of $50. If the total value of all the remaining items is only $20, then you cannot improve this solution enough to beat the current best solution.

At each step, a hill-climbing heuristic would add to the solution the highest-value item that could still fit in the knapsack.

A sorted hill-climbing heuristic might consider the items in order of decreasing weight so that later selections could fill in any remaining room in the knapsack.

Probably a better sorted hill-climbing heuristic would consider the items in order of decreasing value-to-weight ratio, so it would first consider the items worth the most dollars per pound (or whatever the units are).

The decision tree for a knapsack problem with N items contains 2^N leaf nodes, so this isn't an easy problem, but at least you can try some heuristics.

Traveling Salesman Problem

Suppose that you're a traveling salesperson who must visit certain locations on a map and then return to your starting point. In the *traveling salesman problem* (TSP), you must visit those locations in an order that minimizes the total distance covered.

> **NOTE**   TSP has important practical implications for businesses that have fleets of vehicles. For example, the U.S. Postal Service's letter carriers and truck drivers travel 1.3 billion miles per year. If better routing can shave even a fraction of a percent off that total, the savings in fuel and wear on the vehicles could be huge.

To model this problem as a decision tree, the Kth level of the tree corresponds to selecting an item to visit the Kth location in the completed tour. If there are N locations to visit, the root node has N branches, corresponding to visiting each of the locations first. The nodes at the second level of the tree have N − 1 branches, corresponding to visiting any of the locations not yet visited. The nodes at the third level of the tree have N − 2 branches and so on to the leaves, which have no branches. The total number of leaves in the tree would be $N \times (N-1) \times (N-2) \times \ldots \times 1 = N!$.

This tree is so big that you need to use heuristics to find good solutions for all but the tiniest problems.

Satisfiability

Given a logical statement such as "A and B or (A and not C)," the *satisfiability problem* (SAT) is to decide whether there is a way to assign the values true and false to the variables A, B, and C to make the statement true. A related problem asks you to find such an assignment.

You can model this problem with a binary decision tree in which the left and right branches represent setting a variable to true or false. Each leaf node represents an assignment of values to all of the variables and determines whether the statement as a whole is true or false.

This problem is harder than the partition problem because there are no approximate solutions. Any leaf node makes the statement either true or false. The statement cannot be "approximately true." (However, if you use probabilistic logic, in which variables have probabilities of truth rather than being definitely true or false, you might be able to find a way to make the statement probably true.)

A random search of the tree may find a solution, but if you don't find a solution, you cannot conclude that there isn't one.

You can try to improve random solutions. Unfortunately, any change makes the statement either true or not, so there's no way that you can improve the solution gradually. This means you cannot really use the path improvement strategy described earlier. Because you can't improve the solution gradually, you also can't use simulated annealing or hill climbing. In general, you also cannot tell if a partial assignment makes the statement false, so you can't use branch and bound either.

With exhaustive and random search as your only real options, you can solve satisfiability for only relatively small problems.

> **NOTE**   You may wonder why anyone would want to solve SAT. It turns out that you can reduce many other problems to an instance of SAT. For an instance of some other problem, such as the partition problem, you can build a logical expression such that a solution to SAT corresponds to a solution to the partition problem. In other words, if you can solve one, then you can solve the other.
>
> By proving that different problems can be reduced to SAT, you show that they are as hard as SAT. Then the fact that there is no known easy way to solve SAT means that there is no known easy way to solve the other problems.

SAT is related to the *3-satisfiability problem* (3SAT). In 3SAT, the logical statement consists of terms combined with the And operator. Each term involves three variables, or their negations combined with Or. For example, the statement "(A or B or not C) and (B or not A or D)" is in the 3SAT format.

With some work that is far outside the scope of this book, you can show that SAT and 3SAT are equivalent, so they are equally difficult to solve.

Note that the same kind of decision tree will solve either version of the problem.

Swarm Intelligence

Swarm intelligence (SI) is the result of a distributed collection of mostly independent objects or processes. Typically, an SI system consists of a group of very simple objects that interact with their environment and other nearby objects. Most SI systems are motivated by analogies to patterns found in nature, such as ant exploration, bee foraging, bird flocking, and fish schooling.

Swarm intelligence provides an alternative to decision tree searching. Most swarm algorithms provide what seems to be a chaotic search of a solution space, although many of the algorithms use the same basic techniques used by more organized-seeming algorithms. For example, some SI algorithms use hill climbing or incremental improvement strategies.

You can also adapt some SI strategies to work directly on decision trees. For example, you could make a group of ants crawl randomly across a decision tree.

Note that there are often other ways to solve a particular problem. For example, you can use a particle swarm to find the approximate minimum point on a graph, but you may also be able to use calculus to find the minimum exactly.

Swarm intelligence is still useful, however, for several reasons. First, you can apply SI to problems even when an analytical approach is difficult. SI may also apply when you're working with data generated by some real-world process, so a closed-form solution is impossible. SI is also often applicable to a wide range of problems with only slight modification. Finally, swarm intelligence is just plain interesting.

The following sections describe some of the most common approaches for building SI systems.

Ant Colony Optimization

In nature, ants forage by moving in a more or less straight line away from the nest. At some distance, the ant begins making a series of random turns to search for food. When an ant finds a good food source, it returns to the nest.

As it walks, the ant leaves behind a trail of pheromones to aid in navigation. When a randomly wandering ant crosses a pheromone trail, there is some probability that it will turn and follow that trail, adding its own pheromones. If the food source is desirable enough, many ants will eventually follow the trail and build a pheromone superhighway that strongly encourages other ants to follow it. Even if an ant is following a strong pheromone trail, however, there is a chance that it will leave the trail and explore new territory.

General Optimization

One simple ant colony optimization strategy might launch software "ants" (objects) into different parts of a search space. They would then return to the nest (main program) with an estimate of the quality of the solutions they found. The nest would then send more ants to the most profitable-looking areas for further investigation.

Traveling Salesman

The ant colony approach has been used to find solutions to the traveling salesman problem. The algorithm launches ants into the network, and those ants obey the following simple rules:

1. Each ant must visit every node exactly once.

2. Ants pick the next node to visit randomly using the following rules:

   a. Ants pick nearby nodes with a greater probability than farther nodes.

   b. Ants pick links that are marked with more "pheromone" with greater probability

3. When an ant crosses a link, it marks that link with pheromone.

4. After an ant finishes its tour, it places more pheromone along its path if that path was relatively short.

The idea behind the pheromones in this approach is that, if a link is used by many paths, then it is probably an important link, so it should also be used by other paths. The more a path is used, the more pheromone it picks up so the more it is used in the future.

Bees Algorithm

The *bees algorithm* is fairly similar to an ant colony algorithm but without the pheromones. In a beehive, scouts roam randomly around the hive. When a scout finds a promising food source, it returns to the hive, goes to a special area called the *dance floor*, and does a "waggle dance" to tell forager bees where the food is. The bee adjusts the duration of the dance to indicate the quality of the food. Better food sources lead to longer dances and longer dances recruit more foragers.

In a program, scouts (objects) visit different areas in the solution space and assess the quality of the solutions they find. Next, foragers (other objects) are recruited based on the quality of the solutions and they explore the most promising areas more thoroughly.

A group of foragers examines its assigned area looking for an improved solution. The search area shrinks around the best solution found over time. Eventually, when the bees can find no improvement in an area, the best solution is recorded, and that area is abandoned.

During the whole process, other scouts continue exploring other parts of the solution space to see if they can find other promising areas to search.

Swarm Simulation

In a *swarm simulation*, the program uses simple rules to make particles behave as if they are in a swarm or flock. For example, the swarm might mimic the behavior of a flock of birds flying between buildings, a crowd of people running through streets, or a school of fish chasing a food source.

One of the main reasons why swarm simulations were invented was simply to study swarms, although they can be used in optimization problems as a sort of parallel hill climbing technique.

Boids

In 1986, Craig Reynolds built an artificial life program named Boids (short for "bird-oid object") to simulate bird flocking. The original Boids program used three basic *steering behaviors* to control the boid objects.

- *Separation rule*: The boids steer away from their neighbors to avoid overcrowding.

- *Alignment rule*: The boids steer so that they point more closely to the average direction of their neighbors.

- *Cohesion rule*: The boids steer closer to the average position of their neighbors to keep the flock together.

A particular boid only considers flockmates that lie within a certain distance of the boid and that are within a set angular distance of the direction that the boid is facing. (It cannot see boids that are behind it.)

Figure 12.5 shows a boid evaluating its neighbors. The white boid's neighbors are those within the shaded area. Those boids are within the neighborhood distance indicated by the dashed circle and within a specified angle (in this case a 135° span) of the boid's direction.

The separation rule adds vectors, pushing the boid away from its neighbors. In Figure 12.5, those vectors are indicated by the thin arrows pointing away from neighbors toward the boid in the center.

The alignment rule makes the boid point more in the same direction as the neighbors. In Figure 12.5, the center boid should turn slightly to the left as indicated by the curved arrow.

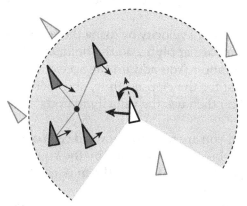

Figure 12.5: A boid can see neighbors only within a certain distance and within a certain angle of the boid's direction.

The cohesion rule makes the boid more toward the average position of the neighbors. In Figure 12.5, the average position is indicated by a small black dot. The heavy arrow pointing away from the center boid shows this vector's direction.

To simulate movement, each boid has a position (x, y) and a velocity vector <vx, vy>. After each time step, the boid updates its position by adding the velocity vector to the position to get its new position $(x + vx, y + vy)$.

In practice, the velocity might be stored in pixels per second. In that case, the program would multiply the vector's components by the elapsed time since the boid was last moved. For example, if 0.1 seconds have elapsed, then the boid's new position would be $(x + 0.1 \times vx, y + 0.1 \times vy)$. That allows the program to update the boids' positions frequently to provide a smooth animation.

To produce a frame in the animation, the program calculates the vectors defined by the separation, alignment, and cohesion rules. It scales those vectors by the elapsed time and then multiplies them by weights. For example, a particular simulation might use a relatively small weight for separation and a larger weight for cohesion to produce a more closely spaced flock. The program would then add the weighted vectors to the boid's velocity and then use the velocity to update its position.

There are many ways that you could modify the original rules used by Craig Reynolds. For example, you could allow a boid to see neighbors behind it. The result is still reasonably good, and the code is simpler.

Pseudoclassical Mechanics

Another approach to flock simulation that has given me good results mimics classical mechanics. Each boid has a mass, and those masses contribute forces in various directions—almost as if the boids were planets interacting with each other gravitationally.

The program uses the forces to update a boid's velocity by using the equation $F = m \times a$. Here F is a force vector that you are applying to the boid, m is the boid's mass, and a is the resulting acceleration. You add up the accelerations because of all the boid's neighbors, adjust for the elapsed time, and then use the result to update the boid's velocity. You then use the velocity to update the boid's position as before.

The cohesion forces point from the boid you are updating toward each of the other boids. The force exerted by another boid is determined by the equation $F = m_1 \times m_2 / d^2$. Here F is the resulting force, m_1 and m_2 are the masses of the two boids, and d is the distance between them.

This equation means that the force exerted by a boid drops off quickly as the distance between boids increases, so boids close at hand exert more force than those that are farther away. This means that in this model you consider all of the other boids, not only those within a certain distance. The boids that are far away contribute little to the net force, so they are effectively ignored anyway.

The separation forces point from another boid toward the boid that you are updating, so it pushes the boids apart. This force is determined by the equation $F = m_1 \times m_2 / d^3$. Because the result is divided by the cube of the distance between the boids, the force drops off quickly. At small distances, the force can be strong (if you give it a large weight). At larger distances, this force shrinks, and the cohesion force dominates so that it can hold the flock together.

This model doesn't use the alignment rule, although you could add it if you like.

Goals and Obstacles

Whichever flocking model you use, it's relatively easy to add goals for the flock to chase and obstacles for it to avoid.

To add a goal, create an object that acts much like a boid but that contributes a strong cohesion component and little or no alignment and separation components. That will make the flock steer toward the object.

Conversely, to create an obstacle, make an object that contributes a strong separation component (at least when a boid is close) and little or no alignment and cohesion components. That will make boids avoid the obstacle.

Summary

Decision trees are a powerful tool for approaching complex problems, but they are not the best approach for every problem. For example, you could model the eight queens problem described in Chapter 9 with a decision tree that was eight levels tall and that had 64 branches per node, giving a total of $648 \approx 2.8 \times 10^{14}$ leaf nodes. By taking advantage of the problem's structure, however, you can eliminate most of the tree's branches without exploring them and examine only 113 board positions. Thinking about the problem as a general decision tree may be a mistake, because it might make you miss the simplifications that let you solve the problem efficiently.

Still, decision trees are a powerful technique that you should at least consider if you don't know of a better approach to a problem. Swarm algorithms may sometimes provide another approach to finding solutions in large solution spaces such as decision trees. They can be particularly effective when the problem doesn't have much structure that can help you narrow the search.

This chapter and the previous two described trees and algorithms that build, maintain, and search trees. The next two chapters discuss networks. Like trees, networks are linked data structures. Unlike trees, networks are not hierarchical, so they can contain loops. That makes them a bit more complicated than trees, but it also lets them model and solve some interesting problems that trees can't.

Exercises

You can find the answers to these exercises in Appendix B. Asterisks indicate particularly difficult problems.

1. Write a program that exhaustively searches the tic-tac-toe game tree and counts the number of times X wins, O wins, and the game ends in a tie. What are those counts, and what is the total number of games possible? Do the numbers give an advantage to one player or the other?

2. Modify the programs you wrote for Exercise 1 so that the user can place one or more initial pieces on a tic-tac-toe board and then count the number of possible X wins, O wins, and ties from that point. How many total games are possible starting from each of the nine initial moves by X? (Do you need to calculate all nine?)

3. Write a program that lets the player play tic-tac-toe against the computer. Let the player be either X or O. Provide three skill levels: Random (the computer moves randomly), Beginner (the computer uses minimax with only three levels of recursion), and Expert (the computer uses a full minimax search).

4. Write a program that uses exhaustive search to solve the optimizing partition problem. Allow the user to click a button to create a list of random weights between bounds set by the user. Also allow the user to check a box indicating whether the algorithm is allowed to short circuit and stop early.

5. Extend the program that you wrote for the preceding problem so that you can perform branch and bound with and without short circuits.

6. *Use the program you wrote for Exercise 4 to solve the partition problem using exhaustive search and branch and bound with the values 1 through 5, 1 through 6, 1 through 7, and so on, up to 1 through 25. Then graph the number of nodes visited versus the number of weights being partitioned for the two methods. Finally, on a separate graph, show the logarithm of the number of nodes visited versus the number of weights for the results. What can you conclude about the number of nodes visited for the two methods?

7. Extend the program that you wrote for Exercise 5 to use a random heuristic to find solutions.

8. Extend the program that you wrote for the preceding problem to use an improvement heuristic to find solutions.

9. What groups would a partitioning program find if it used the hill-climbing heuristic for the weights {7, 9, 7, 6, 7, 7, 5, 7, 5, 6}? What are the groups' total weights and the difference between the total weights? What if the weights are initially sorted in increasing order? In decreasing order? Can you conclude anything about the solution given by the different orderings?

10. Repeat the preceding problem for the weights {5, 2, 12, 1, 2, 1}.

11. Can you think of a group of weights which when sorted in decreasing order does not lead to the best solution?

12. Extend the program that you wrote for Exercise 8 to use a hill-climbing heuristic to find solutions.

13. Extend the program that you wrote for the preceding problem to use a sorted hill-climbing heuristic to find solutions.

14. *Build a program that uses Craig Reynolds' original Boids rules to simulate a flock. Make the mouse position a goal so that the flock tends to chase the mouse as it moves over the drawing area. What do the boids do if the target mouse position remains stationary?

15. *Modify the program that you built for the preceding exercise to add people as obstacles. When the user clicks the drawing area, place a person at that point and make the boids avoid it.

16. *Build a program that uses pseudoclassical mechanics to simulate a flock. Make the mouse position a goal so that the flock tends to chase the mouse as it moves over the drawing area. What do the boids do if the target mouse position remains stationary?

17. *Modify the program that you built for the preceding problem to add people as obstacles. When the user clicks the drawing area, place a person at that point and make the boids avoid it.

18. *Write a program that uses a swarm to minimize the following function:

$$z = 3e^{-r^2} \sin(2\pi r)\cos(3\theta)$$

Here, r and θ are the polar coordinate values for the point (x, y) in the area $-3 \le \{x, y\} \le 3$. You can use the following functions to calculate r and θ:

$$r = \sqrt{x^2 + y^2}$$

$$\theta = \arctan(y, x)$$

Figure 12.6 shows an image of this function taken from my book *WPF 3d: Three-Dimensional Graphics with WPF and C#* (Rod Stephens, 2018).

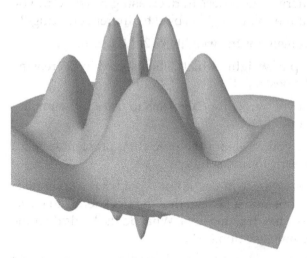

Figure 12.6: Use a swarm of bugs to minimize this strange function.

You can use the following code snippet to calculate this function:

```
// Return the function's value F(x, y).
private double Strange(Point2d point)
{
    double r2 = (point.X * point.X + point.Y * point.Y) / 4;
    double r = Math.Sqrt(r2);

    double theta = Math.Atan2(point.Y, point.X);
    double z = 3 * Math.Exp(-r2) *
        Math.Sin(2 * Math.PI * r) *
        Math.Cos(3 * theta);
    return z;
}
```

To use the swarm, make a `Bug` class. Give it `Location` and `Velocity` properties to track its current position, direction, and speed. Also give it `BestValue` and `BestPoint` properties to keep track of the best solution that the bug has found.

When a timer ticks, the main program should call each bug's `Move` method. That method should use two accelerations to update the bug's position: a cognition acceleration and a social acceleration. The cognition acceleration should point from the bug's current position toward the best position that it has found. The social acceleration should point from the bug's current position toward the global best position found by any of the bugs.

Multiply each acceleration by a weighting factor (set by the user) and a random scale factor between 0 and 1, and then add them to the bug's current velocity. You may need to set a maximum velocity to keep the bugs from running too far away. Then use the result to update the bug's position.

After moving a bug, update its best value and the global best value if appropriate. After a bug has not improved its best value in a certain number of turns, lock its position and don't move it again.

Finally, after each tick, display the bugs, their best positions, and the global best position in different colors. Display locked bugs in a different color. Figure 12.7 shows the SwarmMinimum example program searching for a minimum.

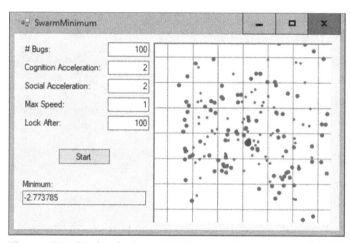

Figure 12.7: Display the bugs, their best positions, and the global best position.

Basic Network Algorithms

Chapters 10–12 explained trees. This chapter describes a related data structure: the network. Like a tree, a network contains nodes that are connected by links. Unlike the nodes in a tree, however, the nodes in a network don't necessarily have a hierarchical relationship. In particular, the links in a network may create cycles, so a path that follows the links could loop back to its starting position.

This chapter explains networks and some basic network algorithms, such as detecting cycles, finding shortest paths, and finding a tree that is part of the network that includes every node.

Network Terminology

Network terminology isn't quite as complicated as tree terminology, because it doesn't borrow as many terms from genealogy, but it's still worth taking a few minutes to review the relevant terms.

A network consists of a set of *nodes* connected by *links*. (Sometimes, particularly when you're working on mathematical algorithms and theorems, a network is called a *graph*, nodes are called *vertices*, and links are called *edges*.) If node A and node B are directly connected by a link, they are *adjacent* and are called *neighbors*.

Unlike the case with a tree, a network has no root node, although there may be particular nodes of interest depending on the network. For example, a transportation network might contain special hub nodes where buses, trains, ferries, or other vehicles start and end their routes.

A link can be *undirected* (you can traverse it in either direction) or *directed* (you can traverse it in one direction only). A network is called a directed or undirected network depending on what kinds of links it contains.

A *path* is an alternating sequence of nodes and links through the network from one node to another. Suppose that there is only one link from any node to any adjacent node (in other words, there aren't two links from node A to node B). In that case, you can specify a path by listing either the nodes it visits or the links it uses.

A *cycle* or *loop* is a path that returns to its starting point.

As is the case with trees, the number of links that leave a node is called the node's *degree*. The degree of the network is the largest degree of any of the nodes in it. In a directed network, a node's *in-degree* and *out-degree* are the numbers of links entering and leaving the node.

Nodes and links often have data associated with them. For example, nodes often have names, ID numbers, or physical locations such as a latitude and longitude. Links often have associated *costs* or *weights*, such as the time it takes to drive across a link in a street network. They may also have maximum *capacities*, such as the maximum amount of current that you can send over a wire in a circuit network or the maximum number of cars that can cross a link in a street network per unit of time.

A *reachable node* is one that you can reach from a given node by following links. Depending on the network, you may be unable to reach every node from every other node.

In a directed network, if node B is reachable from node A, nodes A and B are said to be *connected*. Note that if node A is connected to node B, and node B is connected to node C, then node A must be connected to node C.

A *connected component* in an undirected network is a set of nodes and links in which every pair of nodes is connected by a path through the set's links. The network is called connected if all of its nodes are connected to each other.

If a directed network's nodes are all mutually connected, then the network is called *strongly connected*. If a directed network becomes connected when you replace its directed links with undirected links, then the network is called *weakly connected*.

A subset of a network is called a *strongly connected component* if it contains a path between any two of its nodes, and it is maximal, so you cannot add another node to the set without breaking its strong connectivity.

Figure 13.1 shows some of the parts of a small directed network. Arrows represent the links, and the arrowheads indicate the links' directions. Undirected links are represented either without arrows or with arrows at both ends.

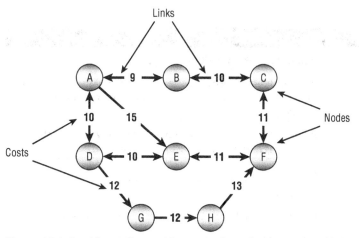

Figure 13.1: In a directed network, arrows show the directions of links.

The numbers on the links are the links' costs. This example assumes that opposite links have the same costs. That need not be the case, but then drawing the network is harder.

The network shown in Figure 13.1 is strongly connected because you can find a path using links from any node to any other node.

Notice that paths between nodes may not be unique. For example, A-E-F and A-B-C-F are both paths from node A to node F.

Table 13.1 summarizes these tree terms to make remembering them a bit easier.

Table 13.1: Summary of Network Terminology

TERM	MEANING
adjacent	If two nodes are connected by a link, then they are adjacent.
capacity	The maximum amount of something that can move through a node or link, such as the maximum current that can flow through a wire in an electrical network or the maximum number of cars that can move through a link in a street network per unit of time.
connected	In an undirected network, nodes A and B are connected if node B is reachable from node A, and vice versa. An undirected network is connected if every node is reachable from every other node.
connected component	A set of nodes that are mutually connected.
cost	A link may have an associated cost. Less commonly, a node may have a cost.

Continues

Table 13-1 (*continued*)

TERM	MEANING
cycle	A path that returns to its starting point.
degree	In an undirected network, the number of links leaving a node. In a directed network, a node has an in-degree and an out-degree.
directed	A link is directed if you can traverse it in only one direction. A network is directed if it contains directed links.
edge	Link.
graph	Network.
in-degree	In a directed network, the number of links entering a node.
link	An object in a network that represents a relationship between two nodes. Links can be directed or undirected.
loop	Cycle.
neighbor	Two nodes are neighbors if they are adjacent.
node	An object in a network that represents a point-like location. Nodes are connected by links.
out-degree	In a directed network, the number of links leaving a node.
path	An alternating sequence of nodes and links that leads from one node to another. If there is only one link from any node to an adjacent node, then you can specify a path by listing its nodes or links.
reachable node	Node B is reachable from node A if there is a path from node A to node B.
strongly connected	A directed network is strongly connected if every node is reachable from every other node.
strongly connected component	A maximal subset of a network that contains a path between every pair of its nodes.
undirected	A link is undirected if you can traverse it in either direction. A network is undirected if it contains only undirected links.
vertex	Node.
weakly connected	A directed network is weakly connected if every node is reachable from every other node when you replace the directed links with undirected links.
weight	Cost.

Network Representations

It's fairly easy to use objects to represent a network. You can represent nodes with a `Node` class.

Exactly how you represent links depends on how you will use them. For example, if you are building a directed network, you can make the links be references to destination nodes that are stored inside the `Node` class. If the links should have costs or other data, you can also add that to the `Node` class. The following pseudocode shows a simple `Node` class for this situation:

```
Class Node
    String: Name
    List<Node>: Neighbors
    List<Integer>: Costs
End Node
```

This representation works for simple problems, but often it's useful to make a separate class to represent the links. For example, some algorithms, such as the minimal spanning tree algorithm described later in this chapter, build lists of links. If the links are objects, it's easy to place links in a list. If the links are represented by references stored in the node class, it's harder to put them in lists.

The following pseudocode shows `Node` and `Link` classes that store links as separate objects for an undirected network:

```
Class Node
    String: Name
    List<Link>: Links
End Node

Class Link
    Integer: Cost
    Node: Nodes[2]
End Link
```

Here the `Link` class contains an array of two `Node` objects representing the nodes it connects.

In an undirected network, a `Link` object represents a link between two nodes, and the ordering of the nodes doesn't matter. If a link connects node A and node B, the `Link` object appears in the `Neighbors` list for both nodes, so you can follow it in either direction.

Because the order of the nodes in the link's `Nodes` array doesn't matter, an algorithm trying to find a neighbor must compare the current node to the link's `Nodes` entries to see which one is the neighbor. For example, if an algorithm is trying to find the neighbors of node A, it must look at a link's `Nodes` array to see which entry is node A and which entry is the neighbor.

In a directed network, the link class only really needs to know its destination node. The following pseudocode shows classes for this situation:

```
Class Node
    String: Name
    List<Link>: Links
End Node

Class Link
    Integer: Cost
    Node: ToNode
End Link
```

However, it may still be handy to make the link class contain references to both of its nodes. For example, if the network's nodes have spatial locations, and the links have references to their source and destination nodes, then it is easier for the links to draw themselves. If the links store only references to their destination nodes, then the node objects must pass extra information to a link to let it draw itself.

If you use a link class that uses the Nodes array, you can store the node's source node in the array's first entry and its destination node in the array's second entry.

The best way to store a network in a file depends on the tools available in your programming environment. For example, even though XML is a hierarchical language and works most naturally with hierarchical data structures such as trees, some XML libraries can also save and load network data.

To keep things simple, the examples that are available for download use a simple text file structure. The file begins with the number of nodes in the network. After that, the file contains one line of text per node.

Each node's line contains the node's name and its x- and y-coordinates. Following that is a series of entries for the node's links. Each link's entry includes the index of the destination node, the link's cost, and the link's capacity.

The following lines show the format:

```
number_of_nodes
name,x,y,to_node,cost,capacity,to_node,cost,capacity,...
name,x,y,to_node,cost,capacity,to_node,cost,capacity,...
name,x,y,to_node,cost,capacity,to_node,cost,capacity,...
...
```

For example, the following is a file representing the network shown in Figure 13.2:

```
3
A,85,41,1,87,1,2,110,4
B,138,110,2,99,4
C,44,144,1,99,4
```

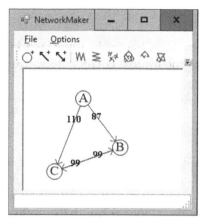

Figure 13.2: This network contains four links—two connecting node A to nodes B and C and two connecting node B to node C.

The file begins with the number of nodes, 3. It then contains lines representing each node.

The line for node A begins with its name, A. The next two entries give the node's x- and y-coordinates, so this node is at location (85, 41).

The line then contains a sequence of sets of values describing links. The first set of values 1, 87, 1 means that the first link leads to node B (index 1), has a cost of 87, and has a capacity of 1. The second set of values 2, 110, 4 means that the second link leads to node C (index 2), has a cost of 110, and has a capacity of 4.

The file's other lines define nodes B and C and their links.

> **NOTE**   Before you can program network algorithms, you need to be able to build networks. You can write code that creates a network one node and link at a time, but it's helpful to have a program that you can use to make test networks interactively. See Exercise 1 at the end of this chapter for instructions on what the program needs to do.

Traversals

Many algorithms traverse a network in some way. For example, the spanning tree and shortest path algorithms described later in this chapter all visit the network's nodes.

The following sections describe several algorithms that use different kinds of traversals to solve network problems.

Depth-First Traversal

The preorder traversal algorithm for trees described in Chapter 10 almost works for networks. The following pseudocode shows the almost correct algorithm modified slightly to use a network node class:

```
Traverse()
    <Process node>
    For Each link In Links
        link.Nodes[1].Traverse
    Next link
End Traverse
```

The method first processes the current node. It then loops through the node's links and recursively calls itself to process each link's destination node.

This would work except for one serious problem. Unlike trees, networks may contain cycles. If a network contains a cycle, this algorithm will end up in an infinite loop, recursively following the cycle.

One solution to this problem is to give the algorithm a way to tell whether it has visited a node before. An easy way to do that is to add a Visited property to the Node class. The following pseudocode shows the algorithm rewritten to use a Visited property:

```
Traverse()
    <Process node>
    Visited = True

    For Each link In Links
        If (Not link.Nodes[1].Visited) Then
            link.Nodes[1].Traverse
        End If
    Next link
End Traverse
```

Now the algorithm visits the current node and sets its Visited property to True. It then loops through the node's links. If the Visited property of the link's destination node is False, the algorithm recursively calls itself to process that destination node.

This version works, but it may lead to very deep levels of recursion. If a network contains N nodes, the algorithm might call itself N times. If N is large, that could exhaust the program's stack space and make the program crash.

You can avoid this problem if you use the techniques described in Chapter 9 to remove the recursion. The following pseudocode shows a version of the algorithm that uses a stack instead of recursion:

```
DepthFirstTraverse(Node: start_node)
    // Visit this node.
    start_node.Visited = True
```

```
// Make a stack and put the start node in it.
Stack(Of Node): stack
stack.Push(start_node)

// Repeat as long as the stack isn't empty.
While <stack isn't empty>
    // Get the next node from the stack.
    Node node = stack.Pop()

    // Process the node's links.
    For Each link In node.Links
        // Use the link only if the destination
        // node hasn't been visited.
        If (Not link.Nodes[1].Visited) Then
            // Mark the node as visited.
            link.Nodes[1].Visited = True

            // Push the node onto the stack.
            stack.Push(link.Nodes[1])
        End If
    Next link
Loop // Continue processing the stack until empty
End DepthFirstTraverse
```

This algorithm visits the start node and pushes it onto a stack. Then, as long as the stack isn't empty, it pops the next node off the stack and processes it.

To process a node, the algorithm examines the node's links. If a link's destination node has not been visited, the algorithm marks it as visited and adds it to the stack for later processing.

Because of the way this algorithm pushes nodes onto a stack, it traverses the network in a depth-first order. To see why, suppose that the algorithm starts at node A and node A has neighbors B_1, B_2, and so on. When the algorithm processes node A, it pushes the neighbors onto the stack. Later, when it processes neighbor B_1, it pushes that node's neighbors C_1, C_2, and so on, onto the stack. Because the stack returns items in last-in, first-out order, the algorithm processes the C nodes before it processes the B nodes. As it continues, the algorithm moves quickly through the network, traveling long distances away from the start node A before it gets back to processing that node's closer neighbors.

Because the traversal visits nodes far from the root node before it visits all the ones that are closer to the root, this is called a *depth-first traversal*.

Figure 13.3 shows a depth-first traversal with the nodes labeled according to the order in which they were traversed.

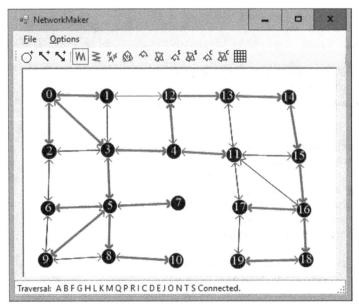

Figure 13.3: In a depth-first traversal, some nodes far from the start node are visited before some nodes that are closer to the start node.

With some work, you can figure out how the nodes were added to the traversal. The algorithm started with the node labeled 0. It then added the nodes labeled 1, 2, and 3 to its stack.

Because node 3 was added to the stack last, it was processed next, and the algorithm added nodes 4 and 5 to the stack. Because node 5 was added last, the algorithm processed it next and added nodes 6, 7, 8, and 9 to the stack.

If you like, you can continue studying Figure 13.3 to figure out why the algorithm visited the nodes in the order it did. At this point, however, you should be able to see how some nodes far from the start node are processed before some of the nodes closer to the start node. For example, node 10, which is four links away from the start node, is visited before nodes 11 and 12, which are only three links away from the start node.

Breadth-First Traversal

In some algorithms, it is better to visit nodes closer to the start node before visiting the nodes that are farther away. The previous algorithm visited some nodes far from the start node before it visited some closer nodes because it used a stack to process the nodes. If you use a queue instead of a stack, then the nodes are processed in first-in, first-out order, and the nodes closer to the start node are processed first.

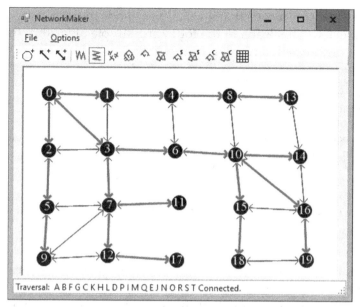

Figure 13.4: In a breadth-first traversal, nodes close to the starting node are visited before those that are farther away.

Because this algorithm visits all of a node's neighbors before it visits any other nodes, this is called a *breadth-first traversal*. Figure 13.4 shows a breadth-first traversal with the nodes labeled according to the order in which they were traversed.

As with the depth-first traversal, you can study Figure 13.4 to see how the algorithm visited the network's nodes. The algorithm started with the node labeled 0. It then added its neighbors labeled 1, 2, and 3 to its queue.

Because the queue returns items in first-in, first-out order, the algorithm next processes node 1 and adds its neighbors to the queue. The only neighbor of that node that has not been visited yet is node 4.

Next the algorithm removes node 2 from the queue and adds its neighbor, marked 5, to the queue. It then removes the node marked 3 from the queue and adds its neighbors 6 and 7 to the queue.

If you like, you can continue studying Figure 13.4 to determine why the algorithm visited the nodes in the order that it did. At this point, however, you should be able to see that all of the nodes closest to the start node were visited before any of the nodes farther away.

Connectivity Testing

The traversal algorithms described in the previous two sections immediately lead to a couple other algorithms with only minor modifications. For example, a traversal algorithm visits all of the nodes that are reachable from the start node.

For an undirected network, this means that it visits every node in the network if the network is connected. This leads to the following simple algorithm to determine whether an undirected network is connected:

```
Boolean: IsConnected(Node: start_node)
    // Traverse the network starting from start_node.
    Traverse(start_node)

    // See if any node has not been visited.
    For Each node In <all nodes>
        If (Not node.Visited) Then Return False
    Next node

    // All nodes were visited, so the network is connected.
    Return True
End IsConnected
```

This algorithm uses the previous traversal algorithm and then checks each node's Visited property to see if it was visited.

You can extend this algorithm to find all of the network's connected components. Simply use the traversal algorithm repeatedly starting at previously unvisited nodes until you visit all of the nodes. The following pseudocode shows an algorithm that uses a depth-first traversal to find the network's connected components:

```
List(Of List(Of Node)): GetConnectedComponents
    // Keep track of the number of nodes visited.
    Integer: num_visited = 0;

    // Make the result list of lists.
    List(Of List(Of Node)): components

    // Repeat until all nodes are in a connected component.
    While (num_visited < <number of nodes>)
        // Find a node that hasn't been visited.
        Node: start_node = <first node not yet visited>

        // Add the start node to the stack.
        Stack(Of Node): stack
        stack.Push(start_node)
        start_node.Visited = True
        num_visited = num_visited + 1

        // Add the node to a new connected component.
        List(Of Node): component
        components.Add(component)
        component.Add(start_node)
```

```
          // Process the stack until it's empty.
          While <stack isn't empty>
               // Get the next node from the stack.
               Node: node = stack.Pop()

               // Process the node's links.
               For Each link In node.Links
                    // Use the link only if the destination
                    // node hasn't been visited.
                    If (Not link.Nodes[1].Visited) Then
                         // Mark the node as visited.
                         link.Nodes[1].Visited = True

                         // Mark the link as part of the tree.
                         link.Visited = True
                         num_visited = num_visited + 1

                         // Add the node to the current connected component.
                         component.Add(link.Nodes[1])

                         // Push the node onto the stack.
                         stack.Push(link.Nodes[1])
                    End If
               Next link
          End // While <stack isn't empty>
     Loop // While (num_visited < <number of nodes>)

     // Return the components.
     Return components
End GetConnectedComponents
```

This algorithm returns a list of lists, each holding the nodes in a connected component. It starts by making the variable num_visited to keep track of how many nodes have been visited. It then makes the list of lists that it will return.

The algorithm then enters a loop that continues as long as it has not visited every node. Inside the loop, the program finds a node that has not yet been visited, adds it to a stack as in the traversal algorithm, and also adds it to a new list of nodes that represent the network's connected components.

The algorithm then enters a loop similar to the one used by the earlier traversal algorithm used to process the stack until it is empty. The only real difference is that this algorithm adds the nodes it visits to the list that it is currently building in addition to adding them to the stack.

When the stack is empty, the algorithm has visited all of the nodes that are connected to the latest start node. At that point, it finds another node that hasn't been visited and starts again.

When every node has been visited, the algorithm returns the list of connected components.

Spanning Trees

If an undirected network is connected, then you can make a tree rooted at any node showing a path from the root to every other node in the network. This tree is called a *spanning tree* because it spans all of the nodes in the network.

For example, Figure 13.5 shows a spanning tree rooted at node H. If you follow the thicker links, you can trace a path from the root node H to any other node in the network. For example, the path to node M visits nodes H, C, B, A, F, K, L, and M.

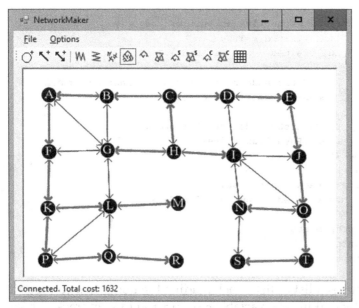

Figure 13.5: A spanning tree connects all of the nodes in a network.

The traversal algorithms described earlier actually find spanning trees, but they don't record the links that are used in the tree. To modify the previous algorithms to record the links used, simply add the following lines right after the statement that marks a new node as visited:

```
// Mark the link as part of the spanning tree.
link.Visited = True
```

The algorithm starts with the root node in the spanning tree. At each step, it picks another node that is adjacent to the spanning tree and adds it to the tree. The new algorithm simply records which links were used to connect the nodes to the growing spanning tree.

Minimal Spanning Trees

The spanning tree algorithm described in the preceding section could use many different combinations of links to connect all of the network's nodes, so many spanning trees are possible.

A spanning tree that has the least possible cost is called a *minimal spanning tree*. Note that a network may have more than one minimal spanning tree.

The following steps describe a simple high-level algorithm for finding a minimal spanning tree with root node R:

1. Add the root node R to the initial spanning tree.

2. Repeat until every node is in the spanning tree:

    a. Find a least-cost link that connects a node in the spanning tree to a node that is not yet in the spanning tree.

    b. Add that link's destination node to the spanning tree.

This is an example of a greedy algorithm because at each step it selects a link that has the least possible cost. By making the best choices locally, it achieves the best solution globally.

For example, consider the network shown on the left in Figure 13.6, and suppose that the bold links and nodes are part of a growing spanning tree rooted at node A. In step 2a, you examine the links that connect nodes in the tree with nodes that are not yet in the tree. In this example, those links have costs 15, 10, 12, and 11. Using the greedy algorithm, you add the least-cost link, which has cost 10, to get the tree on the right.

The most time-consuming step in this algorithm is step 2a, which finds the next link to add to the tree. How much time this step takes depends on the approach you use.

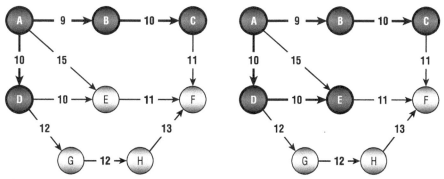

Figure 13.6: At each step, you add to the spanning tree the least-cost link that connects a node in the tree to a node that is not in the tree.

One way to find a least-cost link is to loop through the tree's nodes, examining their links to find one that connects to a node outside the tree and that has minimal cost. This is fairly time-consuming because the algorithm must examine the links of the tree's nodes many times, even if they lead to other nodes that are already in the tree.

A better approach is to keep a list of candidate links. When the algorithm adds a node to the growing spanning tree, it also adds any links from that node to a node outside the tree to the candidate list. To find a minimal link, the algorithm looks through the candidate list for the smallest link. As it searches the list, if it finds a link that leads to another node that is already in the tree (because that node was added to the tree after the link was added to the candidate list), the algorithm removes it from the list. That way, the algorithm doesn't need to consider the link again later. When the candidate list is empty, the algorithm is done.

Euclidean Minimum Spanning Trees

The *Euclidean minimum spanning tree* (EMST) for a set of points is a spanning tree that joins the points with links that have weights equal to their lengths. Another way to think of this is that the EMST connects the points with the smallest total link length. Figure 13.7 shows a program displaying an EMST for a set of points.

The EMST is useful for calculating the least expensive way to connect a collection of points. For example, you could use an EMST to build a network of electrical wires, drainage pipes, or telecommunication lines that connect a set of points. In the real world, however, you might prefer to spend a bit more on extra links to provide better throughput or to make the network fault tolerant so that it can continue working even if one of the links breaks.

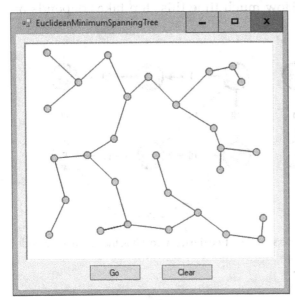

Figure 13.7: An EMST is the cheapest way to connect a set of points.

The most obvious way to build an EMST is to create a network that includes a link between every pair of nodes, set each link's weight equal to its length, and then use the greedy algorithm described in the preceding section to find a minimal spanning tree for the network.

There are faster algorithms for finding an EMST, but they are much more complicated, so I'm not going to describe them here. You can find more information online, for example, at `https://wikipedia.org/wiki/Euclidean_minimum_spanning_tree`.

Building Mazes

You can use a spanning tree to create a maze relatively easily. First, create an area covered in square rooms separated by walls. Place a node in the middle of each room and connect each node to its north, south, east, and west neighbors. Next, generate a random spanning tree for the nodes. Wherever the tree's links cross through a room's wall, remove that wall.

Figure 13.8 shows a program that used this technique to create a maze. The thin, dark lines show the walls between the maze's rooms. The thick, gray lines show the spanning tree.

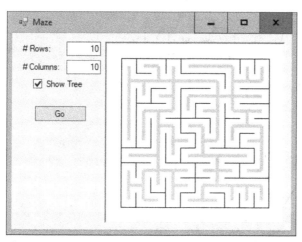

Figure 13.8: You can use a random spanning tree to generate a maze.

You can build the maze's spanning tree almost as you would build any other spanning tree. Pick a random root node and add its links to a candidate list. As long as the candidate list is not empty, pick a random link from the list and add it to the tree as usual.

The only difference between this algorithm and other spanning tree algorithms is that this version picks the next link from the candidate list randomly.

Strongly Connected Components

A subset of nodes in a network is *strongly connected* if every node in the set is reachable from every other node in the set. A *strongly connected component* of a network is a maximal strongly connected subset within the network. In other words, it is strongly connected, and if you add any other node to the subset, it is no longer strongly connected.

A network's strongly connected components partition the network. For example, Figure 13.9 shows a network with its strongly connected components circled with dashes.

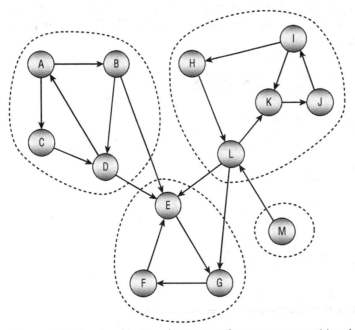

Figure 13.9: A network's strongly connected components partition the network.

The following section describes one algorithm for finding strongly connected components. The section after that one explains why the algorithm works.

Kosaraju's Algorithm

In 1978, Johns Hopkins computer science professor Sambasiva Rao Kosaraju proposed a method for finding the strongly connected components of a network. The algorithm is now known as *Kosaraju's algorithm*. (It's also known as the *Kosaraju–Sharir algorithm*, partially named after Israeli mathematician and computer scientist Micha Sharir, who independently discovered and published the algorithm in 1981.)

The algorithm is reasonably simple, although understanding why the algorithm works is a bit harder. The following steps outline the algorithm at a high level:

1. *Preparation*: Give the Node class the following fields:

   a. Visited: A Boolean field indicating whether the node has been visited in the first part of the algorithm

   b. ComponentRoot: A Node that will represent the strongly connected component to which this node belongs

   c. InLinks: A list of links leading into this node

2. *Initialization*: Loop through the nodes and initialize them as follows:

   a. Set each node's Visited field to false.

   b. Set each node's ComponentRoot field to null.

   c. Add the node's links to the neighboring nodes' InLinks lists.

   d. Create an empty visited_nodes list to keep track of nodes that have been visited.

3. *Visiting*: Loop through the nodes and call the recursive Visit method described shortly for each.

4. *Assigning*: Loop through the nodes in the visited_nodes list and call the recursive Assign method described shortly for each.

The algorithm first performs some setup. The most interesting part of this step is creating an InLinks list for each node. Later the Assign method will use those lists to loop through the nodes' incoming links.

> **NOTE** The InLinks lists essentially let each node find the reverse of its outbound links. Reversed links are called *transpose links*. A network with the direction of every link reversed is called the *transpose network*.

The algorithm then calls the following Visit method for each node:

```
// Recursively visit nodes that are reachable from this one.
Void: Visit(Node: node, List<Node>: visited_nodes)
    If (node.Visited) Then Return
```

```
        node.Visited = True
        For Each link In node.Links
            Visit(link.ToNode, visited_nodes)
        Next link
        visited_nodes.Insert(0, node)
    End Visit
```

The `Visit` method uses a node's `Links` list to traverse recursively all of the nodes that are reachable from that node, skipping any nodes that have already been visited.

Note that the method waits until after it has recursively processed a node's outbound links before it adds the node itself to the *beginning* of the `visited_nodes` list. That places the node closer to the beginning of the list than any nodes that can be reached from it.

After the visiting step, the algorithm loops through the nodes in the `visited_nodes` list and calls the following `Assign` method for each:

```
// Recursively assign nodes to a component root.
Void: Assign(Node: node, Node: root)
    If (node.ComponentRoot != null) Then Return

    node.ComponentRoot = root
    For Each link In node.InLinks
        Assign(link.FromNode, root)
    Next link
End Assign
```

When the method is first called, the node that is passed into it becomes the root node for its connected component. It passes that same root into any recursive calls that the method makes.

For both the initial and recursive calls, the code sets the current node's `ComponentRoot` field to the component's root node. It then recursively traverses the node's incoming links to assign other nodes to the same component.

When the `Assign` method has visited every node, then the algorithm is finished, and each node's `ComponentRoot` field indicates the strongly connected component that contains it.

After executing the algorithm, a program can perform other tasks such as assigning names, numbers, or colors to the nodes in each strongly selected component.

Algorithm Discussion

The key fact that you need to understand to know why Kosaraju's algorithm works is that the nodes in a strongly connected component are exactly those that are reachable both along paths that use forward links and paths that use transpose links. Another way you can state this is by using the following two facts:

Fact 1   If A and B are in the same strongly connected component, then there is a path P_{AB} from node A to node B using forward links, and there is also a reversed path R_{AB} from node A to node B using reversed links. (There are similar paths and reversed paths between *every* pair of nodes in the strongly connected component.)

Fact 2   At least one of the paths P_{AE} or R_{AE} is missing for any node E that lies outside of the strongly connected component that contains node A. In other words, either there is no path P_{AE} or there is no reversed path R_{AE} or there is neither path. (Similarly, there is no path P_{EA} or there is no reversed path R_{EA} or there is neither of those paths.)

To see why Fact 1 is true, suppose that nodes A and B are in the same strongly connected component. Then there must be a path P_{AB} from node A to node B and another path P_{BA} from node B to node A. (That's just the definition of a strongly connected component.) Now let's reverse the paths. The reverse of path P_{AB} gives a reverse path R_{BA} that connects node B to node A along the reversed links. Similarly, the reverse of path P_{BA} gives a reverse path R_{AB} that connects node A to node B along the reversed links. This shows that the paths P_{AB} and R_{AB} exist.

To see why Fact 2 is true, suppose that node E is not in the same strongly connected component as node A. Because the two are not in the same strongly connected component, then there is either no path P_{AE} or there is no path P_{EA}. In that case, either one or both of the reversed paths R_{EA} or P_{AE} must also be missing, and that's what Fact 2 says.

If you look again at Figure 13.9, you'll see that node E is not part of the strongly connected component {A, B, C, D} because while there are paths from those nodes to node E, there are no paths between node E and any of those nodes. If you study the figure a bit more, you can also verify that there are paths and reversed paths between any pair of nodes in the strongly connected component {A, B, C, D}.

All of this leads to an algorithm for finding a strongly connected component. Start at node A and traverse the network as far as possible following forward links. Then start at node A again, this time traversing the network using reversed links. The strongly connected component that contains node A consists of the nodes that you reach in both traversals. The only remaining task is to figure out how to perform those traversals efficiently. That's where Kosaraju's algorithm comes in.

The algorithm first performs a traversal using forward links. It inserts each node at the beginning of the `visited_nodes` list, so it comes before the nodes that were visited starting at that node.

Next, the algorithm visits the nodes in the list and traverses the network using reversed links. Eventually, the `Assign` method reaches a dead end, either because it hits nodes that have already been assigned or because it runs out of transpose links to follow. In either case, it has finished building that strongly connected component.

To get a better idea about how that works, it's worth looking more closely at an example. Consider again the network shown in Figure 13.9 and repeated here in Figure 13.10.

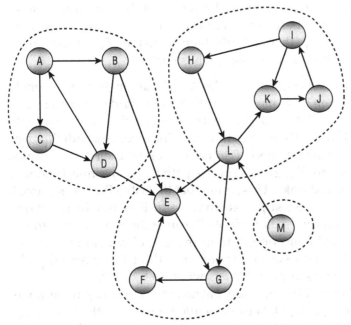

Figure 13.10: Kosaraju's algorithm traverses the network's links forward and then backward.

When the algorithm visits node A, it follows forward links as far as possible. When it finishes that traversal, the `visited_nodes` list contains the following nodes. I've highlighted node A to indicate that it started the traversal:

    A C B D E G F

Notice that these nodes include all the nodes in node A's strongly connected component plus a few extras.

The next nontrivial traversal that the algorithm performs starts at the next unvisited node, which is node H. After that traversal, the `visited_nodes` list contains the following nodes:

    H L K J I **A** C B D E G F

The only remaining nontrivial traversal starts at node M and simply adds that node to the beginning of the list.

    M H L K J I **A** C B D E G F

Now the algorithm uses the `Assign` method to assign nodes. It starts at the first node in the `nodes_visited` list, which is node M, and it performs a traversal using reversed links. That node has no reversed links, so the traversal goes nowhere, and node M is the only node in its strongly connected component.

The algorithm then calls `Assign` for the next node in the list, which is node H. The new traversal follows reversed links to assign nodes I, J, K, and L. (Look again at the figure to see which reversed links it follows.) It would visit node M, but that node has already been assigned.

The algorithm continues moving through the `nodes_visited` list calling `Assign` for the nodes. The nodes L, K, J, and I have already been assigned, so those calls don't do anything interesting. The next nontrivial call is for node A. That reversed traversal assigns nodes D, B, and C.

The algorithm again passes over some previously assigned nodes and then performs a reversed traversal starting at node E. That traversal assigns nodes F and G. That traversal would also visit nodes B, D, and L (and other nodes accessible from them), but those nodes have already been assigned.

The algorithm finishes looping through the `visited_nodes` list, finds no more unassigned nodes, and is done.

If you still have trouble visualizing how the algorithm works, you may want to implement it and step through it in a debugger.

Finding Paths

Finding paths in a network is a common task. An everyday example is finding a route from one location to another in a street network.

The following sections describe some algorithms for finding paths through networks.

Finding Any Path

The spanning tree algorithms described earlier in this chapter gave you a method for finding a path between any two nodes in a network. The following steps describe a simple high-level algorithm for finding a path from node A to node B:

1. Find a spanning tree rooted at node A.

2. Follow the reversed links in the spanning tree from node B to node A.

3. Reverse the order in which the links were followed.

The algorithm builds the spanning tree rooted at node A. Then it starts at node B. For each node in its path, it finds the link in the spanning tree that leads to that node. It records that link and moves to the next node in the path.

Unfortunately, finding the link that leads to a particular node in the spanning tree is difficult. Using the spanning tree algorithms described so far, you would need to loop through every link to determine whether it was part of the spanning tree and whether it ended at the current node.

You can solve this problem by making a small change to the spanning tree algorithm. First, add a new `FromNode` property to the `Node` class. Then when the spanning tree algorithm marks a node as being in the tree, set that node's `FromNode` property to the node whose link was used to connect the new node to the tree.

Now to find the path from node B to node A in step 2, you can simply follow the nodes' `FromNode` properties.

Label-Setting Shortest Paths

The algorithm described in the preceding section finds a path from a start node to a destination node, but it's not necessarily a good path. The path is taken from a spanning tree, and there's no guarantee that it is efficient. Figure 13.11 shows a path from node M to node S. If the link costs are their lengths, then it's not hard to find a shorter path such as M → L → G → H → I → N → S.

A more useful algorithm would find the shortest path between two nodes. Shortest path algorithms are divided into two general categories: label setting and label correcting. This section describes a label-setting algorithm. The next section describes a label-correcting algorithm.

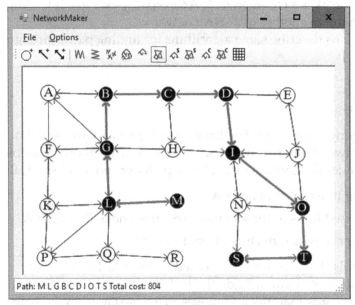

Figure 13.11: A path that follows a spanning tree from one node to another may be inefficient.

The label-setting algorithm begins at a starting node and creates a spanning tree in a manner that is somewhat similar to how the minimal spanning tree described earlier does this. At each step, the minimal spanning tree algorithm selects the least-cost link that connects a new node to the spanning tree. In contrast, the shortest path algorithm selects a link that adds to the tree a node that is the least distance from the starting node.

To determine which node is the least distance from the starting node, the algorithm labels each node with its distance from the starting node. When it considers a link, it adds the distance to the link's source node to that link's cost, and that determines the current distance to the link's destination node.

When the algorithm has added every node to the spanning tree, it is finished. The paths through the tree show the shortest paths from the starting node to every other node in the network, so this tree is called a *shortest path tree*.

The following steps describe the algorithm at a high level:

1. Set the starting node's distance to 0, and mark it as part of the tree.

2. Add the starting node's links to a candidate list of links that could be used to extend the tree.

3. While the candidate list is not empty, loop through the list examining the links.

   a. If a link leads to a node that is already in the tree, remove the link from the candidate list.

   b. Suppose link L leads from node N_1 in the tree to node N_2 not yet in the tree. If D_1 is the distance to node N_1 in the tree and C_L is the cost of the link, then you could reach node N_2 with distance $N_1 + C_L$ by first going to node N_1 and then following the link. Let $D_2 = N_1 + C_L$ be the possible distance for node N_1 that uses this link. As you loop over the links in the candidate list, keep track of the link and node that give the smallest possible distance. Let L_{best} and N_{best} be the link and node that give the smallest distance D_{best}.

   c. Set the distance for N_{best} to D_{best} and mark N_{best} as part of the shortest path tree.

   d. For all links L leaving node N_{best}, if L leads to a node that is not yet in the tree, add L to the candidate list.

For example, consider the network shown on the left in Figure 13.12. Suppose that the bold links and nodes are part of a growing shortest path tree. The tree's nodes are labeled with their distance from the root node, which is labeled 0. The other nodes are labeled with their names.

To add the next link to the tree, examine the links that lead from the tree to a node that is not in the tree and calculate the distance to those nodes. This example has three possible links.

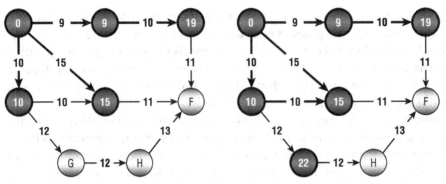

Figure 13.12: At each step, you add to the shortest path tree the link that gives the smallest total distance from the root to a node that is not in the tree.

The first leads from the node labeled 19 to node F. The distance from the root node to the node labeled 19 is 19 (that's why it's labeled 19), and this link has cost 11, so the total distance to node F via this link is $19 + 11 = 30$.

The second link leads from the node labeled 15 to node F. The distance from the root node to the node labeled 15 is 15, and this link has cost 11, so the total distance to node F via this link is $15 + 11 = 26$. Notice that this link leads to the same node as the previous one, node F, but this link gives a shorter path to that node.

The third link leads from the node labeled 10 to node G. The link has cost 12, so the total distance via this link is $10 + 12 = 22$. This is the least of the three distances calculated, so this is the link that should be added to the tree. The result is shown on the right in Figure 13.12.

Figure 13.13 shows a complete shortest path tree built by this algorithm. In this network, the links' costs are their lengths in pixels. Each node is labeled with the order in which it was added to the tree, not its distance from the root. The root node was added first, so it has label 0, the node to its left was added next, so it has label 1, and so on.

Notice how the nodes' labels increase as the distance from the root node increases. This is similar to the ordering in which nodes were added to the tree in a breadth-first traversal. The difference is that the breadth-first traversal added nodes in order of the number of links between the root and the nodes, but this algorithm adds nodes in order of the distance along the links between the root and the nodes.

Having built a shortest path tree, you can follow the nodes' FromNode values to find a backward path from a destination node to the start node, as described in the preceding section.

Figure 13.14 shows the shortest path from node M to node S in the original network. This looks more reasonable than the path shown in Figure 13.11, which used a spanning tree.

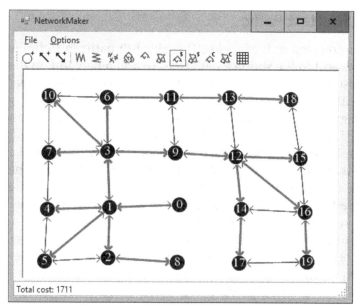

Figure 13.13: A shortest path tree gives the shortest paths from the root node to any node in the network.

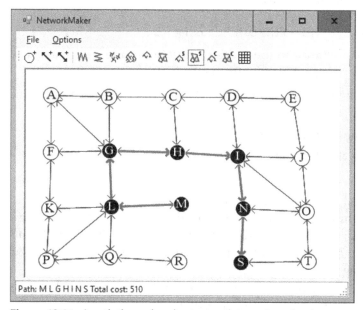

Figure 13.14: A path through a shortest path tree gives the shortest path from the root node to a specific node in the network.

Label-Correcting Shortest Paths

The most time-consuming step in the label-setting shortest path algorithm is finding the next link to add to the shortest path tree. To add a new link to the tree, the algorithm must search through the candidate links to find the one that reaches a new node with the least cost.

An alternative strategy is just to add any of the candidate links to the shortest path tree and label its destination node with its distance to the root as usual.

Later, when the algorithm considers links in the candidate list, it may find a better path to a node that is already in the shortest path tree. In that case, the algorithm updates the node's distance, adds its links back into the candidate list (if they are not already in the list), and continues. Eventually, the algorithm will find no more improved paths and it is done.

In the label-setting algorithm, a node's distance is set only once and never changes. In the label-correcting algorithm, a node's distance is set once but later may be corrected many times.

The following steps describe the algorithm at a high level:

1. Set the starting node's distance to 0, and mark it as part of the tree.

2. Add the starting node's links to a candidate list of links.

3. While the candidate list is not empty:

    a. Consider the first link in the candidate list.

    b. Calculate the distance to the link's destination node: `<distance>` = `<source node distance>` + `<link cost>`.

    c. If the new distance is smaller than the destination node's current distance:

        i. Update the destination node's distance.

        ii. Add all of the destination node's links to the candidate list.

This algorithm may seem more complicated, but the code is actually shorter, because you don't need to search the candidate list for the best link.

Because this algorithm may change the link leading to a node several times, you cannot simply mark a link as used by the tree and leave it at that. If you did and you needed to change the link that leads into a node, you would need to find its old incoming link and unmark it.

An easier approach is to give the `Node` class a `FromLink` property. When you change the link leading to the node, you can update this property.

If you still want to mark the links used by the shortest path tree, first build the tree. Then loop over the nodes, and mark the links stored in their `FromLink` properties.

Figure 3.15 shows the shortest path tree for a network found by using the label-correcting method. Again, in this network the links' costs are their lengths in pixels. Each node is labeled with the number of times its distance (and `From-Link` value) was corrected. The root node is labeled 0 because its value was set initially and never changed.

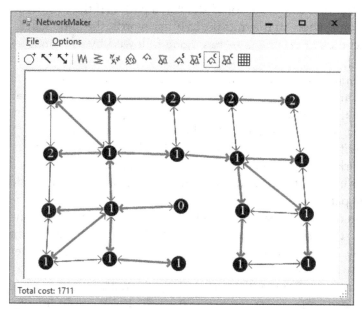

Figure 13.15: In a label-correcting algorithm, some nodes' distances may be corrected several times.

Many of the nodes in Figure 13.15 are labeled 1, meaning that their distances were set once and then never corrected. A few nodes are labeled 2, meaning their values were set and then corrected once.

In a large and more complicated network, it is possible that a node's distance might be corrected many times before the shortest path tree is complete.

All-Pairs Shortest Paths

The shortest path algorithms described so far find shortest path trees from a starting node to every other node in the network. Another type of shortest path algorithm asks you to find the shortest path between every pair of nodes in the network.

The Floyd–Warshall algorithm begins with a two-dimensional array named `Distance`, where `Distance[start_node, end_node]` is the shortest distance between nodes `start_node` and `end_node`.

To build the array, initialize it by setting the diagonal entries, which represent the distance from a node to itself, to 0. Set the entries that represent direct links between two nodes to the cost of the links. Set the array's other values to infinity.

Suppose the Distance array is partially filled, and consider the path within the array from node start_node to node end_node. Suppose also that the path uses only nodes 0, 1, 2, . . ., via_node − 1 for some value via_node.

The only way adding node via_node could shorten a path is if the improved path visits that node somewhere in the middle. In other words, the path start_ node → end_node becomes start_node → via_node followed by via_node → end_node.

To update the Distance array, you examine all pairs of nodes start_node and end_node. If Distance[start_node, end_node] > Distance[start_node, via_node] + Distance[via_node, end_node], then you update the entry by setting Distance[start_node, end_node] equal to the smaller distance.

If you repeat this with via_node = 0, 1, 2, ..., N − 1, where N is the number of nodes in the network, the Distance array holds the final shortest distance between any two nodes in the network using any of the other nodes as intermediate points on the shortest paths.

So far the algorithm doesn't tell you how to find the shortest path from one node to another. It just explains how to find the shortest distance between the nodes. Fortunately, you can add the path information by making another two-dimensional array named Via.

The Via array keeps track of one of the nodes along the path from one node to another. In other words, Via[start_node, end_node] holds the index of a node that you should visit somewhere along the shortest path from start_node to end_node.

If Via[start_node, end_node] is end_node, then there is a direct link from start_node to end_node, so the shortest path consists of just the node end_node.

If Via[start_node, end_node] is some other node via_node, then you can recursively use the array to find the path from start_node to via_node and then from via_node to end_node. (If this seems a bit confusing, it will probably make more sense when you see the algorithm for using the Via array.)

To build the Via array, initialize all of its entries to −1. Then set Via[start_node, end_node] to end_node if there is a direct link between the nodes.

Now when you build the Distance array and you improve the path start_ node → end _ node by replacing it with the paths start_node → via _ node and via_node → end_node, you need to do one more thing. You must also set Via[start_node, end_node] = via_node to indicate that the shortest path from start_node to end_node goes via the intermediate point via_node.

The following steps describe the full algorithm for building the Distance and Via arrays (assuming that the network contains N nodes):

1. Initialize the Distance array:

    a. Set Distance[i, j] = infinity for all entries.

    b. Set Distance[i, i] = 0 for all i = 1 to N − 1.

    c. If nodes i and j are connected by a link i → j, set Distance[i, j] to the cost of that link.

2. Initialize the Via array:

    a. For all i and j:

        i. If Distance[i, j] < infinity, set Via[i, j] to j to indicate that the path from i to j goes via node j.

        ii. Otherwise, set Via[i, j] to −1 to indicate that there is no path from node i to node j.

3. Execute the following nested loops to find improvements:

```
For via_node = 0 To N - 1
    For from_node = 0 To N - 1
        For to_node = 0 To N - 1
            Integer: new_dist =
                Distance[from_node, via_node] +
                Distance[via_node, to_node]
            If (new_dist < Distance[from_node, to_node]) Then
                // This is an improved path. Update it.
                Distance[from_node, to_node] = new_dist
                Via[from_node, to_node] = via_node
            End If
        Next to_node
    Next from_node
Next via_node
```

The via_node loop loops through the indices of nodes that could be intermediate nodes and improve existing paths. After that loop finishes, all of the shortest paths are complete.

The following pseudocode shows how to use the completed Distance and Via arrays to find the nodes in the shortest path from a start node to a destination node:

```
List(Of Integer): FindPath(Integer: start_node, Integer: end_node)
    If (Distance[start, end] == infinity) Then
        // There is no path between these nodes.
        Return null
    End If
```

```
        // Get the via node for this path.
        Integer: via_node = Via[start_node, end_node]

        // See if there is a direct connection.
        If (via_node == end_node)
            // There is a direct connection.
            // Return a list that contains only end_node.
            Return { end_node }
        Else
            // There is no direct connection.
            // Return start_node --> via_node plus via_node --> end_node.
            Return
            {
                FindPath(start_node, via_node] +
                FindPath(via_node, end_node]
            }
        End If
End FindPath
```

For example, consider the network shown at the top of Figure 13.16. The upper arrays show how the Distance values change over time, and the bottom arrays show how the Via values change over time. Values that change are highlighted to make them easy to spot.

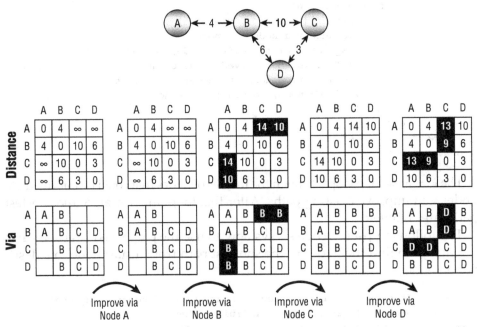

Figure 13.16: The shortest paths between all pairs of nodes in a network can be represented by a Distance array (top arrays) and a Via array (bottom arrays).

The upper-left array shows the initial values in the Distance array. The distance from each node to itself is 0. The distance between two nodes connected by a link is set to the link's cost. For example, the link between node A and node B has cost 4, so Distance[A, B] is 4. (To make the example easier to follow, the names of the nodes are used as if they were array indices.) The remaining entries are set to infinity.

The lower-left array shows the initial values in the Via array. For example, there is a link from node C to node B, so Via[C, B] is B.

After initializing the arrays, the algorithm looks for improvements. First it looks for paths that it can improve by using node A as an intermediate point. Node A is on the end of the network, so it can't improve any paths.

Next the algorithm tries to improve paths by using node B, and it finds four improvements. For example, looking at the second Distance array, you can see that Distance[A, C] is infinity, but Distance[A, B] is 4 and Distance[B, C] is 10, so the path A → C can be improved. To make that improvement, the algorithm sets Distance[A, C] to 4 + 10 = 14 and sets Via[A, C] to the intermediate node B.

If you look at the network, you can follow the changes there. The initial path A → C had distance set to infinity. The path A → B → C is an improvement, and you can see in the network that the total distance for that path is 14.

Similarly, you can work through the changes in the paths A → D, C → A, and D → A.

Next the algorithm tries to improve paths by using node C as an intermediate node. That node doesn't allow any improvements.

Finally, the algorithm tries to improve paths by using node D as an intermediate node. It can use node D to improve the four paths A → C, B → C, C → A, and C → B.

For an example of finding a path through the completed Via array, consider the array on the lower right in Figure 13.16. The following steps describe how to find the path A → C:

- Via[A, C] is D, so A → C = A → D + D → C.
- Via[A, D] is B, so A → D = A → B + B → D.
- Via[D, C] is C, so there is a link from node D to node C.
- Via[A, B] is B, so there is a link from node A to node B.
- Finally, Via[B, D] is D, so there is a link from node B to node D.

The final path travels through nodes B, D, and C, so the full path is A → B → D → C.

Figure 13.17 shows the recursive calls.

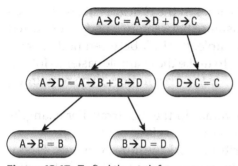

Figure 13.17: To find the path from `start_node` to `end_node` with intermediate point `via_node`, you recursively find the paths from `start_node` to `via_node` and from `via_node` to `end_node`.

After you create the `Distance` and `Via` arrays, you can quickly find the shortest paths between any two points in a network. The downside is that the arrays can take up a lot of room.

For example, a street network for a moderately large city might contain 30,000 nodes, so the arrays would contain $2 \times 30,000^2 = 1.8$ billion entries. If the entries are 4-byte integers, then the two arrays would occupy a combined 14.4 gigabytes of memory.

Even if you can afford to use that much memory, the algorithm for building the arrays uses three nested loops that run from 1 to N, where N is the number of nodes, so the algorithm's total run time is $O(N^3)$. If N is 30,000, that's 2.7×10^{13} steps. A computer running 1 million steps per second would need more than 10 months to build the arrays.

For really big networks, this algorithm is impractical, so you need to use one of the other shortest path algorithms to find paths as needed. If you need to find many paths on a smaller network, perhaps one with only a few hundred nodes, you may be able to use this algorithm to precompute all of the shortest paths and save some time.

Transitivity

Two topics that are closely related to path finding are transitive closure and transitive reduction. In a sense, these ideas are complementary. A networks' *transitive closure* logically adds links to a network to represent all of its connections directly. In contrast, the *transitive reduction* removes as many links as possible without changing the network's connectivity.

The following two sections explain transitive closure and transitive reduction in more detail and describe algorithms for performing each.

Transitive Closure

In the *transitive closure problem*, the goal is to build a data structure that can efficiently determine whether there is a path through a network between any two given nodes. For example, you could construct an array called `PathExists` where `PathExists[A, B]` is true if there is a path through the network from node A to node B.

Conceptually, you can think of the closure as adding links to show which nodes are reachable from other nodes. For example, the left side of Figure 13.18 shows a small network. On the right side of the figure, dashed arrows represent new links added to make the network's transitive closure. If there is a path from node X to node Y in the network on the left, then there is a direct link from node X to node Y in the network on the right.

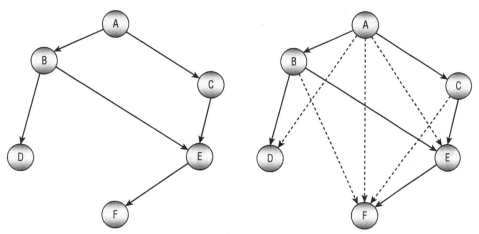

Figure 13.18: In a network's transitive closure, each node is only one link away from every node that it can reach.

There are several methods that you can use to find a transitive closure. The simplest approach is to perform a traversal of the network starting at every node and keep track of all the vertices that the traversal reaches. If the network contains N nodes and E edges, then each traversal takes $O(N + E)$ steps, so the whole process takes $O(N \times (N + E))$ steps. If the network is dense so E is on the order of N^2, then that time is $O(N^3)$. That's fast enough for small networks but impractical for large ones.

A second approach is to use the Floyd–Warshall algorithm described in the section "All-Pairs Shortest Paths" earlier in this chapter, which also runs in $O(N^3)$ time. That algorithm produces an array that gives the shortest distance between every pair of nodes. You can use that array to test reachability between two nodes by checking whether the distance between the nodes is less than infinity.

If the network is relatively dense, then a third approach may be useful. Because the network is dense, many of its nodes should be contained in strongly connected components. In that case, you can find those components and then examine the links between them. If there is a link from component A to component B, then all of the nodes in component B are reachable from all of the nodes in component A.

Transitive Reduction

The *transitive reduction* of a network (which is also known as the *minimum equivalent digraph*) is another network that has the same nodes but with the fewest possible links that give the same reachablity. In other words, if there is a path between two nodes in the original network, then there is also a path between the same two nodes in the reduced network.

Another way to think of this is to remove as many links as possible from the original network without changing the reachability.

Note that the transitive reduction of an acyclic network is unique. For example, Figure 13.19 shows an acyclic network on the left and its transitive reduction on the right.

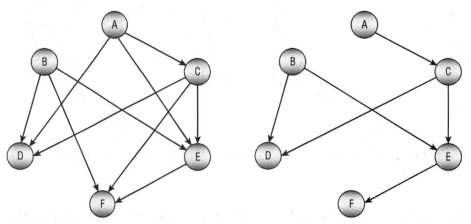

Figure 13.19: An acyclic network's transitive reduction is unique.

If you study the networks shown in Figure 13.19, you'll see that their nodes have the same sets of reachability. Table 13.2 summarizes the networks' reachabilities.

In contrast, a cyclic network may have multiple transitive reductions, and even multiple *minimum reductions* with the fewest possible number of edges. Figure 13.20 shows a cyclic network on the left and two transitive reductions, each containing six links.

Table 13.2: An Acyclic Network's Reachabilities

	A	B	C	D	E	F
A	X		X	X	X	X
B		X		X	X	X
C			X	X	X	X
D				X		
E					X	
F					X	X

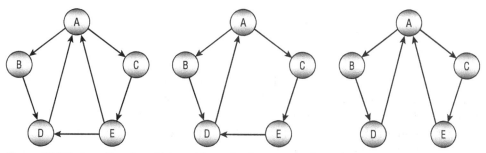

Figure 13.20: A cyclic network's transitive reduction may not be unique.

Note that the transitive reduction of a cyclic network *may* be unique. For example, both of the transitive closures shown in Figure 13.20 are cyclic networks, and they are their own unique transitive closures.

In general, finding a transitive closure for a network can be difficult, but there are a couple of special cases that are manageable. For example, if the network's links are undirected, then finding a minimal transitive closure is equivalent to finding a minimal spanning tree, and you already know how to do that.

The following two sections explain algorithms that you can use to find a transitive closure for other kinds of networks.

Acyclic Networks

Finding a transitive closure for an acyclic network is relatively simple. The basic idea is to remove links that can be replaced with a composite path consisting of two other paths that visit an intermediate node.

For example, consider the link A → B. If there is a node C such that there are paths A → C and C → B, then the link A → B is unnecessary, and we can remove it from the network without changing the network's reachability. That approach gives the following algorithm for acyclic networks:

```
// Find the transitive reduction.
Void: FindTransitiveReduction(Boolean[,]: reachable)
```

```
            // Remove self-links.
            For i = 0 To <Number of nodes>
                reachable[i, i] = False

            // Remove other unnecessary links.
            For i = 0 To <Number of nodes> - 1
                For j = 0 To <Number of nodes> - 1
                    // Consider link i --> j.
                    If (reachable[i, j]) Then
                        // See if there is a node k with paths
                        // i --> k and k --> j.
                        For k = 0 To <Number of nodes> - 1
                            If reachable[i, k] And reachable[k, j] Then
                                Reachable[i, j] = False
                            End If
                    End If
        End FindTransitiveReduction
```

The `reachable` parameter is a Boolean array where `reachable[i, j]` is true if there is a path from node `i` to node `j`. The code first sets `reachable[i, i]` to false for all `i` to remove any self-links between a node and itself.

Next, the algorithm loops over the links between all possible pairs of nodes. For each link i → j, the code loops through all nodes k and checks whether there are paths i → k and k → j. If those paths exist, then the algorithm removes the i → j link.

General Networks

To find a transitive reduction for a general cyclic network, first find the network's strongly connected components. Connect the nodes in each of those components with a directed Hamiltonian cycle. (Basically, make a big loop that connects all of the component's nodes.)

> **NOTE** A *Hamiltonian path* for a set of nodes is a path that visits each of the nodes exactly once. A *Hamiltonian cycle* is a Hamiltonian path that returns to its starting point.

Replace each strongly connected component with a single, condensed node and remove any links that lie within a component. If a link in the original network connected nodes in two different components, add a link connecting the corresponding condensed nodes.

The result is called the original network's *condensation*. The condensed network is acyclic, so you can use the techniques described in the previous section to find its transitive reduction.

Now use the links that remain in the condensed network's reduction to define the reduced links in the original network.

Shortest Path Modifications

Shortest path algorithms are extremely useful and have many obvious and non-obvious uses including data packet routing, financial transaction planning, network flow calculations, robust infrastructure design, social network analysis, movement planning for artificial intelligence applications, and many more. These days, almost everyone with a smartphone has used these algorithms directly to locate nearby restaurants or to find the fastest route to a friend's house.

Because these algorithms are so important, people have come up with a variety of modifications to their basic designs. The following sections summarize a few possible modifications.

Shape Points

Many networks include two kinds of links: those that represent the network's structure and those that represent its shape. For example, the links in a street network in Manhattan may be short, straight segments, but in parts of San Francisco, the streets curve around considerably. Even if a section of road has no intersections, that doesn't mean it's straight.

For example, Figure 13.21 shows two straight vertical roads and two mostly horizontal curvy roads that follow a river (shown in gray). To draw the curved roads, you would need many points spaced closely together, but the network's topology only depends on the connections among the street sections. In the figure, the large dots show the connections that matter to a shortest path algorithm, and the small dots record the shape of the curvy street sections.

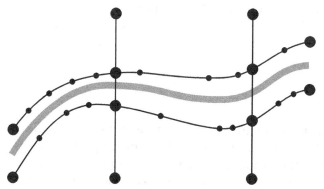

Figure 13.21: Curved streets require many points that don't really matter to the network's connectivity.

To make calculating shortest paths easier, you can build a network that includes only the connections (large dot). For example, each of the curved pieces of road shown in Figure 13.21 would be represented by a single link. An additional ShapePoints list on each link would give the details (small dots) needed to draw the link.

Early Stopping

Label-correcting algorithms are often faster than label-setting algorithms because they don't need to pick the best link to add to the shortest path tree. However, if you know that the destination is relatively close to the starting point, then you may be better off using a label-setting algorithm and then stopping when you reach the destination node.

For example, suppose you want to find a path from your current location in Boston to a restaurant that's about a mile away. A full street network for Boston includes tens of thousands of links, but your path will need to use only a few hundred. In that case, you can use a label-setting algorithm and then stop when you have labeled your destination.

Bidirectional Search

Many shortest path algorithms build a shortest path tree starting at one node and branching out to every other node. Sadly, much of that tree isn't near the shortest path between the start and destination nodes, so a lot of that work is wasted. If the start and destination nodes are close together, then the early stopping strategy described in the preceding section may help. However, if the start and destination nodes are far apart, that method won't help and will probably slow overall performance.

Instead of working outward from a single root node, another approach is to start building shortest path trees from both the start and destination nodes. The searches expand outward from the two nodes in roughly circular patterns until they intersect. At that point, you can find the shortest path through the two trees to connect the two nodes.

Best-First Search

The basic label-correcting, shortest path algorithm adds links to the shortest path tree randomly. Sometimes, you may be able to improve performance if you can quickly pick the best link to add to the tree. For example, you might be able to use the link's direction or the location of the link's end point to get an indication of how well that link will move toward the destination. For example, if the destination node is west of the start node, then you might prefer to use links that point more or less to the west.

In some cases, you might even be able to precalculate link rankings that you can later use to decide which link might be most promising. For example, in a street network, highways tend to be faster than surface streets, so you might give them a higher ranking. Then when the program builds a shortest path tree, it would quickly explore highway links to create paths close to the destination node.

Even then, some prioritized links may be more useful than others. For example, if you're trying to find a path from Los Angeles to Chicago, you probably don't need to explore highway links in Florida.

Turn Penalties and Prohibitions

In many networks, travel is modified by turn penalties. For example, in a street network, left turns generally take longer than right turns, and going straight is usually fastest of all. Left turns are also more dangerous than other maneuvers. UPS even prohibits them (mostly) because they take longer, use extra fuel while the vehicle waits for a chance to turn, and cause more accidents. Giant fleets like those used by UPS, FedEx, and the United States Postal Service drive billions of miles per year, so even a small savings can add up quickly.

Occasionally, a street network will also include turn or direction prohibitions. For example, an intersection may not allow a left turn. Or a turn might be impossible because it would send you down a one-way street in the wrong direction. Sometimes, going straight may even be prohibited if the street is switching from two-way to one-way traffic.

Simple, undirected street networks make it hard for shortest path algorithms to handle turn penalties and prohibitions. For example, if several links meet at an intersection, there's nothing in a simple network to tell the algorithm that it is not allowed to make a particular turn.

The following sections describe some different approaches to handling these situations.

Geometric Calculations

One way to handle turn penalties is to use the network's geometry to add them when you add a new link to the shortest path tree. When the algorithm considers a particular link, it calculates the angle between that link and the one that comes before it in the shortest path tree. For example, it might add a 30-second penalty for right turns greater than 30 degrees and a 60-second penalty for left turns greater than 30 degrees.

This approach has a couple of drawbacks. First, it assumes that all turn penalties can be deduced from the network's geometry. For example, it might assume that a 90-degree left turn deserves a big turn penalty even though the main thoroughfare goes that way, so it should have only a small penalty. This method also cannot handle prohibited turns such as those blocked by a center divider.

A second problem with this method is that this adds a lot of calculations to an otherwise very fast loop, and that will slow performance considerably.

You can work around the second problem (and to an extent the first) by adding a lookup table to each node. When the algorithm wants to use a link out of a node, it uses that table to find the penalty associated with turning from the incoming link to the outgoing link. That table would be large, however, and using it would be relatively slow.

Expanded Node Networks

Another way to model turn penalties is to think of a turn as a separate step while moving through the network. For example, suppose that you want to move from node A to node B, turn left, and arrive at node C. Nodes A, B, and C are already part of the network. What you need to do is to add a new node to represent turning from the A-B link onto the B-C link.

More generally, you can expand a node (in this example, node B) to include subnodes to represent each of the ways that a driver could enter the intersection. You then connect those subnodes with links representing the various turns.

Figure 13.22 shows a simple network on the left. The picture in the middle shows node B expanded to handle turn penalties. The small gray links represent the turns, and their costs give the turn penalties. The extra thick gray link represents the left turn from node A via node B to node C.

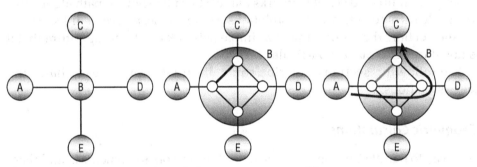

Figure 13.22: You can expand a node to represent turn penalties.

Note that the turn links include two straight links, one vertical and one horizontal, that represent no turn at the intersection. Also note that the links shown here should really be directed links. For example, the thick link represents a left turn from node A to node C, but there should also be a right turn link from node C to node A, and those two links would probably not have the same penalty cost.

This method almost works, but it's not quite restrictive enough to prevent the shortest path algorithm from cheating. The thick path on the right in Figure 13.22 shows how the algorithm can turn left from node A to node C without paying the left turn penalty. The path moves straight through the intersection toward node D, makes a quick about-face, and then follows the link that represents a right turn from node D to node C.

Alternatively, the algorithm could turn right from node A toward node E, make a quick U-turn, and then move straight through the intersection to node C.

To prevent those kinds of shenanigans, you can divide each of the subnodes into two parts: one to represent moving into the original node and one to represent moving out of it. Figure 13.23 shows part of the new structure. Here node B's inbound subnodes are white, and its outbound subnodes are shaded.

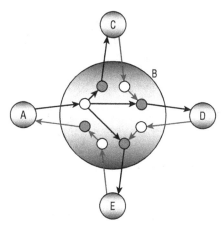

Figure 13.23: Now the algorithm cannot take a shortcut through an intersection and then make a quick about-face.

Figure 13.23 shows only some of the expanded node's links. The paths leading out from node A are dark, and others are gray. There should also be links between every inbound subnode and every outbound subnode that doesn't create a U-turn. For example, there should be links from node D's inbound subnode to the outbound subnodes leading to nodes A and C.

With this new design, if the algorithm tries to move from node A straight through the intersection, then it cannot turn around until it reaches node D.

Interchange Networks

The expanded node technique described in the preceding section allows you to handle turns at a single node. If you want to apply that technique to an entire network, the result will be much larger than the original network.

Another approach is to turn the network inside out so that nodes represent links and links represent turns. This kind of network has many names including *interchange network, line network, covering network, edge/vertex dual, edge graph,* and several others.

Figure 13.24 shows how to convert a network into its interchange network. The picture on the left shows the original network. The first step is to create a new node to represent each of the original network's links, as shown in the middle of the image. To make it easier to see which new nodes represent which original links, I have named the new nodes after the corresponding link end points. For example, the new node A-B represents the old link that connected nodes A and B.

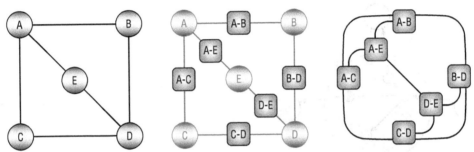

Figure 13.24: You can use an interchange network to represent a network's turn penalties.

The next step is to connect two new nodes if their corresponding original links share a common node in the original network. You can also see that connection in the new nodes' names. For example, new nodes A-B and B-D both have B in their names because their corresponding links in the original network share node B. That means the new nodes should be connected with a link in the interchange network.

That new link represents a turn in the original network starting at node A, moving to node B, and then turning to node D. You could name that link A-B-D to make the turn more obvious.

The picture on the right in Figure 13.24 shows the completed interchange network. The A-B-D link is the one in the upper-right corner of the final network.

Now instead of finding a shortest path tree in the original network, you can find one in the interchange network. When you visit a node, you add that node's cost, which corresponds to a link's cost in the original network. When you cross a link, you add that link's cost, which represents a turn penalty in the original network.

Summary

Many of the algorithms described in this chapter are traversals of networks. The depth-first and breadth-first traversal algorithms visit a network's nodes in different orders. The connectivity, spanning tree, minimal spanning tree, and shortest path algorithms also all traverse the network in various ways. For example, the minimal spanning tree algorithm traverses links in order of their costs, and the label-setting shortest path algorithm traverses links in order of the distances between each node and the root.

The next chapter continues the discussion of networks. It explains more-advanced algorithms that let you solve real-world problems such as task ordering, map coloring, and work assignment.

Exercises

You can find the answers to these exercises in Appendix B. Asterisks indicate particularly difficult problems.

1. *Build a program similar to the one shown in Figure 13.25 that lets you construct, save, and load test networks. The first few tools on the toolbar should let the user add nodes, one-way links, and two-way links (or two links connecting the clicked nodes in both directions). Give the File menu the commands New, Open, and Save As to let the user create, load, and save networks. (If you're using C# or Python and don't want to build the whole program, you can download the example program from this book's website and replace the algorithmic code that it contains with your own code.)

2. Expand the program you wrote for the preceding exercise to let the user perform either a depth-first or breadth-first traversal of the network. If the user selects a traversal tool and then clicks a node, display the appropriate traversal.

3. Expand the program you wrote for the preceding exercise to add a tool that displays the network's connected components.

4. Does the algorithm described for finding a network's connected components work for directed networks? Why or why not?

5. Expand the program you wrote for Exercise 3 to add a tool that finds and displays a spanning tree rooted at a node the user clicks.

6. Can you think of a simple feature of a network that would mean that all of its possible spanning trees are minimal?

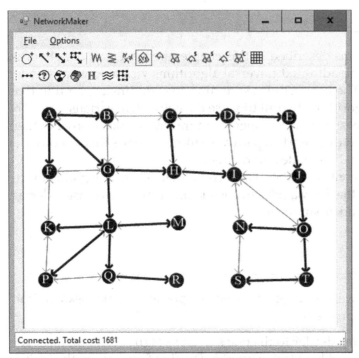

Figure 13.25: The sample program NetworkMaker lets you build, save, and load test networks.

7. Expand the program you wrote for Exercise 5 to add a tool that finds and displays a minimal spanning tree rooted at a node the user clicks.

8. Expand the program you wrote for the preceding exercise to add a tool that uses a spanning tree to find and display a path between two nodes the user selects.

9. Is a shortest path tree always a minimal spanning tree? If so, why? If not, draw a counterexample.

10. Expand the program you wrote for Exercise 8 to add a tool that finds and displays a label-setting shortest path tree rooted at a node the user clicks.

11. Expand the program you wrote for the preceding exercise to add a tool that uses a label-setting shortest path tree to find and display a path between two nodes the user selects.

12. Expand the program you wrote for the preceding exercise to add a tool that finds and displays a label-correcting shortest path tree rooted at a node the user clicks.

13. Expand the program you wrote for the preceding exercise to add a tool that uses a label-correcting shortest path tree to find and display a path between two nodes the user selects.

14. What happens to the label-correcting shortest path algorithm if the network contains a cycle that has a negative total weight? What happens to the label-setting algorithm?

15. Suppose that you want to find the shortest path from your location to a relatively close donut shop in a large street network. How could you make a label-setting algorithm find the path without building the entire shortest path tree? Would the change save time?

16. *For the scenario in the preceding exercise, how could you make a label-correcting algorithm find the path without building the entire shortest path tree? Would the change save time?

17. *Suppose that you're driving to a museum and frequent road construction makes you leave the shortest path. After each change, you need to calculate a new shortest path tree to find the best route from your new location to the museum. How could you avoid those recalculations?

18. *Expand the program you wrote for Exercise 13 to add a tool that finds and displays the Distance and Via arrays for a network. Verify the program on a network similar to the one shown in Figure 13.16.

19. *Expand the program you wrote for the preceding exercise so that the all-pairs shortest path tool uses text output to display the shortest paths between every pair of nodes in the network. Verify the program on a network similar to the one shown in Figure 13.16.

20. Assuming that your computer can execute 1 million steps per second while building the all-pairs shortest path algorithm's Distance and Via arrays, how long would it take to build the arrays for a network with 100 nodes? 1,000 nodes? 10,000 nodes?

21. Using the network shown in Figure 13.26, draw the Distance and Via arrays as they evolve the same way as Figure 13.16 does. What are the initial and final shortest paths from node A to node C?

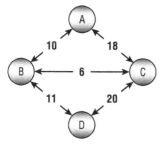

Figure 13.26: Draw the Distance and Via arrays for this network.

22. The section "Depth-First Traversal" in this chapter said that when executed on a network containing N nodes, a simple recursive traversal algorithm might reach a recursive depth of N. Can you think of networks structures for which that happens no matter which node you pick as a starting node?

23. The discussion on general transitive reductions converted a network into a condensation where condensed nodes represented the original network's strongly connected components. The discussion then mentioned that the resulting condensed network was acyclic. Why is that true?

24. In Figure 13.21, how many nodes and links would the network contain if it represented every dot separately? How many would it contain if it represents the connectivity and shape information separately?

25. How many links in total would be required to represent completely every turn in the expanded node shown in Figure 13.23? Draw the fully expanded node.

More Network Algorithms

Chapter 13 focused on network traversal algorithms, including algorithms that use breadth-first and depth-first traversals to find the shortest paths between nodes in the network. This chapter continues the discussion of network algorithms. The first algorithms, which perform topological sorting and cycle detection, are relatively simple. The algorithms described later in the chapter, such as graph coloring and maximal flow calculation, are a bit more challenging.

Topological Sorting

Suppose that you want to perform a complicated job that involves many tasks, some of which must be performed before others. For example, suppose you want to remodel your kitchen. Before you can get started, you may need to obtain permits from your local government. Then you need to order new appliances. Before you can install the appliances, however, you need to make any necessary changes to the kitchen's wiring. That may require demolishing the walls, changing the wiring, and then rebuilding the walls. A complex project such as remodeling an entire house or commercial building might involve hundreds of steps with a complicated set of dependencies.

Table 14.1 shows some of the dependencies that you might have while remodeling a kitchen.

Table 14.1: Kitchen Remodeling Task Dependencies

TASK	PREREQUISITE
Obtain permit	—
Buy appliances	—
Install appliances	Buy appliances
Demolition	Obtain permit
Wiring	Demolition
Drywall	Wiring
Plumbing	Demolition
Initial inspection	Wiring
Initial inspection	Plumbing
Drywall	Plumbing
Drywall	Initial inspection
Paint walls	Drywall
Paint ceiling	Drywall
Install flooring	Paint walls
Install flooring	Paint ceiling
Final inspection	Install flooring
Tile backsplash	Drywall
Install lights	Paint ceiling
Final inspection	Install lights
Install cabinets	Install flooring
Final inspection	Install cabinets
Install countertop	Install cabinets
Final inspection	Install countertop
Install flooring	Drywall
Install appliances	Install flooring
Final inspection	Install appliances

You can represent the job's tasks as a network in which a link points from task A to task B if task B must be performed before task A. Figure 14.1 shows a network that represents the tasks listed in Table 14.1.

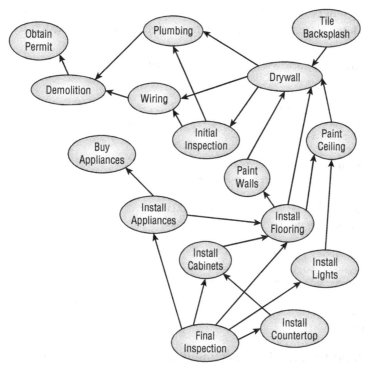

Figure 14.1: You can represent a series of partially-ordered tasks as a network.

A *partial ordering* is a set of dependencies that defines an ordering relationship for some but not necessarily all of the objects in a set. The dependencies listed in Table 14.1 and shown in Figure 14.1 define a partial ordering for the remodeling tasks.

If you actually want to perform the tasks, you need to extend the partial ordering to a complete ordering so that you can perform the tasks in a valid order. For example, the conditions listed in Table 14.1 don't explicitly prohibit you from installing the flooring before you do the plumbing work, but if you carefully study the table or the network, you'll see that you can't do those tasks in that order. The flooring must come after painting the walls, which must come after drywall, which must come after plumbing.

Topological sorting is the process of extending a partial ordering to a full ordering on a network.

One algorithm for extending a partial ordering is quite simple. If the tasks can be completed in any valid order, then there must be some task with no prerequisites that you can perform first. Find that task, add it to the extended ordering, and remove it from the network. Then repeat those steps, finding another task with no prerequisites, adding it to the extended ordering, and removing it from the network until all of the tasks have been completed.

If you reach a point where every remaining task has a prerequisite, then the tasks have a circular dependency so that the partial ordering cannot be extended to a full ordering.

The following pseudocode shows the basic algorithm:

```
// Return the nodes completely ordered.
List(Of Node) ExtendPartialOrdering()
    // Make the list of nodes in the complete ordering.
    List(Of Node): ordering

    While <the network contains nodes>
        // Find a node with no prerequisites.
        Node: ready_node
        ready_node = <a node with no prerequisites>
        If <ready_node == null> Then Return null

        // Move the node to the result list.
        <Add ready_node to the ordering list>
        <Remove ready_node from the network>
    End While
    Return ordering
End ExtendPartialOrdering
```

The basic idea behind the algorithm is straightforward. The trick is implementing the algorithm efficiently. If you just look through the network at each step to find a task with no prerequisites, you might perform O(N) steps each time, for a total run time of $O(N^2)$.

A better approach is to give each network node a new NumBeforeMe property that holds the number of the node's prerequisites. You start by initializing each node's NumBeforeMe value. Now when you remove a node from the network, you follow its links and decrement the NumBeforeMe property for the nodes that are dependent on the removed node. If a node's NumBeforeMe count becomes 0, it is ready to add to the extended ordering.

The following pseudocode shows the improved algorithm:

```
// Return the nodes completely ordered.
List(Of Node) ExtendPartialOrdering()
    // Make the list of nodes in the complete ordering.
    List(Of Node): ordering

    // Make a list of nodes with no prerequisites.
    List(Of Node): ready

    // Initialize.
    <Initialize each node's NumBeforeMe count>
    <Add nodes with no prerequisites to the ready list>

    While <the ready list contains nodes>
```

```
            // Add a node to the extended ordering.
            Node: ready_node = <First node in ready list>
            <Add ready_node to the ordering list>

            // Update NumBeforeMe counts.
            For Each link In ready_node.Links
                // Update this node's NumBeforeMe count.
                link.Nodes[1].NumBeforeMe = link.Nodes[1].NumBeforeMe - 1

                // See if the node is now ready for output.
                If (link.Nodes[1].NumBeforeMe == 0) Then
                    ready.Add(link.Nodes[1])
                End If
            Next link
        End While

        If (<Any node has NumBeforeMe > 0>) Then Return null
        Return ordering
    End ExtendPartialOrdering
```

This algorithm assumes that the network is completely connected. If it is not, use the algorithm repeatedly for each connected component.

Cycle Detection

Cycle detection is the process of determining whether a network contains a cycle. In other words, it is the process of determining whether there is a path through the network that returns to its beginning.

Cycle detection is easy if you think of the problem as one of topological sorting. A network contains a cycle if and only if it cannot be topologically sorted. In other words, if you think of the network as a topological sorting problem, then the network contains a cycle if a series of tasks A, B, C, . . . , K forms a dependency loop.

After you make that observation, detecting cycles is easy. The following pseudocode shows the algorithm:

```
// Return True if the network contains a cycle.
Boolean: ContainsCycle()
    // Try to topologically sort the network.
    If (ExtendPartialOrdering() == null) Then Return True
    Return False
End ContainsCycle
```

This algorithm assumes that the network is completely connected. If it is not, use the algorithm repeatedly for each connected component.

Map Coloring

In *map coloring*, the goal is to color the regions in a map so that no regions that share an edge have the same color. Obviously, you can do this if you give every region a different color. The real question is, "What is the smallest number of colors that you can use to color a particular map?" A related question is, "What is the smallest number of colors that you can use to color *any* map?"

To study map coloring with network algorithms, you need to convert the problem from one of coloring regions into one of coloring nodes. Simply create a node for each region, and make an undirected link between two nodes if their corresponding regions share a border.

Depending on the map, you may be able to color it with two, three, or four colors. The following sections describe these maps and algorithms that you can use to color them.

Two-Coloring

Some maps, such as the one shown in Figure 14.2, can be colored with only two colors.

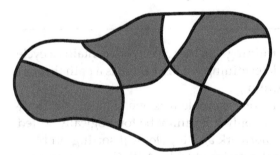

Figure 14.2: Some maps can be colored with only two colors.

> **NOTE** Generating a two-colorable map is easy. Place a pencil on a piece of paper, and draw a shape that returns to your starting point. You can draw any shape as long the curve doesn't follow along an earlier part of itself to make a "doubled edge." In other words, the curve can cross itself at a point but cannot merge with itself for some distance. Figure 14.3 shows such a shape.

> **NOTE** No matter how you make the curve cross itself, the result is two-colorable. If you then draw another shape over the first one in the same way, the result is still two-colorable.

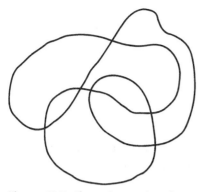

Figure 14.3: If you draw a closed curve without lifting the pencil and without making any "doubled edges," the result is two-colorable.

Coloring this kind of map is easy. Pick any region and give it one of the two colors. Then give each of its neighbors the other color, and recursively visit them to color their neighbors. If you ever come to a point where a node's neighbor already has the same color as the node, the map cannot be two-colored.

The following pseudocode shows this algorithm:

```
TwoColor()
    // Make a queue of nodes that have been colored.
    Queue(Of Node): colored

    // Color the first node, and add it to the list.
    Node: first_node = <Any node>
    first_node.Color = color1
    colored.Enqueue(first_node)

    // Traverse the network, coloring the nodes.
    While (colored contains nodes)
        // Get the next node from the colored list.
        Node: node = colored.Dequeue()

        // Calculate the node's neighbor color.
        Color: neighbor_color = color1
        If (node.Color == color1) Then neighbor_color = color2

        // Color the node's neighbors.
        For Each link In node.Links
            Node: neighbor = link.Nodes[1]

            // See if the neighbor is already colored.
            If (neighbor.Color == node.Color) Then
                <The map cannot be two-colored>
            Else If (neighbor.Color == neighbor_color) Then
                // The neighbor has already been colored correctly.
                // Do nothing else.
```

```
        Else
            // The neighbor has not been colored. Color it now.
            neighbor.Color = neighbor_color
            colored.Enqueue(neighbor)
        End If
    Next link
  End While
End TwoColor
```

This algorithm assumes that the network is completely connected. If it is not, use the algorithm repeatedly for each connected component.

Three-Coloring

It turns out that determining whether a map is three-colorable is a difficult problem. In fact, no known algorithm can solve this problem in polynomial time.

One fairly obvious approach is to try each of the three colors for the nodes and see whether any combination works. If the network holds N nodes, then this takes $O(3^N)$ time, which is quite slow if N is large. You can use a tree traversal algorithm, such as one of the decision tree algorithms described in Chapter 12, to try combinations, but this still will be a very slow search.

You may be able to improve the search by simplifying the network. If a node has fewer than three neighbors, then those neighbors can use at most two of the available colors, so the original node can use one of the unused colors. In that case, you can remove the node with fewer than three neighbors from the network, color the smaller network, and then restore the removed node, giving it a color that isn't used by a neighbor.

Removing a node from the network reduces the number of neighbors for the remaining nodes, so you might be able to remove even more nodes. If you're lucky, the network will shrink until you're left with a single node. You can color that node and then add the other nodes back into the network, one at a time, coloring each in turn.

The following steps describe an algorithm that uses this approach:

1. Repeat while the network has a node with degree less than 3:

    a. Remove a node with degree less than 3, keeping track of where the node was so that you can restore it later.

2. Use a network traversal algorithm to find a three-coloring for whatever network remains. If there is no solution for the smaller network, then there is no solution for the original network.

3. Restore the nodes removed earlier in last-removed, first-restored order, and color them using colors that are not already used by their neighbors.

If the network is not completely connected, you can use the algorithm for each of its connected components.

Four-Coloring

The *four-coloring theorem* states that any map can be colored with at most four colors. This theorem was first proposed by Francis Guthrie in 1852 and was studied extensively for 124 years before Kenneth Appel and Wolfgang Haken finally proved it in 1976. Unfortunately, their proof exhaustively examined a set of 1,936 specially selected maps, so it doesn't offer a good method of finding a four-coloring of a map.

> **NOTE**   The four-coloring theorem assumes that the network is *planar*, which means that you can draw it on a plane with none of the links intersecting. The links need not be straight lines, so they can wiggle and twist all over the place, but they cannot cross.
>
> If a network is not planar, then there's no guarantee that you can four-color it. For example, you could make 10 nodes with 90 links connecting every pair of nodes. Because every node is connected to every other node, you would need 10 colors to color that network.
>
> If you make a network from a normal map, however, you get a planar network.

You can use techniques similar to those described in the previous section for three-coloring.

1. Repeat while the network has a node with degree less than 4:
   a. Remove a node with degree less than 4, keeping track of where the node was so that you can restore it later.
2. Use a network traversal algorithm to find a four-coloring for whatever network remains. If there is no solution for the smaller network, then there is no solution for the original network.
3. Restore the nodes removed earlier in last-removed, first-restored order, and color them using colors that are not already used by their neighbors.

Again, if the network is not completely connected, you can use the algorithm for each of its connected components.

Five-Coloring

Even though there is no simple constructive algorithm for four-coloring a map, there is an algorithm for five-coloring a map, even if it isn't very simple.

Like the algorithms described in the two previous sections, this algorithm repeatedly simplifies the network. Unlike the two previous algorithms, this one can always simplify the network until it eventually contains only a single node. You can then undo the simplifications to rebuild the original network, coloring the nodes as you go.

This algorithm uses two types of simplification. The first is similar to the one used by the two previous algorithms. If the network contains a node that has fewer than five neighbors, remove it from the network. When you restore the node, give it a color that is not used by one of its neighbors. Let's call this Rule 1.

You use the second simplification if the network doesn't contain any node with fewer than five neighbors. It can be shown (although it's outside the scope of this book) that such a network must have at least one node K with neighbors M and N such that:

- K has exactly five neighbors.
- M and N have at most seven neighbors.
- M and N are not neighbors of each other.

To simplify the network, find such nodes K, N, and M, and require that nodes M and N have the same color. We know that they aren't neighbors, so that is allowed. Because node K has exactly five neighbors and nodes M and N use the same color, K's neighbors cannot be using all five of the available colors. This means that at least one color is left over for node K.

The simplification is to remove nodes K, M, and N from the network and create a new node M/N to represent the color that nodes M and N will have. Give the new node the same neighbors that nodes M and N had previously. Let's call this Rule 2.

When you restore the nodes K, M, and N that were removed using Rule 2, give nodes M and N whatever color was assigned to node M/N. Then pick a color that isn't used by one of its neighbors for node K.

You can use techniques similar to those described in the previous section for three-coloring. The following steps describe the algorithm:

1. Repeat while the network has more than one node:
   a. If there is a node with degree less than 5, then remove it from the network, keeping track of where it was so that you can restore it later.
   b. If the network contains no node of degree less than 5, then find a node K with degree exactly 5 and two children M and N, as described earlier. Replace nodes K, M, and N with new node M/N, as described in Rule 2.

2. When the network contains a single node, assign it a color.

3. Restore the previously removed nodes, coloring them appropriately.

If the network is not completely connected, then you can use the algorithm for each of its connected components.

Figure 14.4 shows a small sample network being simplified. If you look closely at the network on the left, you'll see that every node has five neighbors, so you can't use Rule 1 to simplify the network.

You can't use Rule 1 on this network, but you *can* use Rule 2. There are several possible choices for nodes to play the roles of nodes K, M, and N in Rule 2. This

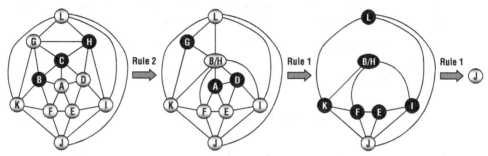

Figure 14.4: You can simplify this network to a single node with one use of Rule 2 and several uses of Rule 1.

example uses the nodes C, B, and H, which are drawn in bold in the network on the left. Those nodes are removed, and a new node B/H is added with the same children that nodes B and H had before. The second network in Figure 14.4 shows the revised network.

After nodes C, B, and H have been replaced with the new node B/H, nodes G, A, and D have fewer than five neighbors, so they are removed. Those nodes are highlighted in bold in the second network in Figure 14.4. For this example, assume that the nodes are removed in the order G, A, D. The third network in Figure 14.4 shows the result.

After those nodes have been removed, nodes L, B/H, K, F, E, and I all have fewer than five neighbors, so they are removed next. Those nodes are highlighted in the third network in Figure 14.4.

At this point, the network contains only the single node J, so the algorithm arbitrarily assigns node J a color and begins reassembling the network.

Suppose that the algorithm gives nodes the colors red, green, blue, yellow, and orange in that order. For example, if a node's neighbors are red, green, and orange, then the algorithm gives the node the first unused color—in this case, blue.

Starting at the final network shown in Figure 14.4, the algorithm follows these steps:

1. The algorithm makes node J red.

2. The algorithm restores the node that was removed last, node I. Node I's neighbor J is red, so the algorithm makes node I green.

3. The algorithm restores the node that was removed next-to-last, node E. Node E's neighbors J and I are red and green, so the algorithm makes node E blue.

4. The algorithm restores node F. Node F's neighbors J and E are red and blue, so the algorithm makes node F green.

5. The algorithm restores node K. Node K's neighbors J and F are red and green, so the algorithm makes node K blue.

6. The algorithm restores node B/H. Node B/H's neighbors K, F, and I are blue, green, and green, so the algorithm makes node B/H red.

7. The algorithm restores node L. Node L's neighbors K, B/H, and I are blue, red, and green, so the algorithm makes node L yellow. (At this point, the network looks like the bottom network in Figure 14.4, but with the nodes colored.)

8. The algorithm restores node D. Node D's neighbors B/H, E, and I are red, blue, and green, so the algorithm makes node D yellow.

9. The algorithm restores node A. Node A's neighbors B/H, F, E, and D are red, green, blue, and yellow, so the algorithm makes node A orange.

10. The algorithm restores node G. Node G's neighbors L, B/H, and K are yellow, red, and blue, so the algorithm makes node G green. (At this point the network looks like the middle network in Figure 14.4, but with the nodes colored.)

11. Now the algorithm undoes the Rule 2 step. It restores nodes B and H and gives them the same color as node B/H, which is red. Finally, it restores node C. Its neighbors G, H, D, A, and B have colors green, red, yellow, orange, and red, so the algorithm makes node C blue.

At this point, the network looks like the original network on the left in Figure 14.4 but colored as shown in Figure 14.5. (The figure uses shades of gray because this book isn't printed in color.)

Other Map-Coloring Algorithms

These are not the only possible map-coloring algorithms. For example, a hill-climbing strategy might loop through the network's nodes and give each one the first color that is not already used by one of its neighbors. This may not always color the network with the fewest possible colors, but it is extremely simple and very fast. It also works if the network is not planar and it might be impossible

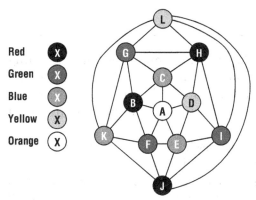

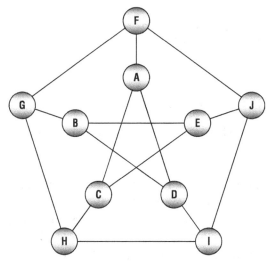

Figure 14.5: This network is five-colored.

Figure 14.6: This network is not planar, but it can be three-colored.

to four-color the network. For example, this algorithm can color the non-planar network shown in Figure 14.6.

With some effort, you could apply some of the other heuristic techniques described in Chapter 12 to try to find the smallest number of colors needed to color a particular planar or nonplanar network. For example, you could try random assignments or incremental improvement strategies in which you switch the colors of two or more nodes. You might even be able to create some interesting swarm intelligence algorithms for map coloring.

Maximal Flow

In a *capacitated network*, each of the links has a maximum capacity indicating the maximum amount of some sort of flow that can cross it. The capacity might indicate the number of gallons per minute that can flow through a pipe, the number of cars that can move through a street per hour, or the maximum amount of current a wire can carry.

In the *maximal flow problem*, the goal is to assign flows to the links to maximize the total flow from a designated source node to a designated sink node.

For example, consider the networks shown in Figure 14.7. The numbers on a link show the link's flow and capacity. For example, the link between nodes B and C in the left network has a flow of 1 and a capacity of 2.

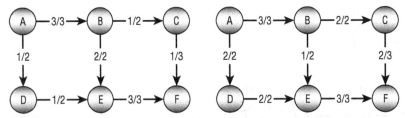

Figure 14.7: In the maximal flow problem, the goal is to maximize the flow from a source node to a sink node.

The network on the left has a total flow of 4 from node A to node F. The total amount of flow leaving the source node A in the network on the left is 1 unit along the A → D link plus 3 units along the A → B link for a total of 4. Similarly, the total flow into the sink node F is 3 units along the E → F link plus 1 unit along the C → F link for a total of 4 units. (If no flow is gained or lost in the network, then the total flow out of the sink node is the same as the total flow into the sink node.)

You cannot increase the total flow by simply adding more flow to some of the links. In this example, you can't add more flow to the A → B link because that link is already used at full capacity. You also can't add more flow to the A → D link because the E → F link is already used at full capacity, so the extra flow wouldn't have anywhere to go.

You can improve the solution, however, by removing 1 unit of flow from the path B → E → F and moving it to the path B → C → F. That gives the E → F link unused capacity so you can add a new unit of flow along the path A → D → E → F. The network on the right in Figure 14.7 shows the new flows, giving a total flow of 5 from node A to node F.

The algorithm for finding maximal flows is fairly simple, at least at a high level, but figuring out how it works can be hard. To understand the algorithm, it helps to know a bit about residual capacities, residual capacity networks, and augmenting paths.

If that sounds intimidating, don't worry. These concepts are useful for understanding the algorithm, but you don't need to build many new networks to calculate maximal flows. Residual capacities, residual capacity networks, and augmenting paths can all be found within the original network without too much extra work.

A link's *residual capacity* is the amount of extra flow you could add to the link. For example, the $C \rightarrow F$ link on the left in Figure 14.7 has a residual capacity of 2 because the link has a capacity of 3 and is currently carrying a flow of only 1.

In addition to the network's normal links, each link defines a *virtual backlink* that may not actually be part of the network. For example, in Figure 14.7, the A $\rightarrow$ B link implicitly defines a backward B $\rightarrow$ A backlink. These backlinks are important because they can have residual capacities, and you may be able to push flow backward across them.

A backlink's residual capacity is the amount of flow traveling forward across the corresponding normal link. For example, on the left in Figure 14.7, the B $\rightarrow$ E link has a flow of 2, so the E $\rightarrow$ B backlink has a residual capacity of 2. (To improve the solution on the left, the algorithm must push flow back across the E $\rightarrow$ B backlink to free up more capacity on the E $\rightarrow$ F link. That's how the algorithm uses the backlinks' residual capacities.)

A residual capacity network is a network consisting of links and backlinks marked with their residual capacities. Figure 14.8 shows the residual capacity network for the network on the left in Figure 14.7. Backlinks are drawn with dashed lines.

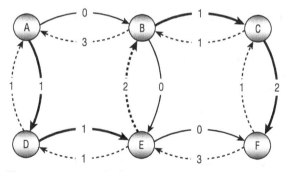

Figure 14.8: A residual capacity network shows the residual capacity of a network's links and backlinks.

For example, the $C \rightarrow F$ link on the left in Figure 14.7 has a capacity of 3 and a flow of 1. Its residual capacity is 2 because you could add two more units of flow to it. Its backlink's residual capacity is 1 because you could remove one unit of flow from the link. In Figure 14.8, you can see that the C → F link is marked with its residual capacity 2. The F → C backlink is marked with its residual capacity 1.

To improve a solution, all you need to do is to find a path through the residual capacity network from the source node to the sink node that uses links and backlinks with positive residual capacities. Then you push additional flow along that path. Adding flow to a normal link in the path represents adding more flow to that link in the original network. Adding flow to a backlink in the path represents removing flow from the corresponding normal link in the original network. Because the path reaches the sink node, it increases the total flow to that node. Because the path improves the solution, it is called an *augmenting path*.

The bold links in Figure 14.8 show an augmenting path through the residual capacity network for the network shown on the left in Figure 14.7.

To decide how much flow the path can carry, follow the path from the sink node back to the source node, and find the link or backlink with the smallest residual capacity. Now you can update the network's flows by moving that amount through the path. If you update the network on the left of Figure 14.7 by following the augmenting path in Figure 14.8, you get the network on the right in Figure 14.7.

This may seem complicated, but the algorithm isn't too confusing after you understand the terms. The following steps describe the algorithm, which is called the *Ford–Fulkerson algorithm*:

1. Repeat as long as you can find an augmenting path through the residual capacity network:

    a. Find an augmenting path from the source node to the sink node.

    b. Follow the augmenting path, and find the smallest residual capacity along it.

    c. Follow the augmenting path again, and update the links' flows to push the new flow along the augmenting path.

Remember that you don't actually need to build the residual capacity network. You can use the original network and calculate each link's and backlink's residual capacity by comparing its flow to its capacity.

> **NOTE** It may be handy to add a list of backlinks to each node so that you can easily find the links that lead into each node (so that you can follow them backward), but otherwise you don't need to change the network's structure.

Network flow algorithms have several applications other than calculating actual flows such as water or current flow. The next two sections describe two of those: performing work assignment and finding minimal flow cuts.

Work Assignment

Suppose that you have a workforce of 100 employees, each with a set of specialized skills, and you have a set of 100 jobs that can only be done by people with certain combinations of skills. The *work assignment problem* asks you to assign employees to jobs in a way that maximizes the number of jobs that are done.

At first this might seem like a complicated combinatorial problem. You could try all of the possible assignments of employees to jobs to see which one results in the most jobs being accomplished. There are $100! \approx 9.3 \times 10^{157}$ permutations of employees, so that could take a while. You might be able to apply some of the heuristics described in Chapter 12 to find approximate solutions, but there is a better way to solve this problem.

The maximal flow algorithm gives you an easy solution. Create a work assignment network with one node for each employee and one node for each job. Create a link from an employee to every job that the employee can do. Create a source node connected to every employee, and connect every job to a sink node. Give all of the links a capacity of 1.

Figure 14.9 shows a work assignment network with five employees represented by letters and five jobs represented by numbers. All of the links are directional, point to the right, and have a capacity of 1. The arrowheads and capacities are not shown to keep the picture simple.

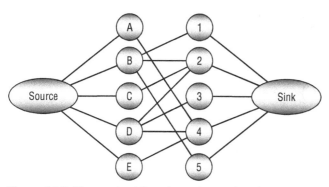

Figure 14.9: The maximal flow through a work assignment network gives optimal assignments.

Now find the maximal flow from the source node to the sink node. Each unit of flow moves through an employee to the job that should be assigned to that employee. The total flow gives the number of jobs that can be performed.

> **NOTE** In a *bipartite network*, the nodes can be divided into two groups, A and B, and every link connects a node in group A with a node in group B. If you remove the source and sink nodes in the network shown in Figure 14.9, the result is a bipartite network.

Bipartite matching is the process of matching the nodes in group A with those in group B. The method described in this section provides a nice solution to the bipartite matching problem.

Minimal Flow Cut

In the *minimal flow cut problem* (also called *min flow cut, minimum cut,* or *min-cut*), the goal is to remove links from a network to separate a source node from a sink node while minimizing the capacity of the links removed.

For example, consider the network shown in Figure 14.10. Try to find the best links to remove to separate source node A from sink node O. You could remove the A → B and A → E links, which have a combined capacity of 9. You can do better if you remove the K → O, N → O, and P → O links instead, because they have a total capacity of only 6. Take a minute to see how good a solution you can find.

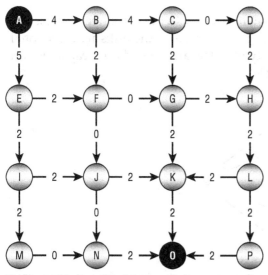

Figure 14.10: Try to find the best links to remove from this network to separate node A from node O.

Exhaustively removing all possible combinations of links would be a huge task for even a relatively small network. Each link is either removed or left in the network, so if the network contains N links, there would be 2^N possible combinations of removing and leaving links. The relatively small network shown in Figure 14.10 contains 24 links, so there are $2^{24} \approx 16.8$ million possible combinations to consider. In a network with 100 links, which is still fairly small for many applications, such as a modeling a street network, you would need to consider $2^{100} \approx 1.3 \times 10^{30}$ combinations. If your computer could consider 1 million combinations per second, it would take roughly 4.0×10^{16} years to consider them all. You could undoubtedly come up with some heuristics to make the search easier, but this would be a daunting approach.

Fortunately, the maximal flow algorithm provides a much easier solution. The following steps describe the algorithm at a high level:

1. Perform a maximal flow calculation between the source and sink nodes.

2. Starting from the sink node, visit all of the nodes that you can visit using only links and backlinks that have residual capacities greater than 0.

3. Place all of the nodes that you visited in step 2 in set A and place all of the other nodes in set B.

4. Remove the links that lead from nodes in set A to nodes in set B.

The algorithm is relatively simple. Unfortunately, the reasons why it works are fairly confusing.

First, consider a maximal set of flows, suppose the total maximum flow is F, and consider the cut produced by the algorithm. This cut must separate the source and sink nodes. If it didn't, then there would be a path from the source to the sink through which you could move more flow. In that case, there would be a corresponding augmenting path through the residual capacity network, so the maximal flow algorithm executed in step 1 would not have done its job correctly.

Notice that any cut that prevents flow from the source node to the sink node must have a net flow of F across its links. Flow might move back and forth across the cut, but in the end F units of flow reach the sink node, so the *net* flow across the cut is F.

This means that the links in the cut produced by the algorithm must have a total capacity of at least F. All that remains is to see why those links have a total capacity of only F. The net flow across the cut is F, but perhaps some of the flow moves back and forth across the cut, increasing the total flow of the cut's links.

Suppose this is the case, so a link L flows back from the nodes in set B to the nodes in set A and then later another link moves the flow back from set A to set B. The flow moving across the cut from set B to set A and back from set A to set B would cancel, and the net result would be 0.

If there is such a link L, however, it has positive flow from set B to set A. In that case, its backlink has a positive residual capacity. But in step 2, the algorithm followed all links and backlinks with positive residual capacity to create set A. Because link L ends at a node in set A and has positive residual capacity, the algorithm should have followed it, and the node at the other end should also have been in set A.

All of this means that there can be no link from set B to set A with positive flow.

Because the net flow across the cut is F and there can be no flow backward across the cut into the nodes in set A, the flow across the cut must be exactly F, and the total capacity removed by the cut is F.

(I warned you that this would be confusing. The technical explanation used by graph theorists is even more confusing.)

Now that you've had time to work on the problem shown in Figure 14.10, here's the solution. The optimal cut is to remove links E → I, F → J, F → G, C → G, and C → D, which have a total capacity of 4. Figure 14.11 shows the network with those links removed.

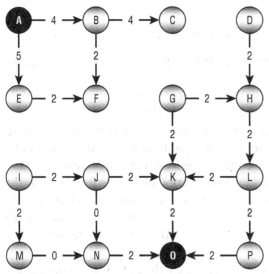

Figure 14.11: This network shows a solution to the min-flow-cut problem for the network shown in Figure 14.10.

Note that the solution to the minimal flow cut problem may not be unique. For example, the links M → N, J → N, K → O, and P → O also have a total cost of 4, and removing them from the network shown in Figure 14.10 also separates nodes A and O.

Network Cloning

Suppose that you want to make a clone of an existing network. A traversal algorithm, such as those described earlier in this chapter, lets you visit the nodes in the network. You could traverse the network and make copies of its nodes, but that wouldn't connect the copied nodes with links that mimic the links in the original network.

After you clone the network's nodes, you need to connect them with appropriate links. To clone a link, you need to find the two cloned nodes that correspond to the link's nodes in the original network.

The following sections explain two simple ways that you can find those nodes so that you can clone the link. Both of these methods assume that you have a list or array containing references to all of the original network's nodes. You can use a traversal to build that list if you don't already have one.

Dictionaries

One way to find the new nodes that correspond to a link's original nodes is to use a dictionary. When you clone a node, store the new node in the dictionary and use the original node as its key. Then you can use the original node later to look up the cloned version.

The following pseudocode shows how you can use this approach to clone a network:

```
// Clone a network.
Node[]: CloneNetwork(Node[]: nodes)
    // Make a dictionary to hold the new nodes.
    Dictionary<Node, Node>: nodeDict = New Dictionary<Node, Node>()

    // Clone the nodes.
    Node[]: newNodes = new Node[nodes.Length]
    For i = 0 To nodes.Length -1
        Node: oldNode = nodes[i]
        Node: newNode = <Clone of oldNode>
        newNodes[i] = newNode
        nodeDict.Add(oldNode, newNode)
    Next i

    // Clone the links.
    For i = 0 To nodes.Length - 1
        Node: oldNode = nodes[i]
        Node: newNode = newNodes[i]
        For Each link In oldNode.Links
            Node: newNeighbor = nodeDict[link.Neighbor]
            <Add link between newNode and newNeighbor>
        Next neighbor
    Next i

    return newNodes
End CloneNetwork
```

The algorithm first creates a dictionary that uses Node objects as both keys and data values. Next, it creates an array to hold the cloned nodes. It then loops through the existing nodes and places clones of them in the new array. It also places the cloned nodes in the dictionary using their original nodes as keys.

After it finishes cloning the nodes, the algorithm loops through the original nodes again and loops through each original node's links. For each link, it finds the node's neighbor at the other end of the link. It then uses the dictionary to find the neighbor's clone. Finally, it makes a new link between the node's clone and the neighbor's clone.

The exact details of how you clone a node depend on the way you are storing the network. When you clone the node, you need to copy any important details from the old node into the clone. For example, you might need to copy the node's name, location, colors, or other attributes.

Similarly, the way that you clone the link depends on how you store links. For example, if a node directly stores references to its neighboring nodes in a list, then you need to add references to the cloned neighbors to the cloned node's list. In contrast, if a node's links are stored in separate Link objects, then you need to make a new cloned Link object, copy any important properties such as cost or capacity into the clone, and set the clone's Node objects to the cloned node and the cloned neighbor.

Clone References

The trickiest part of network cloning is figuring out which cloned node belongs at the end of a cloned link. The algorithm described in the preceding section uses a dictionary to map original nodes to cloned nodes, but there are other options. For example, you could add a new ClonedNode field to the Node class. Then when you clone a node, you can save a reference to the clone inside the original node for later reference.

In fact, that approach is more efficient than using a dictionary because it stores only a single clone reference per node, and it allows you to find a node's clone immediately. In contrast, a dictionary requires a more complicated data structure such as linked lists or a hash table. Those data structures take up additional space and require extra steps to save and retrieve values.

The following pseudocode shows how you could modify the previous algorithm to use a ClonedNode field. The modified code is highlighted in bold.

```
// Clone a network.
Node[]: CloneNetwork(Node[]: nodes)
    // Clone the nodes.
    Node[]: newNodes = new Node[nodes.Length]
    For i = 0 To nodes.Length -1
        Node: oldNode = nodes[i]
        Node: newNode = <Clone of oldNode>
        newNodes[i] = newNode
        oldNode.ClonedNode = newNode
    Next i

    // Clone the links.
```

```
For i = 0 To nodes.Length - 1
    Node: oldNode = nodes[i]
    Node: newNode = newNodes[i]
    For Each link In oldNode.Links
        Node: newNeighbor = link.Neighbor.ClonedNode
        <Add link between newNode and newNeighbor>
    Next neighbor
Next i

return newNodes
End CloneNetwork
```

Instead of storing a cloned node in a dictionary, this version simply stores each node's clone in its `ClonedNode` field. Then it can easily find the node's clone when it needs it later.

An alternative to storing the clone in a node is to store the index of the clone in the `newNodes` array. Then you can use the index to retrieve the clone whenever you need it.

Cliques

A *clique* is a subset of nodes within an undirected graph that are all mutually connected. A *k-clique* is a clique that contains k nodes. A *maximal clique* is a clique that cannot be extended without ruining its clique-ness.

> **NOTE**   Clique is pronounced either "kleek" or "klick." In addition to its graph the-oretical definition, a clique is also a small group of people who do not readily allow others to join them. I don't know why, but I pronounce it "klick" when I'm talking about people and "kleek" when I'm talking about graphs.

Figure 14.12 shows a small network with two maximal cliques circled in dashed lines. One clique includes the nodes { A, B, D }, and the other includes nodes { B, C, D, E }. Both are maximal cliques because they are as large as possible while still being cliques.

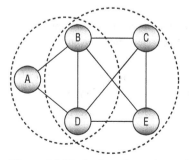

Figure 14.12: A clique is a subset of mutually connected nodes.

There are many different types of clique problems including the following:

- Find a maximum clique (the largest clique in the graph).
- List all maximal cliques (cliques that cannot be enlarged).
- Find a maximum weight clique (with the largest total edge weight).
- Determine whether there is a clique of size K.

For example, { B, C, D, E } is the maximum clique in the graph shown in Figure 14.12 because there are no larger cliques. The clique { A, B, D } is maximal because you cannot add another node to it while keeping all of the nodes mutually connected.

Note that every node forms a single-node clique and any pair of nodes that are connected by a link form a two-node clique.

The following sections describe some algorithms that solve particular clique problems.

Brute Force

A brute-force approach is rarely the best way to attack a problem, but at least it is usually easy to understand. One way to find a clique containing K nodes would be to enumerate every possible selection of K nodes and then check them to see whether they form a clique. If the network contains N nodes, then the number of possible selections is given by the *binomial coefficient*, which is calculated by the following equation:

$$\# \text{Possible K} - \text{Cliques} = \binom{N}{K} = \frac{N!}{K!(N-K)!}$$

For example, if the network contains 10 nodes, then the number of ways that you can select four nodes is the following:

$$\binom{10}{4} = \frac{10!}{4!(10-4)!} = \frac{3,628,800}{24 \times 710} = 210$$

This means you need to check up to 210 selections of four nodes to find four-node cliques.

> **NOTE** In C#, you need to write code to generate the selections. In Python, you can use the `itertools.combinations` method to generate the selections easily.

To see whether a clique is maximal, you can loop through the network's remaining nodes and see whether the selection is still a clique if you add each node to it. If the selection is still a clique after you add one of the remaining nodes, then it is not maximal.

To list all of a network's cliques, you can loop through all of the combinations that include 1 node, 2 nodes, 3 nodes, and so on, and see which combinations are cliques. (If you think that would be a lot of work, you're right!)

To list all of a network's maximal cliques, you can list the cliques and then test each to see whether it is maximal. (The next section describes a better method to do this.)

To find a network's largest clique, simply try to find cliques of sizes 1, 2, 3, and so on, until you find a size for which there is no clique. If a clique contains K nodes, then any subset of K − 1 of those nodes is also a clique. That means if there is no clique containing M nodes, then there is no clique containing more than M nodes either.

All of these methods work and are relatively straightforward, but they are also quite inefficient. The next section describes a better algorithm for performing one of those tasks: finding all of a network's maximal cliques.

Bron–Kerbosch

The *Bron–Kerbosch algorithm* was described by Dutch computer scientists Coenraad Bron and Joep Kerbosch in 1973. It's a recursive backtracking algorithm with a relatively simple idea.

At the very highest level, the algorithm starts with a clique and then tries to grow it by adding other nodes to it. When the clique cannot grow any larger, it is maximal, so the algorithm reports it.

If the algorithm adds a node to the clique that breaks the clique property, the algorithm backtracks to the point before that node was added.

The clever part of the algorithm is the bookkeeping that it uses to expand the cliques efficiently. The details are a bit tricky, so I'll describe them in several sections.

Sets R, P, and X

The algorithm keeps track of the network's nodes in three sets called R, P, and X.

Set R contains nodes that are in the current clique. Set P contains prospective nodes that we will try adding to the clique.

Set X contains nodes that are excluded from consideration because we have already tried using them and reported any maximal cliques that contain the nodes in R plus the nodes in X. In other words, if x is a node in X and there is a maximal clique containing R + x, then we have already reported it. (This is probably the most confusing part of the algorithm, so be sure you understand it.)

> **NOTE** I'm not sure why Bron and Kerbosch decided to name the sets R, P, and X. Perhaps they stand for something in Dutch. In English, we can suppose that R stands for "result," P stands for "possible," and X stands for "excluded."

An important feature of the three sets is that any node that is connected to all of the nodes in R is in one of the three sets. In particular, if node n is not currently in R and n is connected to every node in R, then it is either in P (so we will later try adding it to R) or it is in X (so we have already reported the cliques contain R and n).

Initially R is empty, so the initial clique contains no nodes. Note that you can think of an empty set (or a set that contains a single node) as a clique because it includes a path between every pair of nodes that it contains and there are no such pairs.

Set P begins holding every node in the network. In other words, every node is a candidate to add to the initially empty clique.

Set X begins empty because we haven't tried and discarded any nodes yet.

After the initialization, the algorithm checks sets P and R. If both P and R are empty, then there are no more nodes that we can add to the clique, so it is maximal.

If P is empty but X is not, then there are no more nodes that we can add to the clique. However, because X is not empty, there are cliques that contain the nodes in R and nodes in X. Those cliques are bigger than R (and we have already reported them), so the current clique is not maximal.

Recursive Calls

Now that you understand the three sets R, P, and X, you need to learn how the algorithm calls itself recursively.

Suppose that you have built a clique R. The nodes in P are candidates for expanding the clique, so you loop through those nodes and try adding each to R.

When we add a new node n to R, we should update P so it includes only nodes that we might want to add to the new clique R + n. If node q is in P and it is not a neighbor of node n, then it cannot be used to enlarge the clique further, so we should remove it from P.

We should also update X so that it doesn't include any nodes that we won't consider adding to the clique. If node q is not a neighbor of node n, then it can no longer be in P because we removed node n's non-neighbors. In that case, we don't need to exclude node q by keeping it in set X, so we can remove it.

Pseudocode

The following pseudocode shows the Bron–Kerbosch algorithm:

```
List Of (Set Of Node): BronKerbosch(R, P, X)
    cliques = New Set()
    If (P is empty) And (X is empty) Then cliques.Add(R)
```

```
For Each n In P
    New_R = R + n
    New_P = P ∩ Neighbors(n)
    New_X = X ∩ Neighbors(n)
    cliques.AddRange(BronKerbosch(new_R, new_P, new_X))
    P = P - n
    X = X + n
Next node
return cliques
```

The algorithm returns a list of cliques, each of which is a set of nodes.

The method starts by creating an empty `cliques` list to hold any maximal cliques that it finds.

Next, if the sets `P` and `X` are both empty, the method adds `R` to the list of maximal cliques.

The algorithm then loops through the nodes n in `P` and tries adding them one at a time to `R`. To do that, it creates updated versions of the three sets. It adds the node n to `R` to extend the clique. Then also takes the intersection of sets `P` and `X` with the neighbors of node n.

NOTE The ∩ symbol represents the *set intersection operator*. If A and B are sets, then A ∩ B contains the items that are in both sets.

The code then calls the `BronKerbosch` method recursively, passing it the new sets.

After the recursive call returns, the code removes node n from `P` so that future recursive calls will not include it in the set `new _ P` and thus will not include it in future cliques that contain the nodes in `R`. It also adds node n to set `X` so that the algorithm will not report any more cliques that contain the nodes in `R` plus node n.

After the algorithm has processed all of the nodes in `P`, it returns the maximal cliques that it found.

Example

The Bron–Kerbosch algorithm is remarkably short, but it's also pretty confusing. To make it easier to understand, let's work through an example. Consider the network shown in Figure 14.13.

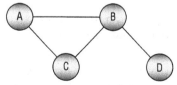

Figure 14.13: You can use the Bron–Kerbosch algorithm to find this network's maximal cliques.

The example is somewhat long even though the network is small, but you should be able to follow it if you work through it slowly and carefully.

The following pseudocode shows the first call to the algorithm:

```
BronKerbosch({ }, {A, B, C, D}, { })        // Level 1
```

The sets P and X are not both empty, so the algorithm loops through the nodes in P.

The order in which items are visited in a set are not clearly defined in most programming languages because a set implies membership but not an ordering. This means that the algorithm will not necessarily visit the nodes in any particular order. For this example, let's assume that the program first visits node A.

To update the sets, the algorithm adds node A to set R and removes the non-neighbors of node A from sets P and X. That means new _ R = {A}, new _ P = {B, C}, and new _ X = { }. The following pseudocode shows the second call to the algorithm:

```
BronKerbosch({A}, {B, C}, { })              // Level 2
```

Sets P and X are still not both empty, so the algorithm loops through the nodes in P. Let's suppose the algorithm tries node B first. It creates the sets new _ R = {A, B}, new _ P = {C}, and new _ X = { }. The algorithm then makes the following call:

```
BronKerbosch({A, B}, {C}, { })              // Level 3
```

Sets P and X are *still* not both empty, so the algorithm calls itself one more time, as shown in the following pseudocode:

```
BronKerbosch({A, B, C}, { }, { })           // Level 4
```

This time P and X are both empty, so R = {A, B, C} is a maximal clique. This call to the algorithm returns that clique and then moves one step back up the call stack to level 3, which was called by the following:

```
BronKerbosch({A, B}, {C}, { })              // Level 3
```

There are no more nodes in P to loop through, so this call returns to the level 2 call:

```
BronKerbosch({A}, {B, C}, { })              // Level 2
```

The recursive call just tried adding node B to the clique. When the recursive call returns, the level 2 call removes node B from P and adds it to X. Now P = {C} and X = {B}.

This is one of the more confusing parts of the example. Each time a recursive call returns, the calling method updates its sets P and X. However, that method is still looping through the nodes that were originally in its set P. For example, set P in the level 2 call original was {B, C}. After returning from the first recursive call, the code sets P = {C}, but it still needs to loop over the remaining node in the original set, which is node C.

In this case, that means the method tries adding node C to the clique. It creates the new sets new _ R = {A, C}, new _ P = { }, and new _ X = {B}. It then makes the following recursive call:

```
BronKerbosch({A, C}, { }, {B})            // Level 3
```

This time P is empty, but X is not. The set X contains node B indicating that we have already reported any maximal cliques that contain the nodes in R plus node B. We did report the set {A, B, C} earlier, so that is correct. This recursive call returns without doing anything interesting. It also returns the earlier level 2 call, so we arrive back at level 1, which we reached through the following call:

```
BronKerbosch({ }, {A, B, C, D}, { })     // Level 1
```

We just tried adding node A to the clique, so the algorithm updates P and X by moving node A from P and to X. Now P = {B, C, D} and X = {A}.

The algorithm then tries adding node B to the clique. To do that, it adds node B to R to get new _ R = {B}. It also removes the non-neighbors of node B from P and X to get new _ P = {C, D} and new _ X = {A}. It then makes the following recursive call:

```
BronKerbosch({B}, {C, D}, {A})            // Level 2
```

Suppose that this call visits node C first. In that case, it adds C to R and removes non-neighbors of C from P and X. That means new _ R = {B, C}, new _ P = { }, and new _ X = {A}. It then makes the following call:

```
BronKerbosch({B, C}, { }, {A})            // Level 3
```

This time P is empty, but X contains node A, indicating that we have already reported any maximal cliques that contain nodes {B, C} plus node {A}. The algorithm again returns without doing anything interesting.

The level 2 call moves node C from P to X and then visits node D. It adds D to R and removes non-neighbors of D from P and X to get the new sets new _ P = { } and new _ X = { }. It then makes the following call:

```
BronKerbosch({B, D}, { }, { })            // Level 3
```

Because sets P and X are both empty, the algorithm reports {B, D} as another maximal clique and returns. (You may not have realized that {B, D} was a maximal clique when you first saw Figure 12.14, but it is.)

The level 2 call has finished visiting the nodes in its original set P (which were C and D), so it returns to the next higher level, which we reached from this call:

```
BronKerbosch({ }, {A, B, C, D}, { })     // Level 1
```

We just tried adding node B to set R, so the algorithm updates P and X by moving B from P to X. Now R = { }, P = {C, D}, and X = {A, B}.

The method must now call itself with the next node in its original set P, which is node C. To do that, it adds node C to set R and removes the non-neighbors of node C from P and X to give new _ R = {C}, new _ P = { }, and new _ X = {A, B}. It then makes the following call:

```
BronKerbosch({C}, { }, {A, B})            // Level 2
```

Set P is empty, but set X is not, so the method returns without doing anything interesting, and we return again to level 1:

```
BronKerbosch({ }, {A, B, C, D}, { })      // Level 1
```

We just tried adding node C to the clique. The algorithm updates its sets by moving C from set P and to set X, so P = {D} and X = {A, B, C}.

The method must now call itself with the next node in its original set P, which is node D. To do that, it adds node D to set R and removes the non-neighbors of node D from P and X to give P = { } and X = {B}. It then makes the following call:

```
BronKerbosch({D}, { }, {B})               // Level 2
```

Again, set P is empty but set X is not, so the method returns without doing anything, and we return once more to the following call:

```
BronKerbosch({ }, {A, B, C, D}, { })      // Level 1
```

We have finished looping over the nodes in the original set P, so this call returns the cliques that it has found and we are done.

The final results include the two maximal cliques {A, B, C} and {B, D}.

Variations

The Bron–Kerbosch algorithm is a big improvement over a brute-force search, but it can still give poor performance for networks that contain many non-maximal cliques. The algorithm calls itself recursively for every clique, so if the network contains many non-maximal cliques, it wastes a lot of time.

There are a couple of modified versions of the algorithm that reduce the number of nodes that must be considered in the set P. You can find descriptions of those variations on the Internet. For example, look at the following URLs:

Wikipedia: https://en.wikipedia.org/wiki/Bron%E2%80%93Kerbosch _ algorithm

University of Glasgow: http://www.dcs.gla.ac.uk/~pat/jchoco/clique/ enumeration/report.pdf

Inria Sophia Antipolis: ftp://ftp-sop.inria.fr/geometrica/fcazals/papers/ ncliques.pdf

Finding Triangles

The previous few sections explained ways to find different kinds of cliques. One particularly simple but interesting type of clique is a triangle. The following sections describe three methods for finding a network's triangles.

Brute Force

An obvious way to find a network's triangles is to use a brute-force approach. Simply enumerate all of the possible triples of nodes and see whether they form a triangle.

One disadvantage to this method is that it considers triples of nodes that might have no chance of forming a triangle. For example, consider a street network. The brute-force approach would check whether nodes at the extreme left, right, and top edges of the network form a triangle, even though that's obviously impossible. This method will spend a lot of time checking triples of nodes that could not possibly form a triangle in any network that has relatively few links compared to the number of nodes.

Checking Local Links

One way to avoid examining triples of nodes that are far apart is to look more locally at each node's neighborhood. Starting at a selected node, you can follow its links to its neighbors. You can then see which neighbors are connected to each other. (You already know that they are connected to the original node because they are its neighbors.)

Even that approach could be confusing as you examine all of the possible pairs of neighbors. A handy way to keep track of the possible pairs is to loop through the neighbors and mark them. Next, loop through each of the neighbors' neighbors. If you find a node that is marked, then you know that the marked node is reachable from one of the other neighbors, so it makes a triangle.

For a more specific example, suppose nodes A, B, and C form a triangle. First, you mark A's neighbors, which includes nodes B and C. Next, you loop through node B's neighbors. When you do that, you will find node C and notice that it already marked. That means the original node, A; the neighbor B; and its neighbor C form a triangle.

All of this leads to the following algorithm for finding a network's triangles:

```
For Each node In AllNodes:
    // Mark the neighbors.
    For Each neighbor In node.Neighbors
        neighbor.Marked = True
    Next neighbor

    // Search for triangles.
    For Each nbr In node.Neighbors:
        // Search for the third node in the triangle.
        For Each nbr_nbr In nbr.Neighbors:
            If nbr.Marked Then <{node, nbr, nbr_nbr} is a triangle.>
```

```
        Next nbr
    Next nbr

    // Unmark the neighbors.
    For Each neighbor In node.Neighbors
        neighbor.Marked = False
    Next neighbor
Next node
```

This algorithm works and doesn't waste time examining widely spaced triples, but it does have one other problem. When you loop through node A's neighbors, you will first find node B and then later you will find node C. This means that you will find, the triangle {A, B, C} and then later the same triangle {A C, B}.

Worse still, you will later use node B as the starting node, so you'll also find triangles {B, A, C} and {B, C, A}. Then when you use node C as a starting node, you'll find triangles {C, A, B} and {C, B, A}. In total, the algorithm finds each triangle six times with different node orderings.

One way to prevent that is to compare the nodes' names, indices, or some other unique feature and only report triangles where the three nodes have a certain ordering. For example, if you compare the nodes' names, you might only report triangles where A.Name < B.Name < C.Name. If each node's name is different, then only one of the six arrangements of items will satisfy the ordering, so the algorithm will generate each triangle only once.

Chiba and Nishizeki

The algorithm described in the preceding section is actually a simplified version of an algorithm described in 1985 by Japanese computer scientists Norishige Chiba and Takao Nishizeki. Their algorithm first sorts the nodes by their degrees. It then examines the nodes in order, largest degree to smallest, and uses the preceding algorithm to find triangles.

When it examines node N, the algorithm works much as the previous one did. It marks N's neighbors and then searches the neighbors' neighbors to find triangles. After it has found all of the triangles that contain node N, it unmarks N's neighbors. It then removes N from the network. That prevents the algorithm from finding the same triangles that contain N again later. It also reduces the size of the network so N's neighbors will have fewer links to search when the algorithm encounters them again.

Of course, Chiba and Nishizeki's algorithm also destroys the network because it removes nodes from it. To avoid that, you might want to work on a copy of the network. Alternatively, you could mark links as removed instead of actually removing them.

Community Detection

Some networks have a noticeable community structure. For example, a social network may have clusters of people who know each other. *Community detection algorithms* try to find those clusters. The following sections describe a few algorithms that you can use to try to find communities in a network.

Maximal Cliques

One way to detect a network's communities is to find its maximal cliques. You already know how to use a brute-force approach or the Bron–Kerbosch algorithm to find maximal cliques, so you can already do this.

Note that communities may not always be cliques. For example, you might play softball with some friends, but you might not be friends on social media with all of them. In that case, the maximal clique that includes you and your softball friends would not include your whole team. In fact, if every team member is not friends with some other member, then this maximal clique might be fairly small even though adding a few more links would make it much larger.

One way to detect the larger community is to consider the members of the maximal clique and look at their neighbors that are not members. If one of those neighbors is a neighbor to most of the clique members, then you might want to add it to the community.

For example, consider the softball team again. Suppose Amanda is Facebook friends with 12 of the 15 players. In that case, she probably belongs to the community, so Facebook could recommend her as a friend to those who are in the clique.

Keep in mind that maximal cliques may overlap. That's good because a node might be a member of more than one community. For example, you might be members of a softball team and a book club.

Girvan–Newman

Maximal cliques detect communities by looking for very tightly connected nodes. Another approach is to look for groups of nodes that are separated by relatively few critical links. If two groups of nodes are separated by only one or two links, then those groups might be communities.

The *Girvan–Newman algorithm* (named after physicists Michelle Girvan and Mark Newman who described it) takes that approach. It assigns each link an *edge betweenness* that indicates how important that link is to the network's structure. The algorithm sets a link's edge betweenness to be the number of shortest paths between all pairs of nodes in the network that pass through that link. The links with the highest edge betweenness are the ones that connect communities.

For a small example, consider the network shown in Figure 14.14. It contains two communities, each of which is a three-node clique. The communities are connected by the bold link.

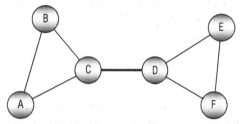

Figure 14.14: Links with high edge betweenness connect communities.

For this example, assume that all of the links have a cost of 1. Table 14.2 shows the shortest paths between each pair of nodes. Each pair is listed only once. For example, the path from node B to node E is the same as the path from node E to node B, so only the first is shown in the table.

Table 14.2: Shortest Paths

	A	B	C	D	E	F
A		A–B	A–C	A–C–D	A–C–D–E	A–C–D–F
B			B–C	B–C–D	B–C–D–E	B–C–D–F
C				C–D	C–D–E	C–D–F
D					D–E	D–F
E						E–F

To calculate a link's edge betweenness, add up the number of times that the link is used in the shortest paths shown in Table 14.2. Figure 14.15 shows the network with the links labeled to show edge betweenness.

Because each community is densely connected (even if it is not a clique), the paths within a community tend to be relatively short. They also tend to use the community's links fairly evenly, so a few links are used much more than others.

In contrast, links like the bold one shown in Figure 14.15 are part of *every* path that connects nodes that lie in two different communities, so they have a relatively high edge betweenness.

That observation leads to the Girvan–Newman algorithm, which is described at a high level in the following:

1. Repeat until the network has no edges:
   a. Calculate the edge betweenness for all links.
   b. Remove the link with the highest edge betweenness.

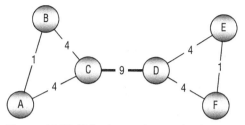

Figure 14.15: This picture shows edge betweenness.

The result is a dendrogram. A *dendogram* is a tree structure that shows hierarchical clustering. In this case, it shows how a network's nodes form communities. The highest nodes in the dendogram represent the largest structures. Branches break the structures into smaller communities. The dendogram's leaves represent the original network's nodes.

Clique Percolation

The *clique percolation method* (CPM) builds communities by combining adjacent cliques. It regards two k-cliques as adjacent if they share k – 1 nodes.

One way to generate a community is to begin with a k-clique, which I'll call the *seed clique*. Remove a node from the clique so that it holds k – 1 nodes. Then look for neighboring nodes that you could add to make a new k-clique. Add that node to the community and repeat the process with the new k-clique.

The result is a community where every member node is linked to many, but not necessarily all, of the other nodes in the community. If you expand the community many times, then some of the nodes added last may not be connected to many of the seed clique's nodes, but every node is connected to at least k – 1 other community members.

Eulerian Paths and Cycles

An *Eulerian path* is a path that visits every link in a network exactly once. An *Eulerian cycle* is an Eulerian path that starts and ends at the same node. A network that contains an Eulerian cycle is called an *Eulerian network*.

Swiss mathematician Leonhard Euler (pronounced "oiler") first discussed finding Eulerian paths and cycles while describing the famous "Seven Bridges of Königsberg" problem in 1736. (See https://en.wikipedia.org/wiki/Seven_Bridges_of_Konigsberg for a description of that problem.) Euler made the following two conclusions:

■ An Eulerian cycle is possible only if every node has an even degree.

- If every node in a connected network has an even degree, then an Eulerian cycle is possible.

Euler proved the first claim, but the second was only proven posthumously by Carl Hierholzer in 1873.

A third interesting property of networks is the following:

- A graph has an Eulerian path if and only if there are at most two vertices with odd degree.

The following sections describe some methods for finding Eulerian cycles.

Brute Force

As is the case with many problems, you can use a brute-force approach to find Eulerian paths. Enumerate all of the possible orderings of the network's nodes and see which ones produce an Eulerian cycle.

If the network contains N nodes, then there are N! possible orderings of its nodes, so this algorithm has O(N!) run time.

Fleury's Algorithm

Fleury's algorithm finds an Eulerian path or cycle.

If the network has two nodes of odd degree, start at one of those. If all of the nodes have even degree, start at any node.

At each step, move from the current node along a link that will not disconnect the network. (A link that would disconnect the network is called a *bridge link*.) If there is no link out of the current node that will not disconnect the network, then move along the node's remaining link. Remove links from the network as you cross them.

When the network has no more links, then the cycle or path is complete.

For an example, consider the network at the top of Figure 14.16. You might want to verify that at most two nodes have odd degree before you try to find an Eulerian cycle or path. In this example, nodes F and G have odd degree, so we start at one of them. I'll arbitrarily pick node G as our starting node.

The algorithm then moves along one of node G's links. The link from node G to node F is a bridge link because removing it from the network would disconnect the network. We must prefer nonbridge links, so we could go to node C or node H. I'll arbitrarily decide to move to node C.

We go from node G to node C and remove the G – C link. The second picture in Figure 14.16 shows the new network. I've replaced the removed link with a dashed arrow to make it easy to see the path that we followed.

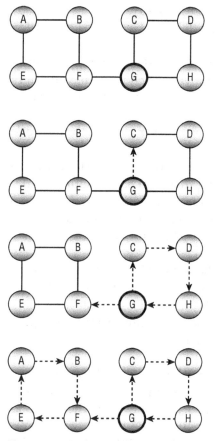

Figure 14.16: Fleury's algorithm follows links, preferring nonbridge links.

We have only one choice for the links to follow at the next few nodes. Following them we visit nodes D, H, G, and F. The third picture in Figure 14.16 shows the new situation.

At this point, we reach a node that has more than one remaining link. We could follow either the link to node E or the link to node B. This time, I'll arbitrarily pick the link to node E.

The remaining moves are predetermined because each node has only one remaining link after we enter it. The final picture in Figure 14.16 shows the complete Eulerian path.

Hierholzer's Algorithm

Fleury's algorithm is fairly straightforward and easy to understand if you're following its steps by hand. Unfortunately, it's relatively hard to detect bridge links. Any time you need to leave a node that currently has more than one link, you need to check for bridge links, so this algorithm is fairly slow. *Hierholzer's algorithm* provides a faster method for finding Eulerian cycles.

Start at any node V and follow links until you return to node V. If every node has even degree, then after you enter a node, it will have at least one link leading out so you cannot get stuck there.

The exception is the start node V. Because you started at that node, it has an odd number of unused links remaining. When you reach it again, you might take up its last link and become stuck. Because you cannot get stuck anywhere else, you must eventually return to node V.

When you return to node V, you may have crossed every link in the network. In that case, you're done.

If you haven't crossed every link, then look back along the loop that you just made from node V to node V. Some node along that loop has remaining links. Pick one of those nodes (call it W) and make another loop starting from that node. When you are finished, join the new loop to the old one at node W.

Repeat this process until the merged loops include all of the original network's links.

For an example, consider the network at the top of Figure 14.17. You might want to verify that all of the nodes have even degree before you try to find an Eulerian cycle in the network. I'll arbitrarily chose node E as our starting node.

We now follow links until we return to node E. For this example, suppose that we move from node E to node B and then back to node E, as shown in the second picture in the figure.

Because we have not visited every link yet, we look back at the nodes along the initial loop E – B – E and look for a node that has unused links. In this case, both E and B have unused links. I'll arbitrarily pick node B to begin the next loop.

Starting from node B, I'll arbitrarily take the link to node C. From then on, we have only one choice at each node, so we quickly build the loop B – C – F – E – D – A – B. The third picture in Figure 14.17 shows the old and new loops. The new loop is black, and the old loop is gray so that you can tell them apart.

The last step is to join loop E – B – E and loop B – C – F – E – D – A – B. We started the second loop at node B, so we break the first loop there and insert the second loop. The first loop becomes the two pieces E – B and B – E. Splicing in the second loop gives the full cycle E – **B – C – F – E – D – A – B** – E. Here I've highlighted the second loop in bold so that you can see where it fits into the first loop. The last picture in Figure 14.17 shows the final Eulerian cycle drawn as one long curve.

Summary

Some network algorithms model real-world situations in a fairly straightforward way. For example, a shortest path algorithm can help you find the quickest way to drive through a street network. Other network algorithms have less obvious uses. For example, not only does the maximal flow algorithm let you determine the greatest amount of flow that a network can carry, but it also lets you assign jobs to employees.

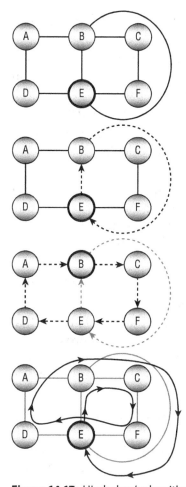

Figure 14.17: Hierholzer's algorithm merges loops.

The edit distance algorithm described in the next chapter also uses a network in a nonobvious way. It uses a network to decide how different one string is from another. For example, the algorithm can determine that the strings "peach" and "peace" are more similar than the strings "olive" and "pickle."

The next chapter discusses algorithms, such as the edit distance algorithm, which let you study and manipulate strings.

Exercises

You can find the answers to these exercises in Appendix B. Asterisks indicate particularly difficult problems. Two asterisks indicate extremely difficult or time-consuming problems.

1. Expand the network program you wrote for the exercises in Chapter 13 to implement the topological sorting algorithm.

2. In some applications, you may be able to perform more than one task at the same time. For example, in the kitchen remodeling scenario, an electrician and plumber might be able to do their jobs at the same time. How could you modify the topological sorting algorithm to allow this sort of parallelism?

3. If you know the predicted length of each task, how can you extend the algorithm you devised in the previous exercise to calculate the expected finish time for all of the tasks?

4. The topological sorting algorithm described in this chapter uses the fact that one of the tasks must have no prerequisites if the tasks can be fully ordered. In network terms, its out-degree is 0. Can you make a similar statement about nodes with an in-degree of 0? Does that affect the algorithm's run time?

5. Expand the program you used in Exercise 1 to two-color a network's nodes.

6. When using Rule 2 to simplify the network shown in Figure 14.4, the example uses the nodes C, B, and H. List all of the pairs of nodes that you could use if you used C for the middle node. In other words, if node C plays the role of node K in Rule 2 terminology, what nodes could you use for nodes M and N? How many different possible ways could you use those pairs to simplify the network?

7. *Expand the program you used in Exercise 5 to perform an exhaustive search to color a planar network using the fewest possible colors. (*Hint*: First use the two-coloring algorithm to determine quickly whether the network is two-colorable. If that fails, you only need to try to three-color and four-color it.)

8. Use the program you used in the previous exercise to find a four-coloring of the network shown in Figure 14.5.

9. Expand the program you used in Exercise 5 to implement the hill-climbing heuristic described in the section "Other Map-Coloring Algorithms." How many colors does it use to color the networks shown in Figure 14.5 and Figure 14.6?

10. For the network shown in Figure 14.18 with source node A and sink node I, draw the residual capacity network, find an augmenting path, and update the network to improve the flows. Can you make further improvements after that?

11. **Expand the program you used in Exercise 9 to find the maximal flow between a source and sink node in a capacitated network.

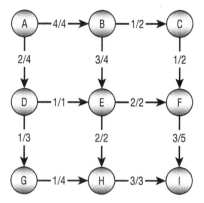

Figure 14.18: Use a residual capacity network to find an augmenting path for this network.

12. Use the program that you built for the previous exercise to find an optimal work assignment for the network shown in Figure 14.9. What is the largest number of jobs that can be assigned?

13. To determine how robust a computer network is, you could calculate the number of different paths between two nodes. How could you use a maximal flow network to find the number of paths that don't share any links between two nodes? How could you find the number of paths that don't share links or nodes?

14. How many colors do you need to color a bipartite network? How many colors do you need to color a work assignment network?

15. **Expand the program you built for Exercise 12 to find the minimal flow cut between a source and sink node in a capacitated network.

16. Use the program you built for the previous exercise to find a minimal flow cut for the network shown in Figure 14.18. What links are removed, and what is the cut's total capacity?

17. Can a network have maximal cliques of different sizes? What if the network is strongly connected?

18. Build a program that uses a brute-force approach to find a clique of a given size entered by the user.

19. *Build a program similar to the one shown in Figure 14.19 that uses the Bron–Kerbosch algorithm to find maximal cliques.

20. Build a program that checks local links to find a network's triangles.

21. Recall the method for building communities by expanding maximal cliques. For example, suppose that you have found a maximal clique containing 15 softball players. You consider the neighbors of those nodes and add those that are adjacent to many of the clique's nodes. For example,

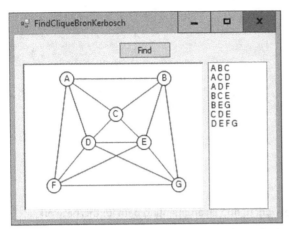

Figure 14.19: This program uses the Bron–Kerbosch algorithm to find maximal cliques.

if Amanda is a neighbor to 12 of the 15 softball player nodes, then she probably belongs in that community.

Now consider two adjacent communities. For example, suppose Amanda is also a member of a book club. Will growing the softball team and book club cliques make them merge into one community? Would that be good or bad?

22. Suppose that you use clique percolation to build communities. You start with a k-clique and expand it M times where M < k.

    a. How many nodes does that community contain?

    b. How far apart could two nodes be in the community?

    c. How close together could the farthest nodes be?

    d. If you expand the community k times, how far apart could two nodes be?

    e. If you expand the community k times, how close together could the farthest nodes be?

23. Explain intuitively why a network cannot have an Eulerian cycle unless all of its nodes have even degree.

24. Explain intuitively why a network cannot have an Eulerian path unless it has two or fewer nodes with odd degree.

25. Can a network have exactly one node with an odd degree?

26. Consider an M × N lattice of nodes where each node is connected by a link to its neighbors to the north, south, east, and west. What values for M and N will allow you to find an Eulerian cycle? What values will allow you to find an Eulerian path?

27. Write a program that uses Hierholzer's algorithm to find an Eulerian cycle in a network.

CHAPTER 15

String Algorithms

String operations are common in many programs, so they have been studied extensively, and many programming libraries have good string tools. Because these operations are so important, the tools available to you probably use the best algorithms available, so you are unlikely to beat them with your own code.

For example, the Boyer–Moore algorithm described in this chapter lets you find the first occurrence of a string within another string. Because this is such a common operation, most high-level programming languages have tools for doing this. (In C#, that tool is the `string` class's `IndexOf` method. In Python, it's a string variable's `find` method.)

Those tools probably use some variation of the Boyer–Moore algorithm, so your implementation is unlikely to be much better. In fact, many libraries are written in assembly language or at some other very low level, so they may give better performance even if you use the same algorithm in your code.

If your programming library includes tools to perform these tasks, use them. The algorithms explained in this chapter are presented because they are interesting, form an important part of a solid algorithmic education, and provide examples of useful techniques that you may be able to adapt for other purposes.

Matching Parentheses

Some string values, such as arithmetic expressions, can contain nested parentheses. For proper nesting of parentheses, you can place a pair of matching parentheses inside another pair of matching parentheses, but you cannot place one parenthesis of a pair inside another matched pair. For example, ()(()(())) is properly nested, but (() and (())) are not.

Graphically, you can tell that an expression's parentheses are properly nested if you can draw lines connecting left and right parentheses so that every parenthesis is connected to another, all of the lines are on the same side (top or bottom) of the expression, and no lines intersect. Figure 15.1 shows that ()(()(())) is properly nested, but (() and (())) are not.

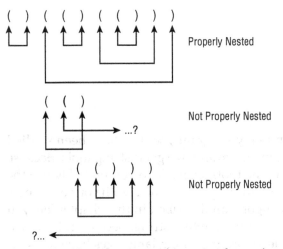

Figure 15.1: Lines connect matching pairs of parentheses.

Algorithmically, it is easy to see whether parentheses are properly matched by using a counter to keep track of the number of unmatched opening parentheses. Initialize the counter to 0, and loop through the expression. When you find an opening parenthesis, add 1 to the counter. When you find a closing parenthesis, subtract 1 from the counter. If the counter ever drops below 0, the parentheses are improperly nested. When you finish checking the expression, if the counter is not 0, the parentheses are improperly nested.

The following pseudocode shows the algorithm:

```
Boolean: IsProperlyNested(String: expression)
    Integer: counter = 0
    For Each ch In expression
        If (ch == '(') Then counter = counter + 1
        Else If (ch == ')') Then
```

```
        counter = counter - 1
        If (counter < 0) Then Return False
    End If
Next ch
If (counter == 0) Then Return True
Else Return False
IsProperlyNested
```

For example, when the algorithm scans the expression ()(()(())), the counter's values after reading each character are 1, 0, 1, 2, 1, 2, 3, 2, 1, 0. The counter never drops below 0, and it ends at 0, so the expression is nested properly.

Some expressions contain text other than parentheses. For example, the arithmetic expression $(8 \times 3) + (20 / (7 - 3))$ contains numbers, operators such as × and +, and parentheses. To see whether the parentheses are nested properly, you can use the previous `IsProperlyNested` algorithm, ignoring any characters that are not parentheses.

Evaluating Arithmetic Expressions

You can recursively define a fully parenthesized arithmetic expression as one of the following:

- A literal value such as 4 or 1.75

- An expression surrounded by parentheses (*expr*) for some expression *expr*

- Two expressions separated by an operator, as in *expr1* + *expr2* or *expr1* × *expr2*

For example, the expression 8×3 uses the third rule, with the two expressions 8 and 3 separated by the operator ×. The values 8 and 3 are both expressions according to the first rule.

You can use the recursive definition to create a recursive algorithm for evaluating arithmetic expressions. The following steps describe the algorithm at a high level:

1. If the expression is a literal value, use your programming language's tools to parse it and return the result. (In C#, use `double.Parse`. In Python, use the `float` function.)

2. If the expression is of the form (expr), then remove the outer parentheses, recursively use the algorithm to evaluate expr, and return the result.

3. If the expression is of the form expr1?expr2 for expressions expr1 and expr2 and operator ?, then recursively use the algorithm to evaluate expr1 and expr2, combine those values appropriately for the operator ?, and return the result.

The basic approach is straightforward. Probably the hardest part is determining which of the three cases applies and breaking the expression into two operands and an operator in case 3. You can do that by using a counter similar to the one used by the `IsProperlyNested` algorithm described in the preceding section.

When the counter is 0, if you find an operator, case 3 applies and the operands are on either side of the operator.

If you finish scanning the expression and you don't find an operator when the counter is 0, then either case 1 or case 2 applies. If the first character is an opening parenthesis, then case 2 applies. If the first character is not an opening parenthesis, then case 1 applies.

Building Parse Trees

The algorithm described in the preceding section parses arithmetic expressions and then evaluates them, but you might like to do other things with an expression after you parse it. For example, suppose that you need to evaluate an expression that contains variables such as X many times for different values of X, perhaps to draw a graph of the equation $(X \times X) - 7$. One approach would be to use the previous algorithm repeatedly to parse and evaluate the expression, substituting different values for X. Unfortunately, parsing text is relatively slow.

Another approach is to parse the expression but not evaluate it right away. Then you can evaluate the preparsed expression many times with different values for X without needing to parse the expression again. You can do this using an algorithm very similar to the one described in the preceding section. Instead of making the algorithm combine the results of recursive calls to itself, however, it builds a tree containing objects that represent the expression.

For example, to represent multiplication, the algorithm makes a node with two children, where the children represent the multiplication's operands. Similarly, to represent addition, the algorithm makes a node with two children, where the children represent the addition's operands.

You can build a class for each of the necessary node types. The classes should provide an `Evaluate` method that calculates and returns the node's value, calling the `Evaluate` method for its child nodes if it has any.

Having built the parse tree, you can call the root node's `Evaluate` method any number of times for different values of X.

Figure 15.2 shows the parse tree for the expression $(X \times X) - 7$.

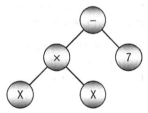

Figure 15.2: You can use parse trees to represent expressions such as $(X \times X) - 7$.

Pattern Matching

The algorithms described in the preceding sections are useful and effective, but they're tied to the particular application of parsing and evaluating arithmetic expressions. Parsing is a common task in computer programming, so it would be nice to have a more general approach that you could use to parse other kinds of text.

For example, a *regular expression* is a string that a program can use to represent a pattern for matching in another string. Programmers have defined several different regular expression languages. To keep this discussion reasonably simple, this section uses a language that defines the following symbols:

- An alphabetic character such as A or Q represents that letter.

- The + symbol represents concatenation. For the sake of readability, this symbol is often omitted, so ABC is the same as A + B + C. However, it may be convenient to require the symbol to make it easier for a program to parse the regular expression.

- The * symbol means that the previous expression can be repeated any number of times (including zero).

- The | symbol means that the text must match either the previous or the following expression.

- Parentheses determine the order of operation.

For example, with this restricted language, the regular expression AB * A matches strings that begin with an A, contain any number of Bs, and then end with an A. That pattern would match ABA, ABBBBA, and AA.

More generally, a program might want to find the first occurrence of a pattern within a string. For example, the string AABBA matches the previous pattern AB * A starting at the second letter.

To understand the algorithms described here for regular expression matching, it helps to understand deterministic finite automata and nondeterministic finite automata. The following two sections describe deterministic and nondeterministic finite automata. The section after that explains how you can use them to perform pattern matching with regular expressions.

DFAs

A *deterministic finite automaton* (DFA), also known as a *deterministic finite state machine*, is basically a virtual computer that uses a set of states to keep track of what it is doing. At each step, it reads some input and, based on that input and its current state, moves into a new state. One state is the *initial state* in which the machine starts. One or more states can also be marked as *accepting states*.

If the machine ends its computation in an accepting state, then the machine accepts the input. In terms of regular expression processing, if the machine ends in an accepting state, the input text matches the regular expression.

In some models, it's convenient for the machine to accept its input if it ever enters an accepting state.

You can represent a DFA with a *state transition diagram*, which is basically a network in which circles represent states and directed links represent transitions to new states. Each link is labeled with the inputs that make the machine move into the new state. If the machine encounters an input that has no corresponding link, then it halts in a nonaccepting state.

To summarize, there are three ways that a DFA can stop:

- *It can finish reading its inputs while in an accepting state.* In that case, it accepts the input. (The regular expression matches.)

- *It can finish reading its inputs while in a nonaccepting state.* In that case, it rejects the input. (The regular expression does not match.)

- *It can read an input that does not have a link leading out of the current state node.* In that case, it rejects the input. (The regular expression does not match.)

For example, Figure 15.3 shows a state transition diagram for a DFA that recognizes the pattern AB*A. The DFA starts in state 0. If it reads an A character, then it moves to state 1. If it sees any other character, then the machine halts in a nonaccepting state.

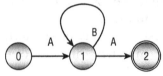

Figure 15.3: This network represents the state transitions for a DFA that recognizes the pattern AB*A.

Next, if the DFA is in state 1 and it reads a B, then it follows the loop and returns to state 1. If the DFA is in state 1 and reads an A, then it moves to state 2. If the DFA is in state 1 and reads any character other than A or B, then it halts in a nonaccepting state.

State 2 is marked with a double circle to indicate that it is an accepting state. Depending on how you are using the DFA, just entering this state might make the machine return a successful match. Alternatively, it might need to finish reading its input in that state, so if the input string contains more characters, the match fails.

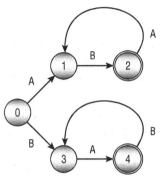

Figure 15.4: This network represents the state transitions for a DFA that recognizes the pattern $(AB)*|(BA)*$.

For another example, consider the state transition diagram shown in Figure 15.4. This diagram represents a machine that matches a string that consists of AB repeated any number of times or BA repeated any number of times.

Programmatically, you can implement a DFA by making an object to represent each of the states in the state transition diagram. When presented with an input, the program moves from the current object to the object that is appropriate for that input.

Table 15.1: A State Transitiotn Table for AB * A

STATE	0	1	1	2
On input	A	A	B	
New state	1	2	1	
Accepting?	No	No	No	Yes

Often, DFAs are implemented with a table showing the state transitions. For example, Table 15.1 shows the state transitions for the state transition diagram shown in Figure 15.3.

> **NOTE**   DFAs aren't useful only for processing regular expressions. You can use them to model the state of any system where it's convenient to specify the system's rules with a transition diagram or transition table.
>
> For example, an order processing system might track the state of the orders in the system. You could give the states intuitive names such as Placed, Fulfilled, Shipped, Billed, Canceled, Paid, and Returned. As events occur, the order's state would change accordingly. For example, if the order is in the Placed state and the customer decides to cancel the order, the order moves to the Canceled state and stops its progress through the system.

Building DFAs for Regular Expressions

You can translate simple regular expressions into transition diagrams and transition tables easily enough by using intuition, but for complicated regular expressions, it's nice to have a methodical approach. Then you can apply this approach to let a program do the work for you.

To convert a regular expression into a DFA state transition table, you can build a parse tree for the regular expression and then use it to generate recursively the corresponding state transitions.

The parse tree's leaves represent literal input characters such as A and B. The state transition diagram for reading a single input character is just a start state connected to an accepting final state with a link labeled by the required character. Figure 15.5 shows the simple state transition diagram for reading the input character B.

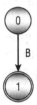

Figure 15.5: This transition diagram represents the simple regular expression B.

The parse tree's internal nodes represent the operators +, *, and |.

To implement the + operator, take the accepting state of the left subtree's transition diagram and make it coincide with the starting state of the right subtree's transition diagram, so the machine must perform the actions of the left subtree followed by the actions of the right subtree. For example, Figure 15.6 shows the transition diagrams for the simple literal patterns A and B on the left and the combined pattern A + B on the right.

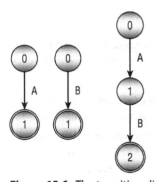

Figure 15.6: The transition diagram on the right represents the regular expression A + B.

To implement the ＊ operator, make the single subexpression's accepting state coincide with the subexpression's starting state. Figure 15.7 shows the transition diagram for the pattern A + B on the left and the pattern (A + B)＊ on the right.

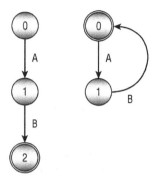

Figure 15.7: The transition diagram on the right represents the regular expression (A + B)＊.

Finally, to implement the | operator, make the starting and ending states of the left and right subexpressions' transition diagram coincide. Figure 15.8 shows the transition diagram for the patterns A + B and B + A on the left and the combined pattern (A + B)|(B + A) on the right.

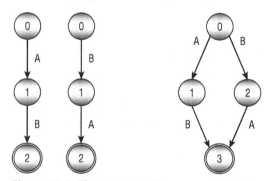

Figure 15.8: The transition diagram on the right represents the regular expression (A + B)|(B + A).

This approach works in this instance, but it has a serious drawback under some conditions. What happens to the | operator if the two subexpressions start with the same input transitions? For example, suppose the two subexpressions are A + A and A + B. In that case, blindly following the previous discussion leads to the transition diagram on the left in Figure 15.9. It has two links labeled A that leave state 0. If the DFA is in state 0 and encounters input character A, which link should it follow?

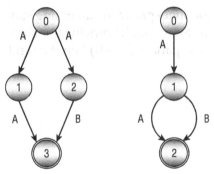

Figure 15.9: These transition diagrams represent the regular expression $(A + A)|(A + B)$.

One solution is to restructure the diagram a bit, as shown on the right in Figure 15.9, so that the diagrams for the two subexpressions share their first state (state 1). This works, but it requires some cleverness—something that can be hard to build into a program. If the subexpressions were more complicated, finding a similar solution might be difficult—at least for a program.

One solution to this problem is to use an NFA instead of a DFA.

NFAs

A deterministic finite automaton is called deterministic because its behavior is completely determined by its current state and the input that it sees. If a DFA using the transition diagram on the right side of Figure 15.8 is in state 0 and reads the character B, it moves into state 2 without question.

A *nondeterministic finite automaton* (NFA) is similar to a DFA, except that multiple links may be leaving a state for the same input, as shown on the left in Figure 15.9. When that situation occurs during processing, the NFA is allowed to guess which path it should follow to eventually reach an accepting state. It's as if the NFA were being controlled by a fortune-teller who knows what inputs will come later and can decide which links to follow to reach an accepting state.

Of course, in practice a computer cannot really guess which state it should move into to eventually find an accepting state. What it *can* do is to try all of the possible paths. To do that, a program can keep a list of states it might be in. When it sees an input, the program updates each of those states, possibly creating a larger number of states.

Another way to think of this is to regard the NFA as simultaneously being in all of the states. If any of its current states is an accepting state, the NFA as a whole is in an accepting state.

You can make one more change to an NFA's transitions to make it slightly easier to implement. The operations shown in Figures 15.6 through 15.9 require that you make states from different subexpressions coincide—and that can be awkward.

An alternative is to introduce a new kind of *null transition* that occurs without any input. If the NFA encounters a null transition, it immediately follows it.

Figure 15.10 shows how you can combine state transition machines for subexpressions to produce more-complex expressions. Here the ø character indicates a null transition, and a box indicates a possibly complicated network of states representing a subexpression.

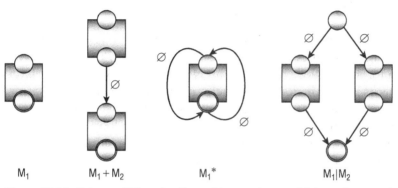

M_1 $M_1 + M_2$ M_1^* $M_1 | M_2$

Figure 15.10: Using an NFA and null transitions makes combining subexpressions more straightforward.

The first part of Figure 15.10 shows a set of states representing some subexpression. This could be as simple as a single transition that matches a single input, as shown in Figure 15.5, or it could be a complicated set of states and transitions. The only important feature of this construct from the point of view of the rest of the states is that it has a single input state and a single output state.

The second part of Figure 15.10 shows how you can combine two machines, M_1 and M_2, by using the + operator. The output state from M_1 is connected by a null transition to the input state of M_2. By using a null transition, you avoid the need to make M_1's output state and M_2's input state coincide.

The third part of Figure 15.10 shows how you can add the * operator to M_1. M_1's output state is connected to its input state by a null transition. The * operator allows whatever it follows to occur any number of times, including zero times, so another null transition allows the NFA to jump to the accept state without matching whatever is inside the M_1.

The final part of Figure 15.10 shows how you can combine two machines M_1 and M_2 by using the | operator. The resulting machine uses a new input state connected by null transitions to the input states of M_1 and M_2. The output states of M_1 and M_2 are connected by null transitions to a final output state for the new combined machine.

To summarize, you can follow these steps to make a regular expression parser:

1. Build a parse tree for the regular expression.
2. Use the parse tree to recursively build the states for an NFA representing the expression.
3. Start the NFA in state 0 and use it to process the input string one character at a time.

String Searching

The previous sections explained how you can use DFAs and NFAs to search for patterns in a string. Those methods are quite flexible, but they're also relatively slow. To search for a complicated pattern, an NFA might need to track a large number of states as it examines each character in an input string one at a time.

If you want to search a piece of text for a target substring instead of a pattern, there are faster approaches. The most obvious strategy is to loop over all of the characters in the text and see whether the target is at each position. The following pseudocode shows this brute-force approach:

```
// Return the position of the target in the text.
Integer: FindTarget(String: text, String: target)
    For i = 0 To <last index of string>
        // See if the target begins at position i.
        Boolean: found_it = True
        For j = 0 To <last index of target>
            If (string[i + j] != target[j]) Then found_it = False
        Next j

        // See if we found the target.
        If (found_it) Then Return i
    Next i
    // If we got here, the target isn't present.
    Return -1
End FindTarget
```

In this algorithm, variable i loops over the length of the text. For each value of i, the variable j loops over the length of the target. If the text has length N and the target has length M, the total run time is $O(N \times M)$. This is simpler than using an NFA, but it's still not very efficient.

The *Boyer–Moore algorithm* uses a different approach to search for target substrings much more quickly. Instead of looping through the target's characters from the beginning, it examines the target's characters starting at the end and works backward toward the beginning.

The easiest way to understand the algorithm is to imagine the target substring sitting below the text at a position where a match might occur. The algorithm compares characters starting at the target's leftmost character. If it finds a position where the target and text don't match, the algorithm slides the target to the right to the next position where a match might be possible.

For example, suppose you want to search the string A man a plan a canal Panama for the target string Roosevelt. Consider Figure 15.11.

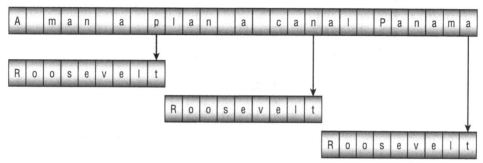

Figure 15.11: Searching A man a plan a canal Panama for Roosevelt requires only three comparisons.

The algorithm first aligns the two strings so that they line up on the left and compares the last character in the target to the corresponding character in the text. At that position, the target's last character is t, and the text's corresponding character is p. Those characters don't match, so the algorithm slides the target to the right to find the next position where a match is possible. The text's character p doesn't appear anywhere in the target, so the algorithm slides the target to the right all the way past its current location, nine characters to the right.

At the new position, the target's last character is t, and the text's corresponding character is n. Again, the characters don't match, so the algorithm slides the target to the right. Again, the text's character n doesn't appear in the target, so the algorithm slides the target nine characters to the right.

At the new position, the target's last character is t, and the text's corresponding character is a. The characters don't match, so the algorithm slides the target to the right. Again, the text's character a doesn't appear in the target, so the algorithm slides the target nine characters to the right.

At this point, the target extends beyond the end of the text, so a match isn't possible, and the algorithm concludes that the target is not present in the text. The brute-force algorithm described earlier would have required 37 comparisons to decide that the target wasn't present, but the Boyer–Moore algorithm required only three comparisons.

Things don't always work out this smoothly. For a more complicated example, suppose that you want to search the text `abba daba abadabracadabra` for the target `cadabra`. Consider Figure 15.12.

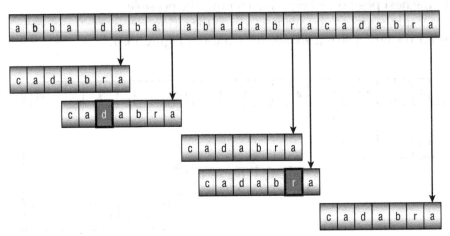

Figure 15.12: Searching `abba daba abadabracadabra` for `cadabra` requires 18 comparisons.

The algorithm starts with the two strings aligned at the left and compares the target character a with the text character a. Those characters match, so the algorithm considers the preceding characters, r and d. Those characters do not match, so the algorithm slides the target to the right. In this case, however, the text's character d *does* appear in the target, so there's a chance that the d is part of a match. The algorithm slides the target to the right until the last d in the target (shown with a dark box in Figure 15.12) aligns with the d in the text.

At the new position, the target's last character is a, and the text's corresponding character is a space. Those characters don't match, so the algorithm slides the target to the right. The target has no space, so the algorithm moves the target its full width of seven characters.

At the new position, the target's last character is a and the text's corresponding character is r. Those characters don't match, so the algorithm slides the target to the right. The character r *does* appear in the target, so the algorithm moves the target until its last r (dark) aligns with the r in the text.

At the new position, the target's last character is a, and the text's corresponding character is a. These characters match, so the algorithm compares the preceding characters to see whether they match. Those characters also match, so the algorithm continues comparing characters backward through the target and text. Six characters match. Not until the algorithm considers the target's first character does it find a mismatch. Here the target's character is c, and the text's corresponding character is b.

The target has a b, but it comes after the position in the target the algorithm is currently considering. To align this b with the one in the text, the algorithm would have to move the target to the left. All leftward positions have already been eliminated as possible locations for the match, so the algorithm doesn't do this. Instead, it shifts the target seven characters to the right to the next position where a match could occur.

At this new position, the target's characters all match the corresponding characters in the text, so the algorithm has found a match.

The following steps describe the basic Boyer–Moore algorithm at a high level:

1. Align the target and text on the left.

2. Repeat until the target's last character is aligned beyond the end of the text:

   a. Compare the characters in the target with the corresponding characters in the text, starting from the end of the target and moving backward toward the beginning.

   b. If all of the characters match, then congratulations—you've found a match!

   c. Suppose character x in the text doesn't match the corresponding character in the target. Slide the target to the right until the x aligns with the next character with the same value x in the target to the left of the current position. If no such character x exists to the left of the position in the target, slide the target to the right by its full length.

One of the more time-consuming pieces of this algorithm is step 2c, which calculates the amount by which the algorithm slides the target to the right. You can make this step faster if you precalculate the amounts for different mismatched characters in different positions within the target.

For example, suppose that the algorithm compares target and text characters, and the first mismatch is in position 3, where the text has the character G. The algorithm would then slide the text to the right to align the G with the first G that appears to the left of position 3 in the target. If you use a table to store the amounts by which you need to slide the target, then you can just look up that amount instead of calculating it during the search.

> **NOTE** Variations on the Boyer–Moore algorithm use other, more complicated rules for shifting the target string efficiently. For example, suppose that the algorithm considers the following alignment:
>
> ```
> ... what shall we draw today ...
>          abracadabra
> ```

The algorithm scans the target `abracadabra` backward. The first two characters, `a` and `r`, match. Then the text's `d` doesn't match the target's `b`. The previous algorithm would shift the target to align the text's mismatched `d` like this:

```
... what shall we draw today ...
          abracadabra
```

But you know that the text matched the following two characters, `ra`, so you know that the text's characters `dra` cannot match the target's characters `dab` at this point.

Instead of shifting to align the text's mismatched `d`, you can shift to align the entire suffix that has been matched so far—in this case, `ra`—to an earlier occurrence of those characters in the target. In other words, you can move the target to place an earlier occurrence of the characters `ra` where the matched suffix is right now, as in the following:

```
... what shall we draw today ...
              abracadabra
```

This lets the algorithm shift the target further so that it can make the search run faster.

For more information on variations on the Boyer–Moore algorithm, see `https://en.wikipedia.org/wiki/Boyer-Moore_string_search_algorithm`.

The Boyer–Moore algorithm has the unusual property that it tends to be faster if the target string is longer because, when it finds a nonmatching character, it can shift the target farther.

Calculating Edit Distance

The *edit distance* of two strings is the minimum number of changes that you need to make to turn the first string into the second. You can define the changes that you are allowed to make in several ways. For this discussion, assume that you are only allowed to remove or insert letters. (Another common change that isn't considered here is changing one letter into another letter. You can achieve the same result by deleting the first character and then inserting the second.)

For example, consider the words *encourage* and *entourage*. It's fairly easy to see that you can change *encourage* into *entourage* by removing the *c* and inserting a *t*. That's two changes, so the edit distance between those two words is 2.

For another example, consider the words *assent* and *descent*. One way to convert *assent* into *descent* would be to follow these steps:

1. Remove *a* to get *ssent*.

2. Remove *s* to get *sent*.

3. Remove *s* to get *ent*.

4. Add *d* to get *dent*.

5. Add *e* to get *deent*.

6. Add *s* to get *desent*.

7. Add *c* to get *descent*.

This requires seven steps, so the edit distance is no more than 7, but how can you tell if this is the most efficient way to convert *assent* to *descent*? For longer words or strings (or, as you'll see later in this section, for files), it can be hard to be sure that you have found the best solution.

One way to calculate the edit distance is to build an *edit graph* that represents all the possible changes that you could make to get from the first word to the second. Start by creating an array of nodes similar to the one shown in Figure 15.13.

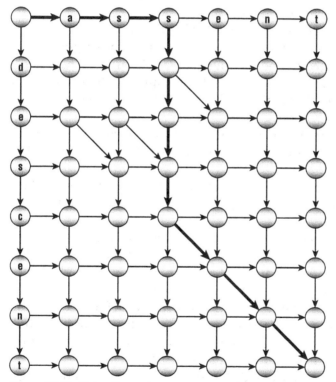

Figure 15.13: This edit graph represents possible ways to convert *assent* to *descent*.

The nodes across the top of the graph represent the letters in the first word. The nodes down the left side represent the letters in the second word. Create links between the nodes leading to their rightward and downward neighbors.

Add diagonal links ending at any locations where the corresponding letters in both words are the same. For example, *assent* has an *e* in the fourth position, and *descent* has an *e* in its second position, so a diagonal link leads to the node below the *e* in *assent* and to the right of the first *e* in *descent*.

Each link represents a transformation of the first word, making it more similar to the second word. A link pointing right represents removing a letter from the first word. For example, the link leading to the *a* on the top row represents removing the *a* from *assent*, which would make *ssent*.

A link pointing down represents adding a letter to the word. For example, the link pointing to the *d* in the first column represents adding the letter *d* to the current word, which would make *dassent*.

A diagonal link represents keeping a letter unchanged.

Any path through the graph from the upper-left corner to the lower-right corner corresponds to a series of changes to convert the first word into the second. For example, the bold arrows shown in Figure 15.13 represent the changes described earlier to convert *assent* into *descent*.

Now finding a path through the edit graph that has the least cost is fairly easy. Give each horizontal and vertical link a cost of 1, and give the diagonal links a cost of 0. Now you just need to find the shortest path through the network.

You can use the same techniques described in Chapter 13, "Basic Network Algorithms," to find the shortest path, but this network has a special structure that lets you use an easier method.

First, set the distances for the nodes in the top row to be their column numbers. To get to the node in column 5 from the upper-left corner, you need to cross five links, so its distance is 5.

Similarly, set the distances for the nodes in the leftmost column to be their row numbers. To get to the node in row 7, you need to cross seven links, so its distance is 7.

Now loop over the rows and, for each row, loop over its columns. The shortest path to the node at position (r, c) comes via the node above at $(r-1, c)$, the node to the left at $(r, c-1)$, or, if a diagonal move is allowed, the node diagonally up and to the left at $(r-1, c-1)$. The distances to all of those nodes have already been set. You can determine what the cost would be for each of those possibilities and set the distance for the node at (r, c) to be the smallest of those.

When you're finished looping through the rows and columns, the distance to the node in the lower-right corner gives the edit distance.

Once you know how to find the edit distance between two words or strings, it's easy to find the edit distance between two files. You could just use the algorithm as is to compare the files character by character. Unfortunately, that could require a very large edit graph. For example, if the two files have about 40,000 characters (this chapter is in that neighborhood), then the edit graph would have about $40,000 \times 40,000 = 1.6$ billion nodes Building that graph would require a lot of memory, and using it would take a long time.

Another approach is to modify the algorithm so that it compares lines in the files instead of characters. If the files each contain about 700 lines, the edit graph would hold about $700 \times 700 = 49,000$ nodes. That's still a lot, but it's much more reasonable.

Phonetic Algorithms

A *phonetic algorithm* is one that categorizes and manipulates words based on their pronunciation. For example, suppose you are a customer service representative and a customer tells you that his name is Smith. You need to look up that customer in your database, but you don't know if the name should be spelled, Smith, Smyth, Smithe, or Smythe.

If you enter any reasonable spelling (perhaps Smith), the computer can convert it into a phonetic form and then look for previously stored phonetic versions in the customer database. You can look through the results, ask a few questions to verify that you have the right person, and begin troubleshooting.

Unfortunately, deducing a word's pronunciation from its spelling it difficult, at least in English. That means these algorithms tend to be long and complicated.

The following sections describe two phonetic algorithms: Soundex and Metaphone.

Soundex

The *Soundex algorithm* was devised by Robert C. Russell and Margaret King Odell in the early 1900s to simplify the U.S. census. They first patented their algorithm in 1918, long before the first computers were created.

The following list shows my version of the Soundex rules. They're slightly different from the rules that you'll see online. I've reformulated them slightly to make them easier to implement.

1. Save the first letter of the name for later use.
2. Remove w and h after the first character.
3. Use Table 15.2 to convert the remaining characters into codes. If a character doesn't appear in the table (w or h), leave it unchanged.
4. If two or more adjacent codes are the same, keep only one of them.
5. Replace the first code with the original first letter.
6. Remove code 0 (vowels after the first letter).
7. Truncate or pad with 0s on the right so that the result has four characters.

Table 15.2: Soundex Letter Codes

LETTER	CODE
a, e, l, o, u, y	0
b, f, p, v	1
c, g, j, k, q, s, x, z	2
d, t	3
l	4
m, n	5
r	6

For example, let's walk through the steps for the name Ashcraft.

1. We save the first letter, *A*.

2. We remove *w* and *h* after the first letter to get Ascraft.

3. Using Table 15.2 to convert the remaining letters into codes gives 0226013.

4. Removing adjacent duplicates gives 026013.

5. Replacing the first code with the original first letter gives A26013.

6. Removing code 0 gives A2613.

7. Truncating to four characters gives the final code A261.

Over the years, there have been several variations on the original Soundex algorithm. Most SQL database systems use a slight variation that does not consider vowels when looking for adjacent codes. For example, in the name Alol, the two *L*s are separated by a vowel. Basic Soundex would convert them into the code, 4, and keep them both. SQL Soundex would remove the vowel, find the two adjacent 4s, and remove one of them.

Another relatively simple variation of the original algorithm uses the character codes shown in Table 15.3.

Table 15.3: Refined Soundex Letter Codes

LETTER	CODE
b, p	1
f, v	2
c, k, s	3
g, j	4
q, x, z	5
d, t	6
l	7
m, n	8
r	9

Still other examples include variations designed for use with non-English names and words. The *Daitch–Mokotoff Soundex* (D-M Soundex) was designed to represent Germanic and Slavic names better. Those kinds of variations tend to be much more complicated than the original Soundex algorithm.

Metaphone

In 1990, Lawrence Philips published a new phonetic algorithm named *Metaphone*. It uses a more complex set of rules to represent English pronunciation more accurately. The following list shows the Metaphone rules:

1. Drop duplicate adjacent letters, except for C.
2. If the word starts with KN, GN, PN, AE, WR, drop the first letter.
3. If the words ends with MB, drop the *B*.
4. Convert C:
   a. Convert C into K if part of SCH.
   b. Convert C into X if followed by IA or H.
   c. Convert C into S if followed by I, E, or Y.
   d. Convert all other Cs into K.
5. Convert D:
   a. Convert C into J if followed by GE, GY, or GI.
   b. Convert C into T otherwise.
6. Convert G:
   a. Drop the G if part of GH unless it is at the end of the word or it comes before a vowel.
   b. Drop the G in GN and GNED at the end of the word.
   c. Convert G into J if part of GI, GE, or GY and not in GG.
   d. Convert all other Gs into K.
7. If *H* comes after a vowel and not before a vowel, drop it.
8. Convert CK into K.
9. Convert PH into *F*.
10. Convert *Q* into K.
11. Convert *S* into *X* if followed by H, IO, or IA.
12. Convert *T*:
    a. Convert *T* into *X* if part of TIA or TIO.
    b. Convert TH into *0*.
    c. Drop the *T* in TCH.

13. Convert *V* into *F*.

14. Convert WH into *W* if at the beginning of the word. Otherwise, drop the *W*s if not followed by a vowel.

15. Convert *X*:

    a. Convert *X* into *S* if at the beginning of the word.

    b. Otherwise convert *X* into KS.

16. Drop *Y* if not followed by a vowel.

17. Convert *Z* into *S*.

18. Drop all remaining vowels after the first character.

Metaphone is an improvement over Soundex, but it also has several variations. For example, *Double Metaphone* is the second version of the original Metaphone algorithm. It is called *Double* Metaphone because it can generate primary and secondary codes for words to differentiate between words that have the same primary code.

Metaphone 3 further refines Metaphone's phonetic rules and provides better results with non-English words that are common in the United States and some common names. It is available as a commercial product. There are also versions that handle Spanish and German pronunciations.

For more information on phonetic algorithms, see the following URLs:

- `https://en.wikipedia.org/wiki/Phonetic_algorithm`

- `https://en.wikipedia.org/wiki/Soundex`

- `https://en.wikipedia.org/wiki/Metaphone`

- `http://ntz-develop.blogspot.com/2011/03/phonetic-algorithms.html`

Summary

Many programs need to examine and manipulate strings. Even though programming libraries include many string manipulation tools, it's worth knowing how some of those algorithms work. For example, using a regular expression tool is much easier than writing your own, but the technique of using DFAs and NFAs to process commands is useful in many other situations. The Boyer–Moore string search algorithm is a well-known algorithm that any student of algorithms should see at least once. Edit distance algorithms let you determine how close two words, strings, or even files are to each other and to find the differences between them. Finally, Soundex and other phonetic algorithms are useful for finding names or other words when you're unsure of their spelling.

One kind of string algorithm that isn't covered in this chapter is algorithms used for encryption and decryption. The next chapter describes some of the more important and interesting algorithms used to encrypt and decrypt strings and other data.

Exercises

You can find the answers to these exercises in Appendix B. Asterisks indicate particularly difficult problems. Problems with two asterisks are exceptionally hard or time-consuming.

1. Write a program that determines whether an expression entered by the user contains properly nested parentheses. Allow the expression to contain other characters as well, as in $(8 \times 3) + (20 \div (7 - 3))$.

2. Write a program that parses and evaluates arithmetic expressions that contain real numbers and the operators +, -, *, and /.

3. How would you modify the program you wrote for the preceding exercise to handle the unary negation operator, as in $-(2 / 7)$?

4. How would you modify the program you wrote for Exercise 2 to handle functions such as sine, as in $3 * \text{sine}(45)$?

5. Write a program that parses and evaluates Boolean expressions such as T&(-F | T), where T means True, F means False, & means AND, | means OR, and – means NOT.

6. **Write a program similar to the one shown in Figure 15.14. The program should build a parse tree for the expression entered by the user and then graph it. (Depending on how your program draws the graphics, the default coordinate system for the picture probably will have (0, 0) in the upper-left corner, and coordinates will increase to the right and down. The coordinate system may also use one unit in the X and Y directions per pixel, which means that the resulting graph will be fairly small. Unless you have experience with graphics programming, don't worry about scaling and transforming the result to fit the form nicely.)

7. Build a state transition table for the DFA state transition diagram shown in Figure 15.4.

8. Draw a state transition diagram for a DFA to match the regular expression ((AB)|(BA))*.

9. Build a state transition table for the state transition diagram you drew for the preceding exercise.

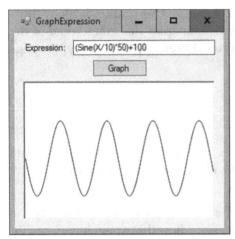

Figure 15.14: This program, GraphExpression, builds a parse tree for an expression and then evaluates it many times to graph the expression.

10. *Write a program that lets the user type a DFA's state transitions and an input string and determines whether the DFA accepts the input string.

11. Do you think it would be better for a DFA to get its state transitions from a table similar to the one shown in Table 15.1 or to use objects to represent the states? Why?

12. How can you make a set of states for an NFA to see whether a pattern occurs anywhere within a string? For example, how could you determine whether the pattern ABA occurred anywhere within a long string? Draw the state transition diagram using a block to represent the pattern's machine (as done in Figure 15.10).

13. Draw the parse tree for the expression $(AB*)|(BA*)$. Then draw the NFA network you get by applying the rules described in this chapter to the parse tree.

14. Convert the NFA state transition diagram you drew for the preceding exercise into a simple DFA state transition diagram.

15. Suppose that you want to search some text of length N for a target substring of length M. Find an example where a brute-force search requires $O(N \times M)$ steps.

16. Study the edit graph shown in Figure 15.13. What rule should you follow to find the least-cost path from the upper-left corner to the lower-right corner? What is the true edit distance?

17. *Write a program that calculates edit distance.

18. *Enhance the program you wrote for the preceding exercise to display the edits required to change one string into another. Display deleted characters as crossed out and inserted characters as underlined, as shown in Figure 15.15.

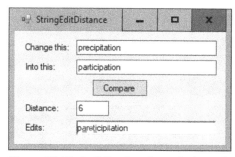

Figure 15.15: By following the path through the edit graph, you can show exactly what edits were needed to change one string into another.

19. Is edit distance commutative? In other words, is the edit distance between word 1 and word 2 the same as the edit distance between word 2 and word 1? Why or why not?

20. *Modify the program you wrote for Exercise 17 to calculate the edit distance between two files instead of the differences between two strings.

21. *Modify the program you wrote for Exercise 18 to display the differences between two files instead of the differences between two strings.

22. Write a program that calculates Soundex encodings. When the program starts, make it verify that the names Smith, Smyth, Smithe, and Smythe all encode to S530. Also make the program verify the encoded values shown in Table 15.4.

Table 15.4: Soundex Encodings for Example Names

NAME	SOUNDEX ENCODING
Robert	R163
Rupert	R163
Rubin	R150
Ashcraft	A261
Ashcroft	A261
Tymczak	T522
Pfister	P236
Honeyman	H555

Cryptography

Cryptography is the study of methods for secure communication in the presence of adversaries who want to intercept information. Early cryptography, which was simply writing, worked because only a few people could read. Later forms of cryptography used special alphabets known only to the message sender and recipient. One of the earliest known instances of this form of cryptography used nonstandard hieroglyphics carved on monuments in Egypt circa 1900 BCE.

Another form of cryptography used by the ancient Greeks and Spartans used a wooden rod called a scytale (rhymes with "Italy"). A strip of parchment was wrapped in a spiral around the rod, and words were written on it. When the parchment was unwrapped, the letters were out of order. To read the message, the recipient would wrap the parchment around a rod with the same diameter.

These forms of cryptography are sometimes called *security through obscurity*, because they rely on the fact that the adversary doesn't know the trick. If the adversary knows the secret alphabet or knows that the message was written on a scytale, it's easy to reproduce the message.

More modern cryptographic techniques assume that the adversary knows all about how the message was encrypted but doesn't know some small, crucial piece of information called the *key*. The message's sender uses the key to encrypt the message, and the recipient uses the key to decrypt it. Because the method of encryption is known, an attacker who can find the key can also decrypt the message.

This form of encryption, in which the attacker knows the encryption method, is more powerful than security through obscurity, because even an attacker who knows the encryption method cannot decrypt the message. This model is also more realistic in the modern world because sooner or later the attacker will discover the encryption method.

This chapter describes some interesting and useful cryptographic techniques. It starts out by describing some classical cryptographic methods. These are no longer considered secure, but they are interesting and demonstrate a few useful concepts such as frequency analysis.

Cryptanalysis, the study of how to break encryptions to recover a message, has been around as long as cryptography. The following sections that describe classical methods also explain the cryptanalysis that lets you break those methods.

The later sections describe more secure techniques, such as permutation networks and public-key encryption. A complete discussion of the latest encryption methods, such as *Advanced Encryption Standard* (AES) and *Blowfish*, is beyond the scope of this book, but the later sections should give you a general idea of how modern approaches work.

Terminology

Before starting the study of cryptography, you should know a few basic terms.

In cryptography, the goal is for a *sender* to send a message to a *receiver* without a third party, usually called an *adversary* or *attacker*, understanding the message. It is assumed that the attacker will intercept the encrypted message, so only the encryption stands between the attacker and understanding the message.

The unencrypted message is called *plaintext*. The encrypted message is called *ciphertext*. Turning plaintext into ciphertext is called *encrypting* or *enciphering* the plaintext. Recovering the plaintext from the ciphertext is called *decrypting* or *deciphering* the ciphertext.

Technically, a *cipher* is a pair of algorithms used to encrypt and decrypt messages.

Cryptanalysis is an attacker's study of methods for breaking an encryption.

To make working with smaller messages easier, they are usually encrypted in all capital letters without spaces or punctuation. That means the sender and receiver don't need to consider more characters than necessary—an important consideration if you're encrypting and decrypting messages by hand. This also removes clues that spaces and punctuation might give to an attacker.

To make encrypted messages a bit easier to read, they usually are written in five-character chunks in a fixed-width font so that characters line up nicely. For example, the message "This is a secret message" would be written as THISI SASEC RETME SSAGE, and it might be encrypted as something like TSRSH AESIS

TASEM GICEE. The receiver may need to spend a little extra time figuring out where to insert spaces and punctuation.

Modern cryptographic algorithms encrypt and decrypt byte streams. Therefore, they can include uppercase and lowercase letters, spaces, punctuation, and even Unicode characters or images, depending on the type of message. Those algorithms are good enough that the attacker shouldn't be able to tell the spaces and punctuation apart from other characters to get extra information about the message.

Transposition Ciphers

In a *transposition cipher*, the plaintext's letters are rearranged in some specific way to create the ciphertext. The recipient puts the letters back in their original positions to read the message.

These ciphers work partly with security through obscurity if the attacker doesn't know what kind of transposition is being used. For example, the scytale method described at the beginning of the chapter uses a transposition caused by winding the parchment around a rod. It relies solely on the fact that the attacker doesn't know that it was the method used to encrypt the message.

Most of transposition ciphers also provide a key that gives some information about the transposition. For example, the row/column transposition cipher described in the next section uses the number of columns as a key. These keys tend to allow a fairly limited set of values, however, so it isn't hard to guess the key and break the encryption, particularly if you use a computer.

These ciphers are fairly easy to work through with paper and pencil and can be a fun exercise. (If they're too easy, try working them out in your head.)

Row/Column Transposition

In a *row/column transposition cipher*, the plaintext message is written into an array by rows. Then the ciphertext is read from the array by columns. For example, Figure 16.1 shows the plaintext "THIS IS A SECRET MESSAGE" written by rows into a four-row, five-column array. (Normally, if the message doesn't fit exactly, you pad it with X's or random characters to make it fit.)

To get the cipher text, you read down each column. In this example, that gives the ciphertext TSRSH AESIS TASEM GICEE. The key is the number of columns used in the transposition.

To decode a ciphertext message, you basically undo the encryption operation. You build the array, write the ciphertext characters into it by columns, and then read the decoded message by rows.

T	H	I	S	I
S	A	S	E	C
R	E	T	M	E
S	S	A	G	E

Figure 16.1: In a row/column transposition cipher, you write the plaintext into an array by rows and then read the ciphertext by columns.

If you're implementing this in a program, you don't really need to write the text into an array. Instead, if the number of columns is num_columns, you can simply read the characters from the plaintext string, skipping num_columns between each character. The following pseudocode shows this approach:

```
String: ciphertext = ""
For col = 0 To num_columns - 1
    Integer: index = col
    For row = 0 To num_rows - 1
        ciphertext = ciphertext + plaintext[index]
        index += num_columns
    Next row
Next col
```

To decipher a message in a program, notice that decoding a message that was originally written in an array that has R rows and C columns is the same as encrypting a message with an array that has C rows and R columns.

The preceding example writes a message into a 4×5 array. Figure 16.2 shows the ciphertext TSRSH AESIS TASEM GICEE written into a 5×4 array by rows. If you look at the figure, you'll see that you can read the plaintext by columns.

T	S	R	S
H	A	E	S
I	S	T	A
S	E	M	G
I	C	E	E

Figure 16.2: Decrypting with an $R \times C$ array is equivalent to encrypting with a $C \times R$ array.

Row/column transposition is easy and makes for a fun exercise, but it's a relatively easy system to break. The secret key is the number of columns in the array. If you factor the length of the ciphertext, you can come up with a few choices for the key.

For instance, the previous ciphertext contains 20 characters. The factors of 20 are 1, 2, 4, 5, 10, and 20, so those are the possibilities for the number of columns. The 1×20 and 20×1 arrays make the ciphertext the same as the plaintext, so there are really only two possibilities to check. If you simply try each value, you'll see that the characters spell gibberish when you use four columns, but they spell words when you use five columns.

The sender can try to make the attacker's life a little harder by adding some extra random characters to the end of the ciphertext so that the array's size isn't exactly determined by the message's length. For example, you could add nine characters to the previous ciphertext to get a message that is 29 characters long. Then it wouldn't be as obvious that the array must have four or five columns.

Even so, you can easily make a program that tries every possible number of columns between 2 and 1 less than the length of the ciphertext. When the program sees that the corresponding decrypted text contains words, it finds the key.

Column Transposition

In a column transposition cipher, the plaintext message is written into an array by rows much as it is in a row/column transposition cipher. The columns are then rearranged, and the message is read out by rows.

Figure 16.3 shows the plaintext "THIS IS A SECRET MESSAGE" written by rows into a four-row, five-column array on the left. The columns are then rearranged. The numbers above the array on the left show the ordering of the columns in the rearranged array on the right. Reading the message by rows from the array on the right gives the ciphertext HTIIS ASSCE ERTEM SSAEG.

2	1	3	5	4
T	H	I	S	I
S	A	S	E	C
R	E	T	M	E
S	S	A	G	E

H	T	I	I	S
A	S	S	C	E
E	R	T	E	M
S	S	A	E	G

Figure 16.3: In a column transposition cipher, you write the plaintext into an array by rows, rearrange the columns, and read the ciphertext by rows.

In this case, the encryption's key is the number of columns in the array plus the permutation of the columns. You could write the key for this example as 21354.

A key that would be easier to remember would be a word with a length equal to the number of columns and with letters whose alphabetical order gives the column permutation. For this example, the key could be CARTS. In this word, the letter *A* comes first alphabetically, so its value is 1, the letter *C* comes second alphabetically, so its value is 2, the letter *R* comes third alphabetically, so its value is 3, and so on. Putting the letters' alphabetical values in the order in which they appear in the word gives the numeric key 21354, and that gives the ordering of the columns. (In practice, you pick the word first and then use it to determine the column ordering. You don't pick an ordering and then try to come up with a word to match.)

To decrypt a message, you write the ciphertext into an array that has as many columns as the keyword has letters. You then find the inverse mapping defined by the letters' alphabetical ordering. In this example, the numeric key 21354 means that the columns move as follows:

- Column 1 moves to position 2.
- Column 2 moves to position 1.
- Column 3 moves to position 3.
- Column 4 moves to position 5.
- Column 5 moves to position 4.

Simply reverse that mapping so that:

- Column 2 moves to position 1.
- Column 1 moves to position 2.
- Column 3 moves to position 3.
- Column 5 moves to position 4.
- Column 4 moves to position 5.

Now you can rearrange the columns and read the plaintext by rows.

As is the case with a row/column transposition cipher, a program that performs row transposition doesn't really need to write values into an array; it just needs to keep careful track of where the characters need to move. In fact, a program can use the inverse mapping described in the preceding paragraphs to figure out which character goes in which position of the ciphertext.

Suppose that mapping is an array of integers that gives the column transposition. For example, if column number 2 moves to position 1, then mapping[2] = 1. Similarly, suppose inverse_mapping is an array that gives the inverse mapping, so for this example, `inverse_mapping[1]` = 2. Then the following pseudocode shows how the program can encrypt the plaintext:

```
String: ciphertext = ""
For row = 0 to num_rows - 1
    // Read this row in permuted order.
    For col = 0 to num_columns - 1
        Integer: index = row * num_columns + inverse_mapping[col]
        ciphertext = ciphertext + plaintext[index]
    Next col
Next row
```

Notice that this pseudocode uses the inverse mapping to encrypt the plaintext. To find the character that maps to a particular column number in the ciphertext, it must use the inverse mapping to find the column from which the character came.

You can use the forward mapping to decrypt the ciphertext.

To attack a column transposition cipher, an attacker would write the message into an array that has the number of columns given by the length of the keyword. The attacker would then swap columns to try to guess the proper ordering. If the array has C columns, then there are C! possible orderings of the columns, so this could require looking at a lot of combinations. For example, 10 columns would result in 3,628,800 possible arrangements of columns.

That seems like a lot of possibilities, particularly if the attacker isn't using a computer, but the attacker may be able to decrypt the message incrementally. The attacker could start by trying to find the first five columns in the plaintext. If the first five columns are correct, then the first row will show five characters of valid words. It may show a complete word or at least a prefix of a word. The other rows may begin with partial words, but after that they will also contain words or prefixes. There are only $10 \times 9 \times 8 \times 7 \times 6 = 30,240$ possible arrangements of five columns chosen from 10, so this is a lot fewer combinations to check, although it would still be a daunting task.

Route Ciphers

In a route cipher, the plaintext is written into an array or some other arrangement and then is read in an order determined by a route through the arrangement.

For example, Figure 16.4 shows a plaintext message written into an array by rows. The ciphertext is read by following the array's diagonals, starting with the lower-left diagonal, so the ciphertext is SRSSE ATATG HSMEI EESCI.

In theory, the number of possible routes through the array is enormous. If the array holds N entries, then there are N! possible routes. The example shown in Figure 16.4 has $20! \approx 2.4 \times 10^{18}$ possible routes.

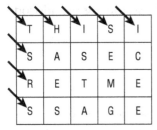

Figure 16.4: In a route cipher, you write the plaintext into an array by rows and then read the ciphertext in some other order.

However, a good route should be reasonably simple so that the receiver can remember it. The diagonal route shown in Figure 16.4 is easy to remember, but if the route jumps randomly all over the array, then the receiver would need to write it down, basically making the key as long as the message. (Later in this chapter you'll see that a one-time pad also has a key as long as the message, and that it also changes the message's letters, so the attacker cannot get extra information such as the frequency of the different letters in the message.)

Some routes also leave large pieces of the message intact or reversed. For example, an inward clockwise spiral starting in the upper-left corner is easy to remember, but the first row of the message appears unscrambled in the cipher-text. These sorts of routes give the attacker extra information and may make it easier to figure out the route.

If you eliminate routes that cannot be easily remembered and routes that include large sections of unscrambled plaintext, then the number of available routes is much smaller than the theoretical maximum.

Substitution Ciphers

In a *substitution cipher*, the letters in the plaintext are replaced with other letters. The following sections describe four common substitution ciphers.

Caesar Substitution

About 2,100 years ago, Julius Caesar (100 BC–44 BCE) used a technique that is now called a *Caesar substitution cipher* to encrypt messages he sent to his officers. In his version of this cipher, he shifted each character in the message by three letters in the alphabet. A became D, B became E, and so on. To decrypt a message, the receiver subtracted 3 from each letter, so Z became W, Y became V, and so on.

For example, the message "This is a secret message" with a shift of 3 becomes WKLVL VDVHF UHWPH VVDJH.

Julius Caesar's nephew Augustus used a similar cipher with a shift of 1 instead of 3. More generally, you can shift the letters in the plaintext by any number of characters.

An attacker can try to decipher a message encrypted using this method by examining the frequencies of the letters in the ciphertext. In English, the letter *E* occurs much more often than the other letters. It occurs about 12.7 percent of the time. The next most common letter, *T*, occurs 9.1 percent of the time. If the attacker counts the number of times each letter is used in the ciphertext, the one that occurs most is probably an encrypted *E*. Finding the number of characters between the ciphertext letter and *E* gives the shift used to encrypt the message.

This attack works best with long messages, because short ones may not have a typical distribution of letters.

Table 16.1 shows the number of occurrences of the letters in the ciphertext WKLVL VDVHF UHWPH VVDJH.

Table 16.1: Number of Occurrences of the Letters in the Example Ciphertext

LETTER	D	F	H	J	K	L	P	U	V	W
Occurrences	2	1	4	1	1	2	1	1	5	2

If you assume *V* is the encryption of the letter *E*, then the shift must be 17. Decrypting the message with that shift gives you FTUEU EMEQO DQFYQ EEMSQ, which does not contain valid words.

If you assume the second-most-used character *H* is the encryption of *E*, you get a shift of 3, and now you can decode the original message.

Vigenère Cipher

One problem with the Caesar substitution cipher is that it uses only 26 keys. An attacker could easily try all 26 possible shift values to see which one produces valid words. The *Vigenère cipher* improves on the Caesar substitution cipher by using different shift values for different letters in the message.

NOTE The Vigenère cipher was originally described by Giovan Battista Bellaso in 1553, but it was later attributed to Blaise de Vigenère in the 19th century, and the name stuck.

In the Vigenère cipher, a keyword specifies the shifts for different letters in the message. Each letter in the keyword specifies a shift based on its position in the alphabet. *A* indicates a shift of 0, *B* represents a shift of 1, and so on.

To encrypt a message, you write the plaintext below a copy of the keyword repeated as many times as necessary to have the same length as the message. Figure 16.5 shows a message below the keyword ZEBRAS repeated several times.

Z	E	B	R	A	S	Z	E	B	R	A	S	Z	E	B	R	A	S	Z	E
T	H	I	S	I	S	A	S	E	C	R	E	T	M	E	S	S	A	G	E

Figure 16.5: In a Vigenère cipher, repeat the keyword as many times as necessary over the plaintext.

Now you can use the corresponding letters to produce the ciphertext. For example, key letter Z represents a shift of 25, so you shift the plaintext letter T by 25 to get S.

To make shifting the letters easier, you can use a "multiplication table" like the one shown in Figure 16.6. To encrypt the plaintext letter T with the key letter Z, you look in row T, column Z.

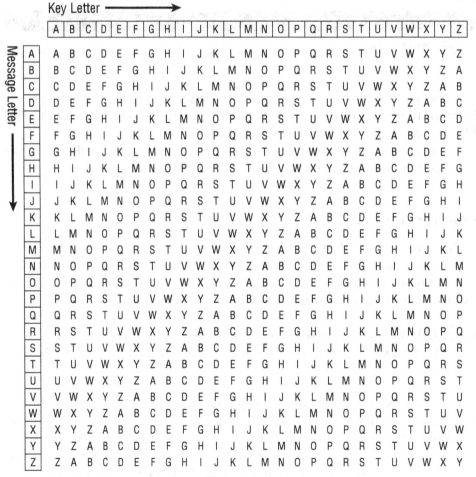

Figure 16.6: This table makes it easier to shift letters in a Vigenère cipher.

To decrypt a ciphertext letter, you look down the key letter's column until you find the ciphertext letter. The row tells you the plaintext letter.

The simple frequency analysis that you can use to attack a Caesar substitution cipher doesn't work with a Vigenère cipher because the letters don't all have the same shift. However, you can use the ciphertext's letter frequencies to attack a Vigenère cipher in a different way.

Suppose the keyword is K letters long. In that case, every Kth letter has the same offset. For example, the letters in positions $1, K + 1, 2 \times K + 1$, and so forth have the same offset. Those letters are not the same as the plaintext letters, but their relative frequencies are the same.

To begin the attack, you try guessing the key's length. You then look at the letters that have the same offset. For example, suppose that you try a key length of 2. You then examine the letters in the ciphertext in positions 0, 2, 4, 6, and so forth. If the key's length actually is 2, then the letters' frequencies should look like those in normal English (or whatever language you're using). In particular, a few letters corresponding to plaintext letters such as *E*, *S*, and *T* should occur much more often than other letters corresponding to plaintext letters such as *X* and *Q*.

If the key's length is not 2, the letters' frequencies should be fairly uniform, with no letters occurring much more often than the others. In that case, you guess a new key length and try again.

When you find a key length that gives a frequency distribution that looks something like the one for English, you look at the specific frequencies, as you did for a Caesar substitution cipher. The letter that occurs most often is probably an encrypted *E*.

Similarly, you look at the other letters with the same offsets to figure out what their offset is. For example, if the key has length 5, then you first look at the group of letters in positions 0, 5, 10, and so on. Next, you look at the group of letters in positions 1, 6, 11, and so on. Different groups will have different offsets, but all of the letters in each group will have the same offset.

Basically, in this step you decrypt a Caesar substitution cipher for each letter in the key.

When you're finished, you should have the offset for each letter in the key. This is more work than the Caesar substitution cipher, but it is still possible.

Simple Substitution

In a simple substitution cipher, each letter has a fixed replacement letter. For example, you might replace *A* with *H*, *B* with *J*, *C* with *X*, and so forth.

In this cipher, the key is the mapping of plaintext letters to ciphertext letters. If the message can contain only the letters *A* through *Z*, then there are 4.0×10^{26} possible mappings.

If you're encrypting and decrypting messages by hand, you'll need to write down the mapping.

If you're using a computer, you may be able to use a pseudorandom number generator to re-create the mapping. The sender picks a number K, uses it to initialize the pseudorandom number generator, and then uses the generator to randomize the letters *A* through *Z* and produce the mapping. The value K becomes the key. The receiver follows the same steps, using K to initialize the random-number generator and generate the same mapping the sender used.

It's easier to remember a single number than the entire mapping, but most random-number generators have far fewer possible internal states than 4.0×10^{26}. For example, if the number you use to initialize the random-number generator is a signed 32-bit integer, then the key can have only about 2 billion values. That's still a lot, but a computer can easily try all possible 2 billion values to see which one produces valid words.

You can also use letter frequencies to make the process a little easier. If the letter *W* appears most often in the ciphertext, then it is probably an encrypted *E*.

One-Time Pads

A *one-time pad cipher* is sort of like a Vigenère cipher where the key is as long as the message. Every letter has its own offset, so you cannot use the letters' frequencies in the ciphertext to find the offsets.

Because any ciphertext letter can have any offset, the corresponding plaintext letter could be anything, so an attacker cannot get any information from the ciphertext (except the message's length, and you can even disguise that by adding extra characters to the message).

In a manual system, the sender and receiver each have a copy of a notepad containing random letters. To encrypt a message, the sender uses the pad's letters to encrypt the message, crossing out the pad's letters as they are used so that they are never used again. To decrypt the message, the receiver uses the same letters in the pad to decrypt the message, also crossing out the letters as they are used.

Because each letter essentially has its own offset, this cipher is unbreakable as long as the attacker doesn't get hold of a copy of the one-time pad.

One drawback of the one-time pad cipher is that the sender and receiver must have identical copies of the pad, and sending a copy securely to the receiver can be as hard as sending a secure message. Historically, pads were sent by couriers. If an attacker intercepted a courier, then the pad was discarded, and a new one was sent.

NOTE If you're implementing a one-time pad in software, you can use the bitwise XOR operator to encrypt each character instead of using letter shifts. If the bytes in the "pad" are random values between 0 and 255, then the encrypted results will also be random values between 0 and 255. This technique lets you encrypt messages other than the letters *A* through *Z* such as images, binary files, or Unicode messages.

Block Ciphers

In a *block cipher*, the message is broken into blocks, each block is encrypted separately, and the encrypted blocks are combined to form the encrypted message.

Many block ciphers also encrypt blocks by applying some sort of transformation to the data many times in rounds. The transformation must be invertible so that you can later decrypt the ciphertext. Giving the blocks a fixed size means that you can design the transformation to work with a block of that size.

Block ciphers also have the useful feature that they let cryptographic software work with messages in relatively small pieces. For example, suppose that you want to encrypt a very large message, perhaps a few gigabytes. If you use a column transposition cipher, the program needs to jump throughout the message's location in memory. That can cause paging, which slows down the program greatly.

In contrast, a block cipher can consider the message in pieces, each of which fits easily in memory. The program may still need to page, but it needs to load each piece of the message into memory only once instead of many times.

The following sections describe some of the most common types of block ciphers.

Substitution-Permutation Networks

A *substitution-permutation network cipher* repeatedly applies rounds consisting of a substitution stage and a permutation stage. It helps to visualize the stages being performed by machines in boxes that are called *substitution boxes* (S-boxes) and *permutation boxes* (P-boxes).

An S-box takes a small part of the block and combines it with part of the key to make an obfuscated result. To obscure the result as much as possible, changing a single bit in the key should ideally change about half of the bits in the result. For example, if an S-box works with 1 byte, then it might use the XOR operation to combine the first bit in the key with bits 1, 3, 4, and 7 in the plaintext byte. The S-box would combine other key bits with the message bits in different patterns. You could use different S-boxes for different parts of the block.

A P-box rearranges the bits in the entire block and sends them to different S-boxes. For example, bit 1 from the first S-box might go to the next stage's bit 7 in the third S-box.

Figure 16.7 shows a schematic for a three-round substitution-permutation network cipher. The S-boxes S_1, S_2, S_3, and S_4 combine the key with pieces of the message. (Note that each round could use different key information.) The

P-boxes all use the same permutation to send the outputs of the S-boxes into the next round of S-boxes.

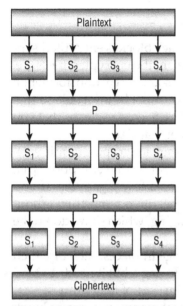

Figure 16.7: In a substitution-permutation network cipher, substitution stages alternate with permutation stages.

To decrypt a message, you perform the same steps in reverse. You run the ciphertext through the inverted S-boxes, pass the results through the inverted P-box, and repeat the necessary number of rounds.

One drawback of this method is that the S-boxes and P-boxes must be invertible so that you can decrypt messages. The code that performs encryption and decryption is also different, so you have more code to write, debug, and maintain.

> **NOTE**   The *Advanced Encryption Standard* (AES), which is probably the most commonly used encryption method today, uses a substitution-permutation network. It uses a block size of 128 bits and a key size of 128, 192, or 256 bits, depending on the level of security you want.
>
> To get a feel for how many possible keys this creates, consider that $2^{128} \approx 3.4 \times 10^{38}$ and $2^{256} \approx 1.2 \times 10^{77}$. If an attacker had a computer that could test 1 billion keys per second (and that seems unlikely for a typical personal computer given how complicated the steps needed to encrypt a message are), it would take about 1.1×10^{22} years to check all possible 128-bit keys and about 3.7×10^{60} years to check all possible 256-bit keys.

AES uses a different number of rounds depending on the key size: 10 rounds for 128-bit keys, 12 rounds for 192-bit keys, and 14 rounds for 256-bit keys. The greater number of rounds for larger keys obscures the message more and makes a brute-force attack slower.

For more information on AES, see https://en.wikipedia.org/wiki/Advanced_Encryption_Standard.

Feistel Ciphers

In a *Feistel cipher*, named after cryptographer Horst Feistel, the message is split into left and right halves, L_0 and R_0. A function is applied to the right half, and the XOR operation is used to combine the result with the left half. The two halves are swapped, and the process is repeated for some number of rounds.

The following steps describe the algorithm at a high level:

1. Split the plaintext into two halves, L_0 and R_0.
2. Repeat:

   a. Set $L_{i+1} = R_i$.
   b. Set $R_{i+1} = L_i$ XOR $F(R_i, K_i)$.

Here K_i is a subkey used for round i. This is a series of values generated by using the message's key. For example, a simple approach would be to split the key into pieces and then use the pieces in order, repeating them as necessary. (You can think of a Vigenère cipher as doing this because it uses each letter in the key to encrypt a single message character and then repeats the key letters as needed.)

After you have finished the desired number of rounds, the ciphertext is L_{i+1} plus R_{i+1}.

To decrypt a message, you split the ciphertext into two halves to get the final values L_{i+1} and R_{i+1}. If you look at the preceding steps, you'll see that R_i is L_{i+1}. Therefore, because you already know L_{i+1}, you already know R_i.

To recover L_i, substitute L_{i+1} for R_i in the equation used in step 2b to get this:

$$R_{i+1} = L_i \, XOR F(R_i, K_i) = L_i \, XOR F(L_{i+1}, K_i)$$

At this point you know L_{i+1}, so you can calculate $F(L_{i+1}, K_i)$. If you combine that with R_{i+1}, then the $F(L_{i+1}, K_i)$ terms cancel, leaving only L_i, so you have recovered L_i.

The following steps describe the decryption algorithm:

1. Split the ciphertext into two halves, L^{i+1} and R^{i+1}.

2. Repeat:

a. Set $R_i = L_{i+1}$.

b. Set $L_i = R_{i+1} \text{ XOR } F(L_{i+1}, K_i)$.

One advantage to Feistel ciphers is that decryption doesn't require you to invert the function F. That means you can use any function for F, even functions that are not easily invertible.

Another advantage of Feistel ciphers is that the code for encryption and decryption is basically the same. The only real difference is that you use the subkeys in reverse order to decrypt the ciphertext. This means that you need only one piece of code for encryption and decryption.

> **NOTE** The *Data Encryption Standard* (DES), which until recently was one of the most commonly used encryption methods, is a Feistel cipher. It is generally no longer considered secure enough for high-security applications, largely because of its relatively short 56-bit key.
>
> A variation of this method called *Triple DES* simply applies DES three times to each block. Triple DES is believed to be secure in practice, although most highly secure applications now use AES instead.
>
> **For more information on DEA, see** https://en.wikipedia.org/wiki/Data_Encryption_Standard.

Public-Key Encryption and RSA

Public-key encryption uses two separate keys: a public key and a private key. The *public key* is published, so everyone (including the attacker) knows it. The *private key* is known only to the receiver.

A sender uses the public key to encrypt the message and sends the result to the receiver. Note that even the sender doesn't know the private key. Only the receiver knows that key, so only the receiver can decrypt the message.

In contrast, other forms of encryption are sometimes called *symmetric-key encryption* because you use the same key to encrypt and decrypt messages.

One of the best-known public-key algorithms is *RSA*, which is named after those who first described it: Ron **R**ivest, Adi **S**hamir, and Leonard **A**dleman.

> **MATH WARNING**
>
> The RSA algorithm is interesting, and some understanding of how it works may be useful in an interview. Unfortunately, the algorithms used by RSA are also very mathematical. If you don't like math, you may want to skip to the section "Practical Considerations."

You follow these steps to generate the public and private keys for the algorithm:

1. Pick two large prime numbers p and q.
2. Compute $n = p \times q$. Release this as the *public key modulus.*
3. Compute $\varphi(n)$, where φ is Euler's totient function. (I'll say more about this shortly.)
4. Pick an integer e where $1 \le e \le \varphi(n)$ and e and $\varphi(n)$ are relatively prime. (In other words, they have no common factors.) Release this as the *public key exponent.*
5. Find d, the multiplicative inverse of e modulo $\varphi(n)$. In other words, $e \times d \equiv 1 \bmod \varphi(n)$. (I'll also say more about this shortly.) The value d is the private key.

The public key consists of the values n and e. To encrypt a numeric message M, the sender uses the formula $C = M^e \bmod n$.

To decrypt a message, the receiver simply calculates $C^d \bmod n$.

> **NOTE** Chapter 2 explains several of the techniques that you need to use to implement RSA. For example, it explains a probabilistic test to determine whether a number is prime. To find a large prime, pick a random large number and see whether it is prime. Repeat until you find one.
>
> Chapter 2 also explains how to perform fast exponentiation and how to use the GCD algorithm to determine quickly whether two numbers are relatively prime.

The strength of RSA relies on the fact that it is hard to factor very large numbers. An attacker who can factor the public modulus n can recover the primes p and q. From p and q, plus the public exponent e, the attacker can then figure out the private key and break the cipher.

This is why the primes p and q must be large—to prevent an attacker from easily factoring n.

> **NOTE** Although factoring is believed to be a hard problem and lots of people have spent a huge amount of effort studying it, there is no guarantee that someone won't eventually come up with a way to factor large numbers quickly.

Euler's Totient Function

Step 3 of the RSA key-generating algorithm requires you to calculate *Euler's totient function* $\varphi(n)$. The totient function, which is also called the *phi function*, is a function that gives the number of positive integers less than a particular number that are relatively prime to that number. For example, $\varphi(12)$ is 4 because there are four numbers less than 12 that are relatively prime to it: 1, 5, 7, and 11.

Because a prime number is relatively prime to every positive integer less than itself, $\varphi(p) = p - 1$ if p is prime.

It turns out that, if p and q are relatively prime, then $\varphi(p \times q) = \varphi(p) \times \varphi(p)$. If p and q are both primes, then they are relatively prime, so in step 3, $\varphi(n) = \varphi(p \times q) = \varphi(p) \times \varphi(q) = (p - 1) \times (q - 1)$. If you know p and q, then this is easy to compute.

For example, suppose $p = 3$ and $q = 5$. Then $\varphi(15) = \varphi(3) \times \varphi(5) = (3 - 1) \times (5 - 1) = 2 \times 4 = 8$. This is true because the positive integers smaller than 15 that are relatively prime to 15 are the eight values 1, 2, 4, 7, 8, 11, 13, and 14.

Multiplicative Inverses

Step 5 of the key-generating algorithm requires you to find the *multiplicative inverse* d of e modulo $\varphi(n)$. In other words, find d so that $d \times e \equiv 1 \bmod \varphi(n)$.

For example, suppose $\varphi(n) = 40$ and $e = 7$. The question now is, "What is the multiplicative inverse of 7 modulo 40?" In this example, $23 \times 7 = 161 \equiv 1 \bmod 40$, so 23 is the multiplicative inverse of 7 modulo 40.

One simple way to find the inverse is to compute $(1 \times d) \bmod \varphi(n)$, $(2 \times d) \bmod \varphi(n)$, $(3 \times d) \bmod \varphi(n)$, and so on, until you discover a value that makes the result 1.

You can also use the extended GCD algorithm described in Chapter 2 to find the value e more efficiently. See the section "Extending Greatest Common Divisors" in Chapter 2 for more information on the extended GCD algorithm. See the following web page for information on using that algorithm to calculate inverses:

    https://en.wikipedia.org/wiki/Extended_Euclidean_algorithm#Computing_
    multiplicative_inverses_in_modular_structures

An RSA Example

First, consider this example of picking the public and private keys:

1. Pick two large prime numbers p and q.
    For this example, let $p = 17$ and $q = 29$. In a real application, these values should be much larger, such as 128-bit numbers when written in binary, so they would have an order of magnitude of about 1×10^{38}.

2. Compute $n = p \times q$. Release this as the public key modulus.
    The public key modulus n is $p \times q = 493$.

3. Compute $\varphi(n)$ where φ is Euler's totient function.
    The value $\varphi(n) = (p - 1) \times (q - 1) = 16 \times 28 = 448$.

4. Pick an integer e where $1 \le e \le \varphi(n)$ and e and $\varphi(n)$ are relatively prime. For this example, you need to pick e where $1 \le e \le 448$ and e and 448 are relatively prime. The prime factorization of 448 is $2^6 \times 7$, so e cannot include the factors 2 or 7. For this example, let $e = 3 \times 5 \times 11 = 165$.

5. Find d, the multiplicative inverse of e modulo $\varphi(n)$. In other words, find d such that $d \times e \equiv 1 \bmod \varphi(n)$.

For this example, you must find the multiplicative inverse of 165 mod 448. In other words, find d such that $d \times 165 \equiv 1 \bmod 448$. In this example, $429 \times 165 \equiv 1 \bmod 448$, so the inverse is 429. (Example program MultiplicativeInverse, which is included in the downloads for this chapter, exhaustively finds inverses such as this one. It tried values until it discovered that 429 worked.)

So, the public exponent $e = 165$, the public modulus $n = 493$, and the secret key $d = 429$.

Now suppose that you want to encrypt the message value 321. The encrypted value C would be $C = M^e \bmod n = 321^{165} \bmod 493$. The ExponentiateMod program, which is available for download on the book's website as part of the solution to Chapter 2, Exercise 12, calculates large exponentials quickly. That program calculates that $321^{165} \bmod 493 = 359$, so the encrypted value is 359.

To decrypt the value 359, the receiver calculates $C^d \bmod n$. For this example, that's $359^{429} \bmod 493$. The ExponentiateMod program from Chapter 2 calculates that $359^{429} \bmod 493 = 321$, so the decrypted message is 321 as it should be.

Practical Considerations

Generating good private keys and calculating big exponents can take some time even if you use fast modular exponentiation. Remember that p and q are very large numbers, so using private-key cryptography to encrypt a long message in blocks small enough to be represented as numbers could take quite a while.

To save time, some cryptographic systems use public-key encryption to allow a sender and receiver to exchange a private key for use with symmetric-key encryption.

NOTE The popular program *Pretty Good Privacy* (PGP) uses public-key encryption for at least part of its computation. To get a good level of obscurity in the ciphertext, a reasonable message length, and acceptable speed, PGP actually processes messages with a series of operations, including hashing, compression, public-key encryption, and private-key encryption. For more information on PGP, see https://en.wikipedia.org/wiki/Pretty_good_privacy.

Other Uses for Cryptography

The algorithms described in this chapter focus on encrypting and decrypting messages, but cryptography has other uses as well.

For example, a *cryptographic hash function* takes as an input a block of data such as a file and returns a hash value that identifies the data. You then can make the file and hash value available publicly.

A receiver who wants to use the file can perform the same hashing function to see if the new hash value matches the published one. If someone has tampered with the file, then the hash values will probably not match, and the receiver knows that the file is not in its original form.

A good hash function should have the following properties:

- It should be easy to compute.
- It should be prohibitively difficult for an attacker to create a file with a given hash value (so the attacker cannot replace the true file with a fake one).
- It should be prohibitively difficult to modify the file without changing its hash value.
- It should be prohibitively difficult to find two files with the same hash value.

One application of cryptographic hashing is password verification. You create a password, and the system stores its hash value. The system doesn't store the actual password, so an attacker who breaks into the system cannot steal the password.

Later, when you want to log into the system, you enter your password again. The system hashes it and verifies that the new hash value matches the one that is saved.

A *digital signature* is a cryptographic tool that is somewhat similar to cryptographic hashing. If you want to prove that you wrote a particular document, you sign it. Later, someone else can examine the document to verify that you have signed it. If someone else modifies the document, that person cannot sign it in your name.

Typically, a digital signature system includes three parts:

- A key-generation algorithm that creates private and public keys
- A signing algorithm that uses the private key to sign a document
- A verification algorithm that uses a public key that you publish to verify that you did sign the document

In a sense, a digital signature is the opposite of a private-key encryption system. In a private-key encryption system, any number of senders can use a public key to encrypt a message, and a single receiver uses a private key to decrypt the message. In a digital signature, a single sender uses a private key to sign a message and then any number of receivers can use a public key to verify the signature.

Summary

This chapter explained a few cryptographic algorithms. The simpler forms, such as transposition and substitution ciphers, are not cryptographically secure, but they provide some interesting exercises. Any student of algorithms should also have some experience with these, particularly Caesar and Vigenère ciphers.

The algorithms described later in the chapter explained how some of the current state-of-the-art cryptographic algorithms work. AES, which uses substitution-permutation networks, and RSA, which uses public-key encryption, are two of the most commonly used algorithms today. Although DES is no longer considered completely secure, it uses a Feistel cipher, which is still interesting and can produce secure encryption schemes such as triple DES.

This chapter covered only a tiny fraction of the cryptographic algorithms that have been invented. For more information, search online or consult a book on cryptography. Two places where you can start your search online include https://en.wikipedia.org/wiki/Cryptography and http://mathworld.wolfram .com/Cryptography.html. If you prefer a book, I highly recommend *Applied Cryptography: Protocols, Algorithms, and Source Code in C*, Second Edition by Bruce Schneier (Wiley, 1996). It describes a huge number of algorithms for encryption and decryption, digital signatures, authentication, secure elections, and digital money. It does not cover the most recent algorithms (and apparently more recent editions do not either), but it contains excellent background information.

All of these encryption algorithms rely on the fact that you can perform some calculations relatively easily if you know the key and an attacker cannot perform the same operation without knowing the key. For example, in RSA, the receiver can easily decrypt messages, but an attacker cannot without factoring the product of two large prime numbers. It is believed that factoring large numbers is difficult, so an attacker cannot break an RSA encryption.

In the study of algorithms, there are two extremely important sets: P and NP. The first set includes problems that are relatively easy to solve, such as multiplying two numbers or searching a binary tree for a piece of information. The second set includes much harder problems, such as solving the bin packing, knapsack, and traveling salesman problems described in Chapter 12.

The next chapter discusses P and NP and explains some of the interesting questions about these important classes of problems that remain unanswered.

Exercises

You can find the answers to these exercises in Appendix B. Asterisks indicate particularly difficult problems.

1. Write a program that uses a row/column transposition cipher to encrypt and decrypt messages.

2. Write a program that uses a column transposition cipher to encrypt and decrypt messages.

3. A column transposition cipher uses the relative alphabetic order of its key's letters to determine the column mapping. What happens if a key contains duplicated letters, as in PIZZA or BOOKWORM? How can you solve that problem? Does this approach have any benefits?

4. A column transposition cipher swaps the columns in a message written into an array. Would you gain extra security by swapping both columns and rows?

5. Write a program similar to a column transposition cipher that swaps both columns and rows.

6. Write a program that uses a Caesar substitution cipher to encrypt and decrypt messages. What is the encryption of "Nothing but gibberish" with a shift of 13?

7. *Write a program that displays the frequencies of occurrence of the letters in a message. Sort the results by frequency, and for each letter, display the offset that would map E to that letter.
   Then use that program and the program you wrote for Exercise 6 to decipher the message KYVIV NRJRK ZDVNY VETRV JRIJL SJKZK LKZFE NRJKY VJKRK VFWKY VRIK. What is the encryption's offset?

8. Write a program that uses a Vigenère cipher to encrypt and decrypt messages. Use the program to decrypt the ciphertext VDOKR RVVZK OTUII MNUUV RGFQK TOGNX VHOPG RPEVW VZYYO WKMOC ZMBR with the key VIGENERE.

9. After you have used all of the letters in a one-time pad, why can't you start over and use the letters again?

10. Suppose that you're using a large one-time pad to send and receive many messages with another person, and one of the messages you receive decrypts into gibberish. What might have happened, and what can you do about it?

11. When using a one-time pad, suppose you send ciphertext messages together with the index of the first letter used to encrypt them. Would that compromise the encryption?

12. Write a program that uses a one-time pad. Rather than making a truly random one-time pad, hard-code a string of random characters into the program. You can generate the characters by hand, use a pseudorandom number generator, or use some other source of randomness such as `http://www.dave-reed.com/Nifty/randSeq.html`.

    As you encrypt and decrypt messages, make the program keep track of the characters that have been used for encryption and decryption.

13. Explain how a perfectly secure cryptographic random-number generator is equivalent to an unbreakable encryption scheme. In other words, if you have a cryptographically secure random-number generator, how could you use it to create an unbreakable encryption scheme and vice versa?

14. The lengths and timing of messages can sometimes give information to an attacker. For example, an attacker might notice that you always send a long message before an important event such as a dignitary visiting or a large stock purchase. How you can avoid giving that sort of information to an attacker?

15. Suppose you're using RSA with the primes $p = 107$, $q = 211$, and $e = 4,199$. In that case, what are n, $\varphi(n)$, and d? What is the encryption of the value 1,337? What is the decryption of 19,905? (You may want to use the ExponentiateMod program from Chapter 2. You may also want to write a program to find inverses in a modulus, or you can use the MultiplicativeInverse program included in this chapter's downloads.)

Complexity Theory

An algorithm's performance is always important when you try to solve a problem. An algorithm won't do you much good if it takes too long or requires too much memory or other resources to actually run on a computer.

Computational complexity theory, or just *complexity theory*, is the study of the difficulty of computational problems. Rather than focusing on specific algorithms, complexity theory focuses on problems.

For example, the mergesort algorithm described in Chapter 6 can sort a list of N numbers in O(N log N) time. Complexity theory asks what you can learn about the task of sorting in general, not what you can learn about a specific algorithm. It turns out that you can show that any sorting algorithm that sorts by using comparisons must use at least N × log(N) time in the worst case.

N LOG N SORTING

To understand why any algorithm that uses comparisons to sort a list must use at least N log N time in the worst case, suppose that you have an array of N unique items. Because they are unique, there are N! possible ways that you can arrange them. To look at this in a different way, depending on the values in the array, there are N! ways that the algorithm might need to rearrange the items to put them in sorted order. This means that the algorithm must be able to follow N! possible paths of execution to produce every possible result.

The only tool the algorithm can use for branching into different paths of execution is to compare two values. So, you can think of the possible paths of execution as

> a binary tree in which each node represents a comparison and each leaf node represents a final arrangement of the items in the array.
>
> There are N! possible arrangements of the items in the array, so the execution tree must have N! leaf nodes. Because this is a binary tree, it has height $\log_2(\text{N!})$. Expanding that expression gives $\log_2(\text{N!}) = \log_2(\text{N}) + \log_2(\text{N}-1) + \log_2(\text{N}-2) + \ldots + \log_2(2)$. Half of these terms (and that makes $\text{N} \div 2$ terms) are at least $\log_2(\text{N} \div 2)$, so $\log_2(\text{N!}) \geq \text{N} \div 2 \times \log_2(\text{N} \div 2)$, which is of the order N log N.

Complexity theory is a large and difficult topic, so there's no room here to cover it fully. However, every programmer who studies algorithms should know at least something about complexity theory in general and the two sets P and NP in particular. This chapter introduces complexity theory and describes what these important classes of problems are.

Notation

One of the first topics covered in this book was Big O notation. Chapter 1 described Big O notation somewhat intuitively by saying that it describes how an algorithm's worst-case performance increases as the problem's size increases.

For most purposes, that definition is good enough to be useful, but in complexity theory Big O notation has a more technical definition. If an algorithm's run time is $f(\text{N})$, then the algorithm has Big O performance of $g(\text{N})$ if $f(\text{N}) < g(\text{N}) \times k$ for some constant k and for N large enough. In other words, the function $g(\text{N})$ is an upper bound for the actual run-time function $f(\text{N})$.

Two other notations similar to Big O notations are sometimes useful when discussing algorithmic complexity. *Big Omega notation*, written $\Omega(g(\text{N}))$, means that the run-time function is bounded *below* by the function $g(\text{N})$. For example, as explained a moment ago, N log(N) is a lower bound for algorithms that sort by using comparisons, so those algorithms are $\Omega(\text{N log N})$.

Big Theta notation, written $\Theta(g(\text{N}))$, means that the run-time function is bounded both above and below by the function $g(\text{N})$. For example, the mergesort algorithm's run time is bounded above by $O(\text{N log N})$, and the run time of any algorithm that sorts by using comparisons is bounded below by $\Omega(\text{N log N})$, so mergesort has performance $\Theta(\text{N log N})$.

In summary, Big O notation gives an upper bound, Big Omega (Ω) gives a lower bound, and Big Theta (Θ) gives an upper and lower bound.

Note that some algorithms have different upper and lower bounds. For example, like all algorithms that sort by using comparisons, quicksort has a lower bound of $\Omega(\text{N log N})$. In the best and expected cases, quicksort's performance actually is $\Omega(N \log N)$. In the worst case, however, quicksort's performance is $O(N^2)$. The algorithm's lower and upper bounds are different, so no function gives quicksort a Big Theta notation. In practice, however, quicksort is often faster than algorithms such as mergesort that are tightly bounded by $\Theta(N \log N)$, so it is still a popular algorithm.

Complexity Classes

Algorithmic problems are sometimes grouped into classes of algorithms that have similar run times (or space requirements) when running on a certain type of hypothetical computer. The two most common kinds of hypothetical computers are deterministic and nondeterministic.

A *deterministic* computer's actions are completely determined by a finite set of internal states (the program's variables and code) and its input. In other words, if you feed a certain set of inputs into the computer, the results are completely predictable. (More technically, the "computer" used for this definition is a *Turing machine* that is fairly similar to the deterministic finite automata or DFAs described in Chapter 15.)

TURING MACHINES

The concept of a Turing machine was invented by Alan Turing in 1936 (although he called it an "a-machine"). The idea was to make a conceptual machine that was extremely simple so that you could prove theorems about what such a machine could and could not compute.

A Turing machine is a simple finite automaton that uses a set of internal states that determine what the machine does as it reads its input. This is very similar to the DFAs and NFAs described in Chapter 15. The main difference is that the Turing machine's input is given as a string of 0s and 1s on a single-ended infinitely long tape that the machine can read from and write to. When the machine reads a 0 or 1 from the tape, the machine's states determine the following:

■ Whether the machine should write a 0 or 1 onto the tape's current position

■ Whether the machine's "read/write head" moves left, moves right, or stays in the same position on the tape

■ The new state the machine should enter

Despite its simplicity, a Turing machine provides a fairly good model of actual computers, although creating a Turing machine program to simulate a complicated real-world program can be quite hard.

Turing machines have several variations. Some use a tape that is infinitely long in both directions. Others use multiple tapes and multiple read/write heads. Some are nondeterministic, so they can be in more than one state at the same time. Some allow null transitions so that the machine can move to a new state without reading anything.

One of the interesting results of studying Turing machines is that all of these different kinds of machines have the same computing power. In other words, they can all perform the same computations.

For more information on Turing machines, see `https://en.wikipedia.org/wiki/Turing_machine`.

In contrast, a *nondeterministic* computer is allowed to be in multiple states at one time. This is similar to how the NFAs described in Chapter 15 can be in multiple states at once. Because the nondeterministic machine can follow any number of paths through its states to an accepting state, all it really needs to do is use the input on all of the possible states in which it could be and verify that one of the paths of execution works. Essentially (and less precisely), that means it can guess the correct solution and then simply verify that the solution is correct.

Note that a nondeterministic computer doesn't need to prove negative results. If there is a solution, the computer is allowed to guess the solution and verify it. If there is no solution, the computer doesn't need to prove that.

For example, to find the prime factors for an integer, a deterministic computer would need somehow to find the factors, perhaps by trying all possible factors up to the number's square root or by using a sieve of Eratosthenes. (See Chapter 2 for more information on those methods.) This would take a very long time.

In contrast, a nondeterministic computer can guess the factorization and then verify that it is correct by multiplying the factors together to see that the product is the original number. This would take very little time.

After you understand what the terms *deterministic* and *nondeterministic* mean in this context, understanding most of the common complexity classes is relatively easy. The following list summarizes the most important deterministic complexity classes:

DTIME(f(N))   Problems that can be solved in $f(N)$ time by a deterministic computer. These problems can be solved by some algorithm with run time $O(f(N))$ for some function $f(N)$. For example, $DTIME(N \log N)$ includes problems that can be solved in $O(N \log N)$ time, such as sorting by using comparisons.

P   Problems that can be solved in polynomial time by a deterministic computer. These problems can be solved by some algorithm with run time $O(N^P)$ for some power P no matter how large, even $O(N^{1000})$.

EXPTIME (or EXP)   Problems that can be solved in exponential time by a deterministic computer. These problems can be solved by some algorithm with run time $O(2^{f(N)})$ for some polynomial function $f(N)$.

The following list summarizes the most important nondeterministic complexity classes:

NTIME(f(N))   Problems that can be solved in $f(N)$ time by a nondeterministic computer. These problems can be solved by some algorithm with run time $O(f(N))$ for some function $f(N)$. For example, $NTIME(N^2)$ includes problems in which an algorithm can guess the answer and verify that it is correct in $O(N^2)$ time.

NP   Problems that can be solved in polynomial time by a nondeterministic computer. For these problems, an algorithm guesses the correct solution and verifies that it works in polynomial time $O(N^P)$ for some power P.

NEXPTIME (or NEXP)   Problems that can be solved in exponential time by a nondeterministic computer. For these problems, an algorithm guesses the correct solution and verifies that it works in exponential time $O\left(2^{f(N)}\right)$ for some polynomial function $f(N)$.

Similarly, you can define classes of problems that can be solved with different amounts of available space. These have the rather predictable names DSPACE(f(N)), PSPACE (polynomial space), EXPSPACE (exponential space), NPSPACE (nondeterministic polynomial space), and NEXPSPACE (nondeterministic exponential space).

Some relationships among these classes are known. For example, $P \subseteq NP$. (The $\subseteq$ symbol means "is a subset of," so this statement means "P is a subset of NP.") In other words, if a problem is in P, then it is also in NP.

To see why this is true, suppose that a problem is in P. Then there is a deterministic algorithm that can find a solution to the problem in polynomial time. In that case, you can use the same algorithm to solve the problem with a nondeterministic computer. If the algorithm works—in other words, if the solution it finds must be correct—that trivially proves the solution is correct, so the nondeterministic algorithm works too.

Some of the other relationships are less obvious. For example, PSPACE = NSPACE and EXPSPACE = NEXSPACE.

The most profound question in complexity theory is, "Does P equal NP?" Many problems, such as sorting, are known to be in P. Many other problems, such as the knapsack and traveling salesman problems described in Chapter 12, are known to be in NP. The big question is, are the problems in NP also in P?

Lots of people have spent a huge amount of time trying to determine whether these two sets are the same. No one has discovered a polynomial time deterministic algorithm to solve the knapsack or traveling salesman problem, but that doesn't prove that no such algorithm is possible.

One way that you can compare the difficulty of two algorithms is by reducing one to the other, as described in the next section.

Reductions

To *reduce* one problem to another, you must come up with a way for the solution to the second problem to give you the solution to the first. If you can do that within a certain amount of time, the maximum run time of the two algorithms is the same within the amount of time you spent on the reduction.

For example, you know that prime factoring is in NP and that sorting is in P. Suppose that you could find an algorithm that can reduce factoring into a sorting problem. In other words, if you have a factoring problem, then you can convert it into a sorting problem that leads to a solution to the sorting problem. If you can convert the factoring problem into the sorting problem and then use the solution to the sorting problem in polynomial time, then you can solve factoring problems in polynomial time. (Of course, no one knows how to reduce factoring to sorting. If someone had discovered such a reduction, then factoring wouldn't be as hard as it is.)

Polynomial time reductions are particularly important because they let you reduce many problems in NP to other problems in NP. In fact, there are some problems to which every problem in NP can be reduced. Those problems are called *NP-complete*.

The first known NP-complete problem was the *satisfiability problem* (SAT). In this problem, you are given a Boolean expression that includes variables that could be true or false, such as (A AND B) OR (B AND NOT C). The goal is to determine whether there is a way to assign the values true and false to the variables to make the statement true.

The *Cook-Levin theorem* (or just *Cook's theorem*) proves that SAT is NP-complete. The details are rather technical (see `https://en.wikipedia.org/wiki/Cook-Levin _ theorem`), but the basic ideas aren't too confusing.

To show that SAT is NP-complete, you need to do two things: show that SAT is in NP, and show that any other problem in NP can be reduced to SAT.

SAT is in NP because you can guess the assignments for the variables and then verify that those assignments make the statement true.

Proving that any other problem in NP can be reduced to SAT is the tricky part. Suppose that a problem is in NP. In that case, you must be able to make a nondeterministic Turing machine with internal states that let it solve the problem. The idea behind the proof is to build a Boolean expression that says the inputs are passed into the Turing machine, the states work correctly, and the machine stops in an accepting state.

The Boolean expression contains three kinds of variables that are named T_{ijk}, H_{ik}, and Q_{qk} for various values of i, j, k, and q. The following list explains each variable's meaning:

▪ T_{ijk} is true if tape cell i contains symbol j at step k of the computation.

- H_{ik} is true if the machine's read/write head is on tape cell i at step k of the computation.

- Q_{qk} is true if the machine is in state q at step k of the computation.

The expression must also include some terms to represent how a Turing machine works. For example, suppose that the tape can hold only 0s and 1s. Then the statement $(T_{001}$ AND NOT $T_{011})$ OR (NOT T_{001} AND $T_{011})$ means that cell 0 at step 1 of the computation contains either a 0 or a 1 but not both.

Other parts of the expression ensure that the read/write head is in a single position at each step of the computation, that the machine starts in state 0, that the read/write head starts at tape cell 0, and so on.

The full Boolean expression is equivalent to the original Turing machine for the problem in NP. In other words, if you set the values of the variables T_{ijk} to represent a series of inputs, the truth of the Boolean expression tells you whether the original Turing machine would accept those inputs.

This reduces the original problem to the problem of determining whether the Boolean expression can be satisfied. Because we have reduced the arbitrary problem to SAT, SAT is NP-complete.

Once you have found one problem that is NP-complete, such as SAT, then you can prove that other problems are NP-complete by reducing them to the first problem.

If problem A can be reduced to problem B in polynomial time, then you can write $A \leq_p B$.

The following sections provide examples that reduce one problem to another.

3SAT

The *3SAT* problem is to determine whether a Boolean expression in three-term conjunctive normal form can be satisfied. *Three-term conjunctive normal form* (3CNF) means that the Boolean expression consists of a series of clauses combined with AND NOT, and that each clause combines exactly three variables with OR and NOT. For example, the following statements are all in 3CNF:

- (A OR B OR NOT C) AND (C OR NOT A OR B)

- (A OR C OR C) AND (A OR B OR B)

- (NOT A OR NOT B OR NOT C)

Clearly 3SAT is in NP because, as is the case with SAT, you can guess an assignment of true and false to the variables and then check whether the statement is true.

With some work, you can convert any Boolean expression in polynomial time into an equivalent expression in 3CNF. That means SAT is polynomial-time reducible to 3SAT (SAT $\leq_p$ 3SAT). Because SAT is NP-complete, 3SAT must also be NP-complete.

Bipartite Matching

A *bipartite graph* is one in which the nodes are divided into two sets and no link connects two nodes in the same set, as shown in Figure 17.1.

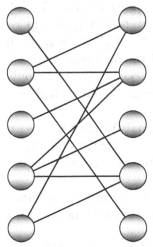

Figure 17.1: In a bipartite graph, the nodes are divided into two sets, and links can only connect nodes in one set to nodes in the other.

In a bipartite graph, a *matching* is a set of links, no two of which share a common end point.

In the *bipartite matching problem*, you are given a bipartite graph and a number k. The goal is to determine whether there is a matching that contains at least k links.

The section "Work Assignment" in Chapter 14 explained how you could use a maximal flow problem to perform work assignment. Work assignment is simply a maximal bipartite matching between nodes representing employees and nodes representing jobs, so that algorithm also solves the bipartite matching problem.

To apply work assignment to this problem, add a source node and connect it to all of the nodes in one set. Next, create a sink node and connect all of the nodes in the other set to it. Now the maximal flow algorithm finds a maximal bipartite matching. After you find the matching, compare the maximal flow to the number k to solve the bipartite matching problem.

NP-Hardness

A problem is NP-complete if it is in NP and every other problem in NP is polynomial-time reducible to it. A problem is *NP-hard* if every other problem in NP is polynomial-time reducible to it. The only difference between NP-complete and NP-hard is that an NP-hard problem might not be in NP.

Note that all NP-complete problems are NP-hard, plus they are in NP.

Being NP-hard in some sense means that the problem is at least as hard as any problem in NP because you can reduce any problem in NP to it.

You can show that a problem is NP-complete by showing that it is polynomial-time reducible to another NP-complete problem. Similarly, you can show that a problem is NP-hard by showing that it is polynomial-time reducible to another NP-hard problem.

Detection, Reporting, and Optimization Problems

Many interesting problems come in three flavors: detection, reporting, and optimization. The *detection problem* asks you to determine whether a solution of a given quality exists. The *reporting problem* asks you to find a solution of a given quality. The *optimization problem* asks you to find the best possible solution.

For example, in the *zero sum subset problem*, you are given a set of numbers. The goal is to find a subset of those numbers that adds up to 0. There are three associated problems:

Detection: Is there a subset of the numbers that adds up to 0 to within some k? (In other words, is there a subset with total between −k and +k?)

Reporting: Find a subset of the numbers that adds up to 0 to within some value k, if such a subset exists.

Optimization: Find a subset of the numbers with a total as close to 0 as possible.

At first, some of these problems may seem easier than others. For example, the detection problem only asks you to prove that a subset adds up to 0 to within some amount. Because it doesn't make you find subsets like the reporting problem does, you might think that the detection problem is easier. In fact, you can use reductions to show that the three forms of problems have the same difficulty, at least as far as complexity theory is concerned.

To do that, you need to show four reductions.

- Detection $\leq_p$ Reporting
- Reporting $\leq_p$ Optimization
- Reporting $\leq_p$ Detection
- Optimization $\leq_p$ Reporting

Figure 17.2 shows the relationships graphically.

Reductions are transitive, so the first two reductions show that Detection $\leq_p$ Reporting $\leq_p$ Optimization, and the second two reductions show that Optimization $\leq_p$ Reporting $\leq_p$ Detection.

Figure 17.2: Detection, reporting, and optimization have the same complexity.

Detection $\leq_p$ Reporting

The reduction Detection $\leq_p$ Reporting is relatively obvious. If you have an algorithm for reporting subsets, then you can use it to detect subsets. For a value k, use the reporting algorithm to find a subset that adds up to 0 to within k. If the algorithm finds one, then the answer to the detection problem is, "Yes, such a subset exists."

To look at this in another way, suppose that ReportSum is a reporting algorithm for the subset sum problem. In other words, ReportSum(k) returns a subset with sum between −k and k, if such a subset exists. Then DetectSum(k) can simply call ReportSum(k) and return true if ReportSum(k) returns a subset.

Reporting $\leq_p$ Optimization

The reduction Reporting $\leq_p$ Optimization is also fairly obvious. Suppose that you have an algorithm for finding the optimal solution. In other words, the algorithm finds a subset with total as close to 0 as possible. Then you can use that algorithm to solve the reporting problem.

Suppose that you want to find a subset with a total that is within k of 0. First use the optimization algorithm to find the subset with total value that is closest to 0. If that subset's total is within k of 0, return it. If the optimal subset's sum is more than k away from 0, then there is no solution for this reporting problem.

To look at this in another way, suppose OptimizeSum(k) returns a subset with a total as close as possible to 0. Then ReportSum(k) can call OptimizeSum(k) and see if the returned subset's total is less than k. If the total is less than k, ReportSum(k) returns that subset. If the total is greater than k, ReportSum(k) returns nothing to indicate that no such subset exists.

Reporting $\leq_p$ Detection

The reduction Reporting $\leq_p$ Detection is less obvious than the previous reductions. First, use the detection algorithm to see whether a solution is possible. If there is no solution, then the reporting algorithm doesn't need to do anything.

If a solution is possible, simplify the problem somehow to give an equivalent problem and then use the detection algorithm to see if a solution is still possible.

If a solution no longer exists, remove the simplification and try a different one. When you have tried all of the possible simplifications and none of them will work, then whatever is left must be the solution that the reporting algorithm should return.

To look at this in another way, suppose DetectSum(k) returns true if there is a subset with total value between –k and k. The following pseudocode shows how to use that algorithm to build a ReportSum algorithm:

1. Use DetectSum(k) on the whole set to see whether a solution is possible. If no solution is possible, then the ReportSum algorithm returns that fact and is done.

2. For each value Vi in the set:

   a. Remove Vi from the set, and call DetectSum(k) for the remaining set to see whether there is still a subset with total value between –k and k.

   b. If DetectSum(k) returns false, restore Vi to the set, and continue the loop at Step 2.

   c. If DetectSum(k) returns true, leave Vi out of the set, and continue the loop at Step 2.

When the loop in step 2 finishes, the remaining values in the set form a subset with total value between –k and k.

Optimization $\leq_p$ Reporting

The final step in showing that the three kinds of problems have the same complexity is showing that Optimization $\leq_p$ Reporting . Suppose that you have a reporting algorithm Report(k). Then the optimization algorithm can call Report(0), Report(1), Report(2), and so on, until it finds a solution. That solution will be optimal.

These reductions show Detection $\leq_p$ Reporting $\leq_p$ Optimization and Optimization $\leq_p$ Reporting $\leq_p$ Detection, so the problems all have the same complexity.

Approximate Optimization

Even though the detection, reporting, and optimization problems have the same complexity, the optimization problem is slightly different from the other two because you can approximate its solutions. The detection problem asks if a certain solution exists. The answer is either "yes" or "no"—it can't be "approximately yes." Similarly, the reporting problem asks you to find a particular solution.

The result is a solution, not an approximation. For example, the reporting version of the subset sum problem should return a subset. It wouldn't make sense for it to return a subset and say, "Most of these items are members of a subset that works."

In contrast, an optimization problem must define some sort of criterion that you can use to evaluate solutions so you can tell which one is best. Even if you cannot find an optimal solution or if you cannot prove that a particular solution is optimal, you can still determine that some solutions are better than others.

All of this means that you can often write a program that searches for an optimal solution. Over time, the program can produce better and better solutions. Depending on the problem, you may not be sure that the latest solution is the best possible, but at least you'll have some sort of approximation to the optimal solution.

In contrast, the detection and reporting versions of the problem can continue to search for solutions, but until they find one, they can only produce the result, "Still haven't found a solution."

NP-Complete Problems

More than 3,000 NP-complete problems have been discovered, so the following list is only a small subset of them. They are listed here to give you an idea of some kinds of problems that are NP-complete.

Remember that NP-complete problems have no known polynomial time solution, so these are all considered very hard problems. Many can only be solved exactly for very small problem sizes.

Because these problems are all NP-complete, there is a way to reduce each of them to every other problem (although that reduction may not be very useful).

- *Art gallery problem*: Given an arrangement of rooms and hallways in an art gallery, find the minimum number of guards needed to watch the entire gallery.

- *Bin packing*: Given a set of objects of different sizes or weights and a collection of bins, find a way to pack the objects into the fewest bins possible.

- *Bottleneck traveling salesman problem*: Find a Hamiltonian path through a weighted network that has the minimum possible largest link weight.

- *Chinese postman problem* (or *route inspection problem*): Given a network, find the shortest circuit that visits every link.

▪ *Chromatic number* (or *vertex coloring*, or *network coloring*): Given a graph, find the smallest number of colors needed to color the graph's nodes. (The graph is not necessarily planar.)

▪ *Clique*: Given a graph, find the largest clique in the graph. (See the section "Cliques" in Chapter 14 for more information.)

▪ *Clique cover problem*: Given a graph and a number k, find a way to partition the graph into k sets that are all cliques.

▪ *Degree-constrained spanning tree*: Given a graph, find a spanning tree with a given maximum degree.

▪ *Dominating set*: Given a graph, find the smallest set of nodes S so that every other node is adjacent to one of the nodes in the set S.

▪ *Exact cover problem*: Suppose you have a set of numbers X, and a collection of subsets $S = \{S_1, S_2, S_3, \ldots\}$ where each S_i contains some of the numbers in X. An *exact cover* is a collection of some of the S's such that every value in X is contained in exactly one of those subsets. The exact cover problem is to determine whether an exact cover exists for a particular X and collection of subsets S.

▪ *Feedback vertex set*: Given a graph, find the smallest set S of vertices that you can remove to leave the graph free of cycles.

▪ *Graph isomorphism problem*: Given two graphs G and H, determine whether they are isomorphic. (The graphs are *isomorphic* if you can find a mapping from nodes in G to nodes in H such that any pair of vertices u and v are adjacent in G if and only if the corresponding nodes u' and v' are adjacent in H.)

▪ *Hamiltonian completion*: Find the minimum number of edges that you need to add to a graph to make it Hamiltonian (in other words, to make it so that it contains a Hamiltonian path).

▪ *Hamiltonian cycle* (or *Hamiltonian circuit, HAMC*): Determine whether there is a path through a graph that visits every node exactly once and then returns to its starting point.

▪ *Hamiltonian path (HAM)*: Determine whether there is a path through a graph that visits every node exactly once.

▪ *Job shop scheduling*: Given N jobs of various sizes and M identical machines, schedule the jobs for the machines to minimize the total time to finish all of the jobs.

▪ *Knapsack*: Given a knapsack with a given capacity and a set of objects with weights and values, find the set of objects with the largest possible value that fits in the knapsack.

- *Longest path*: Given a network, find the longest path that doesn't visit the same node twice.

- *Maximum independent set*: Given a graph, find the largest set of nodes where no two nodes in the set are connected by a link.

- *Maximum leaf spanning tree*: Given a graph, find a spanning tree that has the maximum possible number of leaves.

- *Minimum degree spanning tree*: Given a graph, find a spanning tree with the minimum possible degree.

- *Minimum k-cut*: Given a graph and a number k, find the minimum weight set of edges that you can remove to divide the graph into k pieces.

- *Partitioning*: Given a set of integers, find a way to divide the values into two sets with the same total value. (Variations use more than two sets.)

- *Satisfiability (SAT)*: Given a Boolean expression containing variables, find an assignment of true and false to the variables to make the expression true. (See the section "Reductions" in this chapter for more details.)

- *Subgraph isomorphism problem*: Given two graphs G and H, determine whether G contains a subgraph that is isomorphic to H.

- *Subset sum*: Given a set of integers, find a subset with a given total value.

- *Three-partition problem*: Given a set of integers, find a way to divide the set into triples that all have the same total value.

- *Three-satisfiability (3SAT)*: Given a Boolean expression in conjunctive normal form, find an assignment of true and false to the variables to make the expression true. (See the section "3SAT" earlier in this chapter for more details.)

- *Traveling salesman problem (TSP)*: Given a list of cities and the distances between them, find the shortest route that visits all of the cities and returns to the starting city.

- *Unbounded knapsack*: This is similar to the knapsack problem, except that you can select any item multiple times.

- *Vehicle routing*: Given a set of customer locations and a fleet of vehicles, find the most efficient routes for the vehicles to visit all of the customer locations. (This problem has many variations. For example, the route might require delivery only or both pickup and delivery, items might need to be delivered in last-picked-up, next-delivered order, vehicles might have limited or varying capacities, and so on.)

- *Vertex cover*: Given a graph, find a minimal set of vertices so that every link in the graph touches one of the selected vertices.

Summary

This chapter provided a brief introduction to complexity theory. It explained what complexity classes are and described some of the more important ones, including P and NP. You don't necessarily need to know the fine details of every complexity class, but you should certainly understand P and NP.

Later sections in this chapter explained how to use polynomial-time reductions to show that one problem is at least as hard as another. Those sorts of reductions are useful for studying complexity theory, but the concept of reducing one problem to another is also useful more generally for using an existing solution to solve a new problem. This chapter doesn't describe any practical algorithms that you might want to implement on a computer, but the reductions show how you can use an algorithm that solves one problem to solve a different problem.

The problems described in this chapter may also help you realize when you're attempting to solve a very hard problem so that you'll know a perfect solution may be impossible. If you face a programming problem that is another version of the Hamiltonian path, traveling salesman, or knapsack problem, then you know that you can only solve the problem exactly for small problem sizes.

Having read this chapter, you should now understand one of the most profound questions in computer science: does P equal NP? This question has deep philosophical implications. In a sense, it asks, "What is knowable?" I suspect that most students leave their first programming class thinking that every problem is solvable if you work hard enough and give the computer enough time. Even a brief study of NP destroys that notion.

Just as countingsort and bucketsort "cheat" to sort items in less than $O(N \log N)$ time, someone may someday discover a way to "cheat" and solve NP-complete problems in a reasonable amount of time. Maybe quantum computing will get the job done. Unless someone finally shows that $P = NP$, or someone builds a new kind of computer that can solve these problems, some problems will remain unsolved.

Chapter 12 discusses methods that you can use to address some of these very hard problems. Branch and bound lets you solve problems that are larger than you could otherwise solve by using a brute-force approach. Heuristics let you find approximate solutions to even larger problems.

Another technique that lets you address larger problems is parallelism. If you can divide the work across multiple CPUs or computers, you may be able to solve problems that would be impractical on a single computer. The next chapter describes some algorithms that are useful when you can use multiple CPUs or computers to solve a problem.

Exercises

You can find the answers to these exercises in Appendix B. Asterisks indicate particularly difficult problems. Problems with two asterisks are exceptionally hard or time-consuming.

1. If any algorithm that sorts by using comparisons must use at least $O(N \log N)$ time in the worst case, how do algorithms such as the countingsort and bucketsort algorithms described in Chapter 6 sort more quickly than that?

2. Given a network, the goal of the *bipartite detection problem* is to determine whether the graph is bipartite. Find a polynomial time reduction of this problem to a map coloring problem. What can you conclude about the complexity class containing bipartite detection?

3. Give a network, the goal of the *three-cycle problem* is to determine whether the graph contains any cycles of length 3. Find a polynomial time reduction of this problem to another problem. What can you conclude about the complexity class containing the three-cycle problem?

4. Given a network, the goal of the *odd-cycle problem* is to determine whether the graph contains any cycles of odd length. Find a polynomial time reduction of this problem to another problem. What can you conclude about the complexity class containing the odd-cycle problem? How does this relate to the three-cycle problem?

5. Given a network, the goal of the Hamiltonian path problem (HAM) is to find a path that visits every node exactly once. Show that HAM is in NP.

6. Given a network, the goal of the Hamiltonian cycle problem (HAMC) is to find a path that visits every node exactly once and then returns to its starting node. Show that this problem is in NP.

7. **Find a polynomial time reduction of HAM to HAMC.

8. **Find a polynomial time reduction of HAMC to HAM.

9. Given a network and an integer k, the goal off the network coloring problem is to find a way to color the network's nodes using at most k colors such that no two adjacent nodes have the same color. Show that this problem is in NP.

10. Given a set of numbers, the goal of the zero-sum subset problem is to determine whether there is a subset of those numbers that adds up to zero. Show that this problem is in NP.

11. *Suppose you are given a set of objects with weights W_i and values V_i, and a knapsack that can hold a total weight of W. Then the following list describes three forms of the knapsack problem:

    ■ *Detection*: For a value k, is there a subset of objects that fits into the knapsack and has a total value of at least k?

    ■ *Reporting*: For a value k, find a subset of objects that fits into the knapsack and has a total value of at least k, if such a subset exists.

    ■ *Optimization*: Find a subset that fits in the knapsack and has the largest possible total value.

    Find a reduction of the reporting problem to the detection problem.

12. *For the problems defined in Exercise 11, find a reduction of the optimization problem to the detection problem.

13. **Suppose you are given a set of objects with values V_i. Then the following list describes two forms of the partition problem:

    ■ *Detection*: Is there a way to divide the objects into two subsets A and B that have the same total value?

    ■ *Reporting*: Find subsets A and B that divide the objects and that have the same total value.

    Find a reduction of the reporting problem to the detection problem.

For more practice with the concepts described in this chapter, write a few programs that solve some of the NP-complete problems described in this chapter. Because those problems are NP-complete, you probably won't be able to find a solution that can solve large problems quickly. However, you should be able to solve small problems with brute force. You may also be able to locate heuristics to find approximate solutions for some problems.

Distributed Algorithms

In a paper published in 1965, Gordon E. Moore noticed that the number of transistors on integrated circuits roughly doubled every two years between the invention of the integrated circuit in 1958 and 1965. From that observation, he predicted that the trend would continue for at least another 10 years. This prediction, which is now known as *Moore's law*, has proven amazingly accurate for the last 50 years, but the end may be in sight.

The size of the objects that manufacturers can put on a chip is reaching the limits of the current technology. Even if manufacturers find a way to put even more on a chip (they're quite clever, so it's certainly possible), eventually transistors will reach quantum sizes where the physics becomes so weird that current techniques will fail. Quantum computing may be able to take advantage of some of those effects to create amazing new computers, but it seems likely that Moore's law won't hold forever.

One way to increase computing power without increasing the number of transistors on a chip is to use more than one processor at the same time. Most computers for sale today contain more than one central processing unit (CPU). Often, they contain multiple cores—multiple CPUs on a single chip. Clever operating systems may be able to get some use out of extra cores, and a good compiler may be able to recognize parts of a program that can be executed in parallel and run them on multiple cores. To really get the most out of multiple CPU systems, however, you need to understand how to write parallel algorithms.

> **NOTE**   Some developers also run processes on the computer's graphics processing units (GPUs). Computers often have far more GPUs than CPUs, and they are designed for parallel computation. They are designed for graphics processing, however, so they are not appropriate for all programs.

This chapter explains some of the issues that arise when you try to use multiple processors to solve a single problem. It describes different models of parallel processing and explains some algorithms and techniques that you can use to solve parallelizable problems more quickly.

Some of the algorithms described in this chapter are quite tricky. They can be confusing partly because people normally don't think much in terms of parallel processes. Some are also confusing because they assume that processes can fail in the most tricky and complicated ways possible.

Types of Parallelism

There are several models of parallelism, and each depends on its own set of assumptions, such as the number of processors that you have available and how they are connected. Currently, distributed computing is the most common model for most people. I'll say more about distributed computing shortly.

However, other forms of parallel computing are interesting too, so this chapter spends a little time describing some of them, beginning with systolic arrays. You may not have a large systolic array available to you, but understanding how one works may give you ideas for other algorithms that you might want to write for a distributed system.

Systolic Arrays

A *systolic array* is an array of *data processing units* (DPUs) called *cells*. The array could be one-, two-, or even higher-dimensional.

Each cell is connected to the cells that are adjacent to it in the array, and those are the only cells with which it can communicate directly.

Each cell executes the same program in lockstep with the other cells. This form of parallelism is called *data parallelism* because the processors execute the same program on different pieces of data. (The term *systolic array* comes from the fact that data is pumped through the processors at regular intervals, much as a beating heart pumps blood through the body.)

Systolic arrays can be very efficient, but they also tend to be very specialized and expensive to build. Algorithms for them often assume that the array holds a number of cells that depends on the number of inputs. For example, an algorithm that multiplies NxN matrices might assume that it can use an NxN array of cells. This assumption limits the size of the problem that you can solve to the size of the array that you can build.

Although you may never use a systolic array, their algorithms are fairly interesting, so this section presents one to give you an idea of how they work.

Suppose you want to sort a sequence of N numbers on a one-dimensional systolic array containing N cells. The following steps describe how each cell can process its data:

1. To input the first half of the numbers, repeat the following steps N times:

    a. Each cell should move its current value to the right.

    b. If this is an odd-numbered step, push a new number into the first cell. If this is an even-numbered step, do not add a new number to the first cell.

2. To input the second half of the numbers, repeat the following steps N times:

    a. If a cell contains two values, then it should compare them, move the smaller value to the left, and move the larger value to the right.

    b. If the first cell contains one number, it should move it to the right.

    c. If the last cell contains one number, it should move it back to the left.

    d. If this is an odd-numbered step, push a new number into the first cell. If this is an even-numbered step, do not add a new number to the first cell.

3. To output the sorted list, repeat the following steps N times:

    a. If a cell contains two values, it should compare them, move the smaller value to the left, and move the larger value to the right.

    b. If a cell contains one value, it should move it to the left.

Figure 18.1 shows this algorithm sorting the values 3, 4, 1, and 2 with an array of four cells. The first row in the figure shows the empty array of cells, with the numbers to be sorted on the left. The rows after that show the contents of the cells after each "tick" has finished. The figure calls them *ticks* so that you don't confuse them with the algorithm's steps. For example, after four ticks, the second and fourth cells contain the values 1 and 2.

The first four systolic ticks push the first two values (2 and 1) into the array. These ticks correspond to step 1 in the algorithm. Notice that step 1 only adds a new value to cell 1 during odd ticks, so every other cell is empty, as shown in the second row in Figure 18.1.

The interesting part of the algorithm begins with tick 5 when step 2 of the algorithm begins. During this tick, the algorithm pushes the new value 4 into cell 1. Cell 2 moves its value (1) to the right, and cell 4 moves its value (2) back to the left. After Tick 5, cell 3 contain the values 1 and 2.

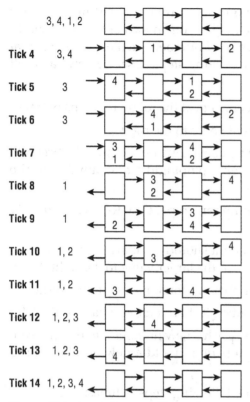

Figure 18.1: A systolic array of four cells can sort four numbers in 14 ticks.

During tick 6, cell 3 compares its two values 1 and 2. It then moves the smaller value (1) to the left, and it moves the larger value (2) to the right. Meanwhile, the first cell moves its value (4) to the right.

During tick 7, the final value in the list of numbers (3) moves into cell 1. Cell 2 compares its values, moves the smaller number (1) to the left, and moves the larger number (4) to the right. Cell 4 moves its single value (2) to the left.

During tick 8, cell 1 compares its values, returns the smaller value (1), and moves the larger value (3) to the right. Similarly, cell 4 compares its values, moves the smaller value (2) to the left, and moves the larger value (4) to the right.

During Tick 9, cell 2 compares its values, moves the smaller value (2) to the left, and moves the larger value (3) to the right. Meanwhile, cell 4 moves its single value (4) to the left.

During tick 10, cell 3 compares its values, moves the smaller value (3) to the left, and moves the larger value (4) to the right. At the same time, cell 1 returns its single value (2).

At this point, the algorithm becomes boring again. Half of the list's values (1 and 2) have been returned in sorted order. The other half of the list's values are stored in the cells in sorted order. They will never collide again in any of the cells, so they simply move to the left until they all pop out in sorted order.

This may seem like a lot of steps to sort four items, but the algorithm would be more impressive if the list of numbers were larger. For N items, the algorithm needs N steps to move half of the numbers into the array (step 1), N more steps to move the rest of the numbers into the array and pull out half of the sorted values (step 2), and N more steps to pull out the rest of the sorted values.

The total number of steps is $O(3 \times N) = O(N)$, which is faster than the $O(N \log N)$ steps required by any nonparallel algorithm that uses comparisons to sort N numbers. Because the numbers are spread across up to $N / 2$ cells, the cells can perform up to $(N / 2)^2$ comparisons at the same time.

This algorithm has a couple of interesting features. First, in tick 7, the last value enters the array. Then, in tick 8, the first sorted value pops out. Because the first sorted value pops out right after the last value is entered, making it seem as if the algorithm is using no time at all to sort the items, this algorithm is sometimes called a *zero-time sort*.

Another interesting feature of this algorithm is that only half of its cells contain data at any one time. That means you could pack values for a second sequence of numbers into the unused cells and make the array sort two lists at the same time.

Distributed Computing

In *distributed computing*, multiple computers work together over a network to accomplish a job. The computers don't share memory, although they may share disks.

Because networks are relatively slow compared to the communication that is possible between CPUs within a single computer, distributed algorithms must try to minimize communication between the computers. Typically, a distributed algorithm sends data to the computers, the computers spend some time working on the problem, and then they send back their results. Two common kinds of distributed environments are clusters and grid computing.

A *cluster* is a collection of closely related computers. Often, they are connected by an intranet or a special-purpose network that has limited access to outside networks. For many practical purposes, you can think of a cluster as a giant computer that has unusual internal communications.

In *grid computing*, the collection of computers is much less tightly integrated. They may communicate over a public network and may even include different kinds of computers running different operating systems.

Communications among the computers in grid computing can be quite slow and may be unreliable. Because the computers are only loosely associated, any given computer may not finish its assigned calculations before its owner shuts it down, so the system needs to be able to reassign subproblems to other computers if necessary.

Despite the drawbacks of relatively slow communications and the unreliability of individual computers, grid computing allows a project to create a "virtual supercomputer" that can potentially apply enormous amounts of processing power to a problem. The following list summarizes some public grid projects:

- Berkeley Open Infrastructure for Network Computing (BOINC), `https://boinc.berkeley.edu`. This open source project is used by many separate projects to study problems in astrophysics, mathematics, medicine, chemistry, biology, and other fields. Its roughly 650,000 computers provide more than 26 petaflops. You can find a list of BOINC projects at `https://boinc.berkeley.edu/projects.php`.

- SETI@home, `https://setiathome.berkeley.edu`. This project uses around 5 million computers producing 892 teraflops to analyze radio signals looking for signs of extraterrestrial intelligence.

- Einstein@Home, `https://einsteinathome.org`. This project uses roughly 2.7 million computers producing 904 teraflops to search gravitational wave data for signs of pulsars.

- Great Internet Mersenne Prime Search (GIMPS), `https://www.mersenne.org`. This project uses around 1.8 million computers producing 615 teraflops to search for Mersenne primes. (A Mersenne prime is a prime number of the form 2^n-1 for some integer n. Currently, the largest known prime number is the Mersenne prime 282,589,933-1, which has 24,862,048 digits.)

- Rosetta@home, `https://boinc.bakerlab.org`. This project uses 1.6 million computers producing 124 teraflops to study protein folding for disease research.

JOINING A GRID

If you're interested in these projects, visit their web pages to download software that will let your computer contribute CPU cycles when it's idle.

FLOPS

Often, the speed of computers that are used to perform intensive mathematical calculations is measured in floating-point operations per second (flops). One teraflop (tflop) is 10^{12} flops, or 1 trillion flops. One petaflop (pflop) is 10^{15} flops, or 1,000 teraflops. For comparison, a typical desktop system might be able to run in the 0.25 to 10 gigaflops range, although by building your own custom system you can get much more power. For example, see the article "Building a 270* Teraflops Deep Learning Box for Under $10,000."

`https://medium.com/intuitionmachine/building-a-270-teraflops-deep-learning-box-of-under-10-000-2d790b0ae2ec`

This article is also linked at `https://tinyurl.com/y4sw3soq`.

Because the processes on distributed computers can execute different tasks, this approach is called *task parallelism*. Contrast this with data parallelism, in which the focus is distributing data across multiple processors.

Multi-CPU Processing

Most modern computers include multiple processors, each including multiple cores on a single chip.

CPUs on the same computer can communicate much more quickly than computers in a distributed network can, so some of the communications problems that can trouble distributed networks don't apply. For example, a distributed network must pass the least possible data between computers so that the system's performance isn't limited by communication speeds. In contrast, CPUs in the same computer can communicate very quickly, so they can exchange more data without paying a big performance penalty.

Multiple CPUs on the same computer can also access the same disk drive and memory.

The ability to exchange more data and to access the same memory and disks can be helpful, but it also can lead to problems such as race conditions and deadlock. These can happen with any distributed system, but they're most common in multi-CPU systems because it's so easy for the CPUs to contend for the same resources.

Race Conditions

In a *race condition*, two processes try to write to a resource at almost the same time. The process that writes to the resource second wins.

To see how this can happen, suppose that two processes use heuristics to find solutions to the Hamiltonian path problem (discussed in Chapter 17) and then use the following pseudocode to update shared variables that hold the best route found so far and that route's total length:

```
// Perform heuristics.
...

// Save the best solution.
If (test_length < BestLength) Then
    // Save the new solution.
    ...
    // Save the new total length.
    BestLength = test_length
End If
```

The pseudocode starts by using heuristics to find a good solution. It then compares the best total route length it found to the value stored in the shared variable BestLength. If the new solution is better than the previous best, the pseudocode saves the new solution and the new route's length.

Unfortunately, you cannot tell when the multiple processes will actually access the shared memory. Suppose two processes happen to execute their code in the order shown in the following pseudocode timeline:

```
// Perform heuristics.
...
                                        // Perform heuristics.
                                        ...


// Save the best solution.
If (test_length < BestLength) Then
                                        // Save the best solution.
                                        If (test_length < BestLength) Then

    // Save the new solution.
    ...
                                            // Save the new solution.
                                            ...
                                            // Save the new total length.
                                            BestLength = test_length
                                        End If

    // Save the new total length.
    BestLength = test_length
End If
```

The timeline shows the actions performed by process A on the left and those performed by process B on the right.

Process A performs its heuristics, and then process B performs its heuristics.

Process A then executes the If test to see whether it found an improved solution. Suppose for this example that the initial best solution had a route length of 100, and process A found a route with a total length of 70. Process A enters the If Then block.

Next, process B executes its If test. Suppose process B finds a route with a total length of 90, so it also enters its If Then block.

Process A saves its solution.

Next, process B saves its solution. It also updates the shared variable Best-Length to the new route's length: 90.

Now process A updates BestLength to the length of the route it found: 70.

At this point, the shared best solution holds process B's solution, which is the worse of the two solutions that the processes found. The variable BestLength holds the value 70, which is the length of process A's solution, not the length of the solution that was actually saved.

You can prevent race conditions by using a mutex. A *mutex* (the name comes from "mutual exclusion") is a method of ensuring that only one process can perform a certain operation at a time. The key feature of a mutex with regard to a shared variable is that only one process can read or write to it at a time.

IMPLEMENTING MUTEXES

Some computers may provide hardware to make implementing mutexes more efficient. On other computers, mutexes must be implemented in software.

The following pseudocode shows how you can add a mutex to the previous algorithm to prevent the race condition:

```
// Perform heuristics.
...

// Acquire the mutex.
...

// Save the best solution.
If (test_length < BestLength) Then
    // Save the new solution.
    ...
    // Save the new total length.
    BestLength = test_length
End If

// Release mutex.
...
```

In this version of the code, the process performs its heuristics as before. It does this without using any shared memory, so this cannot cause a race condition.

When it is ready to update the shared solution, the process first acquires a mutex. Exactly how that works depends on the programming language you are using. For example, in the .NET languages C# and Visual Basic, a process can create a `Mutex` object and then use its `WaitOne` method to request ownership of the mutex.

If a process tries to acquire the mutex after the first process acquires it, the second process blocks and waits until the mutex is released by the first process.

After the process acquires the mutex, it manipulates the shared memory. Because a second process cannot acquire the mutex at this point, it cannot alter the shared memory while the first process is using it.

When it has finished examining and updating the shared solution, the process releases the mutex so that any other process that is waiting for it can continue.

The following code shows what happens if the earlier sequence of events occurs while processes A and B are using a mutex:

```
// Perform heuristics.
...



                                        // Perform heuristics.
                                        ...


// Acquire the mutex.
...

// Save the best solution.
If (test_length < BestLength) Then
                                        // Process B attempts to acquire
                                        // the mutex, but process A already
                                        // owns it, so process B is blocked.

    // Save the new solution.
    ...
    // Save the new total length.
    BestLength = test_length
End If

// Release the mutex.
...



                                        // Process B acquires the mutex, is
                                        // unblocked and continues running.

                                        // Save the best solution.
                                        If (test_length < BestLength) Then
                                            // Save the new solution.
                                            ...
                                            // Save the new total length.
                                            BestLength = test_length
                                        End If

                                        // Release the mutex.
                                        ...
```

Now the two processes do not interfere with each other's use of the shared memory, so there is no race condition.

Notice that in this scenario process B blocks while it waits for the mutex. To avoid wasting lots of time waiting for mutexes, processes should not request them too frequently.

For this example, where processes are performing Hamiltonian path heuristics, a process shouldn't compare every test solution it finds with the shared best solution. Instead, it should keep track of the best solution *it* has found and compare that to the shared solution only when it finds an improvement on its own best solution.

When it does acquire the mutex, a process also can update its private best route length, so it has a shorter total length to use for comparison. For example, suppose process A finds a new best route with a length of 90. It acquires the mutex and finds that the shared best route length is currently 80 (because process B found a route with that length). At this point, process A should update its private route length to 80. It doesn't need to know what the best route is; it just needs to know that only routes with lengths of less than 80 are interesting.

Unfortunately, you can use a mutex incorrectly in several ways.

- Acquiring a mutex and not releasing it
- Releasing a mutex that was never acquired
- Holding a mutex for a long time
- Using a resource without first acquiring the mutex

Other problems can arise even if you use mutexes correctly.

- *Priority inversion*: A high-priority process is stuck waiting for a low-priority process that has the mutex. In this case, it might be nice to remove the mutex from the lower-priority process and give it to the higher-priority process. That would mean the lower-priority process would need to be able somehow to undo any unfinished changes that it was making and then later acquire the mutex again. An alternative strategy is to make each process own the mutex for the smallest time possible so that the higher-priority process isn't blocked for very long.

- *Starvation*: A process cannot get the resources it needs to finish. Sometimes this occurs when the operating system tries to solve the priority inversion problem. If a high-priority process keeps the CPU busy, a lower-priority process might never get a chance to run, so it will never finish.

- *Deadlock*: Two processes are stuck waiting for each other.

The next section discusses deadlock in greater detail.

Deadlock

In a *deadlock*, two processes block each other while each waits for a mutex held by the other.

For example, suppose that processes A and B both need two resources that are controlled by mutex 1 and mutex 2. Then suppose process A acquires mutex 1, and process B acquires mutex 2. Now process A blocks waiting for mutex 2, and process B blocks waiting for mutex 1. Both processes are blocked, so neither can release the mutex that it already holds to release the other process.

One way to prevent deadlocks is to agree that every process will acquire mutexes in numeric order (assuming that the mutexes are numbered). In the previous example, both processes A and B try to acquire mutex 1. One of the processes succeeds, and the other is blocked. Whichever process successfully acquires mutex 1 can then acquire mutex 2. When it finishes, it releases both mutexes, and the other process can acquire them.

The problem is more difficult in a complex environment such as an operating system, where dozens or hundreds of processes are competing for shared resources, and no clear order for requesting mutexes has been defined.

The "dining philosophers" problem described later in this chapter is a special instance of a deadlock problem.

Quantum Computing

A *quantum computer* uses quantum effects such as *entanglement* (where multiple particles remain in the same state even if they are separated) and *superposition* (a particle exists in multiple states simultaneously) to manipulate data.

Currently quantum computing is in its infancy, but laboratories around the world have made amazing progress in the last few years. In fact, IBM has announced the first integrated quantum system called IBM Q System One. You can even run your own programs on IBM Q System One, although the system has only 20 qubits, so the size of the problems it can solve is limited. (*Qubit* stands for quantum bit, the basic unit of information in a quantum computer.)

You can learn more about IBM Q System One at the following URLs:

- ▪ https://quantumexperience.ng.bluemix.net/qx/experience
- ▪ https://www.research.ibm.com/ibm-q/system-one/

Current quantum computers can't do very much, but all advanced technology starts with these sorts of tiny proof-of-concept demonstrations, and there's a chance that quantum computers may eventually become commonplace. In that case, manufacturers may someday be able to build truly nondeterministic and probabilistic computers that can solve problems in NP exactly.

For example, Shor's algorithm can factor numbers in time that is polynomial in the size of the input number. This is much faster than the current fastest-known algorithm, the general number field sieve, which runs in subexponential time. (It's slower than any polynomial time but faster than exponential time.)

Quantum computing is very specialized and confusing, so this book doesn't cover it any further. For more information on quantum computers and Shor's algorithm, see the following:

- ▪ https://en.wikipedia.org/wiki/Quantum_computing
- ▪ https://en.wikipedia.org/wiki/Shor%27s_algorithm

Distributed Algorithms

Some of the forms of parallelism described in the previous sections are rather scarce. Few home or business computers contain systolic arrays (although I could see a case for building a chip to perform zero-time sorting). It may be decades before quantum computers appear in stores—if they ever do.

However, distributed computing is widely available now. Large grid computing projects use hundreds of thousands or even millions of computers to apply massive computing power to complex problems. Smaller networked clusters let dozens of computers work together. Even most desktop and laptop systems today contain multiple cores.

Some of these rely on fast communication between cores on a single chip, and others anticipate slow, unreliable network connections, but all of these cases use distributed algorithms.

The next two sections discuss general issues that face distributed algorithms: debugging and identifying embarrassingly parallel problems.

The sections after those describe some of the most interesting classical distributed algorithms. Some of these algorithms seem more like IQ tests or riddles than practical algorithms, but they are useful for a couple of reasons. First, they highlight some of the issues that may affect distributed systems. They demonstrate ways to think about problems that encourage you to look for potential trouble spots in distributed algorithms.

Second, these algorithms are actually implemented in some real-world scenarios. In many applications, it doesn't matter much if one of a set of processes fails. If a grid computing process doesn't return a value, you can simply assign it to another computer and carry on. However, if a set of processors is controlling a patient's life-support systems, a large passenger plane, or a billion-dollar spacecraft, it may be worth the extra effort to ensure that the processes reach the correct decision, even if one of them produces incorrect results.

Debugging Distributed Algorithms

Because events in different CPUs can occur in any order, debugging distributed algorithms can be very difficult. For example, consider the Hamiltonian path example described earlier. A race condition occurs only if the events in processes A and B happen in exactly the right sequence. If the two processes don't update the shared best solution too frequently, the chance of their trying to update the solution at the same time is small. The two processes might run for a very long time before anything goes wrong.

Even if a problem does occur, you may not notice it. You'll detect the problem only if you notice that process B thinks the best solution is better than the currently saved solution. It's even possible that one of the processes will find a better solution and overwrite the incorrect one before you notice it.

Some debuggers let you examine the variables in use by multiple processes at the same time so that you can look for problems in distributed systems. Unfortunately, by pausing the processes to examine their variables, you interrupt the timing that might cause an error.

Another approach is to make the processes write information about what they are doing into a file so that you can examine it later. If the processes need to write into the file frequently, they probably should use separate files so that they don't fight over access to the file and create yet another possible cause for problems. In that case, they should also write timestamps into the file so that you can figure out the order in which the entries were made.

Even if you have good logs, each process could perform millions of steps over hours or even days before a problem arises.

Possibly your best bet for debugging distributed algorithms is to avoid bugs in the first place. Think carefully about the critical sections of code where multiple processes could interfere with each other and then use mutexes to prevent trouble.

When you write an application, you should also test it as thoroughly as possible. Add extra code to check any shared variables frequently to see if they contain correct values. After you've tested the code and you think it runs reliably, you can comment out the extra logging and value-checking code to get better performance.

Embarrassingly Parallel Algorithms

An *embarrassingly parallel algorithm* is one that naturally breaks into pieces that can easily be solved by separate processes. This kind of algorithm requires little communication among the processes and ideally needs little work to combine the results from different processes.

The following list describes some embarrassingly parallel problems:

Ray Tracing   This is a computer graphics technique that traces a ray from a point of view into a scene to see which objects it strikes. A ray can travel through transparent objects and bounce off of reflective objects. The reason why this is an embarrassingly parallel problem is that the calculations needed for each ray are independent, so you can easily divide them among multiple processors. If you have 10 processors, you can split up the image and make each processor generate one-tenth of the image. Each processor needs to know the scene's geometry, but it doesn't need to know what calculations the other processors are performing. Each process writes its results into different parts of the image, so they may not even need any mutexes to control access to shared memory.

Fractals   Many fractals, such as the Mandelbrot set, require a program to perform a long series of calculations for each pixel in the resulting image. As in ray tracing, the calculations for each pixel are completely separate, so it is easy to divide the problem among as many processors as you have available.

Brute-Force Searches   If you can divide the search space easily, then you can use different processes to search different parts of the search space. For example, suppose that you want to solve a knapsack problem exactly and you want to model the problem as a decision tree, as described in Chapter 12. Suppose also that you have an eight-core computer. Each branch of the decision tree has two branches, representing your putting an item in the knapsack or leaving that item out of the knapsack. In that case, the third level of the tree has eight nodes. You could assign each processor to search one of the eight subtrees at that level and return the best solution that it finds.

Random Searches   If you want to search a solution space randomly, you can make any number of processors search separately and update a shared current best solution. The processors may occasionally examine the same possible solutions and waste some time, but if the solution space is large, this will happen only occasionally. This approach would work well for some kinds of swarm algorithms.

Nonindexed Database Searches   If you need to search a large database that is not indexed, you can partition the database and assign different partitions to different processes. For example, suppose that you have a library of 100,000 photographs of faces and you want to find the best match to a new photograph. You could divide the library into 10 partitions containing 10,000 photographs and then make 10 processes search the partitions.

File Processing   Suppose that you want to perform a slow operation on a large number of files. Say that you have a database containing 100,000 images, and you want to make thumbnails, create embossed versions, or perform some other graphic operation on them. You could divide the files among a group of processors, and they could work separately.

BEWARE OF CONTENTION

The nonindexed database and file-processing examples use a large number of files. Whenever you want multiple processors to handle a large number of files, you need to know how long it will take to read and write the files. Reading and writing files on a hard disk is much slower than processing data in memory. If the operation that you are performing on the files is relatively fast, the processes may spend a lot of time in contention for the disk, waiting their turn until they can read and write files. In the worst case, processes spend so much time waiting for files that the application's speed

is determined by disk access time rather than processing time. (That kind of application is called *disk bound*.)

You can often avoid disk contention by writing the files onto multiple disk drives or
making the processes run on separate computers where each has a disk drive containing part of the database.

Sometimes when you study a problem, you can find a way to address it in
parallel and take advantage of whatever processors you have available. At other
times, you can find pieces of the problem that are naturally parallel. You may
not be able to divide the whole application among a group of processors, but you
may be able to send pieces of the problem to separate processors to save time.

The next section explains how you can use mergesort on multiple processors.
The sections that follow describe some classic algorithms in distributed processing.
Some of them are rather esoteric and may be uncommon in practice, but they
point out some of the low-level problems that may occur in distributed systems.

Mergesort

The mergesort algorithm described in Chapter 6 is naturally recursive. The
following steps give a high-level description of mergesort:

1. Split the values into two, equally sized sublists.

2. Recursively call mergesort to sort the two sublists.

3. Merge the two sorted sublists into the final sorted list.

The following steps describe how you can make mergesort work on P processors, where P is a relatively small fixed number:

1. Split the values into P equally sized sublists.

2. Launch P processes to sort the P sublists.

3. Merge the P sorted sublists into the final sorted list.

Notice that the processors don't necessarily need to use mergesort to sort
their sublists.

Depending on the architecture, splitting the list into sublists in step 1 may
take very little time. For example, if the processors can all access the list in
memory, then you only need to tell each one which part of the list it should sort.

If the processors use a sorting algorithm that uses comparisons to sort, such
as quicksort, then step 2 will take $O\big(N/P\log\big(N/P\big)\big)$ time.

Merging the sorted sublists in step 3 will take $O\big(N\big)$ time.

That means the total time to sort will be $O\big(N/P\log\big(N/P\big)+N\big)$.

Table 18.1 shows the values of $N/P\log(N/P)+N$ when $N=1$ million with different numbers of processors. The final column shows the fraction of time required with the given number of processors. For example, the final row indicates that 16 processors need roughly 0.05 times as long to sort the numbers as 1 processor.

Table 18.1: Run Times with Different Numbers of Processors

P	N/P LOG(N/P) + N	FRACTION OF TIME
1	6,000,000	1.000
2	2,849,485	0.475
4	1,349,485	0.225
8	637,114	0.106
16	299,743	0.050

Dining Philosophers

In the *dining philosophers problem,* N philosophers sit at a table. In front of each is a plate of spaghetti. Between each pair of adjacent philosophers is a fork. The philosophers use a two-handed approach to eating spaghetti, so each needs two forks to eat. The philosophers' goal is to eat, put down both forks for a while to think, and then eat again. They repeat this process until they have fathomed all of the mysteries of the universe. To make the problem harder, the philosophers are not allowed to talk to each other. (Presumably they are too busy thinking.)

NOTE In a real-world application, the dining philosophers problem is really an exercise in distributed processes vying for scarce resources. We're not really concerned about a bunch of bearded men trying to eat spaghetti; we're worried about a group of processes that need to acquire multiple shared resources, such as memory locations.

The following steps describe one algorithm that the philosophers might use:

1. Repeat forever:
   a. Think until the left fork is available. Pick it up.
   b. Think until the right fork is available. Pick it up.
   c. Eat until full.
   d. Put down the left fork.
   e. Put down the right fork.
   f. Think until hungry.

Unfortunately, this algorithm can lead to a deadlock. Suppose that the philosophers are all quite similar, and they all start the algorithm at the same time. Initially, every philosopher finds that the fork on his left is available, so each picks up his left fork. At this point, every fork has been picked up by the philosopher to its right, so every philosopher is stuck waiting for the fork on his right. Because the algorithm does not allow a philosopher to put down his left fork until he has eaten, they are all deadlocked.

This problem has several possible solutions.

Randomization

One way to try to break the deadlock is to have a philosopher put down his left fork and wait for 10 minutes if he has been waiting for the right fork for more than 10 minutes. This prevents a deadlock but may create a livelock. A *livelock* occurs when processes are not blocked indefinitely but still cannot get any work done because of how they try to access the resources. In this example, all of the philosophers could pick up their left forks, all wait 10 minutes, all put down their left forks, all wait another 10 minutes, and then start over.

Sometimes, a simple randomization may break the stalemate. Instead of waiting 10 minutes before giving up on a fork, the philosophers could wait a random amount of time, perhaps between 5 and 15 minutes. Eventually the philosophers will become unsynchronized enough that someone will get to eat.

Depending on the situation, this solution might take quite a while. For example, if many processes are contending over many shared resources, they may need to be very unsynchronized before one of them can get of all the resources it needs.

NOTE You also need to be sure the philosophers' pseudorandom number generators are not synchronized so that they don't pick the same "random" length of time to wait. For example, they could initialize their generators by using their IDs as seeds.

Resource Hierarchy

In a *resource hierarchy* solution, the resources are ranked, and every philosopher must try to acquire the resources in order of their rank. For example, you might number the forks 1 through N, and each philosopher must try to pick up the lower-numbered fork before trying to pick up the higher-numbered fork. If all the philosophers reach for a fork at the same time, most of them pick up the fork on the left (assuming that the fork numbers increase left to right, or counterclockwise).

However, the last philosopher has fork N on his left and fork 1 on his right, so he reaches for the right fork. There are two possibilities, depending on whether he successfully picks up fork 1.

If the last philosopher successfully picks up fork 1, he then reaches for fork N on his left. Meanwhile, the philosopher to his left has already picked up fork N – 1 and now also reaches for fork N. One of the two picks up fork N. Whoever succeeds now has two forks and can eat.

The last philosopher might fail to pick up fork 1 if the philosopher to his right grabbed it first. In that case, the philosopher to his *left* picks up fork N – 1 on *his* left. Because the last philosopher is waiting for fork 1, the philosopher to the left can now pick up fork N unopposed and can eat.

If any of the philosophers eats, the synchronized timing that caused the livelock is broken. Once the philosophers are out of sync, they may occasionally need to wait for a fork, but they shouldn't get stuck in a never-ending livelock.

Waiter

Another solution to the livelock problem is to introduce a waiter as a sort of referee process. Before a philosopher can pick up a fork, he must ask the waiter for permission. The waiter can see who is holding each fork, so he can prevent a deadlock. If a philosopher requests a fork and that would cause a deadlock, the waiter tells him to wait until another fork is freed.

Chandy/Misra

In 1984, Chandy and Misra suggested another solution that allows any number of processes to contend for any number of resources, although it requires that the philosophers talk to each other.

Each fork can be considered clean or dirty. Initially, they are all assumed to be dirty. Then the following steps describe the algorithm:

1. Initially, give each fork to the adjacent philosopher with the lower ID. (If the forks and philosophers are numbered as described in the section "Resource Hierarchy," all but philosophers 1 and N hold their left forks.)

2. When a philosopher wants a fork, he asks his neighbor for it.

3. If a philosopher is asked for a fork, he keeps it if it is clean. If the fork is dirty, he cleans it and gives it to the requester.

4. After a philosopher eats, his forks are dirty. If someone requested a fork while he was using it, the philosopher cleans it and hands it over after he finishes eating.

Suppose that the forks and philosophers are numbered 1 through N in an arrangement, so philosopher K has fork K on his left. Initially, every philosopher has one fork, except for philosopher N, who has no forks, and philosopher 1, who has forks 1 and N. At this point, asymmetry prevents the livelock that can occur with synchronized philosophers.

After this point, the forks' clean and dirty states basically make the philosophers take turns. If you used a fork, it is dirty, so your neighbor can take it from you if he wants it.

The Two Generals Problem

In the *two generals problem*, two generals have armies encamped just outside an enemy city, at opposite ends of town. If the generals both attack the city at the same time, they will win, but if only one general attacks, the enemy will win.

Now suppose that the only way the generals can communicate is to send a messenger through the enemy city; however, the messenger might be captured. The goal is to allow the generals to synchronize their attacks so that they both attack at the same time.

> **NOTE**   Of course, the two generals problem isn't a typical real-world scenario. It's really about distributed processes trying to communicate when messages may randomly disappear. For example, if two players are playing a remote game of chess, then it's important that the players' computers agree on what are each player's moves even if they are communicating over an unreliable network.

An obvious approach would be for general A to send a messenger telling general B that army A will attack at dawn. Unfortunately, general A cannot know if the messenger got through. If general A attacks and general B doesn't, army A will be wiped out. That gives general A a strong incentive not to attack unless he knows that general B got the message.

To tell general A that the message was received, general B can send an acknowledgment message. If general A receives it, then he knows that the two armies are in agreement, and the attack can proceed as planned. However, how does general B know that general A will receive the acknowledgment? If general A doesn't receive the acknowledgment, then general B doesn't know if the attack is still on and whether it's safe to proceed.

The solution, of course, is for general A to send an acknowledgment of the acknowledgment to general B.

By now you can probably see the problem. No matter how many acknowledgments the generals send to each other, there's no way to be sure that the last messenger arrived safely, so there's no way to be certain that the generals agree.

One way around this dilemma is to have the generals send enough copies of the same message to ensure a high probability that one will get through. For example, suppose there's a 1 in 2 chance that a particular messenger will be captured. If one general sends N messages saying "Attack at dawn," then there is a $1/2^N$ chance that all of the messengers will be captured. Perfect certainty is impossible, but the generals can reduce the chances of disagreement to any desired level of certainty.

But how do the generals know the probability that a messenger will be captured? They can figure that out by sending messages to each other. First, general A sends 10 messages to general B saying, "This is message 1 of 10. Attack at dawn." After a reasonable amount of time, general B receives some of the messages. The number of messages received (and the fact that there were 10 of them) tells him the probability of a message's getting through. (The messages' content also tells him to attack at dawn.)

General B uses the probability of capture to calculate the number of acknowledgments that he must send to ensure that at least one will get through with some desired level of confidence.

This works well if general B receives any messages, but what if none of the first batch of messages gets through? In that case, general A never receives an acknowledgment, so he doesn't know if general B got any of the messages.

To solve this problem, general A waits a reasonable amount of time. If he doesn't receive an acknowledgment, he sends a new batch of messages saying, "This is message 1 of 20. Attack at dawn." If he still doesn't get an acknowledgment, he sends another batch of 30 messages, and so on, until he eventually receives an acknowledgment.

Eventually, some of the messages get through, general B calculates and sends an appropriate number of acknowledgment messages, and general A receives an acknowledgment.

Byzantine Generals

In the *byzantine generals problem* (BGP), a set of generals must agree on a plan of action. Unfortunately, some of the generals might be traitors who will spread confusion by giving conflicting signals to the others. The goals are as follows:

- The loyal generals must decide on the same action.

- If the loyal generals really do agree on an action, then the traitors cannot trick some of them into agreeing to the other action.

More generally, you can define the problem so that each general has a value V_i, and all of the loyal generals must learn each other's values. Then the goal for the loyal generals is as follows:

- Learn the V_i values for the other loyal generals.

NOTE   The term *byzantine* comes from the ancient city Byzantium. (The city has had many names including Constantinople, Stamboul, and its current name Istanbul.) Its history is so filled with war, intrigue, and political infighting that the term *byzantine* came to mean characterized by complicated and devious operation. For an introduction to this city and the Byzantine empire that contained it, see https://en.wikipedia.org/wiki/Byzantine_Empire.

Unless you work for the CIA, you probably don't need to worry about actual traitors in your distributed algorithms. The byzantine generals problem is really about assuming that a process might fail in the worst conceivable way. Instead of simply producing an incorrect answer, the process shows different incorrect answers to other processes.

The difficulty arises because the traitors can give other generals conflicting information. A traitor might send general A one value and general B a different value. A traitor could even cast suspicion on general B by telling general A that general B told him something that he didn't.

The problem is easier to solve if you reduce it to the related *general and lieutenants problem*. In this problem, a commanding general gives an order to all of his lieutenants, but either the general or some of the lieutenants might be traitors. The goals for the loyal lieutenants are as follows:

- Decide on a common action.

- If the general is not a traitor, that action must be the one that the general ordered.

Note that you cannot solve the general and lieutenants problem if there are only two lieutenants and one is a traitor. To see why this is true, consider the two situations shown in Figure 18.2.

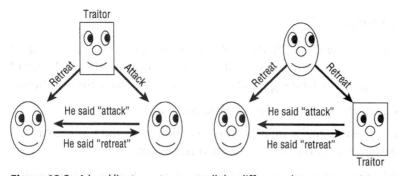

Figure 18.2: A loyal lieutenant cannot tell the difference between a traitor general and a traitor lieutenant.

In the situation on the left, the general is a traitor and gives conflicting instructions to his lieutenants, who honestly report their orders to each other.

In the situation on the right, the general is loyal and tells both lieutenants to retreat, but the lieutenant on the right lies about his orders.

In both of these cases, the lieutenant on the left sees the same result—an order to retreat from the general and an order to attack from the other lieutenant. He doesn't know which order is true.

If there are at least three lieutenants (four people in all) and only one traitor, then a simple solution exists.

1. The general sends orders to the lieutenants.

2. Each lieutenant tells the others what order he received from the general.

3. Each lieutenant takes as his action whatever order is in the majority of those he has heard about (including the one he received from the general).

To see why this works, look at Figure 18.3. If the general is a traitor, as shown on the left, then he can give conflicting orders to the lieutenants. In that case, all of the lieutenants are loyal, so they faithfully report the orders that they receive. That means all of the lieutenants get the same information about the orders they received, so they all come to the same conclusion about which order is in the majority. For the situation on the left in Figure 18.3, all three lieutenants see two orders to attack and one order to retreat, so they all decide to attack and they arrive at a common decision.

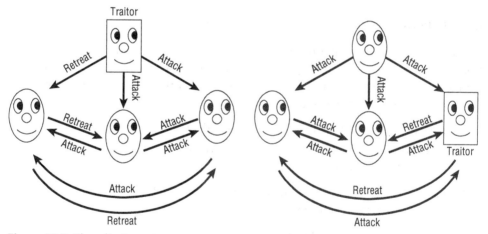

Figure 18.3: Three lieutenants can agree on a common decision no matter who the traitor is.

If a lieutenant is a traitor, as shown on the right in Figure 18.3, then the general gives all of the lieutenants the same order. The traitor can report conflicting or incorrect orders to the other lieutenants to try to confuse the issue. However, the two other lieutenants receive the same order (because the general is loyal) and they faithfully report their identical order. Depending on what the traitor reports, the other two lieutenants may not receive the same set of reported orders, but there are enough loyal lieutenants to guarantee that the true order is the majority decision for every lieutenant.

NOTE The majority vote solution to the general and lieutenants problem works if there are T traitors as long as there are at least 3 × T lieutenants.

After you understand how to solve the general and lieutenants problem, you can reduce the byzantine generals problem to it. Assuming that each of the generals has a value V_i, the following steps give all of the loyal generals the true values of the other loyal generals:

1. For each general G_i:

    a. Run the general and lieutenants algorithm with G_i acting as the commanding general, the other generals acting as the lieutenants, and the value V_i acting as the commanding general's order.

    b. Each of the noncommanding generals should use the majority vote as the value V_i for general G_i.

After all of the rounds of step 1, each general knows the values owned by all of the loyal generals. They may have different ideas about the values held by the traitors, but that's not a requirement of the problem.

Consensus

In the *consensus problem*, a number of processes must agree on a data value even if some of the processes fail. (This is very similar to the byzantine generals problem, in which the generals must agree on a plan of action even if there are traitors.) The specific rules are as follows:

Termination: Every valid process eventually picks a value.

Validity: If all valid processes initially propose value V, then they eventually all decide on value V.

Integrity: If a valid process decides on a value V, then value V must have been proposed by some valid process.

Agreement: All valid processes must agree on the same value in the end.

NOTE The consensus problem applies to distributed computing more obviously than the dining philosophers problem or the byzantine generals problem. This problem is concerned with one or more processes failing. Just to be safe, the problem assumes that a failing process might fail in a byzantine way and produce the worst possible results.

The *phase king algorithm* solves the consensus problem if up to F processes fail and there are at least $4 \times F + 1$ processes. For example, to tolerate one failure, the algorithm requires at least five processes.

Suppose that there are N processes and up to F failures. Initially, each process makes a guess as to what it thinks the final value should be. Let V_i be the guess for process P_i.

To allow up to F failures, the algorithm uses a series of $F+1$ phases. During each phase, one of the processes is designated as the "phase king." You can assign the phase king based on process ID or some other arbitrary value, as long as each phase has a different phase king.

Each of the $F+1$ phases consists of two rounds. In the first round, every process tells every other process its current guess about what it thinks the value should be.

Each process examines the guesses that it receives, plus its own current guess, and finds the majority value. If there is no majority value, then it uses some predefined default value. Let M_i be the majority value for process P_i.

In the phase's second round, the current phase king process P_k broadcasts its own majority value to all of the other processes to use as a tiebreaker. Each process (including the phase king) examines its majority value M_i. If the number of times M_i appears is greater than $N/2+F$, then the process updates its guess by setting $V_i = M_i$. If the number of times M_i appears is not greater than $N/2+F$, then the process sets V_i equal to the phase king's tiebreaker value.

To see how this might work in a simple case, suppose that there are five processes and there could be one invalid process, but in fact all of the processes are working correctly. Let the phase king in phase i be process P_i, and suppose that the processes' initial guesses are *attack, retreat, retreat, attack,* and *attack,* respectively.

Phase 1, Round 1   The processes honestly broadcast their values to each other, so each thinks that there are three votes of attack and two votes of retreat.

Phase 1, Round 2   The phase king broadcasts its majority value attack to the other processes. Each process compares the number of times it saw the majority value (attack) to $N/2+F$. Each process saw the majority value three times. The value $N/2+F=5/2+1=3.5$. Because the majority value did not occur more than 3.5 times, the processes all set their guesses to the tiebreaker value attack.

Phase 2, Round 1   The processes honestly broadcast their values to each other again. Now all of them vote attack.

Phase 2, Round 2   The phase king broadcasts its majority value attack to the other processes. This time, each process sees the majority value five times. The value 5 is greater than 3.5, so each process accepts this as its guess.

Because this example tolerates up to one failure, it finishes after only two phases. In this example, every process votes to *attack,* which happens to be the true majority vote.

For a more complicated example, suppose that there are five processes, as before, but the first fails in a byzantine way (it is a traitor). Suppose that the initial guesses are *<traitor>, attack, attack, retreat, attack*. The traitor doesn't have an initial guess. He just wants to mess up the others.

Phase 1, Round 1   In this phase, the phase king is the traitor process P1. The processes broadcast their values to each other. The traitor tells each process that it agrees with whatever that process's guess is, so the processes receive these votes:

P_1	<The traitor doesn't really care.>
P_2	*Attack, attack, attack, retreat, attack*
P_3	*Attack, attack, attack, retreat, attack*
P_4	*Retreat, attack, attack, retreat, attack*
P_5	*Attack, attack, attack, retreat, attack*

The majority votes and their numbers of occurrence for the processes are <traitor>, attack × 4, attack × 4, attack × 3, and attack × 4.

Phase 1, Round 2   The phase king (the traitor) gives the other processes conflicting tiebreaker values. It tells P2 and P3 that the tiebreaker is attack, and it tells P4 and P5 that the tiebreaker is retreat. Processes P2, P3, and P5 see the majority value attack four times, so they accept it as their updated guess. Process P4 sees the majority value only three times. This is less than the 3.5 times required for certainty, so P4 uses the tiebreaker value *retreat*. The processes' new guesses are <traitor>, attack, attack, retreat, attack. (The traitor seems to be making some headway at sowing confusion.)

Phase 2, Round 1   In this phase, the phase king is the valid process P_2. The processes broadcast their values to each other. In a last-ditch attempt to confuse the issue, the traitor tells all of the other processes that it thinks they should *retreat*, so the processes receive these votes:

P1	<The traitor doesn't really care.>
P2	Retreat, attack, attack, retreat, attack
P3	Retreat, attack, attack, retreat, attack
P4	Retreat, attack, attack, retreat, attack
P5	Retreat, attack, attack, retreat, attack

The majority votes and their numbers of occurrence for the processes are now <traitor>, *attack × 3, attack × 3, attack × 3*, and *attack × 3*.

Phase 2, Round 2   The majority value for the phase king P_2 is attack (seen three times), so it tells all the other processes that the tiebreaker value is *attack*.

All of the valid processes (including the phase king) see the majority value *attack* less than 3.5 times, so they all go with the tiebreaker value, which is *attack*.

At this point, all of the valid processes have *attack* as their current guess.

The reason why this algorithm works is that it runs for $F + 1$ phases. If there are at most F failures, then at least one of the phases has an honest phase king.

During that phase, suppose that valid process P_i doesn't see its majority value more than $N / 2 + F$ times. In that case, it uses the phase king's tiebreaker value.

This means that all valid processes P_i that don't see a value more than $N / 2 + F$ times end up using the same value. But what if some valid process P_j does see a value more than $N / 2 + F$ times? Because there are at most F invalid processes, those more than $N / 2 + F$ occurrences include more than $N / 2$ valid occurrences. That means there is a true majority for that value, so every process that sees a majority value more than $N / 2 + F$ times must be seeing the same majority value. Because there is a true majority value in this situation, the current phase king must see that value as its majority value (even if the phase king doesn't necessarily see it more than $N / 2 + F$ times).

This means that after the honest phase king's reign, all of the valid processes vote for the same value.

After that point, it doesn't matter what an invalid phase king tries to do. At this point, the $N - F$ valid processes all agree on a value. Because $F < N / 4$, the number of valid processes is $N - F > N - (N / 4) = 3 / 4 \times N = N / 2 + N / 4$. Because $N / 4 > F$, this value is $N / 2 + N / 4 > N / 2 + F$. But if a valid process sees more than this number of agreeing guesses, it uses that value for its updated guess. This means that all of the valid processes keep their values, no matter what an invalid phase king does to try to confuse them.

Leader Election

Sometimes, a collection of processes may need a central leader to coordinate actions. If the leader crashes or the network connection to the leader fails, then the group must somehow elect a new leader.

The *bully algorithm* uses the processes' IDs to elect a new leader. The process with the largest ID wins.

Despite this short description, the full bully algorithm isn't quite as simple as you might think. It must handle some odd situations that may arise if the network fails in various ways. For example, suppose that one process declares itself the leader, and then another process with a lower ID also declares itself the leader. The first process with the higher ID should be the leader, but obviously the other processes didn't get the message.

The following steps describe the full bully algorithm:

1. If process P decides the current leader has failed (because the leader has exceeded a timeout), then it broadcasts an "Are you alive?" message to all processes with a larger ID.

2. If process P does not receive an "I am alive" message from any process with a higher ID within a certain timeout period, process P becomes the leader by sending an "I am the leader" message to all processes.

3. If process P does receive an "I am alive" message from a process with a higher ID, it waits for an "I am the leader" message from that process. If P doesn't receive that message within a certain timeout period, it assumes that the presumptive leader has failed and starts a new election from step 1.

4. If P receives an "Are you alive" message from a process with a lower ID, it replies with "I am alive" and then starts a new election from step 1.

5. If P receives an "I am the leader" message from a process with a lower ID, it starts a new election from step 1.

In step 5, when a lower ID process says it's the leader, the higher ID process basically says, "No, you're not," pushes aside the lower ID process, and assumes command. This is the behavior that gives the bully algorithm its name.

Snapshot

Suppose that you have a collection of distributed processes and you want to take a snapshot of the entire system's state that represents what each process is doing at a given moment.

Actually, the timing of when the snapshot is taken is a bit hard to pin down. Suppose process A sends a message to process B and that message is currently in transit. Should the system's state be taken before the message was sent, while the message is in transit, or after the message arrives?

You might want to try to save the system's state before the message was sent. Unfortunately, process A may not remember what its state was at that time, so this won't work (unless you require all processes to remember their past states, which could be quite a burden).

If you store only the processes' states while a message is in transit, the processes' states may be inconsistent. For example, suppose that you want to restore the system's state by resetting all of the processes' states to their saved states. This doesn't really restore the entire system, because the first time around process B received the message shortly after the snapshot was taken, and that won't happen in the restored version.

For a concrete example, suppose processes A and B store the bank balances for customers A and B. Now suppose customer A wants to transfer $100 to customer B. Process A subtracts the money and sends a message to process B, telling it to add $100 to customer B's account. While the message is in transit, you take a snapshot of the system. If you later restore the system from the snapshot, customer A has already sent the $100, but customer B has not yet received it, so the $100 is lost. (This would be a terrible way to manage bank accounts. If a network failure makes a message disappear, the money also will be lost. You need to use a more secure consensus protocol to make sure both processes agree that the money has been transferred.)

So, to take a good snapshot of the system, you need to save not only each process's state but also any messages that are traveling among the processes.

The following steps describe a snapshot algorithm developed by K. Mani Chandy and Leslie Lamport:

1. Any process (called the *observer*) can start the snapshot process. To start a snapshot:

   a. The observer saves its own state.

   b. The observer sends a snapshot message to all other processes. The message contains the observer's address and a *snapshot token* that indicates which snapshot this is.

2. If a process receives a particular snapshot token for the first time:

   a. It sends the observer its saved state.

   b. It attaches a snapshot token to all subsequent messages that it sends to any other process.

3. Suppose process B receives the snapshot token and then later receives a message from process A that does not have the snapshot token attached. In that case, the message was in transit when the snapshot was taken. It was sent before process A started the snapshot process, but it arrived after process B sent its snapshot to the observer. That means it is not taken into account by process B's saved state. To make sure that this information isn't lost, process B sends a copy of the message to the observer.

After all the messages have finished flowing through the system, the observer has a record of every process's state and of any messages that were in transit when the snapshot was taken.

Clock Synchronization

Exact clock synchronization can be tricky because of inconsistent message transmission times that occur in a shared network. The problem becomes much easier if processes communicate directly without using a network. For example, if two computers are in the same room and you connect them with a wire, then you can measure the wire's length and calculate the time it takes for a signal to travel across the wire. Then you can use the result to synchronize the computers' clocks.

This works, but it is cumbersome and may not be possible between computers that are far apart. Fortunately, you can synchronize two processes' clocks fairly well by using a network if you assume that a network's message transmission time doesn't vary too much over a short period of time.

Suppose that you want process B to synchronize its clock to the clock used by process A. Let's call the time according to process A the "true" time.

The following steps describe the messages that the processes should exchange:

1. Process A sends process B a message containing T_{A1} (the current time according to process A).

2. Process B receives the message and sends process A a reply containing T_{A1} and T_{B1} (the current time according to process B).

3. Process A receives the reply and sends process B a new message containing T_{A1}, T_{B1}, and T_{A2} (the new current time according to process A).

Now process B can perform some calculations to synchronize its clock with process A.

Suppose that E is the error between the two clocks so that $T_B = T_A + E$ at any given time. Also suppose that D is the delay required to send a message between the two processes.

When process B records time $T_{B1'}$, the initial message took time D to get from process A to process B, so you get the following:

$$T_{B1} = (T_{A1} + E) + D$$

Similarly, when process A records time $T_{A2'}$, the reply took time D to get from process B to process A, so you get the following:

$$T_{A2} = (T_{B1} - E) + D$$

If you subtract the second equation from the first, you get the following:

$$T_{B1} - T_{A2} = (T_{A1} + E + D) - (T_{B1} - E + D)$$
$$= T_{A1} - T_{B1} + 2 \times E$$

Solving this equation for E gives the following:

$$E = (2 \times T_{B1} - T_{A2} - T_{A1}) / 2$$

Now process B has an estimate of E, so it can adjust its clock accordingly.

This algorithm assumes that the delay remains roughly constant during the time it takes to pass the messages back and forth. It also assumes that a message from A to B takes about the same amount of time as a message from B to A.

Summary

This chapter discussed issues that involve parallel processing. It explained some of the different models of parallel computation and described several algorithms that run in distributed systems. You may not need to use some of the more esoteric algorithms, such as the zero-time sort on a systolic array or the solution to the dining philosophers problem, but all of these algorithms highlight some of the problems that can arise in distributed systems. Those problems include such issues as race conditions, deadlock, livelock, consistency, and synchronization.

Distributed environments range from desktop and laptop computers with multiple cores to huge grid projects that use millions of computers to attack a single problem. Even if Moore's law holds for another decade or two, so much underused processing power is already available that it makes sense to try to take advantage of it with distributed computing. To get the most out of today's computing environments and the increasingly parallel environments that are on their way, you must be aware of these issues and the approaches that you can use to solve them.

Exercises

You can find the answers to these exercises in Appendix B. Asterisks indicate particularly difficult problems.

1. Make a diagram similar to the one shown in Figure 18.1, showing how the zero-time sorting algorithm would sort the two lists 3, 5, 4, 1 and 7, 9, 6, 8 simultaneously. Draw one set of numbers in bold or in a different color to make it easier to keep the two lists separate as the algorithm runs. How many more ticks are required to sort the two lists instead of just one?

2. In many systems, a process can safely read a shared memory location, so it only needs a mutex to write safely to the location. (The system is said to have atomic reads, because a read operation cannot be interrupted in the middle.) What happens to the Hamiltonian path example if the process reads the shared total route length in the If statement and then acquires the mutex as its first statement inside the If Then block?

3. *Consider the Chandy/Misra solution to the dining philosophers problem. Suppose that the philosophers are synchronized, and suppose also that they all immediately attempt to eat. Assume that a philosopher thinks for a long time after eating, so none of them needs to eat a second time before the others have eaten.

In what order do the philosophers eat? In other words, who eats first, second, third, and so on? (*Hint*: It may be helpful to draw a series of pictures to show what happens.)

4. In the two generals problem, what happens if some of the initial messages get through and general B sends some acknowledgments but he is unlucky and none of the acknowledgments makes it back to general A?

5. In the two generals problem, let P_{AB} be the probability that a messenger is intercepted going from general A to general B. Similarly, let P_{BA} be the probability that a messenger is intercepted going from general B to general A. The original algorithm assumes that $P_{AB} = P_{BA}$, but suppose that isn't true. How can the generals figure out the two probabilities?

6. Consider the three-person general and lieutenant problem shown in Figure 18.2. You could try to solve the problem by making a rule that any lieutenant who hears conflicting orders should follow the order given by the general. Why won't that work?

7. Again, consider the three-person general and lieutenant problem shown in Figure 18.2. You could try to solve the problem by making a rule that any lieutenant who hears conflicting orders should retreat. Why won't that work?

8. In the four-person general and lieutenant problem shown in Figure 18.3, can the loyal lieutenants figure out who is the traitor? If they cannot, how many lieutenants would be needed to figure it out?

9. In the four-person general and lieutenant problem shown in Figure 18.3, find a scenario that allows the lieutenants to identify the traitor. In that scenario, what action should the lieutenants take? (Of course, if the traitor is smart, he will never let this happen.)

10. What modification would you need to make to the dining philosophers problem to let the leader algorithm to help with it? How would it help?

11. Would a bully-style algorithm help with the dining philosophers problem?

12. Define a ravenous philosophers problem to be similar to the dining philosophers problem, except this time the philosophers are always hungry. After a philosopher finishes eating, he puts down his forks. If no one picks them up right away, he grabs them and eats again. What problems would this cause? What sort of algorithm might fix the problems?

13. In the clock synchronization algorithm, suppose that the time needed to send a message from A to B differs from the time needed to send a message from B to A. How much error could this difference introduce into the final value for process B's clock?

14. The clock synchronization algorithm assumes that message-sending times are roughly constant during the message exchange. If the network's speed changes during the algorithm, how much error could that introduce into the final value for process B's clock?

15. Suppose that a network's speed varies widely over time. How could you use the answer to the preceding exercise to improve the clock synchronization algorithm?

Interview Puzzles

It's perfectly reasonable for a job interview to include questions that require you to use your skills to solve a problem. Each of this book's chapters contains exercises that might make good interview questions—at least if the candidate is well-versed in algorithms. However, many of those questions would be quite difficult if you hadn't recently been reading about the relevant algorithms.

Not long ago, companies such as Microsoft and Google included certain kinds of puzzles while interviewing job applicants. Some tech companies have discontinued the practice, but you might still find some companies using them.

The puzzles are intended to measure a candidate's creativity and critical-thinking ability. Unfortunately, these sorts of puzzles come with a large set of assumptions that may not be true. Most business situations, even in programming, are not phrased as puzzles involving balance scales, marbles, rickety bridges, and goats. They usually don't involve a clever trick or an amazing insight that is blindingly obvious after you hear it but that is practically impossible to figure out in a 10-minute interview.

It's true that finding the best solution to a real-world problem often requires creativity, but many of these kinds of puzzles don't measure creativity. Instead, they measure whether you've scoured the Internet long enough to find the problem that the interviewer is asking about.

For example, consider the following questions:

1. Why are manhole covers round?

2. On which side of a car is its gas cap?

3. What is the significance of the phrase "dead beef?"

4. What is the next number in the sequence 17, 21, 5, 19, 20, 9, 15?

Take a moment (but only a moment) to think about these questions. Here are the answers, with some comments:

1. So that you can't pick one up, turn it on its edge, and drop it into the manhole. That's clever (although other shapes will work, particularly if the opening is relatively small and the cover is fairly thick), but the question asks you to work backward from the solution to find the problem. How often does that occur in a real programming situation?

2. It's on the side opposite the exhaust pipe (unless the exhaust pipe or the gas cap is in the middle, in which case all bets are off). This question also requires you to work backward from the solution (how to prevent gasoline from spilling on a hot exhaust pipe) to the problem.

3. Back in the days of mainframe and assembly programming, programmers could put the hexadecimal value 0xDEADBEEF in the code to make it easy to spot that particular location. This question doesn't test the applicant's creativity or intelligence; it just determines whether he or she ever programmed in assembly . . . and saw that trick . . . and remembered it. It would be easier just to ask how much experience the applicant has with assembly programming. (For the record, I studied some assembly programming, and I didn't run across this trick.)

4. The answer is 14. If you assign numbers to letters so that A = 1, B = 2, C = 3, and so on, then the sequence in the question spells QUESTIO. If you figure that out, it's fairly easy to guess that the final letter should be N, which is assigned to the number 14. This question fools the applicant into thinking about numbers when he or she should be thinking about letters and encodings. Unless you're hiring a cryptographer, this probably isn't relevant. (If you *are* hiring a cryptographer, then you're probably better off asking the applicant about Laplace transforms and hyperbolic curves.)

The *Journal of Applied Psychology* article "Why Are Manhole Covers Round? A Laboratory Study of Reactions to Puzzle Interviews" questions the usefulness of these kinds of interview questions. The article says this kind of question is not a very effective method for gauging an applicant's reasoning ability. Applicants may also feel that these questions are unfair or arbitrary, and that may cause them to become uncooperative or to turn down the job if it is offered.

Does that mean these questions are worthless in interviews? They certainly are if you use them incorrectly.

The next two sections discuss how to handle these sorts of questions as an interviewer and as an interviewee.

Asking Interview Puzzle Questions

The preceding section gave some examples of bad interview puzzles. They rely on knowledge of trivia or, at best, the ability to work backward from a solution to a problem. Working backward does take creativity, but you can certainly be creative without that ability.

More than anything else, those problems tell you how well the candidate combed the Internet, looking for potential interview puzzles. There's some benefit in knowing that the candidate prepared thoroughly for the interview, but it doesn't really tell you much about his or her creativity or problem-solving ability.

To get useful information from a puzzle, you need a question that the candidate hasn't seen before. On the other hand, the puzzle can't be so impossibly hard that the candidate panics. It shouldn't rely on a trick or point of trivia that only measures whether the candidate happened to see a particular issue of some obscure magazine.

Unfortunately, that rules out a lot of puzzles. Those that remain include puzzles that ask the user to perform a calculation, make an estimate, or otherwise do something that may be straightforward but that gives the candidate room to explore possible approaches.

For example, one popular interview question has a form similar to this: "How many baseballs fit inside a school bus?" The candidate is highly unlikely to have memorized that fact, so this question is really asking the user to come up with an estimate. A good answer will list the assumptions that go into the estimate and perform a calculation. (Suppose a school bus is 36 feet long, the interior is 7 feet high, a baseball is 3 inches in diameter, and so on.) It doesn't really matter whether the assumptions are correct, as long as the process makes sense.

This question determines whether the candidate can perform back-of-the-envelope calculations, which is relevant to software engineering.

Another kind of calculation puzzle comes in a form similar to this: "If I'm three times as old as my brother, and in two years I'll be twice as old as he is, how old am I now?" (See "Appendix B: Solutions to Exercises," Chapter 19, Exercise 6, for the answer to this question.) This is mainly an exercise in translating a word problem into a set of equations. That skill is certainly useful, but many people don't like word problems, and most real-world programming problems don't take this form anyway.

Clock puzzles have this form: "How many times do the hour and minute hands on a clock cross each other between noon and midnight?" (See "Appendix B: Solutions to Exercises," Chapter 19, Exercise 7, for the answer to this question.) This puzzle and other clock puzzles usually can be solved by using a table and plugging in some values. That approach doesn't really showcase the candidate's creativity, but it does show that the candidate can be organized.

Another way that you can get some use out of puzzles is to discuss the puzzle afterward. For example, you could use a relatively simple puzzle that you're pretty sure the candidate can solve. Afterward you can discuss why the solution works, how the candidate found the solution, what other approaches might have been worth trying even if they wouldn't work, and so on.

Alternatively, you could give candidates a very hard puzzle, give them time to think about it so that you're sure they understand the constraints, and then discuss the solution. Now you can talk about different approaches that you might take to reach that solution.

SALVAGING A BAD QUESTION

Giving a candidate an impossible problem with insufficient time to solve it won't help either of you, but what if the candidate fails to solve what you think is an easy problem? You could spend the rest of the interview asking the candidate why he or she failed, pointing out how easy the problem is if you look at it a certain way, and otherwise torturing the poor individual to inflate your ego.

A more productive approach would be to minimize the problem's importance and get on with the rest of the interview. You could say, "That's okay. Almost no one figures out this problem. It's really a test of how you react to difficult situations." Then you can get the interview back on track.

Probably a better approach than a simple puzzle is to describe a situation that resembles one that you might actually encounter in your business. For example, you might say, "Let's design a database to store vacation plans for aliens from other planets." This problem is big enough to give the candidate plenty of room to show his or her database design skills and creativity, but it is silly enough so that the candidate probably won't panic. If you like, you can work through the problem together to see how the candidate interacts with others. You can propose strange twists and ask the candidate what might go wrong under different circumstances to see how creatively he or she handles unexpected problems. This kind of interactive challenge is harder to control, and different candidates may come up with very different solutions, so it may be hard to judge among them. However, this challenge can teach you a lot more than a simple puzzle.

Puzzles can be interesting and entertaining, but they're probably not the best way to measure the qualities that you want in your job candidates.

Answering Interview Puzzle Questions

The preceding section argued that puzzle questions don't really measure the characteristics that an employer wants in a job applicant. Instead of measuring your creativity and critical-thinking ability, they measure your ability to memorize trivia and scour the Internet to find these sorts of problems.

Just because these puzzles don't measure the qualities that they seem to doesn't mean you won't see them in an interview. Some interviewers may use them to see how you handle pressure, respond to unreasonable demands, and cope with impossible problems. These sorts of puzzles may not measure creative thinking ability, but they may provide information about your psychological makeup.

So how should you respond to this kind of puzzle question? First and foremost, don't panic. Whether the interviewer expects you to solve the problem or just wants to see how you react, panicking won't help. Freaking out will make it nearly impossible to solve the problem and will create a bad impression.

Instead, focus on the problem. Once you start working on the problem, you won't have as much time to panic.

Many puzzles at technical interviews are related to programming. They may ask you to reverse the characters in a string, sort objects in an unusual way, copy a data structure, or perform some other straightforward but confusing task. In those cases, think about the algorithmic techniques that you know. Here are some techniques that you should consider:

Divide and conquer: Can you break the problem into pieces that are easier to solve?

Randomization: Does the problem include worst cases that could be avoided with randomization?

Probability: Can you think of a probabilistic method that uses guesses to find a solution or that solves the problem with a given probability?

Adaptive techniques: Can you think of an approach that focuses on specific parts of the problem? Are there really only a few true areas of interest, with the rest of the problem being there to confuse the issue?

Data structures: Does a certain data structure (linked list, array, stack, queue, tree, balanced tree, network) map naturally to the problem? Does a certain data structure have behaviors similar to the ones that you need to solve the problem?

Problem structure: Is the problem's structure naturally recursive, hierarchical, or similar to a network? Can you use tree or network algorithms to search the data?

Decision trees: Can you apply decision tree search methods to the problem? (Often you can, but it would take too long.) You might say, "Well, we could try examining all possible combinations of the data, but that would take forever. Perhaps a divide-and-conquer approach would be better."

If you get stuck, you can also try some of the following general problem-solving tips:

▪ Make sure that you understand the problem. If it contains ambiguities, ask for clarification.

- Restate the problem to be sure that you understand it. If you have made a bad assumption, the interviewer may correct you.

- Compare the problem to other problems that you have seen in the past.

- Break the problem into smaller pieces. If the problem is large, look for pieces that you can solve separately.

- Focus on the details. Sometimes the smaller details are easier to handle.

- Focus on the big picture. Sometimes the details don't make sense except when seen together as a whole.

- Make a list of the facts that you know.

- Make a list of the facts that you would like to know. List ways that you might learn those facts.

- Make a table of values. See if you can extend the table to new values.

- Guess and check. You can solve some problems by making a guess and then adjusting to get the result that you need.

- Think outside the box. If the problem is about numbers, think about letters, shapes, and other nonnumeric values. If the problem is about letters, think about numbers.

- Brainstorm. Talk out loud about the kinds of approaches that you might take. This may be a good time to let the interviewer know what techniques you understand. "Binary subdivision probably won't work. . . . The problem is naturally recursive, but that would lead to an infinite series of operations. . . ." Again, the interviewer may correct you. At a minimum, you'll be telling the interviewer some of the techniques that you know.

- Draw a picture if one makes sense. Sometimes seeing a problem graphically instead of textually can help.

- If you get stuck with one approach, try another. The interviewer doesn't want to see you struggling to use the wrong approach long after it's clear that it won't work.

- Stick with it or give up. If you have the time and the interviewer clearly wants you to spend a lot of time on the puzzle, do so. If it doesn't seem like you have enough time, it may be better to ask the interviewer if you should continue.

Failing to solve an interview puzzle doesn't necessarily mean that you failed the interview. If you try hard, exhaust all of the approaches that you can think of, and are clearly getting nowhere, it may be better to ask whether you should stop. You might say something like, "It seems like a recursive approach would be promising, but I think I'm missing something. Do you want me to keep working on this?" If the interviewer wants you to continue, he or she can say so.

Even if you fail to solve the problem, the interviewer probably will learn something from your attempt. If you talk as you work, the interviewer probably will learn about some of the approaches that you know and something about how you think about problems. The interviewer also will see what you do to understand the problem before trying to solve it and how long you work before giving up.

ONE GLIB ANSWER

You're allowed one glib answer, but then you must be prepared to get to work. For example, one common kind of interview puzzle is the estimation question, such as "How many baseballs fit inside a school bus?" or "How many barbers are there in Tampa, Florida?"

These questions often lend themselves to glib answers. For example, if the interviewer asks, "How much should you charge to clean all the chimneys in Detroit?" you could say "As much as the market will bear" or "$30 per chimney." You can pause for a chuckle, but then you should start working on an estimate. If the interviewer only wants the glib answer, he or she will stop you at that point. More likely, however, the interviewer wants to see how you handle a calculation full of unknown values.

If you have absolutely no clue about some value, leave it in the calculation as a variable. After you come up with an equation, plug in some values just to see what happens and make a guess about whether that seems reasonable. For the chimney example, you might come up with this equation:

$$amount = rate \times time \times population \times percentage$$

where:

- Amount is the total amount to charge.
- Rate is the hourly rate (say, $20 per hour).
- Time is the time required to clean a chimney (say, 1 hour).
- Population is the population of Detroit (say, 1 million).
- Percentage is the percentage of people with a chimney (say, 25%).

The last value may require some further estimates. You might try to estimate the number of people living in each household and the number of people who live in houses as opposed to apartments without chimneys.

When you're done, you plug in your guesses and see what amount comes out. For the values shown here, that would be:

$$amount = 20 \times 1 \times 1,000,000 \times 0.25 = \$5,000,000$$

It doesn't really matter whether the answer is correct; it almost certainly isn't. What's important is the method you use to calculate it.

One thing that you should never do is try to pick apart the interviewer's questions to prove how stupid they are. While looking for websites that contain puzzle-style interview questions, I came across an article in which the author gave a series of "snappy comebacks" to the interview question "How would you design a routine to copy a file?" The article had the applicant ask all kinds of questions about what kind of file it is, whether the file's permissions should be copied, whether the file should be encrypted, whether it should be marked for backup, and other detailed questions until the fictional interviewer was frustrated to the point of saying, "Look, just copy the damn file."

The article's point was that this is a stupid question, because no one writes his or her own routines to copy files. That's true in most cases, although I've worked on projects where copying files was particularly tricky due to file locking issues. In fact, the biggest bottleneck in that customer's whole operation involved copying tens of thousands of files per day multiple times across a series of computers that performed various operations on them. Even a small mistake in copying files resulted in lost files or a backlog of hundreds of thousands of files. Even if a question seems pointless, you can't be sure of that until you know background behind the question.

Proving how smart you are and how stupid the question is won't land you the job. At best, you'll show impatience and a lack of interest when confronted with a problem. At worst, you'll alienate the interviewer, imply that you cannot solve the puzzle, and give the impression that you don't care about the employer's problems.

A much better approach is to inquire why the interviewer is asking the question so that you can understand his or her point of view and come up with an appropriate response.

Summary

Interviewers sometimes use puzzle questions in an attempt to measure a candidate's creativity and critical-thinking skills. Those puzzles don't do a very good job of that, although they may provide some insight into how a candidate deals with frustrating situations.

If you're an interviewer, avoid puzzles that rely on trivia, require the candidate to work backward from a solution to a problem, or are so difficult that the candidate would have to be exceptionally lucky to solve them. Puzzles that make the candidate perform back-of-the-envelope calculations are better and more relevant.

Better still are questions that are similar to those that the candidate may actually encounter at work. You also can use exercises similar to the ones included in this book or other books about algorithms and programming in general.

You should be careful not to pick questions that are too difficult, however. Only someone who has studied algorithms extensively or fairly recently will remember the finer points of balanced-tree rotations or how to show that optimization $\leq_p$ reporting (or even know what that means).

You can usually learn more about what the candidate knows by asking questions and discussing problem-solving approaches than you can by posing a single puzzle that may happen to fall outside of the candidate's realm of experience.

If you're a candidate, try not to panic or be offended by puzzle questions. Make sure that you understand the problem and give it your best shot. Remember, failing to solve a problem doesn't necessarily mean you've also failed the interview.

You can find a huge number of puzzle questions online by searching for "interview puzzle questions." Read a bunch and get a feel for the kinds of things interviewers ask and the kinds of approaches required to solve them. Even if you don't face these sorts of puzzles in an interview, they can be interesting and fun, so you won't have wasted your time.

However, don't forget to work on the other parts of your interview skills. Brush up on your algorithms, database design, architecture, project management, and other relevant skills. Last but not least, don't forget to get a good book or two about how to prepare for interviews more generally.

See the following links for some sites that provide particularly interesting puzzles, puzzles that have been used by companies such as Microsoft and Google, and information about puzzle questions:

- Why Brainteasers Don't Belong in Job Interviews: `https://www.newyorker.com/tech/annals-of-technology/why-brainteasers-dont-belong-in-job-interviews`

- 10 Google interview puzzles: `http://www.mytechinterviews.com/10-google-interview-questions`

- 10 famous Microsoft interview puzzles: `http://www.mytechinterviews.com/10-famous-microsoft-interview-puzzles`

- How to Ace a Google Interview: `https://online.wsj.com/article/SB10001424052970204552304577112522982505222.html`

- techinterview: `http://www.techinterview.org`

- Facebook interview puzzles group: `https://www.facebook.com/interviewpuzzles`

- Haidong Wang's interview puzzles (*note that the answers to many of these are not posted on his site*): `http://www-cs-students.stanford.edu/~hdwang/puzzle.html`

- Top 5 Microsoft interview questions: `http://dailybrainteaser.blogspot.com/2010/08/top-5-microsoft-interview-questions.html`

- A2Z Interviews: puzzles *(these have answers but not explanations)*: http://www.a2zinterviews.com/Puzzles/logical-puzzles

- CoolInterview puzzles: http://www.coolinterview.com/type.asp ?iType=619

- CareerCup: https://www.careercup.com

- Math Olympiads: http://www.moems.org

NOTE The Math Olympiads organization organizes math competitions for students in grades 4 through 8. Many of the problems are similar to interview puzzles, and they're pretty fun.

Many books also cover these sorts of puzzles. Look for them in your favorite bookstore.

NOTE In fact, while working on the first edition of this book, I found these sorts of puzzles so fun and interesting that I wrote and published a book about them: *Interview Puzzles Dissected: Solving and Understanding Interview Puzzles* (Rod Stephens, 2016). It expands on the discussion in this chapter and includes explanations of more than 200 potential interview puzzles.

Exercises

The following exercises are brief examples of some common types of interview puzzles.

1. A man has a dresser drawer containing 10 brown socks and 10 black socks. He gets up early and wants to find a pair of socks without turning on the bedroom light and waking up his wife. How many socks should he take into the living room (where he can turn on the light) to guarantee that he has a matching pair of socks?

2. You are given 10 black marbles, 10 white marbles, and two bowls. You may divide the marbles between the bowls in any way that you like. Then you are blindfolded, the bowls are moved around, and you reach into a bowl and pick out a marble. How should you distribute the marbles to maximize your chances of picking a white marble?

3. If you randomly arrange four red marbles and eight blue marbles in a circle, what are the odds that no pair of adjacent marbles has the same color?

4. If you randomly arrange four red marbles and eight blue marbles in a circle, what are the odds that no pair of adjacent marbles is red?

5. What would be the best data structure for reversing a list of customer records without using additional memory?

6. If I'm three times as old as my brother, and in two years I'll be twice as old as he is, how old am I now?

7. How many times do the hour and minute hands on a clock cross each other between noon and midnight?

8. The people in a certain country particularly value boys, so every couple has children until they get a boy and then they stop having children. Assuming boys and girls are equally likely, what is the total percentage of girls in the population?

9. You hire a consultant who wants to be paid in gold. The job will take between one and seven days (you don't know exactly ahead of time). If the job takes the full seven days, you will give the consultant a small brick of gold. If the job takes less time, you will give the consultant 1/7th of the brick per day worked. What is the fewest number of pieces into which you must cut the brick so that you can pay the consultant no matter how many days the job takes?

10. You have eight golden eggs, but you know that one is only gold-plated so it's lighter than the others. You also have a two-pan balance. How can you find the gold-plated egg in only two weighings?

11. You have five unlabeled pill bottles containing between 10 and 20 pills each. Four of the bottles contain 1-gram pills. The fifth contains placebos that weigh 0.9 grams. How can you use a digital scale (one that shows you a weight in grams, not a two-pan balance) to determine which bottle contains the placebos in a single weighing?

Summary of Algorithmic Concepts

This appendix summarizes the key concepts covered in each of the book's chapters.

Chapter 1: Algorithm Basics

Understanding algorithms: To understand an algorithm, you need to understand certain facts about it, such as the following:

Behavior: Does the algorithm always find the best solution?

Speed: How does speed vary with the number of inputs?

Memory requirements: Are they reasonable? How does memory use vary with the number of inputs?

Main techniques: Can you reuse those techniques?

Algorithms and data structures: A *data structure* holds data in some sort of arrangement. An *algorithm* produces a result. You need an algorithm to build and use a data structure.

Pseudocode: *Pseudocode* is text that looks a lot like code but not in any particular programming language. You need to translate it into an actual programming language such as Python or C# before you can execute it.

Algorithmic goals: To be useful, an algorithm must be correct, maintainable, and efficient.

Big O notation: *Big O notation* describes the relationship between the number of inputs and run time or memory requirements as the problem size grows large. Big O notation ignores constant multiples and considers only the fastest-growing function that describes performance.

Run-time functions: Some common run-time functions in order of increasing speed of growth are 1 (constant), log N, sqrt(N), N, N log N, N^2, 2^N, and N!.

Chapter 2: Numeric Algorithms

Randomization: A program can *randomize* a collection of objects. It can then pick the first items in the randomized collection to make a random selection. For example, to select five cards from a standard deck of 52 cards, a program can randomize the deck and then pick the first five cards. You can use a source of randomness to pick values with a different range (as in using coin flips to pick a number between 0 and 7). You can also use a biased source of randomness to generate fair selections.

Pseudorandom: A *pseudorandom number generator* (PRNG) uses a deterministic process to generate random-seeming values. A *true random number generator* (TRNG) uses some sort of chaotic natural process, such as radio static, to generate values nondeterministically.

Fairness: A pseudorandom process is *fair* if all of the outcomes that it can generate occur with equal probability.

Biased: A pseudorandom process is *biased* if it is not fair. A six-sided die that rolls a 1 half of the time is biased.

Probabilistic algorithm: An algorithm that produces a result with a given certainty is probabilistic. For example, the Fermat primality test detects nonprime numbers at least 50 percent of the time. If you repeat the test many times, you can conclude that a number is prime with great certainty.

Random walks: A *random walk* is a path chosen at random. A *random self-avoiding walk* (or non-self-intersecting walk) is a random walk that is not allowed to intersect itself.

Precalculated values: Some algorithms can use precalculated values to work more quickly. Many programs can be sped up by using precalculated values either calculated on the fly or calculated in advance and saved for later use. The sieve of Eratosthenes uses precalculated values to eliminate numbers as potential primes quickly.

Euclid's algorithm: *Euclid's algorithm* lets you quickly find the greatest common divisor (GCD) of two numbers. A modified version lets you find numbers that satisfy Bézout's identity.

Fermat's little theorem: *Fermat's little theorem* lets you test a number to see if it is prime. If p is prime and $1 \leq n < p$, then n^{p-1} Mod $p = 1$. If you pick a random n and p is not prime, then n^{p-1} Mod $p \neq 1$ with a probability of at least 1/2. (In that case, the number n is called a *Fermat witness*.)

Modeling accuracy: The rectangle and trapezoid rules show that better modeling of a problem can lead to a better result without necessarily requiring a lot of extra work.

Adaptive techniques: Many algorithms can be improved if you focus more work on the parts of the problem that are the most difficult and you spend less work on parts of the problem that are easy to handle.

Monte Carlo simulation: Some algorithms can use pseudorandom values to estimate a result. These methods often don't give the accuracy of deterministic methods unless they perform a huge number of trials, but they often are easy to apply when a deterministic approach is difficult.

Newton's method: *Newton's method* uses an equation's slope to find places where it intersects the x-axis.

Gaussian elimination: *Gaussian elimination* solves a system of linear equations. You can use it to find linear, polynomial, or other least squares fits.

Chapter 3: Linked Lists

Linked lists are built from objects called *cells* that each contain a piece of data plus a link to the next cell in the list.

In a doubly linked list, cells have links to the next and previous cells in the list.

Sentinel: In linked lists, a *sentinel* is a cell that does not contain useful data but that is used to mark the beginning or end of the list.

Basic linked-list operations: It is easy to store a collection of objects in a linked list. The list can grow as needed to hold more objects. It is easy to add and remove items to and from a linked list. Linked lists are not very efficient, however, for sorting or searching for items.

Advanced linked-list operations: More advanced (and interesting) linked-list operations include copying a linked list, using linked lists to sort items, detecting loops in linked lists, and reversing linked lists.

Threaded lists: A *threaded linked list* uses multiple threads of links to allow you to visit cells in multiple orders.

Self-organizing lists: A *self-organizing list* rearranges its items to achieve better than expected performance in the long run. (This idea is also used by *balanced trees*.)

Chapter 4: Arrays

An array is a contiguous piece of memory that holds items.

Basic array operations: *Basic array operations* include calculating statistical values such as the minimum, maximum, average, median, and mode.

Array packing: You can pack items into a piece of memory by mapping array indices to memory locations. For example, to save space you can make a triangular array by mapping indices in the triangular array into positions in a one-dimensional array. Similarly, you can make arrays with nonzero lower bounds by mapping the bounds into a regular, zero-based array. You can map values for one-, two-, and higher-dimensional arrays.

Sparse arrays: You can use linked data structures to build space-efficient *sparse arrays* or matrices.

Chapter 5: Stacks and Queues

A *stack* is a data structure that provides last-in, first-out (LIFO) access to items. You can implement a stack in a linked list or array, although you may need to resize the array if it becomes full.

A *queue* is a data structure that provides first-in, first-out (FIFO) access to items. You can implement a queue in a linked list or circular array, although you may need to resize the array if it becomes full.

In a *priority queue*, items are retrieved in priority order.

Pronounced "deck," a *deque* is a queue that allows you to add or remove items from either end.

Double stack: You can store two stacks in a single array by placing one at each end and making them grow toward the middle. If they become too full, you may need to resize the array.

Uses: Other algorithms often use stacks and queues to hold items while they are being processed.

Chapter 6: Sorting

Insertion: As in *insertionsort*, the algorithm takes an item and inserts it into the correct position in some data structure.

Selection: As in *selectionsort*, the algorithm examines the items that have not yet been processed, finds the best one at that moment, and adds it to some data structure.

Simplicity: Sometimes for small lists simple algorithms such as insertionsort, selectionsort, and bubblesort are faster than more complicated algorithms that have a smaller Big O performance.

Decreasing range of interest: As in bubblesort, the algorithm keeps track of the range of interest and restricts that range over time to reduce the number of items it must consider.

Heap: A *heap* is a tree in which every node has value at least as large as its children's values. A heap can be used as a priority queue.

Storing a complete tree: An algorithm can store a complete tree in an array.

Divide and conquer: An algorithm breaks the problem into smaller pieces and solves the pieces, usually recursively.

Randomization: Quicksort can use randomization to reduce the chance of worst-case behavior because of items initially in a particular order. (This doesn't protect it if there are many duplicate items.)

Parallelization: Quicksort, mergesort, and bucketsort can be parallelized.

External sorting: *External sorting* is sorting data that won't all fit in memory at once. Because of how it moves through memory, mergesort performs external sorting well.

Counting: If items have a limited range, you may be able to count them instead of sorting them as countingsort does.

Partitioning: Pigeonhole sort and bucketsort partitions items to simplify the problem.

Picking the right algorithm: Sorting algorithms provide a good example of when it is important to pick the right algorithm for the problem. Picking the right algorithm can mean the difference between solving a problem in seconds, minutes, or years.

Chapter 7: Searching

A *linear (exhaustive) search* simply loops through all the possible items, looking for a target and giving it O(N) run time. If the list is sorted, the algorithm can stop early if it passes the point where the item would be.

A *binary search algorithm* divides in half the area to be searched at each step, giving it O(log N) run time. This concept applies to many problems.

An *interpolation search algorithm* uses interpolation to guess where a target item is, giving it an O(log(log N)) run time.

Picking the right algorithm: If a list is small, then the simpler linear search may be faster than the more complicated binary and interpolation searches.

Chapter 8: Hash Tables

Hashing requirements: Hashing requires a data structure to hold values, a hashing function to map values into the data structure, and a collision resolution policy.

Mapping: *Hash tables* use a hashing function to map values from one domain (names, employee IDs) to another domain (indices in an array). A good hashing function maps any input values to a random distribution of output values.

Chaining: Using linked lists to hold bucket overflow.

Sorted chaining: Sorting the linked lists improves performance in many algorithms.

Open addressing: Mapping data directly to array entries.

Marking Items as deleted: Many data structures cannot easily remove items. Instead, you may be able to mark items as deleted and then reuse their spots later.

Clustering: In some algorithms, such as linear probing and quadratic probing, the probability of an item's landing in different places may not be equal. This can reduce the algorithm's efficiency.

Randomization: By randomizing data, you can sometimes avoid bad consequences. Double hashing uses a second hash function to avoid clustering.

Ordered hashing: Ordered hashing can improve performance if items are hashed once and then looked up many times.

Chapter 9: Recursion

Recursive metrics: For recursive algorithms, in addition to studying run time and memory requirements, you must consider maximum depth of recursion and use of stack space.

Recursive approach: A *recursive algorithm* calls itself to solve a smaller problem. When the recursive calls reach a point where the problem is small enough, the algorithm solves it without recursion and returns to the calling instance.

Recursive definitions: Some sequences, such as the factorial function and Fibonacci numbers, have natural recursive definitions. Those lead easily to recursive algorithms, although they are not always as efficient as non-recursive algorithms.

Self-similar: *Self-similar fractals* are curves that start with an initiator curve and then recursively replace parts of the curve with a suitably scaled, rotated, and translated generator curve.

Divide and donquer: In a *divide-and-conquer approach,* an algorithm breaks a problem into smaller pieces, recursively solves them, and then combines their results. Examples include mergesort and the skyline problem.

Backtracking: *Backtracking* is a technique where a recursive algorithm considers partial solutions. If it cannot extend a partial solution to a full solution, the algorithm discards the partial solution, backtracks to the previous feasible test solution, and continues searching from there. Examples include the eight queens problem and the knight's tour problem.

Selection: A *selection* is an unordered subset taken from a set of objects. The number of selections without duplicates of k items taken from a total of n items is given by this equation

$$\binom{n}{k} = \frac{n!}{k!(n-k)!}$$

The number of selections with duplicates of k items taken from a total of n items is given by $\binom{n+k-1}{k}$.

Permutation: A *permutation* is an ordered subset of items taken from a set. The number of permutations with duplicates of k items taken from a total of n items is given by n^k. The number of permutations without duplicates is $n \times (n-1) \times (n-2) \times \ldots \times (n-k+1)$. For the special case where k = n, which is what most people think of as a permutation, this is n!

Tail recursion removal: You can replace tail recursion with a loop that resets parameters before the end of the loop.

Dynamic programming: If a calculation such as the Fibonacci numbers must recalculate the same values many times, you can save time by storing values in a lookup table so that you need to calculate them only once.

Bottom-up programming: Sometimes, you can remove recursion by starting with the smallest pieces of data and using them to build larger ones rather than starting at the largest scale and recursively dividing the data.

General recursion removal: You can remove recursion more generally by mimicking how a program calls a method recursively. Push variables onto stacks before recursion, and pop them off afterward.

Chapter 10: Trees

For a review of tree terminology, review the first section in Chapter 10, and see Table 10.1.

Many algorithms use trees, so it's important to remember at least the most basic tree properties.

Logarithmic growth: If a tree is reasonably balanced, its height grows in proportion to the logarithm of the number of nodes it contains.

Lots of leaves: If a binary tree is reasonably balanced, roughly half its nodes are leaves.

Inductive reasoning: Proof by induction is a useful technique for proving tree theorems.

Branches and object references: You can use *object references* or pointers to link a node to its children. You can use similar references to create threads through trees. You also can use similar references to build networks.

Child lists: A node can contain a list of its children. Alternatively, a node might contain a link to its first child, and then the child node can hold a link to its next sibling.

Traversals: Preorder, inorder, postorder, and breadth-first traversals process the nodes in a tree in different orders.

Sorted trees: A *sorted tree* arranges its nodes so that they are processed in sorted order during an inorder traversal.

Deleting nodes: If you delete a node from a sorted tree, you may need to rearrange the tree to keep it sorted.

Threads: You can use special branches or links for threads that let you visit the nodes in a tree or network in unusual orders. A data structure can have as many threads as you find useful, although maintaining threads requires extra work.

Knowledge trees: The animal game uses a knowledge tree to represent questions and the results that answers to those questions give.

Expressions: Expressions can be represented and evaluated as trees.

Spatial trees: Interval trees, quadtrees, and octtrees subdivide one-, two-, or three-dimensional space to make locating objects fast.

Tries: A *trie* or prefix tree stores partial information about strings in its internal nodes and leaf nodes.

Chapter 11: Balanced Trees

Amortized operations: Sometimes you can do a little extra work during common operations such as rebalancing a tree when you add or remove a value to avoid performing much longer operations later.

AVL trees: *AVL trees* use rotations to rebalance the tree, so the heights of two subtrees at any node differ by at most 1.

2-3 trees: Every internal node has either two or three children. If a node has three children and you add a node to it, it splits into two nodes with two children. If a node has two children and you remove one of them, the node rearranges with a sibling node or merges with a value in its parent.

B-trees: Every node holds between K and $2 \times K$ values, where K is the tree's order. A node holding M values has $M + 1$ children. *B-trees* are a generalization of 2-3 trees and use similar node splitting and merging.

Top-down B-trees: When moving down into the tree to add a value, the algorithm splits any full nodes it encounters so that there is room if needed. This is another example of an amortized operation in which the algorithm does some extra work to make later operations easier.

Chapter 12: Decision Trees

You can model many problems with decision trees. A branch in a decision tree represents a single decision.

Game trees are a special kind of decision tree. A minimax strategy lets you minimize your opponent's board position. Game tree heuristics include precomputed initial moves and responses, looking for patterns, and numeric board locations that may change over time.

Types of problems: Many complex problems come in two forms: a yes/no form and an optimization form. Decision trees help model the optimization form. If a decision tree doesn't find a solution to the yes/no form, you cannot conclude that a solution doesn't exist unless you search the tree exhaustively.

Here are some examples:

- To find an ordering of items, a branch at level K in the tree represents selecting one of the remaining items for the Kth position in the ordering. The tree has N! leaf nodes.

- To select a subset of a collection of items, a branch at level K in the tree determines whether the Kth item is in the set. Each node has two branches. The tree has 2^N leaf nodes.

- To select a subset of M items from a collection of N items, a branch at level K in the tree selects one of the $N - K$ remaining items. The tree has $N \times (N - 1) \times \ldots \times K$ leaf nodes.

Branch and bound: As a *branch-and-bound algorithm* searches a tree, it keeps track of the best solution it has found so far and the best possible solution that it can find from the current point in the tree. If the best possible solution from that point cannot beat the current best solution, the algorithm abandons that node and considers other paths through the tree. Branch and bound can be much faster than exhaustive search for finding an optimal solution, but it doesn't change the algorithm's Big O run time.

Difficult problems: Many difficult problems, such as the partition, subset sum, bin packing, cutting stock, knapsack, traveling salesman, and satisfiability problem, can be modeled with decision trees.

Heuristics: Many trees are enormous for large problem sizes, so often they cannot be solved exactly, and you must turn to heuristics. Heuristics that can apply to any decision tree include random search, improving paths, and simulated annealing. Hill climbing and sorted hill climbing often can give good results extremely quickly, although you need to define what *hill climbing* means for a particular problem.

Swarm intelligence: *Swarm intelligence algorithms* such as ant colony, bee, and swarm algorithms provide a framework for randomized searching of a solution space.

Chapter 13: Basic Network Algorithms

For an examination of network terminology, review the first section in Chapter 13 and see Table 13.1.

Some network representations use a separate Link class. Others store link information in the node where the link starts.

Traversals: Depth-first and breadth-first network traversal algorithms work much as tree traversal algorithms do, except that you need to add a property to the node class so that you can tell when you've already visited a node. If you don't do that, then the traversal may get stuck in an infinite loop.

Connectivity: You can determine whether a network is connected starting from a given node by traversing the network from that node and then determining whether the traversal visited every node in the network.

Spanning tree: A *spanning tree* is a tree that connects every node in the network. A minimal spanning tree has the least possible cost. A *Euclidean spanning tree* is one where the links have weights equal to their lengths. The spanning tree algorithm described in Chapter 13 is a good example of a greedy algorithm. You can use a random spanning tree to build a maze.

Strongly-connected components: A subset of a network is strongly connected if it contains a path between any pair of nodes in the subset.

Label setting: A *label-setting algorithm* always adds items to the solution that will remain in the final solution. A *label-setting shortest path algorithm* is a breadth-first traversal of the network.

Label correcting: A *label-correcting algorithm* adds items to the solution that may later be replaced with better items. A *label-correcting shortest path algorithm* is a depth-first traversal of the network.

All pairs: An *all-pairs shortest path algorithm* finds paths between any two nodes in a network. It has polynomial run time, but the $O(N^3)$ polynomial is large enough that the algorithm is slow for big networks. It also takes $O(N^2)$ memory, so it can use a lot of memory for large networks.

Transitive closure: A network's *transitive closure* determines whether there is a path between any pair of nodes. Conceptually, it is similar to adding links between any node and any other that is reachable from that node.

Transitive reduction: A network's *transitive reduction* has the fewest possible links that give the same reachability.

Chapter 14: More Network Algorithms

Topological sorting: *Topological sorting* extends a partial ordering to a full ordering so that you can perform tasks in a feasible order. Topological sorting also lets you determine whether a network contains cycles.

Colorability: If a map is two-colorable, then it is easy to find a two-coloring. Determining whether a map is three-colorable is a very hard problem. You can color any map with at most four colors, but that doesn't mean it will be easy to find a four-coloring. Finding a five-coloring is complicated but reasonably fast. Often, a greedy algorithm finds a coloring without too many extra colors.

Maximal flow: You can find maximal flows by using a (virtual) residual capacity network. An augmenting path shows how to improve the flows. You can use maximal flows to perform work assignment, find a minimum flow cut, and determine the number of disjointed paths from a source to a sink.

Network algorithms: You can model many other problems with networks. For example, you can use a network to perform work assignment.

Other network algorithms: Other network algorithms include network cloning, finding cliques, finding triangles, community detection, and finding Eulerian paths and cycles.

Chapter 15: String Algorithms

Parenthesis matching: You can use parenthesis matching to help parse mathematical, logical, or other parenthesized expressions. You also can use parenthesis matching to build parse trees, which you can then use to evaluate expressions multiple times or to generate data structures.

Regular expressions: *Regular expressions* let a program determine whether a string contains a substring that matches a pattern. The algorithms described for working with regular expressions use DFAs and NFAs to process strings. DFAs and NFAs are also useful in other situations where you want to use a set of simple rules to control a virtual computer.

Substring matching: The *Boyer–Moore algorithm* lets a program check a string for a particular substring without examining every character in the string. In other situations, you may be able to apply the idea that a simple test (checking the end of a target substring) may be able to exclude a large area where the target may appear.

Edit distance: The *edit distance algorithm* determines the similarity of two strings or files. In any situation where you can define the types of changes that are allowed, you can use a similar approach to calculate the similarity of two objects.

Phonetic algorithms: Algorithms such as soundex and metaphone represent a word's pronunciation so that you can search for words that sound similar.

Chapter 16: Cryptography

For most programmers, these algorithms have only academic or entertainment value. They do demonstrate a couple of useful techniques, however.

Transposition ciphers: Even though several of these algorithms treat message text as if it were written into an array, you don't necessarily need to build the array if you can use simple calculations to figure out where a piece of text would be in the array.

One-time pads: *One-time pads* provide provably strong encryption. Their disadvantage is that you safely need to give the same pad to the sender and receiver.

Block ciphers: *Block ciphers* break a message into blocks and then encrypt the blocks separately. Many of them also apply relatively simple operations to blocks repeatedly to increase obfuscation.

Public-key encryption: *Public-key encryption algorithms* essentially publish a partial transformation. Senders apply the partial transformation, and then the receiver finishes the transformation to recover the original message.

Cryptographic algorithms: Other cryptographic algorithms include hashing and document signing.

Chapter 17: Complexity Theory

Complexity classes: Problems (not algorithms) are grouped into complexity classes depending on how difficult they are to solve.

P and NP: P is the set of problems that can be solved in polynomial time by a deterministic computer. NP is the set of problems that can be solved in polynomial time by a nondeterministic computer. The most profound question in computer science is whether P and NP are equal.

DTIME and NTIME: A problem is in DTIME(f(N)) if it can be solved by a deterministic computer in O(f(N)) time. A problem is in NTIME(f(N)) if it can be solved by a nondeterministic computer in O(f(N)) time.

EXPTIME and NEXPTIME: A problem is in EXPTIME if it can be solved by a deterministic computer in exponential time. A problem is in NEXPTIME if it can be solved by a nondeterministic computer in exponential time.

Reduction: You can use polynomial-time reductions to show that a problem is at least as hard as another problem. (In everyday programming you can sometimes reduce one problem to another so you don't need to come up with a completely new solution.)

NP-complete: A problem is NP-complete if it is in NP and all other problems in NP can be reduced to it. Thousands of NP-complete problems have been identified.

Detection, reporting, and optimization: By using reductions, you can show that these forms of problems have equivalent difficulty, at least in terms of complexity theory.

Approximate optimization: Unlike the detection and reporting problems, optimization problems may allow approximation.

Chapter 18: Distributed Algorithms

Kinds of parallelism: There are many kinds of parallelism, including systolic arrays, distributed computing with networked computers, multi-CPU processing with multiple CPUs or cores on a single computer, and quantum computing. Currently, distributed computing with networked computers is the most common form of large-scale parallel computing. Large distributed networks can include millions of computers and generate teraflops or even petaflops of computing power.

Debugging: Debugging parallel algorithms can be very difficult because synchronization issues make it hard to reproduce incorrect behavior.

Embarrassingly parallel algorithms: *Embarrassingly parallel algorithms* are those that naturally break into pieces that can be shared among several processes with minimal communication.

Contention: Some algorithms may be throttled by contention among processes for scarce resources such as disk or memory access.

Mutexes: A mutex can sometimes prevent problems in asynchronous algorithms.

Mergesort: Mergesort has a naturally distributed implementation.

Dining philosophers: The *dining philosophers problem* addresses deadlock and livelock.

Two generals: The *two generals problem* addresses insecure communications.

Byzantine generals: The *byzantine generals problem* and its variants deal with processes that may fail in the worst possible ways, giving incorrect results rather than no results.

Consensus: The *consensus problem* addresses the issue of multiple processes agreeing on a common result.

Leader election: *Leader election* addresses the problem of picking a process to be the leader. The leader can then coordinate to help solve many other distributed problems.

Snapshot: A *snapshot* records the state of a distributed system, including all of the processes' internal states and any messages that are in transit at the time.

Synchronization: *Clock synchronization* attempts to synchronize one process with another in the presence of communication delays.

Chapter 19: Interview Puzzles

Puzzle problems: Interview puzzles don't necessarily do a good job of testing a candidate's reasoning and problem-solving abilities. They often rely on trivia, sneaky tricks, or working backward from a solution to a problem. Candidates who know the trick can often solve these puzzles without much creative thought. Candidates who don't know the trick often have a hard time even if they are creative thinkers.

Programming puzzles: Puzzles that involve programming are better than those that involve marbles or decks of cards. Programming challenges that don't involve clever tricks are even better than programming puzzles.

Difficulty: If an interview includes a puzzle that is too hard, it may rattle the candidate and you won't learn much about his or her normal behavior for the rest of the interview (or day).

Solutions to Exercises

Chapter 1: Algorithm Basics

1. The outer loop still executes $O(N)$ times in the new version of the algorithm. When the outer loop's counter is i, the inner loop executes $O(N-i)$ times. If you add up the number of times that the inner loop executes, the result is $N + (N-1) + (N-2) + \ldots + 1 = N \times (N-1)/2 = (N^2 - N)/2$. This is still $O(N^2)$, although the performance in practice will probably be faster than the original version.

2. See Table B.1. The value Infinity means that the program can execute the algorithm for any practical problem size. The example programs Ch01Ex02 and ch01_ex02, which are available for download on the book's website, generate these values.

Table B.1: Maximum Problem Sizes That Run in Various Times

TIME	LOG$_2$(N)	SQRT(N)	N	N²	2ᴺ	N!
Second	Infinity	1×10^{12}	1×10^{6}	1,000	20	10
Minute	Infinity	4×10^{15}	6×10^{7}	7,746	26	12
Hour	Infinity	1×10^{19}	4×10^{9}	60,000	32	13
Day	Infinity	7×10^{21}	9×10^{10}	293,939	36	14
Week	Infinity	4×10^{23}	6×10^{11}	777,689	39	15
Year	Infinity	1×10^{27}	3×10^{13}	5,617,615	45	17

3. The question is, "For what N is $1,500 \times N > 30 \times N^2$?" Solving for N gives $50 < N$, so the first algorithm is slower if $N > 50$. You would use the first algorithm if $N \le 50$ and the second if $N > 50$.

4. The question is, "For what N is $N^3 / 75 - N^2 / 4 + N + 10 > N / 2 + 8$?" You can solve this in any way you like, including algebra or using Newton's method (see Chapter 2). The two positive solutions to this equation are $N < 4.92$ and $N > 15.77$. That means you should use the first algorithm if $5 \ge N \ge 15$. The Ch01Ex04 and ch01_ex04 example programs, which are available for download on the book's website, graph the two equations and show their points of intersection.

5. Given N letters, you have N choices for the first letter. After you have picked the first letter, you have $N - 1$ choices for the second letter, giving you $N \times (N - 1)$ total choices. That counts each pair twice (AB and BA), so the total number of unordered pairs is $N(N - 1) / 2$. In Big O notation, that is $O(N^2)$.

6. If a cube has side length N, each side has an area of N^2 units. A cube has six sides, so the total surface area of all sides is $6 \times N^2$. If the algorithm generates one value for each square unit, its run time is $O(N^2)$.

    Less rigorously, you could have intuitively realized that the cube's surface area depends on N^2. Therefore, you could conclude that the run time is $O(N^2)$ without doing the full calculation.

7. If a cube has side length N, each of its edges has length N. The cube has 12 edges, so the total edge length is $12 \times N$. However, each of the unit cubes in the corners is part of three edges, so they are counted three times in the $12 \times N$ total. The cube has eight corners, so to make the count correct, you subtract 2×8 from $12 \times N$ so that each corner cube is counted only once. The true number of cubes is $12 \times N - 16$, so the algorithm's run time is $O(N)$.

    Less rigorously, you could have intuitively realized that the total length of the cube's edges depends on N. Therefore, you might conclude that the run time is $O(N)$ without doing the full calculation.

8. Table B.2 shows the number of cubes for several values of N.

    From the way the shapes grow in length, width, and height in Figure 1.4, you can probably guess that the number of cubes involves N^3 in some manner. If you assume that the number of cubes is $A \times N^3 + B \times N^2 + C \times N + D$ for some constants A, B, C, and D, you can plug in the values from Table B.2 and solve for A, B, C, and D. If you do that, you'll find that the number of cubes is $(N^3 + 3 \times N^2 + 2 \times N) \div 6$, so the run time is $O(N^3)$.

Less rigorously, you could have intuitively realized that the total volume of the shapes depends on N^3. Therefore, you might conclude that the run time was $O(N^3)$ without doing the full calculation.

Table B.2: Cubes for Different Values of N

N	CUBES
1	1
2	4
3	10
4	20
5	35
6	56
7	84
8	120

9. Can you have an algorithm without a data structure? Yes. An algorithm is just a series of instructions, so it doesn't necessarily need a data structure. For example, many of the numeric algorithms described in Chapter 2 do not use data structures.

   Can you have a data structure without an algorithm? Not really. You need some sort of algorithm to build the data structure, and you need another algorithm to use it to produce some kind of result. There isn't much point to a data structure that you won't use to produce a result.

10. The first algorithm simply paints the boards from one end to the other. It paints N boards and therefore has a run time of $O(N)$.

    The second algorithm divides the boards in a recursive way, but eventually it paints all N boards. Dividing the boards recursively requires $O(\log N)$ steps. Painting the boards requires $O(N)$ steps. The total number of steps is $N + \log N$, so the run time is $O(N)$, just like the first algorithm.

    The algorithms have the same run time, but the second takes slightly longer in practice if not in Big O notation. It is also more complicated and confusing, so the first algorithm is better.

11. Figure B.1 shows the RuntimeFunctions example program. It plots the Fibonacci function along with the other run-time functions. If you look closely at the figure, you can tell that Fibonacci$(x) \div 10$ curves up more steeply than $x^2 \div 5$ and slightly less steeply than $2^x \div 10$. The shape of its curve is very similar to the shape of $2^x \div 10$, so you might guess (correctly) that it is an exponential function.

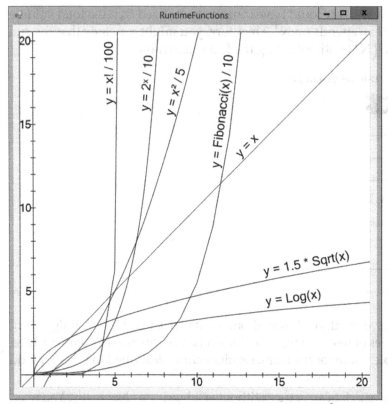

Figure B.1: The Fibonacci function increases more quickly than x^2 but less quickly than 2^x.

It turns out that you can calculate the Fibonacci numbers directly using the following formula:

$$Fibonacci(n) = \frac{\varphi^N}{\sqrt{5}}$$

where:

$$\varphi = \frac{1+\sqrt{5}}{2}$$

So, the Fibonacci function is exponential in φ. The value $\varphi \approx 1.618$, so the function doesn't grow as quickly as 2^N, but it is still exponential and does grow faster than polynomial functions.

Chapter 2: Numerical Algorithms

1. Simply map 1, 2, and 3 to heads and 4, 5, and 6 to tails.

2. In this case, the probability of getting heads followed by heads is $(3/4) \times (3/4) = 9/16$. The probability of getting tails followed

by tails is $(1/4)\times(1/4)=1/16$. Because these are independent outcomes, you can add their probabilities. That means there is a $(9/16)+(1/16)=10/16=0.625$, or 62.5% probability that you'll need to try again.

3. If the coin is fair, the probability that you'll get heads followed by heads is $(1/2)\times(1/2)=1/4$. Similarly, the probability that you'll get tails followed by tails is $(1/2)\times(1/2)=1/4$. Because these are independent outcomes, you can add their probabilities. That means there is a $(1/4)+(1/4)=1/2$, or 50% probability that you'll need to try again.

4. You can use a method similar to the one that uses a biased coin to produce fair coin flips:

```
Roll the biased die 6 times.
    If the rolls include all 6 possible values,
        return the first one.
    Otherwise, repeat.
```

Depending on how biased the die is, it could take many trials to roll all six values. For example, if the die is fair (the best case), the probability of rolling all six values is $6!\div 6^6=720\div 46,656\approx 0.015$, so there's only about a 1.5% chance that six rolls will give six different values. For another example, if the die rolls a 1 half of the time and each of the other five values one-tenth of the time, the probability of getting all six values in six rolls is $0.5\times 0.1^5\times 6!=0.0036$, or 0.36%. So, you may be rolling the die for a long time.

5. You can use the same algorithm to randomize an array, but you can stop after positioning the first M items:

```
String: PickM(String: array[], Integer: M)
    Integer: max_i = <Upper bound of array>
    For i = 0 To M - 1
        // Pick the item for position i in the array.
        Integer: j = <random number between i and max_i>
        <Swap array[i] and array[j]>
    Next i

    <Return array[0] through array[M - 1]>
End PickM
```

This algorithm runs in $O(M)$ time. Because $M\le N,O(M)\le O(N)$. In practice, M is often much less than N, so this algorithm may be much faster than randomizing the entire array.

To give away five books, you would pick five names to go in the array's first five positions and then stop. This would take only five steps, so it would be very quick. It doesn't matter how many names are in the array, as long as there are at least five.

6. Simply make an array holding all 52 cards, randomize it, and then deal the cards as you normally would—one to each player in turn until everyone has five.

It doesn't matter whether you deal one card to each player in turn or deal five cards all at once to each player. As long as the deck is randomized, each player will get five randomly-selected cards.

7. Figure B.2 shows the TwoDiceRolls example program, which is available for download on the book's website. The numbers for each value are the actual percentage of rolls that gave the value, the expected percentage for the value, and the percentage difference.

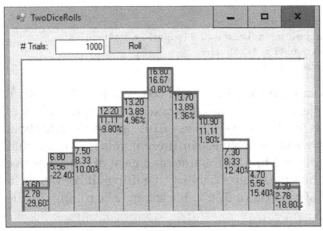

Figure B.2: Relatively small numbers of trials sometimes result in significant differences between observed and expected frequencies of rolls.

The actual results don't consistently match the expected results until the number of trials is quite large. The program often produces more than 5% error for some values until it runs about 10,000 or more trials.

8. The algorithm tries adding a neighboring node to the current path. If that node cannot lead to a complete path, the algorithm removes it from the path and tries again with a new neighbor. That step where the algorithm removes the failed neighbor is the backtracking step, where it undoes a previous move that didn't work out.

9. If the algorithm doesn't randomize the neighbor list, then the algorithm tries the neighbors in the same order each time it reaches a particular point. That means every time the path starts at a particular node, it will produce the exact same path. That won't change its speed; it just makes the result less random and interesting.

10. If $A_1 < B_1$, then A_1 Mod $B_1 = A_1$, so $A_2 = B_1$ and $B_2 = A_1$ Mod $B_1 = A_1$. In other words, during the first trip through the While loop, the values of A and B switch. After that the algorithm proceeds normally.

11. $LCM(A,B) = A \times B / GCD(A,B)$. To see why, suppose $g = GCD(A,B)$, so $A = g \times m$ and $B = g \times n$ for some integers m and n. Then $A \times B / GCD(A,B) = g \times m \times g \times n \div g = g \times m \times n$. The values m and n have no common factors (otherwise that factor would be part of the GCD), so this is the LCM.

12. The following code shows the original fast exponentiation algorithm with changes in bold that make the algorithm perform modular exponentiation:

```
// Perform the exponentiation.
Integer: Exponentiate(Integer: value, Integer: exponent,
   Integer: modulus)
    Integer: result = 1
    Integer: factor = value
    While (exponent != 0)
        If (exponent Mod 2 == 1) Then
            result = (result * factor) Mod modulus
        factor = (factor * factor) Mod modulus
        exponent /= 2
    End While

    Return result
End Exponentiate
```

The ExponentiateMod example program that's available for download on the book's website demonstrates this algorithm.

13. Figure B.3 shows the GcdTimes example program that is available for download on the book's website. The gray lines show the graph of number of steps versus values. The dark curve near the top shows the logarithm of the values. It's hard to tell from the graph if the number of steps really follows the logarithm, but it clearly grows very slowly.

14. You already know that next _ prime * 2 has been crossed out, because it is a multiple of 2. If next _ prime > 3, you know that next _ prime * 3 has also been crossed out, because 3 has already been considered. In fact, for every prime p where p < next _ prime, the prime p has already been considered, so next _ prime * p has already been crossed out. The first prime that is not less than next _ prime is next _ prime, so the first multiple of next _ prime that has not yet been considered is next _ prime * next _ prime. That means you can change the loop to the following:

```
            // "Cross out" multiples of this prime.
            For i = next_prime * next_prime To max_number Step next_
prime Then
                is_composite[i] = true
            Next i
```

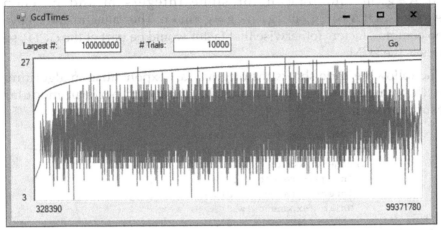

Figure B.3: The GcdTimes example program graphs number of GCD steps versus number size.

15. The following pseudocode shows an algorithm to display Carmichael numbers and their prime factors:

```
// Generate Carmichael numbers.
GenerateCarmichaelNumbers(Integer: max_number)
    Boolean: is_composite[]
    <Make is_composite a sieve of Eratosthenes for
     numbers 2 through max_number>

    // Check for Carmichael numbers.
    For i = 2 To max_number
        // Only check nonprimes.
        If (is_composite[i]) Then
            // See if i is a Carmichael number.
            If (IsCarmichael(i)) Then
                <Output i and its prime factors>
            End If
        End If
    Next i
End GenerateCarmichaelNumbers

// Return true if the number is a Carmichael number.
Boolean: IsCarmichael(Integer: number)
    // Check all possible witnesses.
```

```
                    For i = 1 to number - 1
                        // Only check numbers with GCD(number, 1) = 1.
                        If (GCD(number, i) == 1) Then
                            <Use fast exponentiation to calculate
                            i ^ (number-1) mod number>
                            Integer: result = Exponentiate(i, number - 1,
        number)

                            // If we found a Fermat witness,
                            // this is not a Carmichael number.
                            If (result != 1) Then Return false
                        End If
                    Next i

                    // They're all a bunch of liars!
                    // This is a Carmichael number.
                    Return true
                End IsCarmichael
```

You can download the CarmichaelNumbers example program from the book's website to see an implementation of this algorithm.

16. Suppose that you use the value of the function at the rectangle's midpoint for the rectangle's height. Then, if the function is increasing, the left part of the rectangle is too short and the right part is too tall, so the error in the two pieces tends to cancel out, at least to some extent. Similarly, if the function is decreasing, the left part of the rectangle is too short and the right part is too tall, so again they partially cancel each other out. This reduces the total error considerably without increasing the number of rectangles.

   This method won't help (and may even hurt) if the curve has a local minimum or maximum near the middle of a rectangle. In those cases, the errors on the left and right sides of the curve will add up and give a larger total error.

   Figure B.4 shows the MidpointRectangleRule example program, which is available for download on the book's website, demonstrating this technique. If you compare the result to the one shown in Figure 2.6, you'll see that using the midpoint reduced the total error from about −6.5% to 0.2%, roughly 1/30th of the error, without changing the number of rectangles.

17. Yes. This would be similar to a version of the AdaptiveGridIntegration program that would use pseudorandom points instead of a grid. If done properly, it would be more effective than a normal Monte Carlo integration, because it would pick more points in areas of interest and fewer in large areas that are either all in or all out of the shape.

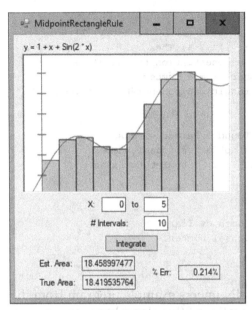

Figure B.4: The MidpointRectangleRule example program reduces error by using each rectangle's midpoint to calculate its height.

18. The following pseudocode shows a high-level algorithm for performing Monte Carlo integration in three dimensions:

```
Float: EstimateVolume(Boolean: PointIsInShape(,,), Integer:
num_trials,
        Float: xmin, Float: xmax, Float: ymin, Float: ymax,
        Float: zmin, Float: zmax)
    Integer: num_hits = 0
    For i = 1 To num_trials
        Float: x = <pseudorandom number between
            xmin and xmax>
        Float: y = <pseudorandom number between
            ymin and ymax>
        Float: z = <pseudorandom number between
            zmin and zmax>
        If (PointIsInShape(x, y, z)) Then
            num_hits = num_hits + 1
    Next i

    Float: total_volume =
        (xmax - xmin) * (ymax - ymin) * (zmax - zmin)
    Float: hit_fraction = num_hits / num_trials
    Return total_volume * hit_fraction
End EstimateVolume
```

19. To find the points of intersection between the functions $y = f(x)$ and $y = g(x)$, simply use Newton's method to find the roots of the equation $y = f(x) - g(x)$. Those roots are the X values where $f(x)$ and $g(x)$ intersect.

20. Sure. You can use least squares with any function if you can take the partial derivatives of the error function, set them equal to zero, and solve them for the function's parameters.

21. If the two points have the same X coordinates, then the calculations of the line's slope and intercept both cause arithmetic errors due to division by zero. To see why, recall that the slope of the line is given by the following equation:

$$m = \frac{\left(S_{xy} \cdot S_1 - S_x \cdot S_y\right)}{\left(S_{xx} \cdot S_1 - S_x \cdot S_x\right)}$$

Here:

$$S_x = \sum x_i$$
$$S_{xx} = \sum x_i^2$$
$$S_1 = \sum 1$$

Suppose that the X coordinate of the two points is x. Then $S_x = 2 \cdot x, S_{xx} = 2 \cdot x^2$, and $S_1 - 2$. That means the denominator in the calculation of m is the following:

$$S_{xx} \cdot S_1 - S_x \cdot S_x = 2 \cdot x^2 \cdot 2 - (2x) \cdot (2x)$$
$$= 4x^2 - 4x^2$$
$$= 0$$

That means the program needs to divide by zero to calculate the slope.

The calculation for the line's Y intercept divides by the negative of the same denominator, so it also tries to divide by zero.

22. If the two data points have X coordinate a, then the line $x = a$ fits them exactly. That line has an infinite slope and no Y intercept, so it makes sense that the equations described in the answer to the preceding exercise cannot calculate those values.

Chapter 3: Linked Lists

1. Assuming that the program has a pointer named `bottom` that points to the last item in a linked list, the following pseudocode shows how you could add an item to the end of the list:

```
Cell: AddAtEnd(Cell: bottom, Cell: new_cell)
    bottom.Next = new_cell
    new_cell.Next = null
```

```
        // Return the new bottom cell.
        Return new_cell
    End AddAtEnd
```

This algorithm returns the new bottom cell, so the calling code can update the variable that points to the list's last cell. Alternatively, you could pass the bottom pointer into the algorithm by reference so that the algorithm can update it.

Using a bottom pointer doesn't change the algorithms for adding an item at the beginning of the list or for finding an item.

Removing an item is the same as before unless that item is at the end of the list, in which case you also need to update the bottom pointer. Because you identify the item to be removed with a pointer to the item before it, this is a simple change. The following code shows the modified algorithm for removing the last item in the list:

```
Cell: DeleteAfter(Cell: after_me, Cell: bottom)
    // If the cell being removed is the last one,
    // update bottom.
    If (after_me.Next.Next == null) Then bottom = after_me

    // Remove the target cell.
    after_me.Next = after_me.Next.Next

    // Return a pointer to the last cell.
    Return bottom
End DeleteAfter
```

2. The following pseudocode shows an algorithm for finding the largest cell in a singly linked list with cells containing integers:

```
Cell: FindLargestCell(Cell: top)
    // If the list is empty, return null.
    If (top.Next == null) Return null

    // Move to the first cell that holds data.
    top = top.Next

    // Save this cell and its value.
    Cell: best_cell = top
    Integer: best_value = best_cell.Value

    // Move to the next cell.
    top = top.Next

    // Check the other cells.
    While (top != null)
        // See if this cell's value is bigger.
```

```
                If (top.Value > best_value) Then
                    best_cell = top
                    best_value = top.Value
                End If

                // Move to the next cell.
                top = top.Next
            End While

            Return best_cell
        End FindLargestCell
```

3. The following pseudocode shows an algorithm to add an item at the top of a doubly linked list:

```
AddAtBeginning(Cell: sentinel, Cell: new_cell)
    // Update the Next links.
    new_cell.Next = sentinel.Next
    sentinel.Next = new_cell

    // Update the Prev links.
    new_cell.Next.Prev = new_cell
    new_cell.Prev = sentinel
End AddAtBeginning
```

4. The following pseudocode shows an algorithm to add an item at the bottom of a doubly linked list:

```
AddAtEnd(Cell: bottom, Cell: new_cell)
    // Update the Prev links.
    new_cell.Prev = bottom.Prev
    bottom.Prev = new_cell

    // Update the Next links.
    new_cell.Prev.Next = new_cell
    new_cell.Next = bottom
End AddAtEnd
```

5. The `InsertCell` algorithm takes as a parameter the cell after which the new cell should be inserted. All that the `AddAtBeginning` and `AddAtEnd` algorithms need to do is to pass `InsertCell` the appropriate cell to insert after. The following code shows the new algorithms:

```
AddAtBeginning(Cell: sentinel, Cell: new_cell)
    // Insert after the top sentinel.
    InsertCell(sentinel, new_cell)
End AddAtBeginning

AddAtEnd(Cell: bottom, Cell: new_cell)
    // Insert after the cell before the bottom sentinel.
```

```
                    InsertCell(bottom.Prev, new_cell)
                End AddAtEnd
```

6. The following pseudocode shows an algorithm that deletes a specified cell from a doubly linked list:

```
    DeleteCell(Cell: target_cell)
        // Update the next cell's Prev link.
        target_cell.Next.Prev = target_cell.Prev

        // Update the previous cell's Next link.
        target_cell.Prev.Next = target_cell.Next
    End DeleteCell
```

Figure B.5 shows the process graphically.

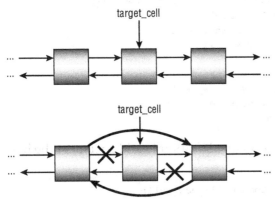

Figure B.5: To delete a cell from a doubly linked list, change the next and previous cells' links to go around the target cell.

7. If the name you're looking for comes nearer to the end of the alphabet than to the beginning, such as a name that starts with N or later, you could search the list backward, starting at the bottom sentinel. This would not change the O(N) run time, but it might cut the search time roughly in half in practice if the names are reasonably evenly distributed.

8. The following pseudocode shows an algorithm for inserting a cell in a sorted doubly linked list:

```
        // Insert a cell in a sorted doubly linked list.
        InsertCell(Cell: top_sentinel, Cell: new_cell)
            // Find the cell before where the new cell belongs.
            While (top_sentinel.Next.Value < new_cell.Value)
                top_sentinel = top_sentinel.Next
            End While

            // Update Next links.
```

```
    new_cell.Next = top_sentinel.Next
    top_sentinel.Next = new_cell

    // Update Prev links.
    new_cell.Next.Prev = new_cell
    new_cell.Prev = top_sentinel
End InsertCell
```

This algorithm is similar to the one used for a singly linked list, except for the two lines that update the Prev links.

9. The following pseudocode determines whether a linked list is sorted:

```
Boolean: IsSorted(Cell: sentinel)
    // If the list has no items, then it's sorted.
    If (sentinel.Next == null) Then Return true

    // Compare the other items.
    sentinel = sentinel.Next;
    While (sentinel.Next != null)
        // Compare this item with the next one.
        If (sentinel.Value > sentinel.Next.Value) Then
            Return false

        // Move to the next item.
        sentinel = sentinel.Next
    End While

    // If we get here, the list is sorted.
    Return true
End IsSorted
```

10. The LinkedSorts example program, which is available for download on the book's website, does this. Selectionsort is generally slower.

11. Insertionsort takes the first item from the input list and then finds the place in the growing sorted list where that item belongs. Depending on its value, sometimes the item will belong near the beginning of the list and sometimes it will belong near the end. The algorithm won't always need to search the whole list, unless the new item is larger than all of the items that are already in the sorted list.

    In contrast, when selectionsort searches the unsorted input list to find the largest item, it must search the whole list. Unlike insertionsort, it can never stop its search early.

12. Insertionsort does not modify the input list. Selectionsort removes items from the input list until that list is empty.

    There are a couple of ways that you can modify selectionsort so that it leaves the input list unchanged. For example, you could use a marking strategy where the algorithm marks each cell when it is moved to the new list. When it searches for the next largest item in the input list, the algorithm would skip any items that were marked.

Another approach would be first to make a copy of the input list and then operate on the copy, leaving the original list unchanged.

13. The PlanetList example program, which is available for download on the book's website, shows one solution.

14. The SelfOrganizingLists example program, which is available for download on the book's website, shows one solution.

15. Performance varies slightly, but in my tests the swapping list didn't start outperforming the MTF list consistently until the program performed around 13,000 searches.

16. The BreakLoopTortoiseAndHare example program, which is available for download on the book's website, shows one solution.

Chapter 4: Arrays

1. The following algorithm calculates an array's sample variance:

```
Double: FindSampleVariance(Integer: array[])
    // Find the average.
    Integer: total = 0
    For i = 0 To array.Length - 1
        total = total + array[i]
    Next i
    Double: average = total / array.Length

    // Find the sample variance.
    Double: sum_of_squares = 0
    For i = 0 To array.Length - 1
        sum_of_squares = sum_of_squares +
            (array[i] - average) * (array[i] - average)
    Next i

    Return sum_of_squares / array.Length
End FindSampleVariance
```

2. The following algorithm uses the preceding algorithm to calculate sample standard deviation:

```
Integer: FindSampleStandardDeviation(Integer: array[])
    // Find the sample variance.
    Double: variance = FindSampleVariance(array)
```

```
        // Return the standard deviation.
        Return Sqrt(variance)
    End FindSampleStandardDeviation
```

3. Because the array is sorted, the median is the item in the middle of the array. You have two issues to think about. First, you need to handle arrays with even and odd lengths differently. Second, you need to be careful calculating the index of the middle item, keeping in mind that indexing starts at 0.

```
    Double: FindMedian(Integer: array[])
        If (array.Length Mod 2 == 0) Then
            // The array has even length.
            // Return the average of the two middle items.
            Integer: middle = array.Length / 2
            Return (array[middle - 1] + array[middle]) / 2
        Else
            // The array has odd length.
            // Return the middle item.
            Integer: middle = (array.Length - 1)/ 2
            Return array[middle]
        End If
    End FindMedian
```

4. The algorithms described in the chapter only return the first mode that they find. To return all modes, you could save the modes in a list such as a linked list. When the algorithm checks a new run length or item count, it would add the new item to the list if the new length matches the current best length. If the new length is greater than the current best length, the algorithm would discard all of the currently saved modes and start a new list containing only the new value.

5. Delaying the comparisons would save some time because you wouldn't need to update counts that are later increased. For example, suppose that the algorithm sees item A, increases its count, and saves it as the new mode. If it then sees item A again, it repeats those steps. In contrast, if the algorithm waits until all of the counts are complete, it only needs to consider item A's count once.

   However, the algorithm needs some way of going back at the end to check the counts that are actually used. If the algorithm keeps a list of the values that are used, then it can do that efficiently. (When it considers a value, it can add the value to the list if that value's count is currently zero so it doesn't add the same value to the list multiple times.)

   In any case, the algorithm still needs $O(N)$ time to loop through the array initially, so this won't change the algorithm's Big O run time. Unless the values cover only a narrow range, it may not be worth the extra complication.

6. The slowest step in the FindModeSort algorithm is sorting the array. If that algorithm uses an $O(N)$ sort, then its run time is also $O(N)$, so its performance is the same as that of the FindModeCounts algorithm, at least in Big O notation.

7. If the values in the array start at vmin, you can simply subtract vmin from each before storing its count in the counts array. In other words, the count for value i would be stored in counts[i - vmin].

8. The following pseudocode removes an item from a linear array:

```
RemoveItem(Integer: array[], Integer: index)
    // Slide items left 1 position to fill in where
    // the item is.
    For i = index + 1 To array.Length - 1
        Array[i - 1] = Array[i]
    Next i

    // Resize to remove the final unused entry.
    <Resize the array to delete 1 item from the end>
End RemoveItem
```

9. There are two basic ways that you can approach this problem depending on whether you store the values in row-major order (the entries in each row are stored adjacent to each other) or column-major order (the entries in each column are stored adjacent to each other).

If you store the values in row-major order, then you need calculate the number of values that come before a particular row and the number of values in that row before a particular column. If the array has N columns, then the number of values in rows before row r is given by the following:

$$\text{Values in previous rows} = r * N - (r^2 - r) / 2$$

The number of elements in row c that come before position c is given by the following:

$$\text{Values before position } c = c - r$$

To find the index where the entry $[r, c]$ should be placed, you add those equations.

$$\text{Index for } [r,c] = r * N - (r^2 - r) / 2 + (c - r)$$

The solution is somewhat simpler if you store the values in column-major order. In that case, all that you really need to do is to use the original method for storing values with the roles of the row and column indices switched. The following pseudocode shows the original method:

```
Integer: FindIndex(Integer: r, Integer: c)
    Return (r * r + r) / 2 + c
End FindIndex
```

The following shows the new version with row and column switched:

```
Integer: FindIndex(Integer: r, Integer: c)
    Return (c * c + c) / 2 + r
End FindIndex
```

10. The relationship between row and column for nonblank entries in an
    N × N array is row + column < N. You could rework the equation for
    mapping row and column to an index in the one-dimensional storage
    array, but it's easier to map the row and column to a new row and column
    that fit the original lower-left triangular arrangement. You can do this by
    replacing r with N − 1 − r, as shown in the following pseudocode:

```
Integer: FindIndex(Integer: r, Integer: c)
    r = N - 1 - r
    Return (r * r + r) / 2 + c
End FindIndex
```

This change essentially flips the array upside-down so that small row
numbers are mapped to the bottom of the array and large row numbers
are mapped to the top of the array. For example, suppose N = 5. Then the
entry [0, 4] is in the upper-right corner of the array. That position is not
allowed in the normal lower-left triangular array, so the row is changed
to N − 1 − 0 = 4. The position [4, 4] is in the lower-right corner, which is in
the normal array.

11. The following pseudocode fills the array with the values ll _ value and
    ur _ value. You can set these to 1 and 0 to get the desired result.

```
FillArrayLLtoUR(Integer: values[,],
  Integer: ll_value, Integer: ur_value)
    For row = 0 To <Upper bound for dimension 1>
        For col = 0 To <Upper bound for dimension 2>
            If (row >= col) Then
                values[row, col] = ur_value
            Else
                values[row, col] = ll_value
            End If
        Next col
    Next row
End FillArrayLLtoUR
```

12. The following pseudocode fills the array with the values ul_value and
    lr_value. You can set these to 1 and 0 to get the desired result.

```
FillArrayULtoLR(Integer: values[,],
  Integer: ul_value, Integer: lr_value)
    Integer: max_col = <Upper bound for dimension 2>
    For row = 0 To <Upper_bound for dimension 1>
        For col = 0 To max_col
```

```
                    If (row > max_col - col) Then
                        values[row, col] = ul_value
                    Else
                        values[row, col] = lr_value
                    End If
                Next col
            Next row
        End FillArrayULtoLR
```

13. One approach is to set the value for each entry in the array to the minimum of its row, column, and distance to the right and lower edges of the array, as shown in the following pseudocode:

```
        FillArrayWithDistances(Integer: values[,])
            Integer: max_row = <number of rows> - 1
            Integer: max_col = <number of columns> - 1

            For row = 0 To max_row
                For col = 0 To max_col
                    values[row, col] =
                        Minimum(row, col, max_row - row,
                            max_col - col)
                Next col
            Next row
        End FillArrayWithDistances
```

14. The key is the mapping between [row, column, height] and indices in the storage array. To do that, the program needs to know how many cells are in a full tetrahedral group of cells and how many cells are in a full triangular group of cells. Chapter 4 explains that the number of cells in a full triangular arrangement is $(N^2 + N) \div 2$, so the following pseudocode can calculate that value:

```
        Integer: NumCellsForTriangleRows(Integer: rows)
            Return (rows * rows + rows) / 2
        End NumCellsForTriangleRows
```

The number of cells in a full tetrahedral arrangement is harder to calculate. If you make some drawings and count the cells, you can follow the approach used in the chapter. (See Table 4.1 and the nearby paragraphs.) If you assume that the number of cells in the tetrahedral arrangement involves the number of rows cubed, you will find that the exact number is $(N^3 + 3 \times N^2 + 2 \times N) / 6$. The following pseudocode uses that formula:

```
        Integer: NumCellsForTetrahedralRows(Integer: rows)
            Return (rows * rows * rows + 3 * rows * rows +
                2 * rows) / 6
        End NumCellsForTetrahedralRows
```

With these two methods, you can write a method to map [row, column, height] to an index in the storage array:

```
Integer: RowColumnHeightToIndex(Integer: row, Integer: col,
    Integer: hgt)
    Return
        NumCellsForTetrahedralRows(row) +
        NumCellsForTriangleRows(col) +
        hgt
End RowColumnHeightToIndex
```

This code returns the number of entries before this one in the array. It calculates that number by adding the entries due to complete tetrahedral groups before this item, plus the number of entries due to complete triangular groups before this item, plus the number of individual entries that come before this one in its triangular group of cells.

15. The sparse array already doesn't use space to hold missing entries, so this isn't a matter of rearranging the data structure to save space. All you really need to do is check that row ≥ column when you access an entry.

16. You can add two triangular arrays by simply adding corresponding items. The only trick here is that you only need to consider entries where row ≥ column. The following pseudocode does this:

```
AddTriangularArrays(Integer: array1[,], Integer: array2[,],
    Integer: result[,])
    For row = 0 To <Upper bound for dimension 1>
        For col = 0 To row
            Result[row, col] =
                array1[row, col] + array2[row, col]
        Next col
    Next row
End AddTriangularArrays
```

17. The following code for multiplying two matrices was shown in the chapter's text:

```
MultiplyArrays(Integer: array1[], Integer: array2[],
    Integer: result[])
    For i = 0 To <Upper bound for dimension 1>
        For j = 0 To <Upper bound for dimension 2>
            // Calculate the [i, j] result.
            result[i, j] = 0
            For k = 0 To <Upper bound for dimension 2>
                result[i, j] = result[i, j] +
                    array1[i, k] * array2[k, j]
            Next k
        Next j
    Next i
End MultiplyArrays
```

Now consider the inner For k loop. If $i < k$, then array1[i, k] is 0. Similarly, if $k < j$, then array2[k, j] is 0. If either of those two values is 0, their product is 0.

The following code shows how you can modify the inner assignment statement so that it changes an entry's value only if it is multiplying entries that are present in both arrays:

```
If (i >= k) And (k >= j) Then
    result[i, j] = result[i, j] + array1[i, k] * array2[k, j]
End If
```

You can make this a bit simpler if you think about the values of k that access entries that exist in both arrays. Those values exist if $k <= i$ and $k >= j$. You can use those bounds for k in its For loop, as shown in the following pseudocode:

```
For k = j To i
    total += this[i, k] * other[k, j];
Next k
```

18. The following code shows a CopyEntries method that copies the items in the ArrayEntry linked list starting at from_entry to the end of the list that currently ends at to_entry:

```
// Copy the entries starting at from_entry into
// the destination entry list after to_entry.
CopyEntries(ArrayEntry: from_entry, ArrayEntry: to_entry)
    While (from_entry != null)
        to_entry.NextEntry = new ArrayEntry
        to_entry = to_entry.NextEntry
        to_entry.ColumnNumber = from_entry.ColumnNumber
        to_entry.Value = from_entry.Value
        to_entry.NextEntry = null

        // Move to the next entry.
        from_entry = from_entry.NextEntry
    End While
End CopyEntries
```

As long as the "from" list isn't empty, this adds a new ArrayEntry object to the "to" list.

The following AddEntries method copies entries from the two lists from_entry1 and from_entry2 into the result list to_entry:

```
// Add the entries in the two lists from_entry1
// and from_entry2
// and save the sums in the destination entry list
// after to_entry.
```

```
AddEntries(ArrayEntry: from_entry1,
   ArrayEntry: from_entry2,
   ArrayEntry: to_entry)
   // Repeat as long as either from list has items.
   While (from_entry1 != null) And (from_entry2 != null)
      // Make the new result entry.
      to_entry.NextEntry = new ArrayEntry
      to_entry = to_entry.NextEntry
      to_entry.NextEntry = null

      // See which column number is smaller.
      If (from_entry1.ColumnNumber <
        from_entry2.ColumnNumber) Then
          // Copy the from_entry1 entry.
          to_entry.ColumnNumber =
              from_entry1.ColumnNumber
          to_entry.Value = from_entry1.Value
          from_entry1 = from_entry1.NextEntry
      Else If (from_entry2.ColumnNumber <
        from_entry1.ColumnNumber)
      Then
          // Copy the from_entry2 entry.
          to_entry.ColumnNumber = from_entry2.ColumnNumber
          to_entry.Value = from_entry2.Value
          from_entry2 = from_entry2.NextEntry
      Else
          // The column numbers are the same.
          // Add both entries.
          to_entry.ColumnNumber =
              from_entry1.ColumnNumber
          to_entry.Value = from_entry1.Value +
              from_entry2.Value
          from_entry1 = from_entry1.NextEntry
          from_entry2 = from_entry2.NextEntry
      End If
   End While

   // Add the rest of the entries from the list
   // that is not empty.
   if (from_entry1 != null)
       CopyEntries(from_entry1, to_entry)
   if (from_entry2 != null)
       CopyEntries(from_entry2, to_entry)
End AddEntries
```

This code loops through both "from" lists, adding the next entry from each list that has the smaller column number. If the current entries in each list have the same column number, the code creates a new entry and adds the values of the "from" lists.

The following code shows how the `Add` method uses `CopyEntries` and `AddEntries` to add two matrices:

```
// Add two SparseArrays representing matrices.
SparseArray: Add(SparseArray: array1, SparseArray: array2)
    SparseArray: result = new SparseArray

    // Variables to move through all the arrays.
    ArrayRow: array1_row = array1.TopSentinel.NextRow
    ArrayRow: array2_row = array2.TopSentinel.NextRow
    ArrayRow: result_row = result.TopSentinel

    While (array1_row != null) And (array2_row != null)
        // Make a new result row.
        result_row.NextRow = new ArrayRow
        result_row = result_row.NextRow
        result_row.RowSentinel = new ArrayEntry
        result_row.NextRow = null

        // See which input row has the smaller row number.
        If (array1_row.RowNumber < array2_row.RowNumber)
        Then
            // array1_row comes first.
            // Copy its values into result.
            result_row.RowNumber = array1_row.RowNumber
            CopyEntries(array1_row.RowSentinel.NextEntry,
                result_row.RowSentinel)
            array1_row = array1_row.NextRow
        Else If (array2_row.RowNumber <
          array1_row.RowNumber)
        Then
            // array2_row comes first.
            // Copy its values into result.
            result_row.RowNumber = array2_row.RowNumber
            CopyEntries(array2_row.RowSentinel.NextEntry,
                result_row.RowSentinel)
            array2_row = array2_row.NextRow
        Else
            // The row numbers are the same.
            // Add their values.
            result_row.RowNumber = array1_row.RowNumber
            AddEntries(
                array1_row.RowSentinel.NextEntry,
                array2_row.RowSentinel.NextEntry,
                result_row.RowSentinel)
            array1_row = array1_row.NextRow
            array2_row = array2_row.NextRow
        End If
    End While

    // Add any remaining rows.
```

```
                    If (array1_row != null) Then
                        // Make a new result row.
                        result_row.NextRow = new ArrayRow
                        result_row = result_row.NextRow
                        result_row.RowNumber = array1_row.RowNumber
                        result_row.RowSentinel = new ArrayEntry
                        result_row.NextRow = null
                        CopyEntries(array1_row.RowSentinel.NextEntry,
                            result_row.RowSentinel)
                    End If
                    If (array2_row != null) Then
                        // Make a new result row.
                        result_row.NextRow = new ArrayRow
                        result_row = result_row.NextRow
                        result_row.RowNumber = array2_row.RowNumber
                        result_row.RowSentinel = new ArrayEntry
                        result_row.NextRow = null
                        CopyEntries(array2_row.RowSentinel.NextEntry,
                            result_row.RowSentinel)
                    End If

                    return result
                End Add
```

The method loops through the two "from" arrays. If one list's current row has a lower row number than the other, the method uses CopyEntries to copy that row's entries into the "to" list.

If the lists' current rows have the same row number, the method uses AddEntries to combine the rows in the output array.

After one of the "from" lists is empty, the method uses CopyEntries to copy the remaining items in the other "from" list into the output list.

19. To multiply two matrices, you need to multiply the rows of the first with the columns of the second. To do that efficiently, you need to be able to iterate over the entries in the second array's columns. The sparse arrays described in the text let you iterate over the entries in their rows but not the entries in their columns.

You can make it easier to iterate over the entries in a column by using a linked list of columns, each holding a linked list of entries, just as the text describes using linked lists of rows.

Instead of building a whole new class, however, you can reuse the existing SparseArray class. If you reverse the roles of the rows and columns, you get an equivalent array that lets you traverse the fields in a column. Of course, the class will treat the rows as columns and vice versa, so this can be confusing.

The following pseudocode shows a high-level algorithm for multiplying two sparse matrices:

```
Multiply(SparseArray: array1, SparseArray: array2,
  SparseArray: result)
    // Make a column-major version of array2.
    SparseArray: new_array2
    For Each entry [i, j] in array2
        new_array2[j, i] = array2[i, j]
    Next [i, j]

    // Multiply.
    For Each row number r in array1
        For Each "row" number c in array2
            // These are really columns.
            Integer: total = 0
            For Each <k that appears in both array1's row
                    and array2's column>
                total = total +
                    <The row's k value> *
                        <the column's k value>
            Next k
            result[r, c] = total
        Next c
    Next r
End Multiply
```

Chapter 5: Stacks and Queues

1. When one of the stacks is full, NextIndex1 > NextIndex2. At that point both stacks are full, NextIndex1 is the index of the top item in the second stack, and NextIndex2 is the index of the top item in the first stack.

2. Simply push each of the items from the original stack onto a new one. The following pseudocode shows this algorithm:

```
Stack: ReverseStack(Stack: values)
    Stack: new_stack
    While (<values is not empty>)
        new_stack.Push(values.Pop())
    End While

    Return new_stack
End ReverseStack
```

3. The StackInsertionsort example program, which is available for download on the book's website, demonstrates insertionsort with stacks.

4. The algorithm doesn't really need to move all of the unsorted items back onto the original stack, because all that it will do with those items is take the next one to insert in sorted position. Instead, the algorithm could just move the sorted items back onto the original stack and then use the next unsorted item as the next item to position. This would save some time, but the run time would still be $O(N^2)$.

5. The fact that the stack insertionsort algorithm works means that you can sort train cars with only one holding track plus the output track. You can use the holding track as the second stack, and you can use the output track to store the car you are currently sorting (or vice versa). This would require more steps than you would need if you have more than one holding track, however. Because moving train cars is a lot slower than moving items between stacks on a computer, it would be better to use more holding tracks if possible.

6. The StackSelectionsort example program, which is available for download on the book's website, demonstrates selectionsort with stacks.

7. You can use the selectionsort algorithm to sort train cars with some small modifications. The version of the algorithm described in this chapter keeps track of the largest item in a separate variable. When sorting train cars, you can't set aside a car to hold in a variable. Instead, you can move cars to the holding track and store the car with the largest number on the output track. When you find a car with a larger number, you can move the car from the output track back to the holding track and then move the new car to the output track.

Of course, with real trains, you don't need to look only at the top car in a stack. Instead, you can look at the unsorted cars and figure out which has the largest number before you start moving any cars. Then you can simply move the cars to the holding track, except for the selected car, which you can move to the output track. That will remove any need to put incorrect cars on the output track and reduce time-consuming shuffling.

8. The InsertionsortPriorityQueue example program, which is available for download on the book's website, uses a linked list to implement a priority queue.

9. The LinkedListDeque example program, which is available for download on the book's website, uses a doubly linked list to implement a deque.

10. The MultiHeadedQueue example program, which is available for download on the book's website, demonstrates a multiheaded queue.

The average wait time is very sensitive to the number of tellers. If you have even one fewer than the optimum number of tellers, the number of customers in the queue quickly grows long, and the average wait time soars. Adding a single teller can make the queue practically disappear and reduce average wait time to only a few seconds. (Some retailers have learned this lesson. Whenever more than a couple of customers are waiting, they pull employees from other jobs to open a new register and quickly clear the queue.)

11. The QueueInsertionsort example program does this.

12. The QueueSelectionsort example program does this.

13. The BinomialHeap example program does this.

Chapter 6: Sorting

> **NOTE** For performance reasons, all of the sorting example programs display at most 1,000 of the items they are sorting. If the program generates more than 1,000 items, all of the items are processed but only the first 1,000 are displayed in the output list.

1. Example program Insertionsort implements the insertionsort algorithm.

2. When the algorithm starts with index 0, it moves the 0th item to position 0, so it doesn't change anything. Making the algorithm's For loop start at 1 instead of 0 essentially makes it treat the first item as already in sorted position. That makes sense, because a group of one item is already sorted. However, starting the loop at position 1 doesn't change the algorithm's run time.

3. Example program Selectionsort implements the selectionsort algorithm.

4. The algorithm's outer For loop could stop before the last item in the array. The final trip through the loop positions the item at position $N - 1$ at index $N - 1$, so it isn't moved anyway. The following pseudocode shows the new For statement:

```
For i = 0 To <length of values> - 2
```

This would not change the algorithm's run time.

5. Example program Bubblesort implements the bubblesort algorithm.

6. Example program ImprovedBubblesort adds those improvements.

7. Example program PriorityQueue uses a heap to implement a priority queue. (This program works directly with the value and priority arrays. For more practice, package the heap code into a class.)

8. Adding an item to and removing an item from a heap containing N items takes $O(\log N)$ time. See the discussion of the heapsort algorithm's run time for details.

9. Example program Heapsort implements the heapsort algorithm.

10. For a complete tree of degree d, if a node has index p, its children are at indices $d \times p + 1, d \times p + 2, \ldots, d \times p + d$. A node at index p has parent index $\lfloor (p - 1) \rfloor / d$.

11. Example program QuicksortStack implements the quicksort algorithm with stacks.

12. Example program QuicksortQueue implements the quicksort algorithm with queues. Stacks and queues provide the same performance as far as the quicksort algorithm is concerned. Any difference would be in how the stacks and queues are implemented.

13. Example program Quicksort implements the quicksort algorithm with in-place partitioning. This version is faster than the versions that use stacks or queues in part because it doesn't move as many items. When dividing part of the array, the other versions move every item onto a stack or queue and then back into the array. This version only moves items that are not already in the correct part (upper or lower) of the array. When it does move an item, it needs to move it only once instead of twice.

14. Instead of dividing the items into two halves at each step, divide them into three groups. The first group contains items strictly less than the dividing item, the middle group contains all repetitions of the dividing item, and the last group contains items greater than the dividing item. Then recursively sort the first and third groups but not the second.

15. Example program Countingsort implements the countingsort algorithm.

16. Allocate a `counts` array with indices 0 to 10,000. Subtract the smallest item's value (100,000) from each item before you increment its count. Then, when you are writing the counts back into the original array, add 100,000 back in. (Alternatively, you could use an array with nonzero lower bounds, as described in Chapter 4.)

17. Example program PigeonholeSort implements the pigeonhole sort algorithm.

18. In this case, bucketsort almost becomes countingsort. Bucketsort would need to sort each bucket, but all of the items in a particular bucket would have the same value. As long as the buckets don't hold too many items, that's not a problem, but countingsort still has a small advantage because it only needs to count the items in each bucket.

19. Example program Bucketsort implements the bucketsort algorithm.

20. If you use only a few buckets, then each will hold many items, and sorting them will take a long time. If you use many buckets, then each will hold only a few items so sorting them will be fast, but you need to allocate more space for the buckets.

21. The following paragraphs explain which algorithms would work well under the indicated circumstances.

    a. 10 floating-point values: Any of the algorithms except countingsort would work. Insertionsort, selectionsort, and bubblesort would be simplest and would probably provide the best performance.

    b. 1,000 integers: Heapsort, quicksort, and mergesort would work well. Quicksort would be fastest if the values don't contain too many duplicates and are not initially sorted or you use a randomized method for selecting dividing items. Countingsort would work if the range of values is limited.

    c. 1,000 names: Heapsort, quicksort, and mergesort would work well. Quicksort would be fastest if the values don't contain too many duplicates and are not initially sorted or you use a randomized method for selecting dividing items. Countingsort won't work. Making bucketsort work might be difficult. (The trie described in Chapter 10 is similar to a bucketsort, and it would work.) Pigeonhole sort might work. For example, you could use 26 buckets to hold names beginning with each of the 26 letters in the alphabet. Of course, the first letters of names are not evenly distributed, so performance might be somewhat limited.

    d. 100,000 integers with values between 0 and 1,000: Countingsort would work very well. Pigeonhole sort and bucketsort would also work well, but not as well as countingsort. Heapsort, quicksort, and mergesort would work but would be slower.

    e. 100,000 integers with values between 0 and 1 billion: Countingsort would not work very well, because it would need to allocate an array with 1 billion entries to hold value counts. Pigeonhole sort and bucketsort would work well. Heapsort, quicksort, and mergesort would work but would be slower.

    f. 100,000 names: Countingsort doesn't work with strings. Making bucketsort work might be difficult. (Again, the trie described in Chapter 10 would work.) Pigeonhole sort would work if you can find a good way to map names into buckets. Heapsort, quicksort, and mergesort would work well, with quicksort being the fastest in the expected case.

g. 1 million floating-point values: Countingsort doesn't work with floating-point values. Pigeonhole sort and bucketsort would work well. Heapsort, quicksort, and mergesort would work but would be much slower.

h. 1 million names: This is a hard one for the algorithms described in this chapter. Countingsort doesn't work with strings. Making pigeonhole sort or bucketsort work with strings could be hard, but would work. Heapsort, quicksort, and mergesort would work but would be slow. The trees described in Chapter 10 can also handle this case.

i. 1 million integers with uniform distribution: Countingsort might work if the range of values is limited. Otherwise, pigeonhole sort or bucketsort would probably be the best choice. Heapsort, quicksort, and mergesort would work but would be slow.

j. 1 million integers with nonuniform distribution: Countingsort might work if the range of values is limited. Pigeonhole sort and bucketsort might have trouble because the distribution is nonuniform. Heapsort, quicksort, and mergesort would work but would be slow.

Chapter 7: Searching

1. Example program LinearSearch implements the linear search algorithm.

2. Example program RecursiveLinearSearch implements the linear search algorithm recursively. If the array holds N items, this method might require N levels of recursion. Some programming languages may be unable to handle that depth of recursion for large N, so the nonrecursive version probably is safer.

3. Example program LinearLinkedListSearch implements the linear search algorithm for a linked list.

4. Example program BinarySearch implements the binary search algorithm.

5. Example program RecursiveBinarySearch implements the binary search algorithm recursively. This method requires more stack space than the nonrecursive version. That could be a problem if the depth of recursion is great, but that would occur only for extremely large arrays, so it probably isn't an issue in practice. That being the case, the better algorithm is the one you find less confusing. (Personally, I think the nonrecursive version is less confusing.)

6. Example program InterpolationSearch implements the interpolation search algorithm.

7. Example program RecursiveInterpolationSearch implements the interpola-
    tion search algorithm recursively. As is the case with binary search, this
    method requires more stack space than the nonrecursive version. That
    could be a problem if the depth of recursion is great, but that would occur
    only for extremely large arrays, so it probably isn't an issue in practice.
    That being the case, the better algorithm is the one you find less confus-
    ing. (Again, I think the nonrecursive version is less confusing.)

8. The bucketsort and pigeonhole sort algorithms use a calculation similar
    to the one used by interpolation search to pick each item's bucket.

9. After you find a target value, you could simply move backward through
    the array until you find the first item that doesn't match the target. In the
    worst case, that would take $O(N)$ time. For example, if a program used
    binary search on an array that contained nothing but copies of the target
    item, the algorithm would find the target halfway through the array and
    then would need to move back to the beginning in $N / 2 = O(N)$ steps.

    A faster but more complicated approach would be to perform a binary
    search or interpolation search starting at the location where the first target
    item was found and expanding outward looking for the next-smaller item.
    This would not change the run time of the original algorithm: $O(\log N)$
    for binary search and $O(\log(\log N))$ for interpolation search.

10. If M occurs in exactly half of the outcomes, the algorithm cannot guarantee
    to produce it. For example, the algorithm performs the following steps for
    the list {A, B, M, M}:

OUTCOME	MAJORITY	COUNTER
A	A	1
B	A	0
M	M	1
M	M	2

In this case, the algorithm returns outcome M.

For the list of outcomes {M, M, A, B}, the algorithm performs the following steps:

OUTCOME	MAJORITY	COUNTER
A	A	1
M	A	0
B	B	1
M	B	0

In this case, the algorithm returns outcome B.

11. After finding a result, simply loop through the items again in $O(N)$ time and count those that match the result. If the number of matches is more than half of the total number of items, then the result is truly a majority.

Chapter 8: Hash Tables

1. Example program Chaining implements a hash table with chaining.

2. Example program SortedChaining implements a hash table with sorted chaining. In one test, when the program's hash table and the hash table from the Chaining program both used 10 buckets and held 100 items, the Chaining program's average probe length was 9.46 positions. The SortedChaining program's average probe length was only 5.55 positions.

3. Figure B.6 shows the average probe sequence lengths for the Chaining and SortedChaining programs. In the figure, the two curves appear to be linear, indicating that both algorithms have an O(1) run time (assuming a constant number of buckets). Sorted chaining has better performance, however, so its run time includes smaller constants.

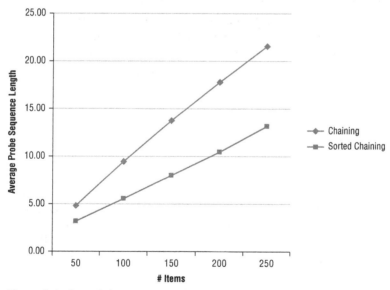

Figure B.6: Sorted chaining gives shorter average probe sequence lengths than chaining.

4. Example program LinearProbing implements a hash table that uses open addressing with linear probing.

5. Example program QuadraticProbing implements a hash table that uses open addressing with quadratic probing.

6. Example program PseudoRandomProbing implements a hash table that uses open addressing with pseudorandom probing.

7. Example program DoubleHashing implements a hash table that uses open addressing with double hashing.

8. The probe sequences used by those algorithms will skip values if their stride evenly divides the table size N. For example, suppose that the table size is 10, and a value maps to location 1 with a stride of 2. Then its probe sequence visits positions 1, 3, 5, 7, and 9 and then repeats. You can avoid this by ensuring that the stride cannot evenly divide N. One way to do that is to make N prime so that no stride can divide it evenly. (That's why the examples shown in this chapter's figures use a table with 101 entries.)

9. Example program OrderedQuadraticProbing implements a hash table that uses open addressing with ordered quadratic hashing.

10. Example program OrderedDoubleHashing implements a hash table that uses open addressing with ordered double hashing.

11. Figure B.7 shows the average probe sequence lengths for the different open addressing algorithms. All of the nonordered algorithms have similar performance. Linear probing generally is slowest, but the others are within about one probe of giving the same performance. Double hashing has a slight advantage.

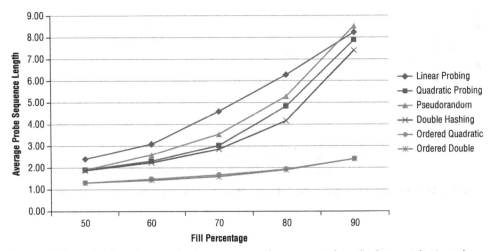

Figure B.7: Double hashing has shorter average probe sequence lengths, but quadratic and pseudorandom probing give similar performance.

It's not obvious from the graph, but the exact values added to the tables make a big enough difference to change which algorithms are faster than the others.

The ordered quadratic probing and ordered double hashing algorithm provide almost exactly the same average probe sequence length. Their values are much smaller than the average lengths of the other algorithms, although inserting items in the ordered hash tables takes longer.

12. The sorted chain is faster because you don't need to search it twice. First you search for the key to verify that it isn't already present. If it isn't, you then insert the key where it would have been if it were present.

13. With unsorted chains, you would need to loop through each chain and move each key into the correct new bucket. You would move every item once, so this would take $O(N)$ steps.

    If a chain is sorted, then the keys that belong in the first new bucket are at the beginning of the chain and the keys that belong in the second bucket are at the end of the chain. You only need to search halfway (on average) through the chain to see where the dividing point is. Then you can move the two halves of the chain into the two new buckets. You don't need to search the second half of the original chain, so this takes roughly $O(N / 2)$ steps. This is still $O(N)$ steps, but it should be faster in practice.

    In fact, you can even reuse the links in the original chain without building new links and that should save time. Again, that won't change the Big O run time, but it should make the process faster in practice.

14. When you insert a new item, you can use a previously vacated spot. Before you can insert the item, however, you need to follow its probe sequence to its end to make sure that the item isn't already in the table somewhere later in its probe sequence.

15. When you insert the second value, there's a $1/N$ chance that it will map to the same position as the first item. There's also a $1/N$ chance that it will map to the following position and a $1/N$ chance that it will map to the preceding position. That means there is a $3/N$ chance that the second item will land adjacent to the first item.

16. You only switch to a new value when that value is larger than the one you are currently adding to the table. Because the new value is larger, you will eventually either deposit the value you're using or you will reach the largest value in the table after which no further switches are possible. In the worst case, you might need to reposition every item in the table.

17. Because ordered hashing algorithms swap smaller items with larger ones, the algorithm might insert the new item but be unable to re-insert a larger one that it swapped essentially losing the previously inserted item.

Chapter 9: Recursion

1. Example program Factorial implements the factorial algorithm. On my computer, a C# version of the program that uses 64-bit integers can calculate 20! = 2,432,902,008,176,640,000, but calculating 21! causes an integer overflow. The BigInteger data type would allow the program to calculate much larger values. A Python version of the program can easily calculate 983! (which is roughly 4.6×10^{2516}), but calculating 984! exhausts the call stack.

2. Example program FibonacciNumbers implements the original recursive Fibonacci algorithm. On my computer, a C# version of the program can calculate Fibonacci(41) = 165,580,141 in roughly 10 seconds. A Python version of the program can calculate Fibonacci (36) = 14,930,352 in around 9.3 seconds.

3. Example program TowerOfHanoi implements the Tower of Hanoi algorithm.

4. Example program GraphicalTowerOfHanoi implements the Tower of Hanoi algorithm graphically. *Hints:*

   a. Make a Disk class to represent disks. Give it properties to represent its size and position, a list of points representing positions that it should visit, a Draw method that draws the disk, and a Move method that moves the disk some fixed distance toward the next point in its points list.

   b. Make stacks to represent the pegs. Initially put Disk objects on the first peg's stack to represent the initial tower of disks.

   c. Make a Move class to represent moves. It should record the numbers of the pegs from which and to which a disk should move. Give it a MakeMovePoints method that gets the top disk from the start peg, builds the Disk's movement points, and moves the Disk to the destination stack.

   d. When the user clicks a button, solve the Tower of Hanoi problem, building a list of Move objects to represent the solution. Then start a timer that uses the Move items in the list to create movement points for the Disk objects and that uses the Disk objects' Move and Draw methods to move and draw the disks.

5. Example program KochSnowflake draws Koch snowflakes. In my versions of the program, you can barely see a difference between the level 6 and level 7 curves. That's just as well because the level 8 curve takes a long time to draw.

6. Example program AngleSnowflake lets the user specify the angles in the generator.

7. Example program Hilbert draws Hilbert curves. *Hint*: If the whole curve should be `width` units wide, set `dx = width / (2^{depth+1} - 1)`.

8. The following pseudocode shows the methods that draw the Sierpiński curve pieces down, left, and up:

```
// Draw down on the right.
SierpDown(Integer: depth, Float: dx, Float: dy)
    If (depth > 0) Then
        depth = depth - 1
        SierpDown(depth, gr, dx, dy)
        DrawRelative(gr, -dx, dy)
        SierpLeft(depth, gr, dx, dy)
        DrawRelative(gr, 0, 2 * dy)
        SierpRight(depth, gr, dx, dy)
        DrawRelative(gr, dx, dy)
        SierpDown(depth, gr, dx, dy)
    End If
End SierpDown

// Draw left across the bottom.
SierpLeft(Integer: depth, Float: dx, Float: dy)
    If (depth > 0) Then
        depth = depth - 1
        SierpLeft(depth, gr, dx, dy)
        DrawRelative(gr, -dx, -dy)
        SierpUp(depth, gr, dx, dy)
        DrawRelative(gr, -2 * dx, 0)
        SierpDown(depth, gr, dx, dy)
        DrawRelative(gr, -dx, dy)
        SierpLeft(depth, gr, dx, dy)
    End If
End SierpLeft

// Draw up along the left.
SierpUp(Integer: depth, Float: dx, Float: dy)
    If (depth > 0) Then
        depth = depth - 1
        SierpUp(depth, gr, dx, dy)
        DrawRelative(gr, dx, -dy)
        SierpRight(depth, gr, dx, dy)
        DrawRelative(gr, 0, -2 * dy)
        SierpLeft(depth, gr, dx, dy)
        DrawRelative(gr, -dx, -dy)
        SierpUp(depth, gr, dx, dy)
    End If
End SierpUp
```

9. Example program Sierpiński draws Sierpiński curves. *Hint*: If the whole curve should be `width` units wide, set `dx = width / (2`$^{depth+2}$` - 2)`.

10. The following pseudocode draws a Sierpiński gasket. This code assumes a `Point` data type that has `X` and `Y` properties.

```
// Draw the gasket.
SierpinskiGasket(Integer: depth,
  Point: point1, Point: point2, Point: point3)
    // If this is depth 0, fill the remaining triangle.
    If (depth == 0) Then
        Point: points[] = { point1, point2, point3 }
        FillPolygon(points)
    Else
        // Find points on the left, right, and bottom
        // of the triangle.
        Point: lpoint = new Point(
            (point1.X + point2.X) / 2,
            (point1.Y + point2.Y) / 2)
        Point: bpoint = new Point(
            (point2.X + point3.X) / 2,
            (point2.Y + point3.Y) / 2)
        Point: rpoint = new Point(
            (point3.X + point1.X) / 2,
            (point3.Y + point1.Y) / 2)

        // Draw the triangles at the corners.
        SierpinskiGasket(depth - 1, gr, point1, lpoint,
            rpoint)
        SierpinskiGasket(depth - 1, gr, lpoint, point2,
            bpoint)
        SierpinskiGasket(depth - 1, gr, rpoint, bpoint,
            point3)
    End If
End SierpinskiGasket
```

11. The following pseudocode draws a Sierpiński carpet. This code assumes a `Rectangle` data type that has `X`, `Y`, `Width`, and `Height` properties.

```
// Draw the carpet.
SierpinskiCarpet(Integer: depth, Rectangle: rect)
    // If this is depth 0, fill the remaining rectangle.
    If (depth == 0) Then
        FillRectangle(rect)
    Else
        // Fill the 8 outside rectangles.
        Float: width = rect.Width / 3
        Float: height = rect.Height / 3
        For row = 0 To 2
            For col = 0 To 2
                // Skip the center rectangle.
```

```
If ((row != 1) || (col != 1)) Then
    SierpinskiCarpet(depth - 1,
        New Rectangle(
            rect.X + col * width,
            rect.Y + row * height,
            width, height))
        End If
    Next col
Next row
End If
End SierpinskiCarpet
```

12. Example program EightQueens solves the eight queens problem.

13. Example program EightQueens2 keeps track of how many times each square is attacked so that it can decide more quickly whether a position for a new queen is legal. In one test, this reduced the number of test positions attempted from roughly 1.5 million to 26,000 and reduced the total time from 2.13 seconds to 0.07 seconds. The more quickly and effectively that you can eliminate choices, the faster the program will run.

14. Example program EightQueens3 only searches the next row for the next queen's position. In one test, this reduced the number of test positions attempted from roughly 26,000 to 113 and reduced the total time from 0.07 seconds to practically no time at all. This program restricts the possible positions for queens even more than the previous version, so it does much less work.

15. The following table shows the number of queen positions examined and the elapsed time on my computer for the programs I wrote for Exercises 12, 13, and 14.

ALGORITHM	POSITIONS	C# TIME	PYTHON TIME
EightQueens	1,502,345	1.05 sec	24.97 sec
EightQueens2	25,943	0.04 sec	2.29 sec
EightQueens3	113	0.01 sec	0.01 sec

16. Example program KnightsTour uses only backtracking to solve the knight's tour problem. The smallest square board that has a tour is 5×5 squares. On my computer, the C# version of the program can find a solution on a 6×6 board in around 0.1 seconds, and the Python version takes around 0.5 seconds. Neither program could find a solution on a 7×7 board after several minutes, so I got bored and stopped them.

17. Example program KnightsTour2 implements Warnsdorff's heuristic. My C# version of the program found a solution on a 54×54 board almost instantly and then crashed with a stack overflow on a 55×55 board. The

Python version worked for a 31×31 board and then crashed with a stack overflow on a 32×32 board.

18. If you take a group of selections and generate all the arrangements of each, you get the original set's permutations. For example, consider the set {A, B, C}. Its selections of two items includes {A, B}, {A, C}, and {B, C}. If you add the rearrangements of those selections (B, A), (C, A), and (C, B), you get the original set's permutations (A, B), (A, C), (B, A), (B, C), (C, A), and (C, B).

19. Example program SelectKofN implements the `SelectKofNwithDuplicates` and `SelectKofNwithoutDuplicates` algorithms.

20. Example program Permutations implements the `PermuteKofNwithDuplicates` and `PermuteKofNwithoutDuplicates` algorithms.

21. Example program NonrecursiveFactorial calculates factorials nonrecursively. My C# version using 64-bit integers can calculate 20! = 2,432,902,008,176,640,000 but causes an integer overflow when calculating 21!. You should be able to calculate much larger values if you use the `BigInteger` data type or Python. For example, my Python program can easily calculate 100,000!, which has 456,574 digits. (It could calculate larger values if I had the patience.)

22. Example program DynamicFibonacci calculates Fibonacci numbers recursively with saved values. My C# version of the program using 64-bit integers can calculate Fibonacci(92) = 7,540,113,804,746,346,429, but calculating Fibonacci(93) causes an integer overflow. The Python version can calculate practically unlimited values. For example, it can calculate Fibonacci(100,000), which has 20,899 digits.

23. Example program NonrecursiveFibonacci calculates Fibonacci numbers nonrecursively. My C# version using 64-bit integers can calculate Fibonacci(92) = 7,540,113,804,746,346,429, but calculating Fibonacci(93) causes an integer overflow. My Python version can calculate Fibonacci(983), which has 206 digits, but calculating Fibonacci(984) causes a stack overflow. (If you use the Python program to calculate increasingly large Fibonacci numbers, the sky's the limit.)

24. Example program NonrecursiveFibonacci2 calculates Fibonacci numbers nonrecursively as needed without a global array. If you use 64-bit integers, then this doesn't change the values that you can calculate. If you use the `BigInteger` data type or Python, then this saves the memory required by the array and that may allow the program to calculate larger values without exhausting the program's memory. Of course, doing anything nontrivial with a 100,000-digit value may be impractical anyway.

25. Example program NonrecursiveHilbert implements the nonrecursive Hilbert curve algorithm.

Chapter 10: Trees

1. No. The number of nodes N in a perfect binary tree of height H is $N = 2^{H+1} - 1$. The value 2^{H+1} is a multiple of 2, so it is always even, and therefore $2^{H+1} - 1$ is always odd.

2. Figure B.8 shows a tree that is full and complete but not perfect.

3. *Base case*: If $N = 1$, the tree is a root node with no branches, so $B = 0$. In that case, $B = N - 1$ is true.

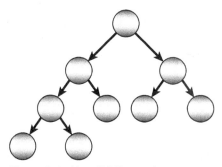

Figure B.8: Not all full complete trees are perfect.

Inductive step: Suppose that the property is true for binary trees containing N nodes and consider such a tree. If you add a new node to the tree, you must also add a new branch to the tree to connect the node to the tree. Adding one branch to the $N - 1$ branches that the tree already had means that the new tree has $N + 1$ nodes and $(N - 1) + 1 = (N + 1) - 1$ branches. This is the statement of the property for a tree with $N + 1$ nodes, so the property holds for binary trees containing $N + 1$ nodes.

That proves $B = N - 1$ by induction.

4. Every node in a binary tree except the root node is attached to a parent by a branch. There are $N - 1$ such nodes, so there are $N - 1$ branches. (This result holds for trees in general, not just binary trees.)

5. *Base case*: If $H = 0$, the tree is a root node with no branches. In that case, there is one leaf node, so $L = 1$ and $L = 2^H = 2^0 = 1$ is true.

Inductive step: Suppose that the property is true for perfect binary trees of height H. A perfect binary tree of height $H + 1$ consists of a root node connected to two perfect binary subtrees of height H. Because we assume the property is true for trees of height H, the total number of leaf nodes in each subtree is 2^H. Adding a new root node above the two subtrees doesn't add any new leaf nodes to the tree of height $H+1$, so the total number of leaf nodes is $(2 \times 2^H) = 2^{H+1}$ and the property holds for perfect binary trees of height $H+1$.

That proves $L = 2^H$ by induction.

6. *Base case*: If $N = 1$, the tree is a root node with no branches. That root node is missing two branches. Then $M = 2 = 1 + 1$, so the property $M = N + 1$ is true for $N = 1$.

Inductive step: Suppose that the property is true for binary trees containing N nodes and consider such a tree. If you add a new node to the tree, that node is attached to its parent by a branch that replaces a formerly missing branch, decreasing the number of missing branches by 1. The new node has two missing branches of its own. Adding these to the tree's original $N + 1$ missing branches gives the new number of missing branches, $M = (N + 1) - 1 + 2 = (N + 1) + 1$. This is the statement of the property for a tree containing $N + 1$ nodes, so the property holds for binary trees containing $N + 1$ nodes.

That proves $M = N + 1$ by induction.

7. The preorder traversal for the tree shown in Figure 10.30 is E, B, A, D, C, F, I, G, H, J.

8. The inorder traversal for the tree shown in Figure 10.30 is A, B, C, D, E, F, G, H, I, J.

9. The postorder traversal for the tree shown in Figure 10.30 is A, C, D, B, H, G, J, I, F, E.

10. The depth-first traversal for the tree shown in Figure 10.30 is E, B, F, A, D, I, C, G, J, H.

11. Example program BinaryTraversals finds the traversals for the tree shown in Figure 10.30.

12. If you use a queue instead of a stack in the depth-first traversal algorithm described in the section "Depth-First Traversal," the result is the reverse of the postorder traversal. You could generate the same traversal recursively by using a preorder traversal but visiting each node's right child before visiting its left child.

13. Example program TextDisplay creates a textual display of the tree shown in Figure 10.31.

14. Example program DrawTree displays a tree similar to the one shown in Figure 10.31.

15. Example program DrawTree2 displays a tree similar to the one shown in Figure 10.31.

16. The following pseudocode shows an algorithm for performing a reverse inorder traversal on a threaded sorted tree. The differences between this algorithm and the algorithm for performing a normal inorder traversal are highlighted.

```
ReverseInorderWithThreads(BinaryNode: root)
    // Start at the root.
    BinaryNode: node = root

    // Remember whether we got to a node via a branch
    // or thread.
    // Pretend we go to the root via a branch so
    // we go right next.
    Boolean: via_branch = True

    // Repeat until the traversal is done.
    While (node != null)
        // If we got here via a branch, go
        // down and to the right as far as possible.
        If (via_branch) Then
            While (node.RightChild != null)
                node = node.RightChild
            End While
        End If

        // Process this node.
        <Process node>

        // Find the next node to process.
        If (node.LeftChild == null) Then
            // Use the thread.
            node = node.LeftThread
            via_branch = False
        Else
            // Use the left branch.
            node = node.LeftChild
            via_branch = True
        End If
    End While
End ReverseInorderWithThreads
```

17. Example program ThreadedTree lets you build threaded sorted trees and display their traversals.

18. Example program ThreadedTree lets you build threaded sorted trees and display their traversals, as shown in Figure 10.34.

19. In the worst case, the FindLcaSortedTree algorithm might need to search from the tree's root to close to its bottom. If the tree contains N nodes and isn't too tall and skinny, then the algorithm has $O(N \log N)$ performance.

20. Example program LcaBinarySortedTree lets you build a sorted binary tree. If you then left- and right-click two nodes, the program finds and displays their LCA.

21. In the worst case, the `FindLcaParentPointers` algorithm might need to traverse the tree from the nodes to the root. That happens if the LCA is the root node. If the tree contains N nodes and isn't too tall and skinny, then the algorithm has $O(N \log N)$ performance.

22. Example program LcaParentPointers implements the `FindLcaParentPointers` algorithm.

23. In the worst case, if the LCA is the root node, the `FindLcaParentsAndDepths` algorithm must traverse the tree from the nodes to the root. If the tree contains N nodes and isn't too tall and skinny, then the algorithm has O(N log N) performance.

24. Example program FindLcaParentsAndDepths implements the `FindLcaParentsAndDepths` algorithm.

25. If `has1` and `has2` are both true, then the recursive call to `ContainsNodes` should have already found the LCA inside the subtree. In that case, the recursive call would have returned the LCA and the calling instance of the algorithm would return it before checking to see whether `contains1` and `contains2` were both true.

26. If the `ContainsNodes` algorithm returns `null`, then the `contains1` and `contains2` variables cannot both be true or else this instance of the algorithm would have found the LCA and returned it instead of `null`.

    If one of the `contains1` and `contains2` variables is true, then we know that the current node is on the path from the root to one of the target values. That means the LCA is one of the current node's ancestors.

    If `contains1` and `contains2` are both false, then we know only that the LCA is not in the current node's subtree. It could be anywhere else and could be either an ancestor of the current node or not.

27. In the worst case, the algorithm needs to search the entire tree to find the target values. For example, suppose that one of the values is in the tree's bottom-rightmost node. In that case the algorithm will visit every node in the tree. Because it visits every node, the algorithm has $O(N)$ performance.

28. Example program LcaTree implements the `ContainsNodes` algorithm.

29. Each node except the root node has a parent branch, so the tree contains $N-1$ branches. An Euler tour crosses every branch twice, once going down and once coming back up, so it visits two nodes for each branch. The one exception is the root node, which is visited an extra time before the tour moves down the first branch. That means the tour visits $2 \times (N-1) + 1 = 2 \times N + 1$ nodes.

    Both the Euler tour algorithm and the ContainsNodes algorithm use $O(N)$ steps. The Euler tour version is much easier to understand, but it also uses $O(N)$ extra storage to hold the nodes' `Depth` and `TourLocation` values and the tour itself.

30. Example program LcaEulerTour uses an Euler tour to find LCAs.

31. Instead of storing a node's first location in the Euler tour, store its first and last positions. When you need to search an interval, compare the first and last positions of the nodes to determine which of the following four situations applies:

    ▪ All occurrences of node1 come before all of the occurrences of node2.

    ▪ All occurrences of node2 come before all of the occurrences of node1.

    ▪ All occurrences of node1 fall between occurrences of node2. In this case, node2 is the LCA.

    ▪ All occurrences of node2 fall between occurrences of node1. In this case, node1 is the LCA.

    ▪ Use the position values to find the shortest interval and search it as before.

32. Example program EulerTour2 implements the approach described in Exercise 31.

33. In the knowledge tree used by the animal game, all internal nodes hold questions and lead to two child nodes, so they have degree 2. All leaf nodes have degree 0. No nodes can have degree 1, so the tree is full.

    The tree grows irregularly, depending on the order in which animals are added and the questions used to differentiate them, so the tree is neither complete nor perfect.

34. Nodes that represent questions are internal nodes that have two children. Nodes that represent animals are leaf nodes, so they have no children. You can tell the difference by testing the node's `YesChild` property to see whether it is `null`.

35. Example program AnimalGame implements the animal game.

36. Figure B.9 shows the expression trees.

$(15 \div 3) + (24 \div 6)$

$8 \times 12 - 14 \times 32$

$1 \div 2 + 1 \div 4 + 1 \div 20$

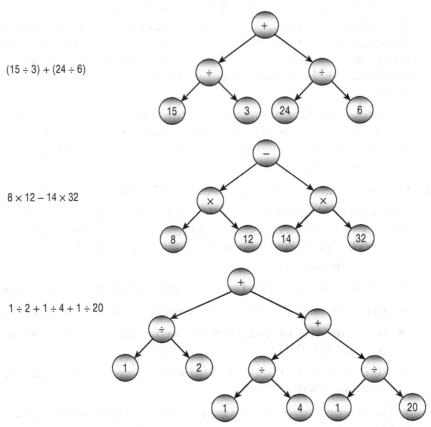

Figure B.9: The expression trees on the right represent the expressions on the left.

37. Example program Expressions evaluates the necessary expressions.

38. Figure B.10 shows the expression trees.

39. Example program Expressions2 evaluates the necessary expressions.

40. Example program IntervalTrees finds intervals that overlap a point.

41. Example program IntervalTrees2 finds intervals that overlap an interval.

42. Example program Quadtree demonstrates quadtrees.

43. Figure B.11 shows a trie for the given strings.

44. Example program Trie builds and searches a trie.

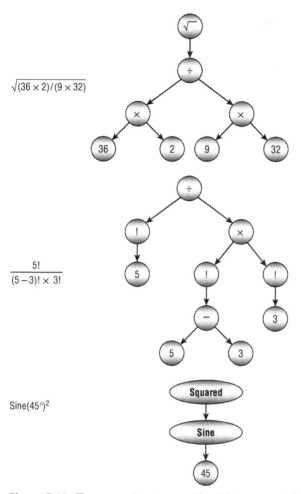

$\sqrt{(36 \times 2)/(9 \times 32)}$

$\dfrac{5!}{(5-3)! \times 3!}$

$\text{Sine}(45°)^2$

Figure B.10: The expression trees on the right represent the expressions on the left.

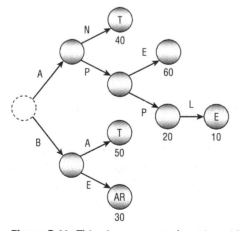

Figure B.11: This trie represents the strings APPLE, APP, BEAR, ANT, BAT, and APE.

Chapter 11: Balanced Trees

1. Figure B.12 shows the right-left rotation.

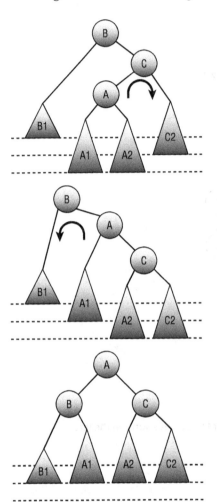

Figure B.12: You can rebalance an AVL tree in the right-left case by using a right rotation followed by a left rotation.

2. Figure B.13 shows an AVL tree as the values 1 through 8 are added in numeric order.

3. Figure B.14 shows the process of removing node 33 and rebalancing the tree. First you need to replace node 33 with the rightmost node to its left, which in this case is node 17. After that replacement, the tree is unbalanced at node 12 because its left subtree has height 2 and its right subtree has

height 0. The tall grandchild subtree causing the imbalance consists of the node 8, so this is a left-right case. To rebalance the tree, you perform a left rotation to move node 8 up one level and node 5 down one level, followed by a right rotation to move node 8 up another level and node 12 down one level.

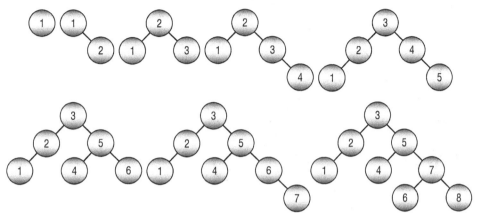

Figure B.13: An AVL tree remains balanced even if you add values in sorted order.

4. Figure B.15 shows the process of adding the value 24 to the tree shown on the left.

5. Figure B.16 shows the process of removing the value 20 from the tree shown on the top. First, replace value 20 with value 13. That leaves the leaf that contained 13 empty. Rebalance by borrowing a value from a sibling node.

6. Figure B.17 shows the process of adding the value 56 to the B-tree on the top. To add the new value, you must split the bucket containing the values 52, 54, 55, and 58. You add the value 56 to those, make two new buckets, and send the middle value 55 up to the parent node. The parent node doesn't have room for another value, so you must split it too. Its values (including the new one) are 21, 35, 49, 55, and 60. You put 21 and 35 in new buckets and move the middle value 49 up to its parent. This is the root of the tree, so the tree grows one level taller.

7. To remove the value 49 from the bottom tree in Figure B.17, simply replace the value 49 with the rightmost value to its left, which is 48. The node initially containing the value 48 still holds three values, so it doesn't need to be rebalanced. Figure B.18 shows the result.

8. Figure B.19 shows a B-tree growing incrementally as you add the values 1 through 11. When you add 11, the root node has four children, so the tree holds 11 values at that point.

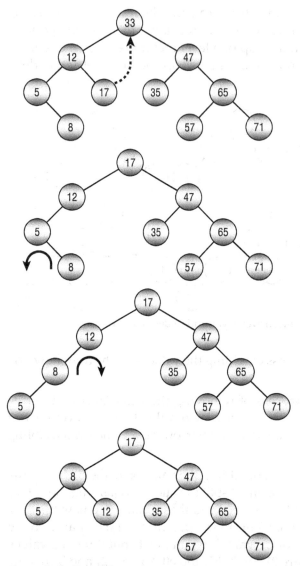

Figure B.14: To rebalance the tree at the top, you need to replace value 33 with value 17 and then perform a left-right rotation.

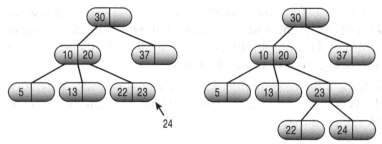

Figure B.15: When you add the value 24 to the tree on the left, the leaf containing values 22 and 23 splits.

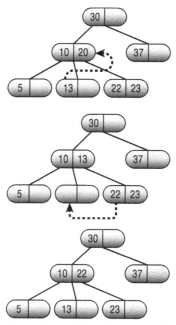

Figure B.16: If you remove a value from a 2-3 tree node and the node contains no values, you may be able to borrow a value from a sibling.

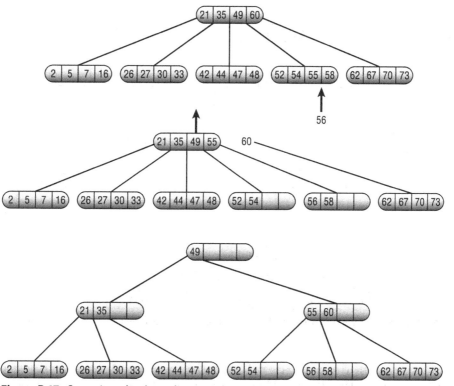

Figure B.17: Sometimes bucket splits cascade to the root of a B-tree and the tree grows taller.

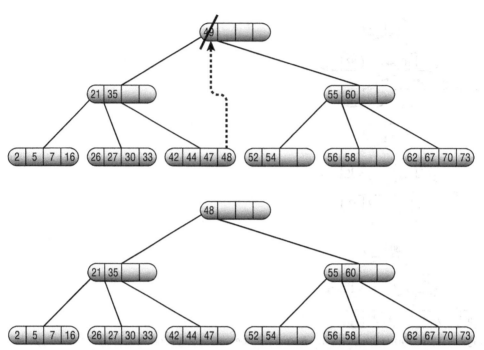

Figure B.18: Sometimes when you remove a value, no rebalancing is required.

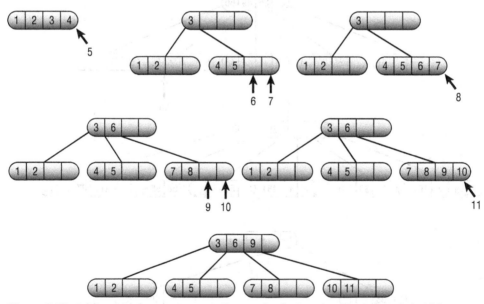

Figure B.19: Adding 11 values to an empty B-tree of order 2 makes the root node hold four children.

9. A B-tree node of order K would occupy $1,024 \times (2 \times K) + 8 \times (2 \times K + 1) = 2,048 \times K + 16 \times K + 8 = 2,064 \times K + 8$ bytes. To fit in four blocks

of 2 KB each, this must be less than or equal to $4 \times 2 \times 1,024 = 8,192$ bytes, so $2,064 \times K + 8 \le 8,192$. Solving for K gives $K \le (8,192 - 8) \div 2,064$, or $K \le 3.97$. K must be an integer, so you must round this down to 3.

A B+tree node of order K would occupy $1,024 \times (2 \times K) + 8 \times (2 \times K + 1) = 200 \times K + 16 \times K + 8 = 216 \times K + 8$ bytes. To fit in four blocks of 2 KB each, this must be less than or equal to $4 \times 2 \times 1,024 = 8,192$ bytes, so $216 \times K + 8 \le 8,192$. Solving for K gives $K \le (8,192 - 8) \div 216$, or $K \le 37.9$. K must be an integer, so you must round this down to 37.

Each tree could have a height of at most $\log_{(K+1)}(10,000)$ while holding 10,000 items. For the B-tree, that value is $\log_4(10,000) \approx 6.6$, so the tree could be seven levels tall. For the B+tree, that value is $\log_{38}(10,000) \approx 2.5$, so the tree could be three levels tall.

Chapter 12: Decision Trees

1. Example program CountTicTacToeBoards does this. It found the following results:

   ▪ X won 131,184 times.
   ▪ O won 77,904 times.
   ▪ The game ended in a tie 46,080 times.
   ▪ The total number of possible games was 255,168.

   The numbers would favor player X if each player moved randomly, but because most nonbeginners have a strategy that forces a tie, a tie is the most common outcome.

2. Example program CountPrefilledBoards does this. Figure B.20 shows the number of possible games for each initial square taken. For example, 27,732 possible games start with X taking the upper-left corner on the first move.

27,732	29,592	27,732
29,592	25,872	29,592
27,732	29,592	27,732

Figure B.20: These numbers show how many possible games begin with X taking the corresponding square in the first move.

Because the tic-tac-toe board is symmetric, you don't really need to count the games from each starting position. All of the corners give the same number of possible games, and all of the middle squares in each edge also give the same number of possible games. You only really need to count the games for one corner, one middle, and the center to get all of the values.

3. Example program TicTacToe does this.

4. Example program PartitionProblem does this.

5. Example program PartitionProblem does this.

6. Figure B.21 shows the two graphs. The graph of the logarithms of the nodes visited is almost a perfectly straight line for both algorithms, so the number of nodes visited by each algorithm is an exponential function of the number of weights N. In other words, if N is the number of weights, then $\langle \text{Nodes Visited} \rangle = C^N$ for some constant C. The number of nodes visited is smaller for branch and bound than it is for exhaustive search, but it's still exponential.

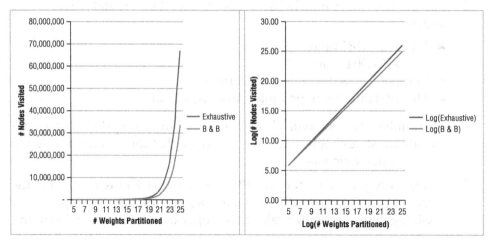

Figure B.21: Because the graph of the logarithm of nodes visited versus number of weights is a line, the number of nodes visited is exponential in the number of nodes.

7. Example program PartitionProblem does this.

8. Example program PartitionProblem does this.

9. The two groups are {7, 7, 7, 5, 5} and {9, 6, 7, 7, 6}. Their total weights are 35 and 31, so the difference is 4.

   If the weights are sorted in increasing order, then the two groups are {5, 6, 7, 7, 7} and {5, 6, 7, 7, 9}. The groups' total weights are 34 and 32, so the difference is 2.

If the weights are sorted in decreasing order, then the two groups are {9, 7, 7, 6, 5} and {7, 7, 7, 6, 5}. The groups' total weights are 34 and 32, so the difference is also 2.

Because this heuristic adds the next weight to the group that is currently smaller, it tends to alternate adding items to one group and then the other. Sorting the weights in either order means the difference between two values added to the groups is relatively small, so adding a pair of adjacent weights tends to make a small change in the weight differences. That produces a good result in this example, but this is still a heuristic so it might not produce as good a result for different weights.

10. With the initial ordering, the two groups are {5, 1, 2, 1} and {2, 12}. The groups have total weights 9 and 14, so the difference is 5.

If the weights are sorted in increasing order, then the two groups are {1, 2, 5} and {1, 2, 12}. The groups' total weights are 8 and 15, so the difference is 7.

If the weights are sorted in decreasing order, then the two groups are {12} and {5, 2, 2, 1, 1}. The groups' total weights are 12 and 11, so the difference is 1.

In this example, sorting the items in decreasing order produces the best result. The differences between adjacent items are still relatively small whether the weights are sorted in ascending or decreasing order, but sorting in decreasing order allows later smaller values to fine tune earlier differences.

11. If you use the weights {30, 20, 20, 30, 20, 1}, then the two groups are {30, 30, 1} and {20, 20, 20}, their total weights are 61 and 60, and their difference is 1.

If you sort the weights in decreasing order {30, 30, 20, 20, 20, 1}, then the two groups are {30, 20, 20} and {30, 20, 1}, their total weights are 70 and 51, and their difference is 19.

12. Example program PartitionProblem does this.

13. Example program PartitionProblem does this.

14. Example program BoidsClassical does this. In my implementation, if the mouse remains stationary, the boids eventually start circling it.

15. Example program BoidsClassicalPeople does this.

16. Example program BoidsGravity does this. In my implementation, if the mouse remains stationary, the boids repeatedly move in close to the target and then bounce away. They don't have a notion of common flock direction, so they don't circle in a group.

17. Example program BoidsGravityPeople does this.

18. Example program SwarmMinimum does this.

Chapter 13: Basic Network Algorithms

1. Example program NetworkMaker does this. Select the Add Node tool and then click the drawing surface to create new nodes. When you select either of the Add Link tools, use the left mouse button to select the start node and use the right mouse button to select the destination node for a new link.

2. Example program NetworkMaker does this.

3. Example program NetworkMaker does this.

4. That algorithm doesn't work for directed networks because it assumes that if there is a path from node A to node B, then there is also a path from node B to node A. For example, suppose a network has three nodes connected in a row $A \to B \to C$. If the algorithm starts at node A, it reaches all three nodes, but if it starts at node B, it only finds nodes B and C. It would then incorrectly conclude that the network has two connected components {B, C} and {A}.

5. Example program NetworkMaker does this.

6. If all of a network's links have the same cost, then all of the network's spanning trees will have the same total cost and will be minimal. If the network contains N nodes and the links have cost C, then every spanning tree will contain $N - 1$ links and have a total cost of $C \times (N - 1)$.

7. Example program NetworkMaker does this.

8. Example program NetworkMaker does this.

9. No, a shortest path tree need not be a minimal spanning tree. Figure B.22 shows a counterexample. The image on the left shows the original network, the middle image shows the shortest path tree rooted at node A, and the image on the right shows the minimal spanning tree rooted at node A.

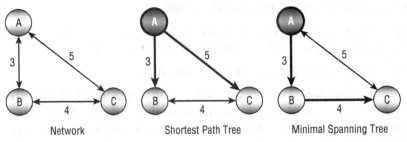

Figure B.22: A shortest path tree is a spanning tree but not necessarily a minimal spanning tree.

10. Example program NetworkMaker does this.

11. Example program NetworkMaker does this.

12. Example program NetworkMaker does this.

13. Example program NetworkMaker does this.

14. If the network contains a cycle with a negative total weight, the label-correcting algorithm enters an infinite loop following the cycle and lowering the distances to the nodes it contains.

    This cannot happen to the label-setting algorithm, because each node's distance is set exactly once and never changes after that.

15. After a node is labeled by a label-setting algorithm, its distance is never changed, so you can make the algorithm stop when it has labeled the donut shop. If the network is large and the start and end destination are close together, this change will probably save time.

16. When a label-correcting algorithm labels a node, that doesn't mean it will not later change that distance, so you cannot immediately conclude that the path to that node is the shortest, the way you can with a label-setting algorithm.

    However, the algorithm cannot improve a distance that is shorter than the distances provided by the links in the candidate list. That means you can periodically check the links in the list. If none of them leads to a distance less than the donut shop's current distance, then the donut shop's shortest path is final.

    This change is complicated and slow enough that it probably won't speed up the algorithm unless the network is very large, and the start and destination nodes are very close together. You may be better off using a label-setting algorithm.

17. Instead of building a shortest path tree rooted at the start node, you can build a shortest path tree rooted at the destination node that uses transpose links (the network's reversed links). Instead of showing the shortest path from the start node to every other node in the network, that tree will show the shortest path from every node in the network to the destination node. When construction makes you leave the current shortest path, the tree already shows the shortest path from your new location.

18. Example program NetworkMaker does this.

19. Example program NetworkMaker does this.

20. Building the arrays would take about 1 second for 100 nodes, 16.67 minutes for 1,000 nodes, and 11.57 days for 10,000 nodes.

21. Figure B.23 shows the `Distance` and `Via` arrays for the network shown in Figure 13.26. The initial shortest path from node A to node C is A → C with a cost of 18. The final shortest path is A → B → C with a cost of 16.

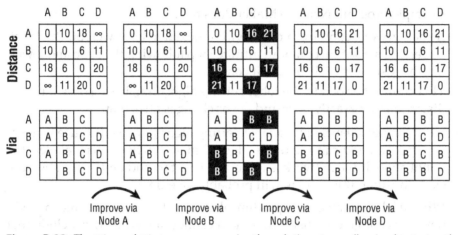

Figure B.23: The `Via` and `Distance` arrays give the solutions to an all-pairs shortest path problem.

22. Full-depth N recursion occurs if there is always an unvisited link out of every node during the traversal. This can happen if all of the network's links form a single big ring. Another type of network where this happens is a *clique*, a group of nodes where every node is connected to every other node.

23. Suppose that there is a cycle in the condensed network. That means there is a path that returns to its starting point. Next suppose that such a path starts at node A, visits node B, and then returns to node A, possibly visiting other nodes on the way. Now suppose that nodes a1 and b1 are nodes in the original network and they are contained in the strongly connected components represented by nodes A and B, respectively. In that case, there are paths a1→b1 and b1→a1 in the original network.

For example, to find a path a1→b1, consider how the condensed network was defined. The link between nodes A and B was created because there were nodes a2 and b2 in A and B, respectively, where the link a2→b2 exists. Because A and B represent strongly connected components, there *are* also paths a1→a2 and b2→b1. That means there is a path from a1 to b1, namely, a1→a2→b2→b1.

You can find a similar path b1→a1 that may pass through other nodes in the condensed network.

Because there are paths a1→b1 and b1→a1, then nodes a1 and b1 are in the same strongly connected component in the original network. That contradicts the assumption that the condensed network contains nodes representing strongly connected components. Because the assumption that the condensation is cyclic leads to a contradiction, the assumption must not be true. Therefore, the condensation is acyclic.

24. If the network includes all of the dots as nodes, then it contains 28 nodes and 28 links. If the network uses separate connection and shape data, then it contains only 12 nodes, 12 links, and 16 shape points.

25. Figure B.24 shows the fully expanded node, which contains 20 links.

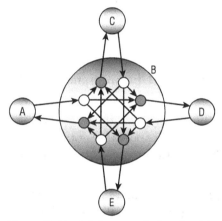

Figure B.24: A fully expanded node with turn penalties contains 20 links.

Chapter 14: More Network Algorithms

1. Example program NetworkMaker does this.

2. When the algorithm adds a node to the output list, it updates its neighbors' NumBeforeMe counts. If a neighbor's count becomes 0, the algorithm adds the neighbor to the ready list. At that point, it could also add the neighbor to a list of nodes that are becoming available for work. For example, when the algorithm adds the Drywall node to the output list, the Wiring and Plumbing nodes both become ready, so they could be listed together. The result would be a list of tasks that become ready at the same time.

3. The algorithm should keep track of the time since the first task started. When it sets a node's NumAfterMe count to 0, it should set the node's start time to the current elapsed time. From that it can calculate the node's expected finish time. When it needs to remove a node from the ready list, it should select the node with the earliest expected finish time.

4. Yes. Just as at least one node must have out-degree 0 representing a task with no prerequisites, at least one node with in-degree 0 must represent a task that is not a prerequisite for any other task. You could add that task to the end of the full ordering. That would let you remove nodes from the network and add them to the beginning and end of the ordered list.

   Unfortunately, the algorithm doesn't have a good way to identify the nodes that have in-degree 0, so it would slow down the algorithm without some major revisions.

5. Example program NetworkMaker does this.

6. You could use the following pairs of nodes for nodes M and N: B/H, B/D, G/D, G/A, H/A, H/B, D/B, D/G, A/G, and A/H. Half of those are the same as the others reversed (for example, B/H and H/B), so there are really only five different possibilities.

7. Example program NetworkMaker does this.

8. Example program NetworkMaker does this. Run the program to see the four-coloring it finds.

9. Example program NetworkMaker does this. In my tests, the program used five colors for the network shown in Figure 14.5 and three colors for the network shown in Figure 14.6. Run the program to see the colorings it finds.

10. The left side of Figure B.25 shows the residual capacity network for the network shown in Figure 14.18, with an augmenting path in bold. Using the path to update the network gives the new flows shown on the right. This is the best possible solution, because the total flow is 7, and that's all of the flow that is possible out of source node A.

11. Example program NetworkMaker does this. Load a network and select the Calculate Maximal Flows tool. Then left-click and right-click to select the source and sink nodes. Use the Options menu's Show Links Capacities command to show the link flows and capacities.

12. Figure B.26 shows example program NetworkMaker displaying maximal flows for the network shown in Figure 14.9. Only four jobs can be assigned. Load or create a work assignment network and select the Calculate Maximal Flows tool. Then left-click and right-click to select the source and sink nodes.

13. To find the number of paths that don't share links, simply give each link a capacity of 1 and find the maximal flow between the nodes. The total flow gives the number of paths.

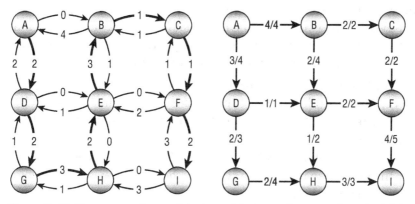

Figure B.25: The augmenting path in the residual capacity network on the left leads to the revised network on the right.

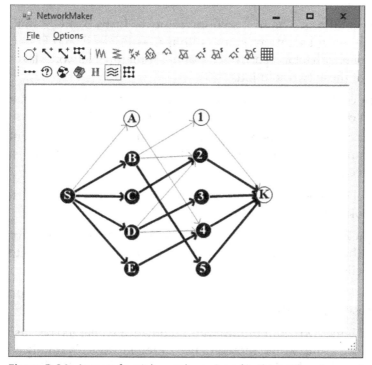

Figure B.26: At most four jobs can be assigned in this work assignment network.

To find the number of paths that don't share links or nodes, replace each node with two nodes—an in-node and an out-node. Connect the two new nodes with a link of capacity 1. Make the links that entered the original node now enter the in-node. Make the links that exited the original node now exit the out-node. Now find the maximal flow. Because each original node is now represented by two nodes connected with a link of capacity 1, only one path can use each in-node/out-node pair.

14. You need only two colors to color a bipartite network. Simply give one color to one set of nodes and a second color to the other set of nodes. Because no link connects a node to another node in the same set, the two-coloring works.

    You can use three colors to color a work assignment network. Use one color for the employee nodes, one color for the job nodes, and one color for the source and sink nodes.

15. Example program NetworkMaker does this. Load a network and select the Minimal Flow Cut tool. Then left-click and right-click to select the source and sink nodes.

16. There are two solutions. The first solution removes links $B \rightarrow C, E \rightarrow F$, and $H \rightarrow I$. The second solution removes links $C \rightarrow F, E \rightarrow F$, and $H \rightarrow I$. Both solutions remove a total capacity of 7. Example program NetworkMaker finds the first of these two solutions.

17. Yes, a network can have maximal cliques of many sizes. For example, a network might consist of several disconnected cliques of different sizes.

    Even a strongly connected network can have maximal cliques of different sizes. For example, Figure 14.12 shows a network with maximal cliques containing three and four nodes.

18. The FindCliqueBruteForce example program, which is available for download on the book's website, does this.

19. The FindCliqueBronKerbosch example program, which is available for download on the book's website, uses the Bron-Kerbosch algorithm to find maximal cliques.

20. The FindTriangles example program, which is available for download on the book's website, does this.

21. It would be bad if the two communities were automatically merged because then the combined group would represent two different, possibly unrelated groups of people. They should be merged only if most of the softball players are also book club members and vice versa. In that case, the groups should merge into a single softball-playing book club group.

    Fortunately, growing cliques into communities will not necessarily merge neighboring cliques. If Amanda is linked to many softball players and many book club members, then she will be added to those communities, but that doesn't mean that the other softball players and book club members will be added to both communities. For example, if Steve is a member of the book club, he will be added to the softball team only if he is also linked to many of its members.

22. Recall that every time you expand the current k-clique, you remove a node from that clique and then add a new node to make a new k-clique. That means every time you expand the community, you add a new node to it.

   a. In this example, the community started with k nodes and you expanded it M times, so at the end the community contains k + M nodes.

   b. Every time you expand the community, the newly added node has a link to every node in the most recent k-clique except possibly for the node that you just removed. Because you expanded the community M < k times, you have only removed at most k − 1 nodes from the original seed clique, so some node (call it node A) still remains from the seed clique. This means that every node is connected to node A. That in turn means that every node is at most two links away from every other node. For example, the path B − A − C connects nodes B and C. That means the farthest apart two nodes could be is two links.

   c. It is possible that every node is connected to every other node. The process started with a k-clique, but it could be that the community is a big clique containing k + M nodes. In fact, the whole network might be a single huge clique. In that case, the nodes that are farthest apart are only one link away from each other.

   d. If you expand the community k times, then it is possible that you have removed all the original seed clique's nodes. However, consider the first expanded community. You have only expanded from that point k − 1 times, so at least one of that second clique's nodes (call it node B) remains until the end. Each of the nodes added after that point is connected to node B.

   Now consider two nodes A and C. If they are both in the seed clique, then they are adjacent. Similarly, if they are both in the second clique, then they are adjacent. The remaining case is when one of the nodes is in the seed clique and the other is not. In that case, the path A − B − C connects the nodes in two links.

   e. As before, the community could be a big clique, so it is possible that every node is adjacent.

23. When the path visits a node, it crosses two of the node's links: one to enter the node and one to leave. Suppose that a node has an odd number of links. Then the number of that node's links is $2 \times K + 1$ for some integer K. The cycle must cross every link in the network to form an Eulerian cycle. After it has visited the node K times, it will have crossed all of the node's

links except one. When it later crosses the node's last link, the path will be stuck with no new link to use when leaving.

24. As I explained in the solution to the preceding exercise, a path crosses two links when it passes through a node: one link to enter and one to leave. If a node has an odd number of links, then one of the path's visits to the node can enter the node or leave it, but it cannot do both. It can enter the node if it is the last node in the path, or it can leave the node if it is the first node in the path. If the network contains three nodes with odd degree, then the path can visit all of the links attached to two of the nodes but one of the nodes will have an uncrossed link.

25. No. In fact, any finite network must contain an even number of nodes that have odd degree. For a proof, see `https://en.wikipedia.org/wiki/Handshaking_lemma`.

26. The only values {M, N} that allow an Eulerian cycle are {1, 1} and {2, 2}.

    The values {1, N} and {M, 1} allow Eulerian paths for any integer values M and N, as do the values {2, 3} and {3, 2}.

    If M and N are both 3 or if either of them is greater than 3, then the edges of the lattice hold more than 3 nodes of odd degree, so Eulerian cycles and paths are impossible.

27. The HierholzersAlgorithm example program, which is available for download on the book's website, does this.

Chapter 15: String Algorithms

1. Example program ParenthesisMatching does this.

2. Example program EvaluateExpression does this.

3. The program would need to look for a fourth recursive case in which the expression is of the form `-expr` for some other expression `expr`.

4. The program would need to look for another recursive case in which the expression is of the form `sine(expr)` for some other expression `expr`.

5. Example program EvaluateBoolean does this.

6. Example program GraphExpression does this.

7. Table B.3 shows a state transition table for a DFA that matches the regular expression $(AB)*|(BA)*$.

8. Figure B.27 shows the state transition diagram.

9. Table B.4 shows a state transition table for the state transition diagram shown in Figure B.27.

Table B.3: A State Transition Table for $(AB)^* | (BA)^*$

STATE	0	0	1	2	3	4
On Input	A	B	B	A	A	B
New State	1	3	2	1	4	3
Accepting?	No	No	No	Yes	No	Yes

Table B.4: A State Transition Table for $\big((AB)|(BA)\big)^*$

STATE	0	0	1	2	2	3	4	4
On Input	A	B	B	A	B	A	A	B
New State	1	3	2	1	3	4	1	3
Accepting?	No	No	No	Yes	Yes	No	Yes	Yes

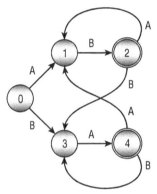

Figure B.27: This DFA state transition diagram matches the regular expression $\big((AB)|(BA)\big)^*$.

10. Example program DFAMatch does this.

11. A table is easy to write down, but it's not easy to look up transitions when you need them. For example, suppose the DFA is in state 17 and it sees the input H. The program would need to search the table to find the appropriate entry before moving to the new state. If the table is large, this could take a while. To speed things up, you might store the transitions in a tree, hash table, or some other data structure to make finding transitions easier. That would take up more memory and complicate the program.

In contrast, suppose that you use objects to represent the states, similar to how you can use node objects to represent locations in a network. Each state object could have a list giving the new state object for various inputs. In that case, state transitions would be relatively quick and simple. If some states can read many possible inputs (in other words, there are many links leaving them in the state diagram), you might still spend some time looking up new states. In that case, you might want to use a tree, hash table, or some other data structure to make finding the new states faster, but at least you won't have to search the whole transition table.

12. Build the NFA states as usual to recognize the pattern. Then add a new start state at the beginning. Add a null transition that connects the new state to the normal states. Add another transition that connects the new start state to itself on every input character. Finally, add a transition that connects the pattern's accepting state to itself on any input character. Figure B.28 shows the transition diagram.

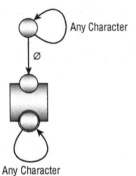

Figure B.28: This NFA state transition diagram matches a pattern anywhere within a string.

13. Figure B.29 shows the solution.

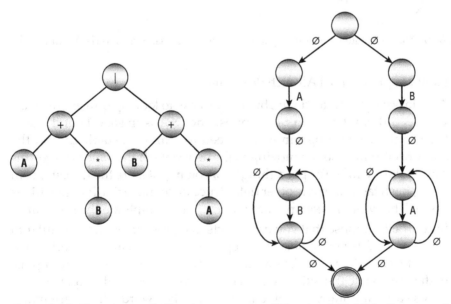

Figure B.29: The parse tree (left) and corresponding NFA network (right) for the expression $(AB*)|(BA*)$.

14. Figure B.30 shows the solution.

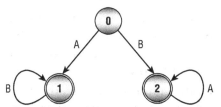

Figure B.30: This DFA state transition diagram matches the same values as the NFA state transition diagram shown on the right in Figure B.29.

15. Let the target consist of a series of A's and the text consist of runs of $M-1$ A's followed by a B. For example, if M is 4, then the target is AAAA, and the text is AAAB repeated any number of times. In this case, the target is not present in the text because there are never M A's in a row. As the outer loop variable i changes, the inner loop must run over $M, M-1, M-2, ..., 1$ values to decide that it has not found a match. Then the sequence repeats. On average, the inner loop runs roughly M / 2 times, giving a total run time of $O(N \times M / 2) = O(N \times M)$.

16. The least-cost path uses as many diagonal links as possible. In Figure 15.13, a path can use at most four diagonal links. A path that uses four diagonal links uses five nondiagonal links, so the edit distance is 5.

17. Example program StringEditDistance does this.

18. Example program StringEditDistance does this.

19. Yes, the edit distance is commutative. To transform word 2 into word 1, you can reverse operations. Instead of deleting a character, insert one. Instead of inserting a character, delete one.

20. Example program FileEditDistance does this.

21. Example program FileEditDistance does this.

22. Example program Soundex does this.

Chapter 16: Encryption

1. Example program RowColumnTransposition does this.

2. Example program SwapColumns does this.

3. If the key contains duplicated characters, then there's no way to know which of the corresponding columns should come first.

    One solution is to use only the first occurrence of each letter, so PIZZA becomes PIZA and BOOKWORM becomes BOKWRM. This actually has the small benefit of increasing obscurity if the attacker doesn't know the rule, because it disguises the number of columns in the encryption array.

4. Swapping both columns and rows greatly increases the number of possible arrangements of rows and columns. For example, if a message contains 100 characters and is written into a 10×10 array, then there are $10! \times 10! \approx 1.3 \times 10^{13}$ possible arrangements of the rows and columns.

   However, if the attacker figures out only the column ordering, the rows will be out of order, but each row in the array will contain valid words. By recognizing the valid words, the attacker can recover the column ordering and then try to swap rows to recover the full message.

   If each row begins with a new word, then finding the row ordering could be difficult. But if words span rows, the pieces of the words will give the attacker extra clues for finding the row ordering. For example, suppose the first row ends with GREA, the second row begins with NT, and the third row begins with TLY. In that case, it's likely that the third row should follow the first row.

   This is an example in which what seems like a perfectly reasonable attempt to add one encryption method to another doesn't really help much. Although adding row transpositions to column transpositions greatly increases the number of possible combinations, it doesn't greatly increase the number of combinations that the attacker must consider.

5. Example program SwapRowsAndColumns does this.

6. Example program CaesarSubstitution does this. The encryption of "Nothing but gibberish" with a shift of 13 is ABGUV ATOHG TVOOR EVFU, which does look like nothing but gibberish.

7. Example program LetterFrequencies displays the relative frequencies of the letters in a message. That program finds the following values for the three most common letters in the ciphertext:

LETTER	FREQUENCY	OFFSET
K	18.5%	6
V	14.8%	17
R	13.0%	13

Using the CaesarSubstitution example program with offset 6 to decipher the message produces gibberish. Using the program again with offset 17 gives the plaintext message THERE WASAT IMEWH ENCAE SARSU BSTIT UTION WASTH ESTAT EOFTH EART. (There was a time when Caesar substitution was the state of the art.)

8. Example program VigenereCipher does this. The decrypted message is AVIGE NEREC IPHER ISMOR ECOMP LICAT EDTHA NCAES ARSUB STITU TION. (A Vigenère cipher is more complicated than Caesar substitution.)

9. If you reuse a one-time pad, you are essentially using a Vigenère cipher where the keyword is the entire pad. You might get away with this for a little while, but eventually, if the attacker knows that you are reusing the pad, the cipher may be broken.

10. This would happen if a message was lost or you received messages out of order so that you're not using the right letters in the pad. You can decrypt the message by starting at different positions in the pad until you find a position that produces a readable message. The number of letters in the pad that you needed to skip tells you how long the message was that you missed. You can either ignore that message or give the sender a message (encrypted, of course) asking for the missing message to be repeated.

11. Not much. It would give the attacker information about the length and frequency of the messages you are sending, but the attacker can learn that anyway by looking at the lengths of intercepted messages (assuming that all messages are intercepted).

12. Example program OneTimePad does this.

13. If you have a perfectly secure cryptographic random number generator, then you can use it to generate one-time pads and use those for encryption. A one-time pad is unbreakable because any message letter could become any ciphertext letter.

    Conversely, suppose that you have an unbreakable encryption scheme. You could use it to encrypt a message consisting of nothing but instances of the letter A to generate a sequence of random letters. You could then use those letters to generate the random numbers for a secure random-number generator.

14. Always send a message of the same length at the same time every day. If you have nothing to say, just say that. Pad the messages to the same length with random characters. If the encryption is secure, the attacker cannot tell when a message contains important information and when it contains random characters.

15. For this scenario, the answers are as follows:

$$n = 22,577$$
$$\varphi(n) = 106 \times 210 = 22,260$$
$$d = 18,899$$
$$C = 1,337^{4,199} \mod 22,577 = 13,400$$
$$M = 19,905^{18,899} \mod 22,577 = 12,345$$

Chapter 17: Complexity Theory

1. Countingsort and bucketsort don't use comparisons. Instead, they perform mathematical calculations to find where in the sorted list each value should go.

2. This can be reduced to the two-coloring problem. If the graph is two-colorable, then it is bipartite. To use a two-coloring algorithm to solve the bipartite detection problem, try to two-color the graph. If a two-coloring is possible, then the graph is bipartite. The two-coloring even gives you the two node sets for the bipartite graph. Just put nodes having one color in one set and nodes having the other color in the other set.

   The two-coloring algorithm described in Chapter 14 runs in polynomial time (it's quite fast), so it's in P, and therefore the bipartite detection is also in P.

3. The odd-cycle problem can be reduced to the bipartite detection problem because a graph has a cycle with odd length if and only if it is not bipartite. To solve the odd-cycle problem, use a bipartite detection algorithm to see whether the graph is bipartite. If the graph is bipartite, then it does not contain any cycles of odd length. If the graph is not bipartite, then it does contain at least one cycle of odd length.

   Exercise 2 shows that the bipartite detection problem is in P, so the odd-cycle problem is also in P.

4. A nondeterministic algorithm for solving HAM is to guess the order in which the nodes can be visited and then verify (in polynomial time) that the ordering gives a Hamiltonian path. To do that, you need to verify that every node is in the ordering exactly once and that there is a link between the adjacent pairs of nodes in the ordering.

5. You can use a nondeterministic algorithm similar to the one described in the solution to Exercise 4: guess the order in which the nodes can be visited, and then verify (in polynomial time) that the ordering gives a Hamiltonian cycle. The only difference is that for this problem you also need to verify that the first and last nodes are the same.

6. HAM and HAMC are very closely related, but they don't instantly solve each other because a network can contain a Hamiltonian path without containing a Hamiltonian cycle. (For example, consider a two-node network with a single link A → B. The ordering A → B gives a Hamiltonian path but not a Hamiltonian cycle.)

   To reduce HAM to HAMC, you must find a way to use a HAMC algorithm to solve HAM problems. In other words, if a network contains a Hamiltonian path, then you must use a HAMC algorithm to detect it.

First, note that a network that contains a Hamiltonian cycle also contains a Hamiltonian path. Simply take a Hamiltonian cycle and remove the final link to form a Hamiltonian path.

Now suppose the network doesn't contain a Hamiltonian cycle, and suppose that it does contain a Hamiltonian path. How could you turn the path into a cycle? Simply add the path's starting node to the end of the path. If a link from the ending node to the starting node was already in the network, then it would have already contained a Hamiltonian cycle, so that link must not be present.

To look for a Hamiltonian cycle, add a new link L_{AB} between two nodes A and B. Now if there is a Hamiltonian cycle, then the same ordering gives you a Hamiltonian path in the original network. Suppose that the Hamiltonian cycle passes through the nodes $N_1, N_2, ..., A, B, N_k, N_{k+1}, ...N_1$. Then the original network contains the Hamiltonian path $B, N_k, N_{k+1}, ...N_1, N_2, ..., A$

The following steps show a complete algorithm for using HAMC to solve HAM:

1. Use the HAMC algorithm to see whether the original network contains a Hamiltonian cycle. If it does, then it also contains a Hamiltonian path and you're done.

2. For every pair of nodes A and B, if there is not already a link from node A to node B:

   a. Add a link L_{AB} between nodes A and B.

   b. Use the HAMC algorithm to see whether the modified network contains a Hamiltonian cycle. If it does, then the original network contains a Hamiltonian path from node A to node B.

   c. Remove link L_{AB} and continue trying other pairs of nodes.

Figure B.31 shows the idea. The original network is on the left. This network clearly has no Hamiltonian cycle, because node L has only one link, so a path that enters that node cannot leave it again.

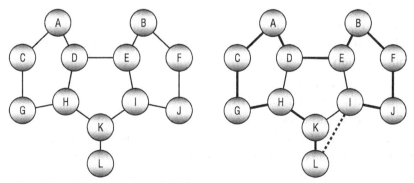

Figure B.31: The network on the left contains a Hamiltonian path but no Hamiltonian cycle.

As the reduction algorithm progresses, it eventually tries adding a link between nodes I and L. The HAMC algorithm finds the Hamiltonian path shown on the right in Figure B.31. If you remove the link between nodes I and L, you get a Hamiltonian path in the original network.

Note that this may be an inefficient algorithm for finding Hamiltonian paths. If the network contains N nodes, you may need to repeat step 2 up to N^2 times. That's still polynomial time, however, so this is a polynomial time reduction.

The HAMC algorithm is NP-complete, so it has no known fast solutions. That means running it N^2 times will be very slow indeed.

7. To reduce HAMC to HAM, you must find a way to use a HAM algorithm to solve HAMC problems. In other words, if a network contains a Hamiltonian cycle, then you must use a HAM algorithm to detect it.

Unfortunately, you can extend a Hamiltonian path to form a cycle only if the last node in the path has a link leading to the first node in the path. A HAM algorithm might find a path that does not have such a link, so it could not form a cycle.

Suppose that the network contains a Hamiltonian cycle that includes the link L_{AB} connecting nodes A and B. Now suppose that you connect a new node A' to node A and a new node B' to node B. Then the new network contains a noncyclic Hamiltonian path starting at node A' and ending at node B'.

Conversely, any Hamiltonian path in the new network must start at node A' and end at node B' (or vice versa in an undirected network). Suppose that the HAM algorithm finds a path that visits the nodes $A', A, N_1, N_2, ..., B, B'$. Then the path $A, N_1, N_2, ..., B, A$ is a Hamiltonian cycle.

The following steps give a complete algorithm for using HAM to solve HAMC:

1. For every link L_{AB} connecting nodes A and B:
   a. Connect a new node A' to node A, and connect a new node B' to node B.
   b. Use the HAM algorithm to see whether the modified network contains a Hamiltonian path. If it does, then the original network contains a Hamiltonian cycle.
   c. Remove the new nodes A' and B' and the links connected to them and continue with another link.

Figure B.32 shows the idea. You can probably find a Hamiltonian cycle easily enough but pretend that you can't. In the image on the right, the reduction algorithm is considering the link L_{QR} connecting nodes Q and

R. It has added node Q′, connected to node Q, and node R′, connected to node R. The Hamiltonian path algorithm finds the path shown in bold in the modified network on the right. Removing the Q′ and R′ nodes and their links and adding the L_{QR} link to the path gives a Hamiltonian cycle.

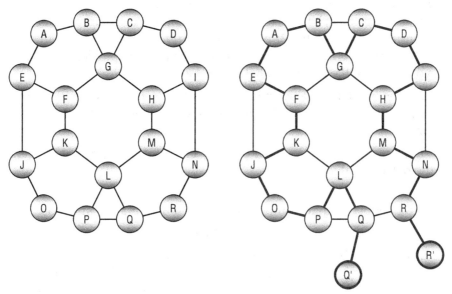

Figure B.32: The bold Hamiltonian path in the network on the right corresponds to a Hamiltonian cycle in the network on the left.

8. A nondeterministic algorithm can guess the coloring. Then, for each node, it can verify that each of its neighbors has a different color from the node.

9. A nondeterministic algorithm can guess the subset and then add up the numbers to verify that their total is 0.

10. The following pseudocode shows one way to reduce the reporting problem to the detection algorithm:

   1. If DetectKnapsack(k) returns false, then no subset with a value of at least k will fit in the knapsack, so the reporting algorithm can return that information and stop.

   2. If DetectKnapsack(k) returns true, then for each object Oi in the set:

     a. Remove object Oi from the set.

     b. Use DetectKnapsack(k) to see whether a solution with value k is still possible.

     c. If a solution with value k is still possible, leave out object Oi and continue the loop in step 2.

     d. If a solution with value k is no longer possible, then restore object Oi to the set and continue the loop in step 2.

When the loop has finished, the items that are still in the set form the solution.

11. The following pseudocode shows one way to reduce the optimization problem to the detection algorithm:

    1. Suppose that Kall is the total value of all of the objects in the set. Use the detection algorithm DetectKnapsack(Kall), DetectKnapsack(Kall – 1), DetectKnapsack(Kall – 2), and so on, until DetectKnapsack(Kall – m) returns true. At that point, Kall – m is the maximum possible value that you can fit in the knapsack. Let Kmax = Kall – m.

    2. Use the reduction described in the solution to Exercise 10 to find ReportKnapsack(Kmax). The result is the outcome of the optimization problem.

12. The following pseudocode shows one way to reduce the reporting problem to the detection algorithm:

    1. If `DetectPartition()` returns false, then no even division is possible, so the reporting algorithm can return that information and stop.

    2. If `DetectPartition()` returns true, then:

       a. Let Omax be the object with the greatest value, and assume Omax is in Subset A. (If a partitioning is possible, then it is possible with Omax in Subset A. If you find a partitioning and Omax in Subset B, just rename the two subsets.)

       b. For each of the other objects Oi:

          i. Remove Oi from the set, and add its value Vi to the value of object Omax.

          ii. Use the `DetectPartition` algorithm to see whether a partitioning is still possible. If it is, then a partitioning of the original set is possible with Oi in Subset A. Leave the set and Vmax as they currently are and continue the loop in step 2b.

          iii. If `DetectPartition` indicates that a partitioning is no longer possible, then object Oi must be placed in Subset B. In that case, subtract the Vi that you added to Vmax, and add Oi back into the set to restore the set to the way it was before step 2b-ii. To represent putting Oi in Subset B, remove object Oi from the set and subtract its value Vi from Vmax. Now continue the loop in step 2b.

    When the loop in step 2b has finished, the set should contain only Omax and Vmax should be 0. The steps that you took to get there tell you which items belong in Subset A and which belong in Subset B.

Chapter 18: Distributed Algorithms

1. Figure B.33 shows the zero-time sort algorithm sorting the two lists. Sorting two lists of numbers takes only one tick longer than sorting a single list.

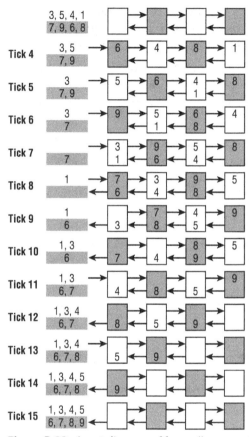

Figure B.33: A systolic array of four cells can sort two lists containing four numbers each in a total of 15 ticks.

2. Suppose that the shared best route length is 100, and process A has a new route with a total length of 80. It reads the shared value and enters its If Then block. Now process B compares the shared value to its new route length of 70, so it also enters its If Then block, and it acquires the mutex first. Process B saves its solution, along with the new total route length of 70, and it releases the mutex. Now process A acquires the mutex and saves its solution with the total route length 80.

In this case, the solution saved by process A is worse than the one saved by process B. The route length saved by process A matches the solution saved by process A, so this is a little better than the original race condition example, but the best solution is still overwritten. Process B also has a local copy of what it thinks is the best route length, 70, so it would not report a new solution with a route length of 70 if it found one.

Process A can save itself if it checks the shared route length again after it acquires the mutex. You can avoid that extra step if you acquire the mutex first, but there may actually be a benefit to checking the value twice.

Acquiring a mutex can be a relatively slow operation, at least compared to checking a memory location. If process A's value isn't as good as the value already stored in the shared variable, then process A can learn that quickly and not bother acquiring the mutex.

3. Figure B.34 shows the situation for four philosophers. Forks with a line through them are dirty. The image on the left shows the initial situation, in which philosopher 4 has no forks, philosopher 1 has two forks, and the other philosophers hold their left forks.

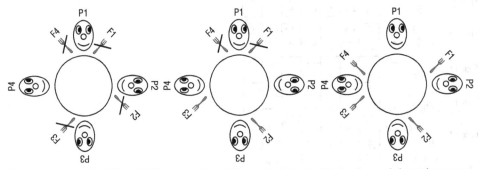

Figure B.34: In the Chandy/Misra solution with synchronized philosophers, philosopher 1 eats first, and philosopher N eats second.

When the philosophers all try to eat at the same time, philosopher 1 already has two forks, so he succeeds and is the first to eat. The others (except for philosopher 4) already hold dirty left forks, so they request right forks. Philosopher N has no forks, so he requests both forks. Because all of the forks are dirty, those who have them clean their left forks and give them away (except philosopher 1, who is eating). The result is shown in the middle of Figure B.34.

In this example, two of the philosophers now have a clean right fork and no left fork, so they ask for the left fork. (In a large problem, most of the philosophers would have a clean right fork and no left fork.) Their neighbors hold clean forks, so they refuse to give them up, and everyone waits.

When philosopher 1 finishes eating, he cleans his forks and gives them to his neighbors, philosophers 2 and 4. The result is shown on the right in Figure B.34. Philosopher 4 now has two forks, so he is the second to eat.

When philosopher 4 finishes eating, he gives his right fork to philosopher 3, who then eats.

When philosopher 3 finishes eating, he gives his right fork to philosopher 2, who then eats last.

More generally, the philosophers eat in the order $1, N, N - 1, N - 2, ..., 2$.

4. In that case, general A never receives an acknowledgment. Therefore, he assumes he didn't send enough messages the first time around, and he sends another batch with more messages. General B receives some of those messages and sends a new batch of acknowledgments (possibly including more this time). Eventually, the generals will go through enough rounds that general A will receive an acknowledgment.

5. General A sends a batch of messages as before. If general B receives any messages, he calculates P_{AB} and then sends a batch of 10 acknowledgments that say, "$P_{AB} = \langle$calculated value$\rangle$. This is acknowledgment 1 of 10. I agree to attack at dawn."

   If general A receives any acknowledgments, he calculates P_{BA}. The content of the acknowledgments tells him P_{AB}. He uses P_{AB} to decide how many messages to send to get a desired level of certainty, and he sends messages saying, "$P_{BA} = \langle$calculated value$\rangle$. Acknowledgment received."

   After the first batch of messages, if general A doesn't receive any acknowledgments (when he sent them, he didn't know P_{AB}, so he didn't know how many to send), he assumes that general B didn't receive any message. In that case, he sends another, larger batch of messages.

   Similarly, if general B doesn't receive a reply to the acknowledgments (when he sent them, he didn't know P_{BA}, so he didn't know how many to send), he assumes that general A didn't receive any acknowledgements. In that case, he sends another, larger batch of acknowledgements.

   Eventually, general A will send enough messages for general B to receive some and calculate P_{AB}. After that, general B will eventually send enough acknowledgments for general A to receive some and calculate P_{BA}. Finally, general A will eventually send enough replies to give general B the value P_{BA}, and both generals will know both probabilities.

6. That would work in the situation shown on the right of Figure 18.2.

   In the situation shown on the left of Figure 18.2, however, each lieutenant makes a decision. In some sense, it doesn't matter what each does, because the general is a traitor and there's no rule that they need to obey a traitorous general. However, there is a rule that two loyal lieutenants must decide on the same action, and in this case they don't.

7. That would work in both of the situations shown in Figure 18.2. In both situations, the lieutenants receive conflicting instructions, so they both retreat.

   However, suppose that the general is loyal (as in the situation on the right of Figure 18.2). The general orders an attack, and the traitorous lieutenant on the right lies about it. In that case, the lieutenant on the left receives conflicting orders, so he retreats, violating the general's orders.

8. No, there isn't enough information for the loyal lieutenants to identify the traitor. For example, consider two scenarios. First, suppose that the general is a traitor who tells the first lieutenant to attack and the other lieutenants to retreat. After the lieutenants exchange information, they believe that they were all told to retreat, except for the first lieutenant.

   For the second scenario, suppose that the first lieutenant is a traitor. The general tells all of the lieutenants to retreat, but the traitor tells the others that the general told him to attack.

   The lieutenants receive the same information in both scenarios, so they cannot tell whether the traitor is the general or the first lieutenant.

   These two scenarios hold no matter how many lieutenants there are, so there is no way to identify the traitor.

   (The traitor could also simply act as if he is loyal and not give conflicting orders. Then there is no way to detect him, although he won't cause any harm that way either.)

9. Suppose that the general tells two lieutenants to attack and two to retreat. After exchanging orders, the lieutenants all believe two attack orders and two retreat orders were given. A single traitor lieutenant could not create that set of orders, so the traitor must be the general.

   If this occurs, the lieutenants don't need to obey the traitor, but they still need to agree on a common decision. They can do that with a predefined rule that says, "If the commanding general is a traitor, retreat."

10. The dining philosophers problem assumes that the philosophers cannot talk to each other. If you let them talk, then they can elect a leader who can act as a waiter.

11. A bully algorithm would let a philosopher remove a fork from a philosopher who has a lower ID. That would help if the philosophers don't eat too often. But if they eat a large percentage of the time, then this might lead to a livelock in which philosophers with lower IDs don't get to eat very often.

12. If the philosophers want to eat too often, then they probably will waste a lot of time waiting for forks. A waiter who allows all odd-numbered philosophers

to eat at the same time and then allows all even-numbered philosophers to eat at the same time would be much more efficient than a free-for-all.

13. Suppose D_{AB} and D_{BA} are the delays for sending a message from A to B and B to A, respectively, and consider the equations the algorithm uses to calculate the clock error:

$$T_{B1} = (T_{A1} + E) + D_{AB}$$
$$T_{A2} = (T_{B1} + E) + D_{BA}$$

Now, if you subtract the second equation from the first, you get this:

$$T_{B1} - T_{A2} = (T_{A1} + E + D_{AB}) - (T_{B1} + E + D_{BA}) = T_{A1} - T_{B1} + D_{AB} - D_{BA} + 2 \times E$$

In the previous analysis where $D_{AB} = D_{BA}$, those two terms cancel. If you leave the terms in the equation and solve for E, you get this:

$$E = (2 \times T_{B1} - T_{A2} - T_{A1}) \div 2 + (D_{BA} - D_{AB}) \div 2$$

The error in E due to the difference between D_{BA} and D_{AB} is half of their difference. In the worst case, where one of these is close to 0 and the other is close to the total roundtrip delay D, the error is $D \div 2$.

After running the clock algorithm, $T_B = T_A \pm D \div 2$.

14. There really isn't any difference between the network speed's changing and it taking a different amount of time for a message to go from A to B or from B to A. In either case, all that matters is that the values D_{BA} and D_{AB} from the answer to the preceding exercise are different. That answer shows that after the clock algorithm runs, $T_B = T_A \pm D \div 2$, where D is the total delay.

15. The answer to the preceding exercise shows that the error in process B's new time is determined by the total round-trip message delay D. If the network's speed varies widely, sometimes D will be short, and sometimes D will be long. To get a better result, perform the algorithm several times and adjust the time according to the trial with the smallest value for D.

Chapter 19: Interview Puzzles

1. If the man brings three socks into the living room, all three can't be different colors, so at least two will be either brown or black.

This problem is simple if you have seen a similar problem before, so it doesn't really test the reasoning ability of anyone who has seen something similar. It's also easy if you write down some possible combinations. Overall it's not too bad a question, but it doesn't really tell the interviewer much.

2. If you put all of the marbles in one bowl, or put half of each color in each bowl, you have a 50% chance of picking a white marble, so that's a quick lower bound for the possible probability. Similarly, if you put all the white marbles in one bowl and all of the black marbles in the other bowl, you have a 50% chance of picking a white marble.

   A better solution is to put a single white marble and no black marbles in one bowl and all the other marbles in the other bowl. When you pick a marble, there is a 50% chance that you'll get lucky and pick the bowl that holds the single white marble. In that case, you are guaranteed to pick a white marble because that's all that this bowl holds.

   If you're unlucky and pick the other bowl, there's still a 9 in 19 chance that you'll get lucky and pull a white marble out of it. That makes your total odds of picking a white marble as follows:

   $0.5 + 0.5 \times (9 \div 19) \approx 74\%$

   This problem involves a little probability but is mostly a clever trick. It would be easier, quicker, and potentially less frustrating to ask the candidate how much he or she knows about probability.

3. At first this seems like a probability or counting question, but it's actually a trick question. There aren't enough red marbles to place one between each pair of blue marbles, so you are guaranteed that there will be adjacent blue marbles.

   This problem is easy if you get the trick, but if you don't, you may waste a lot of time on it. In either case, the interviewer doesn't learn much about the candidate.

   If you don't know the trick, you may be able to discover it if you make a drawing and try a few arrangements of marbles.

4. This is really a counting question. You can find the probability by dividing the number of "good" arrangements by the number of total arrangements.

   First, notice that you don't need to consider arrangements in which you swap marbles of the same color. All red marbles are the same, and all blue marbles are the same.

   Next, to simplify the procedure, assume that you have straightened out the circle of marbles so that you have a row of 12 slots where a marble can be positioned. Now place a blue marble in the first slot. Positioning the other 11 marbles in the remaining 11 slots is equivalent to positioning the original 12 marbles in 12 slots arranged in a circle. This situation is easier to handle because you don't need to worry about the effects of the arrangement wrapping around the circle so that the first marble is adjacent to the last marble. Because a blue marble is in the first position, a blue marble separates the first and last red marbles.

Now you can think of the problem as having 11 slots where you will place the remaining 11 marbles. If you pick slots for the four red marbles, the blue ones will fill in the remaining empty slots. If you think of it this way, then the total number of possible arrangements is as follows:

$$\binom{11}{4} = \frac{11!}{4!(11-4)!} = \frac{11!}{4!7!} = \frac{39,916,800}{24 \times 5,040} = 330$$

To see how many "good" arrangements are possible, start by placing the four red marbles in a row. To ensure that no two red marbles are adjacent, you must put three of the seven remaining blue marbles between each pair of red marbles.

At this point, four blue marbles are left, and they can go anywhere. If you think of the red marbles as defining walls, the remaining blue marbles must go between the walls. (It doesn't matter how the marbles between the walls are ordered, because you can't tell the blue marbles apart.)

One way to think about this is to imagine eight slots where you will put either a blue marble or a wall. Now you can pick slots for the walls and fill in the remaining slots with blue marbles. The number of ways that you can do that is as follows:

$$\binom{8}{4} = \frac{8!}{4!(8-4)!} = \frac{8!}{4!4!} = \frac{40,320}{24 \times 24} = 70$$

The number of "good" arrangements is 70, and the total number of possible arrangements is 330, so the odds that a random arrangement is "good" are $70 \div 330 = 7 / 33 \approx 21\%$.

This problem is pretty interesting, but it's quite difficult. This kind of problem is fairly common in probability and statistics courses, so a candidate who has taken such a course will probably know the basic approach. Even then, it would be a tough calculation, and if the candidate *hasn't* taken that kind of course, this problem will be extremely hard.

All that the interviewer will really learn from this question is whether the candidate has seen a problem like this before or has taken such a course.

5. The most obvious approach is to use a linked list. You could also do this in an array with a For loop. You get bonus points if you mention both methods and say that the better method depends on how the list is already stored for use in performing other operations.

This is actually a relevant question! You may never need to reverse a list of customers in this way, but answering this question shows that you know about at least one type of data structure. Mentioning both the linked list and array solutions shows that you know about at least two data structures and that you can look for more solutions even after you find one. (A skill that many programmers lack!)

6. There are a couple of good approaches for solving this. For the algebraic approach, let M be my current age and let B be my brother's current age. Then we know the following:

$M = 3 \times B$

$(M + 2) = 2 \times (B + 2)$

Plugging the first equation into the second gives you this:

$((3 \times B) + 2) = 2 \times (B + 2)$

Rearranging and solving for B gives you this:

$3 \times B + 2 = 2 \times B + 4$

$3 \times B - 2 \times B = 4 - 2$

$B = 2$

Inserting this value into the first equation gives $M = 3 \times 2 = 6$, so I am 6 right now. (Although I don't know of many six-year-olds who would think to ask this question.)

A second approach is to make a table similar to the following, starting with a guess of age 30 for yourself:

BROTHER'S AGE	MY AGE	BROTHER + 2	MY AGE + 2	2 × (BROTHER + 2)
10	30	12	32	24

After filling in the first row, you compare the last two columns. In this case, My Age + 2 is too big, so you guess again with smaller ages.

BROTHER'S AGE	MY AGE	BROTHER + 2	MY AGE + 2	2 × (BROTHER + 2)
10	30	12	32	24
5	15	7	17	14

In the second row, the difference between the last two columns is closer but still is too big, so you guess again with even smaller ages.

BROTHER'S AGE	MY AGE	BROTHER + 2	MY AGE + 2	2 × (BROTHER + 2)
10	30	12	32	24
5	15	7	17	14
2	6	4	8	8

In this example, the third row finds the solution. (If you overshoot and My Age + 2 turns out too small, try larger ages.)

This problem is almost worth asking because it lets you see whether the candidate is more comfortable using algebra or a table. I'm not sure how useful that information will be, though. Many problems like this one are more involved, so a table won't work well, but just because the candidate used a table doesn't mean that he or she can't use algebra if it's required.

If you use a problem like this, it's probably best to ask the candidate why he or she chose a particular approach and what other approaches might also work.

7. This problem is somewhat relevant for programmers because it involves a *fencepost problem*. Suppose that you're building a fence with rails between posts. There will be one more post than rails, because you need a post on each end of the fence. A fencepost problem (or *off-by-1 problem*) occurs when a programmer accidentally counts some object one too many times or one too few times.

For this problem, the minute hand passes the hour hand a bit after 1:05, a bit longer after 2:10, and so on, up to some time after 10:50. The next time the hands meet after 11:00 is 12:00 midnight. That means the hands cross between 1:00 and 2:00, between 2:00 and 3:00, and so on, up to a time between 10:00 and 11:00. (At this point, you may be able to see the fencepost problem.)

If you only count times strictly between noon and midnight, then the hands cross 10 times. If you also count the times that they cross at noon and midnight, then the hands cross 12 times.

How the candidate approaches this question may tell you a bit about how methodical he or she is, but that may be all it tells you. At least a careful candidate can come up with some solution either right or wrong without knowing a sneaky trick.

8. The following paragraphs describe three ways to look at this problem:

   a. A short, off-the-cuff answer is "50%, because boys and girls are equally likely, so in any given population of children, 50% are girls." That's a good "big picture" answer, but it's not necessarily very intuitive, so the interviewer might ask you to prove it. (That answer actually does prove it, but digging in at this point will probably just annoy the interviewer.)

   b. Another slightly more intuitive way to look at this problem is to consider first children, second children, third children, and so on. All of the couples have at least one child. Half of those are boys, and half are girls, so the population of first children is half boys and half girls.

The couples whose first child is a girl have a second child. Of those children, half are boys and half are girls, so the population of second children is half boys and half girls.

The couples whose first and second children are girls have a third child. Of those children, half are boys and half are girls, so the population of third children is half boys and half girls.

At this point it should be clear that each cohort is half boys and half girls, so the population as a whole must be half boys and half girls.

c. For a third way to look at the problem, consider a couple's first child. There's a 50% chance that it is a boy, and they stop having children, but there's also a 50% chance that they have a girl. After one child, their expected number of children is 0.5 boys and 0.5 girls.

If the couple's first child is a girl, then they have a second child. Again, there's a 50% chance of a girl and a 50% chance of a boy. The expected contribution to the family of this child is the chance of having a second child in the first place (0.5) times the chance of having a boy or a girl. That adds another $0.5 \times 0.5 = 0.25$ expected boys and $0.5 \times 0.5 = 0.25$ expected girls to the family, making a total expected 0.75 boys and 0.75 girls.

I hope at this point you can see a pattern.

In general, to have an Nth child, the couple must previously have had $N-1$ girls in a row. The chance of that happening is $1/2^{N-1}$.

Assuming that they did have $N-1$ girls in a row, there is a 50% chance that the next child is a boy and a 50% chance that the next child is a girl. Therefore, the expected contribution to the family of the Nth child is $0.5 \times 1/2^{N-1} = 1/2^N$ boys and $0.5 \times 1/2^N = 1/2^N$ girls.

If you add up the expected number of children through child N, you get the following:

#Boys: $1/2 + 1/2^2 + 1/2^3 + \ldots + 1/2^N$

#Girls: $1/2 + 1/2^2 + 1/2^3 + \ldots + 1/2^N$

These values are the same. Each couple has the same expected number of boys and girls, and so does the population as a whole.

If you take the limits of these sums as N goes to infinity, then these equations also show that the expected number of children for each family is one boy and one girl.

This is an interesting problem, but it's fairly easy if you've seen it before and rather tricky if you haven't. In the real world, the chances of having a boy or girl are not exactly 50% and even depend on the ages of the parents.

For more information, see the *Psychology Today* article "Why Are Older Parents More Likely to Have Daughters" here:

https://www.psychologytoday.com/blog/the-scientific-fundamentalist/
201104/why-are-older-parents-more-likely-have-daughters

9. Don't make the interviewer mad by pointing out that this is an unrealistic situation. The question basically asks you to cut the brick into pieces so that you can make combinations that add up to 1/7th, 2/7ths, 3/7ths, 4/7ths, 5/7ths, 6/7ths, or the whole brick.

   Clearly you could cut the brick into seven pieces and hand out one for each day worked, but you can do better.

   There are several ways that you can arrive at the best solution. In one approach, you consider how you can pay the contractor after each possible ending day.

   If the job ends after one day, you must give the contractor 1/7th of the brick, so clearly you need a piece that is 1/7th of the brick.

   If the job ends after two days, you must give the contractor 2/7ths of the brick. You could give him another 1/7th piece, but that won't give you any extra flexibility later. A better solution is to give him a piece that is 2/7ths of the brick and keep the 1/7th piece.

   Because you have the 1/7th piece in reserve, you can use it plus the 2/7ths piece to pay the contractor if the job ends after three days. If you had used two 1/7th pieces to pay the contractor after two days, then this solution wouldn't work. You would need a third 1/7th piece, so you would need to have three pieces instead of just two.

   If you remove two pieces from the brick that are 1/7th and 2/7ths of the whole brick, then the remaining brick contains 4/7th of the brick. If the job ends after four days, you can give the contractor that piece and keep the others.

   If the job ends after five days, then you can give the contractor the 4/7ths piece and the 1/7th piece.

   If the job ends after six days, then you can give the contractor the 4/7ths piece and the 2/7ths piece.

   Finally, if the job ends after seven days, you can give the contractor all of the pieces.

   When a problem involves magic numbers such as powers of 2 or 1 less than a power of 2, you should think about binary. In this example, the three pieces of the brick represent 1, 2, and 4 sevenths of the brick. The numbers 1 through 7, which are 001, 010, 011, 100, 101, 110, and 111 in binary, tell you which pieces of the brick to give to the contractor on each day.

A 1 means that you should give the contractor the corresponding piece, and a 0 means that you should keep that piece.

For example, 6 is 110 in binary. That means on day 6 you give the contractor the 4/7ths piece (for the initial 1) and the 2/7ths piece (for the second 1) but not the 1/7th piece (for the final 0). The total payment on that day is $4/7 + 2/7 = 6/7$.

This problem is easy if you've seen it before and can be confusing if you haven't, although you probably can come up with a solution if you work through it starting from day 1. Being aware of magic numbers can also help.

10. This is one of a large family of pan balance puzzles. Whenever you have a tool such as a pan balance that divides a collection of objects into sets, you should think about a subdivision approach. If you can divide a set of objects into two groups and eliminate one group from consideration at each step, then you can use a binary subdivision approach to find whatever you're looking for.

   In this problem, that doesn't quite work. If you put four eggs on each side of the balance, then you can eliminate half of the eggs from consideration in one weighing. Next, you can place the remaining four eggs on the balance, two on each side, and eliminate two more from consideration. At that point, you're still left with two eggs that might be gold-plated, and you've used up your two weighings.

   The key to this problem is to notice that the balance doesn't define only two sets containing eggs in the left pan and eggs in the right pan. It also defines a third set containing eggs that are not in either pan. Instead of using binary division to divide the eggs into two groups and eliminating one, you can use ternary division to divide the eggs into three groups and eliminate two.

   Suppose that you have only three eggs. You could put one in the left pan, one in the right, and omit one. If the two pans balance, then you know that the third egg is gold-plated. If the two pans don't balance, then you know that the egg in the lighter pan is the gold-plated egg.

   That explains how you perform the second weighing to finalize your choice. You still need to figure out how to use the first weighing to reduce the number of remaining eggs to three (or fewer).

   The balance lets you eliminate two of the three groups. After one weighing, the set of eggs still under consideration must include only three eggs. That means the groups that you weigh in the first weighing should contain three eggs each.

   Here's the final solution:

   1. Place three eggs in the left pan, three in the right, and two on the table.

2. If the pans balance:

   a. The gold-plated egg is one of the two eggs that were not weighed the first time. Place one of them in each pan.

   b. The lighter pan contains the gold-plated egg.

3. If the pans don't balance:

   a. Exclude the eggs in the heavier pan and the eggs on the table.

   b. From the remaining three eggs, place one egg in the left pan, one egg in the right pan, and one egg in your pocket.

   c. If the pans balance, then the egg in your pocket is gold-plated.

   d. If the pans don't balance, the lighter pan contains the gold-plated egg.

   Note that, if the pans balance in the first weighing, you have narrowed the number of possibilities to two eggs. The second weighing can find the gold-plated egg in a set of three eggs, so it would work even if you had only narrowed the possibilities to three eggs. That means you can use the same technique even if you start with nine eggs instead of eight. The problem used eight eggs as a red herring. By using eight eggs instead of nine, it encourages you to think about a binary search, which will not lead to the correct solution.

   This is an interesting problem, but it requires you to know the trick. You can use a pan balance to divide objects into three groups—those in the left pan, those in the right pan, and those that are not in any pan. If you have seen this kind of puzzle before, it's fairly easy.

11. Number the bottles 1 through 5. Then place on the scale one pill from bottle 1, two pills from bottle 2, and so on. If all of the pills weighed 1 gram, then the total weight would be $1+2+3+4+5=15$. Subtract the actual weight from 15 and divide by 0.1, which is the difference in weight between a real pill and a placebo. That tells you how many placebos are on the scale, which tells you the number of the bottle containing the placebos.

    The trick to this puzzle is obvious if you've seen a similar puzzle before.

Glossary

2-node — In a 2-3 tree, a node that has two children.

3-node — In a 2-3 tree, a node that has three children.

2-3 tree — A balanced tree structure where every internal node has either two children or three children.

A

accepting state — A state that makes a finite automaton accept its input if it finishes reading the input while in that state.

adaptive quadrature — A technique in which a program detects areas where its approximation method may produce large errors and then refines its method in those areas.

adjacent — Said of two nodes that are connected by a link.

Advanced Encryption Standard (AES) — A symmetric-key encryption algorithm that uses a substitution-permutation network.

adversary — In cryptography, a person trying to intercept and decipher a message sent by a sender to a receiver.

algorithm — A recipe for getting something done.

amortized analysis — Analysis of an algorithm's time, memory use, or other measures over a period of time rather than in the worst case.

ancestor — In a tree, a node's parent, its parent's parent, and so on, to the root node.

array — A chunk of contiguous memory that a program can access by using indices—one index per dimension in the array.

associative array — See *hash table*.

asymptotic performance — The limit of an algorithm's performance as the problem size grows very large.

attacker — In cryptography, a person trying to intercept and decipher a message sent by a sender to a receiver.

augmenting path — A path through a residual capacity network that improves a maximal flow solution.

AVL tree — A sorted binary tree in which the heights of two subtrees at any given node differ by at most 1.

B

B-tree — A balanced tree in which internal nodes (called *buckets*) can hold several values and corresponding branches.

B+tree — Similar to a B-tree, except that the tree's nodes store only key values and pointers to the rest of each record's data instead of holding the data itself.

back substitution — The second part of Gaussian elimination where you successively substitute known values into the matrix to find the values of other variables.

backtracking — A recursive algorithm that considers partial solutions. If it finds a partial solution that cannot be extended to a full solution, the algorithm discards the partial solution, backtracks to the previous feasible test solution, and continues searching from there.

balanced tree — A tree that rearranges its nodes as necessary to guarantee that it doesn't become too tall and thin. This allows algorithms that travel through the tree to run in $O(\log N)$ time.

base case — In recursion, the instance of the recursive method that does not require recursion. In an inductive proof, this is the initial case that you show directly without using induction.

bees algorithm — An algorithm where processes mimic the foraging behavior of bees to try to find an optimal solution in a solution space.

Bézout's identity — An identity that says, "If A and B are integers and $GCD(A, B) = D$, then there are integers x and y such that $Ax + By = D$.

biased — Said of a pseudorandom number generator that does not produce results with equal probability.

Big Omega notation — A lower bound for the algorithm's run time. An algorithm's big omega run time is written $\Omega(g(N))$ if the function $g(N)$ is a lower bound for the algorithm's run time.

Big O notation — An upper bound for an algorithm's run time. An algorithm's big O run time is $O(g(N))$ if the function $g(N)$ is an upper bound for the algorithm's run time.

Big Theta notation — Both an upper bound and a lower bound for an algorithm's run time. An algorithm's big theta run time is $\Theta(g(N))$ if the function $g(N)$ is both a lower and upper bound for the algorithm's run time.

binary search — A search strategy that repeatedly divides the search space into two halves and then searches the half that contains the target item.

binary tree — A tree with degree 2.

binomial coefficient — A coefficient given by the binomial theorem.

binomial heap — A heap constructed out of a forest of binomial trees. The forest can contain at most one tree of any given order, and the trees are stored sorted by order, for example in a linked list.

binomial theorem — A theorem that shows how to calculate the number of ways that you can select n items out of k values. The value $\binom{n}{k}$, pronounced "n choose k," is the number of ways that you can select n items out of k values and is given by the following equation:

$$\binom{n}{k} = \frac{n!}{k!(n-k)!}$$

binomial tree — A balanced tree recursively defined by the two rules: (1) A binomial tree of order 0 is just a root node, and (2) A binomial tree of order k contains subtrees of order $k-1, k-2, \ldots, 0$ stored in that order.

bipartite detection — The problem of determining whether a network is bipartite.

bipartite matching — The process of matching the nodes in one group of a bipartite network with the nodes in the other group.

bipartite network — A network in which the nodes can be divided into two groups, A and B, and every link connects a node in group A with a node in group B.

block cipher — A cipher in which the plaintext is broken into blocks of the same size, each block is encrypted, and the blocks are combined to give the ciphertext.

bottom-up B-tree — A B-tree that performs bucket splits as recursive calls end and move up toward the root.

Boyer–Moore algorithm — A string-searching algorithm.

branch — Connects a parent and child node in a tree.

branch and bound — A tree search algorithm in which the program moves down a branch and then decides whether it is possible to improve its current solution enough to be better than the best solution found so far. If the current solution cannot improve on the best solution so far, the algorithm stops exploring that part of the tree.

breadth-first search — In a tree or network, a search that visits all of a node's children before visiting any other nodes.

breadth-first traversal — In a tree or network, a traversal that visits all of a node's children before visiting any other nodes.

bridge link — In a network, a link that connects two different groups of highly connected nodes.

Bron–Kerbosch algorithm — An algorithm for enumerating all of the maximal cliques in a network.

brute-force — An obvious and nonsubtle algorithm for solving some problem. Many brute-force algorithms enumerate all possible solutions to find the best one. See also *exhaustive search*.

bucket — A data structure used to hold items that are mapped into it. In a hash table, a bucket might be a linked list holding all of the items mapped to the bucket. In a B-tree, a bucket is an internal node that can hold several values and corresponding branches.

bubblesort — A $O(n^2)$ sorting algorithm.

bully algorithm — An algorithm for distributed processes where a process beats any process that has a smaller ID.

byzantine generals problem — A problem in distributed computing problem in which a set of generals, some of whom may be traitors, must reach a consensus on some action.

C

Caesar substitution cipher — A cipher in which each letter in the message is shifted by some amount.

call stack — The sequence of method calls that lead a program to its current state of execution.

capacitated network — A network in which the links have maximum capacities.

capacity — In a network, the maximum amount of something that can move through a node or link, such as the maximum current that can flow through a wire in an electric network or the maximum number of cars that can move through a link in a street network per unit of time.

cell — An object that makes up a linked list. A cell contains data and a link to the next cell in the list.

child — A node connected to a parent in a tree.

Chinese postman problem (CPP) — A problem with the goal of finding the shortest path or closed circuit that visits every edge of a network. Also called the *route inspection problem.*

chromatic number — The smallest number of colors that you need to color a network so that no adjacent nodes have the same color.

cipher — A pair of algorithms used to encrypt and decrypt messages.

ciphertext — In cryptography, a message that has been encrypted to be sent securely.

circular array — An array used to hold a queue in which you treat the last item as if it comes immediately before the first item.

circular linked list — A linked list in which the last link points back to the first item in the list.

clique — A group of nodes that are all directly mutually connected.

cluster computing — Distributed computing that uses a collection of closely related computers, often on an intranet or special-purpose network.

cocktail shaker sort — A version of bubblesort that alternates upward and downward passes through the values being sorted.

collision — In a hash table, the situation when you map a value to a position that is already occupied.

collision-resolution policy — A method that determines how a hash table handles a new value when a collision occurs.

combination — See *selection.*

community detection — The problem of finding subsets of nodes in a network that are closely related.

complete tree — A tree in which every level is completely full, except possibly the bottom level, where all of the nodes are pushed as far to the left as possible.

complexity theory — See *computational complexity theory.*

composite number — A natural number greater than 1 that is not prime.

computational complexity theory — The study of the difficulty of computational problems, focusing on the problems themselves rather than on specific algorithms.

condensation — A representation of a network where you condense the strongly connected components into nodes.

connected — In an undirected network, said of two nodes that are reachable from each other. An undirected network is connected if every node is reachable from every other node.

connected component — In a network, a set of nodes that are mutually connected.

connectivity matrix — A matrix that represents the connections between nodes in a network.

consensus problem — In distributed computing, a problem in which a number of processes must agree on a data value even if some of the processes fail.

coprime — See *relatively prime*.

cost — The price or penalty for using a link. Less commonly, a node may have a cost.

countingsort — An $O(n)$ sorting algorithm that works when the items being sorted are integers that lie between zero and a relatively small upper bound.

covering network — A network built from an initial network by replacing the original's links with nodes, and vice versa. This is also called an *interchange network, line network, edge/vertex dual,* and *edge network*.

cryptanalysis — The study of methods that attackers use to break an encryption system.

cryptography — The study of methods for encrypting and decrypting messages so that a sender can transmit them securely to a receiver without an attacker's recovering the original message.

cryptographic hash function — A method that converts a large piece of data such as a document or file into a small signature form.

CSPRNG — Abbreviation for cryptographically secure pseudorandom number generator.

cutting stock — A problem where you try to cut two-dimensional shapes from pieces of rectangular stock using as few pieces as possible.

cycle — In a network, a path that returns to its starting point.

cycle detection — The process of determining whether a network contains a cycle.

D

Data Encryption Standard (DES) — A symmetric-key encryption algorithm that uses a Feistel network.

data parallelism — A form of parallel processing in which emphasis is placed on distributing data among processors that execute the same or similar programs.

data processing unit (DPU) — Part of the computer that processes a piece of data. Specifically, a cell in a systolic array.

data structure — A way of arranging data to make solving a particular problem easier.

deadlock — In distributed computing, when two processes block each other while each waits for a mutex held by the other.

decipher — See *decrypt*.

decision tree — A tree that lets you model a problem as a series of decisions that leads to a solution.

decrypt — In cryptography, to convert a ciphertext message back into plaintext.

degree — For a node in a tree, the number of children the node has. For a tree, the maximum degree of any of its nodes. For a node in a network or graph, the number of links leaving the node.

dendrogram — A tree diagram that shows taxonomic relationships.

depth — For a tree node, the node's level.

depth-first traversal — In a tree or network, a traversal that visits some nodes far from the starting point before visiting all of the nodes closest to the starting point. Preorder, inorder, and postorder traversals are all depth-first traversals.

deque — Pronounced "deck." This is a queue that allows you to add items to and remove items from either end of the queue.

descendant — In a tree, a node's children, their children, and so on.

detection problem — Asks you to determine whether a solution of a given quality exists.

deterministic finite automaton (DFA) — A virtual computer that uses a set of states to keep track of what it is doing. At each step, it reads some input. Based on the input and its current state, the computer moves into a new state. One state is the initial state where the machine starts. One or more states can be marked as accepting states.

deterministic finite state machine — See *deterministic finite automaton*.

DFA — See *deterministic finite automaton*.

dictionary — Another name for a hash table.

digital signature — A hashing of a document or other piece of data that you can use to verify later that the document's contents have not been changed.

dining philosophers problem — A problem in which N philosophers sit at a table with a fork between each pair. To eat, a philosopher must acquire both adjacent forks without talking to his neighbors.

directed — Said of a link that can be traversed in only one direction. A network is directed if it contains only directed links.

direct recursion — Occurs when a method calls itself directly.

disk bound — An algorithm with performance limited by the speed of disk accesses and not the algorithm itself.

distributed computing — Multiple computers working together over a network to perform a task.

dominating set — In a network, a subset of nodes such that every node in the network is either in the subset or is adjacent to a node that is in the subset.

Double Metaphone — A variation of the Metaphone algorithm. One of its key features is that it provides a secondary encoding (hence the name) to help differentiate among strings that map to the same first encoding.

doubly linked list — A linked list with forward and backward links.

DPU — See *data processing unit*.

DSPACE(f(n)) — The set of problems that can be solved in f(n) space by a deterministic Turing machine.

DTIME(f(n)) — The set of problems that can be solved in f(n) time by a deterministic Turing machine.

dynamic programming — A technique where an algorithm stores previously calculated values for later use so it doesn't need to recalculate them.

E

edge — See *link*.

edge betweenness — In the Girvan–Newman algorithm for community detection, a measure of how many times an edge is used in the shortest paths between every pair of nodes in the network. In some sense, this measures how important the link is.

edge graph — See *covering network*.

edge network — See *covering network*. Also called *edge/vertex dual* and *edge network*.

edge/vertex dual — See *covering network*.

edit distance — For two strings, the number of changes that you need to make to turn the first into the second.

eight queens problem — The problem of positioning eight queens on a chessboard so that none of the queens can attack any of the others.

embarrassingly parallel — When an algorithm naturally breaks into parallelizable pieces that require minimal communication.

encipher — See *encrypt*.

encrypt — In cryptography, to convert a plaintext message into ciphertext.

entanglement — In quantum computing, a condition where multiple particles remain in the same state even if they are separated.

Euclidian algorithm — See *Euclid's algorithm*.

Euclid's algorithm — An algorithm for quickly finding the greatest common divisor of two numbers.

Euler's totient function — Counts the positive integers less than a number n that are relatively prime to n. Written $\varphi(n)$.

Euler tour — See *Eulerian cycle*.

Eulerian cycle — An Eulerian path that starts and ends at the same node. Also called an *Eulerian tour*, *Euler tour*, or *Eulerian circuit*.

Eulerian network — A network that has an Eulerian cycle.

Eulerian path — A path through a network that visits every edge exactly once.

exact cover — If X is a set of numbers and $S = \{S_1, S_2, \ldots\}$ is a collection of subsets of X, then an exact cover C of X is a collection of subsets taken from S such that every value in X is in exactly one of C's subsets.

exhaustive search — Searching all possible items to find a target item or the item that is best according to some metric.

EXPSPACE — The set of problems that can be solved by a deterministic Turing machine using exponential space.

EXPTIME — The set of problems that can be solved by a deterministic Turing machine in an exponential amount of time.

external node — In a tree, a leaf node.

external sorting — Sorting data that cannot fit in memory. Data can be sorted on disk files or tape drives.

F

factorial — For a non-negative integer n, the value $n \times (n-1) \times (n-2) \times \ldots \times 1$. The factorial of n is written n! and pronounced "n factorial."

fair — Said of a pseudorandom number generator that produces all of its possible outputs with the same probability. A PRNG that is not fair is called *biased*.

Feistel cipher — An encryption method where a message is split into two halves, a function is applied to one half, the halves are combined using XOR, the halves are swapped, and the whole thing is repeated.

Fermat liar — If p is not prime, a value n with $1 \le n \le p$ that satisfies the equation $n^{p-1} \bmod p = 1$. The value n is called a Fermat liar because it incorrectly implies that p is prime.

Fermat witness — If p is not prime, a value n where $1 \le n \le p$ and $n^{p-1} \bmod p \ne 1$. The value n is called a Fermat witness because it proves that p is not prime.

Fibonacci numbers — The sequence of numbers defined by the recurrence relation $\text{Fibonacci}(0) = 0$, $\text{Fibonacci}(1) = 1$, and $\text{Fibonacci}(n) = \text{Fibonacci}(n-1) + \text{Fibonacci}(n-2)$ for $n > 1$.

FIFO — Abbreviation for first, in-first-out. Queues are also sometimes called FIFOs. See *queue*.

FIFO list — Another name for a queue. See *queue*.

fill percentage — For a hash table, the percentage of the data structure that is filled. Hash tables with high fill percentages may result in reduced performance.

first common ancestor — For any two nodes, the node that is the ancestor of both nodes that is closest to the nodes.

first-in-first-out (FIFO) — See *queue*.

Fleury's algorithm — An algorithm for finding Eulerian paths.

flops — Also spelled FLOPS, which stands for floating-point operations per second. Calculation speeds are sometimes measured in megaflops, gigaflops, teraflops (one trillion flops), or petaflops (1,000 teraflops).

Floyd's cycle-finding algorithm — See *tortoise-and-hare algorithm*.

Ford–Fulkerson algorithm — An algorithm for calculating maximal flows in a network.

forest — A collection of trees.

forward elimination — The first part of Gaussian elimination where you use row operations to zero out entries in the coefficients in the left columns in a matrix of equations.

four-coloring theorem — A theorem that states that any map can be colored with at most four colors.

full tree — A tree in which every node has either zero children or as many children as the tree's degree.

G

gasket — A type of self-similar fractal in which you start with a geometric shape such as a square or triangle, divide the shape into smaller similar shapes, and then recursively fill some, but not all, of the smaller shapes.

Gaussian elimination — A method for solving a system of linear equations.

GCD — See *greatest common divisor.*

general and lieutenants problem — A problem in which a general gives an order to his lieutenants, but the general or some lieutenants might be traitors. The goal is for the loyal lieutenants to decide on a common action. If the general is not a traitor, that action must be the one the general ordered.

generalized partition problem — The problem of dividing a collection of objects into K sets with equal total weights.

generator — A shape used to create one type of self-similar fractal curve. An initiator sets the fractal's basic shape. At each level of recursion, some or all of the initiator is replaced with a generator.

Girvan–Newman algorithm — An algorithm for detecting communities in a network.

Gordon E. Moore — Cofounder of Intel Corporation and inventor of Moore's law. (See also *Moore's law.*)

graph — A network.

graph isomorphism problem — The problem of determining whether two graphs are isomorphic.

greatest common divisor (GCD) — The largest integer that divides two integers evenly.

grid computing — Distributed computing that uses a collection of loosely related computers that may communicate over a public network. A grid may include different kinds of computers running different operating systems.

H

Hamiltonian — Said of a network that contains a Hamiltonian path.

Hamiltonian circuit (HAMC) — A Hamiltonian path that returns to its starting point.

Hamiltonian completion — The problem of finding the fewest possible links that you must add to a network to make it Hamiltonian.

Hamiltonian path (HAM) — A path through a network that visits every node exactly once.

hashing — The process of mapping a key to a location in a hash table.

hash table — A data structure and algorithms that map data to locations in the data structure.

heap — A complete binary tree in which every node holds a value that is at least as large as the values in all its children.

heapsort — An $O(n \log n)$ sorting algorithm.

height — For a node in a tree, the length of the longest path from the node downward through the tree to a leaf node. For a tree, this is the same as the root's height.

heuristic — An algorithm that often produces a good result but that is not guaranteed to produce the best possible result.

Hierholzer's algorithm — An algorithm for finding Eulerian cycles in a network.

Hilbert curve — A space-filling fractal curve created by starting with an initiator curve and then recursively replacing pieces of the initiator with a suitably scaled, rotated, and translated generator curve.

hill climbing — A heuristic strategy that at each step takes the action that moves the algorithm closest to the best possible solution. This is similar to a hiker trying to find the top of a mountain at night by always moving uphill.

I

in-degree — In a directed network, the number of links entering a node.

independent set — A set of nodes in a network, no two of which are adjacent.

indirect recursion — Occurs when a method calls itself indirectly by calling another method that then calls the first method.

initial state — The state in which a finite automaton starts before reading any input.

initiator — A curve that sets the basic shape for one type of fractal. At each level of recursion, some or all of the initiator is replaced with a generator curve.

inorder traversal — In a tree or network, a traversal that visits a node's left child and then the node and then the node's right child. Also called a *symmetric traversal*.

interchange network — See *covering network*.

internal node — A tree node that has at least one child.

interpolation search — A search algorithm that calculates a target item's likely location.

interval tree — A data structure that makes it easier to determine which interval contains a given point or overlaps with another interval in one-dimensional space.

isomorphic — A one-to-one mapping between two mathematical objects that preserves the objects' operations. Two networks G and H are isomorphic if you can map the nodes in G to the nodes in H such that two nodes in G are neighbors if and only if the corresponding nodes in H are also neighbors.

J

job shop scheduling — The problem of assigning jobs to resources such as machines to minimize the total time needed to complete all jobs.

K

k-clique — A clique containing k nodes.

key — In cryptography, a piece of information that allows the recipient of an encrypted message to decode the message. In modern cryptography, it is assumed that the attacker knows the encryption method, so an attacker who has the key can also decrypt the message.

knapsack problem — Given a set of objects with specified weights and values and given a knapsack that can hold a certain maximum amount of weight, the problem of finding the combination of items that can fit into the knapsack that gives the greatest total value.

knight's tour problem — A problem where the goal is to find a path that a knight can use to visit every position on a chessboard without visiting any square twice. In a closed tour, the final position is one move away from the starting position. A tour that is not closed is open.

Koch curve — A self-similar fractal created by starting with an initiator curve and then recursively replacing pieces of the initiator with a suitably scaled, rotated, and translated generator curve.

Kosaraju's algorithm — An algorithm for detecting a network's strongly connected components.

L

last-in-first-out (LIFO) — See *stack*.

leaf node — A tree node with no children.

least common ancestor — See *first common ancestor*.

least squares fit — A curve-fitting method that minimizes the sum of the squares of the vertical distances between the curve and the data points.

level — The distance between a node and the tree's root node.

level-order traversal — See *breadth-first traversal*.

LIFO — Abbreviation for last-in, first-out. Stacks are sometimes called LIFOs. See *stack*.

LIFO list — Another name for a stack. See *stack*.

line network — See *covering network*.

linear array — A one-dimensional array.

linear congruential generator — A pseudorandom number generator that uses a simple recurrence relation to generate numbers.

linear probing — A technique used to build a hash table in which the collision-resolution policy adds a constant number, usually 1, to each location that is already occupied to generate a probe sequence.

linear search — To search linearly through a linear array or other linear data structure for a value.

link — A reference or pointer from one linked list cell to another, or from one node to another in a tree or network

linked list — A list built of cells connected by one or more links.

list retracing — An algorithm that detects loops in a linked list by looping through the list and tracing the items between the start of the list and each item in it.

list reversal — An algorithm that detects loops in a linked list by reversing the list.

livelock — In distributed processing, a situation similar to a deadlock in which processes are not blocked but still cannot get any work done because of how they try to access resources.

longest path problem — The problem of finding the longest path (measured either in number of edges or in total edge weight) without repeated nodes in a network.

loop — In a network, a cycle. In a linked list, a sequence of cells that returns to its starting point.

lower-triangular array — An array where all of the nondefault entries are in the array's lower-left half.

lowest common ancestor — See *first common ancestor.*

M

majority voting problem — The problem of determining the majority of the values in a list if a majority exists.

map coloring — The process of finding a way to color the regions on a map so that no two adjacent regions have the same color.

matching — The process of pairing objects from one set with objects from another set.

maximal clique — A clique that cannot be enlarged by adding nodes.

maximal flow problem — The problem of finding the maximum possible flow through a capacitated network from a source node to a sink node.

maximum independent set — A largest independent set in a network. (See also *independent set.*)

maximum leaf spanning tree — A spanning tree that has as many leaves as possible.

mergesort — An $O(n \log n)$ sorting algorithm that works particularly well for external sorting or parallel sorting.

Metaphone — A phonetic algorithm.

min flow cut — The problem of finding the minimum total capacity of links that must be cut to separate two nodes in a network.

minimal spanning tree — A spanning tree that has the least possible total cost in the network.

minimax — A strategy for minimizing the worst possible outcome. In games, a minimax strategy minimizes the maximum benefit that your opponent can achieve.

minimum degree spanning tree — A spanning tree with the smallest possible degree.

minimum heap property — The property of a heap that says that a node has a smaller value than the value of any of its children.

minimum k-cut — The problem of finding a minimum cut that will separate a network into k connected components.

minimum reduction — A transitive reduction of a network that has the fewest possible links. (See *transitive reduction*.)

Monte Carlo integration — A numeric integration technique in which a program picks a large number of pseudorandom points and uses the fraction of those that lie within a shape to estimate the shape's area.

Monte Carlo simulation — A probabilistic technique in which the program picks pseudorandom values and determines what percentage satisfies some criterion to estimate the total number of values that satisfy the criterion.

Moore's law — The trend noticed by Gordon E. Moore in 1965 that the number of transistors on integrated circuits doubles roughly every two years.

move to front method — A self-arranging list method that moves the most recently accessed item to the front of the list.

multiple recursion — Occurs when a method calls itself more than once.

multiplicative inverse — The number by which you can multiply another number to get 1. In modular arithmetic, finding the multiplicative inverse can be difficult.

mutex — A method of ensuring that only one process can perform an operation at a time. (The name comes from "mutual exclusion.")

N

natural number — An integer greater than 0.

neighbor — An adjacent node.

network coloring — The process of finding a way to color the nodes in a network so that no two adjacent nodes have the same color.

Newton–Cotes formulas — A numeric integration technique that uses polynomials to approximate a curve to find the area beneath it.

Newton–Raphson method — See *Newton's method*.

Newton's method — A method of finding the roots of a function.

NEXPSPACE — The set of problems that can be solved by a nondeterministic Turing machine using exponential space.

NEXPTIME — The set of problems that can be solved by a nondeterministic Turing machine in an exponential amount of time.

NFA — See *nondeterministic finite automaton*.

node — An object that holds data in a tree or network. Nodes are connected by branches in trees, or links or edges in networks and graphs.

node merge — The process of merging two nodes when rebalancing a 2-3 tree.

node split — The process of splitting a node into two nodes when adding a new value to a balanced tree.

nondeterministic finite automaton (NFA) — Similar to a DFA, except that multiple links may leave a state for the same input. You can think of an NFA as simultaneously being in every possible state for its inputs.

NP — The set of problems that can be solved by a nondeterministic computer in polynomial time.

NP-complete — A problem that is in NP and to which every problem in NP can be reduced in polynomial time.

NP-hard — A problem to which every problem in NP can be reduced in polynomial time.

NPSPACE — The set of problems that can be solved by a nondeterministic Turing machine using polynomial space.

NTIME(f(n)) — The set of problems that can be solved in f(n) time by a nondeterministic Turing machine.

null transition — In a finite automaton, a state transition that can happen spontaneously without reading any new input.

numeric integration — The process of approximating the area under a curve numerically, usually because you can't use the curve's antiderivative and calculus to calculate the area exactly.

numeric quadrature — See *numeric integration*.

O

observer — In a distributed system, a process that initiates a snapshot.

octtree — A tree data structure used to locate objects in three-dimensional space.

odd-cycle problem — The problem of determining whether a network contains any cycles of odd length.

one-time pad cipher — A cipher in which each letter in the message is combined with the corresponding letter in a pad of random letters or offsets. This is similar to a Vigenère cipher, in which the key length is the same as the message length.

open addressing — A method for building hash tables in which keys are mapped into entries in an array. Different versions of open addressing use different hashing functions and collision-resolution policies.

optimization problem — A problem that asks you to find the optimal solution to a particular problem. Optimization problems often have approximate solutions.

order — The value that determines the number of nodes that an internal node in a B-tree can hold. In a B-tree of order K, the internal nodes hold between K and $2 \times K$ values and have between $K + 1$ and $2 \times K + 1$ branches.

ordered tree — A tree in which the ordering of each node's children matters.

out-degree — In a directed network, the number of links leaving a node.

P

P — The set of problems that can be solved by a deterministic computer in polynomial time.

parent node — A node in a tree that has child nodes connected to it by branches. In a tree, every node except the root has exactly one parent.

partial ordering — A set of dependencies that defines an ordering relationship for some but not necessarily all of the objects in a set.

partition problem — Given a set of numbers, the problem of dividing the set into two subsets that have the same total.

path — In a network, an alternating series of nodes and links that leads from one node to another. If there is only one link from any node to an adjacent node, you can specify a path by listing the nodes or links it includes.

perfect tree — A full tree in which all of the leaves are at the same level.

permutation — An ordered subset of items taken from a set.

permutation boxes (P-boxes) — In cryptography, a method that permutes its input bits. See also *substitution-permutation network*.

petaflop (pflop) — 1,000 teraflops.

phase king algorithm — A distributed algorithm that achieves consensus by making each process take a turn being the "phase king" and coordinating information transfer.

phi function — See *Euler's totient function*.

phonetic algorithm — An algorithm that creates a representation of a word's pronunciation.

pigeonhole sort — A sorting algorithm that is extremely fast if the items being sorted span a relatively small range.

plaintext — In cryptography, the message to be sent securely.

planar — Said of a network that can be drawn on a plane with none of its links intersecting.

Polish notation — A mathematical notation that represents equations in prefix order. For example, the standard equation $1*(2+3)$ is written as $*1+23$ in Polish notation.

polygon method — A method for visualizing matchups for a round-robin tournament.

polynomial least squares — A method that fits a polynomial to a set of data points.

polynomial run time — An algorithm with run time dominated by any polynomial function of N. For example, $O(N)$, $O(N^2)$, $O(N^6)$, and even $O(N^{4000})$ are all polynomial run times.

pop — To remove an item from a stack.

postorder traversal — In a tree or network, a traversal that visits a node's left child, and then its right child, and then the node.

prefix tree — See *trie*.

preorder traversal — In a tree or network, a traversal that visits a node, then its left child, and then its right child.

primary clustering — In a hash table that uses open addressing, an effect in which values that map to a cluster of entries end up extending the cluster to form long blocks of occupied entries. That increases average probe sequence length.

prime number — A natural number greater than 1 whose only factors are 1 and itself.

priority inversion — In distributed computing, a situation where a high-priority process is blocked because a lower-priority process holds a mutex.

priority queue — A type of queue where items are removed in priority order.

private key — Used in public-key encryption. In a public-key encryption, anyone can use the public key to encrypt a message. Only the recipient who knows the private key can decrypt the message.

PRNG — See *pseudorandom number generator.*

probabilistic algorithm — An algorithm that produces a correct result with a certain probability.

probe sequence — The sequence of locations that an open addressing hash table algorithm tries for a value.

pseudocode — A language used to describe algorithms that is similar to but not exactly the same as a programming language.

pseudorandom number generator (PRNG) — A number generator that uses calculations to produce numbers that seem random but that are predictable.

pseudorandom probing — A method for collision resolution in a hash table where the probe sequence visits the values $K, K + p, K + 2 \times p, K + 3 \times p, \ldots$ where p is a pseudorandom value generated from the initial location K in the hash table.

PSPACE — The set of problems that can be solved by a Turing machine in a polynomial amount of space.

public key — Used in public-key encryption. In a public-key encryption, anyone can use the public key to encrypt a message. Only the recipient who knows the private key can decrypt the message.

public-key encryption — An encryption method that uses two keys: a private key and a public key. The sender uses the public key to encrypt messages, and the receiver uses the private key to decrypt them.

public key exponent — The exponent that a sender should use to encrypt a message with RSA. If M is the message, e is the public key exponent, and n is the public key modulus, then the sender encrypts the message into ciphertext by using the equation $C = M^e \bmod n$.

public key modulus — See *public key exponent.*

push — To add an item to a stack.

pushdown stack — See *stack.*

Q

quadratic probing — A method for collision resolution in a hash table where the probe sequence visits the values $K, K + 1^2, K + 2^2, K + 3^2, \ldots$.

quadrature — See *numeric integration.*

quadtree — A tree data structure that helps locate objects in two-dimensional space.

quantum computer — A computer that uses quantum effects such as entanglement and superposition to manipulate data.

queue — A data structure in which items are added and removed in first-in, first-out (FIFO) order.

R

race condition — A situation in distributed processing, particularly when a single computer has multiple CPUs, in which two processes try to write to a resource at almost the same time and the process that writes to the resource second wins.

random self-avoiding walk — A random walk that is not allowed to intersect itself.

random walk — A randomly generated path, usually on a lattice.

random solution search — A heuristic for finding a solution to a problem by randomly searching its decision tree.

range minimum query (RMQ) — Given an array of values, a problem where the goal is to find the minimum value in a given subset of the values.

reachable — A property of a node that can be reached from another node by following the network's links.

receiver — In cryptography, the person trying to receive a message sent by a sender.

rectangle rule — A numeric integration technique that uses rectangles to approximate the area below a curve.

recursion — Occurs when a method calls itself either directly or indirectly.

reduce — In complexity theory, the process of using one problem to solve another problem. If you can use problem A to solve problem B, then you have reduced problem B to problem A.

regular expression — A pattern for matching the characters in a string.

relatively prime — The relationship between two integers that have greatest common divisor 1.

reporting problem — A version of a problem that asks you to find a solution of a given quality.

residual capacity — The extra flow you could add to a link in a capacitated network.

residual capacity network — A network consisting of links and backlinks marked with their residual capacities.

resource hierarchy — In distributed computing, a technique that assigns ranks to resources and processes must acquire resources in order of their ranks. This prevents deadlock in the dining philosophers problem.

reverse Polish notation — A mathematical notation that represents equations in postfix order. For example, the standard equation $(2*3)+1$ is written as $2\,3*1+$ in reverse Polish notation.

rod-cutting problem — A problem where the goal is to cut a wooden or metal rod into pieces. Pieces of different lengths have different values, so you must decide the best way to cut the rod to maximize the total value.

root — For a function $f(x)$, the values of x for which $f(x)=0$.

root node — The unique node at the top of a tree that has no parent.

root split — When a series of node splits cascades up a balanced tree until the root node is split.

round-robin schedule — A tournament schedule where every team plays every other team once.

route inspection problem — See *Chinese postman problem*.

row/column transposition cipher — A cipher where plaintext is written into an array by rows and then the ciphertext is read out of the array by columns.

RSA — A public-key cryptosystem invented by Ron Rivest, Adi Shamir, and Leonard Adleman.

S

satisfiability problem (SAT) — Given a Boolean expression containing logical variables, a problem where the goal is to determine whether you can assign the values true and false to the variables to make the expression true.

scytale — A wooden rod used to encrypt messages by ancient Greeks and Spartans.

secondary clustering — In a hash table that uses open addressing with quadratic probing, an effect in which values that map to the same address follow the same probe sequence and produce a long probe sequence.

security through obscurity — A cryptosystem that relies on the fact that the attacker does not know the method used to encrypt the message. Modern cryptosystems assume that the attacker knows how a message was encrypted but does not know the key.

selection — An unordered subset of a set of objects.

self-organizing linked list — A linked list that rearranges its items on the fly to minimize later expected search times.

self-similar fractal — A curve in which pieces of the curve resemble the curve as a whole.

sender — In cryptography, the person trying to send a message securely to a receiver.

sentinel — A cell that is part of the linked list but that doesn't contain any meaningful data placed at either end of the list. It is used only as a placeholder so that algorithms can refer to a cell before the first cell or after the last cell.

shortest path tree — A spanning tree that gives shortest paths from its root node to every other node in the network.

sibling nodes — Two nodes in a tree that have the same parent.

Sierpiński curve — A space-filling fractal curve created by starting with an initiator curve and then recursively replacing pieces of the initiator with a suitably scaled, rotated, and translated generator curve.

sieve of Eratosthenes — A method for finding prime numbers.

Simpson's rule — A numeric integration technique that uses polynomials of degree 2 to approximate the area below a curve.

simulated annealing — A solution improvement heuristic that initially makes large changes to a solution and then over time makes smaller and smaller changes to try to improve the solution.

single recursion — Occurs when a method calls itself exactly once.

skyline problem — Given a collection of rectangles with a common baseline, a problem where the goal is to find an outline for the rectangles.

snapshot — In distributed processing, a picture of the state of the system at a particular moment. A snapshot includes the state of all processes and any messages between them that are in transit.

snapshot token — A value that identifies a particular snapshot.

sorted tree — A tree in which the nodes are arranged so that they are processed in sorted order by a particular traversal, usually an inorder traversal.

Soundex — A phonetic algorithm.

space-filling curve — A curve that, in the limit, approaches arbitrarily closely to every point in the area that it covers.

spanning tree — A tree consisting of some of a network's nodes and links that connects every node in the network.

sparse array — An array data structure that contains very few entries that don't have a default value.

stable sort — A sorting algorithm that preserves the initial order of items that are equivalent.

stack — A data structure in which items are added and removed in last-in, first-out (LIFO) order.

starvation — In distributed processing, when a process cannot obtain the resources it needs to finish.

state transition diagram — A network representing a DFA's or NFA's state transitions.

stride — In a hash table with open addressing and linear probing, the value added to each location in a value's probe sequence.

strongly connected — Said of a directed network where every node is reachable from every other node.

strongly connected component — A strongly connected subset of a network.

subgraph isomorphism problem — Given two graphs (networks) G and H, a problem where the goal is to determine whether G contains a subgraph that is isomorphic to H.

subset sum problem — Given a set of numbers, a problem where the goal is to find a subset of values that adds up to zero. An alternative version of the problem attempts to find a subset of values that adds up to a given nonzero total k.

substitution boxes (S-boxes) — In cryptography, a method that takes a small part of a message block and combines it with part of the key to produce an obfuscated result. See also *substitution-permutation network*.

substitution cipher — A cipher in which the letters in the plaintext are replaced with other letters. Caesar substitution and the Vigenère cipher are two examples.

substitution-permutation network — A cryptographic method that modifies a plaintext message by repeatedly applying rounds of substitution and permutation performed by substitution boxes (S-boxes) and permutation boxes (P-boxes).

subtree — A node and all its descendants in a tree.

superposition — In quantum computing, a condition in which a particle exists in multiple states simultaneously.

swap method — In a self-organizing list, a method that swaps the most recently accessed item with the item before it to move it closer to the top of the list. Also called the *transpose method*.

swarm intelligence (SI) — The result of a distributed collection of simple, mostly independent objects. SI systems are often modeled on real-world swarm patterns such as ant exploration, bee foraging, bird flocking, and fish schooling.

swarm simulation — A program that uses simple rules to mimic the behavior of a swarm or flock.

symmetrically threaded tree — A tree that contains threads forward and backward through the tree's inorder traversal.

symmetric-key encryption — An encryption method that uses the same key to encrypt and decrypt messages. Both the sender and receiver must have the key.

symmetric traversal — See *inorder traversal*.

systolic array — An array of data processing units (DPUs) called *cells* that use data parallelism to provide parallel processing.

T

tail recursion — Occurs when the recursive step is the last thing that a recursive method does.

task parallelism — A form of parallel processing in which emphasis is placed on distributing tasks among processors.

teraflop (tflop) — One trillion floating-point operations per second.

thread — A sequence of links that forms a path through a data structure such as a tree or network.

threaded tree — A tree that contains one or more threads.

three-cycle problem — Given a network, a problem where the goal is to determine whether the network contains a cycle of length three.

three-partition problem — Given a set of numbers, a problem where the goal is to determine whether you can partition the set into groups of three that all have the same total value.

three-satisfiability (3SAT) — Given a Boolean expression in three-term conjunctive normal form, a problem where the goal is to find an assignment of true and false to the variables to make the expression true.

three-term conjunctive normal form (3CNF) — A Boolean expression that is a conjunction of three-term disjunctions. In other words, it consists of pieces that include three variables combined with OR and NOT, and then those pieces are combined with AND. For example, (A or B or not C) and (not A or B or C).

top-down B-tree — A B-tree that performs bucket splits whenever possible as it moves down into the tree looking for a location to place a new value.

topological sorting — The process of extending a partial ordering to a full ordering on a network.

tortoise-and-hare algorithm — An algorithm for detecting and removing a loop from a linked list. (See the section "Tortoise and Hare" in Chapter 3.)

totient function — See *Euler's totient function*.

tower of Hanoi — A puzzle in which the goal is to move a stack of disks from one of three pegs to another peg by moving one disk at a time and never placing a larger disk on a smaller one.

transitive closure — A network augmented with additional links that directly connect nodes that are reachable in the original network. In other words, if there is a path from node A to node B in the original network, then there is a link A → B in the transitive closure.

transitive reduction — A network with as many links as possible removed while still preserving the connectivity of the original network.

transpose link — A link that has been reversed.

transpose method — In a self-organizing list, a method that swaps the most recently accessed item with the item before it to move it closer to the top of the list. Also called the *swap method*.

transpose network — A network with every link reversed.

transposition cipher — A cipher in which the plaintext's letters are rearranged in a specific way to create the ciphertext.

trapezoid rule — A numeric integration technique that uses trapezoids to approximate the area below a curve.

traveling salesman problem (TSP) — Given a network, a problem where to goal is to find the shortest route that visits every node and returns to its starting point.

traversal — To visit all of the nodes in a tree or network in some order.

treesort — A sorting algorithm in which you first build a sorted tree and then use an inorder traversal to produce the sorted items.

triangular array — A two-dimensional array in which the values above the diagonal have some default value, such as 0, null, or blank.

trie — A tree in which nodes represent letters in strings, and the path from the root to a node defines a prefix that all of the strings below the node share.

Triple DES (3DES or TDES) — An encryption algorithm that applies DES three times to each message block.

TRNG — See *true random-number generator*.

true random-number generator (TRNG) — A number generator that uses a source of true randomness, such as radioactive decay or atmospheric noise, to produce truly unpredictable numbers.

Turing machine — A hypothetical computer that manipulates the symbols on a strip of input tape according to a simple table of rules.

two generals problem — A problem in which two generals have armies encamped just outside an enemy city, at opposite ends of town. Using messengers that might be captured by the enemy, the generals must coordinate an attack.

U

unbounded knapsack problem — Similar to the knapsack problem except that you are allowed to place multiple copies of each item in the knapsack.

undirected — In a network, a link that can be traversed in either direction. A network is undirected if it contains only undirected links.

unordered tree — A tree in which the order of each node's children doesn't matter.

upper-triangular array — An array where all of the non-default entries are in the array's upper-right half.

V

vehicle routing — Given a set of customer locations and a fleet of vehicles, a problem where the goal is to find the most efficient routes for the vehicles to visit all of the customer locations.

vertex — See *node*.

vertex coloring — See *network coloring*.

vertex cover — Given a network, a set of nodes in the network such that every edge in the network is connected to at least one of the nodes.

Vigenère cipher — A substitution cipher in which each letter in the message is shifted by an amount determined by a corresponding letter in the key.

virtual backlink — In maximal flow calculations, the virtual reverse of a link over which you can push flow to create an augmenting path.

W

weakly connected — Said of a directed network if every node is reachable from every other node when you replace the directed links with undirected links.

weight — Another name for a link's cost. See *cost*.

work assignment problem — Given a set of people with certain skills and a set of jobs that require someone with certain skills, a problem where the goal is to find an assignment of people to jobs that maximizes the number of jobs that can be performed.

Z

zero subset sum problem — See *subset sum problem*.

zero-time sort — A systolic array algorithm that sorts items in O(N) time. It is called a zero-time sort because the sorted items start popping out as soon as the last item is entered into the cells.

Index

A

A2Z Interviews: puzzles (website), 604
accepting states, 497, 711
acyclic networks, 439–440
adaptive quadrature, 50–53, 711
adaptive techniques, 599, 609
adding
  items, 335–336, 339–341
  nodes, 303–305
AddInterval method, 329
AddItemToChild method, 335–336
AddNote method, 320
Adelson-Velskii, G. M. (mathematician),
  350
adjacent, 405, 711
Advanced Encryption Standard (AES),
  520, 532–533, 711
advanced linked-list operations,
  609
adversary, in cryptography, 520, 711
AES (Advanced Encryption Standard),
  520, 532–533, 711
algorithmic goals, 607
algorithms
  all-pairs shortest paths, 431–436, 617
  backtracking
    about, 252–253
    eight queens problem, 254–257, 718
    knight's tour problem, 257–260, 723

basic exercises, 20–22
basic network
  about, 403
  exercises, 447–450
  finding paths, 425–436
  network representations, 407–409
  network terminology, 403–406
  shortest path modifications, 441–446
  strongly connected components,
    420–425
  transitivity, 436–441
  traversals, 409–420
basic recursion, 228–238
basics of, 607–608
bees, 394, 712
binary search, 203–204, 611
Boyer-Moore, 493, 504–508, 618, 713
branch-and-bound, 616
Bron-Kerbosch, 475–480, 714
Bubblesort, 171–174, 197, 714
Bucketsort, 195–197
bully, 587–588, 714
characteristics of, 607
community detection
  about, 483
  clique percolation method (CPM), 485
  Girvan-Newman, 483–485, 721
  maximal cliques, 473, 483, 724
ContainsDuplicates, 10, 15

ContainsNodes, 313–314
ContainsNodes, 313–314
countingsort, 192–193, 197, 716
cryptographical, 619
data structures and, 2–3
defined, 1, 607, 711
distributed
  about, 561–562, 573, 620
  byzantine generals problem (BGP),
    581–584, 620, 714
  clock synchronization, 589–590, 620
  consensus problem, 584–587, 620, 716
  debugging, 573–574
  dining philosophers problem,
    577–580, 620, 717
  embarassingly parallel, 574–576, 620
  embarassingly parallel algorithm,
    574–576
  exercises, 591–593
  leader election, 587–588, 620
  mergesort, 576–577
  mergesort, 189–191, 197, 576–577, 620,
    725
  mergesort algorithm, 576–577
  snapshot, 588–589, 620, 732
  two generals problem, 580–581, 620,
    736
  types of parallelism, 562–572
Double Metaphone, 514, 718
edit distance, 618
embarassingly parallel, 574–576, 620
Euclidean, 36–37, 608, 719
Euclid's, 36–37, 608, 719
features of, 6–17
FindCellBefore, 75
FindLargest, 8–9, 14
five-coloring, 459–462
Fleury's, 486–487, 720
Floyd-Warshall, 98–100, 431, 437, 735
Ford-Fulkerson, 466, 720
four-coloring, 459, 720
Gaussian elimination, 61–62
Girvan-Newman, 483–485, 721
graphical
  about, 238
  gaskets, 246–247, 720
  Hilbert curve, 241–242, 722
  Koch curve, 239–241, 723

Sierpiński curve, 243–246, 732
skyline problem, 247–252, 732
Heapsort, 175–181, 721
Hierholzer's, 487–488, 722
InsertCell, 88
insertionsort
  about, 18, 197, 610
  in arrays, 168–169
  sorting with, 87–88
interpolation search, 611
Kosaraju's, 421–422, 723
Kosaraju-Sharir, 421–422, 732
label-correcting shortest path, 617
label-setting, 617
LeadsToSolution, 253
linked-list
  about, 86
  copying lists, 86–87
  sorting with insertionsort, 87–88
  sorting with selectionsort, 88–89
list retracing, 94–95
list reversal, 95–97
map coloring
  about, 456, 462–463
  five-coloring, 459–462
  four-coloring, 459, 720
  three-coloring, 458–459
  two-coloring, 456–458
MergeRootsWithSameOrder, 160–161
mergesort, 189–191, 197, 576–577, 620,
  725
Metaphone, 513–514, 725
network
  about, 451, 616–617, 616–618
  cliques, 473–482
  community detection, 473, 483–485,
    721, 724
  cycle detection, 455, 716
  Eulerian cycles, 314–316, 485–488, 719
  Eulerian paths, 314–316, 485–488, 719
  exercises, 489–492
  map coloring, 456–463, 720
  maximal flow, 464–470, 617, 724
  minimal flow cut, 417–418, 468–470,
    725
  network cloning, 470–473
  topological sorting, 451–455, 617, 734
  work assignment, 467–468

numerical
  about, 23, 608–609
  exercises, 68–70
  finding greatest common divisor
    (GCD), 36–40
  finding zeros, 55–57
  Gaussian elimination, 57–62, 609, 721
  least square fits, 62–67, 723
  performing exponentiation, 40–41
  performing numerical integration,
    47–55
  prime numbers, 42–47
  randomizing data, 23–36
O(N log N)
  about, 174
  Heapsort, 175–181, 721
  mergesort, 189–191, 197, 576–577, 620
    725
O(N²)
  about, 168
  Bubblesort, 171–174, 197, 714
  Inserrtionsort in arrays, 18, 87–88,
    168–169, 197, 610
  Selectionsort in arrays, 88–89,
    170–171, 197, 610
parallel, debugging, 620
phase king, 584–585, 728
phonetic, 511–514, 618, 728
PigeonholeSort, 193–195, 197, 728
probabilistic, 47, 608, 729
quicksort, 11, 19, 181–188, 197
recursive, 612
RSA, 534–537, 731
selectionsort
  about, 197, 610
  in arrays, 170–171
  sorting with, 88–89
Shor's, 572
shortest path
  about, 441
  best-first search, 442–443
  bidirectional search, 442
  early stopping, 442
  prohibitions, 443–446
  shape points, 441–442
  turn penalties, 443–446
Soundex, 511–513, 732
specialized tree

about, 322
  animal game, 322–324
  building trees, 328–329
  expression evaluation, 324–326
  intersecting with intervals, 330–332
  intersecting with points, 329–330
  interval trees, 326–328
  quadtrees, 332–337
  tries, 337–342
stable sorting, 191
stack
  about, 141
  reversing an array, 141
  stack insertionsort, 145–146
  stack selectionsort, 146–147
  tower of Hanoi, 143–145, 235–238, 735
  train sorting, 142–143
stack insertionsort, 145–146
stack selectionsort, 146–147
string
  about, 493, 618
  calculating edit distance, 508–511
  exercises, 515–517
  matching parentheses, 494–496
  pattern matching, 497–504
  phonetic, 511–514, 618, 728
  string searching, 504–508
Sub O(N log N)
  about, 192
  Bucketsort, 195–197
  countingsort, 192–193, 197, 716
  PigeonholeSort, 193–195, 197, 728
swarm intelligence, 616
three-coloring, 458–459
tortoise-and-hare, 98–100, 431, 437, 735
train sorting, 142–143
two-coloring, 456–458
alignment rule, 395
all-pairs shortest paths algorithm,
  431–436, 617
amortized analysis, 163, 711
amortized operations, 615
analyzing Quicksort algorithm run
  time, 182–184
ancestors, 286, 288, 712
angle brackets, 4
animal game, 322–324
ant colony optimization, 393–394

Appel, Kenneth (mathematician), 459
append method (Python), 113, 136
approximate optimization, 619
approximate routing, 245–246
arithmetic expressions, evaluating,
    494–496
Array class
    C#, 114
    .NET Framework, 201
array packing, 610
array queues, 148–151
array stacks, 138–139
ArrayEntry class, 121–122
ArrayRow class, 121–122
arrays
    about, 103, 610
    basic concepts, 103–106
    in C#, 104
    circular, 150, 715
    defined, 3, 712
    exercises, 132–134
    Insertionsort algorithm in, 168–169
    lower-triangular, 118, 724
    matrices, 129–131
    nonzero lower bounds, 114–118
    one-dimensional, 105, 106–113, 723
    in Python, 103
    randomizing, 29–30
    Selectionsort algorithm in, 170–171
    sparse, 121–129, 610, 732
    triangular, 118–121, 735
    two-dimensional, 105
    upper-triangular, 118, 736
Array.Sort method, 18–19
art gallery problem, 554
Assign method, 421, 422, 424, 425
associative arrays. *See* hash tables
asymptotic performance, 7–8, 712
attacker, in cryptography, 520, 712
augmenting path, 712
Augustus, 526
average, finding, 107–108
AVL trees
    about, 350
    adding values, 350–352
    defined, 615, 712
    deleting values, 353

B

back substitution, 60–61, 712
backtracking, 35, 613, 712
backtracking algorithms
    about, 252–253
    eight queens problem, 254–257, 718
    knight's tour problem, 257–260, 723
balanced trees
    about, 349, 615
    AVL trees, 350–353, 615, 712
    B-trees, 359–362, 615, 712
    B+trees, 363–364, 712
    defined, 609, 712
    exercises, 365–366
    top-down B-trees, 363, 615, 734
    2-3 trees, 354–358, 615, 711
    variations of, 362–364
base case, 228, 291, 712
basic array operation, 610
basic linked-list operations, 609
basic network algorithms
    about, 403
    exercises, 447–450
    finding paths, 425–436
    network representations, 407–409
    network terminology, 403–406
    shortest path modifications, 441–446
    strongly connected components,
        420–425
    transitivity, 436–441
    traversals, 409–420
bees algorithm, 394, 712
Beginning XML, 5th Edition (Fawcett),
    295
behavior, of algorithms, 607
Bellaso, Giovan Battista (cryptologist),
    527
Berkeley Open Infrastructure for
    Network Computing (BOINC), 566
best-first search, 442–443
Bézout, Étienne (mathematician), 38
Bézout's identity, 38–40, 712
BGP (byzantine generals problem),
    581–584, 620, 714
biased, 712
biased PRNG, 26–29, 608
bidirectional search, 442

Big O notation, 7–11, 544, 607, 713
Big Omega notation, 544, 713
Big Theta notation, 544, 713
BigInteger data type, 41, 276
bin packing problem, 554
binary search, 203–204, 713
binary search algorithm, 203–204, 611
binary tree
  about, 12, 288
  defined, 175, 286, 713
  properties of, 289–291
  storing complete, 175–176
BinaryNode class, 299, 300, 304
Binary-Search method, 201
binomial coefficient, 474, 713
binomial heaps
  about, 152–163
  defined, 713
  merging, 156–161
binomial theorem, 713
binomial trees
  about, 152–154
  defined, 713
  merging, 155–156
bin-packing problem, 388
bipartite detection, 713
bipartite graph, 550
bipartite matching, 713
bipartite matching problem, 550
bipartite network, 467, 713
block ciphers
  about, 531
  defined, 619, 713
  Feistel cipher, 533–534, 719
  substitution-permutation network
    cipher, 531–533
Blowfish, 520
Boids, 395–397
BOINC (Berkeley Open Infrastructure
  for Network Computing), 566
bottleneck traveling salesman problem,
  554
bottom-up B-tree, 363, 713
bottom-up programming, 277, 613
Boyer-Moore algorithm, 493, 504–508,
  618, 713

branch and bound technique, 379–381,
  714
branch-and-bound algorithm, 616
branches, 285, 288, 403, 406, 481–482, 614,
  714, 724
breadth-first search, 714
breadth-first traversals
  about, 301–302
  defined, 714
  for networks, 412–413
bridge link, 486, 714
Bron, Coenraad (computer scientist), 475
Bron-Kerbosch algorithm, 475–480, 714
brute-force approach, 474–475, 481, 486,
  714. See also exhaustive search
brute-force searches, 575
B-trees
  about, 359–360
  adding values, 360–361
  defined, 615, 712
  deleting values, 361–362
B+trees, 363–364, 712
Bubblesort algorithm, 171–174, 197, 714
buckets, 211–213, 359, 714
Bucketsort algorithm, 195–197
building
  complete self-avoiding walks, 34–36
  complete trees, 295–296
  DFAs for regular expressions, 500–502
  mazes, 419–420
  parse trees, 496
  random walks, 31–36
  self-avoiding walks, 33–34
  specialized trees, 328–329
  threaded trees, 318–320
  trees in general, 292–-295
"Building a 270* Teraflops Deep
  Learning Box for Under $10,000," 566
bully algorithm, 587–588, 714
bye, 267–273
byzantine generals problem (BGP),
  581–584, 620, 714

C

C#
  about, 41
  Array class, 114

arrays in, 104
automatic memory management and,
    79
Dictionary class, 209–210
dictionary in, 111
generating selections in, 474
HashTable class, 209–210
IndexOf method, 493
IntegerCell class, 71–72
sorting tools in, 168
Stack class, 136
string class, 493
C programming language, 79
C++ programming language, 79, 129
Caesar, Julius, 526
Caesar substitution cipher, 526–527, 714
calculating
    edit distance, 508–511
    greatest common divisor (GCD), 36–38
call stack, 714
call tree, 190
capacitated network, 464, 714
capacity, 404, 714
CareerCup (website), 604
Carmichael numbers, 630–631
Case statement, 5
cells
    adding at the beginning of linked lists,
        75–76
    adding at the end of linked lists, 76–77
    defined, 71, 609, 715
    deleting from linked lists, 78–79
    finding in linked lists, 73–74
    inserting after other cells in linked
        lists, 77–78
    marking, 92–93
    systolic arrays and, 562
chaining, 211–213, 612
Chandy/Misra, 579–580
checking local links, 481–482
child lists, 614
child node, 286, 288, 715
Chinese postman problem (CPP), 554,
    715
chromatic number, 715
chromatic number problem, 555
cipher, 715. See also specific ciphers
ciphertext, 520, 715

circular array, 150, 715
circular linked lists
    about, 91–92
    defined, 715
    hash tables, 93–94
    list retracing algorithm, 94–95
    list reversal algorithm, 95–97
    marking cells, 92–93
    tortoise-and-hare algorithm, 98–100
classes
    Array
        C#, 114
        .NET Framework, 201
    ArrayEntry, 121–122
    ArrayRow, 121–122
    BinaryNode, 299, 300, 304
    complexity, 545–547, 619
    Dictionary (C#), 209–210
    ExpressionNode, 325–326
    HashTable (C#), 209–210
    IntegerCell (C#), 71–72
    Interval, 328–329
    IntervalNode, 329
    Link, 407, 616
    MatchUp, 272
    Node, 407, 426, 430
    Stack (C#), 136
    string (C#), 493
    TreeNode, 293–294, 310, 311, 312
clique cover problem, 555
clique percolation method (CPM), 485
clique problem, 555
cliques
    about, 473–474
    Bron-Kerbosch algorithm, 475–480, 714
    brute-force approach, 474–475
    defined, 715
    finding triangles, 480–482
clock synchronization, 589–590, 620
clone references, 472–473
closed tour, 723
cluster, 565
cluster computing, 715
clustering, 612
cocktail shaker sort, 173, 197, 715
cohesion rule, 395
collision, 211, 715
collision-resolution policy, 211, 715

colorability, 617

column transposition cipher, 523–525

column-major order, 105

column-ordered sparse matrices, 131

columns, finding, 122–123

combinations. *See* selections

common run time functions, 11–16

community, 483–485

community detection, 715

community detection algorithms

about, 483

clique percolation method (CPM), 485

Girvan-Newman, 483–485, 721

maximal cliques, 473, 483, 724

complete self-avoiding walks, 34–36

complete trees

about, 12, 175–176

building, 295–296

defined, 287, 288, 715

CompleteSelfAvoidingWalk method, 35–36

complexity classes, 545–547, 619

complexity theory. *See* computational complexity theory

composite number, 42, 715

computational complexity theory

about, 543–544, 619

complexity classes, 545–547, 619

defined, 715

detection problem, 551–554, 619, 717

exercises, 558–559

notation, 544–545

NP-complete problems, 554–556

NP-hard, 550–551, 726

optimization problem, 376–377, 551–554, 619, 727

reductions, 548–550, 619

reporting problem, 551–554, 619, 730

condensation, 440, 715

connected, 405, 716

connected component, 404, 405, 716

connectivity, 616

connectivity matrix, 119, 716

connectivity testing, 413–415

consensus problem, 584–587, 620, 716

ContainsDuplicates algorithm, 10, 15

ContainsNodes algorithm, 313–314

contention, 575–576, 620

Cook-Levin theorem, 548

Cook's theorem, 548

CoolInterview puzzles (website), 604

coprime, 730

copying lists, 86–87

costs, 404, 405, 716

count method, 84

counting

combinations, 254–255

defined, 611

permutations with duplicates, 265

permutations without duplicates, 266–267

countingsort algorithm, 192–193, 197, 716

covering network, 445–446, 716

CPM (clique percolation method), 485

cryptanalysis, 520, 716

cryptographic hash function, 538, 716

cryptographical algorithms, 619

cryptographically secure pseudorandom number generator (CSPRNG), 26, 716

cryptography

about, 519–520, 618–619

block ciphers, 531–534, 619, 713, 719

defined, 716

exercises, 540–541

public-key encryption, 534–537, 619, 729

RSA algorithm, 534–537, 731

substitution ciphers, 526–531, 733

terminology for, 520–521

transposition ciphers, 521–526, 618, 735

uses for, 538–539

CSPRNG (cryptographically secure pseudorandom number generator), 26, 716

cutting stock problem, 389–390, 716

cycle, 404, 406, 716

cycle detection, 455, 716

D

dance floor, 394

data, randomizing, 23–36

Data Encryption Standard (DES), 534, 716

data parallelism, 562, 716

data processing units (DPUs), 562, 717
data structures
  algorithms and, 2–3
  defined, 607, 717
data structures technique, 599
deadlock, 571–572, 717
debugging
  distributed algorithms, 573–574
  parallel algorithms, 620
decipher, 520, 717
decision trees
  about, 367–368, 615–616
  defined, 717
  exercises, 398–401
  searching game trees, 368–375
  searching general, 375–392
  swarm intelligence (SI), 392–397
decision trees technique, 599
decrypt, 520, 717
defining heaps, 176–180
degree
  defined, 717
  of nodes, 286, 288, 404, 406
  of polynomials, 65
degree-constrained spanning tree
  problem, 555
DeleteEntry method, 126, 129
deleting
  nodes, 306–309, 614
  values, 127–129
dendogram, 717
depth, of nodes, 287, 288, 311–312, 717
depth-first traversals
  defined, 717
  for networks, 410–412
  for trees, 297
deque, 152, 162–163, 610, 717
Dequeue method, 147–148
DES (Data Encryption Standard), 534,
  716
descendants, 286, 289, 717
detection problem, 551–554, 619, 717
deterministic computer, 545
deterministic finite automaton (DFA),
  497–499, 500–502, 717
deterministic finite state machine. *See*
  deterministic finite automaton (DFA)
dictionary. *See* hash tables

Dictionary class (C#), 209–210
difficulty, 621
digital signature, 538, 717
dining philosophers problem, 577–580,
  620, 717
direct recursion, 718
directed, 718
directed branches, 286
directed link, 404, 406
disk bound, 576, 718
distributed algorithms
  about, 561–562, 573, 620
  byzantine generals problem (BGP),
    581–584, 620, 714
  clock synchronization, 589–590, 620
  consensus problem, 584–587, 620, 716
  debugging, 573–574
  dining philosophers problem, 577–580,
    620, 717
  embarassingly parallel algorithm,
    574–576, 620
  exercises, 591–593
  leader election, 587–588, 620
  mergesort algorithm, 189–191, 197,
    576–577, 620, 725
  snapshot, 588–589, 620, 732
  two generals problem, 580–581, 620,
    736
  types of parallelism, 562–572
distributed computing, 565–567, 718
divide-and-conquer approach, 249–252,
  599, 611, 613
dominating set, 718
dominating set problem, 555
DoSomething method, 5
double hashing, 219
double linked lists, 79–81
Double Metaphone algorithm, 514, 718
double stacks, 139–141, 610
DoubleIt method, 5
doubly linked lists
  defined, 718
  loops in, 100
DPUs (data processing units), 562, 717
DrawRelative method, 242, 244–245
DSPACE(f(n)), 718
DTIME(f(n)), 619, 718
duplicates

permutations with, 265
permutations without, 266–267
selections with, 262–263
selections without, 264
dynamic programming, 275–276, 613, 718

E

early stopping, 442
edge betweenness, 483, 718
edge graph, 445–446, 716
edge network, 445–446, 716
edges, 285, 288, 403, 406, 481–482, 614, 714, 724
edge/vertex dual, 445–446, 716
edit distance
  calculating, 508–511
  defined, 718
edit distance algorithm, 618
edit graph, 509–511
eight queens problem, 254–257, 718
Einstein@Home, 566
Elements (Euclid), 36
embarassingly parallel, 718
embarassingly parallel algorithms, 574–576, 620
EMST (Euclidean minimum spanning tree), 418–419
encipher, 520, 719
encrypt, 520, 719
End While statement, 4
enqueue, 161–162
Enqueue method, 147–148
entanglement, 719
Euclid
  Elements, 36
Euclidean algorithm, 36–37, 608, 719
Euclidean minimum spanning tree (EMST), 418–419
Euclidean spanning tree, 617
Euclid's algorithm, 36–37, 608, 719
Euler, Leonhard (mathematician), 485
Euler tours, 314–316, 485–488, 719
Eulerian cycles, 314–316, 485–488, 719
Eulerian network, 485, 719
Eulerian paths, 314–316, 485–488, 719
Euler's totient function, 535–536, 719
Evaluate method, 496

evaluating arithmetic expressions, 494–496
exact cover, 719
exact cover problem, 555
exercises
  algorithm basics, 20–22
  arrays, 132–134
  balanced trees, 365–366
  basic network algorithms, 447–450
  complexity theory, 558–559
  cryptography, 540–541
  decision trees, 398–401
  distributed algorithms, 591–593
  hash tables, 222–225
  interview puzzles, 604–605
  linked lists, 101–102
  network algorithms, 489–492
  numerical algorithms, 68–70
  recursion, 281–284
  searching, 208
  sorting, 198–200
  string algorithms, 515–517
  trees, 342–348
exhaustive search, 106–107, 202–203, 377–379, 611, 719
ExhaustiveSearch method, 378
expanded node networks, 444–445
exponential functions, 15–16
exponentiation, performing, 40–41
expression evaluation, 324–326
ExpressionNode class, 325–326
expressions, 614
EXPTIME, 619, 719
EXPSPACE, 719
extending greatest common divisor (GCD), 38–40
ExtendWalk method, 35–36
Extensible Markup Language (XML), 295
external node, 286, 289, 719
external sorting, 191, 611, 719

F

Facebook interview puzzles group (website), 603
factorial function, 16, 228–230, 232, 719
fair, 719

fair PRNG, 26–29, 608

fairness, ensuring, 26–28

Fawcett, Joe (author)

  Beginning XML, 5th Edition, 295

feedback vertex set problem, 555

Feistel, Horst (cryptographer), 533

Feistel cipher, 533–534, 719

Fermat liar, 46, 720

Fermat primality test, 46

Fermat witness, 46, 609, 720

Fermat's little theorem, 608–609

Fibonacci function, 231–232, 276

Fibonacci numbers, 230–232, 720

FIFO (first-in-first-out). *See* queues

FIFO list, 720

file processing, 575

fill percentage, 211, 720

find method (Python), 493

FindCellBefore algorithm, 75

FindColumnBefore method, 123–125,
  127, 128

finding

  average, 107–108

  cells in linked lists, 73–74

  columns, 122–123

  greatest common divisor (GCD), 36–40

  items, 106–107, 336–337, 341–342

  maximum, 107–108

  median, 108–109

  minimum, 107–108

  mode, 109–112

  nodes, 306

  paths, 425–436

  prime factors, 42–44

  prime numbers, 44–45

  rows, 122–123

  triangles, 480–482

  zeros, 55–57

FindLargest algorithm, 8–9, 14

FindNode method, 306

FindRowBefore method, 124–125,
  126–127, 128

first common ancestor. *See* lowest
  common ancestor (LCA)

first-in-first-out (FIFO). *See* queues

five-coloring algorithm, 459–462

Fleury's algorithm, 486–487, 720

flops, 566, 720

Floyd, Robert (mathematician), 98

Floyd-Warshall algorithm, 98–100, 431,
  437, 735

For loop, 4, 56–57, 113, 261

Ford-Fulkerson algorithm, 466, 720

forest, 152, 720

forward elimination, 58–60, 720

four-coloring algorithm, 459, 720

fractals, 575

free function (C++), 129

full node, 290

full tree, 287, 289, 720

functions

  cryptographic hash, 538, 716

  defined, 4

  Euler's totient, 535–536, 719

  exponential, 15–16

  factorial, 16, 228–230, 232, 719

  Fibonacci, 231–232, 276

  free (C++), 129

  MoveMemory, 18

  N, 14

  N!, 16

  N log N, 15, 543–544

  N^2, 15

  phi, 535–536, 719

  pow (Python), 41

  RtlMoveMemory, 18

  runtime, 11–16, 608

  Sqrt N, 14

  totient, 535–536, 719

  2^N, 15–16

  visualizing, 16–17

G

game trees, 615–616

gaskets, 246–247, 720

Gauss, Johann Carl Friedrich
  (mathematician and physicist), 58

Gaussian elimination, 57–62, 609, 721

Gaussian elimination algorithm, 61–62

GCD. *See* greatest common divisor
  (GCD)

general and lieutenants problem, 582,
  721

general networks, 440–441

general recursion removal, 277–280, 613

general trees, 312–314

generalized partition problem, 387–388,
  721

generating
  nonuniform distributions, 30–31
  random values, 23–29
  values, 24–26
generator, 239, 721
geometric calculations, 443–444
get method, 115
GIMPS (Great Internet Mersenne Prime
    Search), 566
Girvan, Michelle (physicist), 483
Girvan-Newman algorithm, 483–485,
    721
GPUs (graphics processing units),
    562
graph, 406, 721
graph isomorphism problem, 555, 721
graphical algorithms
  about, 238
  gaskets, 246–247, 720
  Hilbert curve, 241–242, 722
  Koch curve, 239–241, 723
  Sierpiński curve, 243–246, 732
  skyline problem, 247–252, 732
graphics processing units (GPUs), 562
Great Internet Mersenne Prime Search
    (GIMPS), 566
greatest common divisor (GCD)
  calculating, 36–38
  defined, 721
  extending, 38–40
  finding, 36–40
grid computing, 565, 721
grids, joining, 566
Guthrie, Francis (mathematician), 459

H
Haidong Wang's interview puzzles
    (website), 603
Haken, Wolfgang (mathematician), 459
HAM (Hamiltonian path) problem, 440,
    555, 721
HAMC (Hamiltonian circuit) problem,
    555, 721
Hamiltonian, 721
Hamiltonian circuit (HAMC) problem,
    555, 721
Hamiltonian completion problem, 555,
    721
Hamiltonian cycle problem, 440, 555

Hamiltonian path (HAM) problem, 440,
    555, 721
hardware random number generator
    (HRNG), 24
hash tables
  about, 93–94, 111, 209–210, 471–472,
    612
  chaining, 211–213
  defined, 612, 717, 721
  exercises, 222–225
  fundamentals of, 210–211
  open addressing, 213–222
  resizing, 211
hashing
  defined, 210, 721
  double, 219
  ordered, 219–222
HashTable class (C#), 209–210
heaps
  about, 230
  defined, 611, 721
  defining, 176–180
Heapsort algorithm, 175–181, 721
height
  of nodes, 287, 289, 722
  of trees, 153, 287, 289, 305
heuristics
  about, 82
  decision tree, 381–387
  defined, 616, 722
  game tree, 374–375
Hierholzer's algorithm, 487–488, 722
higher dimensions, 115–118
Hilbert, David (mathematician), 241
Hilbert curve, 241–242, 722
hill climbing, 616, 722
hill-climbing heuristic, 385–386
How to Ace a Google Interview
    (website), 603
HRNG (hardware random number
    generator), 24
hybrid methods, 84–85

I
IBM Q System One, 572
If-Then-Else statement, 5
implementing
  Heapsort algorithm, 180–181
  Quicksort algorithm in place, 185–188

`Quicksort` algorithm with stacks, 185
round-robin scheduling, 271–273
improving paths, 382–384
in-degree, 404, 406, 722
independent set, 722
`IndexOf` method (C#), 493
indirect recursion, 722
inductive reasoning, 291, 614
initial state, 497, 722
initiator, 239, 722
inorder traversal, 299–300, 722
`insert` method (Python), 113
`InsertCell` algorithm, 88
inserting items, 112–113
`insertionsort` algorithm
about, 18, 197, 610
in arrays, 168–169
sorting with, 87–88
`IntegerCell` class (C#), 71–72
interchange networks, 445–445, 716
internal node, 286, 289, 722
interpolation search, 204–205, 722
interpolation search algorithm, 611
intersecting
with intervals, 330–332
with points, 329–330
`Interval` class, 328–329
interval trees, 326–328, 722
`IntervalNode` class, 329
intervals, intersecting with, 330–332
interview puzzles
about, 595–596, 621
answering questions, 598–602
asking questions, 597–598
exercises, 604–605
websites, 603–604
Interview Puzzles Dissected: Solving and Understanding Interview Puzzles (Stephens), 604
interview websites, 603–604
isomorphic, 722
iterating, over singly linked lists, 73
`itertools.combinations` method (Python), 474

J
job shop scheduling, 723
job shop scheduling problem, 555
joining grids, 566

K
k-clique, 473, 723
Kerbosch, Joep (computer scientist), 475
key, 723
knapsack problem, 16, 390, 555, 723
knight's tour problem, 257–260, 723
knowledge trees, 614
Koch, Helge von (mathematician), 239
Koch curve, 239–241, 723
Koch snowflake, 241
Kosaraju, Sambasiva Rao (professor), 421
Kosaraju's algorithm, 421–422, 723
Kosaraju-Sharir algorithm, 421–422, 732

L
label-correcting shortest path algorithm, 617
label-correcting shortest paths, 430–431
label-setting algorithm, 617
label-setting shortest paths, 426–429
Landis, E. M. (researcher), 350
last-in-first-out (LIFO). *See* stack
LCM (least common multiple), 69
leader election, 587–588, 620
LeadsToSolution algorithm, 253
leaf node, 286, 289, 290, 723
least common ancestor. *See* lowest common ancestor (LCA)
least common multiple (LCM), 69
least squares fit, 62–67, 723
leaves, 614
left-left case, 350–351
level, of nodes, 287, 289, 723
level-order traversal. *See* breadth-first traversal
LIFO (last-in-first-out). *See* stacks
LIFO lists. *See* stacks
line network, 445–446, 716
linear arrays. *See* one-dimensional arrays
linear congruential generator, 24, 723
linear least squares fit, 62–64
linear probing, 215–217, 724
linear search, 106–107, 202–203, 611, 724
`Link` class, 407, 616
linked lists

about, 71, 609
basic concepts, 71–72
defined, 724
doubly linked list, 79–81
exercises, 101–102
linked lists with loops, 91–100
linked-list algorithms, 86–89
multithreaded linked list, 90
self-organizing linked list, 82–86
singly linked list, 72–79
sorted linked list, 81–82
linked-list algorithms
about, 86
copying lists, 86–87
sorting with insertionsort
    algorithm, 87–88
sorting with selectionsort
    algorithm, 88–89
linked-list queues, 148
linked-list stacks, 136–138
links. *See* branches
list retracing, 724
list retracing algorithm, 94–95
list reversal, 724
list reversal algorithm, 95–97
lists, 86–87, 248–249
livelock, 724
logarithmic growth, 614
logarithms, 12
longest path problem, 556, 724
loops
defined, 404, 406, 724
linked lists with.*See* circular linked
    lists
selections with, 261–262
lower-triangular array, 118, 724
lowest common ancestor (LCA). *See* first
    common ancestor
about, 289, 309
defined, 287, 720
Euler tours, 314–316
general trees, 312–314
pairs, 316
parent pointers, 310–311
parents and depths, 311–312
sorted trees, 309–310
Lucas, Edouard (Mathematician),
    144

M
majority voting problem, 205–207, 724
MakeSkyline method, 250–251
map coloring, 724
map coloring algorithms
about, 456, 462–463
five-coloring, 459–462
four-coloring, 459, 720
three-coloring, 458–459
two-coloring, 456–458
Map2DArray method, 106
mapping, 612
marking cells, 92–93
matching, 724
matching parentheses, 494–496
MatchUp class, 272
Math Is Fun (website), 129
Math Olympiads (website), 604
matrices, 129–131
"Matrix" (website), 129
maximal cliques, 473, 483, 724
maximal flow, 617
maximal flow problem, 464–466, 724
maximum, finding, 107–108
maximum independent set, 724. *See also*
    independent set
maximum independent set problem,
    556
maximum leaf spanning tree, 724
maximum leaf spanning tree problem,
    556
mazes, building, 419–420
median, finding, 108–109
memory requirements, for algorithms,
    607
MergeRootsWithSameOrder algorithm,
    160–161
MergeSkylines method, 251
mergesort algorithm, 189–191, 197,
    576–577, 620, 725
mergesort method, 19
MergeTrees method, 159–160
merging
binomial heaps, 156–161
binomial trees, 155–156
Metaphone algorithm, 513–514, 725
method of gradient ascent, 385–386
method of gradient descent, 385–386

methods
  AddInterval, 329
  AddItemToChild, 335–336
  AddNote, 320
  append (Python), 113, 136
  Array.Sort, 18–19
  Assign, 421, 422, 424, 425
  Binary-Search, 201
  CompleteSelfAvoidingWalk, 35–36
  count, 84
  defined, 4
  DeleteEntry, 126, 129
  Dequeue, 147–148
  DoSomething, 5
  DoubleIt, 5
  DrawRelative, 242, 244–245
  Enqueue, 147–148
  Evaluate, 496
  ExhaustiveSearch, 378
  ExtendWalk, 35–36
  find (Python), 493
  FindColumnBefore, 123–125, 127, 128
  FindNode, 306
  FindRowBefore, 124–125, 126–127, 128
  get, 115
  hybrid, 84–85
  IndexOf (C#), 493
  insert (Python), 113
  itertools.combinations (Python), 474
  MakeSkyline, 250–251
  Map2DArray, 106
  MergeSkylines, 251
  mergesort, 19
  MergeTrees, 159–160
  ModPow (C#), 41
  Newton-Raphson, 55, 609, 726
  Newton's, 55, 609, 726
  passing, 299
  polygon, 728
  pop, 136–137, 728
  push, 136–137, 729
  Rearrange, 85–86
  ReverseList, 97
  ScheduleRoundRobinOdd, 273
  set, 115
  shuffle, 29
  SierpDown, 244–245
  SierpLeft, 244–245
  SierpRight, 244–245
  SierpUp, 244–245
  StartExhaustiveSearch, 378
  swap, 83–84, 733, 735
  transpose, 83–84, 733, 735
  TraverseInorder, 300
  TraversePostorder, 301
  TraversePreorder, 299
  Visit, 422
mi flow cut, 468–470
Microsoft's .NET Framework, 18–19
min flow cut, 725
min-cut, 468–470
minimal flow cut problem, 468–470
minimal spanning trees, 417–418, 725
minimax, 369–372, 725
minimum, finding, 107–108
minimum cut, 468–470
minimum degree spanning tree, 725
minimum degree spanning tree problem, 556
minimum equivalent digraph, 438
minimum heap property, 154, 725
minimum k-cut, 725
minimum k-cut problem, 556
minimum reductions, 438, 725
Mod operator, 4
mode, finding, 109–112
modeling accuracy, 609
ModPow method (C#), 41
Monte Carlo integration, 54–55, 725
Monte Carlo simulation, 609, 725
Moore, Gordon E. (founder of Intel Corporation), 561, 721
Moore's law, 561, 725
move to front method (MTF), 83, 725
MoveMemory function, 18
multi-CPU processing, 567
multiple recursion, 725
multiplicative inverses, 536, 725
multithreaded linked lists, 90
mutex, 569, 620, 725

N
N function, 14
N! function, 16
N log N function, 15, 543–544

N^2 function, 15
natural number, 725
neighbors, 403, 406, 725
.NET Framework (Microsoft), 18–19, 201
network algorithms
  about, 451, 616–617, 616–618
  cliques, 473–482
  community detection, 473, 483–485,
    721, 724
  cycle detection, 455, 716
  Eulerian cycles, 314–316, 485–488, 719
  Eulerian paths, 314–316, 485–488, 719
  exercises, 489–492
  map coloring, 456–463, 720
  maximal flow, 464–470, 617, 724
  minimal flow cut, 417–418, 468–470,
    725
  network cloning, 470–473
  topological sorting, 451–455, 617, 734
  work assignment, 467–468
network cloning, 470–473
network coloring, 556, 726
network coloring problem, 555
network representations, 407–409
networks
  acyclic, 439–440
  bipartite, 467
  capacitated, 464, 714
  covering, 445–446, 716
  Eulerian, 485, 719
  expanded node, 444–445
  general, 440–441
  interchange, 445–446, 716
  line, 445–446, 716
  residual capacity, 730
  transpose, 421, 735
Newman, Mark (physicist), 483
Newton-Cotes formula, 47, 726
Newton-Raphson method, 55, 609, 726
Newton's method, 55, 609, 726
NEXPSPACE, 726
NEXPTIME, 619, 726
Next i statement, 4
NFA (nondeterministic finite
  automaton), 502–504
Node class, 407, 426, 430
node merge, 357, 726
node split, 355, 726

nodes
  about, 406
  adding, 303–305
  child, 286, 288, 715
  defined, 285, 289, 403, 406, 726
  deleting, 306–309, 614
  external, 286, 289, 719
  finding, 306
  full, 290
  level of, 287, 289, 723
  parent, 286, 289, 311–312, 727
  reachable, 404, 406
  root, 286, 289, 731
  sibling, 732
nondeterministic computer, 546
nondeterministic finite automaton
  (NFA), 502–504
nonindexed database searches, 575
non-self-intersecting walk, 33–34,
  608
nonuniform distributions, 30–31
nonzero lower bounds
  about, 114
  higher dimensions, 115–118
  two dimensions, 114–115
Norishige Chiba (computer scientist),
  481
notation, complexity theory, 544–545
NP, 619, 726
NP-complete, 548, 619, 726
NP-complete problems, 554–556
NP-hard, 550–551, 726
NPSPACE, 726
NTIME(f(n)), 619, 726
null transition, 503, 726
numeric integration, 47–55, 726
numeric quadrature, 47–55, 726
numerical algorithms
  about, 23, 608–609
  exercises, 68–70
  finding greatest common divisor
    (GCD), 36–40
  finding zeros, 55–57
  Gaussian elimination, 57–62, 609, 721
  least square fits, 62–67, 723
  performing exponentiation, 40–41
  performing numerical integration,
    47–55

prime numbers, 42–47
randomizing data, 23–36
NumPy library (Python), 114

O

object references, 614
observer, 589, 727
occtrees, 337, 727
odd-cycle problem, 558, 727
Odell, Margaret King (developer of
 Soundex), 511
O(N log N) algorithms
 about, 174
 Heapsort, 175–181, 721
 mergesort, 189–191, 197, 576–577, 620
 725
O(N²) algorithms
 about, 168
 Bubblesort, 171–174, 197, 714
 Inserrtionsort in arrays, 18, 87–88,
  168–169, 197, 610
 Selectionsort in arrays, 88–89,
  170–171, 197, 610
one-dimensional arrays
 about, 105, 106
 defined, 723
 finding items, 106–107
 finding median, 108–109
 finding minimum, maximum, and
  average, 107–108
 finding mode, 109–112
 inserting items, 112–113
 removing items, 113
one-time pad cipher, 530–531, 619, 727
open addressing
 about, 213–214
 defined, 612, 727
 double hashing, 219
 linear probing, 215–217, 724
 ordered hashing, 219–222, 612
 pseudorandom probing, 219, 729
 quadratic probing, 217–218, 729
 removing items, 214–215
optimization problem, 376–377, 551–554,
 619, 727
order, 727
ordered hashing, 219–222, 612
ordered tree, 287, 289, 727
out-degree, 404, 406, 727

P

P, 619, 727
pairs, 316
parallel algorithms, debugging, 620
parallelism
 about, 562
 deadlock, 571–572, 717
 distributed computing, 565–567, 718
 multi-CPU processing, 567
 quantum computing, 572, 730
 race conditions, 567–571, 730
 systolic arrays, 562–565, 734
 types of, 620
parent node
 about, 286, 289
 defined, 727
 depth and, 311–312
parent pointers, 310–311
parenthesis matching, 618
parse trees, building, 496
partial ordering, 453, 727
partition problem, 367, 556, 727
partitioning, 611
passing methods, 299
paths
 about, 404
 all-pairs shortest, 431–436
 augmenting, 712
 defined, 406, 727
 Eulerian, 314–316, 485–488, 719
 finding, 425–436
 improving, 382–384
 label-correcting shortest, 430–431
 label-setting shortest, 426–429
pattern matching
 about, 497
 building DFAs for regular expressions,
  500–502
 deterministic finite automaton (DFA),
  497–499
 nondeterministic finite automaton
  (NFA), 502–504
P-boxes (permutation boxes), 531, 727
perfect tree, 287, 289, 727
performing
 exponentiation, 40–41
 numerical integration, 47–55
permutation boxes (P-boxes), 531,
 727

permutations
  about, 260
  counting, 265, 266–267
  defined, 613, 727
  with duplicates, 265
  without duplicates, 266–267
petaflop (pflop), 566, 728
PGP (Pretty Good Privacy), 537
phase king algorithm, 584–585, 728
phi function, 535–536, 719
Philips, Lawrence, 513
phonetic algorithms, 511–514, 618, 728
PigeonholeSort algorithm, 193–195,
  197, 728
plaintext, 520, 728
planar, 728
points, intersecting with, 329–330
Polish notation, 302, 728
polygon method, 268, 728
polynomial least squares, 728
polynomial least squares fit, 64–67
polynomial run time, 15, 728
polynomials, degree of, 65
pop method, 136–137, 728
popping objects, 136
postorder traversal, 300–301, 728
pow function (Python), 41
practical considerations, 18–19
precalculated values, 608
prefix trees, 337–342, 614, 735
preorder traversal, 297–299, 728
Pretty Good Privacy (PGP), 537
primality, testing for, 45–47
primary clustering, 216, 728
prime factors, finding, 42–44
prime numbers
  defined, 728
  finding, 44–45
  working with, 42–47
priority inversion, 571, 728
priority queues, 151–152, 178, 610, 728
private key, 534, 729
PRNG (pseudorandom number
  generator), 24, 25, 26–29, 608, 729
probabilistic algorithm, 47, 608, 729
probability technique, 599
probe sequence, 213, 729
problem structure technique, 599
procedures, 4

programming puzzles, 621
prohibitions, 443–446
pseudoclassical mechanics, 396–397
pseudocode
  about, 3–6
  Bron-Kerbosch algorithm, 476–477
  defined, 607, 729
  for self-organizing linked lists,
    85–86
pseudorandom number generator
  (PRNG), 24, 25, 26–29, 608, 729
pseudorandom probing, 219, 729
PSPACE, 729
public key, 534, 729
public key exponent, 535, 729
public key modulus, 535, 729
public-key encryption, 534–537, 619,
  729
push method, 136–137, 729
pushdown stack. *See* stack
pushing objects, 136
puzzle problems, 621
Python
  append method, 113, 136
  arrays in, 103
  automatic memory management and,
    79
  dictionary in, 111
  find method, 493
  insert method, 113
  integers on, 82
  itertools.combinations method,
    474
  NumPy library, 114
  pop method, 136, 728
  pow function, 41
  sorting tools in, 168

Q
quadratic probing, 217–218, 729
quadrature, 47–55, 726
quadtrees, 332–337, 730
quantum bit, 572
quantum computing, 572, 730
qubit, 572
queues
  about, 135, 147, 610, 720
  array, 148–151
  defined, 730

linked-list, 148
priority, 151–152
specialized, 151–152
`quicksort` algorithm, 11, 19, 181–188, 197

R
race conditions, 567–571, 730
random searches, 381–382, 575
random self-avoiding walk, 33–34, 608, 730
random solution search, 730
random values, generating, 23–29
random walks
creating, 31–36
defined, 608, 730
randomization technique, 599
randomizing
about, 578
arrays, 29–30
data, 23–36
defined, 608, 612
Random.org (website), 24
`random_trees` program, 25
`RandomTrees` program, 25
range minimum query (RMQ), 730
range minimum query problem, 316
ray tracing, 574
reachable, 730
reachable node, 404, 406
`Rearrange` method, 85–86
receiver, 730
rectangle rule, 48–49, 730
recursion
about, 227–228, 612–613
backtracking algorithms, 252–260
basic algorithms, 228–238
defined, 730
exercises, 281–284
`factorial` function, 228–230
Fibonacci numbers, 230–232
graphical algorithms, 238–252
removal, 273–280
rod-cutting problem, 232–235
selections and permutations, 260–273
Tower of Hanoi, 235–238
recursive algorithm, 612
recursive calls, 476

recursive metrics, 612
reduce, 730
reductions, 548–550, 619
regular expressions
about, 497
building DFAs for, 500–502
defined, 618, 730
relatively prime, 730
remaining node key, 339–340
removing items, 113, 214–215
reporting problem, 551–554, 619, 730
residual capacity, 465, 730
residual capacity network, 730
resizing hash tables, 211
resource hierarchy, 578–579, 731
`Return` statement, 4, 10
reverse Polish notation, 302, 731
`ReverseList` method, 97
Reversi game, 375
reversing an array algorithm, 141
Reynolds, Craig, 395
right rotation, 351
right-right case, 351
rod-cutting problem, 232–235, 731
root node, 286, 289, 731
root split, 355, 731
roots, 55, 731
Rosetta@home, 566
round-robin scheduling
about, 267–268
defined, 731
even number of teams, 270
implementation, 271–273
odd number of teams, 268–270
round-robin tournament, 267
route ciphers, 525–526
route inspection problem. *See* Chinese postman problem (CPP)
routines, 4
row/column transposition cipher, 521–523, 731
row-major order, 105
rows, finding, 122–123
RSA algorithm, 534–537, 731
`RtlMoveMemory` function, 18
runtime, 163, 303
runtime functions, 11–16, 608
Russell, Robert C., 511

S

satisfiability problem (SAT), 391–392, 548, 556, 731
S-boxes (substitution boxes), 531, 733
ScheduleRoundRobinOdd method, 273
scytale, 731
searching
    about, 201–202, 611
    best-first, 442–443
    bidirectional, 442
    binary, 203–204, 713
    breadth-first search, 714
    brute-force, 575
    exercises, 208
    exhaustive, 106–107, 202–203, 377–379, 611, 719
    game trees, 368–375
    general decision trees, 375–392
    interpolation, 204–205, 722
    linear, 106–107, 202–203, 611, 724
    majority voting, 205–207
    random, 381–382, 575
    random solution, 730
    string, 504–508
    traversals and, 296
secondary clustering, 218, 731
security through obscurity, 519, 731
seed, 24
seed clique, 485
Select Case statement, 278
selections
    about, 260
    counting, 254–255
    defined, 613, 731
    with duplicates, 262–263
    with loops, 261–262
    without duplicates, 264
selectionsort algorithm
    about, 197, 610
    in arrays, 170–171
    sorting with, 88–89
self-avoiding walks, creating, 33–34
self-organizing linked lists, 82–86, 731
self-organizing list, 609
self-similar fractal, 239, 613, 732
sender, in cryptography, 520, 732
sentinels, 74–75, 609, 732
separation rule, 395

set intersection operator, 477
set method, 115
Set P, 475–476
Set R, 475–476
Set X, 475–476
SETI@home, 566
setting values, 125–127
"Seven Bridges of Königsberg" problem, 485
shape points, 441–442
Shor's algorithm, 572
shortest path algorithms
    about, 441
    best-first search, 442–443
    bidirectional search, 442
    early stopping, 442
    prohibitions, 443–446
    shape points, 441–442
    turn penalties, 443–446
shortest path tree, 732
shuffle method, 29
SI (swarm intelligence)
    about, 392–393
    ant colony optimization, 393–394
    bees algorithm, 394, 712
    defined, 733–734
    swarm simulation, 394–397, 734
sibling nodes, 732
siblings, 286, 289
SierpDown method, 244–245
Sierpiński, Wacław (mathematician), 243, 247
Sierpiński curve, 243–246, 732
SierpLeft method, 244–245
SierpRight method, 244–245
SierpUp method, 244–245
sieve of Eratosthenes, 44–45, 732
simple substitution cipher, 529–530
Simpson's rule, 50, 732
simulated annealing, 384–385, 732
single recursion, 732
singly linked list, 72–79
skyline problem
    about, 247
    defined, 732
    divide-and-conquer approach, 249–252
    lists, 248–249
snapshot, 588–589, 620, 732

snapshot token, 732
solutions to exercises
    algorithm basics, 623–626
    arrays, 638–648
    balanced trees, 670–675
    basic network algorithms, 678–681
    complexity theory, 692–696
    cryptography, 689–691
    decision trees, 675–677
    distributed algorithms, 697–701
    hash tables, 655–657
    interview puzzles, 701–709
    linked lists, 633–638
    network algorithms, 681–686
    numerical algorithms, 626–633
    queues, 648–650
    recursion, 658–663
    searching, 653–655
    sorting, 650–653
    stacks, 648–650
    string algorithms, 686–689
    trees, 663–669
sorted chaining, 612
sorted hill climbing, 386–387
sorted linked lists, 81–82
sorted trees
    about, 12, 300, 303, 309–310
    adding nodes, 303–305
    defined, 614, 732
    deleting nodes, 306–309
    finding nodes, 306
sorting
    about, 167–168, 610–611
    exercises, 198–200
    with insertionsort algorithm, 87–88
    O(N log N) algorithms, 174–191
    O(N²) algorithms, 168–174
    with selectionsort algorithm, 88–89
    Sub O(N log N) algorithms, 192–197
Soundex algorithm, 511–513, 732
space-filling curves, 245–246, 732
spanning trees
    about, 416
    defined, 617, 732
    minimal, 417–418
sparse arrays
    about, 121–123
    defined, 610, 732

deleting values, 127–129
finding rows/columns, 122–123
getting values, 124–125
setting values, 125–127
spatial trees, 614
specialized queues, 151–152
specialized tree algorithms
    about, 322
    animal game, 322–324
    building trees, 328–329
    expression evaluation, 324–326
    intersecting with intervals, 330–332
    intersecting with points, 329–330
    interval trees, 326–328
    quadtrees, 332–337
    tries, 337–342
speed, of algorithms, 607
Sqrt N function, 14
stable sort, 733
stable sorting algorithm, 191
stack algorithms
    about, 141
    reversing an array, 141
    stack insertionsort, 145–146
    stack selectionsort, 146–147
    tower of Hanoi, 143–145, 235–238, 735
    train sorting, 142–143
Stack class (C#), 136
stack insertionsort algorithm, 145–146
stack selectionsort algorithm, 146–147
stacks
    about, 135–136, 230, 610
    array, 138–139
    defined, 610, 733
    double, 139–141, 610
    implementing Quicksort algorithm
        with, 185
    linked-list, 136–138
StartExhaustiveSearch method, 378
starvation, 571, 733
state transition diagram, 498, 733
statements
    End While, 4
    If-Then-Else, 5
    Return, 4, 10
    Select Case, 278
    Step, 4
steering behaviors, 395

Step statement, 4
Stephens, Rod (author)
    contact information for, 5
    Interview Puzzles Dissected: Solving and Understanding Interview Puzzles, 604
stride, 215, 733
string algorithms
    about, 493, 618
    calculating edit distance, 508–511
    exercises, 515–517
    matching parentheses, 494–496
    pattern matching, 497–504
    phonetic algorithms, 511–514, 618, 728
    string searching, 504–508
string class (C#), 493
string searching, 504–508
strongly connected, 406, 420, 733
strongly connected components
    about, 404, 420
    algorithm discussion, 422–425
    defined, 617, 733
    Kosaraju's algorithm, 421–422, 723
Sub O(N log N) algorithms
    about, 192
    Bucketsort, 195–197
    countingsort, 192–193, 197, 716
    PigeonholeSort, 193–195, 197, 728
subgraph isomorphism problem, 556, 733
subprocedures, 4
subroutines, 4
subset sum problem, 388, 556, 733
substitution boxes (S-boxes), 531, 733
substitution ciphers
    about, 526
    Caesar substitution cipher, 526–527, 714
    defined, 733
    one-time pad cipher, 530–531, 619, 727
    simple substitution cipher, 529–530
    Vigenère cipher, 527–529, 736
substitution-permutation network, 733
substitution-permutation network cipher, 531–533
substring matching, 618
subtree, 287, 289, 733
superposition, 572, 733
swap method, 83–84, 733, 735

swarm intelligence (SI)
    about, 392–393
    ant colony optimization, 393–394
    bees algorithm, 394, 712
    defined, 733–734
    swarm simulation, 394–397, 734
swarm intelligence algorithms, 616
swarm simulation, 394–397, 734
symmetric traversal, 299–300, 722
symmetrically threaded tree, 317, 734
symmetric-key encryption, 534, 734
synchronization, 620
systolic arrays, 562–565, 734

T
tail recursion, 734
tail recursion removal, 274–275, 613
Takao Nishizeki (computer scientist), 481
task parallelism, 567, 734
techinterview (website), 603
techniques
    adaptive, 599, 609
    for algorithms, 607
    branch and bound, 379–381, 714
    data structures, 599
    decision trees, 599
    probability, 599
    problem structure, 599
    randomization, 599
10 famous Microsoft interview puzzles (website), 603
10 Google interview puzzles (website), 603
teraflop (tflop), 566, 734
testing
    connectivity, 413–415
    for primality, 45–47
tflop (teraflop), 566
thread, 90, 317, 614, 734
threaded linked list, 609
threaded trees
    about, 317–318
    building, 318–320
    defined, 734
    using, 320–322
3CNF (Three-term conjunctive normal form), 549, 734

3-node, 354, 711
3-satisfiability problem (3SAT), 392, 549, 556
three-coloring algorithm, 458–459
three-cycle problem, 734
three-partition problem, 556, 734
three-satisfiability (3SAT) problem, 556, 734
Three-term conjunctive normal form (3CNF), 549, 734
Top 5 Microsoft interview questions (website), 603
top-down B-trees, 363, 615, 734
topological sorting, 451–455, 617, 734
tortoise-and-hare algorithm, 98–100, 431, 437, 735
totient function, 535–536, 719
tower of Hanoi, 143–145, 235–238, 735
train sorting algorithm, 142–143
transitive closure, 436, 617, 735
transitive closure problem, 437–438
transitive reduction, 436, 438–441, 617, 735
transitivity
 about, 436
 transitive closure problem, 437–438
 transitive reduction, 436, 438–441, 617, 735
transpose links, 421, 735
transpose method, 83–84, 733, 735
transpose network, 421, 735
transposition ciphers
 about, 521
 column transposition, 523–525
 defined, 618, 735
 route ciphers, 525–526
 row/column transposition, 521–523
trapezoid rule, 49–50, 735
traveling salesman problem (TSP), 16, 391, 393–394, 556, 735
traversals
 about, 296–297, 409
 breadth-first, 301–302, 412–413, 714
 building mazes, 419–420
 connectivity testing, 413–415
 defined, 614, 616, 735
 depth-first, 297, 410–412, 717

Euclidean minimum spanning tree (EMST), 418–419
 inorder, 299–300, 722
 minimal spanning trees, 417–418, 725
 postorder, 300–301, 728
 preorder, 297–299, 728
 run times, 303
 spanning trees, 416, 417–418, 617, 732
 uses for, 302
TraverseInorder method, 300
TraversePostorder method, 301
TraversePreorder method, 299
TreeNode class, 293–294, 310, 311, 312
trees
 about, 285, 614
 AVL, 350–353, 615, 712
 balanced. See balanced trees
 binary, 12, 175–176, 286, 288–291, 713
 binomial, 152–154, 155–156, 713
 bottom-up B-trees, 363, 713
 B-trees, 359–362, 615, 712
 B+trees, 363–364, 712
 call, 190
 complete, 12, 175–176, 287, 288, 295–296, 715
 decision, 367–397, 398–401, 615–616, 717
 Euclidean spanning, 617
 exercises, 342–348
 full, 287, 289, 720
 game, 615–616
 general, 312–314
 height of, 153, 287, 289, 305
 interval, 326–328, 326–342, 722
 knowledge, 614
 lowest common ancestors, 309–316
 maximum leaf spanning, 724
 minimal spanning, 417–418, 725
 minimum degree spanning, 725
 ordered, 287, 289, 727
 parse, 496
 perfect, 287, 289, 727
 prefix, 337–342, 614, 735
 representations, 292–296
 shortest path, 732
 sorted, 12, 300, 303–309, 303–310, 309–310, 614, 732
 spanning, 416, 417–418, 617, 732

spatial, 614
specialized algorithms, 322–326
symmetrically threaded, 317, 734
terminology for, 285–289
threaded, 317–322, 734
top-down B-trees, 363, 615, 734
traversal, 296–303
2-3, 354–358, 615, 711
unordered, 287, 736
treesort, 735
trial division, 44
triangles, finding, 480–482
triangular arrays, 118–121, 735
tries, 337–342, 614, 735
Triple DES (3DES/TDES), 534, 735
true random-number generators
    (TRNGs), 24, 608, 735
TSP (traveling salesman problem), 16,
    391, 393–394, 556, 735
Turing, Alan (mathematician), 545
Turing machine, 545–546, 736
turn penalties, 443–446
two dimensions, 114–115
two generals problem, 580–581, 620, 736
2-3 trees
    about, 354
    adding values, 355–356
    defined, 615, 711
    deleting values, 356–358
2^N function, 15–16
2-node, 354, 711
two-coloring algorithm, 456–458
two-dimensional arrays, 105

U
unbounded knapsack problem, 556, 736
undirected link, 404, 406, 736
unordered tree, 287, 736
upper-triangular array, 118, 736

V
value null, 13
values
    deleting, 127–129
    generating, 24–26
    getting, 124–125
    setting, 125–127

vehicle routing, 736
vehicle routing problem, 556
vertex. *See* nodes
vertex coloring, 556, 726
vertex coloring problem, 555
vertex cover, 736
vertex cover problem, 556, 726
Vigenère, Blaise de (diplomat), 527
Vigenère cipher, 527–529, 736
virtual backlink, 736
Visit method, 422
Visual Basic, automatic memory
    management and, 79
visualizing functions, 16–17

W
waiter, 579
Warnsdorff, H. C. von, 259
weakly connected, 406, 736
websites
    A2Z Interviews: puzzles, 604
    Advanced Encryption Standard (AES),
        533
    Berkeley Open Infrastructure for
        Network Computing (BOINC), 566
    "Building a 270* Teraflops Deep
        Learning Box for Under $10,000,"
        566
    Byzantine Empire, 581
    CareerCup, 604
    Cook-Levin theorem, 548
    CoolInterview puzzles, 604
    Data Encryption Standard (DES), 534
    Einstein@Home, 566
    Euclidean minimum spanning tree
        (EMST), 419
    Extensible Markup Language (XML),
        295
    external sorting on tape drives, 191
    Facebook interview puzzles group, 603
    Great Internet Mersenne Prime Search
        (GIMPS), 566
    Haidong Wang's interview puzzles,
        603
    How to Ace a Google Interview, 603
    IBM Q System One, 572
    Math Is Fun, 129

Math Olympiads, 604
"Matrix," 129
phonetic algorithms, 514
Polish notation, 302
Pretty Good Privacy (PGP), 537
prime factoring, 44
quantum computing, 572
Random.org, 24
reverse Polish notation, 302
Reversi game, 375
Rosetta@home, 566
SETI@home, 566
"Seven Bridges of Königsberg"
     problem, 485
tape drives, 191
techniterview, 603
10 famous Microsoft interview
     puzzles, 603
10 Google interview puzzles, 603
Top 5 Microsoft interview questions,
     603
Turing machine, 546

URLs, 480
Why Brainteasers Don't Belong in Job
     Interview, 603
weights, 404, 406, 736. *See also* costs
wheel factorization, 44
While loop, 4, 38, 74, 179, 188, 221, 275,
     278, 321
"Why Are Manhole Covers Round? A
     Laboratory Study of Reactions to
     Puzzle Interviews," 596
Why Brainteasers Don't Belong in Job
     Interview (website), 603
work assignment problem, 467–468, 736

X
XML (Extensible Markup Language),
     295

Z
zero sum subset problem, 551, 737
zeros, finding, 55–57
zero-time sort, 565, 737